(**Continued on back endsheets**)

American Poets Since World War II
Fourth Series

Dictionary of Literary Biography® • Volume One Hundred Sixty-Five

American Poets Since World War II
Fourth Series

Edited by
Joseph Conte
State University of New York at Buffalo

A Bruccoli Clark Layman Book
Gale Research Inc.
Detroit, Washington, D.C., London

Advisory Board for
DICTIONARY OF LITERARY BIOGRAPHY

Library of Congress Cataloging-in-Publication Data

American poets since World War II. Fourth series / edited by Joseph Conte.
    p. cm. – (Dictionary of literary biography; v. 165)
"A Bruccoli Clark Layman book."
Includes bibliographical references and index.
ISBN 0-8103-9360-3 (alk. paper)
1. American poetry – 20th century – Bio-bibliography – Dictionaries. 2. Poets, American – 20th century – Biography – Dictionaries. 3. American poetry – 20th century – History and criticism.
I. Conte, Joseph Mark, 1960- . II. Series.
PS323.5.A5 1996
811'.5409'03 – dc20   96-12107
                                                              CIP
[B]

For Joy Mara Leighton

Contents

Plan of the Series

The advisory board, the editors, and the publisher of the *Dictionary of Literary Biography* are joined in endorsing Mark Twain's declaration. The literature of a nation provides an inexhaustible resource of permanent worth. We intend to make literature and its creators better understood and more accessible to students and the reading public, while satisfying the standards of teachers and scholars.

To meet these requirements, *literary biography* has been construed in terms of the author's achievement. The most important thing about a writer is his writing. Accordingly, the entries in *DLB* are career biographies, tracing the development of the author's canon and the evolution of his reputation.

The purpose of *DLB* is not only to provide reliable information in a convenient format but also to place the figures in the larger perspective of literary history and to offer appraisals of their accomplishments by qualified scholars.

The publication plan for *DLB* resulted from two years of preparation. The project was proposed to Bruccoli Clark by Frederick C. Ruffner, president of the Gale Research Company, in November 1975. After specimen entries were prepared and typeset, an advisory board was formed to refine the entry format and develop the series rationale. In meetings held during 1976, the publisher, series editors, and advisory board approved the scheme for a comprehensive biographical dictionary of persons who contributed to North American literature. Editorial work on the first volume began in January 1977, and it was published in 1978. In order to make *DLB* more than a reference tool and to compile volumes that individually have claim to status as literary history, it was decided to organize volumes by topic, period, or genre. Each of these free-standing volumes provides a biographical-bibliographical guide and overview for a particular area of literature. We are convinced that this organization – as opposed to a single alphabet method – constitutes a valuable innovation in the presentation of reference material. The volume plan necessarily requires many decisions for the placement and treatment of authors who might properly be included in two or three volumes. In some instances a major figure will be included in separate volumes, but with different entries emphasizing the aspect of his career appropriate to each volume. Ernest Hemingway, for example, is represented in *American Writers in Paris, 1920–1939* by an entry focusing on his expatriate apprenticeship; he is also in *American Novelists, 1910–1945* with an entry surveying his entire career. Each volume includes a cumulative index of the subject authors and articles. Comprehensive indexes to the entire series are planned.

With volume ten in 1982 it was decided to enlarge the scope of *DLB*. By the end of 1986 twenty-one volumes treating British literature had been published, and volumes for Commonwealth and Modern European literature were in progress. The series has been further augmented by the *DLB Yearbooks* (since 1981) which update published entries and add new entries to keep the *DLB* current with contemporary activity. There have also been *DLB Documentary Series* volumes which provide biographical and critical source materials for figures whose work is judged to have particular interest for students. One of these companion volumes is entirely devoted to Tennessee Williams.

We define literature as the *intellectual commerce of a nation:* not merely as belles lettres but as that ample and complex process by which ideas are generated, shaped, and transmitted. *DLB* entries are not limited to "creative writers" but extend to other figures who in their time and in their way influenced the mind of a people. Thus the series encompasses historians, journalists, publishers, and screenwriters. By this means readers of *DLB* may be aided to perceive literature not as cult scripture in the keeping of intellectual high priests but firmly positioned at the center of a nation's life.

DLB includes the major writers appropriate to each volume and those standing in the ranks immediately behind them. Scholarly and critical counsel has been sought in deciding which minor figures to include and how full their entries should be. Wherever possible, useful references are made to figures who do not warrant separate entries.

Each *DLB* volume has a volume editor responsible for planning the volume, selecting the figures for inclusion, and assigning the entries. Volume editors are also responsible for preparing, where appropriate, appendices surveying the major periodicals and literary and intellectual movements for their volumes, as well as lists of further readings. Work on the series as a whole is coordinated at the Bruccoli Clark Layman editorial center in Columbia, South Carolina, where the editorial staff is responsible for accuracy of the published volumes.

One feature that distinguishes *DLB* is the illustration policy – its concern with the iconography of literature. Just as an author is influenced by his surroundings, so is the reader's understanding of the author enhanced by a knowledge of his environment. Therefore *DLB* volumes include not only drawings, paintings, and photographs of authors, often depicting them at various stages in their careers, but also illustrations of their families and places where they lived. Title pages are regularly reproduced in facsimile along with dust jackets for modern authors. The dust jackets are a special feature of *DLB* because they often document better than anything else the way in which an author's work was perceived in its own time. Specimens of the writers' manuscripts are included when feasible.

Samuel Johnson rightly decreed that "The chief glory of every people arises from its authors." The purpose of the *Dictionary of Literary Biography* is to compile literary history in the surest way available to us – by accurate and comprehensive treatment of the lives and work of those who contributed to it.

The *DLB* Advisory Board

Introduction

Dictionary of Literary Biography 165: American Poets Since World War II, Fourth Series, as well as the fifth and sixth series to be published later, is devoted to poets who have made a significant contribution to their art after 1945. Such a criterion allows for the inclusion of poets of different age groups, diverse styles, and competing poetic principles. Some of the poets presented here had already established their careers by the close of World War II; others have only recently begun to attract – or provoke – the critical attention that their talents deserve. The presence of poets accomplished in traditional forms and familiar genres alongside those practiced in a resolutely avant-garde approach is not an accident of this volume but its intention. Readers of *DLB* volumes can naturally choose to read according to their inclinations, but the juxtapositions of poetic careers that either reinforce or contend with one another is perhaps the chief advantage of a book with such variety of subjects and contributors. In the estimation of this editor, the poets included all have a strong claim for their importance in the period, and the thorough critical appraisal, biographical information, and bibliographical support provided by the contributors will enable readers to judge each case for themselves.

In the selection of entries for this volume special consideration was given to its relation to those prior volumes in the *DLB* series that address American poetry after 1945. A particular concern was to supplement the treatment of poets included in the two-volume *DLB 5: American Poets Since World War II, First Series* (1980). In the sixteen years since the publication of *DLB 5,* several of the poets included there have produced major new works or since been the beneficiaries of extensive critical studies. Such changes called for a fresh appraisal. In other instances, it has been deemed sufficient to update and revise the treatment originally afforded the poet to account for less dramatic shifts in a career. The passage of even sixteen years has naturally seen the decline of interest in certain midcentury authors, but it also brings a demand for the augmentation of entries devoted to previously overlooked – but by no means minor – poets. And finally, this volume presents several poets whose work was still in a gestatory stage in 1980 and who thus appear in the *DLB*

for the first time. Such poets may well introduce the poetics that will carry into the next century.

From this vantage point near the close of the twentieth century, the history of postmodern poetry can broadly be described in three generational clusters. The first generation of postmodern poets are those born shortly after the turn of the century. Many of the milestones of high modernism, such as the publication of T. S. Eliot's *The Waste Land* (1922), were written while they were still quite young. In a literal manner they regard the modern poets of their day – Wallace Stevens, Ezra Pound, Eliot, Robert Frost, Gertrude Stein, Marianne Moore, and William Carlos Williams – as both their elders (by some twenty or more years) and as mentors with whom they had extensive personal and epistolary contact. Their early mature work appears between 1929 and 1944, marked by the grinding demands of the Depression and often inflected by leftist politics and economic theory. They are well aware that their writing follows upon the dramatic breach with the genteel aesthetic of late-nineteenth-century poetry as found in Eliot's "The Love Song of J. Alfred Prufrock" (1917), Pound's first gathering of his epic in *A Draft of XXX Cantos* (1930), or Stein's cubist poetry in *Tender Buttons* (1914). In one sense they are late modernists; they regard their work as an extension of the modernist campaign to "make it new." But they also struggle "to witness / and adjust" (adapting Williams's phrase) to the modern condition, interjecting within the revolutionary aesthetic the social, political, and personal concerns of their generation.

In this volume Louis Zukofsky (1904–1978) is a representative type of the first postmodernist, embarking upon his career under the close and sought-after tutelage of Ezra Pound (chronicled in their extensive correspondence between 1927 and 1963). The first half of Zukofsky's own eight-hundred-page epic poem, *"A,"* resembles the canto structure of Pound's "poem including history." After 1951, however, Zukofsky's work becomes increasingly hermetic, procedural in form, and language-oriented. In short, the latter part of his career represents a departure from his modernist mentor and his hortatory manner and culminates in such distinctively postmodern achievements as *80 Flowers* (1978). However different in style and biography, other members of this first generation such as Kenneth Rexroth and George Oppen follow a similar pattern that realizes a slow sundering of the mentor/disciple relationship. Their presence in this volume is not only justified by the substantial work they completed after 1945 but by their continued influence on contemporary poets. Their careers serve as instructive graphs of the transition between a modern and postmodern poetics. In some cases the first postmoderns worked in relative obscurity until discovered, published, and in turn adopted as mentors by members of the postwar generation. Essays on several important poets born in the first decade of this century, including Charles Reznikoff, Edward Dahlberg, Laura Riding Jackson, Langston Hughes, and Stanley Kunitz, can be found in *DLB 45: American Poets, 1880–1945, First Series* and *DLB 48: American Poets, 1880–1945, Second Series.*

Several recent studies, among them Albert Gelpi's *Coherent Splendor* (1987) and Cary Nelson's *Repression and Recovery* (1989), have shown that modern American poetry was hardly the monolithic program that the New Critical canon had suggested. Fissures arising from different relationships with romanticism, in the test of domestic or expatriate affiliations, and in the conflicting political allegiances of the 1930s and 1940s suggest that the spate of movements and groupings that were identified or actively promoted after 1950 were an inevitable result of such disagreements. The postwar generation of postmodern poets are those born in the second quarter of the century, with a particularly distinguished class of 1926–1927 that includes A. R. Ammons, John Ashbery, Robert Bly, Robert Creeley, Allen Ginsberg, James Merrill, W. S. Merwin, Frank O'Hara, and James Wright. Their notable early works appear between 1955 and 1970. It may be judicious to describe the attitude of postwar poets to their modernist forebears as ambivalent, that is, capable of registering strongly positive or negative responses in separate cases. Creeley, for example, rejects the symbolist mode of Eliot for the immediate contact with the real he finds in Williams. This shift from a poetics of transcendence to one of immanence becomes a defining characteristic of midcentury poetry, as Charles Altieri has argued in *Self and Sensibility in Contemporary American Poetry* (1984). Charles Olson, who was the first poet to identify himself as "post-modern" in "The Present is Prologue" (1950), espouses a posthumanism and posthistoricism that runs counter to the romantic ideology found in Stevens. But Ammons and Ashbery have retained a close affinity for the romantic

imagination expressed in Stevens's "poem of the act of the mind." Robert Lowell's first three volumes emulated the dense symbolic language and impersonal registers of Eliot, only to follow Ginsberg's *Howl* (1956) into a confessional mode in *Life Studies* (1959) that made a virtue of traumatic personal revelation. As M. L. Rosenthal and others have noted, the shift from an impersonal to a personal register and the disclosure of the self in the poem are distinguishing aspects of postwar poetry. In the end, the postwar poets neither denied the continuing relevance of the modernist writers nor pledged absolute fealty to their principles.

An additional source of generational tension stems from the longevity of the modernist poets whose major late works appear simultaneously with the important early works of the postwar poets. Creeley's landmark *For Love* was published in the same year as Williams's remarkable *Pictures from Brueghel* (1962). Ashbery's *Some Trees* (1956) closely follows Stevens's *Collected Poems,* published on his seventy-fifth birthday in 1954. Elizabeth Bishop (1911–1979), who was slow to publish and whose reputation accrued gradually, arrives at her *Selected Poems* in the same year as Moore's meticulous edition of her *Complete Poems* (1967).

One finds in the work of these postwar poets many acts of homage to their still-productive modernist predecessors. But these homages are accompanied by profuse statements on poetics that suggest their project was not merely to extend modernism but to advance from it. Olson's "Projective Verse," Denise Levertov's "Some Notes on Organic Form," Ginsberg's "First thought best thought," Kelly's "Notes on the Poetry of the Deep Image," O'Hara's "Personism: A Manifesto," Lowell's autobiographical essay "91 Revere Street," and Adrienne Rich's politically charged "When We Dead Awaken" are among the landmark documents that challenge modernist precepts, add new concepts to the encyclopedia of poetics, and found postmodern schools of poetry. The proliferation of movements and manifestos at midcentury can be read as an attempt by second-generation postmodernists to accentuate their differences from and exploit the fissures within the dominant mode of modernism. Each school challenges the New Critical emphasis on an ironic and distant voice, the mastery of a well-wrought form, and the limitation of decorous language and subject matter in the poem. The proposition of an organic process in poetry by the members of the Black Mountain School, the chatty casualness of the New York School, the reliance upon the intuition among the Beats, and the Confessional provocations of a psyche-in-distress contribute to the expansive modulations of postwar poetry.

If the poets of the 1950s and 1960s suffered somewhat from the anxiety of influence, they also enjoyed the largest and broadest readership for poetry in this century: unofficial tabulation from royalty statements, course enrollments, political rallies in public parks, and the burgeoning popularity of poetry readings in academic lecture halls and bohemian clubs suggest that the cachet of poetry reached its peak in this countercultural era. Books by Bly, Creeley, Sylvia Plath, Anne Sexton, Gary Snyder, and Ginsberg sold tens of thousands of copies. Like many other aspects of American life at midcentury, poetry enjoyed a period of unbridled expansion.

Third-generation postmodern poets are most likely the contemporaries of many readers of this volume. Born during the twenty years after World War II, they count themselves among the baby boomers. They are legion; their achievements are still under evaluation. They are college graduates for whom "Modern Poetry" was a three-credit course in their major; most hold graduate degrees in literature or creative writing; many teach their craft in university writing programs. They have had the opportunity of sitting at a seminar table with acclaimed members of the postwar movements who have been the holders of distinguished professorships and whose papers fetch large sums from Special Collections. But contemporary poets do not identify themselves with postwar movements beyond an acknowledgment of their historical importance. They often feel only slight indebtedness to the prior generation for the battles fought – mostly between the academies and the bohemians, the "cooked" and the "raw" poetries – that are now largely resolved. Few marvel that the renegade poets of the 1960s are now ensconced in the university or in textbook anthologies or that "open" and "closed" forms cohabit in little magazines or in the latest volume by John Ashbery.

The field of contemporary poetry cannot be solely described in terms of movements and schools. Instead one finds a four-sided mandala of less tightly bonded interest groups, or PACs (Poetry Action Committees). In one quarter reside the traditionalists who have assumed the mantle of the academic poets of the postwar generation, though in a more discursive and less intricate language. Aided by recent collections – such as *The Direction of Poetry: An Anthology of Rhymed and Metered Verse Written in the English Language Since 1975* (1988), *Expansive Poetry: Essays on the New Narrative and the New Formalism*

(1989), and *A Formal Feeling Comes: Poems in Form by Contemporary Women* (1994) – an alliance of New Formalists calls for a return to traditional rhyme and meter (to recoup what they view as the slack practice of the 1960s and 1970s) and a renewed emphasis on narrative to foster a general, educated audience for poetry (which the diffuse poetries of the counterculture had supposedly lost). Gjertrud Schnackenberg (b. 1953), Vikram Seth (b. 1952), Brad Leithauser (b. 1953), and Timothy Steele (b. 1948) – all of whom appear in *DLB 120: American Poets Since World War II, Third Series* – revive stanzaic forms and metrical devices fallen into disuse. Though some among their group combine neoconservatism with a return to traditional forms, others do not. The lesbian formalist Marilyn Hacker (b. 1942) addresses the milieu of homosexual life in her sonnets, and businessman-poet Dana Gioia (b. 1950) has successfully resisted both an academic appointment and the Republicanism of the management class.

In the opposite quarter reside the experimentalists whose antiestablishment convictions preclude participation in the "professional verse culture." They are widely published (in small-press books, financially precarious but daring magazines, and on always-warm laser-jet printers) but poorly distributed. They form an underground almost wholly ignored by the Associated Writing Programs and by the prize-selection committees that announce the winners of the latest competition in their newsletters. The Language poets are the most identifiable of this group, attacking the conventions of the personal voice and transparent, "absorptive" language in the lyric. Lyn Hejinian (b. 1941) and Bernadette Mayer (b. 1945), included in this volume, are such poets; others include Susan Howe (b. 1937), Clark Coolidge (b. 1939), Michael Palmer (b. 1943), Ron Silliman (b. 1946), and Charles Bernstein (b. 1950). These poets muster an array of antiabsorptive techniques that provoke self-consciousness about the reading process. Blatant artifice, syntactic disruptions, phonetic play, typographic anomalies, impermeability, and the splicing and co-opting of itinerant texts and popular iterations combine to assert what Bernstein in *A Poetics* (1992) calls the "skepticism, doubt, noise, [and] resistance" of postmodern culture. The Language poet's elaboration of poststructuralist theories of language and their recourse to Marxist attacks on a publishing industry that commodifies referential language have heightened their appeal to a theoretically-aware university readership. A few Language poets, such as Bernstein, Howe, and Bob Perelman (b. 1947) have in fact entered the professoriat. In contrast to the foregrounding of textuality in Language writing, the Performance poetry of Armand Schwerner (b. 1927), Jerome Rothenberg (b. 1931), and David Antin (b. 1932) stresses the improvisation of an oral performance incorporating autobiographical, ethnographic, musical, or other nonliterary sources.

In a third quarter reside poets for whom identity politics are a prominent consideration. Issues of race, gender, ethnicity, and sexual preference constitute the subject matter of their work, which ranges from the most intimate personal revelation to broad public pronouncements. They are less concerned than either traditionalists or experimentalists by debates over poetic form, though they pursue styles that differentiate their work from the speech and experience of white middle America. The espousal of an opaque or overly literary language runs counter to the political statements they feel compelled to make. Their charge is to give voice to those previously repressed segments of American society and therefore to introduce a pluralist concept of community. They speak first to an audience with whom they share their experience of marginality, but they consequently seek the understanding of a larger readership. In the gender and hemispheric politics of Carolyn Forché (b. 1950), in the pan-African rituals and the tonalities of jazz as recorded by Nathaniel Mackey (b. 1947) and Pulitzer Prize winner Yusef Komunyakaa (b. 1947), in the reconciliation of Asian tradition and modern American life in the work of Hawaiian-born Cathy Song (b. 1955) and Indonesian-born Li-Young Lee (b. 1957), and in the bilingual culture of Simon Ortiz (b. 1941), American poetry overcomes its monochromatic and monotonal historical origins.

The fourth quarter is occupied by the practitioners of the most pervasive mode in American poetry today, the personal (or postconfessional) lyric. These poets extend the confessional mode of Lowell, Plath, W. D. Snodgrass, John Berryman, and Sexton, though they are less strident in their attack on decorum and perhaps no longer able to shock through autobiographical revelation in the era of tabloid journalism. Despite the moderation in tone, these poets continue to explore the psyche and emotions in poems that test the propositions of the self against the experience of the world. They exhibit a general disregard for formalist techniques (including meter) that might impede immediate expression, and they refuse to distract from the presentation of the self by calling attention to the language-as-object. Poets such as Robert Hass (b. 1941), Sharon Olds (b. 1942), and Charles Wright (b. 1935), who

is discussed in this volume, as well as James Wright (1927–1980), Stanley Plumly (b. 1939), and Louise Glück (b. 1943), have pursued the family drama and childhood's traumatic incidents, psychic distress and substance abuse, sexual adventuring and marital strife as their common subjects. Beyond the immediate relation to confessionalism, these poets share an exploration of subjectivity that is the legacy of the romantic lyric. Like the odes of William Wordsworth or John Keats – in a language only slightly heightened from the American vernacular and soothing to the contemporary ear – these poems call upon remembrance within a dramatic setting and often reveal the poet's sensibility and identity. Despite Charles Olson's midcentury warning against "the lyrical interference of the individual as ego" in "Projective Verse," the self in the postconfessional lyric once again assumes the role of arbiter of meaningful experience. These are the poems that dominate such verse magazines as *American Poetry Review* (with its author photographs accompanying poems), *Shenandoah, Prairie Schooner,* and the *Denver Quarterly*. And these poems represent the majority of those discussed in writing workshops. The personal lyricists are the most likely to be directors of Writing Programs and to have published award-winning volumes in University Press poetry series.

The four-part mandala of contemporary poetry here described is not intended to locate poets permanently or exclusively in particular quarters. Adrienne Rich (b. 1929), for example, began her career as a formalist in the school of W. H. Auden and underwent a conversion to become one of the foremost exponents (in poetry and prose) of feminist politics. One observes among recent writers a more flexible alliance not permitted by the close-knit movements of midcentury. Poets are often not responsible for the labels attached to their work, and contemporary poets frequently resist the scholar's restrictive and ultimately reductive labels. While LeRoi Jones/Amiri Baraka (b. 1934) abandoned his association with the New York bohemian schools to lead the Black Arts movement, Ishmael Reed (b. 1938), Lorenzo Thomas (b. 1944), and Nathaniel Mackey now move more easily between an African American poetics and an experimental mode. Similarly, female poets such as Denise Levertov (b. 1923) and Carolyn Forché have worked to correlate the terms of the personal lyric and political activism.

The third generation of postmodern poets may also be characterized by outright resistance to the aesthetic and political program of modernism.

In this regard the poets are in alignment with much that has transpired in literary criticism and theory in the past twenty years. The poets of identity politics have been especially critical of the Eurocentric and masculinist bias that permeated modernism. The pluralism that espouses the equal validity and aesthetic worth of disparate cultural experience directly challenges the elitist, sexist, and discriminatory attitudes implicit in modernism. The postmodern lyric's renewed emphasis on personal expression serves as repudiation of the impersonal and objectivist slant of modern verse and reinstates the individual to authority over totalizing systems. Whereas the modernist held the word as sacred and symbolic *Logos,* with intrinsic and incantatory meaning, the postmodern avant-garde regards language as a plastic medium that can be reshaped without lingering impressions. Rather than aspire to a pure, refined art, the postmodern poet appropriates theoretical jargon and demotic speech, the embedded phraseology of commerce and the free signifier. Lastly, there exists a reactionary postmodernism that dubs the modernist revolt against nineteenth-century aesthetics a failure because of its disregard for the general audience and urges a return to traditional forms, public statement, and coherence of narration and setting. On all fronts there is little doubt that the contemporary poet now disdains many of the precepts of modernism. A new literary period has begun.

Contemporary poetry has been even more agitated by debates about the canon than other fields of literary endeavor. Popular acclaim and satisfied booksellers temper judgments as Susan Sontag displaces E. B. White in essay collections, or as Toni Morrison captures the Nobel Prize that eluded Vladimir Nabokov. But because poetry continues to operate within a limited economy and eroding readership outside the university – only a few volumes are published by trade houses, and reviews of poetry in major newspapers and magazines have virtually vanished – arguments as to who the important figures are, how they are identified, and why they should be taught preoccupy the field. The literary canon demands selectivity. It should guide the reader toward works that are significant or rewarding. In the past decade especially, pluralists have argued that such "guides to reading" are neither benign nor impartial. The canon creates a hierarchy of writers, and it traditionally reinforces the dominant culture at the expense of the marginal or disenfranchised. Literary history has a greater obligation to inclusivity, in an attempt to establish a thorough cultural record and to recover unjustly neglected or repressed works. Thus, the canon-reinforcing process of evaluation sometimes clashes with the politics of inclusion and efforts at suitable representation of the diversity of American voices.

In 1929 Ezra Pound asserted in his own effort at canon formation, "How to Read," that poetry should be chosen for an anthology "because it contained an invention, a definite contribution to the art of verbal expression." He argues that one should not "sub-divide the elements in literature according to some non-literary categoric division. You do not divide physics or chemistry according to racial or religious categories" (*Literary Essays*). Although Pound deplored the conservatism of the anthologist of his day, he nevertheless equates the terms of literary selection with the supposedly impersonal and universal truths of science, which is precisely the object of complaint among today's pluralists: the universal category too often turned out to be male and white.

In their efforts to expand the canon, pluralists have introduced a remarkable number of special-interest anthologies that identify poets by gender, race, ethnicity, sexual preference, and nationality, or some combination thereof. Among these are *Breaking Silence: An Anthology of Contemporary Asian American Poets* (1983), *Harper's Anthology of 20th Century Native American Poets* (1987), and *Gay and Lesbian Poetry in Our Time* (1988). As Alan Golding points out in "American Poetry Anthologies," an essay in *Canons* (1984), such collections have the notable virtue of preserving a specific tradition and rehistoricizing our understanding of literary heritage. But they are also symptoms of an increasing literary balkanization through which one reader's familiar figures of contemporary poetry escape the notice of another. And as Charles Bernstein points out in "State of the Art," "Too often, the works selected to represent cultural diversity are those that accept the model of representation assumed by the dominant culture in the first place" (*A Poetics*).

Pound's premise about anthologies should not be considered invalid, but the criteria he posits must evolve as the tradition advances. Inventive writers of all descriptions continue to be neglected by the canon in favor of aesthetically conservative writers. Cultivating those works that, as Pound says, contain "an invention, a definite contribution to the art of verbal expression" is crucial to the survival of poetry in America. The canon of contemporary poetry persists because one must finally discriminate between inventive and stale work. New critiques that persuasively describe daring work to a skeptical readership, in tandem with the poetics of inclusion that represent a panoply of American traditions, make a revised and expanded canon essentially beneficial to American poetry.

The entries in *DLB 165: American Poets Since World War II, Fourth Series* are substantial enough to supply biographical and literary-historical context in addition to an extensive evaluation of the poet's oeuvre. At the same time the entry length limits the number of poets that can be treated. Although each volume contributes to a thorough understanding of the literary history of the genre and period, it cannot offer a complete representation of the work in the field. One should regard this volume a companion and supplement to entries in the earlier volumes of the series. Readers will also find entries on important poets writing after World War II in *DLB 16: The Beats: Literary Bohemians in Postwar America*; *DLB 41: Afro-American Poets Since 1955*; *DLB 82: Chicano Writers, First Series*; and *DLB 122: Chicano Writers, Second Series*. As an incremental series these volumes combine critical selection and comprehensive literary history.

The movements and schools that were so prevalent at midcentury partially depended on the personal association of the poets. The New York School poets were fellow students at Harvard before relocating to Lower Manhattan's art community. Charles Olson and Robert Creeley kept up a voluminous correspondence before they met at Black Mountain in North Carolina. With the institutionalization of creative-writing programs, contemporary poets move singly to jobs at colleges and universities across the country. Among the results of this distribution of talent are the affiliation of poets by publishing venues and by their practice in certain genres and forms.

While the personal lyric is the most prevalent contemporary type of poem in terms of quantity, the meditative poem appears to be growing in importance. The lyric devotes itself to the physical and the passionate; in its intimate voice the lyric provokes an emotional response. The meditative poem retreats from the turbulent desires of the ego; it is cognitive rather than sensual, abstract rather than particular. The lyric is hot; the meditative poem cool. The chief modernist predecessor in the meditative mode is Wallace Stevens, who sought to define modern poetry as "the act of the mind." One finds other late-modern examples, such as George Oppen's *Of Being Numerous* (1968). The major exponents of the meditative mode are now John Ashbery and A. R. Ammons. Their excursions of thought find a comfortable rhythm in longer works such as "Self-Portrait in a Convex Mirror" (1975), "A

Wave" (1984), and *Flow Chart* (1991) by Ashbery and *Tape for the Turn of the Year* (1965), *Sphere: The Form of a Motion* (1974), and *Garbage* (1994) by Ammons. Younger poets at work in meditative poetry include Robert Hass and Ann Lauterbach (b. 1942). One finds a strong meditative vein in the work of performance poet David Antin (b. 1932) and in such demanding works by Clark Coolidge as *The Crystal Text* (1986).

The appeal of the meditative poem resides in the patience with which the mind of the poet deploys, maps, and inscribes itself. As a reaction to the abstract language and indeterminacy of scene in meditative poetry, there have been several recent exponents of a return to narrative verse. With James Merrill's elegant masque, *The Changing Light at Sandover* (1983) now completed, poetic works deploying many characters and eventful linear narratives followed. Vikram Seth (b. 1952) chronicles the foibles of Bay Area yuppies in his 307-page novel-in-verse, *The Golden Gate* (1986). Frederick Turner and Frederick Feirstein issue a manifesto on behalf of the New Narrative in *Expansive Poetry* (1989).

The fizzling of several modernist epic poems and a distaste for the hierarchical structures and belief systems that frame them has led many postmodern poets to serial composition. Poems written in many loosely associated parts also signify the impatience of poets with the short personal lyric demanded by journals. The series is a modular form in which individual sections are both discontinuous and capable of multiple orderings. In contrast to the linear causality of most narrative forms, the serial poem is desultory and polyvalent, accommodating an expanding and heterodox universe. Among the first postmodern examples is George Oppen's *Discrete Series* (1934). Midcentury practice includes the open-ended "Passages" of Robert Duncan (1919–1988) published through several volumes, Robert Creeley's *Pieces* (1969), *The Journals* (1975) of Paul Blackburn (1926–1971), and the later books of Jack Spicer (1925–1965). Among contemporary poets the examples include Leslie Scalapino's (b. 1947) "that they were at the beach – aeolotropic series" (1985), Robin Blaser's (b. 1925) *Pell Mell* (1988), and Robert Kelly's (b. 1935) *flowers of unceasing coincidence* (1988). The serial poem represents postmodern poetry's innovative contribution to the long form.

In contrast to the return to traditional poetic forms espoused by the New Formalists, some postmodern poets have invented their own constricting formal devices. These procedural forms consist of predetermined and arbitrary constraints that are relied upon to generate the context and direction of the poem during composition. Unconvinced by the presence of any grand order in the world, the poet discretely enacts a personal order. Procedural forms present themselves as alternatives to the well-made metaphorical lyric once touted by the New Criticism. Louis Zukofsky composes the dense *80 Flowers* in honor of an eightieth birthday he did not live to see; each "flower" is comprised of eight five-word lines. In such books as *Themes and Variations* (1982) and his Norton "lectures" *I–VI* (1990), John Cage (1912–1992) invents the mesostic, a form of acrostic poem in which he "writes through" a proper name or principle centered vertically in the text. Ron Silliman employs a mathematical sequence to determine the number of sentences in each paragraph of his book-length prose poem, *Tjanting* (1981). Rosmarie Waldrop (b. 1935) has written an abecedarium based on a text by George Santayana. These poets advocate constraint for its paradoxically liberating and generative effect.

Many critics and poets have lamented the increasing marginalization of poetry in American culture and intellectual life, with the postmortem examination performed in essays such as Joseph Epstein's "Who Killed Poetry?" in *Commentary* (1988). Few were disturbed by Epstein's declaration that there were no longer any great poets who spoke of language as an "exalted thing" and went forth as "a kind of priest." The passage of such romantic postures was not lamented because neither American poets nor their readers were any longer comfortable with the production or consumption of a cultural artifact in an elitist or quasi-religious vein. Few contemporary poets wish to see themselves as so detached from the secular and egalitarian American experience; few readers wish to worship much of anything.

Epstein scored more heavily when he attacked poets where they live, challenging the cultural efficacy of "poetry professionals" who are wholly supported as teachers in creative-writing programs and whose publications are largely subvented by grants and foundations. Poetry became irrelevant – or at least marginal – to American life when poets needed only to perform their academic obligations of workshops, readings, and the publication of a quadrennial volume to secure their careers. Epstein's accusations hurt because he pointed to the most prestigious institutions among the society of poets as the culprits of the genre's decline. Responses that prescribed solutions, rather than merely denying that the patient had expired, in-

clude Dana Gioia's "Can Poetry Matter?" in *The Atlantic Monthly* (1991), Jonathan Holden's *The Fate of American Poetry* (1991), and Vernon Shetley's *After the Death of Poetry* (1993). All stop short of suggesting that poets resign their tenured positions. These essays contend that the intensive and self-absorbed "difficulty" of poetry – promoted by modernists as a required response to the complexities of their world, and in disdain for the common reader – has increasingly repelled a general audience. Poetry, these commentators argue, must appeal to and engage the intellectual and cultural concerns of the general reader whose attentions have been captured by prose.

While critics argue over the death of poetry, the writing of poetry has never been more democratically practiced. Gioia estimates that writing programs "will produce about 20,000 accredited professional poets over the next decade." The quantity alone is impressive, and these poets – whether professional or freelance laborers – are surely more diverse in their backgrounds than their predecessors. The result of American pluralism is that there are now many more types of poets and poetry than there were in the homogenized, New Critical 1940s. The absence of a "major" poet may be the price paid for the gradual dissolution of the dominant culture that would have identified and rewarded him. Production has increased with the workforce. As Rochelle Ratner, a reviewer of poetry for *American Book Review*, observed in 1994 with a touch of weariness, "a recent 'Poetry Showcase' at Poets House in New York City had nearly a thousand books on display, all published in 1993." As readership erodes in the relentless surf of popular broadcast media, one wonders whether the chapbooks and small-press publications have not already outnumbered the people who purchase them. But the almost tenfold growth in noncommercial literary presses between 1965 and 1990 documented by Loss Pequeño Glazier in *Small Press* (1992) suggests something important: even as poetry appears to decline in prestige and in the attention paid to it by major markets, there is a thriving "back channel" of writing and exchange that escapes the notice of culturally conservative institutions. This alternative ferment, separate from the résumé-stuffing of some eminent poets and critics, may yet provide the next significant advance in poetics and speak to poetry's role in the next century.

Acknowledgments

This book was produced by Bruccoli Clark Layman, Inc. Karen L. Rood is senior editor for the *Dictionary of Literary Biography* series. George P. Anderson and Kenneth Graham were the in-house editors.

Production coordinators were James W. Hipp and Samuel W. Bruce. Photography editors are Julie E. Frick and Margaret Meriwether. Photographic copy work was performed by Joseph M. Bruccoli. Layout and graphics supervisor is Emily Ruth Sharpe. Copyediting supervisor is Laurel M. Gladden. Typesetting supervisor is Kathleen M. Flanagan. Systems manager is George F. Dodge. Laura Pleicones and L. Kay Webster are editorial associates. The production staff includes Phyllis A. Avant, Ann M. Cheschi, Melody W. Clegg, Patricia Coate, Joyce Fowler, Stephanie C. Hatchell, Kathy Lawler Merlette, Jeff Miller, Pamela D. Norton, Delores Plastow, Lisa A. Stufft, William L. Thomas Jr., and Allison Trussell.

Walter W. Ross and Steven Gross did library research. They were assisted by the following librarians at the Thomas Cooper Library of the University of South Carolina: Linda Holderfield and the interlibrary-loan staff; reference-department head Virginia Weathers; reference librarians Marilee Birchfield, Stefanie Buck, Stefanie DuBose, Rebecca Feind, Karen Joseph, Donna Lehman, Charlene Loope, Anthony McKissick, Jean Rhyne, Kwamine Simpson, and Virginia Weathers; circulation-department head Caroline Taylor; and acquisitions-searching supervisor David Haggard.

The publishers acknowledge the generous assistance of William R. Cagle, director of the Lilly Library, Indiana University, and his staff, who provided many of the illustrations in this volume. Their work represents the highest standards of librarianship and research.

The editor would like to acknowledge the Dean of Arts and Letters, Kerry Grant, and the Chair of the Department of English, Kenneth Dauber, at the State University of New York at Buffalo for providing the sabbatical release time and clerical support that contributed to the timely completion of this volume. I would like to thank the family and friends who tolerated my overly dramatic expressions of exasperation and who offered "life support" in invaluable ways over the past two years, especially Ralph and Ann Conte, Joy Leighton, Charles Jones, and Kerry Maguire. Special thanks is due to those colleagues and contributors who served as unofficial consultants to the project at several stages, including Peter Baker, Elisabeth Frost, Laszlo Géfin, Burt Kimmelman, Patrick Meanor, Diane Middlebrook, Susan Schultz, Willard Spiegelman, Keith Tuma, and Peter Quartermain. Finally, George Anderson and Kenneth Graham at Bruccoli Clark Layman deserve gratitude and praise for their skillful editing of the text and preparation of the materials for the volume.

American Poets Since World War II
Fourth Series

Dictionary of Literary Biography

A. R. Ammons

(18 February 1926 –   )

Roger Gilbert
Cornell University

See also the Ammons entry in *DLB 5: American Poets Since World War II, First Series.*

BOOKS: *Ommateum with Doxology* (Philadelphia: Dorrance, 1955);

Expressions of Sea Level (Columbus: Ohio State University Press, 1963);

Corsons Inlet: A Book of Poems (Ithaca, N.Y.: Cornell University Press, 1965; London: Oxford University Press, 1965);

Tape for the Turn of the Year (Ithaca, N.Y.: Cornell University Press, 1965; London: Oxford University Press, 1965);

Northfield Poems (Ithaca, N.Y.: Cornell University Press, 1966; London: Oxford University Press, 1967);

Uplands (New York: Norton, 1970);

Briefings: Poems Small and Easy (New York: Norton, 1971);

Collected Poems, 1951–1971 (New York: Norton, 1972);

Acceptance Remarks (New York: National Book Awards Committee, 1973);

Sphere: The Form of a Motion (New York: Norton, 1974);

Diversifications: Poems (New York: Norton, 1975);

The Snow Poems (New York: Norton, 1977);

Highgate Road (Ithaca, N.Y.: Inkling X Press, 1977);

Six-Piece Suite (Ithaca, N.Y.: Palaemon, 1978);

Selected Longer Poems (New York: Norton, 1980);

Changing Things (Winston-Salem, N.C.: Palaemon, 1981);

A Coast of Trees (New York: Norton, 1981);

A. R. Ammons (photograph by Lydia R. Johnson)

Worldly Hopes (New York: Norton, 1982);

Lake Effect Country (New York: Norton, 1983);

Sumerian Vistas (New York: Norton, 1987);

The Really Short Poems of A. R. Ammons (New York:
    Norton, 1990);
Garbage (New York: Norton, 1993);
The North Carolina Poems (Rocky Mount, N.C.:
    Wesleyan College Press, 1994);
Brink Road (New York: Norton, 1996);
Set in Motion: Essays and Interviews (Ann Arbor: Uni-
    versity of Michigan Press, 1996);
Strip (New York: Norton, 1997).
Collections: *Selected Poems* (Ithaca, N.Y.: Cornell
    University Press, 1968);
The Selected Poems 1951–1977 (New York: Norton,
    1977); enlarged as *The Selected Poems* (New
    York: Norton, 1987).

OTHER: *The Best American Poetry 1994,* edited by
    Ammons and David Lehman, introduction by
    Ammons (New York: Macmillan, 1994).

A. R. Ammons is the foremost living representative of the American Romantic tradition in poetry.
In an era when most contemporary poets have
abandoned the broad concerns of Romanticism in
favor of more narrowly delimited realms – personal
experience, pop culture, Jungian mysticism, identity
politics – Ammons continues to speak with the kind
of generalizing scope found in such forebears as
Ralph Waldo Emerson, Walt Whitman, Emily
Dickinson, and Wallace Stevens. Yet Ammons is
keenly aware of the pitfalls associated with this tradition, its propensity for afflatus and abstraction, its
seeming remoteness from immediate realities, the
evasiveness behind its transcendental claims. His
great achievement has been to carry the Emersonian line forward into our own skeptical age, devis-
ing a host of formal, stylistic, and rhetorical means
to preserve its essential gestures while firmly root-
ing them in a gritty and scientifically precise vision.
The title of his recent long poem, *Garbage* (1993),
suggests his ongoing effort to incorporate as much
of the sheer dross of living into his work as he can
while still finding room for transcendence.

Archie Randolph Ammons was born on 18
February 1926 on a small tobacco farm near White-
ville, North Carolina. His parents, W. M. Ammons
and Lucy Della McKee Ammons, had previously
begotten three daughters, one of whom died at two
weeks; Archie was followed by two more sons, both
of whom also died, one at birth, the other in infancy. These early deaths had a profound impact on
the poet, as expressed most clearly in his major
poem "Easter Morning" in *A Coast of Trees* (1981).
Another important influence was the farm itself, on
which Ammons worked from an early age, learning

intimacy with natural processes and a grudging tol-
erance for violence and death. His early poem
"Hardweed Path Going" recalls his childhood
chores and ends with the traumatic slaughter of a
beloved hog named Sparkle.

Ammons's literary influences while growing
up were limited chiefly to the family Bible, whose
cadences can be heard in some of his early poems.
In elementary school and high school he received
crucial encouragement from two English teachers,
whom he credits with saving him from oblivion,
awakening his passion for language and learning,
and showing him the extent of his own gifts. Aside
from school exercises, he did not begin writing poetry until he had joined the navy and was serving in
the South Pacific during World War II. Following
his discharge Ammons enrolled at Wake Forest
College in Winston-Salem, where he received a B.S.
in 1949. After marrying Phyllis Plumbo and working briefly as the principal of an elementary school
in Hatteras, North Carolina, Ammons studied literature for three semesters at the University of California, Berkeley. There he formed a friendship with
the distinguished critic and poet Josephine Miles, an
early supporter of his work. After leaving Berkeley
in 1952, Ammons took a managerial job with a medical glassware factory owned by his father-in-law.
He commuted to the factory from his home on the
southern coast of New Jersey, a region that left an
indelible mark on many of his poems for the next
twelve years, including "Corsons Inlet."

During this period from 1952 to 1964
Ammons gradually began to establish his reputation
as a poet, publishing his work in respected journals
such as *The Hudson Review* and making himself
known to the great New Jersey poet William Carlos
Williams and his circle. In 1955 his first book, *Ommateum with Doxology,* a collection of thirty-one
poems, sold only a few copies, most of them bought
by his father-in-law as gifts for South American
business associates. In 1963 his second book, *Expressions of Sea Level,* was published, and a year later he
moved with his wife to the small college town of Ithaca in upstate New York to take a temporary teaching job at Cornell University. The one-year replace-
ment eventually became a permanent position;
Ammons has taught for more than thirty years at
Cornell, where he holds the Goldwin Smith Professorship in Poetry. He and his wife have a son, John
Randolph Ammons.

It was not until the publication of his third
book, *Corsons Inlet: A Book of Poems* (1965), that
Ammons began to receive sustained critical attention, but his work in the next half-dozen years

brought him a resounding volley of recognition, beginning with key essays by critics Richard Howard and Harold Bloom, both of whom proclaimed Ammons to be a major figure. Another burst of praise attended the publication of Ammons's *Collected Poems, 1951–1971* (1972), culminating in the honors of the National Book Award and the prestigious Bollingen Prize, usually awarded to much older poets. Ammons's work has since continued to receive acclaim from influential critics such as Bloom, Howard, and Helen Vendler, and while he has not been as widely read as some poets of his generation, his readership has been unusually devoted. Among his other honors are a MacArthur fellowship bestowed in 1981 and a second National Book Award in 1994 for *Garbage*.

Ammons has led a relatively isolated life, particularly in his first forty years. Even during his tenure at Cornell, where he is a prominent figure in the community, he has given few public readings and done little traveling. It is significant that with the exception of his two years in the San Francisco Bay area when he attended Berkeley, Ammons has never lived in or near a major cultural center. The isolated life that the poet quite deliberately chose for himself may help to explain the paradoxical blend of originality and tradition his work displays. Unlike most other poets of his generation, Ammons has never been closely connected with such recognized schools as the Beats, the Black Mountain poets, the Confessionals, the Deep Image group, or the New York school. And while much of his work is recognizably southern in phrasing, Ammons shows little resemblance to the Fugitive school of John Crowe Ransom, Allen Tate, and Robert Penn Warren. There is something peculiarly self-made, even homemade, about Ammons's style, which is replete with idiosyncrasies of diction, syntax, cadence, and punctuation. Yet no poet writing today is more identifiably American or more a product of his native tradition. One might say that by keeping his distance from the intra- and intergenerational rivalries and disputes preoccupying his contemporaries, Ammons has managed to bypass the more fleeting concerns of the moment and place himself directly into the American tradition.

As a result Ammons's poetry seems as close to nineteenth-century as to twentieth-century sources. In reading his work one does not feel the influence of earlier figures to be filtered through later ones; the poet seems to have a foot in both centuries. Any account of Ammons's relation to literary tradition must begin with Ralph Waldo Emerson, the central voice of the Transcendentalist movement. As has

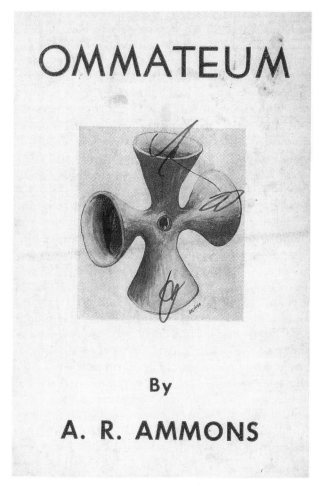

Dust jacket for Ammons's first book of poems, in which his speaker is often a frustrated visionary (courtesy of the Lilly Library, Indiana University)

been abundantly demonstrated by critics such as Bloom, Hyatt Waggoner, and Steven P. Schneider, and as the poet himself cheerfully confirms, Emerson is Ammons's single most crucial literary ancestor. It can be claimed, of course, that Emerson is the ultimate ancestor of virtually all American writers, since Emerson more than anyone else articulated the turbulent and often contradictory vision of self and nature that remains at the heart of the national mythology. But where most twentieth-century writers have absorbed Emerson unconsciously, through the mediation of other texts and authors who qualified and softened his radical vision, Ammons imbibed Emerson at the source, reading him with none of the condescension that so often characterizes the attitude of twentieth-century writers to their nineteenth-century forebears. And unlike most modern readers Ammons has expressed as much admiration for Emerson's poetry as for his major essays. Like Emerson, Ammons has written long narrow poems, diary-like verse accounts of natural phenomena, rapturous lyrics, ironic parables, and poetic conversations with mountains; and while Emerson usually rhymes and Ammons never does, they show a common disdain for excessive regularity and smoothness of form, preferring a raggedness that mimics the intricately varied shapes of nature.

But Ammons's affinities with Emerson run much deeper, centering on a stark, denuded, and deeply ambivalent relation between self and reality or, in Emerson's terms, "Me" and "Not-Me." Like Emerson, Ammons in his poetry moves between asserting the godlike autonomy of the self (though he is never quite as absolute as Emerson in such claims) and advocating a complete surrender of selfhood to the infinite forces of the natural universe. What unites the two writers most fundamentally is a profound and sometimes terrifying sense of solitude, overcome only fitfully and indirectly through verbal acts that create fragile links among individuals. Even more than Emerson, Ammons has shunned the public sphere; large social, political, and cultural issues rarely appear in his work, and when they do they are quickly subsumed by the poet's essentially private vocabulary. Ammons's sense of his audience is correspondingly different from that of poets caught up in public, collective concerns. As he says in a 1980 interview with Cynthia Haythe, "I feel myself to be so peripheral that I don't address groups but look for the single person in his room. He's the person I try to mean something to."

Ammons also shares with Emerson a sense of both internal and external reality as continually changing. What concerns both men is the drama of the isolated self swept up in the act of becoming; and nature rather than human society furnishes the ideal stage for this drama because it offers so many mirrors and metaphors, so many images of flux and process. In his great essay "Circles" Emerson elaborates a subtle and vertiginous view of self and nature forever rippling beyond themselves into new conditions; such a view ultimately proves too dizzying even for Emerson himself, who must fall back on notions of stability to prevent chaos from consuming his discourse. Ammons, with his more intimate knowledge of science and his post-Einsteinian cosmology, allows himself to enter more deeply into the dynamics of flux. His poetry explores the minutest particulars and nuances of a vision Emerson sets forth in a few bold strokes.

Emerson is by no means the only nineteenth-century writer echoed by Ammons. Where Emerson tended in his prose to remain at the level of lofty abstraction, his disciple Henry David Thoreau showed a patient fascination with the concrete facts of nature that Ammons displays as well. Both Ammons and Thoreau believe in the compatibility of scientific knowledge with poetic truth; as writers both are impelled by a faith that no detail of natural occurrence is too small or accidental to yield up matter for reflection. And Ammons has something of Thoreau's uncanny serenity in the face of nature's savagery, its endless cycles of predation and disaster. More obviously, Ammons emulates Walt Whitman, another devoted Emersonian, in his penchant for inclusive forms, for catalogues, chants, and outrageously self-aggrandizing claims, and for a rhetoric of praise that refuses to differentiate between more and less worthy objects. (He also shares Whitman's preoccupation with sex both as act and as metaphor, though Ammons's version of eros remains exclusively heterosexual.) His long poem *Sphere: The Form of a Motion* (1974) represents Ammons's most self-conscious attempt to rival Whitman as a totalizing bard, rolling up the sum of ecstasy and pain. And there are even hints of Emily Dickinson in some of Ammons's shorter lyrics, with their gnomic pronouncements and sharply drawn yet elusive tropes.

For all his manifest ties to these figures, however, Ammons could never be mistaken for a nineteenth-century poet. His style and sensibility are clearly products of his time, reflecting among other things an enlarged sense of what can count as poetic discourse. The twentieth-century poets with whom Ammons has most in common all worked to integrate materials associated with prose into the fabric of their poetry: Robert Frost's emphasis on the rhythms and cadences of ordinary speech, Wallace Stevens's use of philosophical abstraction, and William Carlos Williams's eye for the tawdry and commonplace. In addition, Ammons's work shows occasional affinities with such modernists as Marianne Moore and Ezra Pound, who seems to have furnished an early prosodic model. And he shares aspects of his technique with important postmodernists such as Charles Olson, Robert Creeley, and John Ashbery, the one contemporary poet for whom Ammons has consistently voiced admiration. Again, however, what must be stressed is Ammons's remarkable independence from any single source. His work displays parallels with many key twentieth-century figures without deriving from any of them. Ammons's poetry is unmistakably of his time in its persistent loosening of form and widening of resources, but the routes it takes are mostly discovered, not inherited.

I said, I will find what is lowly
        and put the roots of my identity
        down there;
each day I'll wake up
and ~~look around~~ find the lowly nearby,
        a handy focus and reminder,
a ready measure of my significance,
the voice by which I would ~~want to~~ be heard,
the wills, the kinds of selfishness,
        I ~~would be willing~~ could
freely adopt as my own: ~~I said, whatever~~
~~is lowly will be pure~~

But though I have looked everywhere,
        I can find nothing lowly
        to give myself to:
        everything is

magnificent with existence! everything is
in surfeit of glory,
nothing is diminished
nothing has been diminished for me!

I said, what *more lowly* is lower than the grass:
        ah, underneath,
        a crust of dried-out moss:
        I looked at it closely   *ground-crust*
and said, this can be my habitat: but
nestling in, I looked closer
and found
        (in the brown stems,)
        green mechanisms beyond intellect
awaiting resurrection in rain: so I got up

and ran saying there is nothing lowly in the universe:
I found a beggar:
he had stumps for legs: nobody was paying
him any attention: everybody went on by:
        I nestled in and found his life:
there, love shook his body like a devastation:
and I said
I have looked everywhere
        but I can find nothing lowly
        in the universe:

I whirled through transfigurations up and down,
transfigurations of size and shape and place,
        at one point came still,
        stood in wonder:
moss, beggar, weed, tick, pine, self, magnificent
        with being!

                                5-14-62

First draft for "Still," a poem included in Corsons Inlet *(courtesy of the author)*

One region in which Ammons's original blending of nineteenth- and twentieth-century poetics can be seen is that of diction. Perhaps the first thing to strike a reader becoming acquainted with Ammons's poems is the range of their vocabulary, the sheer variety of words he is able to incorporate. Indeed one can map his poetry with reference to its basic word groups or lexicons. At least four large areas of vocabulary can be identified, forming two distinct polarities. The first could be called the "high," or romantic, word group, comprising terms traditionally associated with transcendent value and sublime feeling, such as *lofty, radiant, glory, beauty, longing, soul, spirit, miracle, splendor,* and *majesty.* Words like these have a perennial place in lyric poetry, but as the twentieth century has continued, the attitudes they imply have come to seem archaic, artificial, even sentimental. Ammons is one of the few contemporary poets still able to deploy this vocabulary convincingly and without irony. In part his romantic vocabulary reflects his unabashed emulation of nineteenth-century models, but his poetry's success also depends on his remarkable agility in leaping from one level of diction to another, creating sudden clashes and jolts that keep his language fresh and surprising.

At the opposite extreme from these "high" words is a wide array of "low," or demotic, terms derived from ordinary speech. These include familiar words such as *fun, bunch, baby* (as a term of address); colorful words such as *bumfuzzlement* and *shenanigans;* southern pronunciations such as *won't* for *wasn't* and *anch* for *inch;* and even vulgar slang like *shit, pussy, pecker.* More generally Ammons's language often approaches a kind of conversational informality that pulls against the transcendentalism at its core, with the result resembling a hybrid of the language of Emerson and Mark Twain. In most of his poetry Ammons represents himself not as a prophet, an orator, or a singer like his nineteenth-century forebears but as a sublimely garrulous talker. His long poems in particular work to sustain the impression of inspired talk, relaxed, meandering, occasionally even vulgar, yet never wholly divorced from the higher matters implied by the first group of words.

This high/low polarity in Ammons's diction is accompanied by another equally crucial division. While many critics have noted Ammons's fondness for scientific terminology, which reflects an ongoing interest in the sciences, his main field of study in college, few have recognized that Ammons's use of scientific language falls into two categories, corresponding to the empirical and theoretical dimensions of science. On the one hand, he draws on the inexhaustible supply of concrete words supplied by empirical science – such words as the names of plants, animals, birds, minerals, organs, cells, microorganisms, chemicals, subatomic particles, and geological and astronomical phenomena. Precise naming is characteristic of Ammons's poetry, which never refers to a tree or a bird when it can speak of a spruce or a grackle, and he extends the same exactness to microscopic and inorganic realms of being. But set against his penchant for particularity is Ammons's fondness for abstractions. His work abounds in terms, usually Latinate, that denote general structures, relations, and processes. Such words as *salience, suasion, configuration, periphery, curvature, engagement, integration,* and *reduction* recur so often that they take on a genuinely thematic weight. This constant interplay in Ammons's work between concrete and abstract diction constitutes an epistemological counterpart to his juggling of high and low words.

One can get a sense of Ammons's management of diction from the opening of his poem "Mechanism," which he published in *Expressions of Sea Level*:

> Honor a going thing, goldfinch, corporation, tree,
>   morality: any working order,
>   animate or inanimate: it
>
> has managed directed balance,
>   the incoming and outgoing energies are working
>   right,
>   some energy left to the mechanism,
>
> some ash, enough energy held
>   to maintain the order in repair,
>   assure further consumption of entropy,
>
> expending energy to strengthen order:
>   honor the persisting reactor,
>   the container of change, the moderator: the yellow
>
> bird flashes black wing-bars
>   in the new-leaving wild cherry bushes by the
>   bay,
>   startles the hawk with beauty[.]

All the areas of vocabulary mentioned above are present in this passage. High words such as *honor* and *beauty* occur beside informal idioms such as *going thing* and *working right;* but more central to the poem is the contrast between abstract notions of order and energy and the particularity of the goldfinch and the wild cherry. The poem's own energy, as in much of Ammons's work, derives from the incongruity between its concrete and abstract perspectives. The very texture of the language alters as the abstractions of the first four stanzas lead into a series of phrases whose clipped syllables and clustered consonants evoke the tangible concreteness of the objects they name.

As the nature of his poetic vocabulary suggests, Ammons is a profoundly dialectical poet, interested less in achieved balances than in the movements of dislocation and disjunction that keep a poem alive. The danger for Ammons, as for Wallace Stevens, is that the structure of ideas he explores can become a closed system to be endlessly — and monotonously — elaborated. Like Stevens, Ammons largely avoids this danger by building a looseness into his poetic forms that allows for unpredictable impingements and digressions. The philosophical structure his poetry engages is not so much his subject as it is a generative device, a kind of landscape or backdrop against which each poem performs its intricate dance of thought, perception, and feeling.

Nonetheless, in reading Ammons it is necessary to keep in mind some of the larger features of his philosophical landscape. Ammons's conceptual vision is built around a series of binary oppositions that include abstract/concrete, general/particular, spirit/matter, unity/diversity (or simply one/many), order/chaos, formlessness/form, permanence/ change, stillness/motion. These oppositions are all familiar motifs in Western philosophy and poetry, of course; what makes Ammons's handling of them original is his readiness to employ abstract terms explicitly in his poems, rather than leaving critics to derive them from his tropes. Many of Ammons's more discursive poems blur the boundary between poetry and criticism — one poem bears the Alexander Pope–like title "Essay on Poetics" and incorporates short lyrics with elaborate commentaries on them. In a representative passage from another essayistic poem, "Extremes and Moderations" from *Collected Poems, 1951–1971,* Ammons criticizes those who never see beyond the particular:

> it's impossible anyone should know anything about the
>   concrete
> who's never risen above it, above the myth of concre-
>   tion
> in the first place: pulverize such, unequal to the synthe-
>   sis,
> the organism by which they move and breathe their
>   particulars:
> and the symbol won't do, either: it differentiates flat
> into muffling fact it tried to stabilize beyond[.]

Although the language of this passage is almost entirely abstract, its syntax has a quirky, darting

movement that distinguishes it from mere prosaic exposition.

But while Ammons displays an unusual appetite for philosophical abstraction in his poems (perhaps the only contemporary poet to approach him in this regard is William Bronk, whose diction is more austerely Heideggerian), he is also able to synthesize the various abstract terms he employs into a few simple spatial figures, chiefly the circle and the sphere. From Emerson's circles to Dickinson's circumferences to Hart Crane's curveship and beyond, American poets have been obsessed with tropes of circularity, but none has elaborated them more fully than Ammons. Key terms in his lexicon are *center* and *periphery,* which correspond in his imaginative system to unifying abstraction and diverse particularity. For Ammons there is a clear trade-off between these mental positions: centers offer a sense of unity and completeness, yet are strangely vacant, while peripheries are partial, accidental, but full of rich detail. Expanding the circle into a three-dimensional form opens a further spatial tension between surface and core, and this figure governs Ammons's book-length poem *Sphere: The Form of a Motion,* which explores the proposition that "a single dot of light, traveling, can memorize the sphere" — that consciousness, by staying in constant motion, can create provisional maps of a totality that exceeds its grasp.

Motion is the most crucial concept of all for Ammons, binding together his various conceptual schemes and establishing vital connections between thematic vision and poetic form. The word *motion* is conspicuous throughout Ammons's poetry and appears in the subtitle of *Sphere: The Form of a Motion;* in the title of a section in *Sumerian Vistas* (1987), "Motion's Holdings"; and in the title of his most recent prose collection, *Set in Motion: Essays and Interviews* (1996). Ammons's commitment to the principle of motion, manifested at all levels of his work from the physical to the verbal and the intellectual, is what rescues him from the schematizing tendencies of his own mind, his propensity for dichotomies, diagrams, and other static constructs — what he calls in "Corsons Inlet" the "straight lines, blocks, boxes, binds / of thought." No idea or proposition can be allowed to stand for more than a moment; all thought must be dissolved in movement, in the continual shiftings and siftings of mind and world. Ammons consciously explores the tradition that reaches back to Emerson, who in "Self Reliance" valorized not "the moment of repose" but "the shooting of a gulf, the darting to an aim." Ammons's rich understanding of natural motions,

Dust jacket for Ammons's 1965 poem, a verse diary in which he
attempts to record experience without imposing artificial
boundaries (courtesy of the Lilly Library,
Indiana University)

with nature more emblematically evoked by Whitman's title *Leaves of Grass* (1855). Despite the fixed nature of the poem on the page, the simple fact for Ammons is that poems move. He aims to intensify and orchestrate the movement of his words by various means, including his inventive use of spacing; restless shifts of topic, pace, and tone; supple syntax that casts off and doubles back incessantly; and most distinctively through his eschewal of conventional punctuation in favor of the colon, which he employs as an all-purpose connective mark much as Dickinson used the dash. The most significant effect of Ammons's colons is to suppress all full stops in favor of continuous forward momentum, while still allowing coherent grammatical units to emerge. In reading Ammons one may miss the sense of completion that periods supply, but in its place one gets a powerful impression of mind, language, and nature in constant flux, sweeping beyond each momentary shape they assume. The provisional, ongoing quality that has been so central to American poetry from Emerson to Stevens receives its most vivid and intimate realization in Ammons's verse, which abandons the very structure of the sentence in its effort to body forth motion.

But while motion often serves in his work to bridge or blur antinomies, Ammons insists that motion must itself be understood in relation to its opposite, stillness. If motion is the vital adhesive principle of nature, mind, and poems alike, stillness allows for the contemplative attention that can synthesize the particulars of movement into a sphere-like whole. Ammons conceives of the relation between motion and stillness in his poems as a temporal one, writing in his essay "A Poem Is a Walk" (*Set in Motion*) that a poem "is a motion to no-motion, to the still point of contemplation and deep realization." The poem moves through time, space, and the reader's awareness until it comes to its last word; then it takes on an autonomy that carries it beyond language, making it apprehensible as an object in its own right. Ammons has developed many formulations for this complex and subtle understanding of how poems work (which bears a family resemblance to Frost's account in his short essay "The Figure a Poem Makes"). In a 1991 interview with Timothy Muskat, Ammons speaks of a poem's movement in terms of a distinction between exposition and disposition, where exposition involves the linear, discursive unfolding of the poem through time, while disposition names the state of completion and repose toward which it moves: "as a disposition [the poem] is similar to any other thing in the world — say, a stone, about which you can write a

however, sets him apart, allowing him to adduce a wealth of evidence for the dynamism of the physical universe while providing him with an inexhaustible supply of metaphors for the less tangible motions of consciousness. This pervasive sense of movement ultimately breaks down all static divisions between spirit and matter, self and world, inside and outside. In his long poem "Hibernaculum" from *Collected Poems, 1951–1971* Ammons proclaims "my little faith, such as it is, is that mind and / nature grew out of a common node and so must obey common / motions." Where Emerson posits a transcendent spirit, or Oversoul, that unites Me and Not-Me, Ammons peels away the transcendentalist metaphysics to expose the immanent reality of motion itself as the force that joins mind to nature.

Motion also serves as a key principle of form and style in Ammons's poetry, allowing him to claim for his work the kind of intimate involvement

great many intelligent papers, though the stone remains silent. . . . [The poem] becomes closed into a disposition that is an untelling, leaving it open and inexhaustible." For all his zest and facility as a talker, Ammons remains fundamentally skeptical of the powers of discourse to circumscribe the real, and so values the poem for its untelling as much as its telling. The title of one poem, "Giving Up Words with Words," collected in *Lake Effect Country* (1983), indicates a fundamental project of his poetry, to move through language to a condition of pure being beyond human speech.

Ammons's use of the stone as a trope for the poem's integrity suggests a key metaphoric polarity that recurs throughout his work and takes as its basic form the relation between stone and wind. The stone is the physical embodiment of stillness – mute, inorganic, singular, and self-contained; magnified it becomes a mountain, a signature image for Ammons. In "Mountain Talk" from *Uplands* (1970), one of many poems in which the poet converses with a rocky eminence, he is envious of the mountain's stability:

> I was going along a dusty highroad
> when the mountain
> across the way
> turned me to its silence:
> oh I said how come
> I don't know your
> massive symmetry and rest:
> nevertheless, said the mountain,
> would you want
> to be
> lodged here with
> a changeless prospect, risen
> to an unalterable view:
> so I went on
> counting my numberless fingers.

The human desire for inhuman certainty and repose must be given voice, but for Ammons the movement, volatility, and inexhaustible variety of experience, wonderfully figured by the poet's "numberless fingers," are finally to be preferred to a mountainous fixity. In the dialectic of motion and stillness that governs Ammons's poetry, motion necessarily has the last word; for while the individual poem may end in stillness, the motion that made it goes on making new poems, carving out new mountains.

Wind is the other privileged trope in Ammons's landscape, signifying a pure motion without visible form or body. In *Garbage* Ammons speaks of "the dispositional axis from stone to wind," a phrase that summarizes both his poetics

and his cosmology. Ammons's wind is just as voluble as his mountains are; indeed in his earlier poems it serves as a kind of muse or guide, initiating the poet into the mysteries of motion, change, and destruction. At the beginning of *The Prelude* (1805) William Wordsworth exclaims, "Oh there is a blessing in this gentle breeze," invoking it as an essentially benign manifestation of natural grace. Ammons heightens the Wordsworthian breeze to a violent gale, as threatening as it is potentially empowering. His first book, *Ommateum with Doxology,* is a virtual rhapsody on the themes of wind and stone. In the blasted, arid landscapes of these first poems, Ammons begins to explore the concerns that will continue to obsess him for the next forty years.

Remarkably self-assured for a beginner, Ammons in *Ommateum with Doxology* shows no hint of the dominant verse fashions of the 1950s. Written in a lean and supple free verse whose shape bends and swerves unpredictably, most of these poems take the form of brief but highly charged narratives in which the first-person speaker figures as aspiring prophet and thwarted quester. They are thus quite self-consciously poems of inception and vocation, yet are already painfully aware of the limitations placed upon all human enterprise. The first poem of the book, "So I Said I Am Ezra" (like many in *Ommateum* titled with its first line), explicitly announces both the ambition and frustration that underlie the volume as a whole:

> So I said I am Ezra
> and the wind whipped my throat
> gaming for the sounds of my voice
>   I listened to the wind
> go over my head and up into the night
> Turning to the sea I said
>   I am Ezra
> but there were no echoes from the waves
> The words were swallowed up
>   in the voice of the surf
> or leaping over the swells
> lost themselves oceanward[.]

The poem continues for another fifteen lines to narrate the confrontation between poet and sea, ending with the figure of Ezra going "out into the night" and dissolving himself in its turbulent elements. The persona of Ezra, invoked in several other poems from *Ommateum with Doxology,* seems to blend biblical prophet and visionary poet and hints at the intensity of the poet's urge toward self-transcendence. Yet all his attempts at prophecy are muffled or stifled by the forces he seeks to master, as his own voice is "swallowed up" by the immeasurably greater voice of the sea. At the beginning of his career Ammons showed none of the easy, relaxed intercourse with natural energies to be found in his mature poems; his point of departure is rather the Romantic topos of a contest or agon with nature, reminding one of Whitman in "Song of Myself" (1855) crying out to the sunrise "See then whether you shall be the master!" Unlike Whitman, however, Ammons stages his own defeat, opening the way for a humbler relation to wind and sea.

The book's title refers to the compound eye of an insect, and in a brief preface Ammons expresses his commitment to the principle of perspectivism, a "many-sided view of reality" refracted through the "numberless radii of experience" (note that the figure of the circle already informs his thinking). But when set beside his later volumes *Ommateum* is perhaps most striking for its uniformity of manner, perspective, and image. With the exception of "Doxology," a strange visionary litany, the poems form an extended narrative sequence whose protagonist, the elusive Ezra, wanders through time and space seeking a "universal word." His search carries him from Strasbourg in the plague year of 1349 to Antioch in 1098, from whaleboat to piney woods to desert plateaus, but the book's primary landscape seems to be the windswept desertlands of the Middle East, and more particularly the ancient Mesopotamian kingdom of Sumer, with which Ammons has had a long standing fascination (his *Sumerian Vistas* was published thirty-two years later). For the most part Ammons shows little interest in human culture and history, preferring the otherness of natural systems; what draws him to Sumer is precisely that it marks the initial moment of differentiation between the human and the natural, city and wilderness. One poem in *Ommateum with Doxology* invokes the Sumerian hero Gilgamesh, protagonist of the oldest known epic, which predates the Old Testament by many centuries. Ammons's first book is a sustained attempt to recover an ancient, shamanistic vision in which the human, the divine, and the elemental are more immediately interwoven than in later stages of culture, as religious orthodoxy sets in.

Motion is already a dominant motif in these early poems, reflected in their restless syntax, the absence of any punctuation, and the heavy preponderance of gerunds — especially at the beginnings of poems, where they enforce a sense of continuous process extending before and after the individual poem. The words *turning, merging, coming,* and *dropping* initiate poems and are followed by similar words such as *whirling, leaping,* and *bristling.* It is important to note, however, that all this motion occurs within a predominantly narrative framework, as part of a represented scene rather than a property of the poem itself. Moreover, the kind of motion that structures *Ommateum with Doxology* as a whole is strongly end-directed; its model is the quest, and while the protagonist never seems to arrive at his goal, the desire for attainment can be felt as a driving force throughout. So intense a commitment to the mythopoeic modes of quest and prophecy, when combined with Ammons's innate skepticism and resistance to dogma, could only lead to the failure prefigured in "So I Said I Am Ezra." During the next ten years Ammons would manage to work free from this early, impossibly ambitious stance, discovering a more relaxed, less focused kind of motion whose characteristic form is that of a walk.

The poems written in the decade after *Ommateum* show Ammons consciously expanding his range. The life-and-death urgency that characterized many of the Ezra poems gives way to a more casual, even playful tone. First-person narrative poems become more anecdotal, less mythically grand; their protagonist is no longer a quester but a prospector, unsure of what he may find but open to all contingencies. Even the colloquies with wind and mountain become downright friendly, as in "The Wide Land" from *Coursons Inlet:* "the wind said / You know I'm / the result of / forces beyond my control / I don't hold it against you / I said / It's all right I understand." Ammons's appetite for natural particulars starts to make itself felt as well; his landscapes are no longer stark and empty, but alive with interesting details of topography and vegetation, as in "Possibility Along a Line of Difference" (*Uplands*):

> At the crustal
> discontinuity
> I went down and
> walked
> on the gravel bottom,
> head below gully rims
>
> tufted with
> clumpgrass and
> through-free roots[.]

Another important poem, "Gravelly Run," initiates a long series of topographical poems that includes "Corsons Inlet," "Cascadilla Falls," and "Triphammer Bridge," all named for some particular place whose spirit is lovingly caught in words. In the late 1950s Ammons also began to explore childhood memories in poems such as "Hardweed Path Going," "Silver," and "Mule Song," evoking a pastoral world of animals and family entirely absent from his first book.

But perhaps the most significant development in this period is Ammons's abandonment of the dramatized first-person speaker and the consequent opening up of formal possibilities. No longer constrained by narrative, Ammons began finding ways to build motion into the structure of his poems. In a series of numbered poems in *Coursons Inlet* under the collective title "Hymn" Ammons's speaker addresses an unspecified "You" that can be understood as God or, more secularly, the principle of motion and life in all things. The first poem in the series wavers between Pascalian extremes, alternately focusing on the microscopic and cosmic manifestations of the divine, and ends with a moving suspension that points to the central dialectic of Ammons's poetry: "and if I find you I must go out deep into your / far resolutions / and if I find you I must stay here with the separate leaves." Another crucial transitional poem from *Coursons Inlet,* "Prodigal," substitutes the more impersonal phrase "the mind" for "I" and in its closing lines definitively announces the change of course that will lead Ammons to his best work:

> the mind whirls, short of the unifying
> reach, short of the heat
>   to carry that forging:
>   after the visions of these losses, the spent
> seer, delivered to wastage, risen
>   into ribs, consigns knowledge to
>   approximation, order to the vehicle
> of change, and fumbles blind in blunt innocence
>   toward divine, terrible love.

The longing for a totalizing knowledge or "universal word" that fueled the questing of *Ommateum with Doxology* is here disowned in favor of approximation, change, and love, three principles that govern the more serene and provisional poetics of Ammons's later work. Yet as the penultimate word *terrible* suggests, the poet remains conscious of what he has given up, and the pain of that concession to mortal limits can also be felt in much of the poetry to come.

The more detached, declarative tenor of this passage marks another shift with far-reaching consequences, as Ammons began to develop a didactic voice to supplement his narrative and descriptive styles. No longer representing himself as an acolyte or thwarted seeker, he now assumes the guise of a skeptical sage, possessing knowledge yet open to discovery. As a result his poems grow more expansive and digressive, better able to gather and syn-

Dust jacket for Ammons's 1966 book of poems (courtesy of the Lilly Library, Indiana University)

thesize facts and concepts; the poet's calmly ruminative voice assigns all things their places. This voice emerges most fully in "Corsons Inlet," the title poem of Ammons's third book. The poem knits together many of the threads Ammons had been following in the ten years since *Ommateum with Doxology* appeared. Its loose, assimilative form and easy blending of concrete description and abstract pronouncement owe everything to its use of a seaside walk both as its narrative frame and formal model.

In his 1967 essay "A Poem Is a Walk," Ammons offers a series of analogies between poetry and the motion of walking:

> First, each makes use of the whole body, involvement is total, both mind and body. . . . A second resemblance is that every walk is unreproducible, as is every poem. . . . The third resemblance . . . is that each turns, one or more times, and eventually *re*turns. . . . The fourth resemblance has to do with the motion common to poems

and walks. . . . There is only one way to know it and that is to enter it. (ellipses added)

"Corsons Inlet" illustrates these insights, not simply describing the poet's walk in a detached, journalistic way, but capturing and reproducing its fine interplay of thought and perception with precision:

> risk is full: every living thing in
> siege: the demand is life, to keep life: the small
> white blacklegged egret, how beautiful, quietly stalks
>   and spears
>   the shallows, darts to shore
>   to stab – what? I couldn't
>   see against the black mudflats – a frightened
>   fiddler crab?

A generalized sense of risk gives way to a sharply realized instance of natural violence as Ammons's language evokes the rhythm and cadence of perception: the initial appearance of the egret in a long, lyrical line that incorporates the spontaneous exclamation "how beautiful," followed by a sudden flurry of movement as the lines contract and move to the right, culminating with a moment of perceptual confusion that reminds readers of the speaker's presence within the scene he describes. Ammons's fluid style effortlessly integrates reflection and mimesis, creating a powerful sense of both mind and world in motion.

A crucial difference between a walk and a quest is that the former is open-ended, not committed in advance to a single outcome. The walk thus figures the kind of curious, pragmatic, experimental stance that Ammons takes up in his mature work, always ready for revelations yet never hurrying them along. The closing lines of "Corsons Inlet" offer a memorable formulation of this attitude:

>   I will try
>   to fasten into order enlarging grasps of disorder,
>   widening
>   scope, but enjoying the freedom that
>   Scope eludes my grasp, that there is no finality of vision,
>   that I have perceived nothing completely,
>   that tomorrow a new walk is a new walk.

The irony, of course, is that these assertions of inconclusiveness are offered in a tone of magisterial assurance. As a didactic poet who believes that human knowledge is a fragile order at best, Ammons often finds himself in this dilemma, yet seems to take it in stride.

As if to illustrate the assertion in the last line of "Corsons Inlet," Ammons a few days later wrote the poem "Saliences," based on a second walk in the same locale but quite different from the previous poem in form, style, and substance. Focusing on his old nemesis the wind, Ammons seeks a final accommodation with the powers of change and dissolution:

> earth brings to grief
> much in an hour that sang, leaped, swirled,
> yet keeps a round
>   quiet turning,
> beyond loss or gain,
> beyond concern for the separate reach.

The turbulent vision of natural process at the heart of both "Corsons Inlet" and "Saliences" parallels many of the concerns of the relatively new science of chaos, one of whose founders, the physicist Mitchell Feigenbaum, has been Ammons's colleague at Cornell since the 1970s. The two men share a fascination with the behavior of systems too complex to be mapped, governed by constantly shifting variables and an intricate, fractal geometry. The image of a shoreline, with its minute irregularities, serves both Ammons and chaos scientists as an illustration of the way natural forms resist linear measurement. "In nature there are few sharp lines," Ammons declares in "Corsons Inlet," and he goes on to evoke a variety of "disorderly orders," "manifold events of sand," and topographical transitions, leading to the marvelous spectacle of

>   thousands of tree swallows
>   gathering for flight:
>   an order held
>   in constant change: a congregation
>   rich with entropy: nevertheless, separable, noticeable
>   as one event,
>   not chaos[.]

Complexity is not chaos; on this point, too, the misleadingly named chaos theorists agree with Ammons. To apprehend nature adequately means recognizing patterns too multiform and volatile for our minds to grasp – what Ammons in his poem calls "the possibility of rule as the sum of rulelessness." Ammons arrived at his poetic understanding of complex systems some ten years before Feigenbaum and others gave it a scientific basis, reminding us that poetry and science often reach the same place by different routes, with poetry perhaps the more light-footed of the two.

Having developed in "Corsons Inlet" and "Saliences" an eloquent, capacious voice, mingling largeness and precision, chattiness and lyricism, Ammons in the late 1960s had essentially found

*Dust jacket for Ammons's second book-length poem, in which he
often alludes to Walt Whitman and* Leaves of Grass *in
self-conscious rivalry (courtesy of Lilly Library,
Indiana University)*

himself as a poet. Henceforth it is difficult to speak of his career in terms of progression or development. His work shows a remarkable consistency in the ensuing decades; every two or three years he published a new book, each with its mix of slighter poems and masterpieces. An intriguing feature of Ammons's work beginning in the mid 1960s has been his tendency to write poems of dramatically varied length, as suggested by his titles *Selected Longer Poems* (1980) and *The Really Short Poems of A. R. Ammons* (1990). More than any other poet of his generation, Ammons has committed himself to exploring extremes of scale, finding in the contrast between concision and expansion a formal counterpart to the philosophical antinomies of one and many, universal and particular, continuity and salience.

Ammons's interest in the long poem was first hinted at in 1960 when he published a series of numbered cantos in magazines and in a privately printed chapbook. This audacious emulation of Pound proved to be a false start, however, and these numbered poems were later included under separate titles in *Expressions of Sea Level.* His impulse toward a sustained utterance was realized spectacularly a few years later when he published *Tape for the Turn of the Year* (1965), a 205-page verse diary written on a single narrow spool of adding machine tape.

Tape for the Turn of the Year is Ammons's first and most extreme attempt to write a poem that plots the continuum of experience and reflection without imposing artificial boundaries on it. Its only divisions are created by the notation of dates. Threading the tape into his typewriter on 6 December, the poet announces his resolve to keep typing until it is full, and the scrolling seamlessness of the tape figures the continuity of life, which is faithfully recorded in all its phases from the mundane to the epiphanic. (Ammons eventually compromised his principle of inclusion, editing out the dullest stretches after the tape had been completed.) As he types,

Ammons periodically describes the poem's coiling progress into a wastebasket set beneath his desk, so *Tape for the Turn of the Year* is quite literally the record of its own composition, its motion through time, space, and typewriter. This conception of the poem-as-process first came into vogue in the 1950s under the influence of Charles Olson's famous essay "Projective Verse." Unlike Olson, however, Ammons remains committed to mimesis, the representation of things external to mind and language; his aim in *Tape for the Turn of the Year* is to register reality and the making of the poem as simultaneous streams that continually impinge on one another.

If *Tape for the Turn of the Year* is flawed, as some readers have felt, this may be due less to its underlying principles than the physical narrowness of its format, which limits the range of prosodic and rhetorical effects available. In poems such as "Corsons Inlet" Ammons makes use of the entire page as a verbal canvas, but in *Tape for the Turn of the Year* he is confined to a width of three inches. The result is a certain diffuseness, as Ammons cheerfully acknowledges toward the end of the poem:

> I've given
> you my
> emptiness: it may
> not be unlike
>   your emptiness:
>   in voyages, there
>   are wide reaches
>   of water
>   with no islands:
> . . . .
>   I've given
> you long
> uninteresting walks
> so you could experience
> vacancy[.]

While these lines rightly suggest that the prosaic has a necessary share in a poem that aspires to take down all of experience, it is nonetheless hard not to feel that *Tape for the Turn of the Year* suffers from too high a proportion of filler, though it also contains many moments of high lyricism. In the end it may be an overly literal attempt to prove that everything passing through consciousness can find its rightful place in the poem.

Ammons gradually refined his approach to the long poem, working to retain the fluidity and inclusiveness of *Tape for the Turn of the Year* while imparting a stronger sense of structure and vision to the whole. As he puts it in "Summer Session 1968" – a thirteen-page poem with slightly wider margins than *Tape for the Turn of the Year,* which it otherwise

resembles – "the problem is / how / to keep shape and flow." One partial solution he developed was to break his discourse into uniform stanzas. Ammons first explores this technique in three middle-length poems from *Collected Poems, 1951–1971*: "Essay on Poetics," which is arranged primarily in three-line strophes; "Extremes and Moderations," cast in groups of four lines; and "Hibernaculum," organized into numbered sections of three three-line stanzas. These experiments culminate in his second book-length poem, *Sphere: The Form of a Motion,* considered by many to be Ammons's finest long poem.

Made up of 155 sections of four three-line strophes, *Sphere,* like *Tape for the Turn of the Year,* shows Ammons's interest in the process of composition, but while he again occasionally notes the date in the poem to mark the passage of time, it is far less diary-like in tone and content than his first book-length poem. *Sphere* touches on a dizzying array of topics, yet all are subordinated to the governing image of the sphere, a traditional metaphor of wholeness and perfection that gives the poem the kind of unifying core that *Tape for the Turn of the Year* lacked but also allows for a great deal of freedom. The poem moves restlessly from one point of interest to another in its effort to engage the reader:

>   this measure moves
> to attract and hold attention: when one is not holding
>   one,
> that is a way of holding: dip in anywhere, go on until
>   the
>
> attractions fail: I angle for the self in you that can be
> held, had in a thorough understanding: not to per-
>   suade you,
> enlighten you, not necessarily to delight you, but to
>   hold
>
> you[.]

As these lines illustrate, Ammons in *Sphere* adopts a Whitman-like stance toward his audience, imploring, seducing, cajoling, but working always to maintain the kind of contact Whitman often figured as an embrace. *Sphere* is full of echoes and invocations of the good gray poet, including one particularly egregious pun: "I am not a whit manic / to roam the globe." Whitman's influence is reflected most clearly in the poem's democratic aspirations. Where *Tape for the Turn of the Year* restricted itself primarily to the poet's own experience, *Sphere* is more expansive both in format and in scope, continually showing an awareness both of its audience and the larger human world beyond. It may be read as Ammons's attempt to extrapolate a working ethics from his ongoing obsessions with the polarities of one and many, center and periphery, identity and difference. More specifically *Sphere* is a meditation on the idea of America as a place where unity and diversity might potentially achieve their ideal calibration:

> with the sense of the continuous
>
> running through and staying all the discretions, differences
> diminished into the common tide of feelings, so that difference
> cannot harden into aggression or hate fail to move with the
>
> ongoing, the differences not submerged but resting clear at
> the surface, as the surface, and not rising above the surface
> so as to become more visible and edgy than the continuum:
>
> a united, capable poem, a united, capable mind, a united capable
> nation, and a united nations! capable, flexible, yielding,
> accommodating, seeking the good of all in the good of each[.]

The undisguised utopianism of these lines is tempered by Ammons's familiar theoretical vocabulary, which gives conceptual rigor to what might otherwise seem a sentimental evocation of universal harmony and love. As the last strophe suggests, *Sphere* is a poem of microcosms and macrocosms, tracing an essential configuration up the ladder of forms from poem to world. If the poem seems idealistic in its faith that the same laws obtain at all levels of being, it nonetheless articulates a powerful vision of things continually flickering between oneness and manyness.

But *Sphere* is not a poem of pure theory; it also contains many fine lyrical and descriptive episodes, such as this comic revision of the myth of Danaë, ravished by Jove in a shower of gold:

> this afternoon I thought Jove had come to get me: I walked
> into a corridor of sunlight swimming showering with turning shoals
> of drift pollen and not yet knowing it was pollen thought perhaps I

> was being taken or beamed aboard but saw over the roof the high swags
> of the blue spruce swaying and felt stabilized from wonder:
> I would still rather beget (though I can't, apparently) than be
> begotten upon, I think I'm almost sure, but I don't know that a vague
> coming of a shimmery gold floating would be so bad: I sneezed: my
> eyes watered: the intimacy was sufficient: nothing is separate[.]

This wonderful mixture of the sublime and the raunchy, part dirty joke and part epiphany, complete with a passing allusion to *Star Trek,* shows Ammons's gift for balancing high and low at its most effective. Passages like this, of which there are many more, prevent *Sphere* from becoming a purely abstract disquisition on moral geometry, giving it a texture and variety that succeed in the poet's stated aim of "holding" the reader. As Ammons writes toward the end of his earlier long poem "Hibernaculum," "if things don't add up they must interest at every moment." Unlike other poets whose exploration of the long poem seems more programmatically based in ideas of process and self-reflexivity, Ammons never loses sight of his primary obligation to be *interesting,* to offer his readers not just language but pleasure, surprise, and insight.

Ammons's next long poem marks another departure in form and procedure. Although in appearance *The Snow Poems* (1977) consists of a series of individual poems, unnumbered and titled with their first lines, Ammons considers the volume to be a single long poem, perhaps because it was composed once again on rolls of paper within a restricted period of time. (The rolls apparently varied in width, as reflected in the changing line lengths over the course of the book.) The organization of *The Snow Poems* into apparently discrete poems derives partly from the fact that during its composition Ammons was also doing a great deal of painting and liked to alternate between poems and paintings. Ammons is more casual and digressive in *The Snow Poems* than in *Sphere,* favoring erratic and whimsical arrangements of lines, sometimes in double columns or emblematic shapes, once even making doodles out of various typographic symbols. In the often entertaining *The Snow Poems* Ammons took a step back from the high seriousness of *Sphere,* returning to the journalistic mode of *Tape for the Turn*

*Dust jacket for the 1977 book that Ammons considers
one long poem*

of the Year, though with a greater sense of playfulness.

Ammons's 1987 volume *Sumerian Vistas* opens with a forty-three-page poem, "The Ridge Farm," which consists of fifty-one numbered, untitled sections of varying length and format. If *Sphere* shows Ammons in his Whitmanian phase, "The Ridge Farm" is his most Thoreauvian work. In keeping with his title Ammons is attuned to the particulars of place and landscape, including in the poem many accounts of walks and vistas, trees and streams, as well as reflections on consciousness, writing, and pedagogy. Some of the playful self-indulgence that characterized Ammons's previous long poems has been restrained, and the result is a more objective, serene vision of the world, lavish with natural detail and for the most part untainted by human presence.

In his fourth book-length poem, *Garbage,* Ammons returns to the human scene at its tawdri-

est, though with his serenity intact. His most ambitious poem since *Sphere, Garbage* constructs an alternative mythos, substituting for the clean, Platonic abstraction of the sphere the messy, pungent concreteness of a huge garbage dump glimpsed from I-95 in Florida. As if challenging himself to envision even the most repugnant of man-made spectacles as an emblem of order, Ammons finds in the mountain of trash slowly smoldering at its peak a manifestation of what he terms "the spindle of energy," the "disposition from the heavy to the light," the ongoing transformation of matter into spirit:

> the
> garbage spreader gets off his bulldozer and
>
> approaches the fire: he stares into it as into
> eternity, the burning edge of beginning and
>
> ending, the catalyst of going and becoming,
> and all thoughts of his paycheck and beerbelly,

even all thoughts of his house and family and
the long way he has come to be worthy of his

watch, fall away, and he stands in the presence
of the momentarily everlasting, the air about
him sacrosanct, purged of the crawling vines
and dense vegetation of desire[.]

It is no coincidence that *Garbage* comes from a man
older than sixty-five; indeed, the start of the poem
includes a brief discourse concerning how to get by
on Social Security by eating boiled soybeans. As
Ammons acknowledges, the aging body itself belongs to the material realm symbolized by the garbage heap. Despite its humor, this is Ammons's
deepest, most sorrowful poem, shot through with
intimations of mortality but informed as well by
what Wordsworth called "a wise passiveness."

Garbage was also composed on a paper roll
slightly wider than the one used in *Tape for the Turn of
the Year.* Divided into eighteen numbered sections,
each several pages in length, the poem is cast mainly
in two-line strophes, with an occasional three-line
stanza thrown in for variety, producing an airier effect
than the three- and four-line blocks Ammons had used
in earlier poems. The result is the most readable of all
Ammons's long poems, full of brilliantly written narrative vignettes, comical rantings, and a densely tex-
tured sense of the material world. The poet's usual
concerns with sex and death find frequent expression, at times juxtaposed to startling effect, as when
Ammons segues from a bawdy, cartoonish portrait
of the commissioner of sanitation and his extremely
large wife to a moving account of a friend's funeral,
within the space of a single line:

> her husband loves
> every bit of her, every bite (bit) round enough to get
> to: and wherever his dinky won't reach, he finds
> something else that will: I went up the road
> a piece this morning at ten to Pleasant Grove
> for the burial of Ted's ashes[.]

Lust and grief, absurdity and pathos are held in
precarious balance here, with Ammons's trademark
colon serving as a makeshift fulcrum. The poem is
full of such non sequiturs, yet the idiomatic even-
ness of Ammons's tone is so engaging that one is
carried along effortlessly. Like all his long poems,
Garbage is a study in motion, an exercise in making
language behave like a fluid rather than a solid; but
that verbal flux still allows local meanings and perceptions to define themselves. Ammons's long poems
succeed by balancing process and substance, assuming "the form of a motion" while offering as well the
content of a vision.

While producing his series of major long
works, Ammons has also written many short lyrics,
ranging in length from two to two hundred lines. In
poems of twelve or more lines Ammons has tended
toward either the celebratory or the elegiac, working
to create the effect of a single strong lyric gesture
carrying steadily through from the first word of the
poem to last. (His colons aid in this aim, since they
effectively make every poem one long sentence.)
Perhaps the most purely rhapsodic of these poems is
the much anthologized "The City Limits," which
first appeared in *Briefings: Poems Small and Easy*
(1971):

> When you consider the radiance, that it does not with-
>   hold
> itself but pours its abundance without selection into
>   every
> nook and cranny not overhung or hidden; when you
>   consider
> . . . .
> the abundance of such resource as illuminates the
>   glow-blue
>
> bodies and gold-skeined wings of flies swarming the
>   dumped
> guts of a natural slaughter or the coil of shit and in no
> way winces from its storms of generosity; when you
>   consider
>
> that air or vacuum, snow or shale, squid or wolf, rose
>   or lichen,
> each is accepted into as much light as it will take, then
> the heart moves roomier, the man stands and looks
>   about, the
>
> leaf does not increase itself above the grass, and the
>   dark
> work of the deepest cells is of a tune with May bushes
> and fear lit by the breadth of such calmly turns to
>   praise.

The impetus for this great poem may come from
a line in Emerson's *Nature*: "There is no object
so foul that intense light will not make beautiful." Like many of Ammons's poems in the high
style, "The City Limits" is written in the three-
line strophes of *Sphere,* which owe something to
Wallace Stevens's meditative tercets. With its
calm, sermonlike declamations and vivid imagery
the poem is certainly one of Ammons's finest lyric
achievements, confirming that the rhetoric of Romanticism, far from a historical relic, can still be a
life-strengthening force.

Another major poem, "Easter Morning," also
takes up the language of Romanticism, though in a
more elegiac key than "The City Limits":

I have a life that did not become,
that turned aside and stopped,
astonished:
I hold it in me like a pregnancy or
as on my lap a child
not to grow or grow old but dwell on[.]

In the first instance the poem grows out of the haunting memory of Ammons's brother who died in infancy; but the trope of the dead child within the self also makes the poem a tragic revision of Wordsworth's "Intimations of Immortality from Recollections of Early Childhood" (1807).

Returning to his scene of origins, the poet finds his extended family gathered in the graveyard and reflects on the unfulfillment of the children gone without trace, the lost lives that failed to perpetuate themselves:

I stand on the stump
of a child, whether myself
or my little brother who died, and
yell as far as I can, I cannot leave this place, for
for me it is the dearest and the worst,
it is life nearest to life which is
life lost: it is my place where
I must stand and fail,
calling attention with tears
to the branches not lofting
boughs into space, to the barren
air that holds the world that was my world[.]

In the poem's closing movement he recovers some of the tranquility he has always taken from natural motion, finding in the spectacle of two eagles coasting and wheeling

a dance sacred as the sap in
the trees, permanent in its descriptions
as the ripples round the brook's
ripplestone: fresh as this particular
flood of burn breaking across us now
from the sun.

"Easter Morning" is perhaps the most traditional of all Ammons's extended lyrics, yet its phased movement from memory to grief to consolation is articulated with a boldness and originality that make the poem more than a simple rehearsal of romantic patterns. A poem like this simultaneously rewrites and renews its poetic sources, keeping a major tradition as fresh and living as the eagles' dance.

Not all Ammons's short poems are first-person lyrics or second-person declamations. Less recognized is his mastery of narrative, apparent in "Parting" from *A Coast of Trees*:

She was already lean when
a stroke or two slapped
her face like drawn
claw prints: akilter, she
ate less and

sat too much on the edge
of beds looking a width too
wide out of windows:
she lessened: getting
out for a good day, she sat

on the bench still and
thin as a porch post:
the children are all
off, she would think, but a
minute later,

startle, where are the children,
as if school had let
out: her husband watched
her till loosened away himself
for care: then,

seeming to know but never
quite sure, she was put in
a slightly less hopeful
setting: she watched her
husband tremble in to call

and shoot up high head-bent
eyes: her mind
flashed clear through, she was
sure of it, she had seen
that one before: her husband

longed to say goodbye or else
hello, but the room stiffened
as if two lovers had just caught
on sight, every move rigid
misfire in that perilous fire.

Much of the impact of this poem has to do with its inventive and surprising diction. The words *akilter, lessened, startle, loosened, tremble, stiffened,* and *misfire* vividly hasten the reader to the poem's poignant conclusion, as husband and wife face each other for the last time with all the intensity and apprehension of new lovers. Even so subtle a touch as the repetition of "fire" in the last line, a purposeful stutter, helps to evoke the jerky, terrified movement, both inward and outward, of the old man and his strickened wife. The economy and precision of this poem are matched only by its empathy; with a handful of other poems "Parting" powerfully refutes the claim that Ammons is too absorbed in nature to notice and record the lives of his fellow humans.

Although his shortest poems – those of fifty words or fewer – have been sprinkled throughout most of his collections, Ammons presented them as a distinct category of his work in the compilation *The Really Short Poems of A. R. Ammons*. The peculiar structure of this book may shed an olique light on Ammons's technique in crafting these poetic miniatures. By his own account, Ammons's procedure in assembling the book involved alphabetizing the poems not by title but by first line, dividing them into odd and even numbered sequences, reversing the order of the even-numbered group, and rearranging the sequences into an extended chiasmus or ABBA pattern, a form that is followed almost obsessively in the poems themselves. (To be accurate, Ammons violates his organizing principle at one point in order to segregate a frivolous set of poems on pages 125–143 that would otherwise distract from more-serious efforts.) Many of the poems are quite explicitly chiastic in structure, such as "Mirrorment":

[A]   [B]
Birds are flowers flying
  [B]   [A]
And flowers perched birds.

Another example is "Small Song":

The reeds give
[A]
way to the

[B]
wind and give
  [B]   [A]
the wind away[.]

A third example is the well-known "Reflective":

I found a
 [A]
weed
that had a

[B]
mirror in it
and that
mirror

looked in at
 [B]
a mirror

in

me that
had a

[A]
weed in it[.]

The first of these poems is a mere figurative jeu d'esprit, the second a haikulike bit of word painting that plays on the several meanings of "give away," the third a more profound meditation on the relation between observer and object. All three poems repeat in their internal structures the pattern that governs the book as a whole. The chiasmus is a figure of symmetry and closure and as such stands at the opposite extreme from the figures of open-ended movement and process that dominate Ammons's longer poems; if the latter emphasize the principle of motion in his poetics, these "really short poems" exemplify the complementary principle of stillness. Because each can easily be grasped in its entirety, one experiences them as instantaneous constructs, existing not in temporal succession but all at once. They are poems of the sharply focused moment rather than the fluid continuum.

Yet motion remains a presence in these poems, in however minimal a form. Many of them resemble the kind of perceptual snapshots in which William Carlos Williams specialized, but Ammons brings a more cinematic eye to the form, as in "Trigger":

I almost step on
a huge spider:
it stalls and
disperses
like oil-beads on water,
baby spiders
shedding radially
till a skinny
mother hardly
shades the
spent center.

Like many others, this poem blends perceptual clarity with subtly implied abstraction. Here the underlying scheme is chiefly carried by the words *radially* and *center,* reminding the reader of Ammons's unending fascination with circles. Another study in radiation, "Winter Scene," posits a very different relation between center and periphery:

There is now not a single
leaf on the cherry tree:
except when the jay

Dust jacket for the 1981 book that includes "Easter Morning,"
Ammons's poem about the death of his brother in infancy
(courtesy of the Lilly Library, Indiana University)

plummets in, lights, and,
in pure clarity, squalls:
then every branch
quivers and
breaks out in blue leaves.

Even in his shortest poems Ammons is able to convey the sense of complex interdependence that poems like "Corsons Inlet" elaborate more fully. "For Louise and Tom Gossett" is a deft and lovely evocation of natural reciprocity:

After a creek
drink
the goldfinch
lights in

the bank willow
which
drops the brook
a yellow leaf.

Yellow leaf and yellow bird change places with perfect ease, a concrete chiasmus that schools readers in the symmetries of nature.

Side by side with these finely etched imagist poems are more openly abstract utterances like "Providence," which might be seen as an attempt to outdo Frost's "Nothing Gold Can Stay" in sheer pithiness:

To stay
bright as
if just
thought of
earth requires
only that
nothing stay[.]

Ammons takes Frost's word *stay* and puts a characteristic double spin on it, hanging his vision of glowing transience on the distinction between its transitive and intransitive uses. But perhaps the most spectacular instance of cosmic vision crammed into Zen-like nutshell is "Pebble's Story," whose text employs a vocabulary of two words:

Wearing away
wears

wearing
away away[.]

Ammons portrays in a mere eleven syllables an act of mind that might have furnished a Romantic poet with the material for an ode: loss gives way to renewal, as seen in a grain of sand. Beyond this level of concision lies that ultimate stillness he frequently invokes as the destination of his poems. If his longer, more ambitious poems lie at the core of his oeuvre, these small gems add an indispensable element of glitter to its surface. Writing them has kept Ammons attentive to the exigencies of language in its most intimate workings as well as its larger motions.

Ammons's work has sometimes been accused of coldness, a dearth of human feeling, an overemphasis on epistemology and other abstract issues. And certainly he has consistently presented himself as a solitary, a man at odds with his society and able to find peace only in isolation. But there is also a strain of communal feeling in Ammons's poetry that runs deep, animating large sections of *Sphere* and other poems but surfacing most movingly in a testamentary passage from *Garbage*. On a visit to an open-air farmers' market, Ammons finds in the gathering of old and young, healthy and afflicted, a positive image of humanity:

we at our best, not killing, scheming, abusing,
running over, tearing down, burning up: why

did invention ever bother with all this, why
does the huge beech by the water come back every

year: oh, the sweet pleasures, or even the hope
of sweet pleasures, the kiss, the letter from

someone, the word of sympathy or praise, or just
the shared settled look between us, that here

we are together, such as it is, cautious and
courageous, wily with genuine desire, policed

by how we behave, all out of eternity, into
eternity, but here now, where we make the most

of it: I settle down: I who could have used
the world share a crumb: I who wanted the sky

fall to the glint in a passing eye[.]

The farmers' market embodies the beloved community that has always been part of Ammons's vision, whether in human or inhuman form. Despite his apparent preference for natural over human affairs, Ammons remains a passionate humanist, in the best sense of that much abused word. His poetic anatomies of solitude, like Emerson's, skirt solipsism by returning always to a shared world in which presence and impermanence, sameness and difference, remain sometimes tragically and sometimes joyfully interlocked.

Interviews:

David I. Grossvogel, "Interview / A. R. Ammons," *Diacritics,* 3 (Winter 1973): 47–54;

Cynthia Haythe, "An Interview with A. R. Ammons," *Contemporary Literature,* 21 (Spring 1980): 173–190;

Richard Jackson, "Event: Corrective: Cure," in his *Acts of Mind: Conversations with Contemporary Poets* (Tuscaloosa: University of Alabama Press, 1983), pp. 32–38;

Jim Stahl, "Interview with A. R. Ammons," *Pembroke Magazine,* 18 (1986): 77–85;

Timothy Muskat, "Reasonable Shapes and Figures: A Conversation with A. R. Ammons," *Bookpress,* 1 (September 1991): 1, 5, 7;

Heather White, "A Talk with A. R. Ammons: The Dynamics of Poise," *Bookpress,* 3 (November 1993): 1, 15–16.

References:

Harold Bloom, "A. R. Ammons: The Breaking of the Vessels," in his *Figures of Capable Imagination* (New York: Seabury Press, 1976), pp. 209–233;

Bloom, "A. R. Ammons: When You Consider the Radiance," in his *The Ringers in the Tower: Studies in Romantic Tradition* (Chicago: University of Chicago Press, 1971), pp. 257–289;

Bloom, "Dark and Radiant Peripheries: Mark Strand and A. R. Ammons," in his *Figures of Capable Imagination* (New York: Seabury Press, 1976), pp. 150–168;

Bloom, "Emerson and Ammons: A Coda," *Diacritics,* 3 (Winter 1973): 45–46;

Bloom, "The New Transcendentalism: The Visionary Strain in Merwin, Ashbery, and Ammons," in his *Figures of Capable Imagination* (New York: Seabury Press, 1976), pp. 123–149;

Bloom, ed., *A. R. Ammons* (New York: Chelsea House, 1986);

Frederick Buell, "'To Be Quiet in the Hands of the Marvelous': The Poetry of A. R. Ammons," *Iowa Review,* 8, no. 1 (1977): 67–85;

Jerald Bullis, "In the Open: A. R. Ammons's Longer Poems," *Pembroke Magazine,* 18 (1986): 28–53;

Miriam Marty Clark, "The Gene, the Computer, and Information Processing in A. R. Ammons," *Twentieth Century Literature,* 38 (Spring 1990): 1–9;

Stephen B. Cushman, "A. R. Ammons, or the Rigid Lines of the Free and Easy," in his *Fictions of Form in American Poetry* (Princeton: Princeton University Press, 1993), pp. 149–190;

Denis Donoghue, "Ammons and the Lesser Celandine," *Parnassus,* 3 (Spring–Summer 1975): 19–26;

John Elder, "Poetry and the Mind's Terrain," in his *Imagining the Earth: Poetry and the Vision of Nature* (Urbana & Chicago: University of Illinois Press, 1985), pp. 136–150;

Thomas A. Fink, "The Problem of Freedom and Restriction in the Poetry of A. R. Ammons," *Modern Poetry Studies,* 11, nos. 1–2 (1982): 138–148;

Charles Fishman, "A. R. Ammons: The One Place to Dwell," *Hollins Critic,* 19 (December 1982): 2–11;

Daniel Fogel, "Toward an Ideal Raggedness: The Design of A. R. Ammons's *Hibernaculum,*" *Contemporary Poetry,* 3, no. 1 (1978): 25–37;

Roger Gilbert, "A. R. Ammons and John Ashbery: The Walk as Thinking," in his *Walks in the*

World: Representation and Experience in Modern American Poetry (Princeton: Princeton University Press, 1991), pp. 209–251;

James Hans, "Ammons and the One: Many Mechanism," in his *The Value(s) of Literature* (Albany: SUNY Press, 1990), pp. 119–156;

Alan Holder, *A. R. Ammons* (Boston: Twayne, 1978);

Richard Howard, "A. R. Ammons: The Spent Seer Consigns Order to the Vehicle of Change," in his *Alone with America: Essays on the Art of Poetry in the United States Since 1950,* enlarged edition (New York: Atheneum, 1980), pp. 1–24;

Josephine Jacobsen, "The Talk of Giants," *Diacritics,* 3 (Winter 1973): 34–39;

David Kalstone, "Ammons's Radiant Toys," *Diacritics,* 3 (Winter 1973): 13–20;

Mary Kinzie, "The Romance of the Perceptual: A. R. Ammons," in her *The Cure of Poetry in an Age of Prose: Moral Essays on the Poet's Calling* (Chicago: University of Chicago Press, 1993), pp. 105–109;

David Lehman, "A. R. Ammons: Where Motion and Shape Coincide," in his *The Line Forms Here* (Ann Arbor: University of Michigan Press, 1992), pp. 121–145;

Hugh Luke, "Gestures of Shape, Motions of Form: On Some Poems by A. R. Ammons," *Pebble,* 18–20 (1980): 79–108;

Jerome Mazzaro, "Reconstruction in Art," *Diacritics,* 3 (Winter 1973): 39–44;

Michael McFee, "A. R. Ammons and *The Snow Poems* Reconsidered," *Chicago Review,* 33 (Summer 1981): 32–38;

Josephine Miles, "Light, Wind, Motion," *Diacritics,* 3 (Winter 1973): 21–24;

Robert Morgan, "The Compound Vision of A. R. Ammons's Early Poems," in his *Good Measure: Essays, Interviews, and Notes on Poetry* (Baton Rouge: Louisiana State University Press, 1993), pp. 45–74;

Linda Orr, "The Cosmic Backyard of A. R. Ammons," *Diacritics,* 3 (Winter 1973): 3–12;

Patricia Parker, "Configurations of Shape and Flow," *Diacritics,* 3 (Winter 1973): 25–33;

Robert Pinsky, "The Discursive Aspect of Poetry II: Ammons," in his *The Situation of Poetry: Contemporary Poetry and Its Traditions* (Princeton: Princeton University Press, 1976), pp. 144–156;

Alfred S. Reid, "The Poetry of A. R. Ammons," *South Carolina Review,* 12 (Fall 1979): 2–9;

Guy Rotella, "Ghostlier Demarcations, Keener Sounds: A. R. Ammons's *Corsons Inlet,*" *Concerning Poetry,* 10 (Fall 1977): 25–33;

Steven P. Schneider, *A. R. Ammons and the Poetics of Widening Scope* (Rutherford, N.J.: Fairleigh Dickinson University Press, 1994);

Willard Spiegelman, "Myths of Concretion, Myths of Abstraction: The Case of A. R. Ammons," in his *The Didactic Muse: Scenes of Instruction in Contemporary American Poetry* (Princeton: Princeton University Press, 1989), pp. 110–146;

Helen Vendler, "A. R. Ammons: Dwelling in the Flow of Shapes," in her *The Music of What Happens: Poems, Poets, Critics* (Cambridge, Mass.: Harvard University Press, 1988), pp. 310–342;

Hyatt H. Waggoner, "The Poetry of A. R. Ammons: Some Notes and Reflections," *Salmagundi,* 22/23 (Spring/Summer 1973): 285–294;

Matthew Wilson, "Homecoming in A. R. Ammons' *Tape for the Turn of the Year,*" *Contemporary Poetry,* 4, no. 2 (1981): 60–76;

Thomas J. Wolf, "A. R. Ammons and William Carlos Williams: A Study in Style and Meaning," *Contemporary Poetry,* 2, no. 3 (1977): 1–16;

Cary Wolfe, "Symbol Plural: The Later Long Poems of A. R. Ammons," *Contemporary Literature,* 30 (Spring 1989): 78–94.

John Ashbery

(28 July 1927 –   )

Thomas Gardner
Virginia Polytechnic Institute & State University

See also the Ashbery entry in *DLB 5: American Poets Since World War II, First Series* and *DLB Yearbook: 1981.*

BOOKS: *Turandot and Other Poems* (New York: Tibor de Nagy Gallery, 1953);

Some Trees (New Haven: Yale University Press / London: Cumberlege, Oxford University Press, 1956);

The Poems (New York: Tiber, 1960);

The Tennis Court Oath (Middletown, Conn.: Wesleyan University Press, 1962);

Rivers and Mountains (New York: Holt, Rinehart & Winston, 1966);

Selected Poems (London: Cape, 1967);

Sunrise in Suburbia (New York: Phoenix Book Shop, 1968);

A Nest of Ninnies, by Ashbery and James Schuyler (New York: Dutton, 1969);

Fragment (Los Angeles: Black Sparrow Press, 1969);

The Double Dream of Spring (New York: Dutton, 1970);

The New Spirit (New York: Adventures in Poetry, 1970);

Three Poems (New York: Viking, 1972);

The Vermont Notebook (Los Angeles: Black Sparrow Press, 1975);

Self-Portrait in a Convex Mirror (New York: Viking, 1975; Manchester, U.K.: Carcanet, 1977);

Houseboat Days (New York: Viking, 1977; London: Penguin, 1977);

Three Plays (Calais, Vt.: Z Press, 1978);

As We Know (New York: Viking, 1979; Manchester: Carcanet New Press, 1981);

Shadow Train (New York: Viking, 1981);

A Wave (New York: Viking, 1984; Manchester: Carcanet, 1984);

Selected Poems (New York: Viking, Penguin, 1985);

April Galleons (New York: Viking, Penguin, 1987);

Reported Sightings: Art Chronicles, 1957–1987, edited by David Bergman (New York: Knopf, 1989);

Flow Chart (New York: Knopf, 1991);

John Ashbery (photograph © 1979 estate of Thomas Victor)

Hotel Lautréamont (New York: Knopf, 1992);

And the Stars Were Shining (New York: Farrar, Straus, Giroux, 1994);

Can You Hear Me, Bird (New York: Farrar, Sttraus, Giroux, 1995).

PLAY PRODUCTIONS: *The Heroes,* New York, Living Theatre, 1952;

The Compromise, Cambridge, Mass., Poets Theatre, 1955.

OTHER: *The Heroes,* in *Artists' Theatre,* edited by Herbert Machiz (New York: Grove / London: Evergreen, 1960);

Jean-Jacques Mayoux, *Melville,* translated by Ashbery (New York: Grove / London: Evergreen, 1960);

Noel Vexin, *Murder in Montmartre,* translated by Ashbery (New York: Dell, 1960);

Geneviève Manceron, *The Deadlier Sex,* translated by Ashbery and others (New York: Dell, 1961);

Jacques Dupin, *Alberto Giacometti,* translated by Ashbery (Paris: Maeght Editeur, 1962);

The American Literary Anthology/1, selected by Ashbery and others (New York: Farrar, Straus & Giroux, 1968);

Frank O'Hara, *The Collected Poems,* introduction by Ashbery (New York: Knopf, 1971);

Painterly Painting, edited by Ashbery and Thomas B. Hess (New York: Macmillan, 1971);

Penguin Modern Poets 24, edited by Ashbery (Harmondsworth, U.K.: Penguin, 1974);

E. V. Lucas and George Morrow, *What a Life!,* introduction by Ashbery (New York: Dover, 1975);

Richard F. Snow, *the funny place,* introduction by Ashbery (Chicago: O'Hara, 1975);

Raymond Roussel, *How I Wrote Certain of My Books,* includes two essays by Ashbery (New York: Sun, 1977);

The Best American Poetry, 1988, edited by Ashbery (New York: Macmillan, 1988);

Joan Mitchell, with a foreword by Ashbery (New York: Robert Miller Gallery, 1993).

In a 1961 piece for *ArtNews* on the murmuring intimacy of Henri Michaux's work, John Ashbery singled out this statement of Michaux's aims:

> Instead of one vision which excludes others, I would have liked to draw the moments that, placed side by side, go to make up a life. To expose the interior phrase for people to see, the phrase that has no words, a rope which sinuously, and intimately accompanies everything that impinges from the outside or inside. I wanted to draw the consciousness of existence and the flow of time. As you would take your pulse.

The ideas in this passage, reprinted in Ashbery's collected art criticism *Reported Sightings: Art Chronicles, 1957–1987* (1989), undoubtedly appealed to his imagination. Years later the desire to make the many sides of consciousness visible – what Michaux calls here the wordless "interior phrase" playing responsively against what "impinges from the outside or inside" – still drives Ashbery's work. In a bold sort of literalism most Ashbery poems, in the name of reflecting what he calls in an interview

collected by William Packard in 1974 "the whole mind," focus on writing, since that is what he is engaged in as he tries to draw consciousness into words. Though other concerns move in and out of his mind, it is the attempt to reflect "the maximum of my experience when I'm writing" that drives most of the colliding analogies and comparisons of his poems.

Ashbery argues in a 1981 interview with Richard Jackson that, far from pulling him away from his experience, "the interests of realism in poetry are actually enhanced in the long run by a close involvement with language; thought created by language and creating it are the nucleus of the poem." That involvement, inevitably bringing him to grips with the limits and frailties of words, often settles him into what he calls a pause or a halt in language's straightforward drive to master or order the world – a pause, however, that generates a new series of concerns or reflections. Most Ashbery poems, as he elaborates in the interview with Packard and in a 1983 interview in the *Paris Review,* both enact and reflect upon the free unfolding of Michaux's many-sided phrase. In the pause, "concentrating attentively in order to pick up whatever is in the air . . . the disparate circumstances that as I say are with us at every moment," elucidating and knocking "a lot of almost invisible currents . . . into some sort of shape," Ashbery is able to "reproduce the polyphony that goes on inside me, which I don't think is radically different from that of other people." At the end, he comments, "a person is somehow given an embodiment out of those proliferating reflections that are occurring in a generalized mind which eventually run together into the image of a specific person, 'he' or 'me' who was not there when the poem began."

Ashbery's poetry to date offers an almost bewildering array of different ways of reflectively involving himself with the limits of language. All of his approaches, however, grow out of a problem embedded in Michaux's aims – the distance between language and consciousness, or between the wordless phrase and what would make it visible. In *The Senses of Walden* (1992) philosopher Stanley Cavell has shown the value in acknowledging that "Words come to us from a distance; they were there before we were; we are born into them. Meaning them is accepting that fact of their condition." He claims, using Thoreau's masterpiece as an example, that such an acknowledgment brings us "back to a context in which [words] are alive" because of their distance or strangeness: "Not till we are lost . . . do we begin to find ourselves, and realize where we are and the infinite extent of our relations. . . . Not till we are completely lost . . . do we appreciate the vastness and strangeness of Nature." Cavell finds in *Walden*'s "endless computation of words," its "puns and paradoxes, its fracturing of idiom and twisting of quotation, its drones of fact and flights of impersonation," a forceful illustration of how that acknowledgment can generate a wide-awake response to one's experience.

Ashbery's work is the strongest contemporary example we have of such an endless computation of language's condition – a deceptively casual pulse-taking that finds, in language's difference from us, an opportunity for making visible some portion of the "infinite relations" of consciousness with its surroundings. His work has become a sourcebook for poets conducting similar investigations. In his poem "Paradoxes and Oxymorons" from *Shadow Train* (1981), Ashbery speaks of poetry as "Bringing a system of them [words] into play," and in the title poem of *A Wave* (1984) he asserts, "By so many systems / As we are involved in, by just so many / Are we set free on an ocean of language." It is that demonstration of freedom, finally, that is his legacy to contemporary poets.

Ashbery was brought up in Sodus, New York, a small town near Lake Ontario. His father, Chester Ashbery, was a fruit farmer. His mother, Helen Lawrence Ashbery, had been a high-school biology teacher before marriage; her father, Henry Lawrence, whose library was to be a powerful influence on the young Ashbery, was a well-known physicist at the University of Rochester. In 1940 Ashbery's nine-year-old brother died of leukemia, a tragedy that suggests his childhood had its share of tensions and sudden, disorienting losses. He attended Deerfield Academy for two years, then enrolled at Harvard in 1945 where his most intense literary friendships were with Kenneth Koch and Frank O'Hara. Ashbery moved to New York in 1949 to begin work on an M.A. at Columbia and soon became part of the explosive postwar arts scene there, his immediate friends including painters Larry Rivers and Jane Freilicher and poets O'Hara, Koch, and James Schuyler. Freilicher illustrated *Turandot and Other Poems* (1953), Ashbery's first, limited-edition publication. In 1955 he and O'Hara submitted work to the Yale Younger Poets series, judged during that period by W. H. Auden. The often-repeated story has it that both manuscripts were rejected, but that Auden, unable to find a suitable winner from the finalists he had been given and having heard about the two poets, asked to see the two manu-

Ashbery at his family's farm in Sodus, New York, in 1944

scripts and chose Ashbery's *Some Trees* (1956), its title poem dating from undergraduate days.

Some Trees is composed of a series of often oblique sketches concerning the problematic nature of expression. The book's first poem, "Two Scenes," for example, presents, as its title suggests, a poem divided into two parts. Beginning "We see us as we truly behave," the poet asserts in the first scene that action might articulate an unspoken relationship. In the second scene the complexity of reading such an articulation dominates, as it concludes "In the evening / Everything has a schedule, if you can find out what it is." Other poems in the collection tend to end with similarly problematic acknowledgments. "Glazunoviana" concludes "In the flickering evening the martins grow denser. / Rivers of wings surround us and vast tribulation." Though the poems share the sentiment of the last lines of "The Picture of Little J. A. in a Prospect of Flowers," that "only in the light of lost words / Can we imagine our rewards," most do not go far with such an imagining.

Two often reprinted poems from this first book do, however, offer some sense of how Ashbery's reflections will develop in his subsequent work. The title poem begins by finding a note of assurance about the possibilities of speech in the way winter trees confidently sketch their alphabets against the sky: "each / Joining a neighbor, as though speech / Were a still performance." Emboldened by that promise and far enough from the world's threatening insistencies to feel safe, the poet turns toward a lover and speaks:

> you and I
> Are suddenly what the trees try
>
> To tell us we are:
> That their merely being there
> Means something; that soon
> We may touch, love, explain.

Even before that speech is quite articulated, however, before the couple actually touches and loves and explains, that still performance gives way and grows multiple and complicated:

> And glad not to have invented
> Such comeliness, we are surrounded:
> A silence already filled with noises,
> A canvas on which emerges
>
> A chorus of smiles, a winter morning.

Like the unreadable "schedule" replacing true behavior in "Two Scenes," this emerging canvas of the day is not what the trees promised. And yet, "Some Trees" suggests by its tone that there is some sort of touching and explaining being accomplished in that nonstill chorus of morning noises. Further, the poem itself – the reference to "[t]hese accents" in the last line echoing a reference to "these ... amazing" trees in the first – claims slyly that though its words seem like self-defense, perhaps they are, in their apparent reticence, freely moving words of love: "Placed in a puzzling light, and moving, / Our days put on such reticence / These accents seem their own defense."

"The Instruction Manual" is a first demonstration of what will become a characteristic feature of Ashbery's work – his entering into the moving puzzlement of words in order to tease out life and freedom. It begins with a speaker bored with his job of

"writ[ing] the instruction manual on the uses of a new metal." He almost immediately wanders away from that straightforward use of language by leaning out his window, looking down at the street, and dreaming of Guadalajara. In this bored pause he plays out a visit never actually made, imagining in the "lost words" of "The Picture of Little J. A. in a Prospect of Flowers" the "City I wanted most to see, and most did not see, in Mexico!" As his daydreaming reflections continue, he works out "the whole network" of the city's colors and neighborhoods and various lovers. He exults: "How limited, but how complete withal, has been our experience of Guadalajara!" In that mapless wandering as language is let loose to play, the poet discovers room to breathe – "a last breeze" before he returns to the instruction manual. One of the important developments in Ashbery's poetry will be his learning how to combine "Some Trees" and "The Instruction Manual" – how to marry an exuberant playing out of "lost words" with an acknowledgment of the finite conditions of his own, never-still "accents."

With his second important collection, *The Tennis Court Oath* (1962), Ashbery took a step toward greater reticence, his accents becoming even more puzzling. Having received a Fulbright Fellowship (1955–1957) to produce an anthology of translations of modern French poetry (never completed), Ashbery moved to Paris, eventually staying there for ten years, living with the poet and journalist Pierre Martory for much of that time and writing for *ArtNews* and the *New York Herald Tribune* to support himself. Most of the poems in *The Tennis Court Oath* were written in France. Although as in *Some Trees* the same desire to find a breathing space is present, this volume forces the reader to deal primarily with what it calls the "wreckage" of language.

The difficulty of the poetry is clear in the first three stanzas of "They Dream Only of America" – apparently an oblique collection of non sequiturs, a heap of fragments:

> They dream only of America
> To be lost among the thirteen million pillars of grass:
> "This honey is delicious
> *Though it burns the throat.*"
>
> And hiding from darkness in barns
> They can be grownups now
> And the murderer's ash tray is more easily –
> The lake a lilac cube.
>
> He holds a key in his right hand.

"Please," he asked willingly.
He is thirty years old.
That was before[.]

The wreckage can be sorted a bit if the reader takes the tense shifts as reliable. Provisionally, one can see in the lines "'Please,' he asked" and "That was before" an event in the past being described, perhaps a first encounter with a lover. The fourth stanza provides more clues – "When his headache grew worse we / Stopped at a wire filling station" – while the fifth stanza pulls these glimpses together: "He went slowly into the bedroom."

The present-tense comments describe a mature stage in a relationship, a time when the actors "can be grownups," where what is delicious also "burns the throat" and where "hiding" is involved. Most strikingly, it is a stage where that initial affair has become a complicated unraveling of signs and gestures – expressed either in the language of pulp fiction ("the murderer's ash tray") or domestic detail ("He holds a key.")

In the fifth stanza, the desire to "touch, love, explain" has apparently become a wearing linguistic adventure:

Now he cared only about signs.
Was the cigar a sign?
And what about the key?

The dark sixth stanza – describing the speaker with a broken leg, back beside his bed, "waiting" in horror for "liberation" – perhaps explains why the poem begins with the "dream" of traveling to "America" and being lost in what might be called a new, expansive way of speaking. The "many uttering tongues" celebrated in Walt Whitman's leaves become here "thirteen million pillars of grass" freely broadcast across a landscape where, as the fourth stanza puts it, "We could drive for hundreds of miles / At night through dandelions." The poem, then, becomes readable as a tentative imagining of freedom in response to a relationship's constricting code. Ashbery attempts to find breathing room within these reflections on how we "touch, love, explain," but, with the rewards of that free space not easily imaginable, the wreckage of "lost words" dominates the poem's presentation.

Equally demanding is Ashbery's notorious collage "Europe," a poem in 111 sections. Many details are cut out from a 1917 British detective novel titled *Beryl of the Bi-plane* and strewn across the page. It seems as if language has exploded. The first section, for example, reads:

To employ her
construction ball
Morning fed on the
light blue wood
of the mouth
                    cannot understand
feels deeply)[.]

As John Shoptaw has pointed out, the World War I story of Beryl and Ronald Pryor and their plane "The Hornet," with its emphasis on codes and disguises and secret agents, has obvious connections to the "paranoid" political atmosphere of the 1950s, and Ashbery might usefully be read here as picking through the wreckage of that decade. But the fragments of the story of Beryl's experimental flying machine may also lead readers to consider Ashbery's reflections on the conditions – the limits, here displayed as wreckage – of language. What "rewards" can be imagined in light of our acknowledgment of the "lostness" of words? What "America" does wrecked "Europe" dream of? How might that wreckage be reassembled?

It is possible to identify two chains of language in "Europe" that speak to just these issues. First, one can find throughout the poem references to wreckage linked with the failure to understand. The first section, for example, juxtaposes a "construction ball" apparently tearing down abandoned structures with phrases that suggest the situation the splintered poem presents – where the gap between what the writer "feels deeply" and what he can express "of the mouth" is filled with tumbling words readers "cannot understand." Sections 13 and 14 link "human waste" to that empty period of waiting "until the truth can be explained." Section 10 describes someone who had "mistaken his book for garbage" while 34 links a similar failure to "understand their terror" to "waste . . . offal." The clearest linkage occurs at the close of the poem, where a plane wreck in *Beryl* is said to be caused by "steel bolts / having been replaced / by a painting of / one of wood!" The result of that misrepresentation results in this stark phrase: "I don't understand wreckage."

At the same time, one can also take note of a second chain of language in which a response is imagined to the wreckage, and life and movement are discovered within the acknowledged failure to understand. Significantly, what emerges is disguised and, like the ending of "Some Trees," reticent – a plane, equipped with a "silencer" rising above the waste and disappearing from view. Section 8 begins with "slight engine trouble" but eventually declares that "All was now ready for the continuance of the

At East Hampton, New York, in summer 1952: Kenneth Koch, Larry Rivers (holding sign), John Ashbery, Jane Freilicher, Lelia Telberg, and Nell Blaine

journey." Successful runs of the disguised, silenced machine, perhaps a metaphor for the reorienting of language, occur in several places. In section 37 the machine "described a half-circle, and, though / still rapidly rising . . . head[ed] eastward in / the direction of the sea," and sections 48, 66, and 68 record variations of the observation: "She followed a straight line leading / due north through Suffolk and Norfolk." The poem's last section completes this chain by describing "a beam of intense, white light" that, mimicking the silenced plane's movements, sweeps the sky with its coded, unreadable reflections. The poem, then, seems to affirm that movement and freedom are possible within the wreckage of language but continues to stress, in the image of the reassembled plane, the feature of reticence.

Ashbery returned to the United States in 1965, after the death of his father, and as an editor at *ArtNews* he continued to support himself as a journalist. His third important collection, *Rivers and Mountains* (1966), marks a turning point in Ashbery's poetry, for he works out first versions of many of his mature approaches to the issues his previous

works raise. The crucial poem is "Clepsydra" – the title refers to a water clock that makes the movement of time visible – for it shows the poet reflecting upon his own act of thinking as he writes. What had been seen in embryonic form in "Some Trees" – an address to a lover shading into a discussion of "these accents" – is here played out at great length. Ashbery addresses a "you," using the tone and terms one would use with a lover and perhaps drawing from actual relationships, but the second person addressed seems clearly to be his wordless consciousness made visible. As both Harold Bloom and Karen Mills-Courts note, this manner of second-person address appears in most of Ashbery's later poems.

The "I" who speaks to "you" in the poem can be said to be reflecting on the richness and limits of language itself. The opportunity, or space, for this reflection is provided by the breaking off of the straightforward movement of consciousness into language. To use the language of versions of this situation rehearsed in previous poems, a kind of wreckage has occurred, or a pause in writing instructions has insinuated itself, or words have become lost. As in ordinary moment-to-moment thought, which cannot be said to have an end or beginning, "Clepsydra" begins in the middle of a thought and does not record the concerns that lie behind its fluid outpouring: "This means never getting any closer to the basic / Principle operating behind it than to the distracted / Entity of a mirage. The half-meant, half-perceived / Motions of fronds out of idle depths." Beginning in the midst of an ongoing reflection will become a favored formal strategy for Ashbery, and one of the pleasures of reading his work is noticing how many different ways — from words cut out of other texts to phrases echoing each other as they march down the page — Ashbery is able to invent for forcing language into the state of "distraction." It is in the pause, where thought is lazily forming and deforming, that reflection occurs.

Despite the inherent difficulty, much of Ashbery's reflection can be worked out. The "I" in the poem is speaking to his being-articulated thoughts about its interaction with the world: "the way / You go," what happened "since / You woke up," and so on, just as in earlier poems Ashbery imagined moving around Guadalajara or tinkering with Beryl's wrecked plane. The poem uses the morning sky — the sun coming up, clouds disappearing, the air growing hazy — to initiate a series of comparisons to that movement of thought. The reader commences following this thought process in the first line without being given the chance to find a beginning before *this* beginning:

> Hasn't the sky? Returned from moving the other
> Authority recently dropped, wrested as much of
> That severe sunshine as you need now on the way
> You go.

Working out more and more implications of the comparison between the poem's movement and the sky's changes, Ashbery, in reflecting on his language, is also demonstrating the "sensation of having dreamt the whole thing, / [And] of returning to participate in that dream, until / The last word is exhausted." Though the dream stays invisible and at a distance, such a return to and unfolding of the words that it prompts, "continu[ing] the dialogue into / Those mysterious and near regions that are / Precisely the time of its being furthered," produces an intricate display of what Ashbery calls "the declamatory / Nature of the distance traveled."

The highlights of Ashbery's reflection are clear and forcefully expressed. Thinking of both the poem's unfolding accents and the hazy filling out of the sky, he writes:

> Each moment
> Of utterance is the true one; likewise none are true,
> Only is the bounding from air to air, a serpentine
> Gesture which hides the truth behind a congruent
> Message, the way air hides the sky, is, in fact,
> Tearing it limb from limb this very moment: but
> The sky has pleaded already and this is about
> As graceful a kind of non-absence as either
> Has a right to expect[.]

That bounding, serpentine gesture — the poem itself, tearing free and displaying the nonspoken whole — is not only graceful but inevitable. It is the only way that consciousness "happens" visibly, a process prompted by the "almost / Exaggerated strictness of the [poem's initial] condition":

> there was no statement
> At the beginning. There was only a breathless waste,
> A dumb cry shaping everything in projected
> After-effects orphaned by playing the parts intended
>   for them,
> Though one must not forget that the nature of this
> Emptiness, these previsions,
> Was that it could only happen here, on this page held
> Too close to be legible, sprouting erasures, except that
>   they
> Ended everything in the transparent sphere of what
>   was
> Intended only a moment ago, spiraling further out, its
> Gesture finally dissolving in the weather.

Ashbery will return, throughout his career, to these orphaned aftereffects "playing the parts" provided by language's ways of shaping, but what is most important to notice at this still-early stage is the way his framing of the poem's conditions — holding the page "too close to be legible" — generates the parts he plays.

Ashbery asserts that the verbal part-playing is both how he sees himself "in this totality" of linguistic possibilities and how he freely enacts some of them:

> a kind of sweet acknowledgment of how
> The past is yours, to keep invisible if you wish
> But also to make absurd elaborations with
> And in this way prolong your dance of non-discovery
> In brittle, useless architecture that is nevertheless
> The map of your desires[.]

A complicated, continually self-reflective investigation, the poem no sooner works out the distance between "I" and "you" and between "you" and the unspoken area it elaborates than it plunges once again into other "stammering" takes on the situation — what Cavell would call "computations of distance":

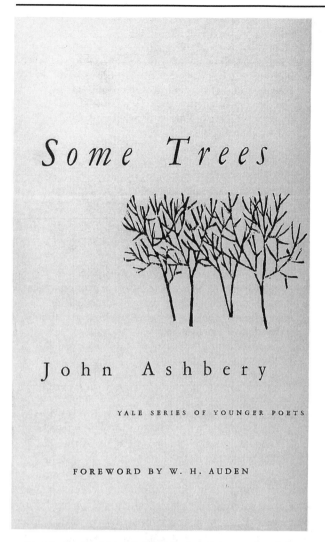

Dust jacket for Ashbery's 1956 book, which was selected for publication in the Yale Younger Poets series by W. H. Auden (courtesy of the Lilly Library, Indiana University)

In this way any direction taken was the right one,
Leading first to you, and through you to
Myself that is beyond you and which is the same thing
    as space,
That is the stammering vehicles that remain unknown,
Eating the sky in all sincerity because the difference
Can never be made up: therefore, why not examine the
    distance?

The other major poem in *Rivers and Mountains* is the long poem "The Skaters." Although the poem records another reflective entry into what it calls the labyrinth, "this mazy business about writing," it is much closer to the exuberant investigation of Guadalajara in "The Instruction Manual" than it is to the intimate self-monitoring of "Clepsydra." The reader can almost overlook that Ashbery is again concerned with the distance of language from what

it would speak for, or as he asserts, "it is you I am parodying, / Your invisible denials." Deliberately echoing the connection between "these trees" and "these accents" in "Some Trees," Ashbery begins the poem by remarking on a bright crowd of skaters in February: "These decibels / Are a kind of flagellation, an entity of sound / Into which being enters, and is apart." This continually surfacing comparison between the way the shouts of the skaters focus and display the day's energy and the way the sounded syllables of language perform a similar focus holds the poem together. Ashbery writes, for example, that when one moves into language, what happens is that "this normal, shapeless entity" of consciousness is "Forgotten as the words fly briskly across, each time / Bringing down meaning as snow from a low sky, or rabbits flushed from a wood."

The most striking part of the comparison is the realization that the brisk mass of flying skaters, that beautiful, dissolving movement into language, continually spins off a series of individual performers:

> skaters elaborate their distances,
> Taking a separate line to its end. Returning to the
>   mass, they join each other
> Blotted in an incredible mess of dark colors, and again
>   reappearing to take the theme
> Some little distance.

The skaters' visible "apart[ness]" provides one way the mass "turns to look at itself." The parallel holds, for the parodies of linguistic performance – "knowing where men *are* coming from . . . hold[ing] the candle up to the album" (ellipses added) – that make up the concluding sections of the poem can be seen as elaborating language's orphaned aftereffects with great high spirits.

The strongest poems in *The Double Dream of Spring* (1970) return to address and reflect upon the consciousness-made-visible found in "Clepsydra." Many of these poems adopt the sort of intimate, murmuring lover's tone that was first evident in "Some Trees." "I've been thinking about you / . . . Reflecting among arabesques of speech that arise," Ashbery whispers in "The Hod Carrier." "You," he promises in "Spring Day," "Gracious and growing thing, with those leaves like stars, / We shall soon give all our attention to you." Ashbery's tone both acknowledges a sense of separation from the world's way of speaking and enters into that difference in "Summer": "life is divided up / Between you and me, and among all the others out there." The first poem of the volume, "The Task," describes "a predicated romance," where "Everyman" will eventually "return unfruitful out of the lightness / That passing time evokes." The poet, however, finds a value in "linear acting into that time." If there are regrets, Ashbery asserts, "they stir only lightly / The children playing after supper, / Promise of the pillow and so much in the night to come. / I plan to stay here a while." The important characteristic of the collection is the way Ashbery begins to describe what is gained in his elaborate reflections. What does it mean to be able to breathe free in an imagined Guadalajara?

In "Soonest Mended" Ashbery's "you" and "I" are "Barely tolerated, living on the margin / In our technological society." The two are "merely spectators" rather than "players," because they refuse to claim a unity between consciousness and its verbal display. They indulge in "fence-sitting / Raised to the level of an esthetic ideal" and cower "in the early lessons, since the promise of learning / Is a delusion." What is gained by this "action, this not being sure, this careless / Preparing, sowing the seeds crooked in the furrow" is an ability to step away from language's blinding inherited drive to master and complete: "To step free at last, minuscule on the gigantic plateau – / This was our ambition: to be small and clear and free." That gigantic plateau, apparently, is nonverbal consciousness, the world outside, the other. One is free from having to hold and own it precisely because one has been forced into the same situation with respect to words:

> The being of our sentences, in the climate that fostered them,
> Not ours to own, like a book, but to be with, and sometimes
> To be without, alone and desperate.

Another poem in *The Double Dream of Spring,* "Rural Objects," adds some detail to this investigation. It begins with the dream that "you" and "I" might share permanently in an understanding (and rendering) of a moment:

> Wasn't there some way in which you too understood
> About being there in the time as it was then?
> A golden moment, full of life and health?
> Why can't this moment be enough for us as we have become?

But "we have become" distant; instead of sharing the moment, "we" share the now-visible stuff of language made accessible because of the "hourglass" that separates us:

> And now you are this thing that is outside me,
> And how I in token of it am like you is
> In place. In between are the bits of information
> That circulate around you, all that ancient stuff,
> Brought here, reassembled, carted off again
> Into the back yard of your dream. If we are closer
> To anything, it is in this sense that doesn't count,
> Like the last few blank pages of a book.

The distance between "you" and "I" has opened a blank space where language "doesn't count" but also where newly visible aspects of it can be freely played out and, as in "Europe," its wreckage be "reassembled."

Ashbery's book-length prose meditation *Three Poems* (1972) works out many of his ideas on language at great length. Made up of three poems titled "The New Spirit," "The System," and "The Recital," it is the work where many of Ashbery's readers first began to get a handle on his issues and his typical ways of conducting his linguistic investigations. Like "Clepsydra" or much of the work in *The Double Dream of Spring,* the poems use the second person, here clearly defined as a portion of consciousness made visible. Ashbery early on comments on the difficulty of capturing consciousness on the page: "I thought that if I could put it all down, that would be one way. And next the thought came to me that to leave all out would be another, and truer way. . . . But, forget as we will, something soon comes to stand in their place. Not the truth, perhaps, but – yourself."

The fact that Ashbery's creation of the you is never "true" provides the grounds for the initial opening up in "The New Spirit" of a pause or gap in language's straightforward flow. With that opening acknowledged, the second person becomes a "System," able to be entered and played out and freely reassembled. If the first poem, then, points to the limits of "these accents," the second poem is a wandering visit through a vast network that convincingly combines the techniques of "Some Trees" and "The Instruction Manual." The third poem performs a brief "Recital" of these visits – a closing that Ashbery often employs in subsequent books. As in the phrases cut out from the detective novel for use in "Europe," Ashbery deliberately adopts language in *Three Poems* that in its worn familiarity and lack of drive serves as a constant reminder of language's limits. The paradox is that Ashbery's playing with this language paradoxically creates an area within which one can be, as if on a gigantic plateau, "small and clear and free."

The acknowledgement of language's inability to adequately represent consciousness in "The New

Spirit" is imagined through the figure of breaking into a largely empty tomb:

> We have broken through into the meaning of the tomb.
> But the act is still proposed, before us,

> it needs pronouncing. To formulate oneself around this hollow, empty sphere ... To be your breath as it is taken in and shoved out. Then, quietly, it would be as objects placed along the top of a wall: a battery jar, a rusted pulley, shapeless wooden boxes, an open can of axle grease, two lengths of pipe ... We see this moment from outside as within.

The discovered objects may be seen as the orphaned aftereffects of expression or "circulating" bits of language, freed by the recognition of them as such and "carted off" to the backyard.

Deliberately adopting language he describes as having "taken on the look of worn familiarity, like pebbles polished over and over again by the sea" and producing "a vast wetness as of sea and air combined, a single smooth, anonymous matrix without surface or depth," Ashbery creates an exaggerated display of consciousness tracked, as it must be, "from outside." He calls it the establishment of an "outer rhythm," an accessing of language's finite, nonideal conditions: "you must grow up, the outer rhythm more and more accelerate, past the ideal rhythm of the spheres that seemed to dictate you, that seemed the establishment of your seed and the conditions of its growing, upward, someday into leaves and fruition and final sap." The tracking of consciousness, it is hoped, will produce not just a version of the poet's speaking self but a reseeing of language as "a medium through which we address one another, the independent life we were hoping to create. . . . A permanent medium in which we are lost, since becoming robs it of its potential." Staying lost with language, then, becomes a demonstration of a place of potential – a "safe vacuum" where one can become "small and clear and free":

> Is it correct for me to use you to demonstrate all this? Perhaps what I am saying is that it is I the subject, recoiling from you at an ever-increasing speed just so as to be able to say I exist in that safe vacuum I had managed to define from friends' disinterested turning away. As if I were only a flower after all and not the map of the country in which it grows. There is more to be said about this, I guess, but it does not seem to alter anything that I am the spectator, you what is apprehended.

Realizing in the poem that though "I hold you. . . . life holds us, and is unknowable," Ashbery in his "mind's suburbs" senses the possibility of establishing a new relationship to language: "a new spirit, commenting on it in their accustomed lilting or droning vernacular." Remarking on the worn, dissolving language of the poem – its "lost words" – the poet describes what freedom might be gained in its display of finite conditions:

> you will have to take apart the notion of you so as to reconstruct it from an intimate knowledge of its inner workings. How harmless and even helpful the painted wooden components of the Juggernaut look scattered around the yard, patiently waiting to be reassembled!

> in place of the panorama that used to be our customary setting and which we never made much use of, a limited but infinitely free space has established itself, useful as everyday life but transfigured so that its signs of wear no longer appear as a reproach but as indications of how beautiful a thing must have been to have been so much prized.

> a prismatic space that cannot be seen, merely felt ... One is aware of it as an open field of narrative possibilities ... There is room to move around in it, which is all that matters. [ellipses added]

Crucially, as is revealed at the end of the first section, all of these possibilities were set into play by the first move of the poem – turning one's back on language's impossible dream of perfection and entering into the give-and-take of its spreading, colliding tongues: "it dawned on him all of a sudden that there was another way, that this horrible vision of the completed Tower of Babel, flushed in the sunset as the last ceramic brick was triumphantly fitted into place, perfect in its vulgarity, an eternal reminder of the advantages of industry and cleverness – that the terror could be shut out – and really shut out – simply by turning one's back on it."

In "The System," one of his most important poems, Ashbery takes on the role of a reflective spectator, working within the open field that language has now become. Reprising the argument of "The New Spirit," Ashbery begins with an almost ritual acknowledgment of limits. Poetry, he notes, is the business of describing how "being" "logically unshuffl[es] into this morning that had to be," a process that involves "mastering the many pauses and the abrupt sharp accretions of regular being in the clotted sphere of today's activities." The poet is expected to accomplish his difficult task, which may be seen as the making of a habitation for the soul: "All of the facts are here and it remains only to use them in the right combinations, but that building will be the size of today, the rooms habitable and leading into one another in a lasting sequence, eternal and of the greatest timeliness."

Ashbery as a poet, however, has come to glory in the fact that such a habitation or completed tower is beyond him; there are always "dry churnings of no timbre, hysterical staccato passages that one cannot master or turn away from." Such a realization means that "the classic truths of everyday life" – the expectation that everyone "really knew what it [truth] *was*" and "life uncurled around it . . . as though innumerable transparent tissues hovered around these two entities and joined them in some way," the truth expressing itself in sentences that "were dry and clear, as though made of wood" – are incomplete. Alongside those confident sentences, there must exist "a residue, a kind of fiction" generated by exploring those nonmasterable sensations and the sentences that result:

> It is this "other tradition" which we propose to explore. . . . other, unrelated happenings that form a kind of sequence of fantastic reflections as they succeed each other at a pace and according to an inner necessity of their own . . . The living aspect of these obscure phenomena has never to my knowledge been examined from a point of view like the painter's: in the round[.]

"The System" both unfolds its own sequence of fantastic reflections and meditates on what is "living" or breathing about them. In a sense, it responds to concerns left hanging in "Some Trees" and "Europe." What is living about such poetry? How could an elaboration of distance offer a place to breathe? Ashbery's reflections in the poem are generated by the disorienting experience of love: "The switches had been tripped, as it were; the entire world or one's limited but accurate idea of it was bathed in a glowing love." Love as an experience produces a "roiling [of] the clear waters of the reflective intellect" with "the bases for true reflective thinking . . . annihilated" and an opportunity presented for following out "idle and frivolous trains of thought leading who knows where." These trains of thought are the objects on the wall or the circulating bits of language discussed in "The New Spirit," what Ashbery describes here as a "cosmic welter of attractions . . . coming to stand for the real thing, which has to be colorless and featureless to be the true reflection of the primeval energy from which it issued forth." In "The System" Ashbery addresses the crucial question of the value of this welter of attractions.

Watching himself think in this ungoverned area, Ashbery reflects on the limits of "ways of speaking" about such openness, elaborating their fi-

Title page for Ashbery's 1960 collection, which was sold in a set with books by Kenneth Koch, Frank O'Hara, and James Schuyler

nitude. He notices, for example, that inevitably the human mind seeks regularity, wants to turn itself off:

> this chaos began to seem like the normal way of being . . . [and] one really felt that one had set one's foot on the upward path, the spiral leading from the motley darkened and lightened landscape here below to the transparent veils of heaven. . . . And even in the darkest night this sense of advancement came to whisper at one's side like a fellow traveler pointing the way. [ellipses added]

He traces out allegories and ways of describing growth that, he admits, can be seen as ways of acknowledging his own need for stability. Among these are an account of "certain young spectators" who, while "correct in assuming that the whole question of behavior in life has to be rethought each second," had, in their quest for "peace," allowed "the generalized shape of this nirvana-like state [to] impose its form on the continually active atoms of the moving forward." A related investigation concerns a figure who, in the constant rush of sensation, assumes the stability of his role as observer, "with the rest of the world as a painted backdrop to his own monodrama of becoming of which he was the lone impassioned spectator." Yet another, watching the way his own wandering thought settles for a series of simple one-liners ("This, then, is surely the way") gets at the limitation of this manner of speaking by questioning its momentary rewards: "The great careers are like that: a slow burst that narrows to a final release, pointed but not acute, a life of suffering redeemed and annihilated at the end, and for what? For a casual moment of knowing that is here one minute and gone the next, almost before you were aware of it? . . . This way of speaking has trapped each one of us."

In a second line of reflection Ashbery explores "two kinds of happiness . . . the frontal and the latent" as ways of talking about and controlling the glowing disruptions of love. Frontal happiness he explains as a taste of "what we were brought into creation for, if not to experience it, at least to have the knowledge of it as an ideal toward which the whole universe tends and which therefore confers a shape on the random movements outside us." From that hint, latent happiness posits a "non-existent center, a fixed point" that, although not yet available, promotes "a growing sense of certainty" – the feeling that "we have only to step forward to be on the right path." Ashbery ultimately declares these two strategies to be merely versions of each other and then, as with his other reflections, dissolves them in an acknowledgment of their limits:

> Let us assume for the sake of argument that the blizzard I spoke of earlier has occurred, shattering the frail decor of your happiness like a straw house, replunging you and your world into the grey oblivion you had been floundering in all your life until your happiness was given to you as a gift. . . . Gazing out at the distraught but inanimate world you feel that you have lapsed back into the normal way things are, that what you were feeling just now was a novelty and hence destined to disappear quickly, its sole purpose if any being to light up the gloom around you sufficiently for you to become aware of its awesome extent, more than the eye and mind can take in.

Watching himself generate ways of living into this new, nonguaranteed space, and watching them give way, has produced a way of becoming aware of the unmasterable whole outside his fragile structures. In becoming small, in seeing his ideas reduced to fragile, disposable variants, he has found a way to enter and move within a great unmasterable complexity. He has found a way to move there without mastering, sensing the reach of that totality and establishing for himself an attitude to take toward it.

One might call this movement into a space where the logos does not hold a development of a new skill, a new way of holding oneself in uncertainty:

> here . . . philosophy broke down completely and was of no use. How to deal with the new situations that arise each day in bunches and clusters, and which resist categorization to the point where any rational attempt to deal with them is doomed from the start? . . . What is required is the ability to enter into the complexities of the situation as though it really weren't new at all, which it isn't . . . How we move around in our little ventilated situation, how roomy it seems!
>
> And it is no longer a nameless thing, but something colorful and full of interest, a chronicle play of our lives, with the last act still in the dim future, so that we can't tell yet whether it is a comedy or a tragedy, all we know is that it is crammed with action and the substance of life. Surely all of this living that has gone on that is ours is good in some way, though we cannot tell why: we know only that our sympathy has deepened, quickened by the onrushing spectacle, to the point where we are like spectators swarming up onto the stage to be absorbed into the play, though aware that this is an impossibility, and that the actors continue to recite their lines as if we weren't there.

One can see in "The System" Ashbery's development of an important new voice, one that sees that the limits of words are the ground for an intimate, awestruck relation to what words would grasp – an other, the world, one's self:

> The person sitting opposite you who asked you a question is still waiting for the answer; he has not yet found your hesitation unusual, but it is up to you to grasp it with both hands, wrenching it from the web of connections to rub off the grime that has obscured its brilliance so as to restore it to him, the pause which is the answer you have been expecting. . . . It needs a new voice to tell it, otherwise it will seem just another awkward pause in a conversation largely made up of similar ones, and will never be able to realize its potential as a catalyst.

The "new voice" of these reflections is the very thing all Ashbery poems seem to be searching for, a reply, finally, to "Some Trees." The ground for touching, loving, and explaining turns out to be an acknowledgment that words shift and grow in puzzling, noncontainable ways; the "pause" becomes "the shortest distance between your aims and those of the beloved, the only human ground that can nurture your hopes and fears into the tree of life."

"The Recital," the short final section, restates many of the discoveries previously made, beginning with a summary acknowledgment of the limits of language. The reason it is so difficult to render the reflections a new emotion sets off is that "not one-tenth or even one one-hundredth of the ravishing possibilities the birds sing about at dawn could ever be realized in the course of a single day." This means, inevitably, that "we cannot interpret everything, we must be selective, and so the tale we are telling begins little by little to leave reality behind. It is no longer so much our description of the way things happen to us as our private song, sung in the wilderness." Ritually pointing to this private song, the poet recites over and over: "Any reckoning of the sum total of the things we are is of course doomed to failure from the start, that is if it intends to present a true, wholly objective picture." But Ashbery has also shown that such an acknowledgment opens up a new relation to "the insistent now that baffles and surrounds you in its loose-knit embrace that always seems to be falling away and yet remains behind, stubbornly drawing you, the unwilling spectator who had thought to stop only just for a moment, into the sphere of its solemn and suddenly utterly vast activities, on a new scale as it were, that you have neither the time nor the wish to unravel." The reader also is drawn in by means of Ashbery's reflective, dramatized sentences that, in their acknowledgment of limits and finitude, generate an appreciation of language's limits: "conjugating . . . the distance and emptiness, transforming the scarcely noticeable bleakness into something both intimate and noble."

The title poem from *Self-Portrait in a Convex Mirror* (1975) dramatizes Ashbery's issues in a more accessible manner, which undoubtedly accounts for the poem's popularity and the collection's sweeping the Pulitzer Prize, National Book Award, and National Book Critics Circle Award. In making sixteenth-century Italian painter Parmigianino's riddling mirror painting the "you" addressed in the poem and the system entered, Ashbery essentially recapitulates the strategies of his work to date while orienting his reader with a concrete reference. As Ashbery notes in the poem Parmigianino created his self-portrait by reproducing on a divided, nine-and-a-half-inch diameter wooden ball what he saw in a barber's mirror. Allowing the painter's reproduction of the distorted face and large, foregrounded hand reflected in his convex mirror to function as a version of the "you" more directly approached, addressed, and described in such poems as "Clepsydra" or "The New Spirit," Ashbery offers the reader what at first may seem closer to art criticism than to his more typical portrayal, in Wallace Stevens's phrase, of the "mind in the act of finding." Also, in

allowing the painting's distortions of hand, head, and background to bring to a halt the poet's attempt at the straightforward business of "Lifting the pencil to [his own] self-portrait," Ashbery recapitulates the way *Three Poems* and all its earlier variants found themselves forced by their own worn language to stop and grasp the pause, searching for a new voice to open and tell it.

The poem is broken into six sections, the first one serving to acknowledge through description the distortions of form or focused consciousness. Parmigianino's painting of his reflection seems to Ashbery to offer a series of comments about entering into form. Working out the implications of the foregrounded hand "protect[ing] / What it advertises," the "sequestered" face peering out from deep within the ball, and the room's background reduced to a few beams and flashes of window surrounding the presentation in a "coral ring," Ashbery "reads" in the painting the "conditions" of its self-presentation. He considers the limits within which "the soul establishes itself," drawing particular attention to what the portrait "says" about the necessary distortions of medium – "its dimensions, / What carries it." The painter's face being so far removed from the apparent surface of the globe seems an argument about the "distance" of a made thing from what it represents. The "soul," according to this reading, is in this form "a captive, treated humanely." It is in many ways "not a soul" at all: it "has to stay where it is, / Even though restless." The foregrounded hand of art seems both to cause the distortion and to be straining, impossibly, to break "out of the globe" and do away with its material means of becoming visible. The reduction of the background to surface seems to assert the medium's limits strikingly:

> The surface is what's there
> And nothing can exist except what's there.
> There are no recesses in the room, only alcoves,
> And the window doesn't matter much, or that
> Sliver of window or mirror on the right[.]

The painting, in its "serene" presentation of such conditions of form as these in a "gesture which is neither embrace not warning / But which holds something of both," seems a rich complex of remarks about language and writing and art.

In the second section, staring at what could be his own reflection, Ashbery opens up what he calls "the straight way out, / The distance between us." He does so by emphasizing the difference between his irregular, multiple-voiced sense of himself – "How many people came and stayed a certain time, /

Dust jacket for Ashbery's only novel, which was begun in 1952 as an amusement on a drive into New York from the Hamptons (courtesy of the Lilly Library, Indiana University)

Uttered light or dark speech that became part of you" – and the "control" exerted by the painting's "curved hand" over "irregular," "windblown" influences. He pulls back from the painting's insistence on reducing multiplicity to a single gesture:

> desks, papers, books,
> Photographs of friends, the window and the trees
> Merging in one neutral band that surrounds
> Me on all sides, everywhere I look.
> And I cannot explain the action of leveling,
> Why it should all boil down to one
> Uniform substance, a magma of interiors.

In *Three Poems* Ashbery proposed that an opened space paradoxically might provide "the shortest distance between your aims and those of the beloved, the only human ground" of live, intimate contact, and here he readies himself to speculate on the life of the "distorted" language in this space.

The next three sections spin out a series of reflections. What is the relation between form and

such uncharted, dreamlike "vacuum[s]" as consciousness that it draws from and necessarily distorts? Through form, "Something like living occurs, a movement / Out of the dream into its codification." And why is seeing oneself in the otherness of form, being conscious of it, important? Why slow or distort the process of self-reflection so that it can be examined? Because, to put it simply, it is how one lives, in and out of poems. The painting, the poem's examined "you," becomes a metaphor or a way to make visible the larger process of moving through life:

> Since it is a metaphor
> Made to include us, we are part of it and
> Can live in it as in fact we have done,
> Only leaving our minds bare for questioning
> We now see will not take place at random
> But in an orderly way that means to menace
> Nobody – the normal way things are done,
> Like the concentric growing up of days
> Around a life[.]

The last section of the poem, as in *Three Poems*, becomes a recital. The poet pulls back from the mirror, insisting that "you can't live there," yet working through some descriptions of the value of its "demonstration." Most powerfully, the painting – or poetry, or consciousness about our mental activity – is valuable because readers are able to feel their way into this most fundamental and generative of human activities:

> Is there anything
> To be serious about beyond this otherness
> That gets included in the most ordinary
> Forms of daily activity, changing everything
> Slightly and profoundly, and tearing the matter
> Of creation, any creation, not just artistic creation
> Out of our hands, to install it on some monstrous, near
> Peak, too close to ignore, too far
> For one to intervene? This otherness, this
> "Not-being-us" is all there is to look at
> In the mirror, though no one can say
> How it came to be that way.

All of Ashbery's poetry makes visible the otherness of all human attempts at order. It reveals them to be finite, as distorted as a convex mirror. And his poetry allows readers to handle a distance that is – as the live, tentative ground of all human activity – the only thing worth being serious about. His work challenges his readers' fundamental approach to language.

In work subsequent to *Three Poems* and *Self-Portrait in a Convex Mirror* Ashbery brings his notion of the generative pause in language much more quickly into play. In *Houseboat Days* (1977) simply calling attention to the lyric — its compression and comparisons, its turn toward meaning — is enough to foreground the distorted hand of art. "What is Poetry," one title asks. Almost every poem in this collection contributes to a discussion of poetics, the "I" of the poem seemingly looking across at the "you" in the lyrics it is accumulating and then reflecting on that distance.

Much of the discussion in *Houseboat Days* is quite straightforward, as if Ashbery is talking with students or responding to an interviewer's questions. What prompts the peculiar slide into private song of a typical Ashbery lyric, poised and listening to itself? The poet provides an answer in "Variant": "Sometimes a word will start it, like / Hands and feet, sun and gloves. The way / Is fraught with danger, you say, and I / Notice the word 'fraught' as you are telling / Me about huge secret valleys." The question of why Ashbery is attracted to "Unctuous Platitudes" is perhaps best answered in the poem of that title:

I like the really wonderful way you express things
So that it might be said, that of all the ways in which to

Emphasize a posture or a particular mental climate
Like this gray-violet one with a thin white irregular line

Descending the two vertical sides, these are those which
Can also unsay an infinite number of pauses

In the ceramic day.

A reader may well feel there is something dangerously self-absorbed about the insistent "unsaying" of one's own "ceramic" intentions and ask about the real world outside of language. Ashbery seems to respond to such a question in "And Others, Vaguer Presences":

It is argued that these structures address themselves
To exclusively aesthetic concerns, like windmills
On a vast plain. To which it is answered
That there are no other questions than these,
Half squashed in mud, emerging out of the moment
We all live, learning to like it.

In Ashbery's work the question of poetry is really a version of all questions. To understand, as is asserted in "Business Personals," that "songs decorate our notion of the world / And mark its limits, like a frieze of soap-bubbles" is to become aware of the tentative ground of all human dealings with the world.

The poems foreground poetry's lyric business as deliberately as Parmigianino's choice of convex mirror and curved painting surface foregrounded the necessary distortions of self-portraiture. "Street Musicians" begins with what seems an account of two companions, separated by death:

One died, and the soul was wrenched out
Of the other in life, who, walking the streets
Wrapped in an identity like a coat, sees on and on
The same corners, volumetrics, shadows
Under trees. Farther than anyone was ever
Called, through increasingly suburban airs
And ways, with autumn falling over everything[.]

The poem gives readers what it calls "beached / Glimpses of what the other was up to" — the figure separated from its companion and wandering soulless through the streets. As the story unfolds, one realizes that death may have been simply a metaphor for separation: "So they grew to hate and forget each other." Every lyric in its use of comparisons proclaims that "dull refrain" and yet, as Ashbery notes, also discovers space to slide and play:

So I cradle this average violin that knows
Only forgotten showtunes, but argues
The possibility of free declamation anchored
To a dull refrain, the year turning over on itself
In November, with the spaces among the days
More literal, the meat more visible on the bone.

In "And *Ut Pictura Poesis* Is Her Name" Ashbery begins by denying Horace's notion of a "poem-painting." Refusing beauty, the poem enters into language's open spaces where odd things occur:

You can't say it that way any more.
Bothered about beauty you have to
Come out into the open, into a clearing,
And rest. Certainly whatever funny happens to you
Is OK.

And yet, as that open space fills with the things of the day handled and discarded — "She approached me / About buying her desk. Suddenly the street was / Bananas and the clangor of Japanese instruments" — a sort of poem-painting does emerge, but is assembled out of

                              an almost empty mind
Colliding with the lush, Rousseau-like foliage of its
     desire to communicate
Something between breaths, if only for the sake

Of others and their desire to understand you and
   desert you
For other centers of communication, so that
   understanding
May begin, and in doing so be undone.

Through its "painting" the poem initiates the reader into the experience of the pause that is the lyric, the generative coming undone of language. Such propositions are offered and debated throughout *Houseboat Days,* making it one of Ashbery's most-quoted collections.

Ashbery prides himself on the inventiveness with which he sets up his explorations of the conditions of language — arrangements designed, as he puts it in "The System," to "restore . . . the pause" and surprise him into telling it with "a new voice." "Litany," a sixty-page poem from *As We Know* (1979), is his most striking improvisation. Written in two sides of a notebook, on different days, the piece was published as a poem in two columns — one roman, one italic — conducting what Ashbery in his "Author's Note" to the poem calls "simultaneous but independent monologues." Although such a form leaves many choices up to the reader and makes a complete account of the poem all but impossible, it seems that the two voices, both the poet's, pursue two different aspects of the same problem. The first voice, rendered in roman type on the left side of the page, calls attention repeatedly to the limits of writing and form. Recalling the voices found in the first sections of "Self-Portrait in a Convex Mirror" and *Three Poems,* in the discussions of wreckage in "Europe" as well as in many other places, it is the voice of acknowledgment, calling attention to the placement of structures "on death's dark river." The poem's second voice, in italic type on the right, describes the landscape opened up in the pause or gap in language. It too is much in evidence in Ashbery's earlier work — in the description of Guadalajara in "The Instruction Manual," offering linguistic versions of skaters' displays in "The Skaters," playing out the implications of Parmigianino's "metaphor made to include us" in "Self-Portrait in a Convex Mirror," or "spectating" in *Three Poems.*

The inventiveness in "Litany" is the presentation of these two concerns simultaneously, with each voice standing at a distance from the other — dramatized by the white space between them — and thus appearing at different times to borrow from, support, contradict, and ignore its neighbor. The presentation, like the worn clichés of *Three Poems* or the deliberately foregrounded distortion of Parmigianino's self-portrait or the display of the lyric's

characteristics in *Houseboat Days,* acts out formally what the poem is about, providing the "system" that the poet and his reader must engage. Both voices seem to talk constantly about the fact of their simultaneous existence — reflecting the easily grasped idea that many potential trains of thought can coexist in the mind — often by taking note of the white space between them. Their simultaneity puts the reader (and perhaps the writer) in a state of heightened uneasiness, for one is often unsure whether the assertions of one voice can stand up to the implied criticism of the other. As John Keeling argues, such reading and writing, with some things always unsettled and not taken in, provides what Ashbery calls an exercise in "not-knowing." But it is a not-knowing native to the conditions of language, its uneasy "human ground." One way of reading "Litany" is to first work out the separate tracks of each voice, which seem to be repeated in each of the poem's three sections, and then to explore the effects of the simultaneous presentation.

In the first section of "Litany," sixteen pages, the poet describes himself in the left-hand column as someone, busy about his "accounts," who likes still performances — things "Kept in one place." That, he assures the reader, is why he is engaging in raising the flowers of this poem: "They do not stand for flowers or / Anything pretty they are / Code names for the silence." Encoding his silent experience, giving it visibility and voice, however, immediately brings him face to face with the limits of his tools. This realization is figured in his noticing "dust blow[ing] through / A diagram of a room":

The dust blows in.
The disturbance is
Nonverbal communication:
Meaningless syllables that
Have a music of their own,
The music of sex, or any
Nameless event, something
That can only be taken as
Itself.

If not all of the "event" can be known, then language becomes a "great implosion" (as is shown in the wreckage of "Europe") testifying to how much of the event it is silent about: "it persists / In dumbness which isn't even / A negative articulation — persists / And collapses into itself." At best, the articulation of a life articulates language's struggle with itself: "The motion by which a life / May be known and recognized, / [Is] a shipwreck seen from the shore, / A puzzling column of figures." Striking analogies for that puzzling wreckage mount, each new linguistic turn itself an example of the impossibility of giving voice to the poem's center-of-the-page blank. Language offers "a rush of disguises / For the elegant truth"; "a talking picture of you" reduced by a ticking clock to "mummified writing / . . . that never completes its curve / Or the thought of what / It was going to say"; "A sheaf of selected odes / Bundled on the waters"; the "zillionth" sampling of the past here, at the "fixed wall of water / That indicates where the present leaves off / And the past begins." To put it bluntly, language produces a feeling of life being "woven on death's loom."

Ashbery's second voice eyes that same blank center space but describes that *"hole"* as a *"cloud /. . . haze that casts / The milk of enchantment / Over the whole town,"* revealing what *"Could be happening / Behind tall hedges / Of dark, lissome knowledge."* And what remains when our ability to know has been erased? It is the stuff of language, the "ways of speaking" displayed in earlier poems: *"Around us are signposts / Pointing to the past, / The old-fashioned, pointed / Wooden kind. And nothing directs / To the present."* But new ways of speaking are found and made available: *"A new alertness changes / Into the look of things / Placed on the railing / Of this terrace."* The terrace here is the center gap, acknowledged by the first voice; the "things" are what other poems have called the linguistic "workings" of you scattered around the backyard, disassembled and known intimately. The backyard of this poem, to give just one of his striking analogies, is a place in language where, like the academy, ways of speaking in the world are held in solution:

> *Certainly the academy has performed*
> *A useful function. Where else could*
> *Tiny flecks of plaster float almost*
> *Forever in innocuous sundown almost*
> *Fashionable as the dark probes again.*

As these two voices in the first section of "Litany" begin to wind down – "You knew / You were coming to the end by the way the other / Would be beginning again, so that nobody / Was ever lonesome" – they begin to take explicit note of what the distortion of the two voices together has produced. The first voice speaks of the way the constant pressure of alternate ways of voicing produces "only picture-making" and no "dramatic conclusion" but comments on the fragile intimacy, aware of the live edges between things, that has been experienced as a result:

A broadside of an early version of a poem that Ashbery revised for inclusion in The Double Dream of Spring *(1970)*

> Under
> The intimate light of the lantern
> One really felt rather than saw
> The thin, terrifying edges between things
> And their terrible cold breath.
> And no one longed for the great generalities
> These seemed to preclude.

The second voice, in tones a little softer, insists that the collapse of sentences, the breaking off of generalities, and the wandering without authority have produced in this section another version of "the shortest distance between your aims and those of the beloved, the only human ground":

> *Two could*
> *Go on at once without special permission*
> *And the dreams were responsible to no base*
> *Of authority but could wander on for*

Short distances into the amazing nearness
That the world seemed to be.

The world is near because of language's acknowledged finitude; "small and clear and free," it leaves the edges between things.

In the long second section of forty pages the play of the voices continues. The first voice becomes concerned with the way the attempt to unfold the complexities of the moment inevitably leads away from singleness to an ever-expanding network. As in "Some Trees," the poem acknowledges the powers of that almost-monstrous expansion:

> There comes a time when the moment
> Is full of, knows only itself.
> . . . .
>   Then there are two moments,
> How can I explain?
> It was as though this thing –
> More creature than person –
> Lumbered at me out of the storm,
> Brandishing a half-demolished beach umbrella,
> So that there might be merely this thing
> And me to tell about it.

As is typical of Ashbery, a series of analogies follows. The loss of the moment is like never being able to catch up with oneself: "All that fall I wanted to be with you, / Tried to catch up to you in the streets / Of that time." It is a pursuit conducted with a certain stylistic charm:

>   Poetry
> Has already happened. And the agony
> Of looking steadily at something isn't
> really there at all, it's something you
> Once read about; its narrative thread
> Carries it far beyond what it thought it was
> All het up about; its charm, no longer
> A diversionary tactic, is something like
> Grace, in the long run, which is what poetry is.

Most forcefully, the loss is a failure of the word:

>   It all boils down to
> Nothing, one supposes. There is a central crater
> Which is the word, and around it
> All the things that have names, a commotion
> Of thrushes pretending to have hatched
> Out of the great egg that still hasn't been laid.
> These one gets to know, and by then
> They have formed tightly compartmented, almost
>   feudal
> Societies claiming kinship with the word.

Across the gap, accompanying this acknowledgment, the second voice points to what is possible

in language, now that the claims of the sentence are derailed and "*the code is ventilated.*" The voice insists it is able now "*to get inside the frame*" or move freely "*inside its space,*" having grown "*aware through the layers of numbing comfort / the eiderdown of materialism and space, how much meaning / Was there languishing at the roots, and how / To take some of it home before it melts.*" An extended analogy linking an acknowledgment of language's gaps – its inability to ever complete its notation of a series of moments – and the life-giving ventilation of its code summarizes many of the concerns of this section:

> *The shops here don't sell anything*
> *One would want to buy.*
> *It's even hard to tell exactly what*
> *They're selling – in one you might*
> *Find a pile of ventilators next*
> *To a lot of cuckoo-clock parts,*
> *Plus used government documents and stacks*
> *Of cans of brine shrimp*
> *. . . . .*
>   *You*
> *Pick up certain things, here, where*
> *You need them, and*
> *Do without the others for a moment,*
> *Essential though they may be.*
> *Every collection is notable for its gaps*
> *As for what's there. The wisest among us*
> *Collect gaps, knowing it's the only way*
> *To realize a more complete collection.*

By taking up gap collecting, Ashbery enables all sorts of things to happen. A little later the second voice exults, "*We can breathe!*" Perhaps most important, though, is that gap collecting establishes a new, intimate ground where, always realizing the incompleteness of the current effort, Ashbery and his reader can keep looking forward to new voices and expansions. Such an unfolding of life in language is, Ashbery would claim, a display of the human condition and allows him to make an ambitious claim for his art:

> *But exactly whom are you aware of*
> *Who can describe the exact feel*
> *And slant of a field in such a way as to*
> *Make you wish you were in it, or better yet*
> *To make you realize that you actually are in it*
> *For better or worse, with no*
> *Conceivable way of getting out?*
> *This is what*
> *Great poets of the past have done, and a few*
> *Great critics as well.*

As with the first section of "Litany," an extensive play goes on between the two voices – quite deliberately unsettling any too-neat readings. For example, the concept of distance is first established and then unsettled as it is passed back and forth between the two voices. The first voice introduces the idea of distance indirectly as part of a lament about its separation from the world it yearns to enter by words: "Supposing that you are a wall / And can never contribute to nature anything / But the feeling of being alongside it, / . . . so that nature / Seems farther apart from itself because of you." The second voice, a few pages later, celebrating this very feeling of language's wandering inability to grasp, observes that the acknowledgment of distance is the very ground of freedom: "*opening landscapes, / New people, mingling in new conversations, / Yet distant, as the back of one's head is distant.*" The first voice, building on that sense of what an acknowledgment of distance might offer in the way of a new approach to the world, both agrees and disagrees some pages later, suggesting one might use such an acknowledgement of distance without continually discussing it as a concept:

In the distance one could see oneself, drawn
On the air like one of Millet's "Gleaners," extracting
This or that from the vulgar stubble, with the roister-
    ing
Of harvesters long extinct, dead for the ear, and in the
    middle
Distance, one's new approximation of oneself:
A seated figure, neither imperious nor querulous,
No longer invoking the riddle of the skies, of distance[.]

The second voice momentarily takes up this invitation, speculating that perhaps a tale could be written so forcefully that "*like gothic / Architecture seen from a great distance, / [It] booms on in such a way / As to make us forget the prodigious / Distance of the waking from the / Thing that was going on.*" The second voice quickly recovers and refuses such a forgetting, but still a larger point is made – that no concept is guaranteed, that the positing of any idea involves a willingness to expose oneself to its hearing and use (across the gap) by others. Finally, both voices do seem to come to rest close to each other: the first claiming darkly that "on death's dark river, / . . . persons / Gesture hurriedly at each other from a distance"; the second insisting that those limited gestures are the heart of the matter, an entering of the "*in between . . . / . . . past the point of conscious inquiry, noodling in the near / Infinite, off limits.*" The off-limits, then, is brought near by the acknowledgment of the limits of "conscious inquiry" created by the dark river of time – an acknowledgment that the whole ("the near infinite") is out of the reach of mastery but open to the play of "noodling."

A lithograph Ashbery made in 1971 incorporating lines from "Variations, Calypso and Fugue on a Theme of Ella Wheeler Wilcox," a poem in The Double Dream of Spring

The last section of "Litany" is another of Ashbery's familiar recitals. It is only ten pages long, with both voices attempting to lay claim to having best demonstrated the implications of the poem's form – that is, in a phrase they both repeat, that poetry "starts out / With some notion and switches to both." Perhaps the best way to note the successful way they seem to chatter at, disarm, and build from each other is simply to notice that the second voice begins, from the first page of this section, by missing the other voice. "*I want him here,*" it states, noting the need for that other voice in order to prompt reflection on the powers of "not-knowing":

The sunset is no reflection
Of its not-knowing – even its knowing
Can be known but is not
A reflection[.]

As the first voice across the gap begins to speak, reflecting and bending the second's investigatory claims, the second voice takes note: "*But the sunset sees its reflection, and / In the curve / Is cured. People, not all, come back / To us in pairs or threes*." The intimate exchange concludes in the poem's last lines with the first voice speaking by itself of that chiming play:

> It would probably be best
> To hang on to these words if only
> For the rhyme. Little enough,
> But later on, at the summit, it won't
> Matter so much that they fled like arrows
> From the taut sting of restrained
> Consciousness, only that they mattered.
> For the present, our not-knowing
> Delights them.

The poem returns to words, finding an attitude that acknowledges both what Elizabeth Bishop in "Poem" calls "the little that we get for free" and the limits of replacing consciousness with matter but understands now that "it won't / matter so much."

Shadow Train, a collection of fifty poems, each in an identical sixteen-line, four-quatrain form, explores the distance between language and the world in yet another way. As Helen Vendler has noted, the opening poem, "The Pursuit of Happiness," explicitly contrasts the method of dramatizing the conditions of language employed in "Litany" with the approach played out in the new collection. "It came about that there was no way of passing / Between the twin partitions that presented / A unified facade," Ashbery begins, leaving unstated the fact that it was precisely the failure to pass through such divisions of the voice that "ventilated the code" and allowed "Litany" to open up the "exact feel and slant of [the] field" that he insists all must find themselves in. What drives his new poems, Ashbery suggests, is the idea of regularity – the form of each poem by its tidy stanzas suggesting language's fierce drive to order and regularize. Like Parmigianino's mirror, the "incisive shadow" of form, "too perfect in its outrageous / Regularity," becomes the acknowledgment that drives the poems. The poems may be read as links of a single meditation – a shadow train – on the conditions of language that their own form visibly foregrounds. Their regularity is Ashbery's means of presenting the tomb or gap or lyric foreshortening that forces readers to pause in their unblinking use of language as a simple, transparent tool.

Many of the poems in *Shadow Train,* expounding Stevens's image in "Of Modern Poetry," are presented as dramatizations of language. References to drama or the stage occur in at least half of them. The second and third poems indicate Ashbery's approach. The first stanza of "Punishing the Myth" suggests that the demands of form quickly foreground the distance between language and what it would grasp:

> At first it came easily, with the knowledge of the
>   shadow line
> Picking its way through various landscapes before
>   coming
> To stand far from you, to bless you incidentally
> In sorting out what was best for it, and most suitable[.]

The imposition of form as a way of knowing, with its sorting through various physical and mental landscapes, can be thought of as a shadow across the hills. As with Emily Dickinson's spring light that "passes and we stay," form holds the world at a distance, and yet Ashbery will argue it "blesses you incidentally" by staging for readers (and making accessible) the ground of their knowing separateness: "So we wiggled in our separate positions / And stayed in them for a time. After something has passed / You begin to see yourself as you would look to yourself on a stage." "Paradoxes and Oxymorons" in the first line explicitly identifies itself as a poem "concerned with language on a very plain level." "Look at it talking to you," Ashbery insists and tugs his reader to see the way these meditations dramatize systems of words:

> Bringing a system of them into play. Play?
> Well, actually, yes, but I consider play to be
>
> A deeper outside thing, a dreamed role-pattern,
> As in the division of grace these long August days
> Without proof. Open-ended. And before you know it
> It gets lost in the steam and chatter of typewriters,
>
> It has been played once more.

Here is a summary of Ashbery's career. Words in formal systems can be played out – their roles or patterns stepped through in exaggerated, visible ways. Quickly lost and abandoned, these played-out systems demonstrate their ungrounded status. There's no "proof" for their claims, no ground for the way they divide up the quotidian world, and an "open-ended" variety of ways they can be used and responded to. But they show Ashbery and his readers themselves, small, clear, and free.

Ashbery's dramatic play is evident in many poems. In such poems as "White-Collar Crime" Ashbery seems to take the role of director giving instructions to an actor:

Now that you've done it, say OK, that's it for a
    while.
His fault wasn't great; it was over-eagerness; it didn't
    deserve
The death penalty, but it's different when it happens
In your neighborhood, on your doorstep[.]

Another example is found in "Everyman's Library":

                              You send someone
Down the flight of stairs to ask after

The true course of events and the answer always
Comes back evasive yet polite: you have only to step
    down . . .
Oops, the light went out.

Often the poems in the volume are built around
a climactic sudden ending, the violent reining in
of a poem's wayward wanderings: "Thus one always reins in, after too much thoughtfulness, the
joke / Prescription. Games were made to seem like
that: the raw fruit, bleeding" ("Breezy Stories").
The constant pressure to conclude is a clear dramatic impetus, as in "Catalpas":

You knew the plot before, and expected to arrive in this
    place
At the appointed time, and now it's almost over, even

As it's erupting in huge blankets of forms and solemn,
Candy-colored ideas that you recognize as your own,
Only they look so strange up on the stage, like the light
That shines through sleep.

"The Vegetarians," the book's final poem,
functions as a ritual summary of how to take and
use these little dramas. If form is a shadowy train or
a series of "long tables leading down to the sun, / A
great gesture building," then these poems, deflating
each verbal gesture by convex-mirror-like exaggeration, "accept it so as to play with it / And translate
when its attention is deflated for the one second / Of
eternity." As always Ashbery insists that his poems
translate and dramatize something already known,
a matter of casual awareness as forms are employed
in daily encounters – a pause, a passing shadow,
that all must adjust to and are spurred on by:

Extreme patience and persistence are required,

Yet everybody succeeds at this before being handed
The surprise box lunch of the rest of his life. But what
    is
Truly startling is that it all happens modestly in the
    vein of

True living[.]

It is that "one second / Of eternity," there in all
sentences that Ashbery, by whatever means possible, would dramatize, for as "attention is deflated"
and as the gap is acknowledged, a new sort of
linguistic breathing occurs, as in "A Prison All the
Same": "Not until someone falls, or hesitates, does
the renewal occur, / And then it's only for a second,
like a breath of air / On a hot, muggy afternoon
with no air-conditioning."

In the six-hundred-line title poem from *A
Wave,* Ashbery, instead of a series of illustrations
to dramatize his issues, uses just one, discovering
yet another way to put language on a near peak
where its sense of "Not-being-us" might be seen
and speculatively entered. It is an elegant proposal:

One idea is enough to organize a life and project it
Into unusual but viable forms, but many ideas merely
Lead one thither into a morass of their own good
    intentions.
Think how many the average person has during the
    course of a day, or night,
So that they become a luminous backdrop to ever-
    repeated
Gestures, having no life of their own, but only echoing
The suspicions of their possessor. It's fun to scratch
    around
And maybe come up with something. But for the ten-
    der blur
Of the setting to mean something, words must be
    ejected bodily,
A certain crispness be avoided in favor of a density
Of strutted opinion doomed to wilt in oblivion[.]

That single idea, which Ashbery describes as
the dense way consciousness "Focuses itself, . . .
the backward part of life that is / Partially coming
into view," offers a way of breaking free of the
blur of already-established, glanced-over thought
patterns that we naturally sink toward, but it is a
break doomed in advance to "wilt" as its distance
from our multiple world becomes clear: "It passes
through you, emerges on the other side / And is
now a distant city, with all / The possibilities
shrouded in a narrative moratorium." It is that
distance that the poem investigates.

Unlike some Ashbery poems, "A Wave,"
though it feints otherwise – "the topic / Of
today's lecture doesn't exist yet" – freely announces its central idea, brought forward and
then lost in "that dream of rubble that was the
city of our starting out." It is the idea of love –
thought about, one supposes, under the shadow

Dust jacket for Ashbery's 1972 book, which includes prose meditations on the limits and possibilities of language (courtesy of the Lilly Library, Indiana University)

of a serious spinal infection that, in 1982, almost killed Ashbery. He describes himself as "putting together notes related to the question of love / For the many, for two people at once, and for myself / In a time of need unlike those that have arisen so far," insisting that his handling of such materials is really intended to demonstrate the course of a single idea and to move about within the space opened up by the inevitably broken-off authority of that system.

Ashbery speculatively enters the ground established by

> the trials and dangerous situations that any love,
> However well-meaning, has to use as terms in the
> argument
> That is the reflexive play of our living together and
> being lost
> And then changed again, a harmless fantasy that must
> grow
> Progressively serious, and soon state its case succinctly
> And dangerously[.]

What he proposes, then, is to keep his eye on this idea as its wave crashes into thought and passes (like "being" in "The Skaters") on through:

> And as the luckless describe love in glowing terms to
> strangers
> In taverns, and the seemingly blessed may be unaware
> of having lost it,
> So always there is a small remnant
> Whose lives are congruent with their souls
> And who ever afterwards know no mystery in it,
> The cimmerian moment in which all lives, all destinies
> And incomplete destinies were swamped
> As though by a giant wave that picks itself up
> Out of a calm sea and retreats again into nowhere
> Once its damage is done.

Ashbery watches that wave, watches himself think in it, and speculatively plays out what he notices about his own system of thinking, proposing to make visible, by means of that "harmless fantasy," the grounds "of our living together."

Ashbery's comments are much more directly focused on his own reflections in "A Wave" than in his previous work. After pronouncing himself "set free on an ocean of language," he notes, "I hadn't expected a glance to be that direct, coming from a sculpture / Of moments, thoughts added on." It is as though his thought (which is never entirely seen) is going on across a gap — as if one of the simultaneous columns of "Litany" is invisibly there, chattering away, while only the other is heard describing it:

> Moving on we approached the top
> Of the thing, only it was dark and no one could see,
> Only somebody said it was a miracle we had gotten
> past the
> Previous phase, now faced with each other's
> conflicting
> Wishes and the hope for a certain peace, so this would
> be
> Our box and we would stay in it for as long
> As we found it comfortable, for the broken desires
> Inside were as nothing to the steeply shelving terrain
> outside[.]

Halfway through this poem of one idea, he declares himself ready:

> the poem, growing up through the floor,
> Standing tall in tubers, invading and smashing the
> ritual
> Parlor, demands to be met on its own terms now,
> Now the preliminary negotiations are at last over.

Ten pages later, as he winds toward a conclusion, he looks at his thoughts about the "invisible current" of that idea and notes, as if looking into the parts yard of *Three Poems* or the network of Guadalajara:

> I feel at peace with the parts of myself
> That questioned this other, easygoing side, chafed it
> To a knotted rope of guesswork looming out of storms
> And darkness and proceeding on its way into nowhere
> Barely muttering. Always, a few errands
> Summon us periodically from the room of our
>   forethought
> And that is a good thing. And such attentiveness
> Besides!

It eventually becomes clear that the not-knowing referred to in the poem's opening line is what "A Wave" is out to describe and measure. As he comments on his thinking about the idea of love, the poet discovers how much not-knowing is involved in his thinking and comes to value it as yet another pause that opens new spaces to speak within. He sees that not-knowing's "stiff standing around, waiting helplessly / And mechanically for instructions that never come, suits the space / Of our intense uncommunicated speculation . . . / . . . and tames it / For observation purposes." Accordingly, Ashbery constantly calls attention to spots in the process where he is able to step back from the idea and, in that "inexpressive void," discover new tools to think with. "Is there something new to see, to speculate on?," he asks at one point. "Dunno, better / Stand back until something comes along to explain it."

Falling away from the idea becomes a tool to see with: "Forgetting about 'love' / For a moment puts one miles ahead, on the steppe or desert / Whose precise distance as it feels I / Want to emphasize and estimate." The moment occurs when

> The machinery of the great exegesis is only
>   beginning
> To groan and hum. There are moments like this one
> That are almost silent, so that bird-watchers like us
> Can come, and stay awhile, reflecting on shades of
>   difference
> In past performances, and move on refreshed[.]

In fact, the poem argues, interruptions are where one begins to feel one's way into the conditions of loving or thinking or being a finite language user. How limited the tools that one has acquired mastery over actually are is very clear in this moment of not knowing, distracted and speechless, when the world begins to show itself and language starts up again:

> But there is something else – call it a consistent
>   eventfulness,
> A common appreciation of the way things have of
>   enfolding
> When your attention is distracted for a moment, and
>   then
> It's all bumps and history[.]
> . . . .
> And they can at last know the fun of not having it all
>   but
> Having instead a keen appreciation of the ways in
>   which it
> Underachieves as well as rages: an appetite
> For want of a better word. In darkness and silence.

The appreciation of understanding's limits provides an opportunity to be alert and attentive to the way touch and love, most alive in the context of limits, really work:

> What were the interruptions that
> Led us here and then shanghaied us if not sincere
>   attempts to
> Understand and so desire another person, it doesn't
> Matter which one, and then, self-abandoned, to build
>   ourselves
> So as to desire him fully, and at the last moment be
> Taken aback at such luck: the feeling, invisible but alert.

A MacArthur Award in 1985 allowed Ashbery to resign from an art critic's position at *Newsweek* that he had held since the early 1980s. Perhaps as a result, the individual lyrics of *April Galleons* (1987) all have to do with the outside world, and the weather, the seasons, the rush of detail outside the "window" of one's consciousness function as the language or "system" of articulation in the collection. The constant circling around to "the moist imprecise sky" or the "rush of season into season" or "the combination of fog and wind" is enough to foreground the issue of articulation, for the weather raises the problem of language's finitude as surely as a discussion of the lyric or a book-long experiment with dueling voices. The landscape outside is so various and unmasterable that in entering it armed with words one necessarily encounters limits: "its pictures / Teasing our notion of fragility with their monumental presence."

Reading Ashbery's poems as a sequence, one recognizes strategies – "listen[ing] to see what words materialize / On the windowpane this time" and "look[ing] out of the window / Past his or her own reflection to the bright, patterned / Timeless unofficial truth hanging around out there" – that have been present throughout Ashbery's career. In "Dreams of Adulthood" "say[ing] it like that . . . / Dream[ing] it like that over landscapes spotted with

cream" inevitably prompts "the feeling that something /
Enormous, like a huge canvas, is happening . . . / . . .
without one single scrap of information being
vouchsafed."

The experience of not-knowing leaves the
reader in a "large, square, open landscape" where
objects are alive in their individual peculiarity, as in
"no I Don't":

> Our fathers, who had so many categories
> For so few things, could have supplied a term
> Like a special brush for bathing, and in due course this
> Peculiarity would have faded into the sum of light,
> An entity no more. But we perceive it as another kind
>   of thing,
> From another order[.]

But also, as is especially clear in Ashbery's work
after *Three Poems,* the experience of being brought
face to face with his distance from storm or sky, his
lack of "assimilation," continually places him in a
position from which words start up again:

> those who lived in a landscape without fully
>   understanding it, may,
> By their ignorance and needing help blossom again in
>   the same season into a new
> Angle or knot, without feeling unwanted again.

This blossoming, in which one is "always . . . quite
conscious of the edges of things," their separate
existence, is perhaps the key experience of
Ashbery's poetry. It is as if, out of silence and one's
imposed muteness, the largeness surrounding one
shatters the monolith of language into a rich shimmer of displayed parts, freed now each to go its own
way:

> I have my notebook ready.
> And the richly falling light will transform us
> Then, into mute and privileged spectators.
> I never do know how to end any season,
> Do you? And it never matters; between the catch
> And the fall, a new series has been propounded
> With brio and elan.

Flow Chart (1991), a poem written over the
course of six months, in six sections, each composed of almost daily, one-to-four page uncoilings
of thought, is Ashbery's boldest attempt to record
"consciousness of existence." His invitation to his
own consciousness this time seems marked by
something close to sheer nerve and desperation:

> Which reminds me:
> when are we going to get together? I mean really – not
>   just for a

drink and smoke, but *really*
invade each other's privacy in a significant way that
   will make sense
and later amends to both of us for having done so, for
   I am
short of the mark despite my bluster and my
   swaggering,
have no real home and no one to inhabit it except you
whom I am in danger of losing permanently as a
   bluefish slips off
the deck of a ship, as a tuna flounders, but say, you know
   all that.

Once again Ashbery's poem takes readers' realization that much of what passes for the union of
speech and the wordless is in fact "bluster and . . .
swaggering," takes their awareness that the "interior phrase" has "no real home," and finds in these
realizations a problem to be struggled with. As in
his previous work Ashbery in *Flow Chart* engages
language in order to demonstrate a new way to
"make sense," promising, if readers follow along,
"amends for having done so." What's new is that
this poem offers Ashbery's most sustained demonstration of *how* one might find in language's pause a
blossoming of new relations.

Ashbery clearly introduces his issues in the
poem's first section. If not a real home, what might
the "I" expect of its uneasy appeal to the wordless
"you"?

> [I]t seems we must
> stay in an uneasy relationship, not quite fitting
> together, not precisely friends or lovers though
>   certainly not enemies, if
> the buoyancy of the spongy terrain on which we exist
>   is to be experienced
> as an ichor, not a commentary on all that is missing
>   from the reflection
> in the mirror. *Did I say that? Can this be me?* Otherwise
>   the treaty will
> seem premature, the peace unearned, and one might as
>   well slink back
> into the solitude of the kennel, for the blunder to be
>   read as anything
> but willful, self-indulgent.

Ashbery proposes here that keeping the uneasiness
of his relationship with the "you" constantly before
his eyes – seemingly surprising himself, for example, with his own language when he asks "*Can this be
me?*" – renders the terrain of language both spongy
and buoyant. Emerson, who in "The Poet" looked
forward to a writer who would be able to step back
from and "articulate" the tropes we inhabit, described the "strange and beautiful" results of such a
project as an "immortal ichor." Though Ashbery's

tongue is firmly in his cheek when he picks up the word, he means it as well, for in handling language, in uneasily working its terrain – Robert Frost's frozen swamp in "The Wood-Pile" where no labor of the mind holds for long – he intends to release and "chart" language's "flow." The trick is to keep the terrain uneasy, the too easy retreat into seeing language as "a commentary on all that is missing from the reflection / in the mirror" as much a threat to that flow as a too easy embrace.

The way Ashbery in *Flow Chart* acknowledges and enters an uneasy relationship with language's conditions is through allowing its sentences to drift, a tendency perhaps encouraged by the great length of the poem. On the book's first page he makes a distinction between "those who ... / ... know enough not to look up / from the page they are reading, the plaited lines that extend / like a bronze chain into eternity" and another reader who acknowledges, "*It seems I was reading something;* / I have forgotten the sense of it or what the small / role of the central poem made me want to feel. No matter." Letting language go its own way, Ashbery describes himself, in his not-knowing, as watching or listening as his sentences "untie / gently, like a knotted shoelace, and then little expressions of relief occur in the whorls." In those pockets of relief, "the subject / going off on its own again," language is reestablished as an area where one can "pause and inspect / the still-fertile ground of our once-valid compact / with the ordinary and the true."

The reader begins Ashbery's poem, then, aware of the limits of and the eventual collapse of expression but aware too that the poem will continue, free to question, free to breathe:

> Still in the published city but not yet
> overtaken by a new form of despair, I ask
> the diagram: is it the foretaste of pain
> it might easily be? Or an emptiness
> so sudden it leaves the girders
> whanging in the absence of wind,
> the sky milk-blue and astringent?

These questions, alive in those whorls where language has been freed of the responsibility of proceeding toward an end, produce exploratory runs of speech whose authority has been "delegated" and dispersed into a myriad of investigations:

> Oh I'm so sorry, golly, how
> nothing ever really comes to fruition. But by the same
> token I am relieved of manifold responsibilities,
> am allowed to delegate authority, and before I know it,
> my mood

Dust jacket for Ashbery's 1975 collection, which won a Pulitzer Prize, a National Book Award, and a National Book Critics Circle Award (courtesy of the Lilly Library, Indiana University)

> has changed, like a torn circus poster that becomes
> pristine again in reverse cinematography,
> and these moments of course matter, and fall by the way-
> side in a positive sense.

The passages cited above are drawn from the poem's first section, and one might legitimately argue that the other sections of the poem, much like Ashbery's collections of lyrics that work over a single problem or shape, simply rework the same concerns, switching from one "channel" or "frequency" to another. To recognize that these repeated concerns are raised in order to keep the relationship between "I" and "you" uneasy, the terrain they share "spongy" and "fertile," is to see that the real interest of the poem is the varied responses to the problem of language rather than the problem itself.

The second section, for example, inspects the uneasy relationship by constantly touching on the notion of "place." In the book's unraveling sentences one's "fog-shrouded destination," under scrutiny, always recedes:

> A sore spot in my memory undoes what
> I have just written
> as fast as I can write; weave, and it shall be unraveled;
> talk, and the listener response
> will take your breath away, so it is decreed. And I shall
> be traveling on
> a little farther to a favorite spot of mine, O you'd like it, but
> no one can go there.

Ashbery puts the reader in a place where the idea of destination becomes irrelevant, which opens up a larger and more interesting problem:

> taking a wrong turning and then after a fretful period
> emerging in some nice
> place we didn't know existed, and would never have
> found without being misled
> by the distracted look in someone's eyes. It's mostly
> green then; the waves are peaceful;
> rabbits hop here and there. And the landscape you saw
> from afar, from the tower,
> really is miniature, it wasn't the laws of perspective
> that made it seem so,
> but for now one must forego it in interests of finding
> an open, habitable space,
> which isn't going to be easy. In fact, it's the big problem
> one was being led
> up to all along under the guise of being obliged to look out
> for oneself [.]

Following the promptings of a "distracted look" rather than a map, Ashbery's spills of language continually take their fretful, attentive ways down a myriad of "wrong turnings." In each case, as destination (viewed from afar) is inevitably abandoned, these runs find themselves worrying the same "big problem": how to find an open space where "you" and "I" can dwell. At every juncture it becomes clear that that open space is in fact the act of questioning — the detour that of course always threatens to cease being a wrong turn and lead somewhere:

> I was appointed to meet you
> and bring you to this place, locus of many diagonals
> without beginning or end except for the sense of them a
> place of confluence
>
> provides. So, as is the custom here, I pulled the hood
> down to cover most of my face.
> In a twinkling the mood had changed. The hiatus in
> the manuscript
> buttoned itself up.

The third section suggests that the way one inhabits the buoyancy of these hiatuses, these fretful

skids of language where many vectors and slants are visible, is by watching oneself in the medium and playing out the parts spread out on the wall:

> one was forced to make snap judgments, though the
> norms unfolded naturally enough,
> constructing themselves, and it wasn't until you found
> yourself inside a huge pen
> or panopticon that you realized the story had disappeared
> like water into the desert sand,
> although it still continued. I guess that was the time I
> understood enough
> to seize one of the roles and make it mine, and knew what
> I heard myself saying

> all the porters have shuffled away, under the erroneous
> impression we haven't the coin
> to pay them no doubt, yet it's not true, we would pay
> them if we could, but just look
> how they have left the funhouse mirror clearly visible
> for perhaps the first time
> and we can at last admire our billowing hips and
> hourglass waists

This pattern emerges frequently throughout the poem's middle sections: forward movement disappears (the story line vanishes; the wind takes over; porters misunderstand; writing is laid aside), leaving one, uneasily, with the language itself in one's hands — its drives and conditions distorted and blown, variously, into visibility.

Becoming aware of such textures, Ashbery asserts in the fourth section, is how we establish a "home" where there is no real one. Dwelling in language, it becomes clear, is different from using or mastering it. Such a home is both hauntingly familiar ("The beloved home with its misted windows, its teakettle, its worn places on the ceiling") and oddly unsettled: "I walked in, not at all sure of myself . . . / . . . [those before me] departed to seek out others and compare notes / on the battle of time being waged in spiral notebooks." Such a home is built, in fact, out of familiarizing oneself with, even exploiting, the uneasiness. Ashbery calls this, at one point, buying in bulk — building not out of language's drive to get somewhere but out of what is simply there in the territory to be handled and tasted and worked: "it's something you can build with. You need no longer inspect the materials / when you buy in bulk; they are as a territory. What gets built happens / to be in that territory, though beside it."

Ashbery labels this nonknowing, nondriven attitude toward language as poetry — and perhaps it is his poem's most important claim:

Any day now you must start to dwell in it,
the poetry, and for this, grave preparations must be
    made, the walks of sand
raked, the rubble wall picked clean of dead vine stems,
    but what
if poetry were something else entirely, not this purple
    weather
with the eye of a god attached, that sees
inward and outward? What if it were only a small,
    other way of living,
like being in the wind? or letting the various settling
    sounds we hear now
rest and record the effort any creature has to put forth
    to summon its spirits for a moment and then
fall silent, hoping that enough has happened?

This, of course, is another sort of poetry than many readers expect, something less grand in its ambitions, lacking the omniscient "eye of a god." It is "only a small, other way of living," one that elevates "effort," not vision. An alive awareness of the attempt to "summon . . . spirits" to visibility, an effort that can be heard and recorded – often, as Ashbery shows, in the creaks and groans of its settling and abandoned structures. What it takes to make poetry out of such a settling is the ability not to force these attempts back on track, but, as he asserts in *Reported Sightings,* rather to listen: "to let things, finally, be."

The last two sections of *Flow Chart* are extended summaries – evaluations in which the poet looks back over his words and listens as they fall silent. "So that's it, really," Ashbery writes, "the proper walk must be aborted / and tangled hope restored to its rightful place in the hierarchy of dutiful devotions." That restoration, that tangled letting be of language, offers not a real home for what is interior but a rich record of awareness:

                    your house or my house,
this time?
            I really think it's my turn,
but the variations don't let you proceed along one footpath
    normally; there are
too many ways to go. I guess that's what I meant. Why
    I was worried,
all along, I mean, though I knew it was superfluous
    and that you'd love me for it
or for anything else as long as I could sort out the
    strands that brought us together
and dye them for identification purposes further on,
    but you
don't have to remain that generalized.

The "I" invites the "you" to its house, conscious that there is no direct way there. The richness of the tangled space between – call it language – is a source of worry, evidently of losing their way, and

yet worry and what it shows about language – that relationship alive and no longer "generalized" – is "what I meant." This is language not as a poet normally moves through it, generating a few strands of complication to be dyed and separated by the figure in charge, but language allowed to be "normal" – language that can only be generated and made visible by the sort of "tangled hope" driving this poem, simultaneously "wanting to know" and accepting "colorful inroads":

            If you can think constructively, cogently,
on a spring morning like this and really want to know
    the result in advance, and can
accept the inroads colorful difficulties can sometimes
    make as well as all the
fortunate happening, the unexpected pleasures and all
    that[.]

Both desires engaged, hope tangles, language spreads, and effort is recorded. Something "exterior" forms and slides and twists into visibility, rendering the medium charged and almost erotically alive:

                    And though the armature
that supports all these varied and indeed desperate
    initiatives has begun
to exhibit signs of metal fatigue it is nonetheless sound
    and beautiful in its capacity to perform
 functions and imagine new ones when appropriate, the
    best model anyone has thought up
so far, like a poplar that bends and bends and is always
    capable of straightening itself
after the wind has gone; in short it is my home, and
    you are welcome in it
for as long as you wish to stay and abide by the rules.
    Still,
the doubling impulse that draws me toward it like
    some insane sexual attraction can
not be realized here.

In *Hotel Lautréamont* (1992) Ashbery continues the exploration of the metaphor of the unending wandering journey in *Flow Chart* but, as in *April Galleons,* he works through a series of single lyrics, almost all of which frame themselves as discussions of movement. One learns, after multiple readings, to listen for the verbs related to movement, a long list that includes *stay, advance, stop, wait, get off, move on, emerge, stumble, trot, wander, travel, walk, ride, march, run, crawl, waltz, plod, backtrack, drift, leave, hover, jiggle, bushwhack, slither, chase, bumble, approach, limp, turn,* and *tour.* One might call this book, as the poem "No Good at Names" puts it, an examination of "Great travel writing" – the repeated words, like the convex mirror, foregrounding certain aspects of

Dust jacket for Ashbery's 1981 collection of fifty poems, each comprising four quatrains (courtesy of the Lilly Library, Indiana University)

the writing process, becoming the system of concerns Ashbery brings into play. In "Light Turnouts" he imagines the entry into language in terms of movement:

> One of us stays behind.
> One of us advances on the bridge
> as on a carpet. Life – it's marvelous –
> follows and falls behind.

As Ashbery's "you" advances, its initial attempts at describing the shared life driven by the demands of description off on its own way, his "I" "stays behind." Life, not seized because of that separation, remains ungrasped and "marvelous" in the not-knowing.

Because there is no end, no "knowing where to stop on an adventure," one is ushered again into an open space where new possibilities can be teased out, or unraveled, as in "A Sedentary Existence":

> This space
> between me and what I had to say
> is inspiring. There's a freshness
> to the air; the crowds on Fifth Avenue
> are pertinent, and the days up ahead,
> Still formless, unseen.

Ashbery's work is perhaps most notable for the inventive ways he allegorizes and describes the pause where the space between the speaker and his speech opens up.

One might read the allegories of *Hotel Lautréamont,* for example, as descriptions of language's conditions scattered and waiting to be reassembled or as new possibilities of utterance suddenly coming within range. "I frequently get off before the stop that is mine / not out of modesty but a failure to keep the lines of communication / open within myself," Ashbery writes in "Autumn Telegram," linking the limits of its language to not reaching a destination. "I am in this street because I was / going someplace, and now, not to be there is here," he writes in "The Whole Is Admirably Composed," eyes on his never-completed chronicle. "There's the well where the message fell apart," comments a voice at the beginning of "Wild Boys of the Road."

Many striking images of "going nowhere" or "hav[ing] no place to go" – "My train is being flagged down"; "in the autumn the roads freeze over"; "An old jalopy with wobbly wheels was seen to limp / into an abandoned filling station" – are generated by the very lack of forward movement that they describe. Writing becomes the place where new imaginings unravel and are experienced. Intertwining the activities of writing and experiencing the world, Ashbery variously figures the writer as having "the courage to know nothing and simultaneously / be attentive"; as knowing "It is from the multiplication / of similar wacko configurations that theses do arise"; as giving up the drive "to contrast the ending / with the articulations that have gone before" and seeing in the space of those lost words "a single and sparing sharpness / that is an education in itself"; and as responding to "the cleft that produced nothing and knowledge, / the freedom to wait."

A good example of a poem in which an imagined experience is unraveled even as it is described is provided in Ashbery's "By Forced Marches." The poem's initial metaphor for the journey into consciousness is the parable of the prodigal son. His mind no longer "wander[ing] daintily as a stream meanders / through a meadow, for no apparent reason," the wandering son returns home from the wil-

*Dust jacket for Ashbery's 1991 book, in which he records the
flow of language through his consciousness during a six-month
period (courtesy of the Lilly Library,
Indiana University)*

derness. Ashbery imagines himself into the story even as he allows the parable to drive the poem, and the son returns to the father's celebration, a "din of slaughtered cattle." The uneasiness with this forced march and arrival having opened up some distance from the parable, Ashbery revises further, placing himself back in "the land we came from" but insisting that he is not met by a welcoming father. The expected end is withheld: "I am all I have. I am afraid. I am left alone."

Opting out of the story, "getting off before the stop that is mine," puts Ashbery in a responsive state of mind as he writes. The moment of departure is likened in the poem to reaching a division between the shallow part of a lake and "the deeper and silenter ship channel," seeing a "still-functioning beacon" flashing but not acting on that sign. It is a realization that in this place, the beacons of language's conditions still operating, "the links we left behind / must be reassembled." And it is a discovery that the reassembly happens simply by being attentive and being freed from having to tell a story. Ashbery's prodigal, loose from the original story, concludes his journey in this way:

> There were many of us at the stream's tip.
> I squatted nearby trying to eavesdrop on the sailors'
> conversations, to learn where they were going. Finally
> one comes to me and says I have the job if I want it.
> Want it! and so in this prismatic whirlpool I am re-
> newed
> for a space of time that means nothing to me.

. . . .
                                    And the old sense of a fullness
is here, though only lightly sketched in.

Ashbery's 1994 collection *And the Stars Were Shining,* like *Hotel Lautréamont* and *April Galleons,* is composed primarily of short lyrics. Ashbery presents the collection as joining what its first and last poems call "the celebration" – a celebration, perhaps, of the conditions that called Ashbery's poems into being as well as the freedom of expression he's discovered in them. "My own shoes have scarred the walk I've taken," Ashbery writes (sounding like Ezra Pound and Robert Lowell) in "Token Resistance. "I look ever closer / into the mirror, into the poured grain of its surface, until another I / seems to have turned brusquely to face me, ready / to reply at last to those questions put long ago," Ashbery asserts in "Bromeliads," eyes on the grain of language that has reflectively distorted him during the years. As always, his tone varies – shifting, for example, in the title poem from the matter-of-fact ("Rummaging through some old poems / for ideas") to the lyric ("O sweetest song / color of berries, that I lied for and extended / improbably a little distance from the given grave"). The poems as a whole form a many-voiced meditation on the inherited "grains" of language's reflective surface. Both their texture and many direct statements claim that the entrance into language breaks an unspoken wholeness into turning, contradictory pieces.

Words "divide the answer among them," the title poem asserts. Notable for "their unique / indifference to each other . . . / . . . and their tendency to fall apart," words defy logical connections:

> if only we weren't old-fashioned, and could swallow
> one word like a pill, and it would branch out thoughtfully
> to all the other words, like the sun following behind
>   the cloud shadow
> on a hummock, and our basket would be full,
> too ripe for the undoing, yet too spare for sleep,
> and the temperature would be exactly right.

In moving into words, one moves into a territory where, as Ashbery puts it in "Not Planning a Trip Back," the soul is never quite found: "The soul isn't engaged in trade. / It's woven of sleep and the weather / of sleep."

Ashbery's litany goes on. How can such an encroachment be seen as a celebration? Part of the answer is provided by the metaphorical furniture of these poems, a majority of which turn out to take place at or near the city or the sea. "You / will have to come up with something, / be it a terraced gambit above the sea / or gossip overheard in the market-place," he writes to himself in "Like a Sentence" concerning the materials available for his metaphorical self-examination. Those two settings forcefully dramatize the multiple, noncoherent elements or pieces from which one's made-visible experience is constructed: people on the street, fragments of overheard conversations (many of the poems contain discordant quotations), grains of sand, and wave washing upon wave. Such details provide material and turns for the poems' picturing of the word trade. The constant references to multiplying details show that art is composed out of what the first poem calls "a common light [that] bathes us, / a common fiction [that] reverberates as we pass" – a storehouse of fragments, worn and anonymous. It is "all the vulgarity / of time, from the Stone Age / to our present."

One can think of Ashbery, then, as looking over his work by engaging in "trade." He "celebrates" what his work has shown him about the freedom of words by embracing, like Whitman, the city and its voices rushing by. He plays those words out by making metaphors, for "comparison shopping is what this place's / all about" ("Spotlight on America"). Among Ashbery's most striking comparisons are accounts of what happens when one enters into words, "dream[s] turned inside out, exploded / into pieces of meaning":

> a slow train from Podunk, the ironed faces
> of the passengers at each window expressing something
>   precise
> but nothing in particular. ("Free Nail Polish")

> So, lost with the unclaimed lottery junk,
> uninventoried, you are an heir to anything.
>   ("The Story of Next Week")

> Shards, smiling beaches,
> abandon us somehow even as we converse with them.
>   ("The Improvement")

>   Count the pigeons, the people,
> townspeople, running fast in all directions.
>   ("Gummed Reinforcements")

> How funny your name would be
> if you could follow it back to where
> the first person thought of saying it,
> . . . .
>   It would
> be like following a river to its source,
> which would be impossible. ("Myrtle")

But finally, one is left with the unmistakable sense that it is the invigorating push and pull of the crowd of words and their formulations that matters most and that is celebrated not only in this collection but also by the whole of Ashbery's career. The title poem clearly argues that in voicing the limits of articulation, Ashbery and his readers enter, through sensing the smallness of their efforts, a grand free territory:

> It was a day, after all. One of those things like a length
>   of sleep
> like a woman's stocking, that you lay flat
> and it becomes a unit of your life – and this is where it
> gets complicated – of so many others' lives as well
> that there is no point in trying to make out, even less
>   read,
> the superimposed scripts in which the changes of the
>   decades
> were rung, endlessly
> . . . .
>   in an instant we realize we are free
> to go and return indefinitely.

Interviews:

John Ashbery and Kenneth Koch: A Conversation (Tucson, Ariz.: Interview Press, 1965);

Louis A. Osti, "The Craft of John Ashbery," *Confrontation,* 9 (Fall 1974): 84–96;

William Packard, ed., *The Craft of Poetry: Interviews from the New York Quarterly* (Garden City, N.Y.: Doubleday, 1974), pp. 111–132;

Richard Kostelanetz, "How to be a Difficult Poet," *New York Times Magazine,* 23 May 1976, pp. 18–26;

Al Poulin, Jr., "John Ashbery," *Michigan Quarterly Review,* 20 (Summer 1981): 243–255;

Richard Jackson, "The Imminence of a Revelation" in his *Acts of Mind: Conversations with Contemporary Poets* (University: University of Alabama Press, 1983), pp. 69–76;

John Koethe, "An Interview with John Ashbery," *subStance,* 37–38 (1983): 178–186;

Piotr Sommer, "An Interview in Warsaw," in *Code of Signals: Recent Writings in Poetics,* edited by Michael Palmer (Berkeley: North Atlantic Books, 1983), pp. 294–314;

Peter Stitt, "The Art of Poetry 33," *Paris Review,* 90 (Winter 1983): 30–59;

Sue Gangel, "John Ashbery," in *American Poetry Observed,* edited by Joe David Bellamy (Urbana & Chicago: University of Illinois Press, 1984), pp. 9–20;

Ross Labrie, "John Ashbery," *American Poetry Review,* 13 (May–June 1984): 29–33;

David Lehman, "John Ashbery: The Pleasures of Poetry," *New York Times Magazine,* 16 December 1984, pp. 62–92;

John Murphy, "John Ashbery," *Poetry Review,* 75 (August 1985): 20–25;

Dinitia Smith, "Poem Alone," *New York,* 24 (20 May 1991): 46–52.

Bibliography:

David K. Kermani, *John Ashbery: A Comprehensive Bibliography* (New York & London: Garland, 1976).

References:

Charles Altieri, "Contemporary Poetry as Philosophy: Subjective Agency in John Ashbery and C.K. Williams," *Contemporary Literature,* 33 (Summer 1992): 214–242;

Altieri, "John Ashbery: Discursive Rhetoric Within a Poetics of Thinking," in his *Self and Sensibility in Contemporary American Poetry* (Cambridge: Cambridge University Press, 1984), pp. 132–165;

Mutlu Konuk Blasing, "John Ashbery: Parodying the Paradox," in her *American Poetry: The Rhetoric of Its Forms* (New Haven: Yale University Press, 1987), pp. 200–213;

Harold Bloom, "The Breaking of Form," in *Deconstruction and Criticism* (New York: Continuum, 1979), pp. 1–38;

Bloom, "Measuring the Canon: John Ashbery's 'Wet Casements' and 'Tapestry,'" in his *Agon: Towards a Theory of Revisionism* (New York: Oxford University Press, 1982), pp. 270–289;

Bloom, ed., *Modern Critical Views: John Ashbery* (New York: Chelsea House, 1985);

David Bromwich, "John Ashbery: The Self Against Its Images," *Raritan,* 5 (Spring 1986): 36–58;

Bonnie Costello, "John Ashbery and the Idea of the Reader," *Contemporary Literature,* 23 (Fall 1982): 493–514;

Stephen Fredman, "'He Chose to Include': John Ashbery's *Three Poems,*" in his *Poet's Prose: The Crisis in American Verse* (Cambridge: Cambridge University Press, 1983), pp. 99–133;

Thomas Gardner, "A Metaphor Made to Include Us: John Ashbery's 'Self-Portrait in a Convex Mirror,'" in his *Discovering Ourselves in Whitman: The Contemporary American Long Poem* (Urbana: University of Illinois Press, 1989), pp. 144–169;

Richard Howard, "John Ashbery," in his *Alone with America: Essays on the Art of Poetry in the United States Since 1950* (New York: Atheneum, 1980), pp. 25–56;

Richard Jackson, "Nomadic Time: The Poetry of John Ashbery" in his *The Dismantling of Time in*

Contemporary Poetry (Tuscaloosa: University of Alabama Press, 1988), pp. 141–186;

David Kalstone, "John Ashbery: 'Self-Portrait in a Convex Mirror,'" in his *Five Temperaments* (New York: Oxford University Press, 1977), pp. 170–199;

John Keeling, "The Moment Unravels: Reading John Ashbery's 'Litany,'" *Twentieth Century Literature,* 38 (Summer 1992): 125–151;

Lynn Keller, *Re-making It New: Contemporary American Poetry and the Modernist Tradition* (Cambridge: Cambridge University Press, 1987);

David Lehman, ed., *Beyond Amazement: New Essays on John Ashbery* (Ithaca, N.Y. & London: Cornell University Press, 1980);

James McCorkle, "John Ashbery's *Artes Poeticae* of Self and Text," in his *The Still Performance: Writing, Self, and Interconnection in Five Postmodern American Poets* (Charlottesville: University Press of Virginia, 1989), pp. 46–86;

Karen Mills-Courts, "The Thing For Which There Is No Name," in her *Representation and Poetic Language* (Baton Rouge: Louisiana State University Press, 1990), pp. 267–314;

S.P. Mohanty and Jonathan Monroe, "John Ashbery and the Articulation of the Social," *Diacritics,* 17 (Summer 1987): 37–63;

Charles Molesworth, "'This Leaving-Out Business': The Poetry of John Ashbery," in his *The Fierce Embrace: A Study of Contemporary American Poetry* (Columbia: University of Missouri Press, 1979), pp. 163–183;

Marjorie Perloff, "Barthes, Ashbery, and the Zero Degree of Genre," in her *Poetic License: Essays on Modernist and Postmodernist Lyric* (Evanston: Northwestern University Press, 1990), pp. 267–284;

Perloff, "'Mysteries of Construction': The Dream Songs of John Ashbery," in her *The Poetics of Indeterminacy: Rimbaud to Cage* (Princeton: Princeton University Press, 1981), pp. 248–287;

Andrew Ross, "Doubting John Thomas," in his *The Failure of Modernism: Symptoms of American Poetry* (New York: Columbia University Press, 1986), pp. 159–208;

Susan M. Schultz, ed., *The Tribe of John: Ashbery and Contemporary Poetry* (Tuscaloosa: University of Alabama Press, 1995);

David Shapiro, *John Ashbery: An Introduction to the Poetry* (New York: Columbia University Press, 1979);

Vernon Shetley, "John Ashbery's Difficulty," in his *After the Death of Poetry* (Durham: Duke University Press, 1993), pp. 103–133;

John Shoptaw, "Investigating *The Tennis Court Oath,*" *Verse,* 8 (Spring 1991): 61–72;

Shoptaw, *On the Outside Looking Out: John Ashbery's Poetry* (Cambridge, Mass. & London: Harvard University Press, 1994);

Richard Stamelman, "Critical Reflections: Poetry and Art Criticism in Ashbery's 'Self-Portrait in a Convex Mirror,'" *New Literary History,* 15 (Spring 1984): 607–630;

Helen Vendler, "John Ashbery, Louise Glück," in her *The Music of What Happens: Poems, Poets, Critics* (Cambridge: Harvard University Press, 1988), pp. 224–261;

Robert von Hallberg, "Robert Creeley and John Ashbery: Systems," in his *American Poetry and Culture, 1954–1980* (Cambridge: Harvard University Press, 1985), pp. 36–61;

Geoff Ward, *Statutes of Liberty: The New York School of Poets* (New York: St. Martin's Press, 1993);

Alan Williamson, "The Diffracting Diamond: Ashbery, Romanticism, and Anti-Art," in his *Introspection and Contemporary Poetry* (Cambridge, Mass.: Harvard University Press, 1984), pp. 116–148;

Harriet Zinnes, "John Ashbery: The Way Time Feels As It Passes," *Hollins Critic,* 29 (June 1993): 1–13.

Robin Blaser

(18 May 1925 –   )

Miriam Nichols
University College of the Fraser Valley

BOOKS: *The Moth Poem* (San Francisco: White Rabbit Press, 1964);

Les Chimères: Translations of Nerval for Fran Herndon (San Francisco: Open Space, 1965);

Cups (San Francisco: Four Seasons Foundation, 1968);

Image-Nations 1–12 & The Stadium of the Mirror (London: Ferry Press, 1974);

Image-Nations 13 & 14, Luck Unluck Oneluck, Sky-stone, Suddenly, Gathering (North Vancouver, B.C.: Cobblestone Press, 1975);

Harp Trees (Vancouver: Sun Stone House & Cobblestone Press, 1977);

Image-Nation 15: The Lacquerhouse (Vancouver: W. Hoffer, 1981);

Syntax (Vancouver: Talonbooks, 1983);

The Faerie Queene and *The Park* (Vancouver: Fissure Books, 1987);

Pell Mell (Toronto: Coach House Press, 1988);

The Holy Forest (Toronto: Coach House Press, 1993).

RECORDING: *Astonishments,* Contemporary Literature Collection, W.A.C. Bennett Library, Simon Fraser University Library, 1974.

OTHER: "Apparators," in *A Poetry Folio* (San Francisco: Auerhahn Press, 1964);

Pacific Nation, no. 1 (1967), edited by Blaser; no. 2 (1969), edited by Blaser and Stan Persky;

"Artaud on Nerval," translated by Blaser and Richard Ross, *Pacific Nation,* no. 1 (1967): 67–78;

"Pindar's Seventh Olympic Hymn," translated by Blaser, *Caterpillar,* 12 (July 1970): 48–53;

"The Fire," in *The Poetics of the New American Poetry,* edited by Donald Allen and Warren Tallen (New York: Grove, 1974), pp. 235–246;

"The Practice of Outside," in *The Collected Books of Jack Spicer,* edited by Blaser (Los Angeles: Black Sparrow Press, 1975), pp. 271–326;

"Kimm," broadside (Prince George, B.C.: Caledonia Writing Series, 1977);

Robin Blaser, 1994 (courtesy of the author)

"Of is the word love without the initial consonant," broadside (Vancouver: Slug Press, 1979);

Mary Butts, *Imaginary Letters,* afterword by Blaser (Vancouver: Talonbooks, 1979), pp. 61–80;

George Bowering, *Particular Accidents: Selected Poems,* edited, with an introductory essay, by Blaser (Vancouver: Talonbooks, 1980);

Art and Reality: A Casebook of Concern, edited by Blaser and Robert Duncan (Vancouver: Talonbooks, 1986);

"Mind Canaries," in *Christos Dikeakos* (Vancouver: Vancouver Art Gallery, 1986), pp. 17–36;

Louis Dudek, *Infinite Worlds: The Poetry of Louis Dudek,* edited by Blaser (Montreal: Véhicule Press, 1988);

"Poetry and Positivisms," in *Silence, the Sacred and the Word,* edited by E. D. Blodgett and Harold Coward (Calgary: Calgary Institute for the Humanities, 1989), pp. 21–50;

"The Elf of It," in *Robert Duncan: Drawings and Decorated Books,* edited by Christopher Wagstaff (San Francisco: Rose Books, 1992), pp. 21–53;

"The Recovery of the Public World" and "Among Afterthoughts on This Occasion," in *Reflections on Cultural Policy, Past, Present and Future,* edited by Blaser, Evan Alderson, and Harold Coward (Waterloo: Wilfred Laurier University Press for the Calgary Institute for the Humanities, 1993), pp. 17–38, 183–190;

"Here Lies the Woodpecker Who Was Zeus," in *A Sacred Quest,* edited by Wagstaff (Kingston, N.Y.: McPherson, 1995), pp. 159–223;

Preface to the Early Poems of Robert Duncan (Toronto & Buffalo: Shuffaloff, 1995), pp. 1–9.

SELECTED PERIODICAL PUBLICATIONS – UNCOLLECTED: "Particles," *Pacific Nation,* no. 2 (February 1969): 27–42;

"The Violets: Charles Olson and Alfred North Whitehead," *Process Studies,* 13, no. 1 (1983): 27–42;

"Hello!," *Sulfur,* 37 (Fall 1995): 84–94;

"Nomad," *Sulfur,* 37 (Fall 1995): 117.

Robin Blaser first emerged as a poet during the late 1940s and early 1950s when he became a key participant with Jack Spicer and Robert Duncan in the Berkeley contingent of the San Francisco Renaissance. While his work has been recognized by writers Robert Creeley, Charles Olson, Louis Zukofsky, Charles Bernstein, George Bowering, B. P. Nichol, and Sharon Thesen and has influenced literary communities in San Francisco and Vancouver, to most American and Canadian critics he is still, as one reviewer put it, "alien exotica." Born and reared in the United States yet having lived in Vancouver since 1966 and become a Canadian citizen, Blaser has struck some critics as too Canadian, others as too American, and many as simply too esoteric to trouble much over; to date, little has been written about his work.

The dearth of criticism is at least partly attributable to the nature of Blaser's poetic project and his mode of composition. Since 1959 Blaser has been working on a long serial poem, *The Holy Forest,* in which he takes on the enormous task of sifting the aesthetic and philosophical implications of modernity. Although sections of the work have appeared as small press publications over the years, the poem generally has been unavailable to a wide readership. The Coach House release of *The Holy Forest* (1993), while not the poet's last word, represents the first opportunity for readers to survey the whole of the work as it currently stands and has generated more critical interest than Blaser has hitherto received. An international conference on his poetry and poetics was held in Vancouver in June 1995, and many of the papers produced for this event are still forthcoming.

Born in Denver, Colorado, in 1925 to Ina Mae McCready Blaser and Robert Augustus Blaser, Robin Blaser grew up in small desert communities in Idaho where his father and maternal grandmother, Sophia Nichols, worked for the railway. On *Astonishments,* a series of autobiographical tapes recorded in 1974, Blaser remembers the resentment and defensiveness of his working-class father toward the "old American" pretensions of Ina Mae's family, who traced their roots to Benjamin West and Harriet Beecher Stowe. In "Sophia Nichols," one of many poems in which his grandmother appears, Blaser acknowledges her efforts to keep "duty and love alive" in what might have been an emotional as well as a physical desert. Sophia's stories opened worlds beyond those of Wapai, Orchard, Blaser, Kimima, or Dietrich, and later it was Sophia who provided the financial support that sent Blaser to college.

After brief stints at Northwestern and the College of Idaho in Caldwell, Blaser entered the University of California, Berkeley, in 1944 to begin an education that had little to do with degrees or academic careers. As Creeley says in his foreword to *The Holy Forest,* this was a "legendary Berkeley, where learning for oneself and discovering the appropriate teacher . . . had still a singular value." Courses with gifted scholars such as Ernst Kantorowicz, a specialist in medieval political philosophy, became full-time jobs, and after meeting Spicer and Duncan, Blaser began to supplement his formal education at Duncan's "anti-university" soirées. The communal residences Duncan lived in at Throckmorton Manor and 2029 Hearst Street were meeting places where poets and students of the various arts took their own counsel on the moderns – William Butler Yeats, Rainer Maria Rilke, James Joyce, Stéphane Mallarmé, Ezra Pound, William Carlos Williams, T. S. Eliot, H. D., and Federico García Lorca. This off-campus apprenticeship in modernity and on-campus study of medieval, Renaissance, and romantic literatures would last nine years.

Blaser emerged from Berkeley in 1955 with an M.A. and an M.L.S.; in 1956 he accepted a position in the Widener Library at Harvard. In his essay "The Fire" (1967) Blaser dates his beginnings as a poet from 1955, the time when he began to distinguish his poetics from those of Spicer and Duncan. Written while he was at Harvard, the eight poems included in *The Holy Forest* under the title *Earlier, 1956–1958: The Boston Poems* are generally the earliest pieces Blaser preserves, although on *Astonishments* Blaser remembers writing volumes of Whitmanesque verse as an eighteen-year-old at Northwestern, and the "Lake of Souls" section in *Syntax* (1983) includes a poem from 1947.

The earliest *Holy Forest* poems introduce some of Blaser's most important recurring images and initiate a meditation on poetic language that runs throughout the poem. Here the first birds and trees, or words and image patterns, of his metaphoric forest begin to appear. Blaser's sense that symbolic language is entangled with a semiotic of nature that can never be fully domesticated to human intention is clear in even his earliest work; words are rhythmic noises as well as conveyors of meaning.

In "The Hunger of Sound," the most impressive of these early poems, Blaser tells a story about the childhood acquisition of language in which he locates poetic discourse between preverbal "measures" of the body and symbolic language. The world that begins to appear to the child as "a tree / first planted in chaos" is both a language system (with Indo-European roots and American branches) and an uncomposed materiality that eludes naming. This thought of the uncomposed — the other of consciousness — is central to Blaser's composition of what he calls the "real." In his essay "The Violets: Charles Olson and Alfred North Whitehead" (1983) Blaser catches the tone and effort of his own poetry:

Poets have repeatedly in this century turned philosophers, so to speak, in order to argue the value of poetry and its practice within the disturbed meanings of our time. These arguments are fascinating because they have everything to do with the poets' sense of reality in which imagery is entangled with thought. Often, they reflect Pound's sense of "make it new" or the modernist notion that this century and its art are simultaneously the end of something and the beginning of something else, a new consciousness, and so forth. It is not one argument or another for or against tradition, nor is it the complex renewal of the imaginary which our arts witness, for, as I take it, the enlightened mind does not undervalue the imaginary, which is the most striking matter of these poetics; what is laid out before us finally is the fundamental struggle for the nature of the real.

And this, in my view, is a spiritual struggle, both philosophical and poetic. Old spiritual forms, along with positivisms and materialisms, which "held" the real together have come loose. This is a cliché of our recognitions and condition. But we need only look at the energy of the struggle in philosophy and poetry to make it alive and central to our private and public lives.

The nearly four-hundred-page *Holy Forest* traces the whole of Blaser's career. In addition to *Earlier, 1956–1958: The Boston Poems* it includes sections titled *Cups* (1959–1960), *The Park* (1960), *The Faerie Queene* (1961), *The Moth Poem* (1962–1964), *Image-Nations* 1–4 (1962–1964), Les Chimères (1963–1964), Charms (1964–1968), Image-Nations 5–14 (1967–1974), *Streams I* (1974–1976), *Syntax* (1979–1981), *Pell Mell* (1981–1988), *Great Companions* (1971, 1988), *Streams II* (1986–1991), and *Exody* (1990–1993). Each part of the book each has its own particular textual history. *The Park* and *The Faerie Queene* appeared in journals well before they were published together as a chapbook in 1987. *Charms* was first published as "The Holy Forest section from *The Holy Forest*" in the July 1970 issue of *Caterpillar,* and *Streams I* was scattered among chapbook and broadside publications during the 1970s. Only *Streams II* and *Exody* include poems that appear for the first time in *The Holy Forest.*

Contrary to the impression given by a table of contents, Blaser's *Holy Forest* is not divisible into discrete units. Single images, poems, or even books are meaningful as elements in an endlessly recombinable series, and it is a distinguishing feature of Blaser's "art of combinations" that seemingly distinct elements are in fact inextricably entangled. Thematic continuity thus gives place to a formal labyrinth that Blaser sometimes refers to as "folded." The trope recalls the "yellow folds of thought" in Mallarmé's *Herodiade* or the pleats of the fan in "Évantail: De Madame Mallarmé" and "Autre Évantail: De Mademoiselle Mallarmé," which continually unfold and refold. Gilles Deleuze comments extensively on this metaphor in *The Fold: Leibniz and the Baroque* (1993), in which he visualizes the shape of Leibniz's baroque world as a draped fabric or "a sheet of paper divided into infinite folds or separated into bending movements, each one determined by the consistent or conspiring surroundings." As Deleuze points out, the "fold" anticipates the emphasis contemporary philosophers have placed on process, interrelationship, and modulation rather than on substance.

Blaser's revisionary understanding of the real is revealed in the way he handles the cultural fragments he inherits from the moderns. The broken

Blaser with his grandparents, Sophia Nichols and "Granpa Auer" (Sophia's second husband), in Idaho in 1926 (courtesy of the author)

mirror of *The Faerie Queene,* the bits of glass on the forest floor in *Charms,* or the wreckage of Atlantis in *The Moth Poem* allude to the ruins of an older worldview based on the primacy of the discrete entity – ruins still discernible in the collage work of modernists such as Pound or Eliot. As *The Holy Forest* unfolds, however, such fragments become better understood as so many lighted curves of a fabric, separated from each other by the dark folds that allow them to appear – the visible entangled with the invisible, the known with the unknown. As Blaser wryly quotes in *Pell Mell* (1988), "'If there's one thing Harry learned / to love more than the sacred, it was / the sacred in ruins.'"

Blaser had studied Mallarmé during his Berkeley years before beginning *The Holy Forest;* Deleuze enters the poem in a quotation from *The Fold* included in *Exody.* Between these two sources, which stand at the beginning and end of *The Holy Forest,* Alfred North Whitehead, Martin Heidegger, Maurice Merleau-Ponty, and Michel Serres (all philosophers of the fold, in Deleuze's view) are among those referenced in poems where *"being is complexity – of reunions – / of act – of quality – / of the world"* (*Pell Mell*) and "the *unfolded fold* is important and

onliest" (*Exody*). Whatever Blaser's subject matter – it ranges from the nature of history, the self, and the sacred to the shenanigans of the neighbors – it is the form of the poem that holds the creativity. In a passage key to his poetics, Blaser writes in *Pell Mell,* "I say or write the Nietzschean brilliance, / who knew that *the best writers understand / form as what others consider content.*"

In "The Fire" Blaser writes that "the real business of poetry is cosmology," and he locates his own poetic project within that Dantean quest for a worldview. However, *The Holy Forest* is always also a story about a man who, like Dante Alighieri, loses his way in a dark wood. This important narrative strand in the poem presupposes Whitehead's definition of subjectivity: the subject is not simply a static entity but a "point of view" and continuing event. In a comment on Whitehead's subject that is relevant to Blaser's work, Deleuze says that a "point of view . . . is not what varies with the subject, at least in the first instance; it is, to the contrary, the condition in which an eventual subject apprehends a variation"; this "perspectivism . . . is not a variation of truth according to the subject, but the condition in which the truth of a variation appears to the subject."

Blaser's hundreds of allusions and quotations in *The Holy Forest* contribute to the composition of an "eventual subject." In "The Art of Combinations" (*Pell Mell*) Blaser writes, "nothing simpler than what I have said because / I didn't say it, nothing simpler than what / I have said, because I said it – ." The narrative component of *The Holy Forest* records the wanderings of the poet toward ever larger areas of exploration – toward inclusiveness, in other words – but always with the awareness that the ripplings of the world exceed any one point of view or even the ideal sum of all. On this last point Blaser takes leave of the theological strand in the philosophical systems of both Leibniz and Whitehead to concur with Mallarmé that the ultimate language or point of view – God's view – is missing.

Blaser's earliest poems are shorter and more cryptic (more tightly "folded up") than his later pieces, but in a condensed manner they lay the groundwork for the larger poem. This is not to imply that *The Holy Forest* follows a preconceived plan but rather that each piece enables the next. Whatever happens in one poem provides possibilities for the next. The form of the poem unfolds as the poet makes choices. *Cups* (1968), the first published book of *The Holy Forest,* consists of twelve short poems written on Blaser's return to San Francisco from Boston in 1959. Woven of images from

Idaho, the poems of *Cups* exemplify the fractured, allusive style that has earned Blaser a reputation for obscurity. Read at the level of form, however, *Cups* simply enacts the formation of an "eventual subject." "Cups 1," for instance, opens with the poet gathering a bouquet of willow, iris, and pepper; this rather mundane activity serves to dramatize a formative interplay between subject and object:

> Inside I brought
> willows, the tips
> bursting,
> 　　　　blue
> iris (I forget
> the legend of long life
> they represent)
> and the branch of pepper tree[.]

The gesture of gathering the willow, iris, and pepper "inside I" implies the interpenetration of "inside" and "outside." The pun on "iris" – flower and iris of the eye – holds this interchange between seer and seen, while the bursting tips of the willows suggest the dynamism of form. As Blaser later says in "The Stadium of the Mirror" (1974), "Form is alive, not a completion of the heart or of the mind."

This opening image of the bursting willows and branch of the pepper tree also marks the poet's entrance into a "forest." In this first series of poems Blaser turns to Dante as a poet who had to compose his way out of a cultural exile. Like Dante's venture into the "dark wood," Blaser's entry into the forest is inspired by Amor. In "Cups 3" "the god / offer[s] with out-stretched hand / the heart to be devoured"; the scene corresponds to the one in *The Vita Nuova* where Amor offers the poet a flaming heart. Love of Beatrice first pulls Dante into a recognition of his lost condition and then into the composition of a world in which both he and the Beloved might be found. But for the poet of *Cups* there is no Virgil to act as a guide, because it is precisely the loss of classical and Christian traditions – an "anthropomorphism in tatters," Blaser later calls them – that has landed the poet in the forest to begin with. Dante could give his cosmos a human shape; Blaser cannot.

The Amor of *Cups* marries the poet not to a human figure but to a tree, an emblem of the human / nonhuman duplicity of word and world as Blaser had first imagined it in "The Hunger of Sound." The ceremony takes place in "Cups 9":

> Upon that tree there was a ring.
> HI　HO　HUM
> The ring surrounded the darkest part.
> HA　HA　HA

> The ring imagined a marriage bout.
> FIRE　FIRE　FIRE

These lines bind the poet to his task: for love of the world, he will recompose it. And lest a pathless forest seem too static a trope of the world, Blaser imagines the forest on fire. As Blaser's signature element, fire recurs throughout his work and signals metamorphosis – sense breaking into nonsense, form in the process of transformation. In "Cups 4," for example,

> The coyotes, burned out of their lairs,
> follow the railroad. Shapes
> of poems
> 　　　　fly out of the dark.

"Cups 11" shows the transforming effects of Blaser's fire as it fuses the personal and public, the poetic and political. The poem turns on an autobiographical fragment: the "Uncle Mitch" (Mitchell West) of this piece did, as the poem says, write westerns. On *Astonishments* Blaser recalls that his father burned a wicker trunkful of these manuscripts when Mitch was institutionalized for eccentricities that included the punctuation of his conversations with whistles. Blaser's own "western" moves from the memory of Mitch to a frontier story about the Mormon component of the family (Ina West Johnson, Blaser's great-grandmother, traveled west with Brigham Young). This family history then modulates into a fragmented account of the Mountain Meadows Massacre of 1857, in which a group of Mormons attacked a caravan of undesirable emigrants from Arkansas and Missouri, hoping to blame the incident on the Indians. The massacre, as presented in the poem, points to the consequences of building cultural "stockades":

> the stockade grew in our hearts –
> supperless – we hid
> in the brush – the colour
> of raspberries – the fire
> consumed – [.]

In the lines that immediately follow, musical notes, indicative of Mitch's whistles, puntuate the story and disturb the sense of it. The form of the poem thus enacts the breaking open of enclosures, whether they be the metaphorical enclosures of linear narratives or actual stockades. The poet's openness to what in "Cups 11" he calls the "dark" has a destabilizing effect on cultural grammars that claim totality – a claim that the poem implies can result in mental barricades and actual massacres.

In "The Practice of Outside," an essay written for *The Collected Books of Jack Spicer* (1975), Blaser argues the necessity of a poetic language that continually rends open completions of thought and feeling to admit an Otherness that cannot be administered by reason or corralled by belief. Citing Michel Foucault, Blaser argues that human constructions of the world are provisional and therefore always accompanied by an "unthought." If the poem is to reenact this temporality accurately, it must be situated on that imaginary border between the "already" and "not yet" of thought, where the known shatters and re-forms.

In *The Park* and *The Faerie Queene,* both first published in 1961, Blaser begins to work through the formal possibilities of the understanding achieved in *Cups. The Park* opens in Idaho, with "Cleo on the Section Gang / 75 miles of railroad Checking / the ties Repairing the washouts." On *Astonishments* Blaser recalls being nine years old when he met Cleo Adams, a young railroad worker who would spin tales about the rocks he collected to polish. Cleo's stories, as they later appear in "Image-Nation 4," were mythopoeic narratives or "ties" between the human world of discourse and a material world of brute facts ("rocks"). The traditional function of such myths is to create a world that is humanly meaningful – in the language of the poem to turn the wilderness into a park. But as *Cups* implies, the real is not reducible to the human narration of it. Blaser reverses the usual mythopoeic process through which events of the everyday become significant insofar as they can be made to exemplify existing cultural myths or patterns of meaning; in *The Park* the intrinsic ambiguity of common events displaces these patterns. Like the memory of Cleo, the autobiographical components of the poem become elements in a revisionary kind of narrative, indeterminate with respect to meaning and limited by point of view.

In *The Faerie Queene* "The gods written on paper flare up" in a transformational fire that signals a metamorphosis of older mythic forms (the "already thought"). What remains is "A mirror of leaves and noise" that is neither a transparency (a window on the world) nor a simple reflection of consciousness (a mirror of the self). Instead, the mirror-window – poetic language – becomes the locus of an event through which self and world take shape; language is form. This is poetry performing its traditional function as cosmogony, but here the creation of the world is a form of *poiesis* and hence a renewable event.

With *The Moth Poem* (1964) Blaser refolds his work on poetic language into a complex theory of translation. The blind flutterings of the moth represent the movements of the mind as it "translates" between the material and the intelligible. In *After Lorca* (1959) Spicer had focused on the sound, rhythm, and unrepeatable historical context of Lorca's poems. In "Letters" to the Spanish poet, he proposes to find correspondences in English for the untranslatable component of Lorca's Spanish: "that lemon may become this lemon, or it may become this piece of seaweed. . . ." *The Moth Poem* offers several tropes for this art of translation-as-correspondence." *Paradise Quotations,*" for instance, is a poem composed entirely of quotations. The decontextualized passages produce what might be construed as the body of a moth, as if the original texts could be made to release a materiality hitherto suppressed by the "content" or message.

"The Borrower" provides a translation of Nathaniel Hawthorne's "Artist of the Beautiful." It transports the story from the nineteenth to the twentieth century, from a romantic to a contemporary aesthetic, and from prose to poetry. In Hawthorne's tale a gorgeous mechanical butterfly is reduced to fragments in the careless grasp of a child. The exposure of the work of art as merely a material object destroys the illusion of life that was the artist's greatest achievement. In "The Borrower" a moth is crushed by "the one loved," but the exposed cavity of the body suggests a point of departure for the artist rather than defeat. In the "red water," "white threads," and "ghost of his thigh" the poet sees a "highway."

Blaser's meditations on translation come together in "The Translator: A Tale," a poem that tells the story of the poet's translation of the Attis myth from the Roman poet Gaius Valerius Catullus's Latin into English. Blaser frames his translation of the myth with a tale that corresponds to the original, juxtaposing a conventional translation from Latin to English, with a translation of the Spicerian kind:

> last night's coffee spoon sticks to the drainboard
> under it the clear print of a brown moth, made of sugar,
> cream, coffee with chicory, and a Mexican spoon of blue
> and white enamel

> The ashtray is full and should be emptied before working that translation[.]

The myth of Attis's self-castration in the service of the goddess Cybele follows, but in the last verse,

the mound of cigarette butts moves, the ashes shift,
fall back on themselves like sand, startle out of
the ashes, awakened by my burning cigarette, a brown
moth noses its way, takes flight[.]

The framing tale suggests the action of the Attis myth, not the sense. Attis is "translated" from man to woman. His male and female selves correspond to each other as a text in one language might correspond to that in another; the difference is literally material. The story of the moth emerging from the ashtray is a "translation" of this order: from the ash of a Latin myth about translation, a living emblem in English of the translator's art.

While writing *The Moth Poem* Blaser began to work on a translation of French poet Gérard de Nerval's sonnet sequence *Les Chimères* (1854). *Les Chimères: Translations of Nerval for Fran Herndon* (1965) marked a major shift in his career. Since Nerval's allusions to the death of the gods and the loss of traditional cultural grammars suggest an understanding of modernity close to that which informs *The Holy Forest,* Blaser's choice of Nerval may be seen as strategic. He treats the French text as a complex poetic event to be answered by a corresponding event specific to his own time, place, and language. The completed translations brought about a confrontation with Robert Duncan, who for different reasons considered *Les Chimères* as vital to his own work as Blaser felt it to be to his. In a 19 November 1965 letter Duncan attacked Blaser for "rejecting Nerval's source in his life (biography!) experience (mysticism!) or in his studies" and for eliminating "basic concepts at work in Nerval's poetics." The resulting quarrel is partially recorded in a special Duncan issue of *Audit* (1967), where Duncan presents his own version of *Les Chimères* and argues that Blaser sacrifices fidelity to Nerval's symbolic architecture for personal style. "Style," of course, constitutes for Blaser a point of view; the acknowledgment that one has a position is a mark of the honest poet.

The quarrel between Blaser and Duncan over *Les Chimères* marked a new low in a friendship already under stress from rivalries and dangerous liaisons within the fractured poetry community they shared. (Duncan and his companion, Jess Collins, did not care for Spicer's North Beach crowd; Blaser seems to have had a foot in both camps.) When Spicer died in the alcoholic ward of the San Francisco General Hospital in 1965, Berkeley had already begun to pale. In 1966 Blaser accepted a timely offer from Simon Fraser University in Vancouver. The newly established university was ac-

quiring a reputation for radical student politics, and the city offered a community of young writers who had already welcomed such "new American poets" as Duncan, Olson, Creeley, and Ginsberg to the Vancouver Poetry Conference at the University of British Columbia in 1963. Blaser would remain at Simon Fraser for the next twenty years, teaching in the Department of English and at the Centre for the Arts. Outside the university he would become a touchstone for several generations of Vancouver poets. The move, as Creeley says, allowed Blaser to come into "his own power without distraction or compromise."

In 1962 Blaser had begun an ongoing series of poems he intended to intersperse throughout his evolving *Holy Forest.* With the *Image-Nations* poems Blaser unfolds another facet of his work on translation through an investigation of the aesthetic and ethical implications of a post-Mallarméan world. The question for Blaser is how to "translate" or negotiate between divergent points of view. In the Leibnizian system each "monad" (Leibniz's term for a simple, indivisible substance) expresses the same world, although not all portions of it with equal clarity. The apparent disjunction between monads is a matter of point of view and in fact is a continuity from God's point of view. In such a world, ethical questions may be referred to natural law, since the existing world is an expression of the best possible world despite local dissonances. This thought of the whole – a form of humanism in Blaser's view – allows Duncan to affirm in "what is" an ethical as well as aesthetic imperative, and herein lies a major difference between Duncan and Blaser. In Blaser's Mallarméan modernity chance displaces principle; there is no transcendent point of view and hence no reconciliation of disjunctive positions. The world need not be unified, logically consistent, harmonious, nor compatible with human values and therefore cannot provide a foundation for ethical thought.

In the *Image-Nations* Blaser assembles hosts of images and voices, many of them conflicting. To borrow a line from *Pell Mell,* the poems are analogous to "a large, crowded reception / in a private house" – private because they are limited by the amplitude of the poet's point of view; public because they are open to whoever or whatever might come by. The ethics of this poetic lie in the possibility the poems enact of cohabitation within a space where differences may be sounded out. By listening to other voices Blaser signals a companionable willingness to share the earth as well as the textual space of the poem.

Blaser visiting a cemetery in Oakland, California, in 1955 (courtesy of the author)

In "Image-Nation 5 (erasure," composed after the *Les Chimères* episode, Blaser refers to the "quarrel over the immortal Word" with Duncan and then turns to the thought of divergent points of view. In one particularly dense passage, Imr Al-Qais, Jalal al-Din Rumi, Nerval, and Mallarmé are brought into the poem through quotation and allusion as poets who share Blaser's sense of the dynamics of poetic form. The passage opens with an allusion to the *Mu'Allaqa,* an eighth-century collection of seven Arabic poems sometimes called "the golden poems":

> traces the old Bedouin poets
> called them encampments of
> what was
>   a movement
> the seven poems, called golden
> give the same pattern
> of this movement[.]

Blaser goes on to quote Al-Qais, who is credited with the oldest of the seven poems; in the Arabic

poet's account of love and the nomadic life, Blaser finds a formal movement that corresponds to that in his own poetry. In Al-Qais's poem there is "a torrent / and then traces / *of wild beasts drowned / in the watercourse*"; in the context of Blaser's poem the image seems to allude to a poetic drama about the dissolution and emergence of form. Blaser answers with a corresponding image of the transformational fire that began to burn in *Cups:*

> the day lightning split the last
> big Douglas fir on this street
> all the houses filled with
> a pale-green, luminous
> movement
> I stood up from my work table
> waiting
> for the house to flame[.]

In the lines that follow this evocation of fire, the images suggest a movement from an inside ("house") to an outside ("falls, like rain"), from form-as-static to form-as-dynamic (dance, music), from the poet's point of view to that of others:

>   this co-herence   falls, like rain,
>   into the syllables
>   this in-herence
>   of a golden poem
>   translating
>   blood, dancers,
>   and whirling
>   drunken lives
>   into a tense
>   music
>   of a hollyhock[.]

The lines contain a suggestion of Rumi, the thirteenth-century Persian mystic credited with initiating the ecstatic whirling dance of the Mevlevi dervishes. Rumi's lyrics praise a divine Beloved who takes many forms but is ultimately beyond definition. Blaser later confirms the presence of the Persian poet with a quotation. Nerval is also present in Blaser's reference to "a golden poem," an allusion that conflates "the seven poems, called golden" with "Vers Dorés." In his *Les Chimères* Blaser translates the latter as "Golden Poem" and hears in the original a rebuke to human narcissism: "free of the dead, / what can be thought / seems to be yours in this world / where *it all coheres* / free to spend some powers, / but the universe is absent / from all your plans[.]" The implication of this passage is that the kind of thinking that would make all things cohere represents a false ideality. The voices of Blaser, Nerval, Rumi, and Al-Qais converge with that of Mallarmé on the elusive dynamism of the real:

>   Mallarmé said *l'immortelle*
>   *parole is* missing from our speech
>   the constant
>   movement
>   of a finitude
>   which re opens[.]

The poets Blaser assembles in this section of "Image-Nation 5" join a conversation about the nature of poetic form. Each poet presents the "movement / of a finitude" from his own point of view, and each unwittingly "translates" the others. However, the juxtapositioning of these voices also draws attention to the differences among them. Blaser makes no effort to reconcile Rumi's divine Beloved with the Mallarméan God who plays dice or the cultural grammar of Al-Qais's "golden poem" with that of Nerval's "Vers Dorés." The lightning-struck Douglas fir captures the imminent divergence of

these voices in an image and proclaims the destruction of organic wholes. The meeting of worlds Blaser effects is tentative and temporary, indicative of multiple and conflicting orders rather than coherent wholes.

Blaser's evocation of divergent worlds is key to the formal as well as the ethical significance of the "fold" in his serial poem. In contrast to the linear seriality implicit in the Leibnizian concept of one world expressible by many points of view, Blaser's seriality is close to what Deleuze calls a "nomadology," in which each unit ("nomad," point of view, or subject) may refer to more than one world. For Blaser the image is nomadic in this way — a point of intersection and divergence, exerting both a centrifugal and a centripetal force. The lightning-struck fir, for instance, would mean something different to each of the poets Blaser gathers: to Mallarmé, it might signify chance; to Rumi, the presence of the Beloved; to Blaser it could be an emblem of Duncan's attack on the aesthetic roots of *The Holy Forest*. As an element in each of these diverging worlds, the tree acts as a means of correspondence between them. In his 1969 essay "Particles" Blaser credits Hannah Arendt with influencing his politics, and from her he takes the notion that "To live together in the world means essentially that a world of things is between those who sit around it; the world, like every in-between, relates and separates men at the same time." The *Image-Nations* creates a world of things that in turn sustains discourse. As Blaser argues in "Particles," what can be shared is not a point of view but particularity as such.

Syntax, the next book-length installment of *The Holy Forest,* develops this work on diverging points of view through an investigation of word and world orders. This book takes its directive from a comment by Olson, which Blaser records in the poem "Diary, April 11, 1981":

>   Olson said, "I'd trust you
>   anywhere with image, but
>   you've got no syntax" (1958)

The irony, of course, is that Blaser's apparent lack of syntax is a considered element of his poetics. Dense with quotations and found poems, *Syntax* shows that no one "syntax" accounts for the world. *The Truth is Laughter* poems, an ongoing series of poems Blaser introduces in this book, draw attention to idiosyncrasies in human efforts to achieve complete systems or universal truths, dissolving the high seriousness of such pretensions into laughter as in "The Truth is Laughter 11":

> *Time* magazine said he used
> a screwdriver to divine the reason
> Moses took the long way around
> and a spell in Arabic: *some days*
> *it's honey, some days*
> *it's onions*[.]

Syntax also includes an exploration of human violence – an issue implicit in the idea of incompatible points of view. In "Image-Nation 17 (opercula" Blaser draws on Bernard-Henry Lévy's *Barbarism with a Human Face* to suggest that the expulsion of the sacred from contemporary thought has resulted in "this societal dream of itself as absolute / reality, then practiced as uniformity and barbarism." Although Blaser has always insisted that the Other is a necessary corollary of finitude, in this and other poems of *Syntax* he focuses more directly on the connection between the Other and the sacred. Like the Foucauldian "unthought" to which Blaser refers in "The Stadium of the Mirror" and "The Practice of Outside," the Other is not before or after conscious thought, but coeval with it – like a silence made audible by sound or a vacant lot made visible by the buildings that surround it.

While Blaser's evocation of the Other, which he capitalizes to distinguish it from the various othernesses referenced in *Syntax,* has sometimes been read as mysticism, the poet defines it as a space of accommodation. The Other enables divergent thought systems to coexist because it implies a limit on the claims of any one of them; no thought world is ultimate, and hence there is always room for others. To the extent that the Other invades syntaxes through silence or semiotic disruption, it not only destabilizes them but also gestures toward their mortality. Death is the Other that accompanies consciousness and which gives to others an elusiveness that resists appropriation. Such a figuration of the sacred qualifies the arguments of René Girard in *Violence and the Sacred* (1977), a text Blaser brings into "Lake of Souls." Girard contends that without some reference to a transcendent authority that can be used to mediate and arrest potentially endless rounds of vengeance, civil orders will simply dissipate into uncontrollable violence. Alternatively, Blaser develops the position he takes in "The Stadium of the Mirror": the Other is "not an object, but acts chiasmatically . . . [it is] the opposite and companion of any man's sudden form."

Begun in 1981, the year Blaser finished writing *Syntax, Pell Mell* was seven years in the making.

At 114 pages in the original Coach House publication of 1988, it is the largest book of the Holy Forest series and the one that most directly addresses the many discourses that have shaped contemporary thought about culture. The juxtapositions of such past thinkers and writers as Dante, Nicolaus Copernicus, Michel Eyquem de Montaigne, Sigmund Freud, and Karl Marx with Julia Kristeva, Jacques Derrida, Michel Serres, Geoffrey Hartman, and Cornelius Castoriadis bring a historical perspective to the contemporary discussion – a move on Blaser's part that enacts the premise of *Syntax* and distinguishes his compositional practice from that of other postmoderns. While many postmodern writers discard or deconstruct traditional cultural narratives as ideologically suspect – patriarchal, theological, hierarchal – Blaser rejects the truth claims of these narratives but contends that cultural memory is essential to an understanding of the historicity of the contemporary. As he says in the essay "The Recovery of the Public World" (1993):

> We need to know how old we are. We need to trace the consciousness of that ageing. In order to gain "an attitude that knows how to take care and preserve and admire the things of the world." Perhaps then we could turn with greater assurance and finer judgment to the modern project which is devoted to change.

"Fousang," a poem exemplary of Blaser's approach in *Pell Mell,* argues the political significance of cultural memory. A Chinese name for the northwest coast of North America, "Fousang" stands for the ahistorical fantasies of both East and West:

> You made the past
> a myth of nature
> or history
>
> you said the future
> would be this or
> that, devouring
> the unpredictable
>
> you fell into the East
> destroying an alphabet
> the future disappeared
> for a myriad
>
> millenial silliness
> at the heart of your notation – [.]

Whether conceived as a primordial golden age or an ultimate historical destiny, the utopianism represented by "Fousang" suggests at once a forgetting of history and a closure of the future into cultural narratives that have taken themselves as the only reality. Blaser argues that this amnesia conceals a bid for totality that forecloses the operations of chance:

> the whole
> light-body, unpredictable
> terrible, sexual, torn heart
> of the matter is not there
> matter is not there,
>
>   for that
>
> we can thank Soviets
> and U.S.'s alike, who alike stand
> for nothing
>
> matter is not there – turning,
> the birds of paradise grow
> feet and claws – the terror
> becomes elegant as in your grammar
> we are cast into nothing[.]

In recent history the efforts of revolutionaries in China and the former Soviet Union to erase a "decadent" past in the name of social justice has resulted in coercion ("feet and claws"). China offers the example of a cultural revolution that literally destroyed an alphabet by simplifying the written character ("you fell into the East / destroying an alphabet"). Similarly, Euro-American history includes a western advance (the "western" referenced in *Cups*) that thinly veils the destruction of aboriginal cultures in the name of destiny.

Against the forgetfulness of history represented by such "millenial silliness," Blaser poses the Memory Theatre. As early as his essay "The Fire" Blaser refers to Frances Yates's *The Art of Memory* (1966) to describe "the Memory Theatre, a box with tiers, where the initiate would take the place of the stage and look out on the tiers, which in an ordinary theatre would hold the audience, – here there are images upon images, so that a man could hold the whole world in view." Yates's Memory Theatre is a Renaissance version of a classical mnemonic device. The student of the classical art of memory would select a building or create one imaginatively and then mentally place mnemonic images in each room. The student would learn to trigger the desired memories by mentally walking through the building. The Memory Theatre of *Pell Mell* holds the histories of those sacred, social, and political narratives that have laid claim to the real; it functions both as a means of historicizing these grammars and of measuring those of the contemporary. This "fold" in *The Holy Forest* reveals the poem as both a site of reception and a public space for the

Blaser at the launch of The Holy Forest, *4 November 1994 (courtesy of the author)*

practice of ethical and aesthetic judgment. The poet stages a play of various worlds, against which the reader is invited to measure his or her own.

In the most recent additions to *The Holy Forest*, *Streams II* and *Exody*, Blaser begins to take the measure of popular culture and contemporary politics through the Memory Theatre. In "Of the Land of Culture" in *Streams II* Blaser juxtaposes a chilling description of our sorry civilization to Friedrich Nietzsche's voice: "*You are half-open doors at which grave-diggers wait. And this is / your reality: 'Everything is worthy of perishing.'*" In "Even on Sunday," a poem from *Exody* written for Vancouver's Gay Games (1990), Blaser takes on the homophobia of fundamentalist religious groups. He provides a historical perspective on "that blasphemy which defines god's / nature by our own hatred and prayers for vengeance and / dominance" by positioning homophobia within traditions of thought that have created "normed existence," thereby dividing insiders from outsiders.

It would be misleading to leave the impression that these later poems are given over to social criticism. Like Blaser's earlier work, they unfold the poet's delight in form. In *Exody* Blaser provides a space for the voices of Serres, Mark C. Taylor, and Deleuze in his meditation on the possibilities for a contemporary ontology, but the heart of the piece is a section on Hieronymus Bosch's painting *The Garden of Delights,* which Blaser reads through Michel de Certeau's *The Mystic Fable* (1982). This phantasmagoria of Bosch, as Blaser calls it, is made of "indeterminate realities and imaginings – / no entrance – no exit" – an *"unintelligibility that extinguishes / itself,* like Igitur or Thereupon, old friends."

In *The Mystic Fable* de Certeau speaks of Bosch's *Garden of Delights* as a visual presence that invites interpretation but also eludes it. The same might be said of *The Holy Forest;* the poem brings to momentary and partial presence an "eventual subject" that is also always a labyrinthine world. The garden of Bosch, the Memory Theatre, the work on translation, or the story of the poet who loses his way in a forest are not simply discrete moments in Blaser's poetic venture, but tropes that interpret and reshape each other. There is no transcendent point of view in this poem, and hence "no entrance – no exit." In "Image-Nation 25" the poet appears as a wanderer in this forest-garden of his own making. But Blaser tells us that the image he has in mind here comes from a "portrait of the / wandering Jew or nomad" on the "leather backrest" of an old rocking chair from the railcar the family called home in Idaho. The nomad in the rocker is a trope of the poet who is most at home wandering in the "yellow folds of thought" – the only home, the poem implies, that the human mind has ever had.

In *The Holy Forest* Blaser radicalizes the historical sensibility of Pound and Eliot beyond the modernist deference to tradition and historicizes the humanist strand in the poetries of immediate peers such as Duncan. Through his handling of divergent systems of thought, he also contributes to contemporary debates surrounding the aesthetic and ethical issues of pluralism. But most notably, Blaser reopens a discussion about the sacred at a time when many intellectuals have abandoned the debate; in the process he lays bare the theologisms that continue to inhabit secularity. Blaser argues that the real is not only what we say it is but also a chancy matter that eludes the human will.

Since his retirement from Simon Fraser University in 1986, Blaser continues to live and work in Vancouver with David Farwell, his companion since 1975. For years a private man, Blaser recently has given readings and talks in Canada and the United States and has participated in events organized by Vancouver's gay community. *The Holy Forest* is a life work, and Blaser is presently working on new additions. He is also preparing a collection of his essays for publication.

References:

Charles Bernstein, "Robin on His Own," *West Coast Line,* 17 (Fall 1995): 114–121;

Joseph Conte, "Seriality and the Contemporary Long Poem," *Sagetrieb,* 11 (Spring & Fall 1992): 35–45;

Kevin Killian, "Blaser Talk," *West Coast Line,* 17 (Fall 1995): 126–131;

Daphne Marlatt, "Erratic/Erotic Narrative: Syntax and Mortality in Robin Blaser's 'Image-Nations,'" *West Coast Line,* 17 (Fall 1995): 136–141;

Miriam Nichols, "Independent Realities: Notes on Robin Blaser's *Pell Mell,*" *Sulfur,* 27 (Fall 1990): 222–226;

Nichols, "Robin Blaser's Poetics of Relation: Thinking without Bannisters," *Sagetrieb,* 9 (Spring & Fall 1990): 121–145;

Nichols, "Robin Blaser's *Syntax*: Performing the Real," *Line,* no. 3 (Spring 1983): 64–77;

Nichols, "Three for Public: Steve McCaffery, Nicole Brossard, Robin Blaser," *Public* (Spring 1995);

Sherman Paul, "Serial Poems from Canada," in his *Hewing to Experience* (Iowa City: University of Iowa Press, 1989), pp. 37–48;

Peter Quartermain, "The Mind as Frying Pan: Robin Blaser's Humor," *Sulfur,* 37 (Fall 1995): 108–116;

Jed Rasula, "Taking Out the Tracks: Robin Blaser's Syncopation," *Sulfur,* 37 (Fall 1995): 95–107;

Charles Watts, "Foreword," *Sulfur,* 37 (Fall 1995): 81–84;

Phyllis Webb, "Robin Blaser's 'Image-Nations,'" *Nothing But Brush Strokes, The Writer as Critic: V,* edited by Smaro Kambaureli (Edmonton: NeWest Publishers, 1995), pp. 55–73.

William Bronk

(17 February 1918 –   )

John Ernest
University of New Hampshire

BOOKS: *Light and Dark* (Ashland, Mass.: Origin, 1956);

the World, the Worldless (New York & San Francisco: New Directions – San Francisco Review, 1964);

The Empty Hands (New Rochelle, N.Y.: Elizabeth, 1969);

That Tantalus (New Rochelle, N.Y.: Elizabeth, 1971);

To Praise the Music (New Rochelle, N.Y.: Elizabeth, 1972);

Utterances (Providence, R.I.: Burning Deck, 1972);

Looking at It (Rushden, U.K.: Sceptre, 1973);

The New World (New Rochelle, N.Y.: Elizabeth, 1974);

A Partial Glossary: Two Essays (New Rochelle, N.Y.: Elizabeth, 1974);

Silence and Metaphor (New Rochelle, N.Y.: Elizabeth, 1975);

The Stance (Port Townsend, Wash.: Greywolf, 1975);

Finding Losses (New Rochelle, N.Y.: Elizabeth, 1976);

The Meantime (New Rochelle, N.Y.: Elizabeth, 1976);

My Father Photographed with Friends and Other Pictures (New Rochelle, N.Y.: Elizabeth, 1976);

Twelve Losses Found (Lumb Bank, U.K.: Grosseteste Press, 1976);

That Beauty Still (Providence, R.I.: Burning Deck, 1978);

The Force of Desire (New Rochelle, N.Y.: Elizabeth, 1979);

The Brother in Elysium: Ideas of Friendship and Society in the United States (New Rochelle, N.Y.: Elizabeth, 1980);

Life Supports: New and Collected Poems (San Francisco: North Point, 1981);

Light in a Dark Sky (Concord, N.H.: Ewert, 1982);

Six Duplicities (Brooklyn, N.Y.: Jordan Davies, 1982);

William Bronk (photograph © Layle Silbert)

Vectors and Smoothable Curves: Collected Essays (San Francisco: North Point, 1983);

Careless Love and Its Apostrophes (New York: Red Ozier, 1985);

Manifest; and Furthermore (San Francisco: North Point, 1987);

Death Is the Place (San Francisco: North Point, 1989);

Living Instead (San Francisco: North Point, 1991);

Some Words (Mount Kisco, N.Y.: Asphodel, 1992);

The Mild Day (Hoboken, N.J.: Talisman, 1993);
Our Selves (Hoboken, N.J.: Talisman, 1994);
Selected Poems (New York: New Directions, 1995).

RECORDING: "William Bronk: A Selection," Watershed Signature Series, 1979.

SELECTED PERIODICAL PUBLICATION –
UNCOLLECTED: "The Actual and the Real in Thoreau," *Thoreau Quarterly: A Journal of Literary and Philosophical Studies,* 14 (Spring 1982): 26–27.

Although William Bronk received the American Book Award for his *Life Supports: New and Collected Poems* (1981), it was still possible for Beverly Schlack Randles to observe in 1988 that "this poet who can provoke such praise, and justly claim to be among America's finest, is virtually unknown, even to those who count themselves serious readers of poetry." Randles notes also that "Bronk is not altogether an innocent victim of his state of obscurity," for "most assuredly *not* constructing a literary life, nor housing himself in a recognizable package called The Poet, William Bronk has rejected compromise and costume." For almost all of his life Bronk has lived in the same Victorian house in the quiet upstate New York town of Hudson Falls. He has been an outsider to most literary circles, an occasionally active participant in few, and a disciple of none.

His work is characterized by a singular and persistent focus on the distinction between human perceptions of the world and a "real" world always beyond those perceptions, a reality that both invites and frustrates comprehension; as Norman M. Finkelstein argues in 1982, "The single great constant in the poetry of William Bronk is desire; specifically, desire for *the world,* which can never be known as a totality." So persistent is Bronk's focus that the most common comment on his work – and the most frequent complaint – is that he writes, as Gilbert Sorrentino put it in the spring 1972 *Grosseteste Review,* "the same poem over and over again, exploring the quality and reality of despair." Repeating this observation twenty years later in a 1992 review essay, Susan Schultz perhaps speaks for many in suggesting that Bronk's thematic persistence "can be seen as a virtue, if indeed it be the truth, but the reader may grow impatient, finally, with so many approaches to the same impasse." Still, readers patient and impatient continue to discover the unassuming but demandingly intimate power of Bronk's work.

The singularity of Bronk's style has led Finkelstein and others to find in his work a "formal and intellectual integrity unmatched in contemporary poetry." The poem "Music That Sees Beyond the World" from *Light and Dark* (1956) indicates Bronk's belief in "a world beyond our world which holds our world," and Bronk surely sees himself less as a poet than as a vehicle for poetry engaged in a mystical relationship with that greater world. In a 1988 "conversation" with Bronk (Bronk prefers the word *conversation* to *interview*) appearing in the special issue of *Sagetrieb* devoted to the poet, Henry Weinfield, responding to Bronk's assertion that he has little control over the poems he writes, suggests that "it's as if the poem exists outside of you and you're transcribing it," to which Bronk responds, "Of course, where else?" So complete is this process of transcription that Bronk's workbooks of poems are virtually free of revision; the poems appear as they are received. And so intimate is this process that Bronk often insists, as in a 4 April 1983 letter, "my work is concerned only with the relationship between me and the work." Weinfield argues in an essay appearing in the same 1988 issue of *Sagetrieb* that Bronk's body of work "represents what is perhaps the most radical confrontation with the limits of poetry in our time," the individual poems echoing one another and collectively marking the boundaries of an understanding that refuses a merely aesthetic relief from the limits.

In an exchange recorded in poet Cid Corman's 1976 essay, Bronk responds to Corman's contention that Bronk's poetry is "doomed" by an approach that relies at once on the contradictory demands of belief and reason. Bronk explains, "Belief and reason, God help us, are the only game in town" and argues that doomed approaches are precisely the point:

> My poetry is about all of those things of which we have concepts but which we find non-existent or unapproachable, and about our experience of finding them so. It would appear you would like me to forget about that experience – to mature out of it – as boys are exhorted to do – and go on to other things. But to me there are no other things to go on to and to pretend that there are would be the most desperate kind of evasion, the dreariest escapism and eccentricity.

With reason and belief at times working against each other the limits of both are exposed. Bronk's poetry reveals this paradoxical reality that he insists exists apart from him. In "The Poems: All Concessions Made," from *The Meantime* (1976), he writes of his poems, "It is as though they wait – as if there."

Through the years Bronk's relationship with his work has developed to the point that he sees it as a relationship between the work and itself, an ongoing conversation before which Bronk stands as a reverent audience. As he writes in the recent poem "Of Poetry" from *Death Is the Place* (1989),

> The work is what speaks
> and what is spoken
> and what attends to hear
> what is spoken.

The stark simplicity and directness of these lines are characteristic of Bronk's poetry throughout his career, even of his longer, earlier poems where he examines his subject in some detail. Bronk is a poet who looks to the silences that lie waiting behind and beyond his poems. Instead of searching for what Whitman in the preface to the 1855 *Leaves of Grass* conceives as "the medium that shall well nigh express the inexpressible," Bronk leaves the inexpressible unexpressed and works instead to indicate the limits of expression and thereby to suggest what he cannot hope to say.

Bronk was born in 1918 in Fort Edward, New York, just down the road from Hudson Falls, to William M. and Ethel (Funston) Bronk. His paternal family line connects to Jonas Bronck, whose farm provided the Bronx with its name; Bronk's branch of the family moved upstate in the mid 1600s, where it has been ever since. Bronk's father founded a retail fuel and building supply business, the management of which Bronk was later to assume following his father's death. Bronk attended public school in Hudson Falls and then studied at Dartmouth, graduating in 1938. He endured a single frustrating semester of pursuing graduate studies in English at Harvard, where, he asserted in a 1989 conversation, he found the dry conventions of approaching literature as "a scholarly subject" at odds with his sense of literature as an art.

Drafted into the army in 1941, he reached the rank of lieutenant and served as historian, writing *A History of the Eastern Defense Command and of the Defense of the Atlantic Coast of the United States in the Second World War* (1945). At the completion of his military service in 1945, Bronk taught for a year at Union College in Schenectady, New York, before taking over the family business – as he thought, temporarily. This temporary position lasted until the mid 1970s, providing Bronk with the economic security and the freedom of mind to write.

Bronk's experiences at Dartmouth and Harvard were both, in their different ways, formative. His frustrations at Harvard led him to write essays on Herman Melville, Walt Whitman, and Henry David Thoreau – later included in *The Brother in Elysium: Ideas of Friendship and Society in the United States* (1980) – that he could not write in accordance with formal academic conventions. Bronk completed all but one of the essays before he entered the army. At the end of his military service he finished the book and added a dedication to his former teacher at Dartmouth, "Epistle Dedicatory to Sidney Cox, among many," in which he writes, "This is partly a book about friendship; and I address you, Sidney, as a friend among many friends." The book thus serves partly as a reaction against Harvard and partly as a fulfillment of Bronk's experiences at Dartmouth, where the young writer began a long and intimate friendship with Cox, an unusually gifted teacher devoted to his students and to intellectual independence.

It perhaps is not too great an exaggeration to characterize the whole of Bronk's career as a response to Cox's teaching. In a 1976 conversation Bronk credited his teacher with his decision to become a poet: "I'm fairly sure there wouldn't have been anything without Sidney, or at least I can't imagine it really – maybe, maybe, I would have been writing anyway, but he was so much an influence on me, and had so much to do with my writing poetry at all, and being interested in poetry, that I simply can't think in terms of his not being there." Moreover, one can hear in Bronk's poetry the rhythms and diction of Cox's own style and can follow an eye similarly attuned to the conjunctions of the familiar and the unknown.

Bronk's work both echoes and extends the belief Cox asserted in his well-known text *Indirections: for those who want to write* (1947): the artist's desire should include "all genuine spiritual forces, ignoring for the present ideal veils and sops or patterns in the sky that no more determine action than Cassiopeia's Chair." From the beginnings of his career, Bronk has quite deliberately held to the demands of this desire. In poems such as "The Abnegation," from *That Tantalus* (1971), he challenges what he refers to as "handouts, makeshifts, sops / for creature comfort." In doing so, he has risked the critical disapproval and misapprehension Cox suggested an artist should expect:

> when desire is strong enough to force the skyey web apart, the writer always meets resistance. The timid want dreams left intact. They want facts and what they call ideals kept apart. And though the writer's patience, deviousness, and humanness may eventually get around repudiation, his patterns woven in the warp of

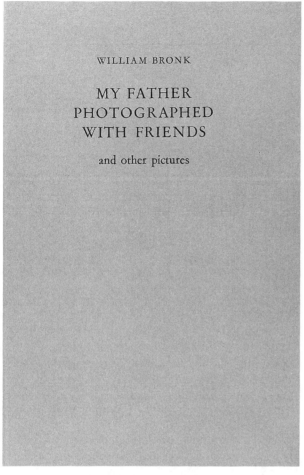

WILLIAM BRONK

MY FATHER
PHOTOGRAPHED
WITH FRIENDS

and other pictures

*Dust jacket for the book of poems Bronk unsuccessfully submitted
for the Yale Younger Poets series in 1948. It was finally
published in 1976 (courtesy of the Lilly Library,
Indiana University).*

days are generally labeled as "ideal" and used as ornamental hangings well away from muddy boots.

Bronk, who seems at times to go out of his way to challenge ideals not only of the world or even of the world of poetry but also of poets themselves, has met with resistance both passive and active throughout his career. Even with success Bronk clearly has feared having his work transformed into literary ornaments. He seems determined to keep his poetry close to the muddy boots.

Although Bronk did not begin to publish his poetry regularly until the 1950s, his earlier poems indicate significant promise. Three of his poems were included under the heading "Dartmouth College" in *An Anthology of New Hampshire Poetry* (1938); two poems were published in *Five Cummington Poems* (1939); another poem was chosen for *Four Dartmouth Poems* (1940), edited by Sidney Cox. In 1948 Bronk submitted his manuscript *My Father Photographed*

with Friends and Other Pictures (1976) to the Yale Younger Poets series, and although W. H. Auden did not select the collection, he wrote Bronk of his interest in his work. In his most prestigious early publication, his poem "March, Upstate" appeared in *The New Yorker* in 1949.

But promise did not evolve into recognition, and during the years between his graduation from Dartmouth and his 1982 American Book Award or again from 1982 to 1991, when he received the Lannan Literary Award for Poetry, Bronk has lived true to Cox's credo in *Indirections:*

> Yet one whose special quirk is product of strong desires and a few deep delights will not dicker for publication and approbation, even after many disillusions, by ironing out his meaning. He cannot damp his dangerous desires. . . . He writes because he is lonesome, but his loneliness will accept no substitutes. He must make a contact between the shy, striped, and crooked self and something corresponding in his readers. His individualness is a holding out for sociability that is real.

Bronk presents his own version of this desire for genuine contact in the first essay in the first section of *The Brother in Elysium,* a meditation on Thoreau titled "Friendship." Bronk's understanding of Thoreau might equally well be applied to the life that emerges from his own work:

> Thoreau, who was deeply sensible of his relationships to others and so honest with himself and them in facing the true worth of the relationship, and so exacting moreover, demanding that friendship be based on and maintain a mutual respect and independence, has led people from his own time to ours to say that he lacked feeling for his fellow men and lacked the desire and capability for friendship. He refused to pretend to that which had no existence and indeed could not have cheapened real friendship, for which he had the deepest regard and desire, by accepting something else as though it were indistinguishable from what he really wanted, or had equal value with it.

Bronk has similarly refused to accept something else, and much of his career can be viewed as an ongoing insistence on intimacy.

Particularly important is the friendship that began with Cid Corman, the editor of the journal *Origin,* one of the most influential literary periodicals of the 1950s and 1960s. Samuel French Morse, another student of Cox, recommended Bronk's poetry to Robert Creeley, who was planning a small literary review. After Creeley abandoned his plans, Corman asked for the poems for his own new literary journal. As Corman recalls in his introduction to *The Gist of Origin, 1951–1971: An Anthology* (1975),

"The poetry I shortly received from Bronk (who was and remains shy of sending his work around to be rejected) struck me at once as the real thing, the work of a particular, a unique poet." Looking back, Corman, who began featuring Bronk's work in *Origin* in the 1950s, considered it "the thread that binds all the issues together." Origin Press published Bronk's first book-length collection, *Light and Dark*. Bronk's poems in *Origin* also attracted the poet George Oppen, who encouraged New Directions to publish *the World, the Worldless* (1964).

Light and Dark and *the World, the Worldless* together offer a striking introduction to Bronk's poetry, for though published eight years apart, the poems in the two books seem to talk back and forth to each other across time. The tensions implicit in the deceptively calm philosophical tone of the first book seem to unravel by the end of *the World, the Worldless* into the poem "The Outcry," with its concluding line, "What I want to do is shout! Break! Shout!" When Bronk reads this poem aloud in the reading recorded for the Watershed Signature Series in 1979, his voice rises to a shout that echoes in the listener's ear.

Light and Dark begins with one of Bronk's many stirring meditations on music, "Some Musicians Play Chamber Music for Us." In the opening lines Bronk characteristically responds to his title:

Well, that's a proposition well composed;
the very justice of it states a demand
for some response, a further phrase, its tone
asking perhaps, or adding, or simply "yes."

In the beginning lines of "The Truth as Known," the first poem in *the World, the Worldless,* Bronk examines directly the impulse to respond or to look to responses:

Isn't it true though, we could ask
– who? – almost anybody, what's
it all about? Yet, asking, not
wait for an answer, or getting one, part
of one, suspect it, scoff, know it was false.

In this response disrupted by the question "who?" the reader sees the mind catching itself in the act of looking for its correspondent. In Bronk's second book another poem, "The Nature of Musical Form," ends where "Some Musicians Play Chamber Music for Us" begins: "as though we could say of music only, it is."

While one can readily understand why Oppen, in a letter written just before the publication of *the World, the Worldless* in January 1963, ventured

that "the purport of the poems, of course, is the solipsist position," Bronk in fact works to deconstruct solipsism, to disrupt the very operations of the mind that most distinctively characterize his poetry. As Oppen observes of another poem in *the World, the Worldless*, "Not My Loneliness But Ours," "once said, as it is here said, it seems inescapable. The loneliness not of the individual, but of the group. The poem moves quietly, patiently, as if with a scalpel, disclosing what is there."

The patient and often impatient disclosures of *the World, the Worldless* speak to the studied delusions of poems such as "The Rain of Small Occurrences" from *Light and Dark:*

We watch to see our lives come true.
Not as a dream might come, for who could dream it?
More maybe as we say this house is true,
true square and plumb. We, angled as no square
was ever made, so slight the subtlest plummet
cannot line us as it lines the air,
on whom the small occurrences rain in until
the template of our lives seems made of time,
watch for the shape not wholly shaped by time,
that one, that shape, almost that solid man.

Seeming to turn away from that search for the solid man, Bronk in *the World, the Worldless* tells readers not to abandon the world in their awareness of the worldless. In the poem "The Body" he begins breathlessly, "Watch it." The watching leads fervently to the final line: "But it's fascinating. There's always something new."

Bronk's third collection, *The Empty Hands,* was published by the Elizabeth Press in 1969. This strangely undervalued book contains some of Bronk's most significant work, poems that seem to emerge from the desperate shout at the end of *the World, the Worldless*. As he insists in "Not to Cry Out, 'How Long, Oh Lord, How Long,' " "What I mean to include is our helplessness," for it is in this helplessness that Bronk searches for a hint of grace. If he asserts in "Colloquy on a Bed" that "this universe, / in any rational sense is hopelessly / insane," he follows immediately by pressing against the boundaries of that observation: "Hopelessly: the saving word."

In "On *Credo Ut Intelligam*" the saving grace of hopelessness becomes an expression of faith that "Reality is what we are ignorant of." Arguing against Saint Anselm's approach to religious mystery – "Anselm believed in order to understand" is the poem's opening line – Bronk turns resolutely to the face of hopelessness for an awareness of the reality beyond:

How should I turn my head away to look
at anything other than that I am ignorant of,
it being all; or make belief invent
a world or a life besides, it being there?

Increasingly, Bronk's poems would turn toward "that I am ignorant of" and look to the silences beyond human expression. He amplifies the statements of previous poems in the lines that close the last two poems of the collection. "The Difference" concludes: "Some of the things we think and say of the world / are reasonable, but none of them is true." He takes this recognition further in the last line of "On Divers Geometries," the final poem of *The Empty Hands:* "There is no limited truth: there is no truth." If some took Bronk's early poems on the fictiveness of human understanding to be interesting excursions into one among many philosophical and poetic regions, Bronk would make it clear that he meant what he said, that he believes there are no other regions worth exploring.

The important sequence of books published by the Elizabeth Press in the 1970s offers various attempts to meet the demands of the reality beyond the "truths" humans claim. In an 18 June 1974 letter to New Directions publisher James Laughlin, Oppen worried that "Elizabeth Press . . . has printed a somewhat damaging amount of [Bronk's] lesser work," but it is in this work that one encounters the heart of Bronk's identity as a poet. Apparently working to identify and emphasize the limitations of human understanding and expression, Bronk writes less for the sake of the poem than for the sake of the world from which the poem seems to arrive.

In *That Tantalus* Bronk examines unrealizable desires, as in the poem "I am," to face deliberately a "despair" that is "all," a fundamental condition neither separate nor distinct from a "joy," which is neither cause nor result. In this collection also appears one of Bronk's most oft-quoted poems, "The Plainest Narrative," which begins,

I am William Bronk, have been raised to believe
the personal pronoun plus the verb to be
and a proper name said honestly is fact
from which the plainest narrative begins.
But it isn't fact; it comes to this. Is it wrong?
Not wrong. Just that it isn't true.

Life, like a sentence, holds together for sense. Bronk here and in a series of poems about and against biography over the years creates his sentences to show clearly both the effort of construction and the desire for coherence. Awareness of self begins be-

yond the period that marks the limits of the sense that the sentence makes.

In subsequent books Bronk's narratives of understanding would become increasingly plain and direct. In the fourteen-line poems of *To Praise the Music* (1972) – written, he noted in 1988, after he had "spent a long time intensively reading Shakespeare's sonnets" – Bronk works with and against the form, breaking the lines in one poem and regrouping them in another, drawing out both the promise and the limitations of form. In *Silence and Metaphor* (1975) Bronk writes only eight-line poems and opens with an untitled poem that begins, "*Here is the silence; it is everywhere.*"

The two collections published in 1976, *The Meantime* and *Finding Losses,* become more silent still. *The Meantime,* which begins with "The Poems: All Concessions Made," contains only fifteen poems, all but two of which are either fourteen-line or eight-line poems, echoing the previous collections. *Finding Losses* contains sixty-five four-line poems, one poem of eight lines, and one of just two lines. In the two-line poem, "He Importunes the God," Bronk complains, "Why do I have to do this? I've got / a poem I'd rather write than this one." *The Force of Desire* (1979) is a series of untitled three-line poems, including what has been called Bronk's funniest poem (for all of their despair, many of Bronk's poems are funny):

Ultimate reality has its own
zip code: 12839.
This is all it is. Write to me. Here.

Far from being his "lesser" work, the Elizabeth Press books of the 1970s are part of a body of work in which the collections are best read with and against one another. Through his poems that reach back and forth across zip codes of impersonal maps and intimate addresses Bronk emphasizes both the cohesiveness and boundaries of his approach to poetry.

The Elizabeth Press published not only Bronk's new collections of poetry but also his previous collections and essays. In 1974 the press published Bronk's important essays on the Mayan and Incan ruins, *The New World,* and also brought out *A Partial Glossary: Two Essays. Light and Dark* was republished in 1975, and the next year saw the publication of *My Father Photographed with Friends and Other Pictures,* the collection that Bronk had submitted to the Yale Younger Poets series in 1948. In 1980 the Elizabeth Press published the long-completed *The Brother in Elysium.*

In 1981 North Point Press included Bronk's ten previously published collections with his new work, *Life Supports,* in *Life Supports: New and Collected Poems.* Gathered together chronologically, Bronk's poetry shows progressive experimentation as well as unity; even the seemingly slight poems converse eloquently with the poems that first drew attention to his work. As Joseph M. Conte notes in *Unending Design: The Forms of Postmodern Poetry* (1991), "*Life Supports . . .* is something of a constant, and each poem rings its changes." The new poems in the final section of the collection are lengthier, more expansive in their treatment than the poems he published toward the end of the 1970s, as if the laconic insistence of *The Force of Desire* had led Bronk back to a voice that had to be sounded and still contained. The tensions of *That Tantalus* are addressed in "Unsatisfied Desire"; the early meditations on Thoreau find their way into "Flowers, the World and My Friend, Thoreau"; and whereas in "Home Address," from *My Father Photographed with Friends,* Bronk had written of "Leaving an empty room to disrepair," he returns in "The Strong Room of the House" to find "horror" in the room.

Although *Life Supports* marked the beginning of a wider appreciation of Bronk's achievement – Finkelstein, for example, argued in 1982 that the collection "finally confirms what a small but evergrowing number of readers has known for some time: that Bronk is one of the most significant poets writing in English today" – Bronk had not entirely escaped significant notice before. His earlier work had received high-profile reviews in *The New York Times Book Review* and been the subject of a special issue of the English journal *Grosseteste Review* in 1972. He had been interviewed by Robert Bertholf for the journal *Credences* in 1976. His poems had also been anthologized. In 1970 five of Bronk's poems from *the World, the Worldless* were included in Hayden Carruth's *The Voice That Is Great Within Us: American Poetry of the Twentieth Century.* Corman reprinted many of Bronk's poems in his 1975 anthology *The Gist of Origin, 1951–1971: An Anthology* and in 1976 published *William Bronk: An Essay,* a book largely composed of Bronk's published poems and his letters to Corman. Beginning in the 1970s Bronk's work was used in New York's Poetry in Public Places Program, and his short poems appeared, for example, on small billboards next to advertisements on buses. Some of these poems were still being used in the 1990s.

WILLIAM BRONK

TO PRAISE THE MUSIC

Dust jacket for Bronk's book of fourteen-line poems, which he wrote after intensive study of William Shakespeare's sonnets (courtesy of the Lilly Library, Indiana University)

In 1983 North Point Press brought Bronk's prose together in *Vectors and Smoothable Curves: Collected Essays,* in which the two short essays that constitute *A Partial Glossary,* "Costume as Metaphor" and "Desire and Denial" (together only five pages), serve as a bridge between his longer works, *The New World* and *The Brother in Elysium.* In "Costume as Metaphor," which was inspired by a conversation with a friend about Ingmar Bergman's 1972 film *Cries and Whispers,* Bronk looks to the tangible metaphors of reality – costumes physical and otherwise – that become performances of identity by which one negotiates with "the world," which "is a silence," by talking "of it and to it." Bronk concludes that none of these performances "is the world nor are they all together the world. Songs only that sing its praise, the earnest entreaties and importunities of our desire." In "Desire and Denial" Bronk explores the importunities of desire: "we are denied those shapes and spaces of desire by our desire which rejects them. Shapeless and impalpable ourselves, we want that reality which has no shape to occupy."

The desire that rejects its own objects is very much the point in Bronk's *New World* essays on the fascinating appeal of the Mayan and Incan ruins, which have value for him because they are ruins, because they force us to acknowledge the fiction of our own world. In *The Utopian Moment in Contemporary American Poetry* (1988), Finkelstein views these essays as critiques of history, arguing that "The fate of a 'primitive,' 'alien' culture, which at first seems, in its historical and geographic specificity, to be radically *other,* is made to appear no more or less meaningful or consequential than our own: the revenge of the universal against the particular." But the revenge leads to affirmation by reminding us, as Bronk puts it in "Copan: Historicity Gone," that "it is by our most drastic failures that we may perhaps catch glimpses of something real, of something which is." "There are things which we feel," Bronk asserts in "Copan: Unwillingness, the Unwilled," the last of the essays in *The New World,* "certain angers, rejoicings, fears": "We learn at last, and accept the learning at last, that these feelings come to us without our willing or acceding or inventing. They come from beyond our skin like approaches to us, like messages."

In the world of *The Brother in Elysium* Bronk looks for such messages in his fellowship with Thoreau, Whitman, and Melville. Finding close friendship with Thoreau, acknowledging a grudging respect for Whitman but distrusting deeply that poet's desire "to regain a world which had had no imperfections, and thereby to so far simplify the problem of his identity," Bronk seems in some ways closest to Melville, the two essays about whom conclude *The Brother in Elysium.* In a conversation with Edward Foster, Bronk said, "I suspect that it was probably Melville more than the others that got me dealing more with philosophical problems." He also noted that the second essay on Melville was the only one that he did not write before the war, maintaining that he "could not have written" it earlier though he knew what he wanted to say.

Echoing what many have asserted, Bronk says of Melville that "Horror, barrenness, and negativism were inescapable aspects of reality in that polar world in which [he] found himself." But just as the despair in Bronk's work unfolds into affirmation, so Bronk finds the same "cry of affirmation and acceptance" in Melville. In discussing the character Billy

Budd's haunting blessing on the man who ordered him executed, Bronk seems to anticipate his own ability as an artist as he reveals Melville's:

> For that little moment, in an irreparably evil and ambiguous world, ambiguity and evil with all their consequences were acquiesced in, and Jackson and Bland, Ahab, Claggart, and Ishmael, and the evil Whale itself, were drawn up and absorbed in a clear act of conviction and faith. Herman Melville was at peace. God bless Captain Vere!

As Edward Halsey Foster notes in his 1988 essay on *The Brother in Elysium* in the special issue on the poet in *Sagetrieb,* "there is often in Bronk's work a tone of necessary and resolute acceptance" that corresponds to what Bronk finds in Melville. Foster concludes that Bronk's collected essays on nineteenth-century literary figures "is a very personal book, through which its author was able to argue his way into an aesthetic which has for more than forty years sustained one of the great poetries of this century."

After winning the American Book Award in 1982, Bronk was more widely noticed as a important presence in the world of poetry. His work began to attract the attention of those looking for, one might say, "that one, that shape, almost that solid man," but Bronk showed little inclination to perform such a role. As Randles notes, even, or perhaps especially, after receiving wide recognition, "Bronk refused to grant interviews and reiterated an earlier comment of his that the serious poet disappears in the work." In 1983 Bronk served as inaugural poet for Mario Cuomo, and his comment to the press, as reported in the 2 January *New York Times,* is characteristic: "He said the inaugural poem, 'Waterland,' was 'not a poem in praise of Mario Cuomo,' and quickly added: 'I've got nothing against him, I voted for him, but I don't really know that much about him. It's a poem about the state and how water is a key factor in the state.'"

Bronk followed the acclaim with characteristic silence; his next collection of poems, *Careless Love and Its Apostrophes,* was published four years after *Life Supports.* Perhaps as a commentary on the disquietingly public notice his work had received, the first half of the collection includes "Poems: Way to Go," in which Bronk ruefully admits, "I sent them out; I wish I could have them back." The second half of the book is made up of "Apostrophes" – what Bronk referred to in 27 September 1984 letter as "a series of flat-out statements" – presented in lines spaced apart from one another. Bronk's tone is at once calm and impatient, and the work is unlike anything he had published before.

The need to state the case plainly and then to "cast about," as Bronk put it in a 9 September 1986 letter, for a sense of what lies beyond the statement is implicit in the title of Bronk's next book, *Manifest; and Furthermore* (1987). The first part of the collection ends with the poem "Manner of Speaking," and the second half ends with "More or Less." As Michael Heller notes in an essay on this book for the special Bronk issue of *Sagetrieb* in 1988, the word "manifest" refers not only to "what is obvious, clearly apparent," but also to "a listing of the goods, . . . the inventories by which we make ourselves 'real' "; and it refers as well to the manifestation of power. "Bronk's ironies," Heller argues, "are all in the byplay between these senses of the word, senses which Bronk is able to place in contradiction." The other half of the book's title, "and furthermore," "which is almost like a clearing of one's throat prior to attempting eloquence," serves as "an invocation to the offices of poetry, the need to speak the thing out."

This book, to which Heller refers as "Bronk's Winter Tale," begins a series of meditations on winter, aging, and death – not new subjects for Bronk but ones brought increasingly to the foreground of his work. In a poem bearing the title of Bronk's birthplace, "Fort Edward," the poet watches a train passing, its cars "firmly articulated," and perhaps alludes to the inexorable passing of one's years in the final line: "The conductor checks his watch. The schedule is sure." The poem "Foresight" speaks of death in stark terms: "I lie in bed / practicing dead." But as Bronk approaches the subject of death more directly, he also approaches the awareness of a reality emphasized by the finality of life. If he revels in "the glory of the world" in the poem "Aura," his revelations seem heightened by the fact, as he writes in "The Informer," that "Our minds are directed otherwhere / by death." In "Winter Evening" he seems to celebrate that "otherwhere" direction when he writes, "All I can think of is praise: its desire." In *Manifest; and Furthermore* Bronk looks for "what doesn't satisfy," as the book's closing words have it, perhaps to open to a keener desire.

Bronk's meditations on finality continue in his next two books, *Death Is the Place* and *Living Instead* (1991). The poet seems to return to the concerns of the conductor for his schedule in "The Time Observed," the first poem of *Death Is the Place,* though instead of the conductor with his watch, time is observed by "The days and nights." In the poem "Holy Ghost" Bronk speaks of the unknown presence known in "the feel of desire," a presence for which

one writes books and builds houses: "Times that he comes," the poem concludes, "we can hear him read." Death itself emerges in "Elder Brother" as "the one immortal, he that / fraternal *in utero*" will be "chief of mourners to mourn our dying." What comes of this anticipated mourning in *Living Instead* is a heightened awareness of life's tenuousness and insupportable illusions but also the quiet grace to realize that "the frail world goes on / unmastered, unmastering, and so do we." When Bronk, as he does in all of his books, returns to his house as subject and metaphor in "House Tour," a generally unused room again attracts his attention, in part for its uniform appearance through the years – holding to the appearance of "old parlors" that often "*looked* unused" and "even unusable" – and in part for the presence of an item said to be an old clock, though "it doesn't tick / and no numerals on the face. If this is the face." The other rooms in the house, unusable rooms that invite and resist living in them, do not even present the opportunity to stare into the face of time. In the final poem of *Living Instead,* "Debriefing," life itself becomes a tour "into time / and space" where "you get a body of your own" and experience "Needs and pleasures." "Quite a trip," Bronk concludes in the last lines; "Good though, to get back."

At the tail end of the 1980s *Talisman* (1989) and *Sagetrieb* (Winter 1988) devoted special issues to Bronk's work. Both journals contain significant appraisals of Bronk's career and conversations with the poet. Both also include poems written to honor Bronk by friends, former publishers, and other poets, well known and some still unknown, that together suggest the depth and extent of his influence on contemporary poetry. The *Sagetrieb* essays serve as a useful introduction to Bronk's work and to the variety of responses that it inspires – from Louise Chawla's meditations on the task of writing the biography of a self-described "antibiograph," to Burt Kimmelman's reconsideration of the connections between Bronk and Wallace Stevens that dominated the minds of early reviewers of Bronk's work, to meditations by Weinfield and John Ernest on the mysticism in and of Bronk's poetry. These subjects all come up as well in the conversations, as the antibiograph both answers and resists questions about his life, acknowledges his influences while holding to the singularity of his relationship with his work, and discusses his own mystified response to the process and results of poetry. "[I]t doesn't seem that I am working at it," Bronk says toward the end of the conversation in *Sagetrieb,* when the discussion turns

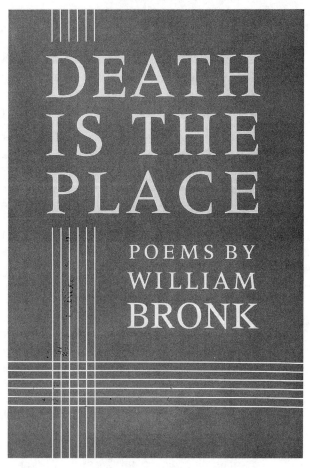

*Dust jacket for Bronk's 1989 book, in which Death is
personified as an "Elder Brother" who will be the "chief
of mourners to mourn our dying" (courtesy of the Lilly
Library, Indiana University)*

to the craft of poetry; "it seems that I am trying to
hear some conversation that is in the next room or
through a radio turned down too low or something
like that."

The conversations and the poems dedicated
to Bronk indicate the intimate tone of his work and
the response to it, the unforced flow of ideas implicit in the poems and provoked by them. The *Talisman* issue, for example, reprints a poem by
Weinfield, "The Lives of the Poets," and directs the
reader to Bronk's poem "The Lives of Poets"
(from *Life Supports*) dedicated to Weinfield. In the
Talisman conversation Bronk chides Foster's attention to language as an approach to Bronk's poetry.
"There you go on language again," Bronk remarks.
When Foster observes, "I would assume that you believe that language has no final authority, and so I ask
then how you feel a poem is possible," Bronk skepti-
cally responds, "It isn't. Oh, I don't know, Ed." In "Fos-

tering," a poem dedicated to Foster in *Death Is the
Place*, Bronk begins,

Ed asks me
does the poem depend
on what is said
or language saying[.]

The poem and Bronk both conclude by responding
less to the question than to the act of conversation
itself. Presenting the poems as "acts of love," Bronk
asserts simply, "they depend."

Bronk insists implicitly in *Some Words* (1992)
that the fragile but binding acts of dependence are
the stuff not only of human experience but also of
poetry. Directly addressing the subject of reading
and writing itself, Bronk invites the reader to enter
his complex and dependent world (the life one lives,
as the title of one poem asserts, "As If"). "Come
into the poem, reader," begins the poem "Bid." In

poems such as "The Writer," "Writing," and the title poem, which concludes the collection, Bronk connects acts of writing and understanding to the symbolic world everyone creates for him- or herself, identifying the fundamental dependencies of that world.

The sequence of the poems is significant ("Pride" goeth before "Research"), suggesting the general progression of an archetypal story, a communal spiritual autobiography with its own delusions and illusory rebirths: "Premises," "Visionary," "Belief in Our Biographies," "Placement," "Realization," "Curriculum," "Community," "Representations," "These Constructs," "Freedom," and "Penance." But the stories, Bronk insists, are fictions, and the words used to construct the stories depend not on the belief in their reality but on the recognition of their fictionality; "There aren't any stories that are true," he insists in "The Writer." In "All Told" Bronk echoes the point: "The mortal part wasn't much. We made / history: stories."

Those who think of Bronk as a poet of despair will find that poet on the first page in "Being Symbol," where he concludes a discussion of the love of sports, "Why not? It's not as though there were something to do." But there too is the desire that despair engenders, the belief that one can do without comforting fictions of significance because "solace is trivial: none is enough." Bronk seems to celebrate his work's temporality while looking anxiously for some sign of communion with the real. If in "Dating," musing on his own poetic career, he recognizes that "Time is what the work was most about," in the collection's title poem he seems to plead for the possibilities of expression and awareness that open when fictions are treated as fictions: "Bring some words together toward a real."

Bronk's awe for the real is still strong in his most recent collections. In "Bare Boards at the Globe," from *The Mild Day* (1993), he writes, "Sit witness of life's power. We attend." Bronk's strength throughout his career has been to serve as such a witness, letting nothing distract him from his sense of the sacredness of the task. His power has been to stand in time and attend, finding the subjects worthy of his attention as fully realized in mild days and expressions of careless love as in grand achievements and singular desires. Like Thoreau he draws his readers to worlds that require no travel, worlds that he delineates only to show that they cannot be captured by the mind except in the act of resisting understanding. As witness he has focused less on that which he would witness than on the act by which witnessing becomes possible, an act of de-

sire that remains unsatisfied. His poetry continues on the same course, as if to emphasize that the course leads to no destination and cannot be completed.

In an extended reading of one of Bronk's early poems, "The Arts and Death: A Fugue for Sidney Cox," Conte notes that although the poem is about the death of an important friend, ultimately and "in keeping with the generic rules" of elegy, Bronk "offers something other than despair at the close – not redemption, but not oblivion either. Our lives are part of the real, and as such persist; only our language closes, only forms have an end." Throughout his career Bronk has brought himself and his readers to a usually calm but always insistent confrontation with despair's demanding gaze. Refusing to turn away from that gaze, Bronk has again and again disclosed the closure upon which his own reliance on language depends; writing "the same poem over and over again," he has worked to keep his forms from having an end; and in doing so he has suggested something beyond and other than despair. This poetry seems part of the real, and one suspects that it will persist, regardless of whether Bronk is ever widely recognized for what he is: one of our most intimate, haunting, and important poets.

Interviews:

Robert Bertholf, "A Conversation with William Bronk," *Credences*, 1, no. 3 (1976): 9–33;

Henry Weinfield and Burt Kimmelman, eds., "A Conversation with William Bronk," *Sagetrieb*, 7 (Winter 1988): 17–43;

Edward Foster, "Conversations with William Bronk," in *Postmodern Poetry: The Talisman Interviews* (Holooken: Talisman, 1994), pp. 1–19.

Bibliography:

Edward Foster, "A William Bronk Checklist (A Selected Bibliography)," *Sagetrieb*, 7, no. 3 (1988): 153–156.

References:

Rober Bertholf, "On William Bronk, His Silence and Metaphor," *Credences*, 1, no. 3 (1976): 34–41;

Joseph M. Conte, "Constant and Variant: Semantic Recurrence in Harry Matthews, William Bronk, and Robert Creeley," in *Unending Design: The Forms of Postmodern Poetry* (Ithaca, N.Y.: Cornell University Press, 1991), pp. 214–238;

Cid Corman, *William Bronk: An Essay* (Carrboro, N.C.: Truck Press, 1976);

John Ernest, "Fossilized Fish and the World of Unknowing: John Ashbery and William Bronk," in *The Tribe of John: John Ashbery and Contemporary Poetry,* edited by Susan M. Schultz (Tuscaloosa: University of Alabama Press, 1995), pp. 168–189;

Norman M. Finkelstein, *The Utopian Moment in Contemporary American Poetry* (Lewisburg, Pa.: Bucknell University Press, 1988), pp. 96–111;

Finklestein, "William Bronk: The World as Desire," *Contemporary Literature,* 23 (Fall 1982): 480–492;

Ruth Grogan, "'Talk is what it's about': William Bronk's Colloquiality," *Sagetrieb,* 11, nos. 1–2 (1992): 85–102;

Kevin Oderman, "Undone, Undoing: William Bronk's Pre-Columbian Things," *North Dakota Quarterly,* 55, no. 4 (1987): 276–285;

Oderman, "William Bronk: In Conceptual Thicket," *Credences,* 3, no. 3 (1985): 138–150;

Beverly Schlack Randles, "A Poetics of Space: William Bronk's Unhousing of the Universe," in *Analecta Husserliana: The Yearbook of Phenomenological Research, Vol. 23: Poetics of the Elements in the Human Condition,* edited by Anna-Teresa Tymieniecka (Dordrecht: Kluwer Academic Publishers, 1988), pp. 323–341;

Sagetrieb, special issue on Bronk, edited by Burt Kimmelman and Henry Weinfield, 7 (Winter 1988);

Susan Schultz, "Impossible Music," *Postmodern Culture,* 2 (January 1992): 1–14;

Gilbert Sorrentino, "William Bronk," in his *Something Said* (San Francisco: North Point, 1984), pp. 77–80;

John Howland Spyker, *Little Live's* (New York: Grosset & Dunlap, 1978);

Felix Stefanile, "Praising the Music," *Parnassus: Poetry in Review,* 5, no. 2 (1977): 222–234;

John Taggart, "Reading William Bronk," *Songs of Degrees: Essays on Contemporary Poetry and Poetics* (Tuscaloosa: University of Alabama Press, 1994), pp. 25–50;

Talisman, special issue on Bronk, no. 2 (Spring 1989).

Papers:

Collections of Bronk's letters, manuscripts, rare publications, and other documents are at the University of New Hampshire and Columbia University.

Gwendolyn Brooks

(7 June 1917 –)

Farah Jasmine Griffin
University of Pennsylvania

See also the Brooks entries in *DLB 5: American Poets Since World War II, First Series* and *DLB 76: Afro-American Writers, 1940–1955.*

BOOKS: *A Street in Bronzeville* (New York & London: Harper, 1945);
Annie Allen (New York: Harper, 1949);
Maud Martha, a novel (New York: Harper, 1953);
Bronzeville Boys and Girls (New York: Harper, 1956);
The Bean Eaters (New York: Harper, 1960);
Selected Poems (New York: Harper & Row, 1963);
In the Mecca (New York: Harper & Row, 1968);
Riot (Detroit: Broadside Press, 1969);
Family Pictures (Detroit: Broadside Press, 1970);
Aloneness (Detroit: Broadside Press, 1971);
The World of Gwendolyn Brooks (New York: Harper & Row, 1971);
Report From Part One (Detroit: Broadside Press, 1972);
The Tiger Who Wore White Gloves: Or What You Are You Are (Chicago: Third World Press, 1974);
Beckonings (Detroit: Broadside Press, 1975);
Primer for Blacks (Chicago: Black Position Press, 1980);
Young Poet's Primer (Chicago: Brooks Press, 1980);
To Disembark (Chicago: Third World Press, 1981);
Black Love (Chicago: Brooks Press, 1982);
Mayor Harold Washington; and, Chicago, the I Will City (Chicago: Brooks Press, 1983);
Very Young Poets (Chicago: Brooks Press, 1983);
The Near-Johannesburg Boy and Other Poems (Chicago: David, 1986);
Blacks (Chicago: David, 1987);
Winnie (Chicago: Third World Press, 1988);
Children Coming Home (Chicago: David, 1991).

OTHER: "The Life of Lincoln West," in *Soon One Morning: New Writing By American Negroes,* edited by Herbert Hill (New York: Knopf, 1963): 317-319;
A Broadside Treasury, edited by Brooks (Detroit: Broadside Press, 1971);

Gwendolyn Brooks (circa 1970)

Jump Bad; A New Chicago Anthology, edited by Brooks (Detroit: Broadside Press, 1971);
A Capsule Course in Black Poetry Writing, edited by Brooks and others (Detroit: Broadside Press, 1975).

SELECTED PERIODICAL PUBLICATIONS –
UNCOLLECTED: "Poets Who Are Negroes," *Phylon,* 2 (December 1950): 312;

"Why Negro Women Leave Home," *Negro Digest,* 9
   (March 1951): 26–28;
"How I Told My Children About Race," *Negro Digest,* 9 (June 1951): 29–31;
"They Call It Bronzeville," *Holiday* (October 1951):
   60–67;
"Perspectives," *Negro Digest,* 15 (July 1966): 49–50;
"In Montgomery," Photographs by Moneta Sleet
   Jr., and captions by Brooks, *Ebony,* 26 (August
   1971): 42–48.

Throughout her career Gwendolyn Brooks
has been committed to a political vision of black liberty and equality while refusing to sacrifice the complexity and sheer beauty of her art. In light of her
achievement she has become considered by many to
be one of the most significant poets of the twentieth
century. For a body of work that draws from various traditions, but is circumscribed by none, Brooks
has been widely recognized. With her volume of
poems *Annie Allen* (1949), she became in 1950 the
first African American to receive the Pulitzer Prize.
She was named poet laureate of the state of Illinois
in 1978 and consultant in poetry to the Library of
Congress. In 1987 Brooks became the first black
woman to be elected an honorary fellow of the
Modern Language Association. In 1994 she was
chosen to deliver the Jefferson Lecture of the National Endowment for the Humanities, the highest
honor bestowed by the U.S. government for intellectual achievement in the humanities. Brooks has
also received honors usually bestowed upon poets
after their deaths, as cultural centers, literary prizes,
and at least one school have been named after her.

Brooks is also a dedicated teacher and a
source of encouragement for younger poets. Since
1963 she has taught at various institutions, including Columbia College, Chicago; Elmhurst College,
Elmhurst, Illinois; and Northeastern Illinois State
College. She was named the Rennebohm Professor
of English at the University of Wisconsin–Madison
and Distinguished Professor of Arts at City College
at the City University of New York. In 1969 she established the Illinois Poet Laureate Award to encourage younger writers.

Her commitment to nurturing younger poets
recalls the encouragement Brooks received from her
parents. Born on 7 June 1917 in Topeka, Kansas, to
David and Keziah Brooks, Gwendolyn soon moved
to Chicago with her mother. Keziah Brooks recognized her daughter's talent early and encouraged
her by promising she would become the "lady Paul
Laurence Dunbar." Having grown up in a creative
and loving environment, Brooks credits both par-

ents with having given her the courage and support
to pursue her desire to write. The young poet was
also encouraged by established poets such as
Langston Hughes, who recommended she listen to
and learn from the blues, blues poets, and the
voices of the street, and James Weldon Johnson,
who introduced her to modernist poets such as T. S.
Eliot and Ezra Pound. The Chicago socialite and
patron of the arts Inez Cunningham Stark, who conducted a workshop in modern poetry at Chicago's
South Side Community Center in 1941, was another important influence on Brooks's development
as a poet.

Following her graduation from Wilson Junior
College in 1936, Brooks worked as a maid and secretary for a "spiritual adviser" who sold patent med-
icines. These experiences would later appear in her
work, especially *Maud Martha* (1953) and *In the
Mecca* (1968). On 17 September 1939 Brooks married Henry Lowington Blakely II. Their first child,
Henry L. Blakely III, was born in 1940 and a
daughter, Nora, was born in 1951. During the early
years of her marriage to Blakely, Brooks first experienced life in Chicago's infamous kitchenette buildings, which provided the settings for her first collection of poems, *A Street in Bronzeville* (1945).

Published by Harper in 1945, the volume
marked Brooks as one of the most significant writers of her generation. Harper sent the original
manuscript to Richard Wright, who wrote that
Brooks's poems in *A Street in Bronzeville* "are hard
and real, right out of the central core of Black Belt
Negro life in urban areas. I hope she can keep on
saying what she is saying in many poems. . . . Miss
Brooks is real and so are her poems." In this first
collection, themes of enduring importance to
Brooks appear: community, domesticity, black female rage, racial injustice, intraracial color prejudice, and most important, the complexity of the
lives of poor black people – their tragedy as well as
their exuberant sense of joy. Brooks sensitively delineates the extraordinariness of ordinary black people and their daily lives. Her collection is filled with
a myriad of poetic forms ranging from ballads to
sonnets to the blues. In *The Wicked Sisters: Women
Poets, Literary History & Discord* (1993), Betsy Erkkila
writes:

> In the poems of *A Street in Bronzeville* . . . the relation
> between Brooks's black content and her use of white
> literary forms is never simple or static. The irony of T. S.
> Eliot merges with the tragic comedy of Langston
> Hughes's laughter amid tears; the allusive and elliptical
> mode of modernist verse merges with the oblique and
> cryptic utterance of black folk forms; and the traditional

sonnet is transformed into a vehicle of contemporary black protest and irresolution, as the social consciousness of the Harlem Renaissance and the technical experimentation of literary modernism are joined in a dynamic interaction.

A Street in Bronzeville is divided into three sections. The first presents a community of poor black inhabitants of Chicago's South Side, who include Pearl May Lee, de Witt Williams, and Satin-Legs Smith. These and the other kitchenette characters become dreamers, possible artists, whose dreams are thwarted because of the mundane reality of their existence: " 'Dream' makes a giddy sound, not strong / Like 'rent,' 'feeding a wife,' / 'satisfying a man.' "

The act of dreaming seems a waste of time in light of the realities confronting these people – realities of providing food, shelter, and some degree of sensual pleasure – but they dream nonetheless. The remainder of the poem is a meditation about the dream's attempt to escape, its struggle with the reality of the tenement, the smells and sounds.

> But could a dream send up through onion fumes
> Its white and violet, fight with fried potatoes
> And yesterday's garbage ripening in the hall,
> Flutter, or sing an aria down these rooms[.]

In the second and third stanzas there is a mounting tension that leads to an anticlimactic intrusion of reality: "Even if we were willing to let it in, / Had time to warm it, keep it very clean, / anticipate a message, let it begin? / We wonder. But not well! not for a minute! / Since Number five is out of the bathroom now, / We think of lukewarm water, hope to get in it." The kitchenette dwellers attempt to nurture and sustain dreams and to create a community with the others who share their station in life. More often than not, their efforts fail and the dreams die; but Brooks records the humanity of these attempts with grace and beauty.

One of the most poignant poems of this section is "The Mother," a dramatic monologue in which the poem's persona speaks directly to the reader about her aborted children. Opening with the line, "Abortions will not let you forget," the first stanza is filled with tightly controlled rhymed couplets, which yield to the emotion-filled longings of the second stanza: "I have heard in the voices of the wind the voices of my dim killed children." The final stanza releases the apology: "Believe me, I loved you all."

The second section of *A Street in Bronzeville* is composed of five portraits, the first of which is "The Sunday of Satin-Legs Smith," the longest poem of the book at 159 lines. This section also includes "Negro Hero," and the "Ballad of Pearl Mae Lee." Satin-Legs Smith is a zoot-suited dandy dressed in "wonder-suits in yellow and in wine / Sarcastic green and zebra-striped cobalt. / All drapes. With shoulder padding that is wide / And cocky and determined as his pride; / Ballooning pants that taper off to ends / Scheduled to choke precisely." Satin-Legs Smith ends his day of rest enveloped in the body of his lover: "Her body is like new brown bread . . . / Her body is a honey bowl / Whose waiting honey is deep and hot."

While Satin-Legs Smith's zoot suits show his defiance of wartime rationing of fabric, the persona of "Negro Hero" is a patriotic hero in spite of, perhaps because of, the racism he encounters: "I had to kick their law into their teeth in order to save / them." The poem gives voice to the thousands of black soldiers who fought to defend an American democracy of which they were not the beneficiaries – a theme that emerges again in the final section of the Bronzeville portraits in the twelve-sonnet sequence titled, "Gay Chaps at the Bar."

Following the success of *A Street in Bronzeville,* Brooks won several awards, including the Mademoiselle Merit Award in 1945 and a Guggenheim Fellowship in 1946. She continued to write poetry and began to write fiction and book reviews as well, but her most significant work would be her second collection of poems, *Annie Allen.* In this collection, the kitchenette dweller-dreamer is a woman who, like Brooks's earlier characters, is a keeper of the dream, despite the prosaic reality that often intrudes her life.

Nowhere is this characteristic more apparent than in "The Anniad," the difficult mock epic poem that marks the center of *Annie Allen* and that carries Annie from a wishful, dreamy childhood to the realization of the limitations of her life: "Think of thaumaturgic lass / Looking in her looking-glass / At the unembroidered brown; / Printing bastard roses there; / Then emotionally aware / Of the black and boisterous hair, / Taming all that anger down." Here Annie tries to brighten her ordinary brown face with makeup and straighten her hair. "Taming all that anger down" suggests the resistant possibilities of black hair in its natural state – a theme that reemerges in Brooks's poem, "For My Sisters Who Kept Their Naturals." Despite her efforts to change her appearance, however, Annie's lover does not cherish her as she dreamed he might; instead, he leaves her to her children, her books, and her dreams. "Think of twinked and twenty-four. /

*Brooks with her husband, Henry Lowington Blakely II, and
their son, Henry Lowington Blakely III, in 1945
(courtesy of the author)*

Fuschias gone or gripped or gray, / All hay-colored that was green. / Soft aesthetic looted, lean."

Of *Annie Allen,* Brooks has said, "I wanted to prove that I could write well"; and indeed, the collection represents Brooks's mastery of Western literary forms. The poems document the life of a young, poor, black woman, Annie Allen, from childhood through marriage and motherhood. Annie finds the fullest expression of her being comes in motherhood, because it brings the realization of the injustices that await her poor black children. It is this realization that provokes Annie Allen's biting critique of and challenges to American racism. The sonnet sequence of the third part, "The Womanhood," is titled "The Children of the Poor," and articulates the concerns and visions of the black mother: "What shall I give my children? who are poor, / Who are adjudged the leastwise of the land." Because Annie Allen seeks to make a home space out of her dilapidated living conditions, and because she gives birth to and nurtures "the children of the poor," she continues to dream, and

her dreams are at best spaces of resistance and at least spaces of sustenance and survival, as necessary as food, clothing, and shelter. Annie Allen tells her "children of the poor" to "First fight. Then fiddle." She sees a place for dreaming and for the creation of art, but it is a hard-won place: "Carry hate / In front of you and harmony behind. / Be deaf to music and to beauty blind. / Win war. Rise bloody, maybe not too late. For having first to civilize a space / Wherein to play your violin with grace."

The themes of *Annie Allen* find their prose voice in Brooks's novella, *Maud Martha,* published in 1953. Like Annie Allen, Maud Martha grows from a dreamy little girl to a pragmatic mother. Themes of intraracial color prejudice and infidelity among the kitchenette dwellers also reemerge. The novella is filled with the same nuanced rage that characterizes *Annie Allen,* but there is an unending hopefulness in Maud Martha's character. The novella concludes with the end of World War II and with Maud Martha's new pregnancy. "The sun was shining, and some of the people in the world had been left alive and it was doubtful whether the ridiculousness of man would ever completely succeed in destroying the world."

Maud Martha, Brooks's first and only novella, has not yet earned its place in the canon of African American fiction, perhaps because it does not easily fall into the categories typically expected from books by other black writers. There is no evocation of southern folk life, nor is there the harsh realism of the race prejudice of many urban whites. Indeed, *Maud Martha* is as lyrical, metaphorical, and concise as Brooks's poetry. *Maud Martha,* which appeared in the same era as James Baldwin's *Go Tell It on the Mountain* and Ralph Ellison's *Invisible Man,* did not receive the critical attention of either of those novels. With the emergence of black feminist criticism in the 1970s and 1980s, however, Brooks's novella was brought to the attention of a larger audience, and it is now widely recognized as an important and pioneering text in the tradition of black women writers.

Bronzeville Boys and Girls (1956) is one of several books Brooks has written for and about children. The poems and the children whose lives they depict are deceptively simple. These children are mature, aware, and creative. Thirty-four poems introduce thirty-seven young people with names such as Andre, Ella, Towanda, and Narcissa. There is also the poverty-ridden John, who is "so lone and alone," and Cynthia, who revels in the wonder of newly fallen snow. "It SUSHES. / It hushes / The loudness in the road. / It flitter-twitters, / And laughs away from me. / It laughs a lovely whiteness / And whitely whirs away, / To be / Some other where, / Still white as milk or shirts. / So beautiful it hurts." The onomatopoeia of these lines evokes a child's sensibility; however, the image of the beautiful white snow suggests not only the color and texture of the snow, but also the stifling standards of beauty that surely hurt this brown child. Like their adult counterparts, the children of Bronzeville are not only specifically black and poor, but also universal children, who find joy and complexity in their daily lives.

In 1960 Brooks published her fourth volume of poems, *The Bean Eaters,* which contains some of her best known poems, including "We Real Cool," "A Bronzeville Mother Loiters in Mississippi, While, A Mississippi Mother Burns Bacon," and "The Lovers of the Poor." While Brooks was finishing the poems for *The Bean Eaters,* her father died, and the collection opens with a poem dedicated to him, "In Honor of David Anderson Brooks, My Father": "He Who was Goodness, Gentleness and Dignity is Free / Translates to public love / Old Private Charity." This dedication creates the image of a gentle and generous man, while the much anthologized "We Real Cool" embodies the image of young, short-lived, inner-city men. Several poems in *The Bean Eaters* are more explicitly about political subjects than Brooks's previous poems, particularly "The Chicago *Defender* Sends a Man to Little Rock," a bitterly ironic piece about a reporter who is sent to cover the school desegregation troubles in Little Rock, Arkansas.

In *The Bean Eaters* Brooks is as concerned with class as she is with race. In fact, there is no mention of race at all in poems such as "The Crazy Woman" and "Pete at the Zoo." Instead, Brooks focuses on the fears, questions, and desires that haunt humankind. Not only do the the poems tend to be more political, but *The Bean Eaters* also signals a transition of form. The meter is freer; there are fewer sonnets. In *Gwendolyn Brooks: Poetry and the Heroic Voice* (1987), D. H. Melhem notes of *The Bean Eaters,* "The form registers the content, and the content expresses activism, the quest for leadership and the emergence of folk heroes." One of those folk heroes is M. Till, mother of Emmett Till, the fourteen-year-old Chicago boy who was brutally beaten and lynched while visiting family members in Mississippi. In "The Last Quatrain of the Ballad of Emmett Till," "Emmett's mother is a pretty-faced thing; / the tint of pulled taffy." She possesses the dignity and grace of the many black women who have lost sons, husbands, and lovers to America's

racial violence. With the final lines of the poem, "Chaos in windy grays / through a red prairie," the mother becomes an indelible part of the Illinois landscape. Her tears, her mourning, and her dignity set the tone for its symbolic geography.

The poem that precedes "The Last Quatrain" is "A Bronzeville Mother Loiters in Mississippi, While a Mississippi Mother Burns Bacon." This poem centers on a white Mississippi woman, an heiress of the tradition of white southern chivalry that countenances the murders of black boys to "protect" white ladies. The only form the woman has to make sense of the brutal murder is the romanticized ballad tradition that she learned in school. "From the first it had been like a / Ballad. It had the beat inevitable. It had the blood." She sees the roles southern society has carved out for her in the themes and characters of the ballad: "Herself: the milk-white maid, the 'maid mild' / of the ballad. Pursued / By the Dark Villain. / Rescued by the Fine Prince." While the woman constructs her narrative to fit her form, she burns the bacon she is trying to cook and quickly hides it, because burnt meat doesn't fit her perfect breakfast of eggs, sour-milk biscuits, and quince preserves. Similarly, the burnt, beaten, and murdered body of the black boy does not fit the neat form of her ballad. She hides the bacon, just as she tries to subdue the harsh reality of the child's murder.

By stanza four, this reality comes to the forefront of her consciousness, refusing to be repressed. As this happens, the form begins to shift – it bursts out of the precise, measured form of earlier stanzas. "But there was a something about the matter of the Dark Villain. / He should have been older, perhaps." "The fun was disturbed, then all but nullified / When the Dark Villain was a blackish child / Of fourteen, with eyes still too young to be dirty." As she begins to question the act of killing the boy, she also questions her own perception: "So much had happened, she could not remember now what / that foe had done / Against her, or if anything had been done."

In stanza eight the myth of the pure white maiden confines and constricts the real white woman. She feels she must "be more beautiful than ever," so that her husband will believe her worthy of his crime. "He must never conclude / That she had not been worth it." The violence that murders the young black boy infiltrates her own home when one of her children throws a molasses pitcher in his brother's face and his father smacks him. The molasses, the syrupy sweet image of southern hospitality, becomes an instrument of terror. The disci-

Cover for Brooks's 1969 book, which was written in the aftermath of the Chicago riots. Its epigraph is a quotation from Martin Luther King Jr.: "A riot is the language of the unheard."

plined small white child, "the small and smiling criminal," is not unlike the dead black boy. As her husband tries to comfort her, she imagines that "a red ooze was seeping, spreading darkly, thickly / slowly, Over her white shoulders, her own shoulders," and at his kiss she feels only "a sickness" and "a hatred for him."

Reaction to *The Bean Eaters* was mixed. Some critics lamented the political content of the poems, suggesting that Brooks's lyricism gave way to political didacticism. However, most contemporary reviewers, like most later critics, agreed that *The Bean Eaters* marked a significant shift in Brooks's artistry.

George Kent, a Brooks's biographer, notes that *The Bean Eaters* "registers the complete achievement of Gwendolyn's sensibility in embracing both the autobiographical world and the main strands of the larger universe."

The political implications of *The Bean Eaters* came to fullest realization in Brooks's later period. The 1967 Writers' Conference at Fisk University in Nashville, Tennessee, marked a turning point in Brooks's politics and her craft. At Fisk, Brooks encountered the newer black nationalist poets, such as Don L. Lee (Haki R. Madhubuti) and Amiri Baraka. Encouraged by their defiance and powerful articulation of black rage (a subject significant in her earlier works), Brooks decided to write more accessible poetry that would speak more directly to those black people in the "tavern . . . the street . . . [and] the halls of a housing project." She also decided to depart from the standard Western literary forms and "to create new forms" that she felt would be more suited to black life.

Throughout the 1970s Brooks also decided to publish her poems in pamphlet form, making them easier to distribute. During this period she left her old publisher for the black-owned Broadside Press. Throughout the decade she published with Broadside and with Madhubuti's Third World Press. In addition to continuing her artistic growth, Brooks also gained greater ownership of her material. In 1980 she founded the David Company so that she could publish her own books.

The publication of *In the Mecca* in 1968 heralds Brooks's new political and aesthetic sensibility. The Mecca of the book's title is an apartment building inhabited by Sallie Smith and her many children, as well as numerous other characters, including Alfred the poet, Prophet Williams, and Jamaican Edward. In the title poem Sallie Smith's youngest daughter, Pepita, is a creative child who loves to write rhymes. When Sallie Smith comes home to find Pepita missing, she sets off on a desperate search for the little girl. The poem narrates Sallie's search for Pepita among apathetic neighbors and indifferent police officers: "The Law arrives – and does not quickly go / to fetch a Female of the Negro Race." At last, Pepita's dead body is found under Jamaican Edward's cot. "She never went to kindergarten. / She never learned that black is not beloved. / Was royalty when poised, / sly, at the A and P's fly-open door. / Will be royalty no more. / 'I touch' – she said once – 'petals of a rose / A silky feeling through me goes!'"

With these lines, Brooks identifies herself with the murdered Pepita. Like Pepita, she, too, did not learn that black was not loved until she went to kindergarten and, like the rhyming Pepita, she, too, was a poetic prodigy. The kitchenette building that housed poetic dreamers in Brooks's work of the 1940s and 1950s now houses the murderers of poetic little girls in the Mecca. Little boys of *In the Mecca,* like the one in "Boy Breaking Glass," say, "I shall create! If not a note, a hole. / If not an overture, a desecration." For many who live in the neighborhood's grimness, artistic possibility is thwarted at every turn. And yet there are heroes here, too, especially in the poems dedicated to Medgar Evers, Malcolm X, and martyred Black Panther leaders.

In "The Chicago Picasso" Brooks warns artists against creating art that does not speak to people, and in "The Second Sermon on the Warpland," she reminds black poets of the dignity and grandeur of ordinary black life: "A garbage man is dignified / as any diplomat. / Big Bessie's feet hurt like nobody's business, / but . . . / she is a citizen, / and is a moment of highest quality; admirable."

Following the assassination in 1968 of Martin Luther King Jr., Bronzevilles across the nation exploded in violence and rioting. Within days of Chicago's riots, Madhubuti commissioned Gwendolyn Brooks's poem "Riot" for the magazine *Black Expression.* "Riot" contains three parts: "Riot," "The Third Sermon on the Warpland," and "An Aspect of Love, Alive in the Fire and Ice." The first poem is a satiric verse inhabited by John Cabot, "once a Wycliffe" – a white Chicagoan, driver of a Jaguar, who frequents elegant restaurants such as Maxim's and Maison Henri. Cabot's life of luxury is disrupted by "Negroes" "coming down the street . . . / In seas. In windsweep. They were black and loud." The Negroes become a mobile mass. Melhem notes that Brooks's choice of the name John Cabot links the character to John Wycliffe, "an English forerunner of the Protestant Reformation," and the name Cabot also links him to the European settlers of Massachusetts. The contemporary Cabot inherits the name but not the heroism of his forefathers. While they helped to create a Christianity that led to greater individual freedom, his notion of religion and freedom is a mockery of their ideals. As he burns in the fires of the riot, the poem ends in his voice: "Forgive these nigguhs that know not what / they do."

From Cabot's ashes arises the "The Third Sermon on the Warpland," subtitled "Phoenix." As is the case with the boy of "Boy Breaking Glass," destruction in this poem has a creative dimension: "Fire. / That is their way of lighting candles in the / darkness." The phrase echoes the epigraph that opens this collection, a quotation from Martin Luther King: "A riot is the language of the unheard."

The last poem of "Riot," "An Aspect of Love, Alive in the Fire and Ice," subtitled "LaBohem Brown," evokes what is perhaps the real phoenix that arises out of the ash of the burning city – an equal, loving relationship between a black man and a black woman. Although this poem embodies Brooks's assertion of her black nationalism, it also alludes to the works of white male poets, such as Robert Frost's "Fire and Ice," and John Donne's "The Sunne Rising." Like the persona of Donne's poem, the persona of "An Aspect of Love" resents the encroachment of day and the outside world. "Because the world is at the window / we cannot wonder very long." The lovers, together in the house, "in Camaraderie," go their separate ways, to pursue their separate lives, sure to return to the mornings "of [their] love."

While Brooks's poetry of the late 1960s and 1970s, *Riot* (1969), *Beckonings* (1975), and *Primer for Blacks* (1980), continued her search for newer forms in which to portray black life, her poems of the 1980s moved beyond urban America to the African Diaspora. This change is especially true in the collections *The Near-Johannesburg Boy and Other Poems* (1986) and *Winnie* (1988). In the poems of this period emerge new heroes such as Steve Biko, the children of Soweto, and Winnie Mandela, as Brooks carves out a Pan-Africanist vision that links the black subjects of her imagined Africa to those of her Bronzeville. This Pan-Africanist vision is especially clear in "Primer for Blacks." "The word Black / has geographic power, pulls everybody in: / Blacks here — / Blacks there — / Blacks wherever they may be." This inclusive vision returns Brooks to the theme of color difference among blacks that so preoccupied her in her earlier work; here she gathers blacks of every shade and hue in her celebration of "blackness."

The blacks in these poems are linked by a common history of oppression and a shared grandeur. The young male persona of the title poem, "The Near-Johannesburg Boy," might be heralding Annie Allen's admonition to "fight first, then fiddle." Joined by "a hundred of playmates," he walks into white-only areas and declares "we shall forge with the Fist-and-the-Fury," and the poem ends with the affirmation, "we shall." The title of the second section of the collection, "Early Death," brings to mind both the African American males of "We Real Cool" and the young people murdered by South African police. The association is reinforced in poems such as "Of the Young Dead" and "To the Young Who Want to Die." In the latter poem Brooks might be speaking to young black gang bangers or those contemplating suicide. "You need not die today . . . Stay here. See what the news is going to be tomorrow."

Winnie — a poem in two parts — was published in pamphlet form in 1991. In the first part *Winnie* seems to be written in the third person and presents the reader with a Winnie Mandela not unlike Annie Allen in her youth. This Winnie "would like to be a little girl again." But unlike Annie, this Winnie is the "founding mother" of an unrealized black nation. Where in Annie Allen, the reader is encour-

aged to "Think of thaumaturgic lass," here the reader is urged to "Think of plants and beautiful weeds in the Wilderness." Like the plants and weeds, Winnie wants simply to grow free; both she and the trees have trash "dumped at their roots." In the poem's last line, the speaker reveals himself to be "I Nelson the Mandela," Winnie's husband.

Part two, "Song of Winnie," is spoken or sung in her voice. Like the trees of the first part, Winnie is beautiful, sensual, wild, and defiled by garbage. "But Ladyhood. . . . / Ladyhood eludes me: nor shall favor me ever. / When Botha's lieutenants / spit in my face, and pinch me, / Ladyhood eludes me." She cannot afford the luxury of ladyhood. She must be "reformer / revolutionary / pioneer." This Winnie is also a poet — a poet who, like her creator Brooks, is "not a tight-faced poet." Winnie as poet creates a "big poem" for black people. She directs the final stanzas to other black women who love their men as equals, as revolutionaries, as strategists, and visionaries. In this poem Brooks returns to the female vision that was largely absent from her nationalist work. Yet unlike the females in the earlier women-centered poems, Winnie stands poised and proud, defiant and indignant, capable of bringing her vision into existence.

Nevertheless, while Brooks lauds the heroism of Africans, she does not romanticize the relationship between black Americans and their African cousins. In her autobiography, *Report from Part One* (1972), Brooks notes that black Americans can never "return to Africa," because the Africans consider them Americans, not Africans. "THE AFRICANS! They insist on calling themselves Africans and their little traveling brothers and sisters 'Afro Americans' no matter how much we want them to recognize our kinship." Brooks's Pan-Africanist vision is not a particularly romanticized one. Her poetry is too sophisticated for crude nationalist ideology, too complex to be dismissed as nonfeminist, and too socially engaged to be dismissed as "art for art's sake."

Until recently, the critical response to Brooks has not been as sophisticated or complex as her work demands. Early white critics were pleased with her use of modernist forms but often perturbed by her black subject matter; black nationalist critics applauded Brooks's material while questioning her modernist aesthetic. She did not fit neatly into the categories into which either group wanted to place her. With her turn toward black nationalism, however, nationalist critics initiated a celebration of her life and work. In 1969 the actress Val Gray Ward organized a "Living Anthology" to honor her. At

Brooks presenting novelist Nelson Algren a $6,000 check on behalf of the Illinois Arts Council

this celebration black writers, painters, photographers, dancers, actors, and musicians paid tribute to Brooks in an evening of poetry, speeches, and music. Participants included Madhubuti, Nikki Giovanni, Carolyn M. Rodgers, Lerone Bennett, and Margaret T. G. Burroughs. Much of the program— with additions sent from artists who could not appear – was collected and published in *To Gwen with Love: An Anthology Dedicated to Gwendolyn Brooks* (1971), edited by Patricia Scott Brown, Don L. Lee, and Francis Ward. The collection is one of many examples of the various ways black artists and intellectuals have illustrated their appreciation for Brooks's life and work.

More recently, black feminist critics such as Claudia Tate, Hortense Spillers, and Mary Helen Washington have initiated sophisticated critical readings of Brooks's earliest works. Betsy Erkkila has also provided a sustained feminist reading of much of Brooks's entire oeuvre. To date there are three books about Brooks: George E. Kent's biography, *A Life of Gwendolyn Brooks* (1990), D. H.

Melhem's critical biography, *Gwendolyn Brooks: Poetry and the Heroic Voice,* and a collection of essays gathered in *A Life Distilled: Gwendolyn Brooks, Her Poetry and Fiction* (1987), edited by Maria K. Mootry and Gary Smith. This collection presents the broad range of Brooks criticism through essays that explore the feminist, modernist, and black nationalist elements of her writing.

Throughout her prolific career, Brooks has used her writing to explore the poetic dimensions of the lives of black people. Since the 1960s, she has also used her writing, lectures, readings, and teaching as a means of communicating with and touching the lives of those about whom she writes. In her many forums, she listens to the voices of the kitchenette dwellers, the gang members, the woman pregnant with an unwanted child; she remains attentive to the sounds and sights of the larger world, as well. Finally Brooks is a public poet, a democratic poet, and a word activist who has a passionate and ongoing commitment to working with young people. Whether they be college students, elementary-school students, or members of the Blackstone Rangers gang, Brooks believes that poetry has the ability to transform people's lives. Critic Houston Baker sums up Brooks's work with insight when he observes that "Gwendolyn Brooks's characters . . . are infinitely human because at the core of their existence is the imaginative intellect." As one who is herself "infinitely human," Brooks continues to create work and follow her own advice: "Conduct your blooming in the noise and whip of the whirlwind."

Interviews:

Paul M. Amgle (Paul McClelland), "We Asked Gwendolyn Brooks about the Creative Environment in Illinois" (Chicago: Community Development Division, Illinois Bell Telephone, 1966);

Hoyt Fuller, "Interview with Gwendolyn Brooks," in *In the Memory and Spirit of Frances, Zora and Lorraine: Essays and Interviews on Black Women and Writing,* edited by Eugenia Collier and Juliette Bowles (Washington, D.C.: Institute for the Arts and Humanties, 1979), pp. 1–5;

Susan Elizabeth Howe and Jay Fox, "A Conversation with Gwendolyn Brooks," *Literature and Belief,* 12 (1982): 1-12.

Bibliography:

R. Baxter Miller, *Langston Hughes and Gwendolyn Brooks: a reference guide* (Ann Arbor: University of Michigan Press, 1966).

Biographies:

D. H. Melhem, *Gwendolyn Brooks: Poetry and the Heroic Voice* (Lexington: University Press of Kentucky, 1987);

George Kent, *A Life of Gwendoyn Brooks* (Lexington: University Press of Kentucky, 1990).

References:

Gayle Addison, "Gwendolyn Brooks: Poet of the Whirlwind," in *Black Women Writers (1950–1980): A Critical Evaluation* edited by Mari Evans (Garden City, N.Y.: Anchor/Doubleday, 1984), pp. 79–87;

Patricia Scott Brown, Don L. Lee, and Francis Ward, eds., *To Gwen with Love: An Anthology Dedicated to Gwendolyn Brooks* (Chicago: Johnson Publishing, 1971);

Eugenia Collier, "With a Womanliness Shining Through: The Poetry of Gwendolyn Brooks" in *In the Memory and Spirit of Frances, Zora and Lorraine: Essays and Interviews on Black Women*

and Writing, edited by Eugenia Collier and Juliette Bowles (Washington, D.C.: Institute for the Arts and Humanities, 1979), pp. 68–71;

Emma Waters Dawson, "The Vanishing Point: The Rejected Black Woman in the Poetry of Gwendolyn Brooks," *Obsidian II: Black Literature in Review,* 4 (Spring 1989): 1-11;

Betsy Erkkila, *The Wicked Sisters: Women Poets, Literary History & Discord* (New York: Oxford University Press, 1993);

Ekaterini Georgoudaki, *Race, Gender, and Class Perspectives in the Works of Maya Angelou, Gwendolyn Brooks, Rita Dove, Nikki Giovanni, and Audre Lorde* (Thessaloniki: Aristotle University of Thessaloniki, 1991);

Brooke Kenton Horvath, "The Satisfactions of What's Difficult in Gwendolyn Brooks's Poetry," *American Literature: A Journal of Literary History, Criticism, and Bibliography,* 62 (December 1990): 606–616;

Gertrude Hughes, "Making It Really New: Hilda Doolittle, Gwendolyn Brooks, and the Feminist Potential of Modern Poetry," *American Quarterly,* 42 (September 1990): 375–401;

Patricia Lattin and Vernon E. Lattin, "Dual Vision in Gwendolyn Brooks's *Maud Martha,*" *Critique: Studies in Contemporary Fiction,* 25 (Summer 1984): 180–188;

D. H. Melhem, "Cultural Challenge, Heroic Response: Gwendolyn Brooks and the New Black Poetry," in *Perspectives of Black Popular Culture,* edited by Harry B. Shaw (Bowling Green, Ohio: Bowling Green University Popular Press, 1990), pp. 71–84;

Melhem, *Gwendolyn Brooks: poetry & the heroic voice* (Lexington, Ky.: University Press of Kentucky, 1987);

Maria K. Mootry and Gary Smith, eds., *A Life Distilled: Gwendolyn Brooks, Her Poetry and Fiction* (Chicago: University of Illinois Press, 1987);

Dee Seligman, "The Mother of Them All: Gwendolyn Brooks's *Annie Allen*" in *The Anna Book: Searching for Anna in Literary History,* edited by Mickay Perlman (Westport, Conn.: Greenwood Press, 1992), pp. 131–138;

Harry B. Shaw, *Gwendolyn Brooks* (Boston: Twayne, 1980);

Smith, "Gwendolyn Brooks's *A Street in Bronzeville:* The Harlem Renaissance and the Mythologies of Black Women," *MELUS: The Journal of the Society for the Study of Multi Ethnic Literature of the United States,* 10 (Fall 1983) 33–46;

Spillers, "'An Order of Constancy:' Notes on Brooks and the Feminine," *The Centennial Review,* 29 (Spring 1985): 223–248;

Ann Folwell Stanford, "Dialectics of Desire: War and Resistive Voice in Gwendolyn Brooks's 'Negro Hero' and 'Gay Chaps at the Bar,'" *African American Review,* 26 (Summer 1992): 197-211;

Henry Taylor, "Gwendolyn Brooks: An Essential Sanity," *The Kenyon-Review,* 13 (Fall 1991): 115-31;

Mary Helen Washington, "Plain, Black and Decently Wild: The Heroic Possibilities of Maud Martha," in *The Voyage in Fictions of Female Development,* edited by Elizabeth Abel and Marianne Hirsch (Hanover, N.H.: University Press of New England for Dartmouth College, 1983), pp. 270–286;

Washington, "Taming All that Anger Down: Rage and Silence in Gwendolyn Brooks's *Maud Martha,*" *Massachusetts Review,* 24 (Summer 1983): 453–466;

Stephen Caldwell Wright, ed., *On Gwendolyn Brooks: reliant contemplation* (Ann Arbor: University of Michigan Press, 1996).

Papers:

Gwendolyn Brooks's papers (1954–1967) are held in the Manuscripts, Archives and Rare Books Division of the Schomburg Center for Research in Black Culture, the New York Public Library.

Hayden Carruth

(3 August 1921 –   )

David W. Landrey
Buffalo (N.Y.) State College

See also the Carruth entry in *DLB 5: American Poets Since World War II, First Series.*

BOOKS: *The Crow and the Heart, 1946–1959* (New York: Macmillan, 1959);

In Memoriam: G. V. C. 1888–1960 (Pleasantville, Iowa: Privately printed, 1960);

Journey to a Known Place (Norfolk, Conn.: New Directions, 1961);

The Norfolk Poems: 1 June to 1 September 1961 (Iowa City: Prairie, 1962);

Appendix A (New York: Macmillan / London: Collier-Macmillan, 1963);

North Winter (Iowa City: Prairie, 1964);

After the Stranger: Imaginary Dialogues with Camus (New York: Macmillan / London: Collier-Macmillan, 1965);

Nothing for Tigers: Poems 1959–1964 (New York: Macmillan / London: Collier-Macmillan, 1965);

Contra Mortem (Johnson, Vt.: Crow's Mark, 1967);

The Clay Hill Anthology (Iowa City: Prairie, 1970);

For You (New York: New Directions, 1970; London: Chatto & Windus, 1971);

From Snow and Rock, from Chaos (New York: New Directions, 1973; London: Chatto & Windus, 1973);

Dark World (Santa Cruz, Cal.: Kayak, 1974);

The Bloomingdale Papers (Athens: University of Georgia Press, 1975);

Loneliness: An Outburst of Hexasyllables (West Burke, Vt.: Janus, 1976);

Aura: A Poem with a Paperwork by Claire Van Vliet and Kathryn and Howard Clark (West Burke, Vt.: Janus, 1977);

Brothers, I Loved You All: Poems, 1969–1977 (New York: Sheep Meadow, 1978);

Almanach Du Printemps Vivarois (New York: Nadja, 1979);

Working Papers: Selected Essays and Reviews (Athens: University of Georgia Press, 1982);

Hayden Carruth (courtesy of the author)

The Mythology of Dark and Light (Syracuse, N.Y.: Tamarack Editions, 1982);

The Sleeping Beauty (New York: Harper & Row, 1982; Toronto: Fitzhenry & Whiteside, 1982; revised edition, Port Townsend, Wash.: Copper Canyon, 1990);

Effluences from the Sacred Caves: More Selected Essays and Reviews (Ann Arbor: University of Michigan Press, 1983; Rexdale, Canada: John Wiley & Sons Canada, 1983);

92

If You Call This Cry a Song (Woodstock, Vt.: The Countryman, 1983);

Asphalt Georgics (New York: New Directions, 1985; Toronto: Penguin, 1985);

Lighter Than Air Craft (Lewisburg, Penn.: Press of Appletree Alley, 1985);

The Oldest Killed Lake in North America: Poems, 1979–1981 (Grenada, Miss.: Salt-Works, 1985);

Mother (Syracuse, N.Y.: Tamarack Editions, 1985);

Sitting In: Selected Writings on Jazz, Blues, and Related Topics (Iowa City: University of Iowa Press, 1986; expanded edition, Iowa City: University of Iowa Press, 1993);

Sonnets (Lewisburg, Penn.: Press of Appletree Alley, 1989);

Tell Me Again How the White Heron Rises and Flies Across the Nacreous River at Twilight Toward the Distant Islands (New York: New Directions, 1989; Toronto: Penguin, 1989);

Suicides and Jazzers (Ann Arbor: University of Michigan Press, 1992);

Scrambled Eggs & Whiskey, Poems 1991–1995 (Port Townsend, Wash.: Copper Canyon, 1996);

Selected Essays and Reviews (Port Townsend, Wash.: Copper Canyon, 1996).

Collections: *The Selected Poetry of Hayden Carruth* (New York: Collier Books, 1985; London: Collier-Macmillan, 1985);

Collected Shorter Poems, 1946–1991 (Port Townsend, Wash.: Copper Canyon, 1992);

Collected Longer Poems (Port Townsend, Wash.: Copper Canyon, 1994).

OTHER: *A New Directions Reader,* edited by Carruth and James Laughlin (New York: New Directions, 1964);

The Voice That Is Great Within Us: American Poetry of the Twentieth Century, edited by Carruth (New York, Toronto & London: Bantam, 1970);

The Bird/Poem Book: Poems on the Wild Birds of North America, selected by Carruth (New York: McCall / Toronto: Doubleday Canada, 1970);

The Collected Poems of James Laughlin, with an introduction by Carruth (Wakefield, R.I.: Moyer Bell, 1994).

Hayden Carruth first published a poem in 1946, and his poetry, essays, and anthologies now approach forty volumes with no sign of abatement. He has, moreover, by his own estimate written several thousand pieces for newspapers, magazines, and anthologies. He is often called a poet's poet, and his aid to and promotion of others has been remarkable. His eclectic anthology, *The Voice That Is*

Great Within Us (1970), a survey of American poetry from Robert Frost to its date of publication, has been widely used and continues to be highly regarded. Carruth's influence and importance have grown markedly in the last decade, especially with the publications of his historical/mythical epic, *The Sleeping Beauty* (1982); *Collected Shorter Poems* (1992), which won the National Book Critics Circle Award in 1993; and *Collected Longer Poems* (1994). Furthermore, his essays and reviews, now collected in four volumes, including *Suicides and Jazzers* (1992), constitute a major overview of the craft of American poetry since World War II.

Carruth has been an editor of *Poetry* (1949–1950), associate editor at the University of Chicago Press (1950–1952), the project administrator for Intercultural Publications of the Ford Foundation (1952–1954), the poetry editor of *Harper's* magazine (1977–1981), and advisory editor for *The Hudson Review* (1970–present). His many prizes, grants, and honors include the University of Chicago's Harriet Monroe award (1960), Guggenheim Fellowships in 1965 and 1979, National Endowment for the Arts fellowships in 1968 and 1974, the Shelley Prize of the Poetry Society of America (1979), Senior Fellow of the National Endowment for the Arts (1988), and the Ruth Lilly Poetry Prize (1990). Carruth is a member of American P.E.N., the Poetry Society of America, and the Academy of American Poets.

Born in Waterbury, Connecticut, Carruth's primary formative experience was of small-town and country life. He reports in an interview with David Weiss in *In the Act: Essays on the Poetry of Hayden Carruth* (1990) that his father, Gorton Veeder Carruth, a newspaperman, editor, and writer of verse, once told him, "Don't ever take any job that isn't a service to the community." Carruth has heeded this advice. His mother, for whom he wrote a long elegy in 1985, was Margery Barrow Carruth. His education includes a B.A. in journalism from the University of North Carolina (1942) and an M.A. in English from the University of Chicago (1948). Before his emergence on the literary scene, he served two years in Europe during World War II as a member of the Army Air Corps.

Carruth has been married four times, the first three ending in divorce. He married Sara Anderson on 14 March 1943. He has a daughter by that marriage, Martha Hamilton. He married Eleanore Ray on 29 November 1952. His third marriage, to Rose Marie Dorn on 28 October 1961, produced his son, David Barrow, whom he calls "the Bo." The family lived for eighteen years in Johnson, Vermont, a period Carruth in *Suicides and Jazzers* recalls "afforded

Dust jacket for Carruth's 125-stanza poem, which uses the fairy-tale princess to explore the history of beauty in culture

emanate from the center of my poems. . . . Poetry for me was, and is, second-best to jazz." Carruth's sorrow also has other powerful roots. He writes of the decline of the nation, especially of family farming, of the distraught lives of ordinary people, and of the destructive history of power politics; in the process, he often proclaims himself a "philosophical anarchist." To convey the starkness of these issues he recurs to such aspects of hard natural beauty as the stone, winter, birds, and trees as well as to the idea of "nothing," his own continuing struggle with psychological problems, and the voices of the men and women of his milieu. An abiding interest in philosophy, especially existentialism, underpins Carruth's thought. He has special interests in Søren Kierkegaard, Arthur Schopenhauer, Jean-Paul Sartre, Martin Heidegger, Immanuel Kant, and Albert Camus. Although he says in *Suicides and Jazzers,* writing with passion of his own attempted suicide in 1988, that "every artist of the second half of the twentieth century knows that his or her working life is in at least one sense a resounding defeat," he maintains an elemental love of life.

In November 1953, after six years in Chicago, followed by his first divorce and second marriage, Carruth entered Bloomingdale psychiatric hospital in White Plains, New York, where he remained for fifteen months. He has often said that the time there did not help and may have made matters worse, but it clearly became a central issue in his early poetry and has never quite disappeared from his work. Part of his treatment consisted of his writing about the experience between November 1953 and January 1954, an effort that resulted in *The Bloomingdale Papers,* a volume not published until 1975 when his friend, the artist Albert Christ-Janer, persuaded Carruth to let the University of Georgia Press publish it. Despite the depth of his personal despair, Carruth was sensitive to the problems of his fellow inmates and to the madness of the larger world. "I think of it as a paradigm of the general quality of life in this country during the 1950s," he says in his preface, "Explanation and Apology, Twenty Years After." Taking "exile as the experience *par excellence* of the mid-twentieth century," Carruth writes:

> The bitcheries of Madison Avenue
> Where I lost my mind, where pigs that learned to read
> Talk moneywise around the urn of love; . . .
> The catalogue of our misfortunes, oh
> How long it is, so have the false men prospered!

While he had not been able to function in the face of the "false men," he ends the book with a plea for his daughter:

me the opportunity to put everything together, the land and seasons, the people, my family, my work, my evolving sense of survival (for when I'd been in the hospital the doctors had told me I'd never again have anything like a normal life), in one tightly integrated imaginative structure. The results were my poems, for what they're worth, and in my life a very gradual but perceptible triumph over the internal snarls and screw-ups that had crippled me from childhood on." Carruth married poet Joe-Anne McLaughlin on 29 December 1989. The couple resides in Munnsville, New York.

Although Carruth has said that he abhors repetition and has always employed a diversity of forms, some of his own invention, he has almost methodically examined and reexamined a cluster of themes and concerns. In "Influences: The Formal Idea of Jazz," an essay collected in *Sitting In: Selected Writings on Jazz, Blues, and Related Topics* (1993), Carruth writes that having poetry rather than music as his articulation of his lifelong absorption in jazz may account, "in part for the sorrow that appears to

That some small wisdom always may endure
Amidst your weariness; that lovers may
Be kind to you; that beauty may arouse
You; that the crazy house
May never, never be your home: I pray.

After emerging from the hospital Carruth settled in New England, where for the next twenty-four years he spliced together a bare living. From 1955 to 1960 he lived a secluded life in his parents' house in Pleasantville, New York. From 1960 to 1962 he lived in Norfolk, Connecticut, in a place provided by poet and publisher James Laughlin, who also provided Carruth with many writing and editorial tasks. (Carruth's friendship with Laughlin has been an enduring one. In 1994 Carruth wrote a warmly appreciative introduction to Laughlin's *Collected Poems*.) Besides working the land, the insomniac Carruth did reviews, ghostwriting, and editing at all hours. He fitted writing his own poems into spare moments.

The products of these years were his first three published volumes and the creation of his special form, the paragraph. In 1990 he explained that his invention of this fifteen-line form was

> influenced by a sonnet of Paul Goodman . . . in which he displaced the final couplet and put it in the middle after the octet. . . . So when I invented the paragraph I put a rhymed couplet in the middle, a tetrameter couplet, and in a way the whole history of what I did with the paragraph was to get around that terrible barrier, that terrible problem I'd given myself, because having a rhymed couplet in the middle tends to break up the poem terribly and I had to find ways to flow through that.

Carruth's first collection, *The Crow and the Heart, 1946–1959* (1959), includes poems written before, during, and after his Bloomingdale stay. The most important poem is the thirteen-part "Asylum," written in 1957 and later revised as the first section of *For You* (1970), his first effort using the paragraph form. Gaining perspective on his experience at Bloomingdale and musing on its relationship to the century's problems, Carruth plays on the meanings of *asylum*. He notes that "The nation was asylum when we came" and asks "is not the whole earth / Asylum? Is mankind / In refuge?" In the penultimate section, he asserts that "ultimately asylum is the soul"; but he ends the poem on a cryptic note: "Here am I – drowned, living, loving, and insane."

Journey to a Known Place (1961), written in 1959, takes a large step away from what Carruth calls in the introduction to *The Bloomingdale Papers* his "spirit caged and struggling." The four-part poem depicts a Dantean movement of the spirit through the primal elements, cast as a journey across a frozen land, a descent to the depths of the sea, an awakening on shore, and a soaring guided by an eagle and its song. The poem concludes, "Aspiring now in sun's cascading element,"

>   we make
> Each in his only ascertainable center,
> The world of realization, the suffered reality,
> Through which comes understanding.

The understanding attained, however, is not presented as a permanent haven.

The Norfolk Poems, 1 June to 1 September 1961 (1962) completes Carruth's Connecticut period. In this third collection he begins to examine his neighbors, to grapple with their fading world, and to make contact with the land. Disparaging the proclivity to make "the stone a thing that is less than stone, / A dolmen, a god," Carruth writes,

> the stone is a greatness, itself in its grain,
> Meaning more than a meaning, and more than a mind
> May diminish.

Thus Carruth moves to new stages of his thought, holding tightly to the forms of the natural world yet seeking a personal transcendence.

The first books published by Carruth during his long Vermont sojourn were *North Winter* (1964) and *After the Stranger: Imaginary Dialogues With Camus* (1965), both of which he worked on at the same time in 1963. The experimental nature of each book no doubt fed the other. In *After the Stranger* a painter named Aspen (Carruth is fascinated by the shimmering qualities of the aspen tree) recognizes his entrapment in his loft and in his work. Rather like the painter in Franz Kafka's *The Trial* (1925) or like Joseph Grand in Camus's *The Plague* (1947) Aspen is obsessed by a single motif, in his case a stone, which he constantly reconceives on canvas. To begin his liberation, he moves to Paris and engages for the balance of the book in conversation with Camus, mostly about the motives of the character Meursault in *The Stranger* (1942) and what, if anything, he attains. The result is Aspen's gradual emergence into painting things other than the stone and his finding love in the person of Dora. Instrumental in his change is Dora's former lover, D'Arrast, who bears the name of the protagonist of Camus's short story, "The Growing Stone," which was published in America in 1958.

In her contribution to *In the Act,* Maxine Kumin describes "North Winter" as "a tone poem in 57 strophes, subtly modulated here and there with little skips and riffs of typographical invention. Not 'concrete' poetry, but lightly shaped, like a homemade loaf." The blending of form, subject, and precise language is stunning. Carruth, who points out that he used no personal pronouns in the poem, leads his reader through winter's stages to a rebirth. In strophe 12 he urges the reader not to think of snow as chaste but to think

> of stags raging down
> the rutting wind and of northern
> passion crackling like naked trumpets
> in the snow under the blazing aurora.

In strophe 57, the poet emerges in spring, "brushing the / mist from his shoulders" to discover

> water water
> the pools and freshets
> wakening
>   earth glistening
> releasing the ways of
>   the
> words of
>   earth long frozen.

A section titled "AFTERWORD: / WHAT THE POET HAD WRITTEN," inspired by the 1909 arctic expedition of Commdr. Robert E. Peary and Matthew Henson, concludes the poem:

> north is the aurora north is
> deliverance emancipation . . .
>   . . . north is
> nothing. . . .

For Carruth existential acceptance is essential, but like Aspen in *After the Stranger* he has grown to new realms.

During the next decade Carruth settled in to his milieu, restructuring his Vermont home, enjoying family life, listening to the voices of those around him, and infusing his spirit with jazz. Building toward the major work *Brothers, I Loved You All: Poems, 1969–1977* (1978), he yet had to take some important soul-searching steps. "The Smallish Son" from *Nothing for Tigers: Poems 1959–1964* (1965) underscores the pain that continued to flow from Carruth's early years:

> Listen,
> I who have dwelt at the root of a scream forever,
> I who have read my heart like a man with no hands
> reading a book whose pages turn in the wind,
> I say listen, listen, hear me

in our dreamless dark, my dear. I can teach you complaining.

But Carruth also heeds his own command to listen, as his close friend and fellow poet David Budbill points out in *In the Act*: "This ability to *listen* to the world both outside and inside the self and then attempt to articulate what you hear is rife throughout Hayden's work." In *Nothing For Tigers* Carruth goes on to speculate on "Freedom and Discipline," addressing "Saint Harmony" and discovering that

> Freedom and discipline concur
> only in ecstasy, all else
>
> is shoveling out the muck.
> Give me my old hot horn.

In "Fragments of Autobiography" from *Suicides and Jazzers* Carruth recalls, "Once in 1965 I was able to give myself a whole month. I don't remember how this came about, but I wrote 'Contra Mortem,' a poem in thirty parts, doing one part a day for thirty days. . . . This poem remains my personal favorite among all the poems I've written." Published by Carruth's own Crow's Mark Press *Contra Mortem* (1967) is a reflection on "Being" and "Nothing" that concludes:

> Such figures if they succeed are beautiful
> because for a moment we brighten in a blaze of rhymes
> and yet they always fail and must fail
> and give way to other poems
> in the endless approximations of what we feel
> Hopeless it is hopeless Only the wheel
> endures It spins and spins winding
> the was the is the willbe out of nothing
> and thus we are Thus on the wheel we touch
> each to each a part
> of the great determining reality How much
> we give to one another Perhaps our art
> succeeds after all our small song done in the faith
> of lovers who endlessly change heart for heart
> as the gift of being Come let us sing against death.

In this poem Carruth arrives at his clearest statement of the absurdist paradox and sets forth the terms of the rest of his work.

After revising five of his previously published long poems in *For You* — a book that traces the poet's journey from the asylum outward into the world — Carruth took his last major step toward *Brothers, I Loved You All* in the collection *From Snow and Rock, from Chaos* (1973). In poems such as "Emergency Haying" he identifies with his close friends, in this case Marshall Washer, and expresses the agony of work on the diminished farms of Ver-

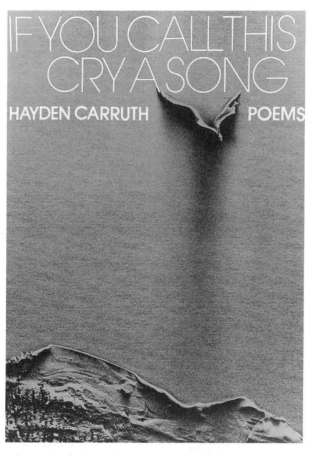

*Dust jacket for Carruth's 1983 book of poems, a varied collection
that includes jazz-inspired verse as well as "Loneliness: An
Outburst of Hexasyllables"*

mont. His role as poet-participant is clear in "The Ravine":

> These are what I see here every day,
> not things but relationships of things,
> quick changes and slow. These are my sorrow[.]

In the entry on Carruth in *DLB 5* William Koon called *Brothers, I Loved You All* by far his best work. He adds, "Carruth seems to have endured his personal agony, his Bloomingdale, and emerged a more complete poet." Carruth opens the volume with "The Loon on Forrester's Pond," hearing the bird's cry:

> it came from inside the long wilderness
> of my life.

He realizes that the bird's laugh is

> a vestige, the laugh that transcends
> first all mirth
> and then all sorrow
> and finally all knowledge, dying

into the gentlest quavering timeless
woe. It seemed
the real and only sanity to me.

In this and other poems of the collection Carruth shows a deep understanding of both his spirit and surroundings. In the long poem "Vermont" he captures the geography, language, and feeling of the state in a cascade of wit.

Galway Kinnell's praise of *Brothers, I Loved You All* in his "Foreword" to *The Selected Poetry of Hayden Carruth* (1985) could apply to much of Carruth's later work:

> One of the most striking things about his work is his ability to enter the lives of other people . . . and tell their tales. . . . I think this is so because he knows them through their speech. There is a reciprocity in all this, however. In telling their tales, he finds a means to express his own inner life. He gives them a voice, they give him a language.

The voices are those of his "brothers," in one sense all of humankind but particularly the jazz musicians who have given music to his language.

In the twenty-eight-part "Paragraphs" from *Brothers* he loosens (as he calls it) his invented form. The poem concludes with a vision of the recording session of "Bottom Blues" by Albert Ammons, Lips Page, Vic Dickenson, Don Byas, Israel Crosby, and Big Sid Catlett that occurred while the poet was fighting in World War II:

> A day   very solid   February 12th, 1944
> cheerless in New York City (while I kneedeep
> elsewhere in historical war
> was wrecking Beauty's sleep
> and her long dream)[.]

He conveys "a moment ecstatic / in the history / of creative mind *and* heart" and prays,

> Ah,
>   holy spirit, ninefold
> I druther've bin a-settin there, supernumerary
> cockroach i' th' corner, a-listenin, a-listenin,,,,,,
>   than be the Prazedint ov the Wurrurld.

In *If You Call This Cry a Song* (1983) Carruth continues his exploration of others' voices, deepens his analysis of political and social corruption, and enlarges his use of jazz rhythms. "Marvin McCabe" is the dramatic monologue of a man rendered inarticulate by an auto accident who is now thought to be "good for nothing" by his father. McCabe says of Carruth,

> He's listened to me so much
> he knows not only what I'm saying but what
> I mean to say, you understand? – that thought
> in my head. He can write it out for me.

The poem is a bitter portrait of the failure of community. At its conclusion Carruth and McCabe seem to be speaking as one:

> It isn't because we're a joke, no,
> it's because we think we aren't a joke – that's
> what the whole universe is laughing at. It makes
> no difference if my thoughts are spoken or not,
> or if I live or die – nothing will change.
> How could it? This body is wrong, a misery,
> a misrepresentation, but hell, would talking make
> any difference? The reason nobody knows me

is because I don't exist. And neither do you.

Seemingly in the same spirit of negation is "On Being Asked to Write a Poem Against the War in Vietnam." He says he has done so and has written against many other wars as well,

> and not one
> breath was restored
> to one
>
> shattered throat[.]

But, as Wendell Berry observes in *In the Act,*

> Mr. Carruth's protest poem is a poem against reduction. On its face, it protests – yet again – the reduction of the world, but its source is a profound instinct of resistance against the reduction of the poet and man who is the poet. By its wonderfully sufficient artistry, the poem preserves the poet's wholeness of heart in the face of his despair. And it shows us how to do so as well. That we would help if we could means that we will help when we can.

While the collection also features rollicking, jazzy poems such as "A Little Old Funky Homeric Blues for Herm" and "Who Cares, Long As It's B-Flat," perhaps its masterpiece is "Loneliness: An Outburst of Hexasyllables," another powerful poem of anguish. The poem was written, Carruth recalls in *Effluences from the Sacred Caves: More Selected Essays and Reviews* (1983), "in extreme emotion – agitation, depression, bitterness" – that is evident in its concluding lines:

> I know that
> I am a fool and all
> men are fools. I know it
> and I know I know it.
> What good is it to know?

And yet Carruth's artistic integrity convinces the reader that the poet's spirit will prevail. His loneliness is like the snow-sculpted tree, "made by / the whole of motioning, / all in a concert."

Throughout the 1970s Carruth worked on the verses of his long poem *The Sleeping Beauty,* in which he reveals a sweeping vision of human history. He begins the 125-paragraph sequence in his favorite setting:

> Out of nothing.
>
>   This morning the world was gone;
> Only grayness outside, so dense, so close
> Against the window that it seemed no season,
> No place, and no thought almost,

Except what preys at the edge of thought, unknown;
But it was snow.

From "A presence gathering," at once beauty –
"which is also love" – and his own consciousness,
the poem begins.

Carruth identifies three principal "persons" in
the poem, beginning with the princess from the
fairy tale:

> Oh, begin
> In all and nothing then, the vision from a name,
> This Rose Marie Dorn,
> Woman alive exactly when the Red Army came
> To that crook of the Oder where she was born,
> Woman who fled and fled in her human duty
> And bore her name, meaning Rose in the Thorn,
> Her name, the mythologos, the Sleeping Beauty.

In a note included in *Collected Longer Poems* Carruth explains the allusion to his wife – "Because their
family name was Dorn, her parents named her intentionally after the story of *Dornröschen,* and from this
the poem sprang" – though he asserts that "nothing
beyond this in the poem should be construed as a personal reference." The second person is the prince who
would in his arrogance awaken Beauty but who
"knows the horror of being / Only a dream."

> Third is the poem, who must make
> Presence from words, vision from seeing,
> This no one that uniquely in sorrow rejoices
> And can have no pronoun.

Throughout the poem, one may also hear "the
echo of coincidental voices" as Carruth traces "this
beauty in its centuries of wrong," *beauty* meaning
not only the princess but the quality, especially as it
is manifested in the spirit of art. As Sleeping Beauty
dreams, the prince appears in many guises, as historical figures and events and as abstract entities –
all beginning with the letter *H*. From Homer to
Hayden, Carruth reveals Beauty's exploitation "In
this history of the Slaughter / Of the Innocents." In
section 108, where "Its peculiar name is Hydrogen
Bomb," Carruth asks,

> Yet was not each
> Dream always precisely made for this power
> At the heart of darkness, this violence, this beast
> Of non-existence hulking beyond your horror?

Among the counterpoints of the poem are a
woman's face in stone looking upward through the
water of a brook and the voice of Amos, a Vermont
farmer long dead. Carruth uses such images to gain
perspective on the centuries of horror.

*Cover for Carruth's 1992 book of poems, of which he remarks,
"At times I think this collection is everything of its kind I
wish to save. At other times I think it is simply all I
dare to offer."*

Sleeping Beauty is certainly a masterpiece. In his
essay from *In the Act* Sam Hamill describes the poem
as "perhaps Hayden Carruth's grandest achievement. It is astonishingly inclusive, making use of
his enormous narrative skills as in *Brothers, I Loved
You All,* formal without being awkward or self-
conscious, lyrical in its execution and epic in its proportion, sweeping in its broad affections and horrors. Squarely in the American romantic-mytho-
poeic tradition, *The Sleeping Beauty* is a sustained visionary icon of our culture. It returns to us a spirit
now too often missing in our poetry, one which
dares the sustained experience, a spirit which encourages as many literary lions as housecats."

In 1979, as he relates in "Fragments of Autobiography," Carruth was worn out from the Vermont
years of hard labor and needed money to send his
son to the university. "The system had snagged me
after all," he admitted. Although he somewhat reluc-

tantly accepted a professorship at Syracuse University, where he would work until his retirement in 1991, he was entering into a new era of productivity.

The first published result of the Syracuse period was *Asphalt Georgics* (1985), a collection in which Carruth incorporates a whole new cast of voices – with names such as Septic Tanck, Capper Kaplinski, and Art and Poll – in an examination of urban life. Carruth exposes the vacuity of life caused by strip malls and housing subdivisions, but as in his earlier work his characters emerge with a stubborn dignity. The quirky quatrains of his "Georgics" seem suited to capture a diminished modern life. The poem "Cave Painting," for example, reviews the progressive extinction of species, down to "our own / fixed and impoverished being":

> We were with them. They went away.
>   And now every bell in
> every tower in every vil-
>   lage could toll the tocsin
>
> of our sorrow forever and
>   still not tell how across
> all time our origin always
>   is this knowledge of loss.

The theme of loss dominates *The Oldest Killed Lake in North America: Poems, 1979–1981* (1985), titled after Syracuse's Onondaga, dead from pollution. Also lost are clean air and most human values. In "The Sleeping Beauty (Some Years Later)," Carruth writes that "The face in the water is gone" and records that the brook in which the face appeared is filled with the "damp dregs / of all the world."

Against the ubiquitous decay of life Carruth in his most recent verse and essays takes his stand mainly in two alternatives: love and cynicism. *Sonnets* (1989) presents a long sequence about rediscovered eroticism and political anger. Even though he knows "our country has no use for how / value survives" and lives "in a system more absolute / than any kingdom, for now the State is god," he is sustained by physical love and the love expressed in the act of writing. "The kiss is one and egoless," he proclaims; and although "my poems too are incorporated" in the system, he writes:

> Always I wanted to give and in wanting was
> the poet. A man now, aging, I know the best
> of love is not to bestow, but to recognize.

In *Tell Me Again How the White Heron Rises and Flies Across the Nacreous River at Twilight Toward the Distant*

Islands (1989), Carruth argues that "The poem is a gift, a bestowal" and "is for us what instinct is for animals, a continuing and chiefly unthought corroboration of essence." In this volume of mostly long-line poems, he adopts his posture as cynic. In "The Incorrigible Dirigible," the opening meditation on the alcoholism he has shared with Raymond Carver and John Cheever (a condition conquered by all three), he depicts Cheever and himself in a long discussion: "We were men buoyant in cynicism." In "Suicide" from *Suicides and Jazzers* he reveals a new joy in life after his 1988 suicide attempt: "My dictionary says: 'The Cynics [in ancient philosophy] taught that virtue is the only good, and that its essence lies in self-control and independence'. . . . For me virtue is indeed the only good." The act of creation is his virtue, for "the artist must not only work but *live* in a state of devotion to things greater than himself."

In his influential essay, "The Act of Love: Poetry and Personality," collected in *Working Papers: Selected Essays and Reviews* (1982), Carruth defines *personality* as "the whole individual subjectivity, the spirit-body-soul." When that personality has been realized in a poem, he asserts, "It is no longer an object; it transcends objects." That realization he calls love. In "Sometimes When Lovers Lie Quietly Together, Unexpectedly One of Them Will Feel the Other's Pulse" from *Tell Me Again How the White Heron Rises and Flies Across the Nacreous River at Twilight Toward the Distant Islands* he presents a moment in mid August when he feels no less than the pulse of the world itself, his ultimate lover: "And for a while I was taken away from my discontents / By this rhythm of the truth of the world, so fundamental, so simple, so clear."

Carruth currently is working with David Budbill to revive the reputation of the turn-of-the-century writer of sketches and stories Rowland Robinson. His *Collected Shorter Poems* includes a concluding section titled "New Poems, 1986–1991" in which he has written passionate elegies for friends George Dennison and Raymond Carver, and he has recently published *Scrambled Eggs & Whiskey, Poems 1991–1995* (1996) and *Selected Essays and Reviews* (1996).

Interviews:

David Weiss, "An Interview With Hayden Carruth," in *In the Act: Essays on the Poetry of Hayden Carruth,* 20th Anniversary Issue of *Seneca Review,* edited by Weiss (Geneva, N.Y.: Hobart & William Smith Press, 1990);

Anthony Robbins, "Hayden Carruth: An Interview," *American Poetry Review,* 22 (September/October 1993): 47–55.

References:

Dick Allen, "The Gift to Be Simple," *Poetry,* 124 (May 1974): 103–116;

Wendell Berry, "On Carruth's Poetry," *American Poetry Review,* 3 (January/February 1974): 39;

James Dickey, *Babel to Byzantium* (New York: Farrar, Straus & Giroux, 1968), pp. 127–131;

William Dickey, "The Poet and the Moment," *Hudson Review,* 24 (Spring 1971): 159–170;

Lillian Feder, "Poetry from the Asylum: Hayden Carruth's *The Bloomingdale Papers,*" *Literature and Medicine,* 4 (1985): 112–127;

R. W. Flint, "The Odyssey of Hayden Carruth," *Parnassus: Poetry in Review,* 11 (Spring/Summer 1983): 17–32;

Geoffrey Gardner, "The Real and Only Sanity," *American Poetry Review,* 10 (January/February 1981): 19–22;

Jim Harrison, "The Northness of North," *Nation,* 200 (15 February 1965): 180;

Richard Howard, "To a Known Place," *Poetry,* 107 (January 1966): 253–258;

Paul Ramsay, "American Poetry in 1973," *Sewanee Review,* 82 (1974): 393–406;

Adrienne Rich, "A Tool or a Weapon," *Nation,* 213 (25 October 1971): 408–410;

Roger Sale, "New Poems, Ancient and Modern," *Hudson Review,* 18 (Summer 1965): 299–308;

David Shapiro, "Into the Gloom," *Poetry,* 128 (July 1976): 226–232;

David Weiss, ed., *In the Act: Essays on the Poetry of Hayden Carruth,* 20th Anniversary Issue of *Seneca Review* (Geneva, N.Y.: Hobart & William Smith Press, 1990) – includes essays by Philip Booth, Wendell Berry, Geof Hewitt, W. S. Di Piero, David Rivard, Maxine Kumin, David Weiss, Anthony Robbins, Stephen Kuusisto, Sam Hamill, William Matthews, Geoffrey Gardner, Carolyn Kizer, and David Budbill.

Papers:

Carruth materials are held at the library of the University of Vermont.

Lyn Hejinian

(17 May 1941 –)

Juliana Spahr
State University of New York at Buffalo

BOOKS: *a gRReat adventure* (Self-published, 1972);
A Thought Is the Bride of What Thinking (Willits, Cal.: Tuumba Press, 1976);
A Mask of Motion (Providence, R.I.: Burning Deck, 1977);
Gesualdo (Berkeley, Cal.: Tuumba Press, 1978);
Writing Is an Aid to Memory (Berkeley, Cal.: The Figures, 1978);
My Life (Providence, R.I.: Burning Deck, 1980; revised and enlarged, Los Angeles: Sun & Moon Press, 1987);
The Guard (Berkeley, Cal.: Tuumba Press, 1984);
Redo (Grenada, Miss.: Salt-Works Press, 1984);
Individuals, by Hejinian and Kit Robinson (Tucson, Ariz.: Chax Press, 1988);
Leningrad: American Writers in the Soviet Union, by Hejinian and Michael Davidson, Ron Silliman, and Barrett Watten (San Francisco: Mercury House, 1991);
The Hunt (La Laguna, Canary Islands: Zasterle Press, 1991); revised and enlarged as *Oxota: A Short Russian Novel* (Great Barrington, Mass.: The Figures, 1991);
The Cell (Los Angeles: Sun & Moon Press, 1992);
The Cold of Poetry (Los Angeles: Sun & Moon Press, 1994);
Two Stein Talks (Santa Fe, N.M.: Wenselsleeves Press, 1995).

RECORDING: *Guess Language,* by Hejinian and Charles Bernstein, Madison, Wis., Audio Muzixa Qet, 1986.

OTHER: Arkadii Dragomoshchenko, *Description,* translated by Hejinian and Elena Balashova (Los Angeles: Sun & Moon Press, 1990);
Dragomoshchenko, *Xenia,* translated by Hejinian and Balashova (Los Angeles: Sun & Moon Press, 1994).

SELECTED PERIODICAL PUBLICATIONS – UNCOLLECTED: "The Rejection of Closure," *Poetics Journal,* 4 (May 1985): 134–143;
"Strangeness," *Poetics Journal,* 8 (1989): 83–99;
"Language and 'Paradise,'" *Line,* 6 (Fall 1995): 32–45.

An unusual lyricism and descriptive engagement with the everyday world crucially establish Lyn Hejinian as a forceful contemporary poet. Hejinian is a founding figure of the language writing movement of the 1970s, and her work, like most language writing, enacts a poetics that is theoretically sophisticated, one that comments on and discusses such philosophical ideas as poststructuralist and deconstructive theory as it refigures the poem as information system or argument. While language writing is stylistically diverse and, as a movement, difficult to reduce to a particular style, most writers in this group are concerned with writing in nonstandardized, often nonnarrative, forms. Language writing is community-centered and often takes as its subject progressive politics and social theory. Hejinian's work, for example, is resolutely committed to exploring the political ramifications of the ways that language is typically used. But her work differs importantly from the traditional, identity-affirming political poem of most left-wing writers. It is easier to trace the influence of language philosopher Ludwig Wittgenstein's aphoristic statement that "the limits of my language mean the limits of my world," or to apply Viktor Shklovsky's theory of "making strange" to Hejinian's work than it is to relate her work to the contemporary poetry usually anthologized in the Norton or Heath anthologies of American literature.

But while language writing tends to be anti-confessional and antirealist, Hejinian's work does not reject these forms. Rather, it insists that alternative means of expression are necessary to truly represent the confessional or the real. Her work, repeatedly concerned with biography or autobiography, explores the relationship between alternative writing practices and the subjectivity that the normal practices of biography and autobiography often obscure. The alternative form that Hejinian uses most frequently is what has come to be called the "new sentence." Hejinian has said that her "major goal has been to escape *within* the sentence, to make an enormous sentence – not necessarily long ones, but capacious ones."

Hejinian was born in 1941 to Chaffee Earl Hall Jr. and Carolyn Frances Erskine in Alameda, California, and grew up in an academic family. Her father was a high school teacher and aspiring novelist who served in World War II and later became an academic administrator at the University of California and at Harvard University. He died in 1968. Erskine remarried and is a homemaker.

Hejinian attended Harvard University and graduated with a B.A. in 1963. In 1961 she married John P. Hejinian and had two children – Paull, born in 1964, and Anna, born in 1966. In 1968 Hejinian moved back to the West Coast, settling in the San Francisco Bay area. She was divorced in 1972. In 1973 she returned to rural California and began writing poetry seriously. In July 1977 Hejinian returned to the San Francisco Bay area. This same year she married Larry Ochs, a well-known composer and jazz musician. It was in San Francisco that Hejinian met Rae Armantrout, Steve Benson, Carla Harryman, Tom Mandel, Bob Perelman, Kit Robinson, Ron Silliman, and Barrett Watten. This loosely formed community began at that time to formulate the aesthetic and theoretical discourses of language writing through various journals, such as *This, Miam, Tottel, Ou*, and presses, such as Tuumba Press, which Hejinian founded in 1976.

From 1976 to 1984 Hejinian was the editor of Tuumba Press, producing fifty books. Tuumba Press was responsible for establishing and disseminating the early works of a large number of San Francisco Bay language writers. Beginning in the 1970s, as major houses published less and less poetry, small presses proliferated, and the innovative editing of these presses caused the current renaissance of experimental writing. Tuumba Press, run solely by Hejinian, provides an excellent example of the innovative possibilities of small press publishing. Through Tuumba Hejinian involved herself in a means of literary distribution that was mainly outside the limitations of the economic marketplace and controlled by a member of the community the literature helped define. Hejinian's work with Tuumba Press was, as she remarks in an interview with Manuel Brito, "simply an extension of my writing, of my being a poet. Small presses, magazines,

poetry readings are the constructs of our literary life and provide conditions for writing's meanings." Hejinian is currently on the faculty of the graduate Poetics Program at the New College of California and works part-time as an assistant to a private investigator for capital crime defense and death row appeals.

Crucial to understanding Hejinian's work is the realization that it cultivates, even requires, an act of resistant reading. Her work is deliberately unsettling in its unpredictability, its diversions from conventions, the ways it is out of control. In her essay "The Rejection of Closure" (1985), she develops a theory of an "open text" that defines both her earlier and her current work. An "open text," she writes, "is open to the world and particularly to the reader. . . . [It] invites participation, rejects the authority of the writer over the reader and thus, by analogy, the authority implicit in other (social, economic, cultural) hierarchies."

For the open text to reject the authority of the writer over the reader, it engages in a series of disruptive techniques that expose the reader to the possibilities of meaning that he or she brings to the text. In Hejinian's work the disruptive technique most often used is what fellow poet Ron Silliman has called the "new sentence." The new sentence is a form of prose poem, composed mainly of sentences that have no clear and definite transitions. When reading the new sentence, Hejinian writes, "the reader (and I can say also the writer) must overleap the end stop, the period, and cover the distance to the next sentence. . . . Meanwhile, what stays in the gaps, so to speak, remains crucial and informative. Part of the reading occurs in the recovery of that information (looking behind) and the discovery of newly structured ideas."

The gap created by a text that moves from subject to subject invites the reader to participate, to bring his or her own reading to the text. Hejinian guides her readers to moments where they are required to recognize and use their own interpretive powers in the reading act, but, at that point, the work is neither passive nor full of signifiers that the reader can merely fill as he or she wants. Hejinian's work does not resist the fact that reading carries with it the tendency to appropriate from the written words of the text but, indeed, capitalizes on that tendency.

In 1972 Hejinian self-published her first work, *a gRReat adventure*, a mixed-genre collage that includes drawings, poems, and a collaboration with Doug Hall, who was then working as a performance artist. Few copies of this work exist because

Cover for Lyn Hejinian's first book-length collection of poems, in which she depicts the "raw confusions" of memory

Hejinian destroyed most of them. The pursuit of an "open text" informs Hejinian's early chapbooks: *A Thought Is the Bride of What Thinking* (1976), a collection of three essays on narrative, knowledge, and communication; *A Mask of Motion* (1977), a chapbook-length poem on the breakdown of subjectivity and history; and *Gesualdo* (1978), a chapbook-length annotated prose poem. It is *Gesualdo,* which, by using the biography of the composer Don Carlo Gesualdo (1560–1613) as a context for an exploration of literary and sexual passion, perhaps best prefigures the attention to forms of life writing that define Hejinian's later work. In this poem the life of Gesualdo weaves through first-person observations about the nature of subjectivity and the relationship between the narrator and Gesualdo.

Hejinian's first book-length collection, *Writing Is an Aid to Memory* (1978), continues her wrestlings with the confessional systems of memory and the difficulties of portraying these systems without smoothing over the questions they raise. As she writes in the preface, "memory cannot, though the future return, and proffer raw confusions." Instead, in this poem about memory Hejinian presents an excess of information. The poem is composed of forty-two sections of loosely gathered phrases. These phrases, usually five to eight words, are spread out over the page. In the diverse content of these poems, memories, details from everyday life, and scientific information are combined and connected by a narrative voice that self-reflexively questions the poem's construction and its narrator's role. *Writing Is an Aid to Memory* intends, as Hejinian writes, to portray the way that, "though we keep company with cats and dogs, all thoughtful people are impatient, with a restlessness made inevitable by language." The portrayal of such a restlessness, a primary condition of our postmodern world that is defined more and more by the remote-induced, constantly changing images of mass media, is a central concern throughout Hejinian's work.

While the rhetoric around Hejinian's "open text" is common to the language poetry movement, her application of this rhetoric to the genre of autobiography, as in *My Life* (1980), usefully complicates models of subjectivity and the role language has in shaping subjectivity. A good example of just how "open" Hejinian intends her open text to be is evident in the fact that there are two editions of *My Life* (and there is a rumor that Hejinian continues to add to this poem). *My Life* was published in 1980, and then a revised expanded edition was published in 1987. The 1980 edition sold out quickly and the 1987 edition is in its third printing. *My Life* is currently the most important of Hejinian's work and has attracted much scholarly attention. The first edition, written in 1978 when Hejinian was thirty-seven, has thirty-seven sections, each with thirty-seven sentences. In the second edition, eight new sentences were interpolated into each of the previous thirty-seven sections, and eight new sections, each with forty-five sentences, were added.

The form of *My Life* is that of the prose poem. In it the full sentence has replaced the phrasal unit of *Writing Is an Aid to Memory*. Each section begins with a sentence or phrase that is later repeated at some time in the book (although at times the phrase or sentence is slightly altered). The autobiography, with its two editions, is a work characterized by its multiplicity; it is written as a mix of autobiographical confession and language-centered aphorism, of poetry and prose. Its content moves through reminiscence and observation, moves nonsynchronically through the past and the present.

While *My Life* is undeniably autobiographical, Hejinian crucially refuses to adopt a stable-subject position and to indulge in a rhetoric of self-propaganda or self-restoration. This work, through its attention to alternative and multiple ways of telling, refuses to invoke the transparent language conventions that often compose autobiography. It does not allow its readers to ask and then decide who Lyn Hejinian is, but rather, it places them squarely within a representational crisis that forces them to attend to and interrogate their customary ways of interpreting and reading themselves. Hejinian's emphasis is more on the roles the self of *My Life* wants to play than it is on an absolutely gendered, or otherwise subjected, narrative. As she writes, referencing the title, "My life is a permeable constructedness." An example of the subject's "permeable constructedness" can be seen in Hejinian's frequent repetition of the phrase "I wanted to be . . ." This phrase takes many forms in the "early years" of her book: "In any case, I wanted to be both the farmer and his horse when I was a child, and I tossed my head and stamped with one foot as if I were pawing the ground before a long gallop." Or, "I wanted to be a brave child, a girl with guts." Or "If I couldn't be a cowboy, then I wanted to be a sailor." Or, "she pretends she is a blacksmith. . . . Now she's a violinist." Gradually the declaration of "I wanted to be . . ." changes into a new form, into the "I am. . . ." But Hejinian's "I am . . ." differs radically from the repetitive tautology of "I am I," a statement that speaks to a grammatical connection between the subject and the object of identity. Instead, Hejinian writes, "I am a shard, signifying isolation – here I am thinking aloud of my affinity for the separate fragment taken under scrutiny."

My Life pushes the reader into an act of choosing among multiplicities. In *My Life* a resignified, fluctuating subjectivity is accompanied, ideally, by the resistance of the reader. Hejinian's model of subjectivity denies essentialist notions of the subject at the same time that it cultivates the powers of the reader by opening an anarchic space for reader response. By writing an autobiography, a genre that in its most clichéd form claims a representative relationship between author and narrator, as an open text, Hejinian directs attention to the role language has in shaping subjectivity. *My Life* provokes useful and important questions: for example, how might the very linear structure of narrative, which in autobiography centers most detail around the subject, further perpetuate essentialist notions of the subject? How might the grammatical structures of our language, in which being is continually bestowed on

Dust jacket for Hejinian's 1980 book of poems that rejects the authority of the autobiographical persona (courtesy of the Poetry Collection, State University of New York at Buffalo)

the subject by its primacy in the hierarchy of the sentence, do the same? While *My Life* does not directly answer these questions, it usefully complicates any answers that we might have.

In 1983 Hejinian traveled to Leningrad and Moscow with Ochs, her husband, who was on tour with the Rova Saxophone Quartet. In these cities she met some contemporary, samizdat Russian poets such as Vladimir Aristov, Arkadii Dragomoshchenko, Aleksei Parshchikov, Ilya Kutik, Nadezhda Kondakova, Viktor Krivalin, Olga Sedakova, Marianne Zoschenko, and Ivan Zhdanov. She also began a friendship with Leningrad poet Dragomoshchenko that continues to influence her work. From Dragomoshchenko she learned Russian and began, with Elena Balashova, to translate his and other Russian poets' works. She returned to Russia again in 1989 with the American poets Michael Davidson, Ron Silliman, and Barrett Watten. Together they wrote *Leningrad: American Writers in the Soviet Union* (1991), a book that is part travel narrative, part political commentary, part cultural studies.

Leningrad is very much a text of the language movement. The collaborative nature of the piece is common to language writers, many of whom enact their theoretical concerns with questions of community through communal writing practices. Further, its theoretically astute discourse reflects the current philosophical trends that encourage a fragmented subjectivity, especially in relation to East European nationalism and racism. The four poets in this collection alternate voices and discuss various ways post-Glasnost society forces them to confront their own politics of encounter. The possibilities and manifestations of community play a major role in this book. Hejinian, for instance, describes her interest in things Russian as an "exterior passion, or desire" that is "stirred by an insatiable identity. Being there is to be in a state of incommensurability and hence of inseparability, as if that were the status or 'human' nature of Not-me." But while Russia is often posed as the space of the "Not-me," Hejinian's work transcends this dichotomy. Her statement on Russia as the place of identity-centered difference concludes with her losing herself "in the crowds flowing on the Nevsky."

The dissolution of national boundaries also defines Hejinian's next works, *Oxota: A Short Russian Novel* (1991), a revised version of a novel originally titled *The Hunt* and *The Cell* (1992). *Oxota, The Cell,* and *Leningrad* are in many ways an interconnected trilogy, and often a story will appear in more than one book, although always in a different form. *Oxota* was written by Hejinian during her many visits to Russia, and *The Cell* was written concurrently from October 1986 to November 1988. Both works are sentence-based.

Oxota is to some extent novelistic, composed of short chapters that often read as if they were an independent scene or comment. Each chapter is composed of a very free adaptation of the fourteen-line stanza form used by Aleksandr Pushkin in *Eugene Onegin*. While *Oxota* is in many ways an autobiography in which fragments of conversation overlie a narrative continuum involving the author, Dragomoshchenko, his wife, Zina, and other friends of the author's, *Oxota* extends the work Hejinian began in *My Life*. *My Life* is more an internal text than an external. In contrast, the concerns of *Oxota* spill outward toward the global, as is evident in its attention to things like nationalism, art, and identity in Russia and the United States.

Oxota opens with the statement "This time we are both," indicating just how all persuasive both the tensions of an "insatiable identity" and Hejinian's friendship with Dragomoshchenko are. While a linguistic division separates the United States and Russia, and Hejinian and Dragomoshchenko, as well, this division in *Oxota* is "not a displacement but relocation" of the difficult permeabilities of identity. Hejinian, for example, reverses the cliché "lines of state" in the sentence "Our language was divided into states of line" to speak to the various possible states of the poetic or grammatical line. *Oxota* then plots, as Hejinian writes, the way that "Our experiences achieve pathos when they force us to acknowledge that the significances and meanings of things – things we've known, it would seem, forever, and certainly since early childhood – have changed – or rather, when we are forced to absorb the memory of being utterly unable to catch or trace or name the moment of transition when one meaning changed to another – the moment of interruption in the course of our knowing such things."

In *The Cell,* a book-length collection of poems with their dates of composition, the line is shorter – most often five words – than in Hejinian's previous work, giving the poems a sort of formal hesitancy. The writing here is involved with the daily, the everyday encounter, but, at the same time, continues to examine *Oxota*'s global concerns with nation and identity. Hejinian's interest in biographical questions continues in the poem "The Cell" in its examination of subjectivities. But here the biographical figure has been replaced by the biological cell, which highlights the inability to isolate the smallest part of anything from its context. As Hejinian writes, "there are no / single notes, no unique gender," and further, "the question 'who?' disappears." Processes of identification instead are skewed in this collection, crossing even human/animal boundaries: "Feeling female in identification with / a male animal."

The most recent book in Hejinian's varied, developing career is *The Cold of Poetry* (1994), a collection of previously published and now out-of-print shorter works. The movement from the internal to the external that occurs between *My Life* and *Oxota* suggests a trend in Hejinian's poetry toward a rethinking of the language writing movement's emphasis on the form as being the primary location of the politics of the piece. Her work seems to be moving toward a merging of the formal concerns of language poetry with the social concerns of cultural studies. In Hejinian's work, then, social reformation interacts with global transformation. She is currently writing several collaborative works – one with Dragomoshchenko and another with Carla Harryman, a long, picaresque book on eros and sex; she is also writing a feature-length film with the American cinematographer Jackie Ochs.

Interviews:

Andrew Schelling, "Interview with Lyn Hejinian," *Jimmy's and Lucy's House of K,* 6 (May 1986): 1–17;

Tyrus Miller, "Interview with Lyn Hejinian," *Paper Air,* 4, no. 2 (1989): 33–40;

Manuel Brito, "Interview with Lyn Hejinian," in *A Suite of Poetic Voices* (Santa Brigida, Spain: Kadle Books, 1992), pp. 71–93.

References:

Rae Armantrout, "Feminist Poetics and the Meaning of Clarity," *Sagetrieb: A Journal Devoted to Poets in the Imagist/Objectivist Tradition,* 11 (Winter 1992): 7–16;

Charles Bernstein, "Hejinian's Notes," in his *Content's Dream* (Los Angeles: Sun & Moon Press, 1986), pp. 284–285;

Hilary Clark, "The Mnemonics of Autobiography: Lyn Hejinian's *My Life,*" *Biography,* 14 (Fall 1991): 315–335;

Michael Davidson, "Approaching the Fin de Siecle," in his *The San Francisco Renaissance* (New York: Cambridge University Press, 1989), pp. 200–218;

Michael Greer, "Ideology and Theory in Recent Experimental Writing of, the Naming of 'Language Poetry,'" *Boundary 2,* 16 (Winter/Spring 1989): 335–355;

David R. Jarraway, "My Life through the Eighties: The Exemplary LANGUAGE of Lyn Hejinian," *Contemporary Literature,* 33 (Summer 1992): 319–336;

Marjorie Perloff, "The Return of the (Numerical) Repressed," in her *Radical Artifice: Writing Poetry in the Age of Media* (Chicago: University of Chicago Press, 1991), pp. 162–170;

Perloff, "The Word as Such: L=A=N=G=U=A=G=E Poetry in the Eighties," *American Poetry Review* (May–June 1984): 15–22;

Peter Quartermain, "Syllable as Music: Lyn Hejinian's *Writing Is an Aid to Memory,*" *Sagetrieb: A Journal Devoted to Poets in the Imagist/Objectivist Tradition,* 11 (Winter 1992): 17–31;

Stephen Ratcliffe, "Private Eye/Public Work," *American Poetry,* 4 (Spring 1987): 40–48;

Ratcliffe, "Two Hejinian Talks: 'Writing/One's Life' and 'Writing/Re:Memory,'" *Temblor,* 6 (1987): 141–147;

Rosmarie Waldrop, "Chinese Windmills Turn Horizontally: On Lyn Hejinian," *Temblor,* 10 (1989): 219–222;

Barrett Watten, "The World in the Work: Toward a Psychology of Form," in his *Total Syntax* (Carbondale: Southern Illinois University Press, 1985), pp. 146–149.

Papers:

Hejinian materials, primarily correspondence and papers up to 1984, and especially information related to Hejinian's editing of Tuumba Press, are in the Archive for New Poetry at the University of California, San Diego.

Michael Heller

(11 May 1937 –   )

Burt Kimmelman
New Jersey Institute of Technology

BOOKS: *Two Poems* (Mount Horeb, Wis.: Perishable Press, 1970);

Accidental Center (Fremont, Mich.: Sumac Press, 1972);

Figures of Speaking (Mount Horeb, Wis.: Perishable Press, 1977);

Knowledge (New York: Sun, 1979);

Conviction's Net of Branches: Essays on the Objectivist Poets and Poetry (Carbondale: Southern Illinois University Press, 1985);

Marginalia in a Desperate Hand (Great Britain: Pig Press, 1986);

In the Builded Place (Minneapolis: Coffee House Press, 1989);

Wordflow: New and Selected Poems (Hoboken, N.J.: Talisman House, forthcoming 1997).

OTHER: *Marble Snows, Origin* (9 October 1979);

Carl Rakosi: Man and Poet, edited, with an introduction, by Heller (Orono, Maine: National Poetry Foundation, 1993);

"The Uncertainty of the Poet," *American Poetry Review,* 24 (May/June 1995): 11–15.

Michael Heller (courtesy of the author)

Within the world of contemporary poetry Michael Heller has staked out a territory all his own. His is the most important of many attempts to elaborate an "Objectivist" poetics, first described as such by Louis Zukofsky in a 1931 issue of *Poetry* magazine. Heller is faithful to the Objectivist desire for a poetry deriving from the senses, from fact and directness, yet he aspires to a more complex aesthetic. His poems are marked by an acute and highly original sensitivity to contemporary concerns about voice, language, history and knowledge. Henry Weinfield has noted in them the "penetration of the immediate, lived experience by something that [they refuse] to call 'eternity.' " They articulate a sublime uncertainty as well as absolute tangibility.

Heller was born in Brooklyn, New York, on 11 May 1937, to Peter and Martha Rosenthal Heller. Heller's father, the son of a rabbi and writer, was brought as a child to the United States from the Belorussian city of Bialystok, now part of Poland. In the early 1940s, while Heller was still a boy, his mother developed a serious heart condition, and the family moved to Miami Beach, Florida. He has an older brother, Avrom, and a younger sister, Tena. He has a son, Nicholas, a musician and composer, from his first marriage, to Doris Whytal in 1962.

That marriage ended in divorce in 1978. Heller remarried in 1979, to the poet and literary scholar Jane Augustine.

Heller graduated from high school in Miami Beach and returned north to attend Rensselaer Polytechnic Institute where, in 1959, he earned a B.S. in mechanical engineering. While working in New York City as an engineer and technical writer for various corporations, he began to write poetry. In 1964 he won the Coffey Poetry Prize for his work at the New School for Social Research. In the mid 1960s he lived and wrote in Europe, residing for a year and a half in a small village on Spain's Andalusian coast. He returned from Spain to New York in 1966. In 1967 he joined the faculty of the American Language Institute, a part of New York University, where in 1986 he earned an M.A. in English.

Heller's achievements include three major verse collections – *Accidental Center* (1972), *Knowledge* (1979), and *In The Builded Place* (1989) – three chapbooks of poetry, and a novella, *Marble Snows, Origin* (1979). Portions of his memoir, "Living Root," an ongoing project, have been published in various magazines. Heller is also widely recognized as an important critic and essayist on contemporary American poetry. His critical prose includes *Conviction's Net of Branches: Essays on the Objectivist Poets and Poetry* (1985), which won the Alice Fay Di Castagnola Award of the Poetry Society of America; *Carl Rakosi: Man and Poet* (1993), which he edited and introduced; scores of essays published individually; and "Uncertain Poetries: Essays 1985 to 1991 on Contemporary Poets and Poetry," a collection as yet unpublished. In addition, his poetry has been set to both dance and music, and he is presently completing a libretto for an opera.

Heller has received many honors for his work, including awards and fellowships from the National Endowments for the Arts and Humanities, the New York Foundation on the Arts, and Yaddo. He has served on the editorial boards of such important literary magazines as *Origin, Montemora, Pequod,* and *Sagetrieb* and as a consultant for the National Endowment for the Humanities, the Ucross Foundation, and the Poetry Society of America. He is on the advisory board of Poets House and is a former board member of Poets in Public Service.

Heller's poetry is intimately autobiographical, which is remarkable when one considers how deeply it is a poetry of ideas. These two aspects of his work are in some measure due to the influences of writers and poets he admires. The works of John Donne and other metaphysical poets resound in much of his work. Zukofsky, Charles Reznikoff, and George Oppen – who along with Carl Rakosi and Lorine Niedecker made up the core of the Objectivist movement – can be heard especially in Heller's early writings. Another influence was Oppen's acquaintance, William Bronk, who was published along with most of the Objectivists in journals such as *Origin* and the *Black Mountain Review*.

Heller has said that he greatly values a life of writing defined by an intuition about poetry shared with others; such a community affords him the opportunity to evolve within and further a poetic tradition. The address to a dying, senile father in a hospital – in the poem "Miami Waters," from *In the Builded Place* – reveals both Heller's individual voice and his use of the tradition that he claims for himself:

> In the night
> Outside, the arc lamps burn
>
> And under the bridge the canal
> Runs light and dark. The palms gleam
> Like silvery feathers. I try to follow
> Into the spillway of your words,
> Meanings as loose upon the world
> As this powdery effect of the light's particles.

Heller's gripping line, "Meanings as loose upon the world," recalls the Yeatsian chaos of "Mere anarchy is loosed upon the world" from "The Second Coming," but it is also meant to intermingle love and sickness in a way reminiscent of Williams Carlos Williams's hospital and doctor poems. Heller's echoing emphasizes the speaker's feelings of loss. The final line of the passage, furthermore, suggests Heller's preoccupation with the question of vision. Sight, here, the "powdery effect of the light's particles," is presented as a metaphor for knowledge and empathy – a common trope in the works of Oppen, Bronk, and Williams.

Indeed, the importance of sight in Heller's poetic tradition is apparent in a line that passes from Williams to both Oppen and Heller. Oppen, in his poem "The Little Hole," openly acknowledges Williams:

> The little hole in the eye
> Williams called it, the little hole
>
> Has exposed us naked
> To the world
> And will not close.

The line is recalled by Heller in "4:21 P.M. on St. George's Clock: Film," from *Accidental Center:*

solitary park
solitary benchers

still air, still branches

the green footage stopped
– matter, call it matter
perceived as light, corpuscles of light
in the "little hole
of the eye[.]"

    One of Heller's chief concerns throughout his poetry is the act of perception. He often speaks of perception as an act in which the world impinges on a consciousness that continually interprets a sensorium of act and event. In this sense, his use of the process of photography ("a woman's face known to me by photons // photons burnt onto a photographic plate," in "4:21 P.M.") or the tecnology of the telescope, mirror and lens, is meant to suggest that one's framings of phenomena are devices for containing, and yet, more important, for releasing, hopes and passions. For Heller the world coheres in an art such as poetry because of a radical element in nature, while paradoxically a frame or lens may serve as a secondary force that can create a unity of composition as the field of perception comes alive.

    Just as Bronk writes in his poem "The Various Sizes of the World" of how "the sensitive plate / of a telescope [fixes], a light so far / we never knew," Heller, in his work, contemplates the relationship between percept and knowledge. In "Telescope Suite" from *Accidental Center* he writes

of astral tides
lifting lovers to their wants
the world's sore wants

that nakedly confront
– but in star-light
star-crust
diadem
out which being looks
hidden behind Heraclitian signs

they were small
& gathered

on the silvered glass[.]

Heller's interest in the percept, as it comes into existence through the coalescence of world and seer, is a constant throughout his poetry and can be seen in the title poem of *Knowledge:*

To think a man might dream against this
This something simpler than metaphor

The world

Which spoke back
In facts, to him

That heavy pageantry[.]

Heller's notion of the world, another trope shared with Oppen and Bronk, becomes his own when he insists that life be unmediated by figure or anything else. The world somehow resists being known, yet Heller must try to know it – and ultimately its secrets are revealed to him as a kind of genetic code of the world's resistance. By the time of *In the Builded Place* the description of Heller's quest has fully matured. In "With a Telescope in the Sangre de Cristos" Heller speaks of the possibility for unity, of a "fine life of bonds and connections" in which there can be belief, even in the face of a void whose existence must also be acknowledged:

Again and again that night
The glass checked
In its round frame

The nebula's thumbprint swirls:
This fine life of bonds and connections . . .

Then
I looked in
At another's eyes

Looked past that image
Of the self,
In at the pupil's black hole

Where light gives up
The granular,
Becomes a maelstrom
Grinding
Beyond the phenomenal
To a lightless, frightening depth.

    Heller has also acknowledged Ezra Pound and Wallace Stevens as influences on his work. There is a Stevens-like musical and intellectual strain, for instance, in the title poem from *In the Builded Place,* one of Heller's many forceful evocations of city life. The poem begins by describing the effects of a streetlamp's light and ends with the light having become a figure for life that is described as "flimsy beatitudes of order." The ornate language of this phrase, its extravagance, is characteristic of Stevens, but the phrase is also indebted to Zukofsky, as are such lines as "Disprove us least as things of love appearing / In a wish gearing to light's infinite focus."

Although Heller's connections to the works of other writers are clear, his poetry can be easily distinguished from his forebears by his tendency, increasing as his career has progressed, to make language itself the subject of his writing. Like Reznikoff, Heller has also explored his Jewish heritage, at the heart of which lies the concept of textuality. At times he explicitly contemplates not only the meaning and substance of texts but also the meaning of making and using texts, which includes his own process of writing poetry. Language is seen by Heller as sometimes synonymous with, sometimes separate from, a text that might embody it. References to and discussions of language, even the use of language as a figure to signify other subject matter, are ubiquitous in his later work.

In a May/June 1995 essay for the *American Poetry Review* titled "The Uncertainty of the Poet" Heller asserts that creating poetry has more to do with awareness than with speech. "At root," he writes, "the poetic act begins, not in expression but in recognition, in the gaze into the deep abyss of not knowing." What the poet finally recognizes is a fundamental uncertainty about the possibility of apprehending the world, and this recognition becomes "the very ground one stands on"; further, uncertainty extends to the act of writing about it. It "is dizzying – and this is the thrill of it – to ask, as Holderlin had once asked, the question of questions, why to write a poem at all?" Although the posing of such a question may suggest to some a poetry of bloodless cerebration, Heller's work is remarkable for its rich poignancy.

His early interest in science has been combined with a poet's sensitivity to the ambiguity involved in all utterance. His poetry's emotional depth derives from an ongoing investigation into the likenesses and antinomies of science and beauty. Writing of *Accidental Center* James Guimond suggests that Heller's "universe is an animated, vitalistic one . . . continually presenting entities moving and acting upon one another." He likens Heller's poetry to that of the "Renaissance and Neo-classical poets who speculated on the Great Chain of Being and micro-macrocosm relationships." In a 1992 interview Heller said that "science at its best, at its most experimental, at the frontier, in some way [is] a quest very similar to poetry. Poetry and science have certain kinds of aspirations and longings in common." In a letter written that same year Heller speaks of his "practice as a writer" and maintains that "poetry does not establish 'facts' (the validity

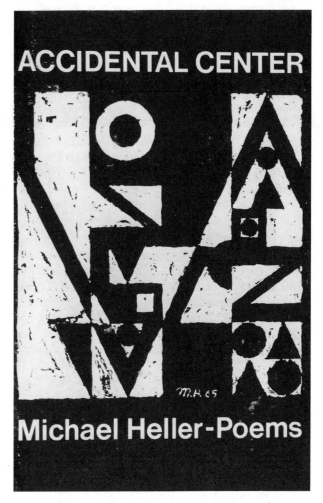

Dust jacket for Heller's 1972 book, which includes "Telescope Suite," a poem that indicates his interest in the act of perception (courtesy of the Poetry Collection, State University of New York, Buffalo)

of the Big Bang, creation, etc.) but is a spiritual (I wish there were a better word) response to the facts or data of the mind."

Heller's first major collection, *Accidental Center,* consolidates his enduring poetic and philosophical concerns and demonstrates a fundamental approach to his overall interpretation of experience, one grounded in the terms of science. The book's controlling impulse is to comprehend the role of language in human affairs. Yet his contemplation of language is meant to get at something deeper. He creates a world in which persons, landscapes, and language coexist. His ultimate subject is the subtleties experienced in the consciousness of otherness – not as an alienating phenomenon but as a creative and generative difference. In 1992 he explained the title *Accidental Center* and described this sense of difference:

What I felt in choosing that as a title was that we live in a world in which we are the center. I mean everything, all our experience radiates out from us. There's this flow, yet there's a certain dimension to that experience of not belonging, of distance, of unease. That has always struck me as the poetic dimension – bridging that dimension constantly. Language, itself, simply furthers that another way by forcing us to constantly come to grips with the otherness of the world, of the universe.

The changes in Heller's life – the birth of his son, his marriage headed toward divorce – are reflected in a dialectic he explores between solitude and community.

Heller's poetics and his beliefs about how life is to be lived found their first comprehensive articulation when he was studying to be an engineer. He uses science in order to talk about daily events while at times seeing in it a false comfort. Jeffrey Peterson has written that

> Heller's poetics of "building," the "place" of the poem comes to matter only insofar as its solemnity is undergirded by uncertainty, its solidity informed by fragility. The poem finds its ground, for Heller, only through a questioning of its own foundations. . . . Heller's poetic dwellings thus admit their uncertain moorings, routing us [as Heller has said] "back into possibility": whether the structure in question is the intimately "accidental center: home" in *Accidental Center* or the "flimsy beatitudes of order" in *In the Builded Place.*

The poetic focus of *Accidental Center* is notably revealed in its vocabulary. Certain words are repeated frequently, as Heller from one poem to the next turns ideas on their various sides so to gain their full appreciation. The book's key terms are *world, mind, center, home, empty, sight, signal, photon, wave, image, lens, mirror, camera, emulsion, stellar, dust, fix, web, stone, rock,* and *beauty.* Heller tests and transforms the assumptions about reality he acquired in his scientific training through their application in human, ultimately inexplicable circumstances such as illness and death, sex and the complications of love. In talking about such circumstances through the language of precision, Heller raises basic questions, such as How do we know what we know? and Can what is known be adequately spoken of?

The title of Heller's next important collection, *Knowledge,* suggests both insight and communal transmittal. As in *Accidental Center,* these poems address the question of whether or not poetry can assuage solitude. Poetry is perceived as the imagination's resistance to pure factuality and rationality. *Knowledge,* however, is a more earthbound volume than its predecessor. Its poems take as their

locales the human spaces of New York's City streets, summer mountain retreats, and resort beaches of Florida and Eastern Long Island, where Heller has lived. One of Heller's great strengths in these poems is his ability to express, in precise and yet loving terms, the details of the landscapes and the infiltration of their beauty and strangeness into daily life.

The book has a more conversational tone than *Accidental Center,* as if its "knowledge" were only valid as a shared substance and no longer private or privileged when transmitted as poetry and language. In his spring 1980 review in *Sagetrieb* Laszlo Géfin observed that "Most of [Heller's poems] germinate from a particular experience at a particular place, as their titles indicate, but the poet is rarely alone in nature; nearly always, the experience is shared." This archetypal scenario is in keeping with Heller's need to construct a view of his life within larger contexts, personal, historical, cultural, philosophical, and aesthetic.

Géfin remarks that "in the poem 'At Albert's Landing' the poet gently warns [his son] not to coerce the reality of things to conform to the shapes of the human mind." Essentially, Heller is posing a contrast between "aloneness" and communion, suggesting at the same time that the world must be taken on its own terms. Simple observation and description in the poem do the work of philosophy as Heller's sense of otherness takes on a palpably human dimension:

> Matted leaves
> Beneath which lie
> Dirt, bones, shells.
> Late April: milky light
> And warmth. Thinnest odors rise.
> In the middle of one's life
> More things connect
> With dying, what's come,
> What's over.

Heller here attempts to put the realization of death into a perspective that includes solitude and language. In a world of transient being where "what exists is like the sky / through which clouds pass," the poet senses his own work as a "poetry of clouds," an attempt to grasp at unmediated existence, "the naked very thing."

Heller is led in the poem to a vision of a "fugal world," which in its constant interrelatedness presents a working definition of what Heller means by *knowledge:*

Here we are in some fugal world.
And the squirrel, when he eats,
Looks like a little man. And here
You fling your arms out
Whirling around at the frightened
Skimming ducks. The duck's eye,
Like ours, must be at its center. We
Are alone, rooted in our aloneness.
And yet things lean and lean,
Explaining each other and not themselves.
I call you; it's time to go.

The gentle last line of this passage is tinged with a sense of dispossession, for the poet has been ruminating on the visceral yet ephemeral cycle of life. Still, Heller's vision of a "fugal world," with its endless, ramifying counterpoint between reality and the imagination, between fact and the possibilities of poetry, is finally hopeful, as he says in the poem's conclusion:

Things lean and lean, and sometimes
Words find common centers in us
Resonating and filling speech.
Let me know a little of you.

Knowledge also introduces a themes that will occupy much of Heller's later work. Heller now begins to merge his secular Judaism with his poetic and philosophic concerns. The book's longest poem, "Bialystok Stanzas," is a meditative sequence reflecting on Heller's family origins and the fate of Jews both in the Holocaust and in America. Like some poems of the earlier *Accidental Center,* the sequence is a response to photographs, to a life and history of "posthumous shocks," as Walter Benjamin phrased it in *Illuminations.* Norman Finkelstein describes the overall effect of this group of poems when he writes that "[t]aken from 'a book of old pictures,' this sequence embodies the delicacy and horror, the precarious comfort and certain doom of European Jewry. We view these pictures through two lenses, that of the photographer and that of the next generation, the American generation, the fortunate children of those who got away. Impossibly remote, the poet still tries to get as close as he can."

In the opening poem of the sequence, Heller writes of "Light – / The scene filled with photographer's light" that captures

This sparsely furnished room
In the corner of which
A china-closet Ark

The old men
Under green shaded bulbs

Reading Torah

The prayers are simple,
To what they think larger
Than themselves
 – the place almost bare,
Utterly plain[.]

The poet, as with the natural world in "At Albert's Landing," attempts to recuperate a lost community, not in terms of a modern day ethnic sentimentality but as an act of respect for its otherness and ultimate irretrievability. Finkelstein describes this distinction as that of "reverie" and "nostalgia, its close attendant." Reverie, in the poem's concluding lines,

is implicitly understood as the inevitable violation of historical space, a psychic zone which can maintain its dignity only in mute memory. The photograph having been taken, reverie follows its course, which leads, sooner or later, to poetry. And poetry, in order to maintain its dignity, must restrain itself as much as possible, so that like the photographer's "flat white light," it "adds no increment / But attention."

The "Terrible Pictures" section of the sequence focuses on photographs of Jews who died in the Bialystok ghetto. Heller can respond to them only by repeating their captions – "died in the ghetto," "fell in battle ... 1944," "killed" – as though any attempt to recapture their living faces would be an obscene violence to their history. Contemplating Bialystok's synagogue, burnt to the ground by the Nazis while filled with people, Heller insists on the duty of witnessing:

Here, look, look, this is but
Its mirror

Only the mirror remains

And gone –
Whole peoples are gone
To horror beyond remonstrance
. . . .
Words can add nothing
That flame was without a light[.]

Heller asserts historical consciousness in the identical rhyme of "mirror" along with its off-rhyme with "horror." Memory and imagination for Heller become poles for a poetry that joins rhyme and imagery with larger "fugal worlds" to yield a complex unity.

The title *In the Builded Place* signifies a world of overmediated information, a world hemmed in by, as Heller remarked in a 1993 interview, "the mecha-

Dust jacket for Heller's 1979 book, which includes the
"Bialystok Stanzas," a long poem on the Jewish
experience of the Holocaust and its aftermath
(courtesy of the Poetry Collection, State
University of New York, Buffalo)

our imagination are contaminated by fear and greed, "making ideas as political as sliced pie / or Psyche's credit-card sorting of seeds . . . for the dim video game of winter."

In the Oppenesque "At Beaches Again" the sea as a kind of grand meditation on time's endlessness comes to stand for history itself, which is in danger of extinction. The poem addresses the question of present-day science's influence in the world as humanity teeters on its own self-destructive edge between technology and nature:

> We have come to the time
> Of the accurate missile, of concern for such
> Accuracy in the world, of all that we call terror.
>
> Even love is poised on that pelvic
> Terror, on the wave and its sparkling foam
> One barely hears in the world.
>
> We have yet to hear that wave break,
> Hoping we are shoreward enough
> But that we are overheard.
>
> For speech, speech comes with ease to us,
> Yet what if there is more of that wave in man
> Than speech.

A macabre dance takes place here; the prototype for all technology, language meets the physicality of experience step for step. The waves of the sea, the human body, the missiles loaded with warheads, and love are all equipoised with language. The poem asks whether humanity contains within itself the capacity to avoid self-destruction.

In the Builded Place also reinvestigates the cosmological themes of Heller's earlier work. "With A Telescope in the Sangre De Cristos" speaks of "town and ranch lights" that make "shallow bowls / Into other heavens." The framings of the natural world through metaphor or scientific instrument, which in the earlier books signaled the tension points for Heller's poetry, seem almost benign before the wildness of the depths of human nature. For Heller the "builded place" where we create our "bonds and connections" is mainly linguistic and the basis for the only hope of community. Central to Heller's poetics are the questions of how the world is to be considered a linguistic construct and who are to be its authors. Such questions dominate "Heteroglossia on Fifty Third." As the poet walks among New York City's "museums and limousines," he is invaded both externally and internally:

nistic logic or machinery of conceptualization." According to Bill Tremblay in his review in the November/December 1990 *American Book Review* this machinery amounts to a "vast codependency." But Heller is not merely mirroring "a Modernist diagnosis of the sick industrial soul"; instead, he is possessed by an "ambition to embody a reassociation of sensibilities," to "locate an emotional or spiritual or intellectual need at the heart of his experience and to use that core of feeling as a way to integrate fragmentary impressions . . . to make connections in his poems."

In "Asthma," a poem dealing variously with his "child's cough" and a civil defense training film in which "the shock-waved halfway house of hope de-domesticates to splinters," Heller says that we live now "where in this century most air is stolen." The words with which we write, the very breaths of

A bag lady shouts "I am entitled!" I also
am entitled to my thoughts at least, yet all day,
dream or nightmare do my talk, undo my walk,
so I let talk pitch self into doze or dream or chat:
man, woman, testicle, dessert. The language falls,
a chunk of disembodied sound through space.

The "talk of street people is a groaning, each to
each," part of the inescapable intrusion of multiple
voices that drive the poet out of his private dream
state as though he were possessed by them:

> Ghost words, ghost fuckers!
> They utter their words right out to do their ravaging
> in me, joining my dead lords of speech like animals
> granted province over those on whom they prey.

The variegated cityscape becomes a dynamic text, a
site of numberless textual beings whose voices claim
their own authority. The overmediated world is
represented by the modern city's inheritance of
complex traditions of speaking and writing; the
world has its own insistence, as various textualities
blend with, compete with, and sometimes diametri-
cally oppose the poet's singular voice.

All of Heller's work, as Géfin has pointed out,
eventually turns to the question of language's "duplicity and unreliability" and involves Heller in "a
desire to redefine the poetic function in the light of
language conceived as a system of signs signifying
man's age-old metaphysical longing." The longing
is both complex and celebratory, charged with
imaginative presences and awe. In "Water, Heads,
Hamptons," for example, memory, love, and "our
unimaginable gods" of natural phenomena are gathered and transmuted into an extraordinary vision of
great depth and brilliance.

Central to all emotional and physical places
Heller visits is singularly his memorable elegiac
tone. The evocation of keen personal loss in much
of his verse is haunting. "In a Dark Time, On His
Grandfather," for instance, Heller brings together
his conception of language in the abstract with that
of language as the very substance of the quotidian.
He treats the memory of Zalman Heller, who died
in 1956, asking whether or not language survives
the visceral, mortal language user.

There's little sense of your life
Left now. In Cracow and Bialystok, no carcass
To rise, to become a golem. In the ground

The matted hair of the dead is a mockery
Of the living root. Everyone who faces

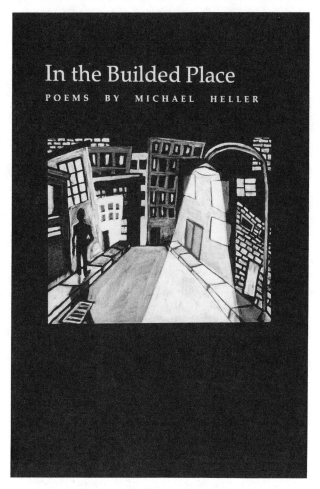

*Dust jacket for Heller's 1989 book, which represents his attempt
to create a place with language to stand against "the
mechanistic logic or machinery of conceptualization"
(courtesy of the Poetry Collection, State
University of New York, Buffalo)*

Jerusalem is turned back, turned back.

It was not a question of happiness
Nor that the Laws failed, only
That the holy or sad remains within.

The survival of language is not just a philosophical
idea here. Against logic Heller must hope that language remains when the person is gone. His hope is
literal, in the sense that his grandfather had purport-
edly written a book called *The Just Man and the
Righteous Way,* which is recalled in the poem's concluding stanza:

The just man and the righteous way
Wither in the ground. No issue,
No issue answers back this earth.

The poem accounts for the grim fact of mortality,
yet for Heller, language has everything to do with

history and law, with the ways in which people come to know them and all things including death, especially his own family lineage and cultural heritage. This complex understanding informs his imagination into the sweeping, catastrophic history of twentieth-century European Jewry, its law, morality, and epistemology. Language is bound up with his grandfather's writings and his family experiences, where he first encountered the ancient Hebrew (and Greek and Roman) texts. These associations are in turn part of his realization of historical loss in the Holocaust and of the spiritual decimation of contemporary secular life and discourse. As Heller consigns his grandfather to memory he realizes that as a poet and author he bears the sadness of death and the burden of speech.

In "Born in Water" Heller shows his ability to balance mourning and celebration perfectly. Even in this elegy about his own family he creates a riveting yet quiet heroism that carefully sidesteps sentimentality. The poem invokes great dignity and ceremony by employing unassuming language and imagery:

Born in water. I was born in
my mother's water and washed out
into the world from the burst sac.

When my mother died, we respected her wishes,
collected her ashes at the crematorium,
then spread them on the grass over my father's grave.

And because the wind was blowing,
we poured water from a plastic pitcher,
and added water from our eyes
so the ashes wouldn't blow away
but seep into the ground.
Mother and father, as on the day
I was conceived, mingled together.

The poem's grief and praise are stately, without pomp. Every elegy exploits, perhaps, a basic rhetoric, but Heller has inherited from the Objectivists a sensitivity to the ways in which the sensual world and language intertwine. This poem is typical of Heller's extraordinary metaphysics. Underlying the scene of mourning and renewal is a communication between the material realm and the suprasensory.

Heller goes beyond the Objectivist aesthetic, however. For him, as Ruby Riemer has noted, "facts have a stronger moral – as opposed to scientific or empirical – edge than for the Objectivists, a moral edge carrying him more in the direction of self than of the world." Riemer finds that this "self" is ultimately viewed as essentially constructed out of language whose "independent status" Heller ac-

knowledges. Heller's explorations of language in and of itself also show his desire to extend himself beyond Objectivism's purview. His reach is remarkable because unlike most contemporary poets who share his philosophical concerns – including those of the L=A=N=G=U=A=G=E school such as Charles Bernstein and Lyn Hejinian – Heller rejects "obfuscation and enigma, the loss of self and the distortions of history." He has a need for clarity, historical and otherwise.

Nevertheless, "in poem after poem," as Thomas Gardner observes, Heller "relentlessly" brings up "the issue of our uncertain grasp on our experience," which happens when the reader apprehends the "sheer dailiness" of his poems. In a 1991 interview Heller spoke of the "double edge of community" in which there is a "desire to be entangled and to escape entanglement simultaneously"; he confronts "solitude, unbridgeability, otherness." It is in this context that he can speak of "a whole series of transpositions of self-other . . . which has been the thematic of my work from the start." But always another, related dialectic, self-other, emerges out of an essential experiential dualism: the world of the senses and the urge to speak of it, science and poetry.

Heller's work combines a sense of grandeur and difficulty. In trying to show forth the equivocal nature of literary texts, he creates multivalent poetic statements that often allude to their own ambiguous natures. In so doing he exposes a possible gap between knowledge and articulation. It is under the sign of this uncertainty concerning language that Heller strives to come to terms with his family history and Jewish heritage. These two interests are profoundly connected for him, since, to be a Jew, even one who is paradoxically also an atheist, means to be able to read the great Hebrew texts as well to see oneself as their inheritor and caretaker. Not unrelated to the rabbinic tradition is his concern for the meaning and substance of texts and of the textual act itself, including the processes by which he creates his own poetry. Reflecting in "Some Anthropology" from *In the Builded Place* on poetic making, the possibly fictionalized Philippine tribe of the Tasaday, and on his own "lost tribe of Jews," Heller writes about "the anthropology of the poet who must build his poems out of the myths he intends to falsify."

Heller's major work in progress, parts of which have appeared in various magazines, is a memoir titled "Living Root," a line taken from "In a Dark Time, on His Grandfather." The memoir weaves prose, poetry, and commentary into a complex narrative of spiritual journey, personal history,

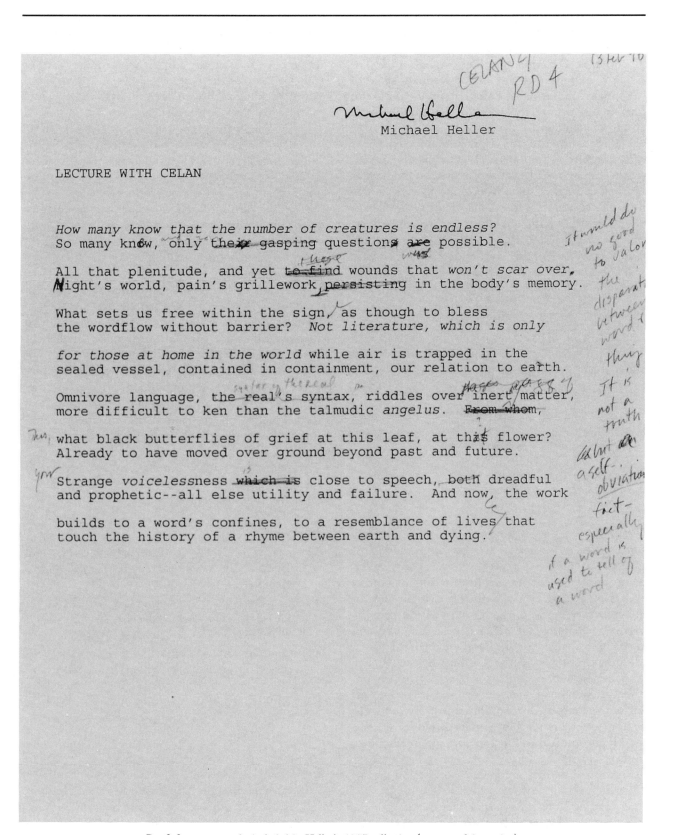

Michael Heller

LECTURE WITH CELAN

How many know that the number of creatures is endless?
So many know, only their gasping questions are possible.

All that plenitude, and yet to find wounds that won't scar over,
Night's world, pain's grillework, persisting in the body's memory.

What sets us free within the sign, as though to bless
the wordflow without barrier? Not literature, which is only

for those at home in the world while air is trapped in the
sealed vessel, contained in containment, our relation to earth.

Omnivore language, the real's syntax, riddles over inert matter,
more difficult to ken than the talmudic angelus. From whom,

what black butterflies of grief at this leaf, at this flower?
Already to have moved over ground beyond past and future.

Strange voicelessness which is close to speech, both dreadful
and prophetic—all else utility and failure. And now, the work

builds to a word's confines, to a resemblance of lives that
touch the history of a rhyme between earth and dying.

Draft for a poem to be included in Heller's 1997 collection (courtesy of the author)

reflections on language, and religious tradition. The memoir is both autobiography and ars poetica. Through recollection and poetic invention Heller hopes to achieve a profound and resonant sense of the human condition, to comprehend the nature of poetry per se and its relationship both to one's life and to knowledge.

Continuing to explore the thematic concerns raised in his earlier books, Heller's memoir recontextualizes such previously published poems as "Bialystok Stanzas" from *Knowledge* and those touching on Jewish themes from *In the Builded Place*. These poems underline the often bitter historical connection between Judaism and writing. In a passage from "Terrible Pictures" Heller describes Jews who will soon be executed, their photographs taken by the Nazis with their penchant for record keeping:

Snow –
A group of people
Awkwardly caught

They have just discovered
The photographer, and he, them

The old man with the sack
Who has turned
Shrugs his disbelief into the lens

No sense of emergency
In the pose
Could be as real[.]

Humans are set apart from the rest of life by their capacity for reflection, an activity that is made possible to the greatest degree by texts. The simultaneous intervention into and historicizing of human events by record keeping – in this case the lens of the camera records as significantly as the pen – is part of Heller's overall belief system. The past animates his struggle to understand the nuanced power of language. Heller draws on the work of Walter Benjamin (whom he proclaims as the "patron saint" of his memoir) and Gershom Scholem as well as on ancient writings such as the Torah and Talmud. He demonstrates his kinship with such works as they shed light on his own life and writing, especially as concerns his shift toward secularism and away from the stricter doctrines of his father and rabbi grandfather.

"Living Root" also makes clear that Jewish immigration to America, its thematics of resistance and assimilation, are keys to understanding Heller's life in relation to these inherited texts. In the Bible the Diaspora first emerges as an idea, and it is the Diaspora, Heller emphasizes, that marks the Jew as

Other. What finally unites him with the Jews and their texts is the question of literacy. At times Jews have been persecuted for their learning, at other times either for their ignorance or blasphemy, but always at the heart of such conflicts is the question of the Jewish reverence for texts.

Through the juxtapositions in "Living Root" of reflective prose with poetry – poetry that in his collections already has a certain "pastness" – Heller attempts to create a unity out of his life, to literalize into meaning its themes and occasions. The "Bialystok Stanzas" and the other poems in their new surroundings, embedded in an almost midrashic structure of word, gloss, and commentary, become part of an overall elegy for the life of the Jews and the life of texts.

Heller's poetry, especially when appreciated in conjunction with his prose, has created a system of signs complexly wrought and freighted with human history and desire. His extraordinary achievement is that he handles both language and the notion of language with great intellectual rigor and equally great tenderness and compassion. His poems communicate his rigor of thought in the most human of terms. Heller's poetry and prose are noble in gesture and intent, superbly rich and profoundly emotional. They should be considered a unique and vital part of the contemporary canon. Widespread recognition of his accomplishments can only sustain a healthy literary culture.

Interviews:

Thomas H. Johnson, "An Interview with Michael Heller," *Contemporary Poetry: A Journal of Criticism* (Spring 1978): 1–24;

Thomas Gardner, "An Interview with Michael Heller," *Contemporary Literature,* 32 (Fall 1991): 297–311;

Keith Baughman, "Michael Heller: Interview," *Reflector* (Shippensburg University) (1992): 16–29;

Edward Halsey Foster, "An Interview with Michael Heller," *Talisman: A Journal of Contemporary Poetry and Poetics,* 11 (Fall 1993): 48–64.

References:

Norman Finkelstein, "Dy-Yanu: Michael Heller's 'Bialystok Stanza,'" *Talisman: A Journal of Contemporary Poetry and Poetics,* 11 (Fall 1993): 77–80;

Richard Frye, "The Poet as Phenomenologist," *Talisman: A Journal of Contemporary Poetry and Poetics,* 11 (Fall 1993): 90–91;

Thomas Gardner, "'Speaking the Estranged of Things': Michael Heller," *Talisman: A Journal of Contemporary Poetry and Poetics,* 11 (Fall 1993): 94–95;

Laszlo K. Géfin, "Michael Heller's Personae," *Talisman: A Journal of Contemporary Poetry and Poetics,* 11 (Fall 1993): 81–85;

Géfin, "Review of *Knowledge,*" *Sagetrieb,* 3 (Spring 1980): 143–147;

James Guimond, "Moving Heaven and Earth," *Parnassus,* 1 (Fall/Winter 1972): 106–115;

Burt Kimmelman, "The Autobiography of Poetics: Michael Heller's Living Root," *Talisman: A Journal of Contemporary Poetry and Poetics,* 11 (Fall 1993): 67–76;

Jeffrey Peterson, "The Builder's Art of Michael Heller," *Talisman: A Journal of Contemporary Poetry and Poetics,* 11 (Fall 1993): 96–99;

Ruby Riemer, "Michael Heller: A Poet's Quest," *Talisman: A Journal of Contemporary Poetry and Poetics,* 11 (Fall 1993): 100–102;

Armand Schwerner, "'Taking Up the Thread' ('Father Studies'): On the Poetry of Michael Heller," *Talisman: A Journal of Contemporary Poetry and Poetics,* 11 (Fall 1993): 65–66;

Hugh Seidman, "Eye : Void : Matter," *Talisman: A Journal of Contemporary Poetry and Poetics,* 11 (Fall 1993): 105–109;

Nathaniel Tarn, "A Letter to Michael Heller," *Talisman: A Journal of Contemporary Poetry and Poetics,* 11 (Fall 1993): 86–89;

Marc Weber, "Heller's Realm: The Overlook," *Talisman: A Journal of Contemporary Poetry and Poetics,* 11 (Fall 1993): 103–104;

Henry Weinfield, "Fragment of an Imaginary Dialogue with Michael Heller on *In the Builded Place,*" *Talisman: A Journal of Contemporary Poetry and Poetics,* 11 (Fall 1993): 110–112;

Alan Williamson, "At, Borders, Think," *Parnassus,* 9 (Fall/Winter 1981): 247–254.

Robert Kelly

(24 September 1935 –)

Patrick Meanor
State University of New York College at Oneonta

See also the Kelly entry in *DLB 5: American Poets Since World War II, First Series,* and *DLB 130: American Short-Story Writers Since World War II.*

BOOKS: *Armed Descent* (New York: Hawk's Well, 1961);

Her Body Against Time (Mexico City: Corno Emplumado, 1963);

Round Dances (New York: Trobar, 1964);

Lunes, published with *Sightings,* by Jerome Rothenberg (New York: Hawk's Well, 1964);

Enstasy (Annandale-on-Hudson, N.Y.: Matter, 1964);

Lectiones (Placitas, N.Mex.: Duende, 1965);

Map of Annandale (Bennington, Vt., 1965);

Words in Service, For the Marriage of P. Adams Sitney & Julia Adams (New Haven, Conn.: Robert Lamberton, 1965);

Weeks (Mexico City: Corno Emplumado, 1966);

Devotions (Annandale-on-Hudson, N.Y.: Salitter, 1967);

Twenty Poems (Annandale-on-Hudson, N.Y.: Matter, 1967);

Axon Dendron Tree (Annandale-on-Hudson, N.Y.: Matter, 1967);

Crooked Bridge Love Society (Annandale-on-Hudson, N.Y.: Salitter, 1967);

A Joining: A Sequence for H.D. (Los Angeles: Black Sparrow, 1967);

The Scorpions (Garden City, N.Y.: Doubleday, 1967; London: Calder & Boyars, 1969);

Alpha (Gambier, Ohio: Fisher, 1968);

Finding the Measure (Los Angeles: Black Sparrow, 1968);

A Play and Two Poems, by Kelly, Diane Wakoski, and Ron Loewinsohn (Los Angeles: Black Sparrow, 1968);

Sonnets, 1967 (Los Angeles: Black Sparrow, 1968);

Songs I-XXX (Cambridge, Mass.: Pym-Randall, 1968);

Statement (Los Angeles: Black Sparrow, 1968);

Robert Kelly, 1992 (photograph by Charlotte Kelly)

The Common Shore, Books I–V (Los Angeles: Black Sparrow, 1969);

A California Journal (London: Big Venus, 1969);

Kali Yuga (London: Cape Goliard / New York: Grossman, 1970);

Flesh: Dream: Book (Los Angeles: Black Sparrow, 1971);

Cities (West Newbury, Mass.: Frontier, 1971);

In Time (West Newbury, Mass.: Frontier, 1971);

Ralegh (Los Angeles: Black Sparrow, 1972);

The Pastorals (Los Angeles: Black Sparrow, 1972);

Reading Her Notes (Uniondale, N.Y.: Salisbury Printers, 1972);

The Mill of Particulars (Los Angeles: Black Sparrow, 1973);

The Tears of Edmund Burke (Annandale-on-Hudson, N. Y.: Printed by Helen in Annandale, 1973);

A Line of Sight (Los Angeles: Black Sparrow, 1974);

The Loom (Los Angeles: Black Sparrow, 1975);

Sixteen Odes (Santa Barbara, Cal.: Black Sparrow, 1976);

The Lady Of (Santa Barbara, Cal.: Black Sparrow, 1977);

The Convections (Santa Barbara, Cal.: Black Sparrow, 1978);

The Book of Persephone (New Paltz, N.Y.: Treacle, 1978);

Wheres (Santa Barbara, Cal.: Black Sparrow, 1978);

Kill the Messenger Who Brings Bad News (Santa Barbara, Cal.: Black Sparrow, 1979);

The Cruise of the Pnyx (Barrytown, N.Y.: Station Hill, 1979);

Sentence (Barrytown, N.Y.: Station Hill, 1980);

Spiritual Exercises (Santa Barbara, Cal.: Black Sparrow, 1981);

The Alchemist to Mercury, edited by Jed Rasula (Richmond, Cal.: North Atlantic, 1981);

Mulberry Women (Berkeley, Cal.: Hiersoux, Powers, Thomas, 1982);

Under Words (Santa Barbara, Cal.: Black Sparrow, 1983);

Thor's Thrush (Oakland, Cal.: Coincidence, 1984);

A Transparent Tree (New Paltz, N.Y.: McPherson, 1985);

Not This Island Music (Santa Rosa, Cal.: Black Sparrow, 1987);

The Flowers of Unceasing Coincidence, edited by George Quasha (Barrytown, N.Y.: Station Hill, 1988);

Oahu (Rhinebeck, N.Y.: St. Lazaire, 1988);

Doctor of Silence (Kingston, N.Y.: McPherson, 1988);

Cat Scratch Fever (Kingston, N.Y.: McPherson, 1990);

Ariadne (Rhinebeck, N.Y.: St. Lazaire, 1990);

A Strange Market (Santa Rosa, Cal.: Black Sparrow, 1992);

Queen of Terrors (Kingston, N.Y.: McPherson, 1994);

Mont Blanc (Ann Arbor, Mich.: OtherWind Press, 1994);

Red Actions: Selected Poems 1960–1993 (Santa Rosa, Cal.: Black Sparrow, 1995).

PLAY PRODUCTIONS: *The Well Wherein a Deer's Head Bleeds,* New York, 1964;

Eros and Psyche, with music by Elie Yarden, New Paltz, N.Y., 1971.

OTHER: *A Controversy of Poets,* edited by Kelly and Paris Leary (Garden City, N.Y.: Doubleday/Anchor, 1965);

Paul Blackburn, *The Journals,* edited, with a foreword, by Kelly (Los Angeles: Black Sparrow, 1975).

Robert Kelly is perhaps the most prolific major poet in contemporary American literature. He is also one of the country's most respected short-fiction writers and teachers of creative writing. The founder of three distinguished literary magazines — *Chelsea Review, Trobar,* and *Matter* — he has also been a contributing editor to such respected journals as *Conjunctions, Caterpillar, Los, Alcheringa: Ethnopoetics,* and *Sulfur.* Associated with Bard College for more than thirty-five years, Kelly has been the Asher B. Edelman Professor of Literature since 1986. In the early 1980s he became known as a skillful and creative administrator as he helped to organize the Milton Avery Graduate School of the Arts," a program that serves as a model for other M.F.A. programs that wish to avoid academic rigidity in developing the artistic capabilities of their students. In the 4 October 1992 *New York Times* Anthony DePalma named Kelly, along with poet John Ashbery, composer Joan Tower, and African novelist Chinua Achebe, one of the "stars" that Bard College "is ablaze with."

Most important, though, is that Kelly is a cofounder along with the poet Jerome Rothenberg of what has come to be recognized as a uniquely American school of poets who at first chose to identify their concerns as the poetry of Deep Image. Borrowing a term from psychology and linguistics, they propounded the creation of a poetry that eschews "the cult of personality" and the practices of a prevailing poetic establishment that fostered a poetry of "private complaint." The Deep Image poets worked to move beyond so-called confessional poetry and into an exploration of the richness and diversity of the world which they designate as "the Other." As a practitioner of archetypal poetry, Kelly has become a recognized and highly influential literary figure around whom a number of like-minded writers, musicians, and artists have gathered. There is little question that since the death of the poet Robert Duncan in 1988 Kelly has become one of the most prominent poets in an ever-growing group of nonacademic writers usually associated with what were called the Black Mountain and New York schools.

When he was asked by *Contemporary Poets* to help the general reader understand his complex work, Kelly in 1991 described his stance as a poet: "First, tell him it is not *my* work, only Work, itself, somehow arisen through (or in spite of) my instrumentality. My personality is its enemy, only distracts." Defining his aim as a poet Kelly remarked that because "we are human in the world" the "sharing of thought, perception, is what becomes the world. The world is our shared thought."

In *In Time* (1971) Kelly writes that the writer should be "a scientist of holistic understanding, a scholar . . . to whom all data whatsoever are of use." One of the original projects of the Deep Image poets was to explore the varieties of archetypal/mythic content beyond that found in American culture. Their sources of inspiration included the Dogon of West Africa, the images in the primitive caves at Lascaux and Altamira, alchemical wisdom, the wisdom traditions found in the Cabala and the Zohar, the hermetical writers and scientists of the Middle East, and the many forms of spirituality in non-Western traditions such as Hinduism and, especially, Tibetan Buddhism. In short, Kelly and his colleagues have been creatively tapping the spiritual resources of multiculturalism long before there was a word for it.

In fulfilling the request of the Contemporary Authors Autobiography Series in 1994 for an article on his life, Kelly's ambivalence is clear in his repeated statement "My life is not my past." He early on explains: "When I think about my life, I think of how I hated it when I was younger, and love it now. Then it was curse and now it is bless. What I wanted to curse was how cut off I felt from everyone, mostly from those I wanted to be close to, wanted to like me." In his poetry Kelly largely avoids nostalgic reveries and treating the destructiveness of time because he believes thinking of the past too personally can tie the imagination down unnecessarily to a historical/autobiographical stance toward life. Kelly maintains that there are as many lives as there are "selves who come calling," an attitude that suggests his life philosophy cannot be understood merely through a linear tracing of autobiographical events.

Kelly's interest in language and in tracing the evolution of individual words through their etymologies leads him early in his article to consider the Greek etymologies embedded in the components of the word *biography*:

> My autobiography is the writing (*graphein*) of my life, my bios. Now Greek knows two words like that, two words the ancients surmised had at first been one: *bíos,* "life," and *biós,* "a bow" to shoot with as the hunter takes the life of things and turns them into his own life, the life of the tribe.
>
> Writing my life is writing my instrument, my strength.
>
> My life is not my past.

Since Kelly's work is so steeped in Greek and Roman mythology, particularly the work of Homer,

one can hardly overlook the way one of Kelly's major poetic and spiritual influences, Robert Duncan, used the word *bow* in the title of his 1968 volume of poetry, *Bending the Bow*. The bow in that poem alludes not only to Odysseus's famous bow but also to the bow that the ancient bards used to bend and string into a lyre or harp to play with their poetry. The lyre has subsequently become one of the principal symbols for the creative act. Kelly transforms the bow into a metaphor for the imagination in the act of creation: "Real autobiography is *the life that writes itself.* That is what a writer's works are, in truth. Look no further: self-written, self-begotten, the poems I have spent most of my life writing are my actual autobiography. . . . But my life is not my past; my life is my strength, my instrument ('my bow')."

Robert Kelly was born on 24 September 1935 in Brooklyn, New York, "on Brown Street, in Marine Park, near Gerritsen Beach, the coal docks and conduits." He is always specific because geography plays such a crucial role in building and recording the many "conduits" that make up his life. All connections are important to Kelly, and there are connections that link together all of his fifty volumes of poetry and four collections of fiction. His father, Samuel Jason Kelly, provided for the family with the help of Kelly's mother, Margaret Rose Kane, a public-school teacher all her life; the small salaries were spent frugally. Because both parents worked all day, the boy was mostly alone. He preferred reading to talking and talked with great reluctance. He enjoyed listening to his father, who possessed a wonderful tenor voice and sang "formally and deliberately."

Kelly writes that his great-grandfather on his father's side, Samuel Marles, "presided over the fantasy-of-the-past for me as I grew up, so much so that when I first was publishing in college, I used his name as my pseudonym." The figure of Marles, who left England for America, joined the Union army, and fought in the Civil War, surfaces throughout Kelly's work. Wounded at Gettysburg, he never returned home to his family, instead traveling to Australia and what is now Pakistan, where he settled and disappeared from view. Kelly retains some of his letters, his journals, and a number of his well-crafted poems. A painter as well as a poet, Marles served to ground Kelly's imagination in a genealogical and geographical history: "In any case, Samuel Marles has been a vital figure for me, establishing at once whatever authenticity it is to have connections with history (Gettysburg) and Over There (Somerset, Bristol), and at the same time pointing me to Asia." This great-grandfather is also the prototype of the major character in one of Kelly's most renowned short stories, "Samuel Naked," the longest and final story in *A Transparent Tree* (1985).

During the years 1943 and 1944 two traumatic events occurred that caused the young Kelly great apprehension. When he seemed to be losing his sight his parents forbade him to read books for fear of overstraining his eyes and going blind, though the condition was later diagnosed as simple myopia. A greater trauma, however, was the loss of the family's comfortable home on Brown Street and their moving to a shabby part of town on "Crescent Street in the Old Mill district, east of Brownsville and New Lots, south of Cypress Hills, west of Ozone Park." It was Kelly's fall from the Edenic happiness and security of childhood that awoke him to poetry, and he would often return to the Brown Street house "not so much for the friends I had there, but for the house, the place – and the garden, which still, in its modesty, defines what flowers mean: the pansies in the windowbox on the garage, the pussywillow by the picket fence, the aisle of deep red roses, the huge blue blossoms of the hydrangea that always seemed wet with dew no matter how hot the day." Readers familiar with Kelly's work will recognize in this memory the origin of the profusion of flowers and the Jungian "house" – the symbolic place/space one can spiritually inhabit – that inform both his poetry and prose.

Though the new neighborhood was shabby, Kelly was able to explore the great marshlands that bounded the south shore of Long Island: "In those marshes I walked a lot, losing and finding myself. Black mud, wild birds, luminous byways of water, sea creeks, endless acres of timothy and marsh grass.... And this was the place for me, these marshes, gulls, and sky. My place." Again, these autobiographical details suggest the origin for the dozens of species of birds that are found throughout Kelly's poems and the primary importance of water – rivers, lakes, and seas – which sometimes structures the poems. The act of "walking" is also a recurring motif throughout his work.

Kelly's reputation for reading made him one of his elementary school's stars: "The first day in school, the nun took me around from classroom to classroom, making me read from some book in front of other students. I didn't understand what was happening. I did what I was told. I read aloud. I was uncomfortable being dragged around but I did what I was told. I almost always have." In 1949 he went to a Jesuit high school, where he could study

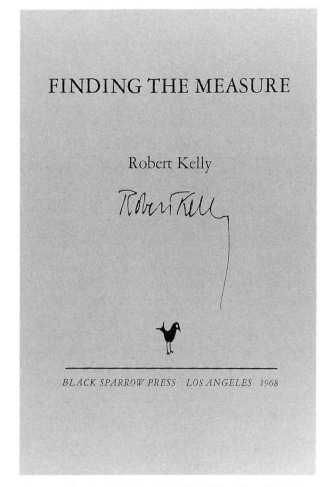

FINDING THE MEASURE

Robert Kelly

BLACK SPARROW PRESS   LOS ANGELES   1968

Signed title page for the book in which Kelly defines his aim as "the natural articulation of ideas"

Greek and Latin, which Kelly enjoyed immensely. It was there that he also began his study of German, a subject that he later taught at Bard College. Concurrent with his classical studies were his first venturings into the underworld of adolescence and New York City. He began to miss classes and eventually dropped out of school.

Kelly calls the years from 1950 to 1952 his *Wanderjahre,* in which he "fell through the cracks, absenteeism gradually turning into dropoutism, wandered the city, got no further than Philadelphia ... mostly Manhattan: the Village and the subways and hanging around Columbia. Era of nosleepism, no eatism, weird mentalisms, seehowfarIcangoism." However, he had begun his own educational discipline when he discovered, at the age of eleven, Samuel Taylor Coleridge's "Kubla Khan," then at fourteen the work of T. S. Eliot (especially the *Four Quartets*), Ezra Pound, the French surrealist poet Guillaume Apollinaire, and the German visionary poet Rainer Maria Rilke – influences that would remain with him for the rest of his life. He discovered his other "house" – a spiritual/aesthetic one – in these writers and in his wanderings: "Poetry I sought, and fame, feeding, noise, Viennese music, the secular roar of history. Kulchur, said Pound, and I carried his vade mecum with me in Times Square at fourteen, he was my author and my book was yet to be. Pound and Mahler, Joyce and the girl across the subway car, the girl in the wind . . . the blue distances, Italian bread, white cheese, Pepsi-Cola, IRT – these were my house."

Music also began to assume a large role in his evolving intellectual and emotional life. The composer whose sense of structure felt to Kelly strangely like his own was Anton Bruckner: "When I first began to listen to Bruckner's symphonies, I understood that 'structure' in music was not about construction but about housing, interiority, carving out a space in the rock of the world we could live in, or defining by some masterstroke, the templum, *space defined as ours* – a place we can live in. Hearing is a house." Undoubtedly, his lesson from Bruckner helped Kelly in his development of larger and longer structures as his work moved from the Olsonian *The Common Shore, Books I–V* (1969) to Kelly's longest masterpiece, *The Loom* (1975), particularly in the way the latter work concludes with the poet-architect building an Orphic Temple around a sacred altar.

There is no contemporary American poet who possesses a better sense of the architectonics of the long/large poem than Kelly, precisely because his knowledge and love of music are so obvious throughout his work. His deep love of composers such as Bruckner, Gustav Mahler, and Alban Berg and the operas of Richard Wagner, Giuseppe Verdi, Vincenzo Bellini, and especially Richard Strauss inform not only the melodic figurations and lyrical sweep of his poetic lines but also his unerring sense of the movement and juxtaposition of the controlling elements of his poetry. Kelly has stated that he views all of his work as a kind of operatic drama: "I think I am writing a great play all of my life and every poem a speech in it. Only to find the right mouth, the right shadow. Come, speak me. Come be my mouthed verities and bellow tendernesses. Come be me. Every poem is a cry that matches exactly its lewd or sacred juncture in the play. Every story a precis or stage direction."

The only way Kelly's parents could bring their son back into the habit of schooling was to pressure him to enroll in college. He started attending City College of New York (CCNY) at the age of fifteen "and went sedately enough through four years of mostly immemorable required classes." He continued working with Greek and Latin poetry as well as Romantic and modern German authors, while studiously avoiding almost all contemporary English language work. He remembers arguing vehemently with classmate and future poet David Antin about the quality of the poems of William Carlos Williams; Kelly was appalled by Williams's bleakness, a criticism he later disavowed as he came to love and be deeply influenced by Williams's work, especially *Paterson* (1963) and his late poetry. Another poet whose influence was beginning to make itself felt in Kelly's verse was the Jesuit poet Gerard Manley Hopkins. He was drawn especially to Hopkins's syntactical virtuosity and his love for building poems on Celtic-Welsh and Anglo-Saxon etymological bases. He described his own early work in a 31 July 1994 letter to Patrick H. Meanor as "high-rhetorical, largely free verse – a strange (it seems now) blend of modernist versecraft with something older and haughtier. Clearly I had not found the measure." Kelly became friends with Antin and poet Jack Hirshman, among others, and fell in love with Joan Lasker, who, as "Joby," became the dedicatee of many of Kelly's early poems.

After graduation from CCNY in 1955, Kelly married Lasker and moved back to Brooklyn, where he worked translating medical and pharmaceutical texts from German and Spanish. He also enrolled in the Columbia University Graduate School to pursue work in seventeenth-century studies with Marjorie Nicholson and Pierre Garay. Kelly's most important work in terms of immediate influences were his studies in medieval literature in a department formed by Roger Loomis. These readings led him to research the legend of the Grail with particular emphasis on the work of Sir Thomas Malory, "answering an intuition that Malory had somehow – in his sullen art, his strange isolation, his feral apartness – enlarged nonetheless the notion of the Grail company, the sacred committee of holy knowing." He did all the course and exam work for the doctorate but never bothered to write a master's essay.

At Columbia, Kelly, along with his friend and fellow poet George Economou and novelists Ursule Molinaro and her husband Venable Herndon, edited a journal they called the *Chelsea Review*. Kelly at this time also fell in love with the poetry of Dylan Thomas, the Welsh bard who fathered the Beat poets but destroyed himself with drink in 1953. The work of Thomas thrilled him with its linguistic brilliance. The influence of Thomas and Hopkins caused Kelly's poetry to become more technically innovative; he experimented with Celtic measures, fancy meters, and Hopkinsian compactness. But he continued to read widely, still looking for someone besides Pound whose work both thrilled and taught him poetic craft. "Poetry had to be exaltation. It still does," Kelly wrote in his 31 July 1994 letter. "I could find no American poetry that thrilled me – it was pompous and imitative, or raw and graceless. I wanted Titania in the kitchen." He was certainly not the only young American poet who found little to respond to emotionally in the poetry coming out of the academy that had been fashioned by the poet-critics of the New Criticism.

The most profound experience, not only of 1958 but of Kelly's life up to his twenty-third year, was a spiritual awakening that took him by surprise while he was walking home from work on Lexington Avenue on a lovely October evening. He was feeling "tired and absurd":

> It seemed that the sky opened quietly and an Under-standing spoke in me, saying that if I dedicated myself to writing, if I gave myself to that truth I knew as somehow the sky and the voice that speaks inside and the good of the world, if I gave myself over to writing and for the good of the world, it would be well, and it would be well with me.

Kelly felt called to the vocation of the poet in a visionary experience, and like the Grail knight who dedicates himself to serve the Lady, he made a vow: "That October commitment is the story. To write every day was the method. To attend to what is said. To listen. To prepare myself for writing by learning everything I could, by hanging out in languages and enduring overdetermined desires, by tolerating my own inclinations as if they had the physical accuracy of gravity. To listen, and say what I heard." Kelly believes deeply in the vocation of writing, that "while language does not tell all the truth or the whole truth there is some truth that only language tells." Nowhere does Kelly elucidate more simply his commitment to the priesthood of the word by his willingness to enter "wholly into language." Upon returning home he described his vision to his wife, Joan, and she immediately agreed that he should quit his twelve-hour-a-day job and devote himself to writing full time.

Concurrent with his increased efforts at writing poetry were new discoveries of contemporary American writers who for the first time offered Kelly some real hope for American literature. He wrote in his 31 July 1994 letter that he found in Jonathan Williams's *The Empire Finals at Verona* (1959) the voice of "someone who knew the Real World of Poetry (Old England, Rome, etc.) but who spoke it

in American." Kelly calls the work "a crisis book" that drew him closer to some of the writers of the Black Mountain School such as Charles Olson and Robert Duncan. Duncan's *Selected Poems* (1959) convinced him that it was possible for an American poet to live in Stinson Beach, California, while creating a world informed by Eliot, Pound, Hopkins, and Dante – the continuous river of poetry as revelation.

The late 1950s also brought other significant contacts for Kelly. Louis Zukofsky and his wife, Celia, welcomed both the Kellys and George Economou into their home for evenings of not so much discussion of the latest trends in literature as intense scrutiny of the minute particulars of some poem, studying it aloud as if Zukofsky were trying to see its breath. As editors of a new journal called *Trobar,* Kelly and Economou were able to publish one of Zukofsky's least-known small books called *I's (pronounced* eyes) in 1963. Years later Kelly was able to honor Zukofsky by proposing him for an honorary doctor of letters from Bard College.

Kelly also became close to the poet Jerome Rothenberg and his anthropologist wife, Diane, and through them the poet Paul Blackburn, whose journals Kelly edited after his death. The work of the Rothenbergs in connecting anthropological and poetic concerns began to reveal to Kelly the real and sensuous impact of what he knew abstractly from linguistics, that it is the community that gives language power. The Rothenbergs' influence – particularly their interest in Native American poetry, song, and ritual and in finding "a current English/American voice for Native American and other tribal poetics" – contributed to Kelly's developing sense of his need for community, which may have saved his work from becoming overly interiorized. The Rothenbergs and poets Economou, Diane Wakoski, and Armand Schwerner and a few others founded The Blue Yak, a bookstore in Manhattan exclusively devoted to poetry from small presses. It was a cooperative run by poets for poets and managed to break even for a while.

Kelly had two other seminal encounters with fellow poets in 1959. That year he began an enduring correspondence with the poet Gerrit Lansing, whose mind and work were first revealed in the journal *Set.* Lansing's deep knowledge of the occult and of Gnostic and hermetic texts would have a lasting effect on Kelly's work, providing Kelly with alternate sources of spiritual sustenance. Later that year Kelly first met Robert Duncan at "the old Figaro, a sleazy and comfortable cafe on Bleecker," at a time of despondency when he "felt neglected, ignored, unknown." Duncan's recognition gave

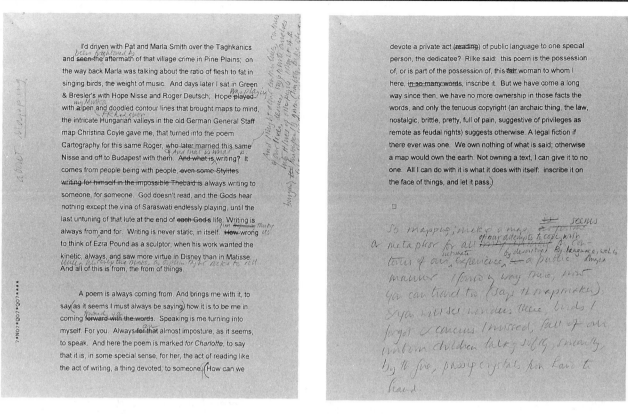

Pages from Kelly's notebook revised by the author

Kelly a much-needed boost: "This man had recognized me! This man, whom I regarded as the greatest living poet in my language, had spoken my name, known me. Always a knower, Duncan had deftly, simply, saved my life, literally." What attracted Kelly to Duncan's work was "the power of his attention to the dance of words that – so attended to – always would make sense of the body and all its pivots with the world. Social as Auden, fierce as [George] Barker, incantatory as Thomas, learned as Lansing, honest as Olson, adventurous as Mac Low, musical as Zukofsky, Duncan struck me as the complete poet and one whose grace let him play and comfort and be gone. And part of his grace was his strict, sometimes even humorless, fidelity to dream and vision – which made him the key in my own struggles on the side of the surreal against the neo-classic."

Kelly's poems began to show signs of both thematic purpose and technical security. Prophetically, a poem published in the first issue of *Trobar* (and never reprinted) was a predictive poem titled "The Flight of the Dalai Lama." Little did he suspect that he would, twenty years later, become a Buddhist himself. Kelly in his 31 July 1994 letter considered

this poem his watershed – "the gathering of all the registers." What many critics would consider his first mature poem, though, was published in 1961, "The Alchemist," a piece Kelly concedes was "the first poem I was sure of . . . in the sense of getting out of school." Though an early poem, "The Alchemist" addresses the impossibility of his task – that of transforming the materialism of so-called "civilization" into something resembling a human habitation. Kelly forcefully confronts the military-industrial complex of the powers that be:

if we do not get up and destroy all the congressmen
turn them into naked men and let the sun shine on
　　them
set them down in a desert & let them find their way
　　out,
north, by whatever sexual power is left within them, if
　　we do not
seize the president and take him out in daytime and
　　show him
the fire & energy of one at least immediate star, white
　　star
hammer that down in his skull till he can hear only that
rhythm & goes and enters the dance or makes his own,
we will walk forever down the hallways into mirrors
　　and

stagger and look to our left hand for support & the sun
will have set inside us & the world will be filled with
Law,
  and it is that exchange we must sweep out of the temple,
  the changing of gold and power & the figure of Christ into
  Law.

The poetic voice shows no sign of weakness and
makes its statement directly and without hysteria.
The poet is the alchemist whose job it is to awaken
and transform the world in a Blakean way to a
visionary consciousness that might save it from self-
destruction.

After a short teaching assignment at Wagner
College, Kelly began his long career at Bard College. He first taught German there in 1961, beginning with a seminar in Goethe's *Faust*: "What was I
doing? Exhausting, draining, almost nightmarish –
yet I wrote more than I had ever written in my
life – an instruction that activity is itself stimulating
to the prophetic faculty, not the reverse. Lazy people have nothing to say."

In 1961 Kelly's first book of poems, *Armed Descent,* was published by the Rothenbergs' Hawk's
Well Press. Discussing the volume's origin and significance some thirty years later, Kelly expostulates
on its title: "I proposed in my first book an armed
descent – Valéry's mot, 'who would descend into
the self must go armed to the teeth.' And that is
what I have tried to do, if do is the word for it, if
tried is true. To go down into the self, armed with
everything I have of flesh or dream or information.
Armed, but not armored. To go down into the self,
not especially my self but the sense of, steady beat-
ing pulsing beautiful soon lost forever physiology of
the, self." *Armed Descent* includes Kelly's first major
long poem, "The Exchanges," and is the clearest example of Kelly's poetry coming directly out of the
poetics of the Deep Image.

The theory of the Deep Image was partially intended as a delicate corrective to Charles Olson's
famous manifesto "Projective Verse" (1950), in
which he defines a poem as "a high energy construct and, at all points, an energy discharge. . . . It
is by their syllables that words juxtapose in beauty."
Olson further posits that a poem's syllabic measures
should be derived from the natural rhythm of the
creating poet's breathing. Though a great admirer
of Olson's work, Kelly proposed in "Notes on the
Poetry of Deep Image" in the 1961 *Trobar* a less
mechanistic metaphor for the genesis of poetry –
the image rather than the syllable: "Projective verse . . .
offers a method of resolving breath and line, and
my concern with it here seeks to substitute the cen-

trality of image for the centrality of syllable & line as
a way of access to the happening of the poem. Thus
a poem involves the fundamental rhythm of the images (fundamental because more complexly present), a rhythm which is at once intellectual and sensuous, and also the structural, more directly sensual, rhythm of the breath expressed in line. The
counterpoint of these two rhythms is a principal
source of fullness and complexity in the poem."
While Olson had little passion for music except in
discussions of aesthetic/philosophical battlefields,
Kelly's poetry from the beginning is infused with
obvious musical rhythms.

Armed Descent can be understood as a descent
directly into the source of deep images, the archetypal, mythic sources buried in both the individual
and the collective unconscious. Deep Imagism
comes directly out of the interest of both Kelly and
Rothenberg in the surrealism of Federico García
Lorca, Apollinaire, Pablo Neruda, André Breton,
and others. The disaster of World War I and its virtual destruction of western European culture that
Eliot's *The Waste Land* (1922) so brilliantly documented also engendered surrealism and its desperate reliance on the only available source of "truth"
left in such a world – the individual unconscious,
the repository of the deep images that might save
humanity from itself. All other intellectual, religious, and philosophical traditions had been called
into question.

Critic Edward N. Schelb notes Kelly's indebtedness to surrealism in many of these early poems:
"As in dreams, images form their own context, yet
that context determines their meaning . . . Kelly's
primary rhythm of images corresponds to the structural displacements in dream-work . . . *Armed Descent*
notably establishes a number of standard themes –
the hidden light of revelation, the carnality of perception, the violence of alchemical change. Like
Pablo Neruda, Kelly strips away the vestiges of ordinary perception, sacrificing himself, burrowing
into the earth, embracing his animal nature, and
singing of the Muse." In "How It Fell" images of the
body, nature, and the Divine intermix surrealistically:

here
turning remorselessly
into an animal
and in
the next town he closed his eyes
hearing the good news grow
feet moving in her body
being able to run faster than God
hearing the babies cry in the fields
the rooted bodies

twisted roots of their legs
alive.

Schelb designates "The Exchanges" as "the purest expression of the deep image. It's a full-blown dreamscape – its images are animistic, elemental, free of personal associations – and it moves through the mechanisms of dream-work, condensation and displacement. Images are charged with multiple meanings and operate with a type of autonomous dream logic." The opening of "The Exchanges" is one of Kelly's most haunting and archetypal:

where the spirit feeds
under the green trees, their
leaves falling in sunlight
red now yellow now
black pitch of the pine tree
& give it a name
& call it her
offer to become one with it in the moss
between tree roots
hollow the trunk.

"The Exchanges" is also full of Christian-Grail images and transformations of pagan phallic worship into sacramental Christian rituals of communion, all of which are variations on the alchemical changes brought about by language deriving its energy from the deep structures:

the currency of exchange
. . . .
language we learn with our fingers
deep in the ground,
language of hunger, syllables of pure animal vowel
since that continues, that
endures
and sings through all form
as it sings in dream
unforgotten.

Under its original title "Spiritum," "The Exchanges" was also published in Cid Corman's *Origin* of 1962, an issue that was devoted largely to Kelly's work. The many letters between Kelly and Corman were the beginning of a lengthy correspondence between the two poets.

Kelly wrote in his 31 July 1994 letter that he had in these early poems "gathered the exaltation and the domestic, the real work of poetry, to exalt the presences and empower the absences." Kelly's poetic palette is so inspiriting that he can, as James Breslin said of painter Mark Rothko, transform absence "into a luminous, sensuous, diffused and hovering *presence.*" After his first book, his activities

multiplied, and he wrote as much during his first year at Bard as in his previous ten years. He had finally hit his stride, and his productivity rarely waned thereafter.

The year 1963 saw the publication of a dual-language edition in English and Spanish of Kelly's next major volume of poetry, *Her Body Against Time,* his first dramatic celebration of the body electric. The syntax in this collection is much less elaborate than in the first as Kelly consciously strives for a stripped-down, pastoral quietude. Schelb notes the intertwining of sensuality and spirituality: "Kelly prowls in search of sexual intensity and redemptive orgasms . . . and the most profound vision of God is through women . . . carnal bliss." In "Statement," a 1962 essay in *Nomad,* Kelly wrote of the body as the primary vehicle of transcendence: "The discovery is ourselves through the visible, of the visible through ourselves. The gateway is the visible; but we must go in." Much of the poetry in this volume can be viewed as an ecstatic, Dionysian variation on the key line in Wallace Stevens's "Sunday Morning": "Death is the mother of beauty." From this volume onward it is clear that for Kelly woman is unquestionably the principal mediator to the Other.

In *Round Dances* (1964) Kelly used complicated twists of syntax as he attempted to combine something of Williams's ecstatic dance of the body with Dante's music of the spheres – the Dionysian merging with the Apollonian. The tone and direction of many of these almost experimental lyrics would animate much of Kelly's poetry from then onward. *Lunes* (1964) contains poems written in a three-line, thirteen-syllable form Kelly had developed. The designation of thirteen represents the thirteen months of the lunar year, Kelly explained in the preface, for these "small poems . . . spend half their lives in darkness & half in light." In the same year Kelly met Helen Belinky, whom he would marry and live with for many years. Many of the books of the 1970s, including *The Loom,* were dedicated to her as she became not only Helen Kelly but also embodied the mythic, Homeric Helen and other feminine divinities.

From 1965 through 1967 Kelly published several collections of poetry, including *Weeks* (1966), the first of his long serial poems, and his first novel, *The Scorpions* (1967). His most important work of the period was perhaps *Axon Dendron Tree* (1967), one of his successful long poems. No modern or contemporary poet has produced as many long poems as Kelly. For a proper understanding of Kelly's range and varied accomplishments, critic Jed Rasula created four distinct categories: book-length works, meditations, narratives, and assemblies/series. Rasula classifies *Axon Dendron Tree* as the third of Kelly's seven book-length poems. The title alludes to a tree being the mythic axis of the cosmos – Yggdrasil, or the World Ash Tree. There is, however, a major shift of Kelly's attentions away from his earlier preoccupation with deep image to a new figure of the tree of language as a linguistic tree.

According to Schelb *Axon Dendron Tree* marks "a transition from [Kelly's] earlier expressionist 'deep image' poetry, whose imagistic intensity was a poor vehicle for the long poem, to a poetics of elaborate syntax and structural complexity." In the poem Kelly treats many of the mythic trees in ancient and modern religious traditions, including the tree of knowledge in the Garden of Eden, the tree of Calvary, the tree that became both Odysseus's bed and his bow, and the tree of the Cabala's Adam Kadmon. But it is the tree of language uniting all of these trees that becomes the *axis mundi* of Kelly's mythos. Kelly moves into what Schelb calls an "incarnational poetics" – a poetics of the Word as *word* and not representational of any specific entity but instead the root, the ground of all of them. He develops his ideas much more thoroughly in his perhaps most important work, *Finding the Measure* (1968).

Formally, too, *Axon Dendron Tree* is a radical shift for Kelly. The poem is a conscious response to Zukofsky's *"A"-15* (1963), whose work along with that of Pound played a crucial role in moving Kelly's poetry into new and tighter forms. Imitating Zukofsky's short one- or two-word lines, Kelly strives to ground his poetics in natural rhythms. The result, as Schelb points out, is that "instead of the visual image or allegory of depth, the word is foregrounded. The visual axis no longer dominates. Instead, the linguistic play offered by phonemes and morphemes offers a musical, processual structure devoid of a dominant ethos of objective representation. . . . Instead of isolated images, there are multiple linkages of sound and metonymic associations. Discourse on the structure of language now redefines the nature of Kelly's poetics. The self and the body are seen as linguistic structures."

During the years 1965 through 1967 Kelly was also working on another long poem, a meditation on America titled *The Common Shore,* the first five books of which were published in 1969. The influence of Olson – whom Kelly had met through Gerrit Lansing in Gloucester, Massachusetts, in 1962 – on both the structure and content of this work is clearly evident. Kelly had visited more with Olson during the summer of 1964, when Olson in-

vited him to join him, Edward Dorn, Amiri Baraka, and Robert Creeley in teaching at the State University of New York at Buffalo. Kelly describes Olson's influence as overwhelming: "Olson, who overpowered me and my kind with the fervor with which he, sometimes breathless and in doubt, sustained what seemed – too easily – the mind's argument against the heart. Amazing man, that such flesh and tune and ballsiness should doubt Lord Plato." *The Common Shore* also owes some of its inspiration to Pound's *Cantos* and Williams's *Paterson.* Though Kelly moved in a different direction with his masterpiece *The Loom,* he admits that he still feels close to certain sections from *The Common Shore.* The sixth book of *The Common Shore, The Winthrop Poems,* was published in the Autumn 1969 issue of *Massachusetts Review,* and the seventh book was published as *The Pastorals* (1972).

Though Rasula warns readers to be careful when entering the historical labyrinths of *The Common Shore,* Schelb sees the work as having a clear purpose and goal:

> In *The Common Shore,* Kelly confronts the breakdown of social order and the corresponding default of narrative forms. He perceives the present as a perpetual crisis – Vietnam, phantoms of the Civil War, the riots in Newark and Watts give the play of love and strife a murderous literalism. The nation for Kelly was like the sterile lands of chivalric romance, suffering from "the agonies of blind justice." The nature of democracy was in danger of forfeiture. . . . By constructing a form – or allowing a form to emerge – in which meaning can be generated as if beyond conscious intention, Kelly seeks a poetic methodology equal to the shifting patterns of history, patterns to be embodied in an incarnation of meaning.

The Common Shore offers healing through a reintegration with America's origins. For Kelly, though, the personal is the historical and the political as he seeks to combine his family's history with the history of the nation in a mythic descent into origins. Kelly seeks regeneration through language: "Only language heals the rift in order to 'settle our strife / & set home / over the whole span, groundlings again.'" The movement in the poem's first five books is from discord to a vision of a unified, redeemed America.

In writing *The Common Shore* Kelly discovered that what worked for Olson did not suit his own more open imagination, one that innately distrusted the temporal constraints of historical theory. Kelly's mythopoeic imagination, his ability to entertain multiple fictive approximations of "reality," functioned closer to that of Wallace Stevens. Kelly's

Kelly at work in 1988

imagination might also be likened to that of Percy Bysshe Shelley. Indeed, Kelly used Shelley's "Mont Blanc" some twenty-five years later in his vision of the same mountain in a poem of the same title.

Kelly produced four major collections of poetry from 1968 to 1973: *Finding the Measure, Kali Yuga* (1970), *Flesh: Dream: Book* (1971), and *The Mill of Particulars* (1973). He was also composing *The Loom* during his residency at the California Institute of Technology (1971–1972). This five-year period is certainly one of the most productive of Kelly's entire career and, because of the variety of the work, one of its richest.

Some critics consider *Finding the Measure* to be the book that most clearly articulates the movement of Kelly's poetics toward a linguistic basis. Rasula cites its "prefix" as the most definitive statement to date of the way Kelly has synthesized language, the poet, and the world into the poem:

Finding the measure is finding the mantram,
is finding the moon, as index of measure,
is finding the moon's source;
if that source
is Sun, finding the measure is finding
the natural articulation of ideas.

The enemy of the "natural articulation of ideas" is what Kelly calls "style" – the rigid adherence to proscribed ways of writing. Rejecting "the workshop poem" and the kind of highly polished artifacts that an artist becomes identified with, Kelly asserts, "Style is death. Finding the measure is finding / a freedom from that death, a way out, a movement / forward." Nothing will kill the creative spark more quickly than for a poet to fall into a style, a tradition validated by a past that impedes an open imagination from moving forward.

For Kelly, the poem is never a finished product; instead it is a process. What keeps the poet from falling into hopeless solipsism is that the poetic process is always grounded in the cycles of nature:

> Finding the measure is finding the
> specific music of the hour,
> the synchronous
> consequence of the motion of the whole world.

Rasula interprets Kelly's quest to find the measure as "a process of modulating the rhythms of both language and attention.... The measure thus found is a mode of tuning or attunement, as well as a mode of address."

Although *Finding the Measure* is full of zodiacal symbolism, cycles of Gnostic poems, and alchemical transformations, Christian figures, especially the suffering Christ, surface most frequently. The passional Christ elicits one of the major "findings" not only in this collection but in all of Kelly's work:

> in front
> of the agony of any being
> we are stupid mute
>
> what is important to each man
> he never says,
> never learns it till the light
> walks out of the sky
> & he is left
> alone with his failed utterance
> impossibly clear in the dark
>
> *write everything*
> the oracle said,
> . . . .
> let what is natural
> say what it can
>
> *what is not here*
> *is nowhere.*

Kelly does not conclude the poem in despair at the seeming insignificance of the human enterprise. Instead, he offers language as a redemptive agent that imbues life with meaning:

> for all we see we know nothing,
> our utterance alone makes
>
> something of this death[.]

These lines from "Last Light," one of the gems in this collection, perhaps offer a response, not a corrective, to Robert Duncan's opening poem in his *The Opening of the Field* (1960), titled "Often I Am Permitted to Return to a Meadow." Both poems are about the origins of the poetic process, and each

opens in a mythic meadow resembling the Garden of Adam Kadmon from the Cabala.

In its title *Flesh: Dream: Book* articulates the central trinity of sources for Kelly's complex mythopoesis. Glyn Pursglove sees the poem as explicating "'the three great sources of human information' named in the book's title. The flesh – the universe as accessible to sensual experience; the dream – the associations and fusions of dream and vision; the book – human learning. The excitement of Kelly's work, at best, is the effectiveness with which he integrates all these sources of 'information,' how the poetry refuses to exclude any of the three, and finds language and form for all."

In *The Mill of Particulars* Kelly descends into the labyrinths of language as it is enacted in painting, music, mythology, and architecture. In the book's "prefix" Kelly again explores the issues raised in his earlier "prefix" in *Finding the Measure*. In the first sentence Kelly affirms that "Language is the only genetics"; it is a

> Field
> 'in which a man is understood & understands'
> & becomes
> what he thinks,
> becomes what he says
> following the argument.

That "field" has become all fields of human inquiry and experience, even the baseball field in which Kelly places his "Centerfielder" from a poem of the same title. But that centerfielder is the poet trying to make sense out of the demythologized or fallen world of the twentieth century. The poet must, by the alchemical power of his imagination, transform that emptiness into a "Field of Flashing Lights" and restore the broken world:

> the image
> leaps & shatters
>
> & all that's left is you
>
> Enlarge this altar!

Nowhere does Kelly so clearly map out the task of poet-as-priest as he does in the poems of *The Mill of Particulars*. The poet is the maker of ways of envisioning "The World," the title of one of the collection's most important poems.

The poet makes the world whole, a word that shares the same etymological root with "holy." An illustration of the way Kelly sacramentalizes the world and acts as a thaumaturge is a long poem titled "A Book of Building," in which he gives significance to the banal images of famous buildings on the backs of American matchbook covers. Considering "such trivial things, such degraded images, as obligations," Kelly in his thirty-page serial poem turns the images of the Leaning Tower of Pisa, Big Ben, the Eiffel Tower, the Arc de Triomphe, and the Sphinx into meditations on the nature of architecture and how it re-creates orders and categories of perception and knowledge. The Leaning Tower "balances our attention" and reminds us humorously of Martin Luther's dictum: "we are not responsible for horizontal mistakes." The Eiffel Tower becomes the structure that's "the easiest / building for birds" while the Arc de Triomphe is transformed into

> a keyhole
> at the end of the street.
> Though I saw it
> I have little memory of the aperture
> just what I saw through it.

In the special summer 1974 issue of *Vort 5* devoted to Kelly, Christopher Wagstaff sees *The Mill of Particulars* as an attempt to continue the task of Ludwig Wittgenstein insofar as "Kelly appears to be concerned with discovering the true nature of objects and situations from a perspective outside of the objects and situations themselves." Wagstaff defines Kelly's concept of "measure" as an activity of "opening one up to the abundance of life and experience. . . . Like Pound, Kelly cannot accept the supposition that men lack the inner capacity to constructively shape and form their own experience. He affirms that the creative individual [the poet] essentially fashions his own environment out of the materials provided to him from the exalted moments of his own creative life." But Kelly does not believe that there must be a "holy" moment for this process to occur. With Walt Whitman, Kelly holds that all anyone has to do is to open his/her eyes and ears to the particulars that the Mill — the world — is eternally grinding out.

Kelly began writing *The Loom,* a 415-page poem that became the culmination of all of his work up to that time, while he was poet in residence at the California Institute of Technology: "In the fall of 1971, I turned thirty-six, thus in some literal sense outliving the predictions I had lived with since my childhood, that I would die at thirty-five. In the overwhelming gush of survival energy, I began *The Loom* and finished it, for the most part, in two months, sometimes composing (at the second-hand Olympia we had just bought) for twenty hours at a stretch." Part of the success of the poem is the

genius of its structure. Both long and large, *The Loom* could be accurately described as a sacramentalized hypertext. Because he uses the figure of a loom, Kelly is able to cross-weave or stitch together the warp of his autobiography with the woof of important spiritual and intellectual traditions. The structure of *The Loom* enables it to grow both vertically *and* horizontally simultaneously. He interweaves seeming dichotomies such as time and place, inside and outside, narrative and soliloquy, self and Other, knowing and being into a unified field of discourse that he defines in the poem's opening lines:

> To find a place
> to talk to you
> or find
> a talk
> to place you in,
> natural contexts
> growth & form
> fold, calm hands
> of a man
> hearing music,
> hears it
> as it is, fold & unfold, two rhythms two
> motions,
> place
> & talk.

Out of the weaving emerges the fabric of Kelly's life, since the poems he has spent his life writing are his "actual autobiography." *The Loom* is Kelly's version of Stevens's *Notes Towards a Supreme Fiction.*

The fabric and fabrication of *The Loom* — form and content become one process — are consonant with Kelly's perpetual quest to move to origins, not only his own, personal ones but the origins of poetic utterance. Some of the first Western European poetry came into being to enliven the routine of weaving, giving birth to the expression "spinning a yarn or tale." Also conversant with Eastern mythology and religions, Kelly would certainly have known that the Sanskrit word for *thread* is *sutra,* a word that comes to mean discourse, a series of aphorisms, or a continuous teaching (the *Kama Sutra* is a collection of sutras). Schelb provides a further analysis of these linguistic associations: "The image of the loom is in fact tantric — *tantra* means variously loom, web, discipline, as well as book and the way — and the poem's dominant melodic line is constructed of images of sexual release, the splendor of objects, and the eroticization of language." Kelly's proposition throughout the poem — especially during the construction of the Temple at the poem's magnificent conclusion — is to sacramentalize the re-

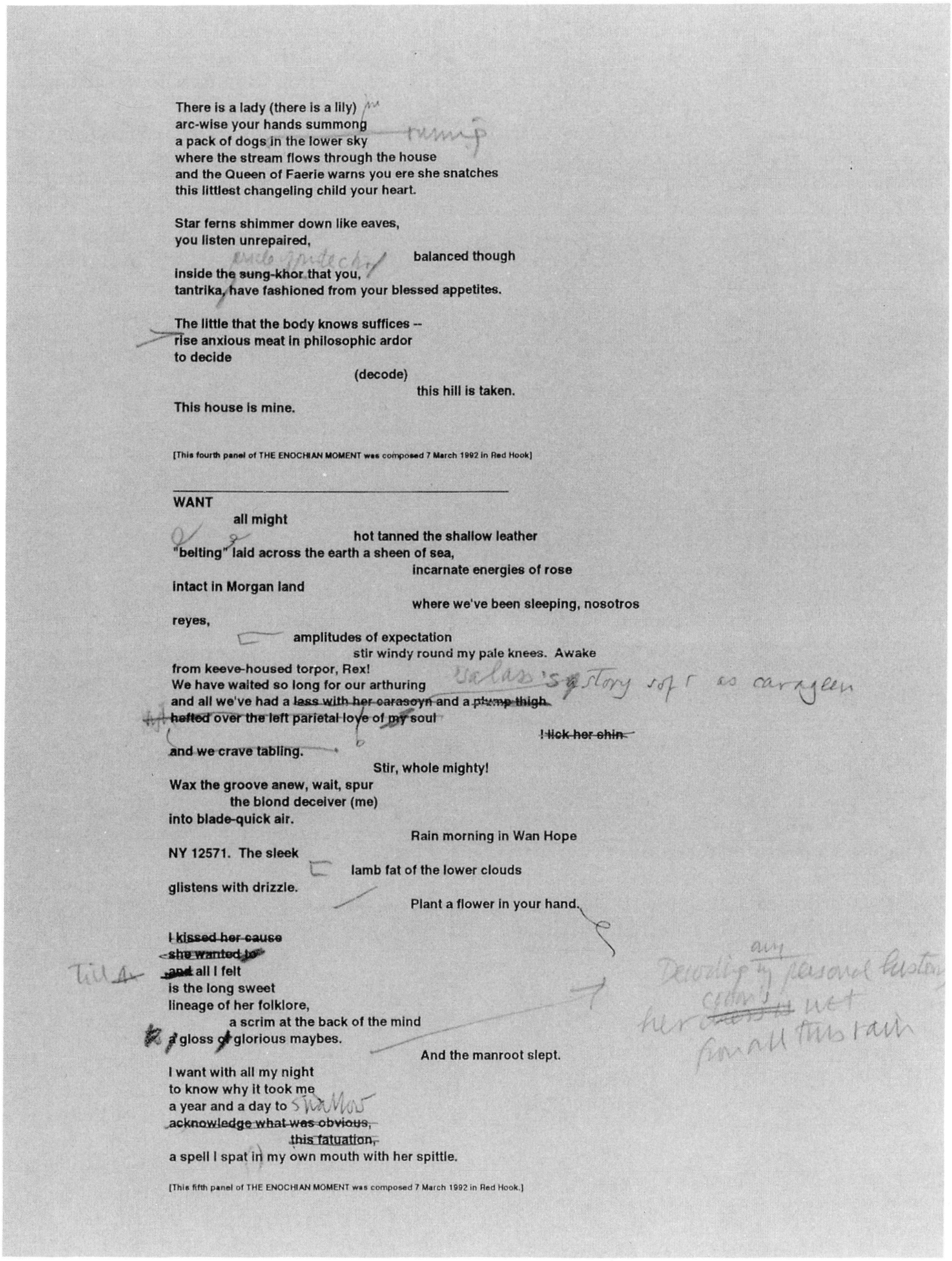

There is a lady (there is a lily)
arc-wise your hands summong
a pack of dogs in the lower sky
where the stream flows through the house
and the Queen of Faerie warns you ere she snatches
this littlest changeling child your heart.

Star ferns shimmer down like eaves,
you listen unrepaired,
balanced though
inside the sung-khor that you,
tantrika, have fashioned from your blessed appetites.

The little that the body knows suffices --
rise anxious meat in philosophic ardor
to decide
(decode)
this hill is taken.

This house is mine.

[This fourth panel of THE ENOCHIAN MOMENT was composed 7 March 1992 in Red Hook]

_____

WANT
all might
hot tanned the shallow leather
"belting" laid across the earth a sheen of sea,
incarnate energies of rose
intact in Morgan land
where we've been sleeping, nosotros
reyes,
amplitudes of expectation
stir windy round my pale knees. Awake
from keeve-housed torpor, Rex!
We have waited so long for our arthuring
and all we've had a lass with her carasoyn and a plump thigh
hefted over the left parietal love of my soul
I lick her chin
and we crave tabling.
Stir, whole mighty!
Wax the groove anew, wait, spur
the blond deceiver (me)
into blade-quick air.
Rain morning in Wan Hope
NY 12571. The sleek
lamb fat of the lower clouds
glistens with drizzle.
Plant a flower in your hand.

I kissed her cause
she wanted to
and all I felt
is the long sweet
lineage of her folklore,
a scrim at the back of the mind
gloss of glorious maybes.
And the manroot slept.
I want with all my night
to know why it took me
a year and a day to
acknowledge what was obvious,
this fatuation,
a spell I spat in my own mouth with her spittle.

[This fifth panel of THE ENOCHIAN MOMENT was composed 7 March 1992 in Red Hook.]

Draft for a section of "The Enochian Momet," 7 March 1992 (courtesy of the author)

curring image of the "table," or place of conversation, into an "altar," or place of communion.

The structure of *The Loom* is neither a journey nor a calendar; nor is it a chronology or a sequence; it is not linear, cyclic, or circular. It is, rather, a field of fields, modeled somewhat on the Visionary Recitals of Avicenna in which Kelly employs the Arabic concept of *ta'wil,* a Sufi technique of reading that carries the soul back to its origins. For Kelly origins always mean, as George Quasha observes in the *Vort 5* special issue, language events or events in consciousness. The structure of *The Loom* is built on recitals of visionary events in consciousness that Kelly elaborates throughout its thirty-six sections.

Kelly's cantos invoke such figures as Siegfried, Theseus, Odysseus, Arjuna, the Dogon wise man Ogotemmêli, Kore, Kali, Christ, and the Blessed Virgin Mary. The most important mythic figure is Hephaistos, the lame god of the Underworld who tends the alchemic furnace Athanor, out of which change may come. The poem culminates in the building of a vast Orphic Temple and altar, where an oracular skull-self speaks to the seeker, the words revivifying the wasteland desert. The grail-loom regenerates Eden by the sacramental power of the imagination. Dante's "Rosa Mystica" in Kelly's poem becomes "small, very bright red" flowers upon which he walks to "get to the well." The vast poem ends at a well, the source of the Gnostic and Hermetic wisdom traditions that *The Loom* celebrates.

In his 1978 collection *The Convections* Kelly continues his search for clarity and purpose. The poems treat such mythological figures as Orpheus and Persephone as well as eighteenth-century philosophical and scientific personages such as Edmund Burke and Isaac Newton. The volume also contains intermittent discussions of his changing poetics woven through some of the poems. In "Purity," for example, the poet defines the poem in terms of its reader:

> For years I hated Lot's wife, who was the Reader
> Looking Back through the Text. The woman reliving
> her memories. Rereading the poem
>
> It must come to this: the line becomes line, as the
> Word becomes Flesh
> . . . .
> A line is the breath's take on the heart's grasp of the
> senses' senses, burnt up in an instant on the altar of
> the poem.

The title poem shows Kelly's understanding of poems as "convections," acts or processes of trans-

ferring energy, specifically heat, which for Kelly always suggests passion and love and anger. Though many of the poems are dedicated to Helen, Kelly's relationship with his wife was falling apart. The couple divorced in 1977.

The failure of his second marriage may have led Kelly to reconsider his depiction of idealized love and woman in his poetry. The knowledge that such love could really only exist within the fictive realm of the poet's imagination is evident in his rich collection *Kill the Messenger Who Brings Bad News* (1979). In the poem "The Queen of Between" the women are clearly of the imagination:

> Women
> of within
> from dream
> I call them
> roses
>
> of an inner
>
> springtime
> . . . .
> they are
> interior
> commissars
> of every order
> whose summons
> is this caress.

Archetypal women, however, continue to surface in the poems. They appear as versions of Beatrician mediators or Parisian women of the night in one of the gems of this collection, "Women of the Bois de Boulogne."

Although Kelly was moving toward Buddhism at this time, several poems in *Kill the Messenger Who Brings Bad News* concern themselves with the Virgin Mary, including "Six Marian Hymns" and "Queen of Heaven Variations." Kelly also seems to be trying to make sense of the Christ presence; that figure recurs throughout this collection, especially in "The Agony in the Garden," "Easter," "INRI," and "The Dismembered." The opening poem, "East River," perhaps provides an apt metaphor for Kelly's imagination during this transitional period. The river is transformed into a goddess who contains the multiple texts of Kelly's life: "He could remember / when he was a child he prayed to it." *Kill the Messenger Who Brings Bad News* won the prestigious *Los Angeles Times* prize for the best book of poetry for the year 1979.

Spiritual Exercises was published in 1981, the year Kelly became a Buddhist. By taking the title of Saint Ignatius of Loyola's sixteenth-century master-

MAN SLEEPING

for Charlotte

He had been sleeping for an hour and the ocean changed

he had been dreaming towers and the sand stretched west

trying to ~~engage~~ *enlist* him in one more continent.

Elephants and equipoise. ~~Entrain.~~ *Marker towers, minarets.*

~~They wanted him to be England, they wanted his France.~~

They wanted his sleeve full of doves

~~and~~ his desires *must be* ~~to be as~~ delicate as frog spawn

dry in the noon time heat.

He wanted nothing of what they wanted of him,

slept again like the barque *Unparalleled*

ran aground off this shoaly island

full of bibles and Dutch cheese *and gaberdine.*

Red skulls of it wedged in rocks for weeks

till gulls and weather woke him

reeling from the Carpenter's embrace

—whose tongue was talking so fast in his mouth?—

am I wood or water? Shanks of maple,

hips of seaside roses, he was heaven.

A woman reading close to color of jute. A color of buys.

And woke some more. Mostly fire.

Mostly air. Air was first of all

elements, the moving *will* before somethingness.

Mornings before a single man has gone to work—

he woke and woke, a few things *almost* clear.

There is no creator, though a Making Spirit

Draft for the beginning of a long poem Kelly included in his 1995 collection (courtesy of the author)

piece for his own, Kelly suggests his focus. He addresses his Jesuit education (Saint Ignatius founded the Jesuits) and, by extension, the entire Christian substructure upon which his life and work had been built. While not rejecting Roman Catholicism, Kelly moves away from its structure and strictures and tries to understand the meaning of spirituality in other contexts and traditions. In a sense he is exorcising the harmful Christian influences so that he may more fully exercise his own spiritual powers. The etymological root of the words *exercise* and *exorcise* is the same, but as the words developed *exercise* came to mean expanding one's inner spiritual energy while *exorcise* came to mean expelling demonic energies from the soul. Only with Kelly's movement toward a much older spiritual tradition, Buddhism, was he able to place his formative Catholic education and influences in their proper perspective and free himself from the guilt and self-abnegation that so frequently stifle the imaginations of Catholic authors.

Two long poems from *Spiritual Exercises* stand out as indicators of new directions for Kelly. The speaker in "Sentence" submits to the voice of the text and lets the wisdom of language guide the imagination. "The Emptying" is an experiment in what Kelly calls polysyntaxis – a combining of the many possibilities of utterance that an emptying of self permits. The poem works in a manner analogous to and imitative of orthodox Christian *kenosis* in which Christ empties himself of his divine form by becoming man and suffering death. The priest-poet now "bends to drink / chaliced in eternal emptying / self into no-self till the sound / we are empties out into his hands." Each of Kelly's later books moves even further away from the egoistic poetry of private complaint that had dominated American poetry for more than thirty years.

At the end of 1981 Kelly needed a change: "beginning to be tired of what had begun to look like persistent patterns of greed and aggression in what I thought was my innocent behavior, I took refuge in the Buddha, Dharma, and Sangha." He traveled to India, returned to America, and began working with the spiritual guides Kalu Rinpoche and Lama Norlha. The particular tradition of Buddhism that Kelly practices is called tantric, a belief foreshadowed in *The Loom* ten years earlier. The connection is clear in Kelly's explanation of the term: "tantra means continuity. At root, the word means something like loom, and the seamless continuity of what is woven. The Tibetan word is clearer: *rgyud,* the thread, the line, the lineage, the continuity."

Possibly because of the serenity that Buddhism brought to him, Kelly in the poems in *Under Words* (1983), as in *Spiritual Exercises,* seems more free to move in different directions than his earlier poems. There is considerable playfulness in *Under Words,* especially in prose-poems such as "The Nature of Metaphor" and "Detective Story." Consistent with his desire to dig under everything, Kelly admitted that he wanted to explore in these pieces "what lay beneath . . . the things I said and meant and used . . . to build poems." The volume documents his interest in "spiritual etymology, to lead the word back – but not now to some Indo-European root, but to its root in my experience, mind in action, tree in the world. Words are narratives intact in themselves, and all the narrations and sequences here (more story-prone than before in my work) unpack the primal narrative each word tacitly persists in laying before me." The book is a journey to what Kelly calls "my personal underworld," and his aim is to "report the word I heard there." One of the volume's longest poems is "Postcards from the Underworld," a charming narrative that echoes somewhat Stevens's "A Postcard from the Volcano." Kelly's poem carefully and at times humorously creates a vaguely familiar mythopoeic world, one drawn from the myths of several cultures, not just Judeo-Christian ones. Kelly acknowledges an indebtedness to "Starobinski's account of Saussure's long, subtle studies of anagrams in Lucretius and Virgil, *Les Mots sous les Mots.*"

In 1985 Kelly met Mary Moore Goodlett, with whom he worked and lived till her death in 1990. Her effect on him was profound: "As a fourteenth generation American from Kentucky, she made me, somehow, more American than I knew I could be." In 1986 Kelly received an award for distinction from the American Academy and Institute of Arts and Letters. The citation recognized Kelly's work both in poetry and fiction, which he had begun to publish with some regularity in the 1980s.

In *Not This Island Music* (1987) and *A Strange Market* (1992) Kelly gathers together many varied poems, and as collections they do not seem to have identities as distinct as do books such as *Spiritual Exercises* or *Kill the Messenger Who Brings Bad News.* In major long poems from the 1987 collection such as "The Man Who Loved White Chocolate," "Anything Naturally Its Opposite," and "A Language" Kelly uses language as both subject and form in portraying his Blakean visions. Gertrude Stein mixes with Wallace Stevens and Ludwig Wittgenstein in the comic probing of these poems into how words create realities and the ecstasy that consciousness of that process produces.

The opening poem of *Not This Island Music,* "Vampire," and the epilogue of the volume, "To the Reader (2)," suggest the range in style and substance as well as something of the evolution of Kelly's poetics. The poet-as-vampire in the opening poem comically defines Kelly's relationship with language and the things of the world in sacramental terms:

How can he make his move among these sacraments?
So language is in permanent détente
always with gleaming fangs
scared of its proper meat. The virgin neck of things
persists to lure me. That
is my Europe and my Orient
. . . .
I make my prey
into a word I can speak.

In "To the Reader (2)" Kelly develops a kind of biopoesis after that articulated by poet–molecular biologist Harvey Bialy in the 1970s: "For the benefit of all, not just the talker, the poem shapes itself in syllables, breath patterns, deep metabolic rhythms it borrows from the writer – signal of what is personal (body) transcending itself into what is sharing, shared. . . . Then the musical powers of syntax, all our listening, line structure, sound begin to act: the poem. A poem is activity, a nest of deeds which reader and writer share, transpersonal, unpossessed. . . . My obscurations are my wisdoms. My needs are my permissions. What I hear is sacred: in one ear and out the mouth." The culmination of Kelly's lean toward biopoesis is the brilliant long poem "The Physiology of William Blake" that appeared in *Conjunctions 21* in 1993. Kelly anatomizes Blake in terms of the geography of England and the human body in ways similar to James Joyce's mapping of Finn MacCool in *Finnegans Wake* (1939) as both the mythic and geographic body of Ireland.

Kelly calls the period between 1988 through 1990 the years of sickness and death, for he lost Robert Duncan; his teacher Kalu Rinpoche; his first wife, Joby; his companion Mary Goodlett; and both his mother and father. *A Strange Market* reflects Kelly's personal concerns, moving away from the ecstatic celebrations of *Not This Island Music* into darker, more serious work. "In the Light," the opening and greatest poem in the collection, provides a Stevens-and-Whitman-like panoptic cataloguing of every conceivable kind of light. But Kelly descends to near despair in "A Baltic Tragedy." There is a firmer balancing and recovery in "Studying Horses" and the poems in the section "Afterdeath."

A human form of light and love came to Kelly with his marriage on 3 June 1993 to Charlotte Mandell, a writer, translator of French, and fellow music devotee. As a result of Kelly's regularly spending time with his wife in southeastern France, Kelly has written one of his greatest poems, *Mont Blanc* (1994). In many ways the forty-five-page, thirty-four-stanza poem is a culmination of every long poem he has ever written. It goes beyond culmination, though, for Kelly's work joins Shelley's "Mont Blanc" in its recognition of what constitutes the sublime and maps new directions for the poet's imagination. Kelly's *Mont Blanc* is built upon Shelley's poem and is faithful to its every word. On the page following the title page, Kelly writes: "Inscribed in the spaces of Shelley's 'Mont Blanc.'"

Nowhere has Kelly taken so seriously his own proposition that "Language is the only genetics." Kelly's poem resembles technically the way Guy Davenport "writes over" or interscribes every word of Franz Kafka's first published newspaper article, "The Aeroplanes of Brescia," transforming it into his own story of the same title fifty years later. However, *Mont Blanc* also participates in William Wordsworth's "vast ventriloquism" by becoming Kelly's version of "Tintern Abbey," which along with Shelley's "Mont Blanc" became definitive articulations of the relationship of the imagination to the objects of its attention.

Echoes of many of the major English and American Romantic poets resonate in Kelly's line "Only by voice with nature reconciled / we stand our ground," but he develops a postmodern gloss of the sentiment: "as if there is (there is) a kind of knowing / impossible except when being said." Kelly gives the mountain a voice that directs the poet to "Come speak me" and whose utterance, then, speaks the poet also. Stevens's great, late poem "The Rock" – another homage to Shelley's "Mont Blanc" – resonates within Kelly's poem in that both poets reinvent linguistic avenues into the "holy" that go beyond the limiting theological strictures of Western organized religion. In both Stevens's and Kelly's worlds words do more than record meaning: they create it. The poet's words reach

all the way
to the bottom of perceiving – these words
mute meaning. In the lone glare of sound
we almost sense. In day we snow. Descend
further and the crystalline conversation
fuses to amorphous glaze.

As he has often done before, Kelly uses alchemy as a metaphor for the creative process but also redefines as clearly as he ever has what measure is: "There is only one measure. We are it." The act of poetic transformation in and of itself creates significance by the power of its articulated attention. The poet "minds out loud" – conjoins perception and mind "in the eye's mind" – by means of language and generates the poem capable of redeeming us from the vacancy of solipsistic despair. Extending his formulation of the major office of the poet from *In Time* – "THE DISCOVERER OF RELATION, / redintegrator, / explorer of ultimate connection . . . for our use / at-one-ing / the world" – Kelly in *Mont Blanc* offers his most comprehensive proposition to date concerning the healing power of the imagination fusing the mind and the world through language.

The spring of 1995 saw the publication of *Red Actions: Selected Poems 1960–1993,* a four-hundred-page selection from thirty-two collections. A year before, on 21 May 1994, the State University of New York at Oneonta awarded Kelly the honorary degree of doctor of letters for the richness of his contribution to the body of contemporary American literature. Guy Davenport, one of American literature's most respected writers and critics, commented on the significance of Kelly's accomplishment:

> Like Valéry, he fills volumes of notebooks. He has published a shelf of books. He gets a lifetime of work into a year. He has Picasso's energy and fertility of invention. . . . No American poet except perhaps Wallace Stevens has his sense of balance in a line. . . . Such skill frees his mind to meditate, to think, to play. . . . What Eliot and Pound slaved over Kelly seems to have an innate gift for balancing out. . . . He turns a subject with grace and delicacy, as if he must be careful not to smash it with the lover's touch – paintings, flowers, a woman's voluptuousness, glass, fruit, things that bruise, break, or withdraw if handled roughly. . . . You do not read a Kelly poem, you dance it. He is the most musical poet of our time except Zukofsky, from whom he must have

learned that the language in a poem treads a measure as prime duty.

There is little question that Kelly belongs in the august company of poets such as Charles Olson and Robert Duncan. His voice, like theirs, possesses an authority derived from his consistent and devoted efforts to explore the process of language probing itself for its deepest and most profound truths.

Interviews:

David Ossman, *The Sullen Art* (New York: Corinth, 1963), pp. 33–38;

Dennis Barone, "Nothing but Doors: An Interview with Robert Kelly," *Credences,* 3 (Fall 1985): 100–122;

Bradford Morrow, "An Interview with Robert Kelly," *Conjunctions,* 13 (1989): 137–166.

References:

Paul Christensen, *Minding the Underworld: Clayton Eshleman & Late Postmodernism* (Santa Rosa, Cal.: Black Sparrow, 1991), pp. 10, 33–38;

Patrick H. Meanor, "Robert Kelly: An American Thaumaturge," *Threshold,* 34 (Winter 1983/ 1984): 26–32;

Jed Rasula, "Ten Different Fruits on One Different Tree: Reading Robert Kelly," *Credences,* 3 (Spring 1984): 127–175;

Edward N. Schelb, "*Mirroring an Altogether Different Set of Lights*": *The Early Poetry of Robert Kelly* (N.p., 1994);

Vort, special issue on Kelly, 5 (Summer 1974).

Papers:

Most of Kelly's journals, correspondence, and manuscripts are in the Lockwood Memorial Library at the State University of New York at Buffalo. Some early manuscripts are at Kent State University. Letters to Charles Olson are in the Robert Kelly File at the University of Connecticut.

Li-Young Lee

(19 August 1957 –   )

Ruth Y. Hsu
University of Hawaii

BOOKS: *Rose* (Brockport, New York: BOA Editions, 1986);

The City in Which I Love You (Brockport, New York: BOA Editions, 1990);

The Winged Seed: A Remembrance (New York: Simon & Schuster, 1995).

Gerald Stern, in his foreword to *Rose,* describes Li-Young Lee's poetry as having "the large vision, the deep seriousness and the almost heroic ideal, reminiscent more of John Keats, Rainer Maria Rilke and perhaps Theodore Roethke than William Carlos Williams on the one hand or T. S. Eliot on the other." Lee lists among his influences such writers as John Keats, Robert Frost, Emily Dickinson, Walt Whitman, Bruno Schulz, Emily Brontë, Cynthia Ozick, Li Bai, Tu Fu, Su Tung Po, and Yang Wan Li.

Critical reaction to Lee's collections has been favorable. One reviewer wrote in the *Bloomsbury Review* that *Rose* "was created by a young voice whose fire is only beginning to burn." Another reviewer for the *Pennsylvania Review* observed, "Here is a poet unafraid of exceeding tenderness, and agile enough to walk the tightrope between anger and fear." Of Lee's second book, *The City in Which I Love You* (1990), Pat Monaghan wrote in *Booklist* (1 October 1990) that Lee's poetry had a "rare emotional intensity . . . whose passion mounts to incendiary pitch. But he's a philosophic poet, too, asking profound questions." David Daniel in the *Harvard Book Review* describes Lee's book as "a powerful, often ecstatic pursuit of a background . . . against which what he has to say has its meaning."

Lee's poetry has already attracted much attention. In the December 1990 meeting of the Modern Language Association in Chicago, he, Kyoto Mori, and David Mura were the featured writers of the Asian American Reading Group. Since then, Lee's standing among the Asian American and the larger American writing community has continued to grow. His work is admired because of its intensity

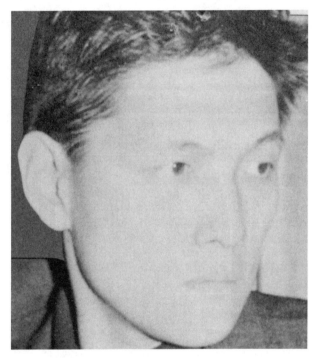

Li-Young Lee

and power, and because it represents so well the aspirations and concerns of post-1965 Asian Americans. The Asian immigrants arriving on United States shores as a result of the 1965 immigration reforms come from a multitude of distinct cultures, so that today the term Asian American can include Laotians, Indonesians, Vietnamese, Thai, Hmong, Indians, Sri Lankans, and Chinese from Hong Kong or Taiwan, as well as those from traditional immigrant countries such as Korea and China. Lee's poetry reflects the new reality of a global power structure developed and perpetuated by transnational capital. The "philosophy" that Lee ponders in his writing explores the question of individual identity in a world where vast numbers of people have been uprooted from ancestral cultures but are not totally accepted in their adopted lands. In a sense Lee's poetry is about the desire to establish boundaries in a world where some boundaries – such as a nation's – no longer exist; it is also about discovering where his father's identity ends and his own begins; it is about locating his cultural and artistic lineage.

Li-Young Lee was born 19 August 1957 in Jakarta, Indonesia, to Richard K. Y. Lee and Joice Yuan Jiaying. Richard Lee was a personal physician to Mao Zedong in China before leaving for Indonesia, where he helped found Gamaliel University, a small college in Jakarta. He was a professor of English and philosophy at Gamaliel until his arrest in 1958 by then-dictator President Sukarno during a wave of government-sponsored, anti-Chinese agitation. In 1959 he and his family escaped from Indonesia, embarking on a five-year trek through Hong Kong, Macau, and Japan, arriving finally in the United States in 1964. According to Jessica Greenbaum, writing in the 7 October 1991 issue of *The Nation*, Richard Lee became a "Presbyterian minister in a tiny Pennsylvanian town, full of rage and mystery and pity, blind and silent at the end." He died in 1980.

Li-Young Lee attended Kiski Area High School in Vandergrift, Pennsylvania; the Universities of Pittsburgh (1975–1979) and Arizona (1979–1980); and the State University of New York at Brockport (1980–1981). He has taught at several universities, including Northwestern and the University of Iowa. *Rose*, his first book of poetry, won New York University's Delmore Schwartz Memorial Poetry Award in 1986. *The City in Which I Love You* was the 1990 Lamont Poetry Selection of the Academy of American Poets. Other honors and awards include grants from the Illinois Arts Council, the Commonwealth of Pennsylvania, the Pennsylvania Council on the Arts, and the National Endowment for the Arts. In 1987 Lee received a Ludwig Vogelstein Foundation fellowship, followed the next year by a Writer's Award from the Mrs. Giles Whiting Foundation. Lee has appeared with Bill Moyers in the PBS series *The Power of the Word*. In 1989 Lee won a fellowship from the prestigious Guggenheim Foundation. He currently lives in Chicago, Illinois, with Donna, his wife, and their two children. They were married on 25 November 1978.

Several issues recur in Lee's poetry, namely his sense of being part of a vast, global Chinese diaspora; his desire to understand and accept his father, whom he both loves and fears; and his identity's dimensions and textures, at least to the extent that those can be garnered from his relation to words, to the sensual, to love and passion. These themes often merge, informing each other, so that,

while it is possible to delineate distinct issues that the poet returns to time and again, any attempt to place his work in strict, impermeable, thematic categories is to ignore the fact that individual poems are often a synthesis of multiple and varied life experiences. A poem on the rose is also a poem about the family and about a fearful past; a poem about persimmons flows seamlessly into a desire for the presence of the father. Gerald Stern, in his preface to *Rose*, describes Lee's poetry as "a search for wisdom and understanding." If so, the poetry also reveals a passionate wish to make language, as Lee has said, "say the unsayable," a wish that sometimes results in startling images. For example, in his poem to the prosaic indigo, he writes, "It's late. I've come / to find the flower which blossoms / like a saint lying upside down." Lee's writing is a searching for answers – to the past, to his father, to the forces that drive his work. If this desire to plumb profound depths infuses his work with a contemplative tone, it can also imprint his poems with a childlike perplexity and wonderment about life and its strange twists.

"Epistle," the first poem in *Rose*, sets the tone for the collection. The short, three-line stanzas are a counterpoint to the poem's topic – painful childhood memories that the adult speaker remembers and now tries to understand. Wisely, the adult knows that true wisdom is beyond attainment so he begins the poem lightly enough, with the humble disavowal: "Of wisdom, splendid columns of light / waking sweet foreheads, / I know nothing." Neither does he hope for "daydreams / Of a world without end." Instead, what this speaker remembers is that as a boy he heard "the sound of weeping / coming from some other room of his father's house." The boy notices the noon sunlight and "how the monotonous sobs resembled laughter," while realizing fully that the sounds were not laughter. The description of the noon sunlight in his room ironically echoes the idea in the first stanza: of wisdom, of "splendid columns of light," he knows nothing. However, Lee's evocation of light and shadow not only expresses artistic considerations but it also clearly illustrates the Christian influences on his writing. His reference to "columns of light" is a reminder of Paul in the New Testament, who, after being struck and blinded by a shaft of divine light, came to "see" the godly nature of Jesus Christ. Notably, the poem is titled "Epistle." However, in this modern world devoid of miracles, the grief that the young boy hears is incomprehensible, composed of the silence of an otherwise sleeping house and an unmoving clock, interposed with memories of shadows that delineate the light in a "vaulted room." Still, the boy is surely father to the man, because somehow the speaker has gleaned from those boyhood remembrances the "wisdom" contained in that hour when "the sun grew terrible, the clock stopped, / and melancholy gave up to grief." Because in that suspended hour, in images seared into the child's mind, the grown man comes to learn that wisdom often contains paradox, that

> It is not heavenly and it is not sweet.
> It is accompanied by steady human weeping,
> and twin furrows between the brows.

Similarly, "My Indigo" shows the poet envisioning profound worlds in the most negligible and unremarkable of occurrences and everyday objects. Instead of a shaft of light recalling painful memories, Lee sees "a saint lying upside down" in the small indigo. "My Indigo" reminds one of William Wordsworth, another poet who contemplates nondescript flowers. However, if Lee has any intention of evoking a quintessentially romantic poem such as "The Daffodils," he does so only with a sense of irony, because what this poet sees in the indigo is a part of nature that is the exact opposite of the bright, yellow flowers in Wordsworth's poem. This little blue flower is "the moody one, the shy one / downcast, grave, and isolated." "Blackness" gathers where it grows. Just as strikingly, the speaker sees the blossom as sensual, primal: "vaginal and sweet / you unfurl yourself shamelessly / toward the ground." In another poem the sensuality of irises takes a slightly different form. For the speaker, the flowers in "Irises" carry the imprint of a woman, who "lay by them awhile, / then woke, rose, went." The tenderness implied in those lines is contrasted in the next stanza by an image that often recurs in this collection, the image of one frantic to know, to possess the essence "of their beauty and indifference." The speaker will "tear these petals with [his] teeth," because "I'd like to investigate these hairy selves . . . They hold / their breath all their lives / and open, open." Again, as in "My Indigo," a flower is not simply a flower but calls up in the speaker a desire to possess life's secrets, to know the logic behind paradox — "we waken dying." The speaker's contemplation of the irises itself contains a paradox, for even while life — "thought and desire" — expires, he still wishes to know what makes an iris an iris, its living essence.

Lee's writing often displays this capacity to call up and interweave, always from the simplest objects, painful or happy memories, musings about his father or the past, and to make the association of object and profound yearnings seem natural. In "Always a Rose," with his usual ability to draw attention to the paradoxes of life, the poet describes how the rose, that "doomed, profane" and also "Odorous and tender" flower, marks his life, reminding him of his arrivals and departures, of lying next to his wife, of a loved one "dragging her steel hip" — "Always a rose for her" — as well as of the brother who "inherited / worm-eaten rose / of his brain, rose / of ruin in his poor life." Most striking in this poem are the strong feelings that the rose invokes in him of his father, a major influence in his life, a figure who occurs often in his poetry. To the poet, his father will always be "one I love," one for whom he feels great sadness and sympathy for his being "exiled from one republic and daily defeated in another" and one "who was shunned by brothers and stunned by God, / who couldn't sleep because of voices." The tenderness for the father is echoed in poems such as "Water" and "Eating Together." In the former, the poet hears splashing water in the swaying of pine trees and recalls the time when

> The sound of washing
> is the sound of sighing,
> is the only sound
> as I wash my father's feet —
> those lonely twins
> who have forgotten one another.

As the son ministers to the father, he remembers how the latter endured torture at the hands of a vengeful victor: "1949, he's 30 years old, / his toenails pulled out, / his toes beaten a beautiful / violet that reminds him of Hunan, barely morning." In "Rain Diary" the poet writes about his father's "sleepless nights and stories / of camps where his spit turned to blood." The son remembers the "rocking ship" and the "melancholy of trains" as the family fled from country to country in the wake of political upheaval in China and oppression in Indonesia. In recounting his father's suffering, the poet apparently feels both sadness for what he had endured as well as respect for his father's strength in the face of such hardships. "Eating Together" was apparently written after the father's death. Lee's love and feelings of tenderness for the father have turned into a yearning for one who will not return. The poem describes the mother, sister, and brothers preparing lunch — a trout, steamed the Cantonese way, with ginger, onions, and sesame oil. However, having the family together, and the elaborate preparations themselves, remind the poet that the father is no longer with them, because one day "he lay

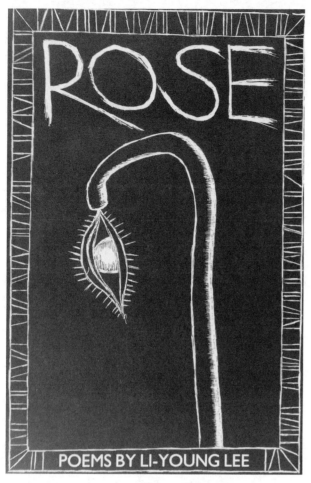

Dust jacket for Lee's first book, which includes several poems about his father, a man he both loved and feared (courtesy of the Poetry Collection, State University of New York, Buffalo)

tains a wish for some sign of affection from the father, a wish that the father could have said, "Forgive me. Why do I die? Hold me, hold me." In "Mnemonic," the son's admiration for the father is evident; he fears that his father will be ashamed of him for lacking his orderly, logical mind, for not being the man his father was. To the poet, his mind contains memories that are

> . . . a heap
> of details, uncatalogued, illogical.
> For instance:
> God was lonely, so he made me.
> My father loved me. So he spanked me.
> It hurt him to do so. He did it daily.

The father's perceived brilliance is evidently a burden to the son; yet, the pressure that comes from feeling that he must live up to another's unattainable standard is often tempered by the enduring memories of a father's tenderness and love. Thus, although the poet often remembers his father as a hard man, he also knows him as capable of sweetness. In "Mnemonic," Lee writes: "I was cold once. So my father took off his blue sweater, / He wrapped me in it. . . ." And in "Early in the Morning," the poet, with moving simplicity, describes his father's love for his mother. The most significant poem about his father's capacity to love is "The Gift," in which Lee credits his father for teaching him tenderness and love. Lee's feelings toward his father – strong and contradictory – are best represented by these lines from "Always a Rose":

> My father the Godly, he was the chosen.
> My father almighty, full of good fear.
> My father exhausted, my beloved.
> My father among the roses and thorns.
> My father rose, my father thorn.

In *Rose* Lee reveals a diasporic consciousness that is frequently inextricably woven into the memories and feelings he holds for his father and the rest of the family. The sense of uprootedness, loss, the vague yearning for a return to some lost existence is sometimes the overt topic of his poetry; at other times, a sadness from some unspecified source pervades his work. "Rain Diary" is a lyrical poem that seeks to honor the father by honoring the suffering he underwent as an exile from his native China, forced to live as a stranger in a foreign land. The rain in the night reminds him of another time when rain had marked their lives: "Where did the rain go? . . . / Straight down / to my father / in his boat, with a lamp." Rain also marked the family's stay in Pittsburgh in 1964, under a leaky roof, and

down / to sleep like a snow-covered road / winding through pines older than him, / without any travelers, and lonely for no one."

The poet reveals emotions, however, that are never simply of one dimension. Hence, his love for his father is laced with fear and awe. In "Always a Rose," for example, the father is one who has great power, who "put his hand on my crown and purified me / in the name of the Father, of the Son, and of the Holy Ghost." The poet also remembers a father who struck his children, who grew angry and told him that he no longer was welcome in his father's home. Lee's poetry is painful to read at times because so much of it is about pain. Yet, as one reviewer has noted, the honesty with which Lee tells "what I know" is an indelible characteristic of his writing. He seemingly hides little, revealing even his aching desire for the love and approval of a father reticent about displays of affection. In "Always a Rose" the poet's love for his father also con-

"his father leaning / into his own hands." When his father died, everything was "perforated by rain." The last two stanzas of "Rain Diary" contain some of the most compelling lines of the poem:

Rain falls and does not
break. Neither does it stop, but just pulls up
the gangplank and is gone . . .
Rain knocks at my door and
I open. No one
is there, and the rain marching in place.

The sadness that is part of the exile's existence is powerfully rendered in "I Ask My Mother to Sing." The grandmother joins in the mother's song about old China, and this singing is the only way that the poet will ever come close to regaining a sense of what the China of his parents was. He "loves to hear it sung; / how the waterlilies fill with rain until / they overturn, spilling into water, / then rock back, and fill with more." And although the poet recalls how both women cried at the song, neither stopped their singing, because those memories, painful though they are, are often all that they have of the past.

The poet's understanding of the exile's experience derives from more than his parents' lives. In "Persimmons," a poem widely anthologized, he recounts how his sixth-grade teacher, Mrs. Walker, slapped the back of his hand and banished him to a corner of the classroom for failing to differentiate *persimmon* from *precision, fight* from *fright, wren* from *yarn.* The sixth-grade teacher thus constructs him as the outsider, the one who lacks the native's "natural" grasp of the language. She pronounces him inferior because he cannot mimic exactly his classmates' accent or place words in reproductions of "proper" English sentences. Nevertheless, the boy understands at a far more fundamental and significant level the difference between *fright* and *fight:* "Fight was what I did when I was frightened, / Fright was what I felt when I was fighting." As for persimmons, the teacher shows an unripe persimmon to the class, calling it a "Chinese apple," while, with great precision, the poet describes how one would know that a persimmon is ripe, how one would savor its fragrance and meat, "so sweet, / all of it, to the heart," and how *persimmon* means more than simply fruit. Persimmons can also be, for the poet, as he contemplates the painting of persimmons that his father did after he became blind, that which is "swelled, heavy as sadness, / and sweet as love." Those persimmons measure a profounder precision, as the father tells the son:

Oh, the feel of the wolftail on the silk,
the strength, the tense
precision in the wrist. . . .
Some things never leave a person:
scent of the hair of the one you love,
the texture of persimmons,
in your palm, the ripe weight.

Lee's second collection, *The City in Which I Love You,* was honored as the Lamont Poetry Selection of the Academy of American Poets for 1990. This collection contains works that evince a remarkable sense of peace and stillness, such as "Goodnight," "Waiting," and "A Final Thing" – poems about his love for his wife and son. Nevertheless, Lee's preoccupation remains his attempt to deal with a life marked by profound loss, including the loss that scarred his father's life. These poems are filled with intense passion, but passion born of suffering and the realization that life sometimes permits no return from exile.

In the first group is "Goodnight," which begins with a haunting sense of stillness: "You've stopped whispering / and are asleep. I go on listening / to apples drop in the grass / beyond the window." It ends with a sense of peace as well:

. . . Now
I no longer hear the apples fall. But how

they go! Incessantly, though
with no noise, no

blunt announcements of their gravity.
See!

There is no bottom to the night, no end
to our descent.
We suffer each other to have each other a while.

This silent communion with the son asleep beside him reminds the poet of another father's love for the son and the son's love for his father. He recalls an incident when he himself was a young boy: he falls from the roof while trying to pluck a flower for the father, who, horrified, "yelled / my name, ran out to find me sprawled, dazed, gripping his crushed gift, thrust / at him in my bloody fist." Just as the father must have cradled him in his arms, the poet now enfolds his own son in his arms, feels the young boy's "shoulders, knees, elbows, hands, / lumpy like sacked fruit." In this poem, as in many others, Lee deftly suggests that one's life in the present is strongly colored by the memories that one contains. Indeed, in "Furious Versions," he writes,

"Memory revises me." One senses from Lee's writing that memories are not simply a recapitulation of a time gone by; they affect how one lives in the present and are part of the present, shaping one's actions, feelings, beliefs, and outlook on life. In "Goodnight," for example, tactile perceptions act as a catalyst toward the spiritual realm, and the son asleep next to the poet brings to mind his own childhood – that painful fall and a father's solicitousness – that creates in the poet the sense of bonding, an image of multigenerational community that also serves as a road map for living. Lee writes, "He plunges below us now, as we / fall soundless toward him, our bodies / crowded on your narrow bed."

"A Final Thing" is a similarly tender poem about the poet's wife and son, and yet it is also very much a work about memories that shape and sustain the present. The poem begins with the poet waking up to the voices of mother and son. The mother is telling the child a story, her voice "weighted with that other's attention, / and avowing it / by deepening in intention." Then he hears his son ask a question, his voice "an invitation to be met, stirring anticipation." For the poet, being able to listen is in itself a kind of participation, and he finds comfort in it. The experience is a moving and humbling one for the poet. Most important, he realizes that this morning, composed mostly of sound – transitory, fragile – will become the memory that in the future will serve to sustain him. Lee concludes the poem in plain but compelling language:

> . . . the first
> sound I hear
> is the voice of one I love
> speaking to one we love.
> I hear it through the bedroom wall;
>
> something, someday, I'll close my eyes to recall.

Although the figure of Lee's father is still an important aspect of this collection, the father does not seem to loom as large as he did in *Rose*. The father has lost some of his imposing power, the capacity to paralyze his son; he seems more human. In "Here I Am," the poet is able to say he misses the father without seeing him at the same time as a Godlike figure to be feared. The poem is also an apt illustration of what Gerald Stern has called Lee's "love of plain speech." Indeed, in *The City in Which I Love You,* the poet works less with what Jessica Greenbaum has called "unorthodox imagery." He also reveals less his sense of awe and perplexity at the paradoxes of life. In "Here I Am," the poet writes simply and directly about missing his father:

"I wait. I don't go. He will come, the one / who waited for me each day / at the edge of the schoolyard." The poet waits, knowing full well that "Such waiting is impossible," that the father will not be coming; for death has made him "small as the rain / and as many." Indeed, remembrances of a stern, intellectual father, distant and all-powerful, are now leavened much more unreservedly with memories of a lonely, vulnerable man. In *Rose* sympathy for the father carries the tendency to maintain a worshipful stance – the father in those poems is, after all, able to absolve one's sins. In this second collection, the son sees the father much more as his own equal, someone who had to battle his own fears and insecurities. The speaker wonders:

> Maybe he fears he is forgotten,
> the way I am forgotten,
>
> each of us the one
> who, in that childhood game, shouts,
> though no one hears, *Here I am*!

"My Father, In Heaven, Is Reading Out Loud" is the poem most representative of the poet's change in attitude toward the father. He is able to measure clearly the effect that the older man has had upon his life; yet he does so now without seeing the father as a distant, Godlike figure. The speaker's words are uttered without passion, almost objectively. He understands that the father's ways permeate his own outlook on life, have become part of his walk, the way he holds his shoulders. Nevertheless, the son retains sufficient sense of the father's power to imagine still that he himself was a "remarkable disappointment to him, / I am like anyone who arrives late / in the millennium and is unable / to stay to the end of days." However, these words are spoken with regret and sadness but not an oppressive feeling of guilt. The poem echoes "Always a Rose," when the poet writes that his father "put his hand on my crown and purified me / in the name of the Father, of the Son, and of the Holy Ghost." The crucial difference is that in "My Father, In Heaven, Is Reading Out Loud" the father remembered is not one who stands in majestic judgment but one who is gentle and will "run to save a child's day from grief." The most marked difference in the poet's memory of the older man is that now the son sees both the father and the son as being alike in many ways, in what they see of life, in their helplessness when confronted with overwhelming tragedy:

At the doorway, I watched, and I suddenly
knew he was one like me, who got my learning
under a lintel; he was one of the powerless,
to whom knowledge came while he sat among
suitcases, boxes, old newspapers, string.

Memory can provide succor during times of distress; the past that one endeavors to remember certainly defines who one is. Still, the act of remembering can be also a heavy burden to bear, one that the poet takes up only with great reluctance. In "The Interrogation" the speaker dreams about a stream gone dry because it "was clogged with bodies." His mind contains a jumble of memories about avenues and doors, a burning house, and fires in the streets. He remembers that "We stood among men, at the level / of their hands, all those wrists, dead or soon to die." The speaker reports that he grows "leaden with stories." He is "through with memory" and will no longer let "my survival / depend on memory." But the poet's litany of denial fails to dispel the images of the past and, indeed, is in itself a way to call up those memories, a reminder that there is no escape from remembering.

Although Lee's portrayal of his father in *The City in Which I Love You* is of a gentler man, it is also of someone who has been in a sense broken by his hardships. Lee shares with his father memories of the soldiers, the threats, the boat in the night. He pities the older man for what he has had to endure. Yet, what Lee identifies most with in the father is the sense of alienation and marginality that comes from living in a society in which people of color have been and continue to be defined as the outsiders. *The City in Which I Love You* consists of poems haunted by recollections of imprisonment and death; but perhaps, some of the most haunting poems are ones about not being able ever to belong truly to the country in which one lives, of never being able to consider the present without seeing how the past will always intrude into that present. Dark, uneasy visions pervade Lee's second book, none more dark perhaps than the first poem in the collection, "Furious Versions." The poet writes that "The past / doesn't fall away, the past / joins the greater / telling, and is." He continues in the next stanza, "At times its theme seems / murky, other times, clear. Always, death is a phrase." This speaker will "measure time by losses and destructions" and with memories:

I hear
interrogation in vague tongues,
I hear ocean sounds and a history of rain.
Somewhere a streetlamp,

Dust jacket for Lee's 1990 collection of poems, in which he writes "Memory revises me" (courtesy of the Poetry Collection, State University of New York, Buffalo)

and my brother never coming
Somewhere a handful of hair and a box of letters.
And everywhere, fire,
corridors of fire, brick and barbed wire.

Those memories and losses at times seem to merge the poet's life into his father's, so that Lee is moved to note, "These days I waken in the used light / of someone's spent life . . . I feel dismantled," and in lines that seem to echo T. S. Eliot he asks, "Will I rise and go / out into an American city? / Or walk down to the wilderness sea?" Or perhaps, he will be the one "to bribe an officer for our lives / and perilous passage . . . and I'd answer / in an oceanic tongue / to *Professor, Capitalist, Husband, Father*." The scars in his father's life have so marked the poet's, he wonders where his own scars begin and the other's end:

But if I waken to a jailer
rousting me to meet my wife and son . . .

> ... did I stand on a train from Chicago to Pittsburgh
> so my fevered son could sleep? Or did I
> open my eyes
> and see my father's closed face
> rocking above me?

His identification with his father goes beyond what escape from tyranny and death have wrought to include the older man's sense of alienation in "an American city," a feeling that has been reinforced by his own experiences. The sense of loss – of an ancestral culture, of the country of one's parents – pervades section 5 in "Furious Versions." Lee writes, "My father wandered, / me beside him, human . . . unlike Paul, we had no mission." Lee remembers encountering his father's old friend, and "The way he stared and spoke my father's name . . . Here was the sadness of ten thousand miles . . . after twenty years / on a sidewalk in America." The poet's feeling of being a stranger in someone else's home is only partially alleviated by seeing, on the same American streets,

> Li Ba and Tu Fu, those two
> poets of the wanderer's heart. . . .
> Gold-toothed, cigarettes rolled in their sleeves,
> they noted my dumb surprise:
> *What did you expect? Where else would we be?*

According to Gerald Stern, Lee's poetry evinces the influence of Keats and Rilke; however, the poet here is surely also claiming both his Chinese as well as his Western artistic forebears. He welcomes their company in his exile; yet, the incongruity of this scene is also evident and indicates the poet's failure to dispel totally the sense of his otherness. Carol Muske has described Lee's work as "pairing Walt Whitman with the great Tang dynasty poet Tu Fu." Whether Li-Young Lee's artistic influences have been Rilke or Whitman, this poet's published work has already made a considerable impact upon the poetry scene. At this writing, Lee is working on an epic-length poem. His autobiography, *The Winged Seed: A Remembrance*, was published in 1995.

References:

Judith Kitchen, Review of *The City in Which I Love You, Georgia Review,* 45 (Spring 1991): 154–169;

Roger Mitchell, Review of *Rose, Prairie Schooner,* 63 (Fall 1989): 129–139;

David Neff, "Remembering the Man Who Forgot Nothing," *Christianity Today,* 32 (2 September 1988): 63;

Sanford Pinsker, Review of *Rose Literary Review,* 32 (Winter 1989): 256–262;

Marilyn Nelson Wanisk, Review of *The Cry in Which I Love You, Kenyon Review,* 13 (Fall 1991): 214–226.

Denise Levertov

(24 October 1923 –   )

Anne Day Dewey
Saint Louis University, Madrid, Spain

See also the Levertov entry in *DLB 5: American Poets Since World War II, First Series.*

BOOKS: *The Double Image* (London: Cresset Press, 1946);

Here and Now (San Francisco: City Lights Pocket Bookshop, 1957);

5 Poems (San Francisco: White Rabbit Press, 1958);

Overland to the Islands (Highlands, N.C.: J. Williams, 1958);

With Eyes at the Back of our Heads (New York: New Directions, 1959);

The Jacob's Ladder (New York: New Directions, 1961);

City Psalm (Berkeley, Cal.: Oyez, 1964);

O Taste and See (New York: New Directions, 1964);

Psalm Concerning the Castle (Mount Horeb, Wis.: Perishable Press, 1966);

The Sorrow Dance (New York: New Directions, 1967);

A Marigold from North Vietnam (New York: Albondocani Press & Ampersand Books, 1968);

A Tree Telling of Orpheus (Los Angeles: Black Sparrow Press, 1968);

In the Night: A Story (New York: Albondocani Press, 1968);

The Cold Spring & Other Poems (New York: New Directions, 1968);

Three Poems (Mount Horeb, Wis.: Perishable Press, 1968);

Embroideries (Los Angeles: Black Sparrow Press, 1969);

A New Year's Garland for My Students / M.I.T. 1969–1970 (Mount Horeb, Wis.: Perishable Press, 1970);

Relearning the Alphabet (New York: New Directions, 1970);

Summer Poems, 1969 (Berkeley, Cal.: Oyez, 1970);

To Stay Alive (New York: New Directions, 1971);

Footprints (New York: New Directions, 1972);

Conversation in Moscow (Cambridge, Mass.: Hovey St. Press, 1973);

Denise Levertov (photograph by David Geier)

The Poet in the World (New York: New Directions, 1973);

The Freeing of the Dust (New York: New Directions, 1975);

Chekhov on the West Heath (Andes, N.Y.: Woolmer/Brotherson, 1977);

Modulations for Solo Voice (San Francisco: Five Trees Press, 1977);

Life in the Forest (New York: New Directions, 1978);

Collected Earlier Poems 1940–1960 (New York: New Directions, 1979);

Light Up the Cave (New York: New Directions, 1981);

Mass for the Day of St. Thomas Didymus (Concord, N.H.: William B. Ewert, 1981);

Pig Dreams: Scenes from the Life of Sylvia: Poems (Woodstock, Vt.: Countryman Press, 1981);

Wanderer's Daysong (Port Townsend, Wash.: Copper Canyon Press, 1981);

Candles in Babylon (New York: New Directions, 1982);

Poems 1960–1967 (New York: New Directions, 1983);

Two Poems (Concord, N.H.: William B. Ewert, 1983);

El Salvador: Requiem and Invocation (Concord, N.H.: William B. Evert, 1983);

The Menaced World (Concord, N. H.: William B. Ewert, 1984);

Oblique Prayers: New Poems with 14 Translations from Jean Joubert (New York: New Directions, 1984);

Selected Poems (Newcastle upon Tyne: Bloodaxe Books, 1986);

Poems 1968–1972 (New York: New Directions, 1987);

Breathing the Water (New York: New Directions, 1987);

Seasons of Light, by Levertov and Peter Brown (Houston, Tex.: Rice University Press, 1988);

A Door in the Hive (New York: New Directions, 1989);

New and Selected Essays (New York: New Directions, 1992);

Evening Train (New York: New Directions, 1992);

Tesserae: Memories and Suppositions (New York: New Directions, 1995);

Sounds of the Well (New York: New Directions, 1996).

OTHER: "Biographical Note," in *The New American Poetry,* edited by Donald Allen (New York: Grove Press, 1960), pp. 440–441;

"A Personal Approach," in *Parable, Myth, and Language,* edited by Tony Stoneburner (Cambridge, Mass.: Church Society for College Work, 1967);

Out of the War Shadow: An Anthology of Current Poetry, edited by Levertov (New York: War Resisters League, 1967);

Penguin Modern Poets 9, edited by Denise Levertov, Kenneth Rexroth, and William Carlos Williams (Harmondsworth, U.K.: Penguin, 1967);

In Praise of Krishna: Songs from the Bengali, translated by Levertov and Edward C. Dimock (Garden City, N.Y.: Doubleday, 1967);

Jules Supervielle, *Selected Writings,* translated by Levertov (New York: New Directions, 1968);

Eugene Guillevic, *Selected Poems,* translated by Levertov (New York: New Directions, 1969);

Rainer Maria Rilke, *Where Silence Reigns,* translated by T. G. Craig Houston, with a foreword by Levertov (New York: New Directions, 1978);

Contribution to *The Bloodaxe Book of Contemporary Women Poets* (Newcastle upon Tyne: Bloodaxe Books, 1984);

Poets of Bulgaria, edited by William Meredith and translated by Levertov and others (N.p.: Unicorn Press, 1985);

Alain Bosquet, *No Matter No Fact,* translated by Levertov, Sam Beckett, and Edouard Roditi (New York: New Directions, 1988);

Jean Joubert, *Black Iris: Selected Poems by Jean Joubert,* translated by Levertov (Copper Canyon, Wash.: Copper Canyon Press, 1988);

Beatrice Hawley, *The Collected Poems of Beatrice Hawley,* edited by Levertov (N.p.: Zoland Books, 1989);

Jean Joubert, *White Owl and Blue Mouse,* translated by Levertov (N.p.: Zoland Books, 1990).

In her prolific, highly regarded, sometimes controversial career, Denise Levertov has created a multidimensional body of poetry that is pervaded by her strong belief in her poetic vocation and by her ideals of personal integrity. Her meticulously crafted work involves a variety of genres — nature lyrics, love poems, poems of political protest, and Christian poetry — that converge and diverge throughout her career. In book after book, she explores such themes as domesticity, romantic love, the erotic, parenting and other family relations, political change, the poet's relation to artistic tradition, and aging — nearly always with reference to contemporary issues central to women. Born in England, Levertov eventually shed the neoromanticism popular in that country during World War II and, moving to the United States in 1948, embraced the experimentation of American poetry in the 1950s. The poetic community that she joined included the Beats, the New York School, the San Francisco Renaissance, and the Black Mountain poets, all of whom were identified by Donald Allen as "New American" poets in his influential anthology *The New American Poetry* (1960). This highly diverse community had grown from a counterculture movement that challenged the traditional meter and elevated diction of the New Critics in little magazines. It was to become the vanguard of a major strand of postmodern American poetry, whose writings appeared by the 1960s in such magazines as Henry Rago's *Poetry.*

Closely allied during the 1950s and 1960s with the Black Mountain poets, especially Robert Duncan and Robert Creeley, Levertov was energetically involved in the contemporary discussion of poetry and poetics. Her sensual evocation of an epiphanic vision that arises from the strikingly concrete, everyday world and her poetics of "organic form" were both influential in the attempts to formulate a positive alternative to the poetic theories of the New Critics. Meanwhile, her poetry assimilated and transformed the modernist legacy of Ezra Pound, William Carlos Williams, and D. H. Lawrence. During the 1960s Levertov's work, like that of many of her contemporaries, became intensely political. Much of her controversial poetry of this period criticized American involvement in the Vietnam War and aligned her with the various movements for social reform prevalent in that decade.

The increasingly romantic style of her later poetry distanced Levertov from Creeley and Duncan and the experimental avant-garde. Since her gradual conversion to Christianity in the late 1970s and early 1980s, Levertov's belief in the poet's vocation as a visionary who enriches the imaginative life of society has strengthened. Many recent poems are meditations on historical artifacts and biblical texts that attempt to render artistic and religious tradition as a vital presence in contemporary life. Levertov's luminous vision of nature, her unconventional love poems, her theory and practice of political poetry, and her Christian vision – as well as her attempts to weave these various strands of her work together – all represent significant contributions to postmodern poetry.

Born in England in 1923, Levertov grew up in Ilford, Essex, near London. Her immediate family included her Welsh mother, Beatrice Spooner-Jones Levertoff, a teacher who sang, painted, and wrote; her Russian-born father, Paul Levertoff, an Anglican priest and scholar who had converted from Hasidic Judaism as a student; and a musically talented sister Olga, nine years her senior, who devoted much of her adult life to political activism. (Levertov changed the spelling of her name to distinguish herself from her sister, who published a book of poetry in 1949.) An older sister Philippa died twelve years before Levertov was born. Levertov's intensely intellectual and artistic home life included reading aloud, attending musical performances, walking in the countryside with her older sister Olga and being surrounded by adults who espoused various political causes (particularly protesting fascism in Spain and Germany) and who provided aid to political refugees during World War II. Levertov was educated at home, primarily by her mother, until the age of twelve, when she began ballet, piano, French, and art lessons. An avid and independent reader, she became familiar with fairy tales and also with the works of English poets such as George Herbert, John Donne, William Wordsworth, John Keats, and Alfred Tennyson. Although she studied ballet seriously and

hoped as a teenager to become a dancer, Levertov entered nurses' training when she was nineteen and worked as a civilian nurse in London during the war.

Having started writing poems at the age of five, she felt a strong sense of poetic vocation by the time she was nine or ten years old. By the age of twelve, she had written to T. S. Eliot, from whom she received a response that included a critique of her poems. Herbert Read became an early friend and correspondent, occasionally offering advice and encouragement about her writing. In her late teens and early twenties, Levertov published her first poems in Charles Wrey Gardiner's *Poetry Quarterly* and in other British magazines such as *Outposts* and *Voices*. Following the acceptance of her first book of poetry, *The Double Image* (1946), she remembers entering a church "to kneel in awe because my destiny, which I had always known as a certain vague form on the far horizon, was beginning to *happen*."

The Double Image emulates the "new romantic" style that was prevalent during World War II in England. Poets such as those presented in Kenneth Rexroth's anthology *New British Poets* (1948) rejected the severity and experimental meters of the modernists for lush musicality in traditional meters and a melancholy beauty pervaded by a consciousness of death. Many were influenced by the poetry of Rainer Maria Rilke, whom Levertov began to read in 1946 and who remains a lifelong influence in her work. Crossing the threshold from adolescent innocence to adulthood, Levertov expressed in new romantic conventions the loss of youthful illusions. Sexual love and nature promised a worldly knowledge that is both desired and feared and that is represented by the recurrent image of a flame whose warmth and brilliance attract the moth, only to consume its fragile life. Innocence and experience yield double, contradictory knowledge. The romantic child's trust in nature's "caressing grasses" and rejuvenating power seem "tender vanity" in a harsh and disenchanting adult world. Failed communion in love brings the isolating recognition of a narcissistic projection of the self that prevents authentic communication. "Each, in the hardening crystal / a prisoner of pride, abstractedly caresses / the stranger at his side."

While *The Double Image* treats issues specific to Levertov's personal and historical circumstances during the war, she transmutes these issues to consider them in terms of the universal themes of "death," "time," "history," and "desire." Her nature imagery evokes a psychological rather than a physical landscape:

Cover for Levertov's 1972 book of poems, which shows a strong anti–Vietnam War sentiment

At Durgan waves are black as cypresses,
clear as the water of a wishing well,
caressing the stones with smooth palms, looking
into the pools as enigmatic eyes
peer into mirrors, or music echoes
out of a wood the waking dream of day,
blind eyelids lifting to a coloured world.

The succession of contradictory images – black and clear, visual and aural, sensitive and unable to sense – dissolve the sea into an insubstantial fantasy generated by the mind in its isolation. Meditating on the eternal themes of poetry and in search of her self, Levertov finds self, the world, and even words increasingly unreal. Her poems claim a wraithlike existence. Words that for her are "valid symbols" are unable to bridge "the distance and the veil" that separate her from others. Images that tend to the Gothic, such as death as an opulent bridegroom, and susurrant blank verse that is rich with assonance and alliteration intensify the theme of dreamy self-absorption. Both theme and meter remain, however, part of an inherited conception of poetry into

which the poet seeks to grow and that she does not yet question.

In 1947 Levertov married Mitchell Goodman, a former soldier who had recently completed graduate work at Harvard in economics and labor relations. They moved to New York City, where their son, Nikolai, was born in 1949. With the exception of a year and a half in Europe and two in Mexico, New York City remained their home until the late 1960s. During the eleven years that separate *The Double Image* from her next book, *Here and Now* (1957), Levertov adapted to a new culture, to motherhood, and to a new poetics, retraining herself as a poet of the post–World War II American avant-garde and assimilating the modernist legacy rejected by the neoromantic milieu in England. Although she did not publish a book during this time, she continued to write and publish poems in magazines.

Meanwhile, she met Robert Creeley in 1949, William Carlos Williams in 1951, and Robert Duncan shortly thereafter. The four formed enduring friendships fueled by an enthusiasm for and a criticism of each other's work. Levertov also joined the poetic discussions that appeared in Cid Corman's little magazine *Origin* and Creeley's *Black Mountain Review*. Contributors to these magazines were attracted by the artistic possibilities of Charles Olson's essay "Projective Verse" (1950). Olson's "composition by field," an idea based on his borrowing from field theory in physics, suggested metaphysical and formal foundations with which to replace the formal standards promulgated by the New Critics. Challenging what he termed, in reference to Keats, the "Egotistical sublime" of Western humanism, Olson advocated a poetry that rendered the artist one object among others and the poem a record of the moment-by-moment interaction of consciousness with other forces in the environment. Creeley, Duncan, and Levertov had read Pound, Williams, and D. H. Lawrence early. From these common interests and their assimilation of Olson's "composition by field," the three writers developed the shared conception of poetry and poetics for which they became known as the Black Mountain poets in the late 1950s.

Levertov's next volumes record the experiments inspired by her new environment. Although published at different times, *Here and Now* and *Overland to the Islands* (1958) are composed of poems written during the same period. Publishers Lawrence Ferlinghetti of City Lights and Jonathan Williams of Jargon Press approached Levertov at roughly the same time and chose from her stock of poems at hand, Ferlinghetti first, and Jonathan Williams from the rest. The third volume, *With Eyes at the Back of Our Heads* (1959), was published by James Laughlin's New Directions, initiating Levertov's close publishing relationship with this press, one that has continued to the present. *With Eyes at the Back of Our Heads* extends her new apprenticeship, as Levertov's later decision to group it with her *Collected Earlier Poems 1940–1960* (1979) indicates, but also demonstrates her assimilation of the new influences into an independent style.

The influence of Williams is primary in these experiments, although Levertov also names Wallace Stevens and Pound – particularly in his book *ABC of Reading* (1934) – as significant to her conceptions of the poet's craft and technical precision. These volumes strip away the Gothic dreamworld of *The Double Image* to explore nature, love, and art through the colloquial language of Williams's American idiom and the immediacy of sensual presence. "Tomatlan (Variations)" reveals a visual clarity, a sexual response to nature, and a counterpoint of physical description and grammatical structure characteristic of Williams:

> The green palmettos of the
> blue jungle
> shake their
> green breasts, their stiff
> green hair –
> the wind, the sea wind is come
> and touches them
> lightly, and strokes them, and
> screws them.

"The Departure" explores the energetic rhythms of American colloquial speech as Levertov perceives it:

> Have you got the moon safe?
> Please, tie those strings a little tighter.
> This loaf, push it down further
> the light is crushing it – such a baguette
> golden brown and so white inside
> you don't see every day
> nowadays.

In addition to Williams's influence, some poems assimilate the themes and vocabulary of "Projective Verse" in ways similar to the early experiments by Creeley and Duncan, structuring the poem around the interaction of elements in a particular environment and using line breaks and spacing to identify the agents that produce a particular moment. "Everything that Acts Is Actual" adopts Creeley's abstract language of the "act" to represent the relationship between two people. "A Silence"

seems to revise Keats's "Ode on a Grecian Urn" by describing a vase and a broken rose in the irregular spatial dispersion and antiromantic themes typical of early Black Mountain experiments:

> Phoenix-tailed
> slateblue martins pursue
>   one another, spaced out
> in hopeless hope, circling
>   the porous clay vase, dark from
> the water in it. Silence
> surrounds the facts. A language
> still unspoken.

Although adopting Williams's visual precision, the poem's lineation distinguishes the agents that compose the moment. The extra space between *one* and *another* enacts the separation between the martins, while a new line divides the clay and water. Whereas Keats's urn fused the elements on it into a transcendence of time in the eternal moment of art, Levertov accentuates the instability and chance conjunction of a broken flower, water, and clay. The double meaning of *still* as "motionless" or "yet" suggests that language can merge with concrete "facts"; but it also suggests doubts about the ability of language to represent these facts accurately, an ambivalence about objectifying language that pervades contemporary poems by Creeley and Olson.

Just as she rejected romantic notions about nature, Levertov also rejects romantic notions about love and art. "The Third Dimension" apparently translates the feeling of ecstatic union with nature, a feeling associated with love, into colloquial and concrete terms: "Who'd believe me if / I said, 'They took and / split me open from / scalp to crotch, and / still I'm alive, and/ walk around pleased with / the sun and all the world's bounty?'" Other poems portray idiosyncratic moments in unidealized love and marriage. "I give up on / trying to answer my question, / Do I love you enough?" "Attention" and "commitment" replace the idealized love of *The Double Image*.

The appeal to a transcendent source of inspiration recedes before Levertov's evolving interest in the artist's materials and tools. "An Innocent (II): (*1st version*)" links the artist to a destitute man poking through garbage with "the calm intense look of a craftsman." This "prince of scavengers" who "makes / some kind of life from [an endless city of refuse]" shares Levertov's satisfaction in the found or overlooked object and in attention to the materials and tools that make art. "The Hands" likewise refuses escape into an ethereal beauty of music by focusing the pianist's "crablike / hands, slithering / among the keys" with "almost painful / movement." Even when Levertov describes inspiration as possession by a force more powerful than the individual, a part of her experience of creativity throughout her life, she presents her muse in concrete terms. In "The Goddess," a deity of honesty and truth expels her violently from "Lie Castle," throwing her facedown to force immediate contact with nature in the taste of mud and seeds.

The early 1960s marks Levertov's transition from her apprenticeship period to the achievement of an independent poetic vision. *The Jacob's Ladder* (1961) and *O Taste and See* (1964) add a spiritual dimension to the vivid description she learned from Williams. At the same time, her work begins to depart from the early Black Mountain emphasis on the idiosyncratic to discover moments of epiphanic beauty or coherence in everyday experience. Sensual images become a "Jacob's ladder" that extends from earth to heaven and permits commerce between the two regions. The sensual world both enables perception of a spirit beyond material fact and becomes the medium through which the poet represents her own spiritual experience. This spirit life does not cohere into a specific cosmology; Levertov seeks rather to represent the particular vitality of each unique being. The last two stanzas of "Six Variations," for example, contrast the animating power of light with that of human consciousness.

v
The quick of the sun that gilds
broken pebbles in sidewalk cement,
and the iridescent
spit, that defiles and adorns!
Gold light in blind love does not distinguish
one surface from another
. . . .

vi
Lap up the vowels
of sorrow,
            transparent, cold
water-darkness welling
up from the white sand.
. . . .
Through the hollow globe, a ring
of frayed rusty scrapiron,
is it the sea that shines?
Is it a road at the world's edge?

Light, capable of "blind love," reveals the "quick" beauty and life of the concrete. In contrast, the human awareness of loss or absence discovers the limits of sensual being. The contrasting short *i* and long *o* sounds reinforce the sharpness of the vis-

ible world and the flowing, inchoate quality of desire. While Levertov does not abandon the colloquial, this more crafted music becomes an important technique through which she communicates the coherence and beauty that she finds in the everyday world.

This intensified musicality is one element of an increasingly literary emphasis in Levertov's work of the early 1960s, an emphasis that she shared with Creeley and Duncan in this period. Through her deepening friendship with Duncan and their mutual admiration for the then nearly forgotten poet H. D. (Hilda Doolittle), Levertov began to see poetic tradition as a resource that sustains the life of the imagination by providing examples of a richer vision that enhances ordinary perception. In the 1962 essay "H. D.: An Appreciation," Levertov writes that she admires in H. D.'s writing "the play of sound," "the interplay of psychic and material life," "[t]he interpenetration of past and present, of mundane reality and intangible reality," a description that fits her own poetic concerns. Mythological figures such as Ishtar, angels, elves, literary epigraphs and dedications, as well as natural objects, inspire the poems. Daily events are framed as rituals evoking the divine presence in the ordinary fact. Through her exploration of tradition, Levertov began to rediscover her European roots. Joan Hallisey has traced the influence of Martin Buber's *Tales of the Hasidim* (1948) in the mystical appreciation of the immediate and everyday world in *O Taste and See*. Boris Pasternak and Henrik Ibsen join Williams and Pound as literary ancestors. Although Levertov develops its significance in different contexts throughout her life, her epiphanic experience of the everyday world in its immediate and concrete particularity forms the core of her mature poetic vision.

The early 1960s brought the increased recognition of the poets of the "New American" poetry, who gained wider exposure in poetry readings; in the proliferation of little magazines such as *Evergreen, Kulchur,* and *Floating Bear;* and in the publication of their work in mainstream magazines such as *Poetry* during Henry Rago's editorship. During this time Levertov began her professional career as a poet, supporting herself by reading, writing, and teaching. In addition to reading more frequently, she served as poetry advisor to Norton Publishing Company and as the poetry editor of *The Nation* in the 1960s. During this decade she also held part- and full-time teaching positions at Drew, the City College of New York, Vassar, Berkeley, and the Massachusetts Institute of Technology. She taught at Tufts in the 1970s and at Brandeis and Stanford in the 1980s.

Although appreciating the work of poets as diverse as Allen Ginsberg, Gary Snyder, and Adrienne Rich, Levertov felt her closest affinity with Creeley and Duncan. Their commitment to poetry as a means to intensify and purify ordinary language became the hallmark of Black Mountain poetry in the 1960s. Within the discussion of poetry among the New American poets, this emphasis distanced them from what Levertov termed the "confessional" tendency of the Beats to publicize the private realm and to employ the chatty or ironic tone of New York poets such as Frank O'Hara and John Ashbery. The emphasis also drew critical fire. In his magazine *The Sixties,* Robert Bly attacked Duncan's and Levertov's literary allusions as an artificial and inauthentic inducement of vision.

During the 1960s Levertov formulated and refined a theory of poetry that underlay her luminous epiphanies from the concrete realities of the world, epiphanies that remain at the core of her poetics. Her 1965 essay "Some Notes on Organic Form" was one of many poetic theories developed at this time, as Levertov and her contemporaries sought to explain their departures from traditional forms. Seeking to refute the equation of "free verse" with arbitrary meter, Levertov's essay defines "organic" form as fidelity to a form that is inherent in a thing or in an interplay among several things – "inscape" – or in an experience – "instress." *Inscape* and *instress* are terms borrowed from Gerard Manley Hopkins, and Levertov's use of the word *organic* indicates her indebtedness to the work of Samuel Taylor Coleridge and Ralph Waldo Emerson.

For Levertov, poems emerge from "an intuition of order, a form beyond forms, in which forms partake, and of which man's creative works are analogies, resemblances, natural allegories." Although her emphasis on the interplay among things and the process of experience derives from Williams and from a Black Mountain emphasis on the process of perception, her Wordsworthian conception of a single form unifying human and natural life departs from both. Levertov thus modifies Creeley's process-oriented "form is never more than the extension of content" with the assertion that "Form is never more than a *revelation* of content." This conception of form remains the basis of her critical and theoretical writings. Later essays such as "On the Function of the Line" (1979) describe poetic form as a visual and musical "score" or performance guide through which the reader may grasp the poet's experience. Her essay "On the

Dust jacket for Levertov's book of essays, which includes "Some Notes on Organic Form"

Need for New Terms" (1986) replaces the overused *organic* with *exploratory* and reiterates Levertov's "passion . . . for the vertebrate and cohesive in all art."

In the 1960s the events of the war in Vietnam introduced one of the major contexts in which Levertov developed the significance of her poetic epiphanies – the political – when, like many of her contemporaries, she found both her life and her poetry politicized by American engagement in the war in Southeast Asia. Involved in the mid 1960s in RESIST, a movement to encourage draft resisters, she grew increasingly active politically, attending peace rallies, organizing readings and other protest events, participating in 1969 in the People's Park in Berkeley (a grassroots effort to create a park on abandoned university land), and visiting North Vietnam with Muriel Rukeyser and Jane Hart in 1972. The years of the late 1960s brought both personal and political crises as Levertov struggled with tensions in her marriage, depression, and the strain of her continuous involvement in political activism.

This time of crisis triggered an effort by Levertov to rethink her poetic vision – the progress and growing pains of which are recorded in her remarkably prolific output of the next few years: *The Sorrow Dance* (1967), *Relearning the Alphabet* (1970), *To Stay Alive* (1971), and *Footprints* (1972).

The first and last sections of *The Sorrow Dance*, "Abel's Bride" and "Life at War," locate Levertov's poetic crisis in the inadequacy of her poetics of the luminous concrete to express suffering. "A Lamentation" opens with the question: "*Grief, have I denied thee?*" and describes Levertov's childhood theatrical performance as "Summer" as a betrayal of her "autumn birthright." Celebrating the fullness of the presence of nature now seems insufficient, "[h]ypocrisies / of seemly hope ... if the day / is no day for miracles." While "Abel's Bride" presents Levertov's sorrow as a vaguely defined woman's sorrow, "Life at War" describes the war's horror as a crippling intrusion into her search for beauty, "the imagination / filmed over with the grey filth of it." Levertov's early war poems extend rather than depart from her poetics of presence, using vivid representation to make the war's brutality immediate to her readers and to render human the media's impersonal statistics and demonized "enemy."

Relearning the Alphabet achieves a shaky resolution of Levertov's crisis of vision. Although discovering renewed joy in the colorful concreteness and sensuous particularity of things, the poet remains conscious of the limitations of this vision. "Reduced to an eye / I forget what / I / was." While looking occasionally to her poetics of the 1940s to recover her subjective voice, she finds as yet no access to her inmost self. In her long poem "A Tree Telling of Orpheus," she dramatizes the tranformation of nature into words not as escape into the impersonal life of things but as an agonized awakening into human consciousness:

He told of the dreams of man, wars, passions, griefs,
        and I, a tree, understood words – ah, it seemed
my thick bark would split like a sapling's that
                        grew too fast[.]

Levertov's search for a language of self seems most successful when she returns to the interpersonal source of her poetic vision that was prominent in her exploration of love in *The Double Image* but developed only intermittently throughout the 1950s and 1960s. Commemorating her sister's death in 1964, the "Olga Poems" of *The Sorrow Dance* powerfully render her passionate, tormented sister. As Levertov is alternately "the little sister / beady-eyed in the bed ... My head / a camera," watching her

sister, Olga " kneeling / to undress, / scorching luxuriously, raking / her nails over olive sides," and then the adult analyzing her sister's frustrated idealism, the "rage for order / [that] disordered her pilgrimage," the sister becomes a presence whom Levertov creates from a wealth of memory and cultural allusion that is focused by deep personal emotion. In the same way, Levertov's renewed joy in daily existence in *Relearning the Alphabet* is awakened through renewed love in her marriage, as her relation to nature becomes grounded in human community. The cycle *A New Year's Garland for my Students/ M.I.T.: 1969–1970* (1970) continues a playful exploration and an expansion of imagery and poetic conceit that emphasizes the relationships between people rather than things.

Levertov's exploration of Olga's personality – passionate, manipulative and even demonic in her political frustration as an adult – begins the poet's effort to define the relation between an ideal vision and political activism. Much of Levertov's political vision hinges on the opposition of peace to war, nature to technology, and communism to imperialist capitalism, in a sort of political dualism that typified many political reform movements in the 1960s. Her most controversial volume, *To Stay Alive,* composed almost entirely of the long poem, "Staying Alive," places her short lyric visions in a long documentary-diary of her political experiences from late 1967 to 1970, including such events as de Courcy Squire's hunger strike, political rallies, waiting for her husband's trial for aiding draft resisters, the People's Park protests, and her travels in Europe.

Embedded in a collage of verbatim newscasts, revolutionary slogans, conversations, diary entries, letters from others, and memories, Levertov's lyric passages become a part of the society from which poetic vision springs and to which it, in turn, speaks. "Staying Alive" seeks to give substance to the protesters' ideal of peace abroad and social revolution at home, the same ideal to which Levertov committed herself. The poem's concrete instances of communal harmony, poetic images of harmony in nature, of childhood memory, and of poetic tradition all contribute to an explication of the popular slogan, "Revolution or death." Levertov presents the slogan's meaning as one defined by a democratic consensus that provides for the interplay between the individual and collective, an interplay that governs both her poetry and the group's language. Her preface to *To Stay Alive* locates her poetics not in extraordinary vision but in the typicalness of her experience as a citizen of her era. So completely does she fuse personal and political history that the poem is at once a record of her changing self-conception as a political activist and a vivid history of the protest movement.

The poems Levertov wrote about the Vietnam War received a mixed reception. Dorothy M. Nielson and Paul Lacey praised their discovery of forms and their use of language as being fully appropriate to the political issues they explored, and Hayden Carruth hailed Levertov's political and antiwar poems as work that approached the status of an epic. Other poets and critics, however, attacked Levertov's poetry about the Vietnam War as crude and unpoetic. In the judgment of Duncan, Levertov accepted too readily the problematic language of public debate and thus denied the poet's responsibility to stretch language and the imagination to their full potential; she did this by employing disclaimers such as that concerning her use of *revolution* as "[t]he wrong word / . . . / But it's the only / word we have." Other critics faulted the documentary emphasis in the poetry. Charles Altieri criticized Levertov's "aesthetics of presence," with its focus on the concrete image, as being inadequate to represent the complex political and ethical issues and their contexts. While "Staying Alive" lacks the intensive phonetic and verbal play of Levertov's short lyrics, this long poem attempts to root the value of poetic language in its audience (as represented in the poem), rather than in its formal autonomy.

Levertov herself reconsidered the politics of her poetics, questioning her love for "surfaces that are their own / interior life" and questioning, too, the life of poetry among its readers and its audience. She records that Chuck Matthei read "A Man," a poem from *The Sorrow Dance* that is about the personal wisdom gained from experience, at a rally. In the charged context it acquired an overtly political tone. In "Staying Alive" Levertov's image of social harmony as a communion chalice is stripped of its inspirational power by the anger of the revolutionaries "shattering / the patient wineglasses / set out by private history's ignorant / quiet hands." New, seemingly inchoate images gain substance when embraced by the crowd, however. Like "islands" in muddy "floodwaters," they lead her to suggest that "[m]aybe what seems / evanescent is solid." While such an explanation may not justify Levertov's poetic choices, unresolved images like that of water — alternately the all-embracing sea as unity, crystalline ice as a sign of natural order, and a torrential stream as a metaphor for history — dramatize the absence of a poetic coherence and a fixed truth in the historical process.

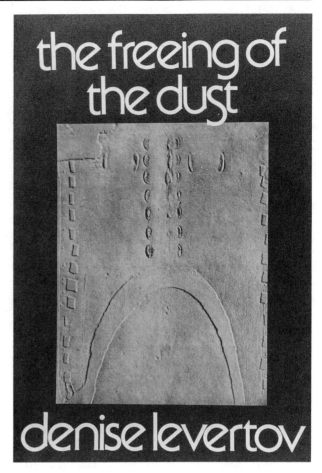

Dust jacket for Levertov's 1975 collection, in which she treats personal subjects while avoiding the "overuse of the autobiographical"

The end of "Staying Alive" conveys Levertov's exhaustion from her sustained political activity and the painful loss of self that resulted from her commitment to a group effort. While she remained active in peace rallies and antinuclear protests and she continued to write political poetry, she began at this time to focus more and more on the individual, rather than the group, as the source of political change. Levertov's intensive involvement in public politics and the changes in her poetic practices alienated her from Duncan, and she and Creeley also drifted apart, ending the close friendships and shared poetic concerns that earlier identified the three as Black Mountain poets. An angry exchange of letters between Levertov and Duncan after the publication of her book *To Stay Alive* demonstrated their diverging poetics and foreshadowed the different strains of political poetry that emerged in the 1970s and 1980s. Whereas Levertov moved toward a romantic voice and a commonly understood language as the vehicles of protest poetry, Creeley and

Duncan continued to maintain that political critiques and poetic originality emerged only from experimental poetry that challenged the norms of syntax and poetic form.

Levertov's participation in an international struggle for peace and her increasingly international reputation in the late 1960s widened her interest in and contact with an international community of poets and revolutionaries. Her increased engagement in an international poetic tradition led, among other things, to several experiments in translation. In 1967 she collaborated with Edward C. Dimock in the translation of Bengali love songs. She also published translations of Rilke, Jules Supervielle, Eugene Guillevic, Jean Joubert, Alain Bosquet, and a collection of Bulgarian poets. Although a fairly literal translator, Levertov sometimes altered the original texts to accentuate her own poetic preferences. Whereas Joubert, for example, frequently uses long, flowing lines to establish a rhythmic momentum independent of meaning, Levertov breaks some lines to achieve the scoring of concrete detail and the visual clarity that is characteristic of her own poems. Levertov's contact with an international community also reinvigorated her engagement of European literary traditions, her reading of which increasingly lent her visions authority and provided examples for experimentation.

Retreating from the attempt to embed poetic language in political language, Levertov's next two volumes, *Footprints* and *The Freeing of the Dust* (1975), accentuate the distance between the poet's poetic and political visions. Lacking the social context that was provided in *To Stay Alive*, the glowing moments of *Footprints* seem spare and isolated. Many poems are sequences of brief, unconnected images, as in "Brass Tacks":

i

The old wooden house a soft
almost-blue faded green
embowered in southern autumn's
nearly-yellow green leaves,
the air damp after a night of rain.

ii

The black girl sitting alone in the back row
smiled at me.

While "Brass Tacks" presents such images as consoling essentials of experience, Levertov pares them to independent glowing presences rather than weaving them into a larger scheme in the poem.

Many of the political poems are structured by the stark opposition between the images of beauty that strengthen her and the horror of war, presenting a simultaneity of opposites that remains a recurrent theme in her writing.

Near Saigon,
in a tiger-cage, a woman
tries to straighten her
          cramped spine
and cannot.

Unclenched fist
cinnamon warmth of winter light,
revelation, communion.

While the book introduces Levertov's ecological concerns into her representation of natural beauty, it also turns to the private realm to speak of childhood memories and Levertov's divorce from her husband. Although these poems explore the imaginative vision for its own sake, they frequently make the speaker's position explicit. The opening series of poems on views from an airplane, for example, expresses a consciousness of the technologies that frame vision and that are less prominent in Levertov's earlier work.

If this poetry records a growing distance between the personal and political dimensions of her life, Levertov's theoretical writings of the mid 1970s seeks to reunite them in a refined conception of political poetry. Motivated by her desire to defend the possibility of political poetry, both traditional and contemporary, against its critics, she rethought the relation between the personal and political. In her 1975 essay "On the Edge of Darkness: What is Political Poetry?" she asserts the compatibility of lyricism and political message, arguing that the personal testimony of a lyric voice is the most powerful tool of political advocacy. She writes that the goal of politically committed writers should be "such osmosis of personal and public, of assertion and song, that no one would be able to divide our poems into categories." Levertov's subsequent political poetry locates the source of change in the development of individual vision, in developing the role of the imagination in constructing a community where individual and collective growth coincide.

Like *The Freeing of the Dust*, *Life in the Forest* (1978) develops deeply personal subjects, including the death of Levertov's mother in 1977 and Levertov's growth in the love relationships that followed her divorce. She attempts, however, to give these themes a significance that transcends their personal dimension. The book's introductory note describes her desire to emulate the antifascist Italian poet Cesare Pavese, whose poems about his local Piedmont area and its people in *Lavorare Stanca (Hard Labor)* (1943) reveal his character through his bond to the land and community. Following Pavese's model, Levertov seeks to use landscape and portrait to "avoid overuse of the autobiographical, the dominant first-person singular of so much of the American poetry – good and bad – of recent years." Levertov's poems about her mother's death portray her mother's character by describing such works as her garden. The poems suggest an acceptance of the finality of death and change, evoking the Mexican landscape as it reclaims the garden as wilderness. The very different selves that emerge in two cycles of love poems also explore the relationship between character and natural and social environment. The playful, self-mocking "Modulations for Solo Voice" dissects the various traditional and nontraditional stances Levertov adopts as she attempts to find communion in a new love relationship. Titles such as "The Phonecall," "Psyche in Somerville," and "A Woman Pacing Her Room, Rereading a Letter, Returning Again and Again to Her Mirror" expose the destructive cultural forms that importantly mediate interpersonal relations.

"Metamorphic Journal," however, describes the growth of self that may be gained from the experience of love, in the lovers' mutual reflection. In this sequence the images of trees, rivers, and flame, through which Levertov attempts to grasp the lovers and their relationship, develop a cosmology that invests the lovers' whole environment with meaning. For Levertov the imagination originates in the agency through which people make sense of their world and their interpersonal relations. On the other hand, certain images convey an uncertainty about this process of growth through mutual reflection. The image of water as a mirror suggests narcissism, and a final image of the imagination's creations as fire-cast shadows on a cave wall alludes to Plato's illusory knowledge of mere opinion. Still, the poem begins to envision the more fruitful relationships between individuals that emerge in Levertov's mature politics of the personal.

Levertov's next volume, *Candles in Babylon* (1982), integrates more closely the subjects of nature, politics, and love, each of which had been for the most part developed separately since the early 1970s. The book's five sections establish a new significance to Levertov's romantic identification with nature. While some poems abjure a romantic innocence of perception, considered inappropriate given both her own aging and experience and the horrors of contemporary history, nature comes to play a new role in Levertov's poetic portrayal of her contemporary social context. The book's second section, "Pig Dreams," is a playful Wordsworthian *Prelude* of the pet pig, Sylvia. Here Levertov traces the growth of Sylvia's specifically porcine "culture" and religious reverence for nature to her natural needs and pleasures and her friendships with other farm animals. Sylvia's empathetic extension into their lives produces the interplay of similarity and difference through which she comes to know herself and her place in the farm community.

While Sylvia's Vermont farm represents an idyll of harmonious, intimate community, Levertov uses this ideal to criticize the alienating "Babylon" of mass culture in which she finds herself. Images of this culture, presented as a dark movie theater that isolates individuals while holding them in passive thrall to its visions of technological power and Cold War ideology, convey a social environment that prevents the individual from growth and authentic engagement in the world. In the rest of *Candles in Babylon*, the poems seem to explore the means by which imaginative vision can take root in a world that is politically alienating. The characteristic of empathy, embodied in the flexible octopus for whom *"any shelter it can find is home,"* becomes a means to social and poltical connectedness. Identifying with the "steadfast ranks" of mountains or the "alertness of red rooftiles," the octopus not only anchors its own existence in the world by rendering the alien familiar, but it also provides an example for others to do the same. Increasingly, Levertov's poems on nature and art suggest ways in which individuals may "domesticate" seemingly alien aspects of their environment and reconstruct social institutions on the basis of genuine and intimate personal relations. For the poet, empathetic reflection is a virtue that both increases one's sensitivity toward fellow beings and also enriches the individual through his or her act of imagining the lives of others.

The final section of *Candles in Babylon* introduces Levertov's Christian beliefs as another major context in which she develops the varied meanings of her concrete epiphanies. As a logical outgrowth of the book's political ideal, a belief in the Christian God who is presented in a "Mass for the Day of St. Thomas Didymus" becomes the basis for a potential social harmony that recognizes the metaphysical unity of all beings as creatures of a benevolent deity. Represented as the weak, newborn lamb of Christ, Levertov's Christian God is also a fragile vision of innocence and goodness whose very existence depends on its protection by all. As an element of the collective imagination, Christianity thus provides what Albert Gelpi has called "the transcendent third term that bridges the rupture between individual epiphany and public calamity" in Levertov's poetry.

In her treatment of gender issues, Levertov states quite clearly that as a poet she is not a feminist. Her 1982 essay "Genre and Gender v. Serving an Art" treats gender as one aspect of the specific and immediate situations from which the poet develops meanings that "will transcend gender." Denying the existence of a poetics that is specific to women, she writes, "I don't believe I have ever made an aesthetic decision based on my gender." Although she frequently portrays women's experiences and writes explicitly in a woman's voice, many of her poetic choices may be attributed to other interests. Her frank exploration of sexuality, for instance, is typical of many poets of the 1950s and 1960s, and she shares her emphasis on themes of domesticity with Creeley and Duncan. Linda A. Kinnahan argues persuasively that Levertov's attention to the specifics of women's lives develops a legacy of Williams's attention to the local and the sexual aspects of experience, a legacy that provided an enabling model for contemporary women poets to write as women.

Levertov's love poems reflect a variety of concerns that develop throughout her writing – from her early love lyrics, written in the dreamy unreality of her neoromanticism, to her frankly erotic poems and her poems on marriage, replete with the antiromantic sensual immediacy of the 1950s and 1960s. Likewise, her poems about the personal growth that is achieved through the transformations of love illustrate her interest in the interpersonal realm as an integral part of her political vision in the 1970s and 1980s. Her most recent love lyrics examine the conflicts between sexual and romantic love and the process of physical aging. Frequently writing directly from her particular sexual and socioeconomic situation, Levertov, nevertheless, also adopts other women's voices – such as those of Ishtar, Rose White and Rose Red, and the much-traveled, wine-drinking old soothsayer – not to critique them as models of a particular kind of femininity but rather, as she does with other cultural themes, to reveal them as familiar cultural influences that live in and shape her imagination.

Because she writes as a daughter, lover, wife, mother, and sister, Levertov's poetry explores various aspects of women's sexuality, their domestic culture, their poetic identity, and their roles in the cultural imagination of myth and fairy tale. Then,

Cover for Levertov's 1982 book, in which the final section shows her integration of Christian faith and political idealism

too, her relation to Olson's phallic theory of "projective" verse and the "objectifying" poetics that undergird the Black Mountain poetics is significant for her poetic development. Perhaps unconsciously, her *Collected Earlier Poems 1940–1960* presents the transition to the Black Mountain style as a shift from women portrayed as subject to women seen as object. "Who He Was," the last of the poems strongly grounded in iambic pentameter, describes a woman feeling the movements of her unborn child and wondering who the child will become. In contrast, the next two poems, which adopt the shorter lines and less regular meter of her new American environment, describe the woman from the outside. "Kresch's Studio" describes the artist's model "in taut repose, intent / under violent light that pulls / the weight of breasts to answer the long/ shadow of thighs, / confronts angles with receding / planes." "A Woman" attempts to understand a woman's unsettled emotions in her "remote," glittering green eyes but finds no key in this specific physical detail.

In *With Eyes at the Back of Our Heads,* "A Ring of Changes," a poem written to reconcile an argument between husband and wife, dramatizes an early version of Levertov's interpersonal poetics as a feminine transgression. While the man sits alone like the creator God of Genesis "forming darkness into words," the woman wishes to shed her angry pride, "to dig shame up, a buried bone / and tie it to my breast − / (would it change, in time, / to an ornament?)." Although this beginning generates a poem of reconciliation, the bone's resemblance to Hester Prynne's embroidered *A* in *The Scarlet Letter* explains an ambivalence about the interpersonal, rather than the autonomous source of poetic vision, in terms of gender. Levertov's vision of interpersonal relationships develops fully only when she engages her love for the impersonal life of things, learned from Williams, in a social context, whether that context be interpersonal or publicly political.

Levertov's images of women challenge conventional conceptions of women's creativity. Deborah Pope and Sandra Gilbert have studied the tension between two women, one wholesome, charitable, and domestic, the other artistic, glamorous, and non-nurturing. Poems such as "In Mind" and "The Earthwoman and the Waterwoman" dramatize the tension between the housewife or mother, on the one hand, and the artist, on the other, with biological and artistic creativity frequently presented as mutually exclusive options for the female artist. In contrast, Kinnahan and Susan Stanford Friedman have explored Levertov's construction of a matrilinear tradition of poetic vision that was inherited from her mother and that seems to reconcile this tension.

Levertov's political vision tends to be colored by the political romanticism of the 1960s and the feminist critiques of patriarchy that present a female-dominated culture as a positive alternative to a violently destructive male-dominated public world. Levertov's political ideals, grounded in a domesticity and harmony with nature traditionally associated with women, contrast with the public world of technology, rationality, and politics associated with men. While rarely involved in detailed critiques of the social institutions that shape gender roles in society, Levertov nevertheless explores the powerful ways in which institutions shape the cultural imaginations of both men and women.

Levertov in *Oblique Prayers* (1984) uses brief images and short lines to praise the wisdom to be gained from the fragmentary fact: "half a loaf / reveals / the inner wheat: / leavened / transubstantiation." Levertov focuses on the individuality of particular beings, attempting to approach God by grasping the particular "divinity," or spirit, of a tree, river, flower, and even of herself, in "Of God and of the Gods." This intensive focus on the individual creature in its unique reality stems both from a reverence for all nature as divine creation and from a heightened consciousness of the changing meaning of experiences.

Felt life
grows in one's mind:
each semblance

forms and
reforms cloudy
links with
the next

and the next.

Increasingly tolerant of contradictions, Levertov represents her life as composed of patterns or threads of a fabric whose order she herself cannot grasp. In contrast to the weak lamb of "Mass for the Day of St. Thomas Didymus," the God of *Oblique Prayers* is a remote weaver whose purpose the individual cannot fathom: "our eyes, / our lives, too close to the canvas, / enmeshed within / the turning dance, / to see it [perfection]."

Levertov's ecological concerns find expression in poems in which she delves into the actual relationship between human and natural beings. The sequence "Gathered at the River" employs techniques that recur in Levertov's later nature poetry. Personifying trees as fearful of their extermination by a nuclear holocaust, the poem extends Levertov's interpersonal poetics to include the nonhuman beings in nature. Levertov frequently uses images of a family or a single organism to signify the interdependence of human and natural life in the single ecosystem of the earth; she also evaluates human actions in terms of their impact on the earth and its inhabitants, and she seeks to awaken a sensitivity to and respect for the creatures and the patterns of life that are seemingly independent of human interest, yet worthy of equal respect.

Oblique Prayers thus blends the Christian and ecological visions that enlarge the field of the poet's earlier poetic concerns. In her 1991 essay, "Some Affinities of Content," Levertov describes the reading she prefers at this time to be "a certain kind of poem about the world of nature written predominantly by poets of the Pacific Northwest, and poems of various provenance that were concerned more or less with matters of religious faith," primarily al-

Dust jacket for Levertov's 1989 book, which exhibits the intensely mystical vision found in her later work (courtesy of the Lilly Library, Indiana University)

though not exclusively in a Christian or Jewish context. Among the latter, she includes Ben Sáenz, Lucille Clifton, and Czeslaw Milosz, in whose work spiritual longing includes "the quest for or the encounter with God." The "affinities" between these two groups lie for Levertov in their sense of life "'on pilgrimage,'" "in search of significance underneath and beyond the succession of temporal events." In her later poetry, Nature and God are the subjects that provide frameworks for a moral and spiritual understanding, one that surpasses the restrictive, human-centered views offered by technology and political history.

Breathing the Water (1987) and *A Door in the Hive* (1989) retain the focus on the concrete world exemplified in *Oblique Prayers,* but these books introduce the stronger mystical vision that informs much of Levertov's later poetry. Grounded in the visionary traditions of Rilke's conception of poets as "bees of the invisible," creatures that distill pollen

into honey, and also in a Christian reverence for each object as a miraculous creation capable of providing knowledge of God, this heightened vision focuses increasingly on those moments of perception when physical matter is somehow transformed into a spiritual essence. As Levertov's poetic vision deepens, she moves from a pure meditation on the natural object to the creation of artistic moments or patterns that serve as the "doorkey" or "embrasure" to a fuller and larger vision. In "Athanor," for example, a dogfood bag gilded by light becomes a "fleeting conjugation / of wood and light, embrace that leaves wood / dizzying and insubstantial." In "From the Image Flow – Death of Chausson, 1899" the poet imagines the death of the composer as a synesthesia of a mauve stream of music and green leaves, culminating in silence.

For Levertov, the composed rather than the found poetic object becomes central in stimulating the imagination. Occasionally, poems in these volumes express an uncertainty about what seems to be Levertov's new relation to nature, with the speaker dramatized in "The Spy" as a spy and in "Captive Flower" as a jailer. Two sections titled "Spinoffs" establish the spinoff's quasi-generic character as "a verbal construct which neither describes nor comments but moves off at a tangent to, or parallel with, its inspiration."

While Levertov's Rilkean visions delight in description and imaginative vision for their own sake, her poems on Christian themes frequently contemplate the relation of the poetic illumination to personal life, history, and cosmology. In *Breathing the Water,* the sequence "The Showings: Lady Julian of Norwich, 1342–1416" explores the mystic's visions elicited by the everyday world by employing rich biographical and historical detail, such as the child's wonder at a newly laid egg or a hazelnut, even in the "dark times" of war and plague in the late Middle Ages. Levertov emphasizes Julian's desire to experience the Crucifixion of the flesh as a compassionate act of empathy with all human suffering. Julian's clinging to joy amid such suffering, "like an acrobat, by your teeth, fiercely," represents a faith that is foreign yet admirable to Levertov. In direct address, Levertov conjures Julian as a model of a faith alien to the modern mind yet empowering in the struggle toward goodness – after deeds, quoting Julian, "*so evil / . . . / it seems to us / impossible any good / can come of them.*"

Levertov's "El Salvador: Requiem and Invocation," a libretto written for the composer Newell Hendricks and included in *A Door in the Hive,* seeks a Julian-like way to heal suffering. Taking as its occasion the murder of Archbishop Romero, three Mary Knoll sisters, and a lay volunteer in El Salvador, the "Requiem" attempts to render those murdered or silenced by the oppressive regime as a sustaining source of resistance. The poem returns to the collage style of *To Stay Alive,* using the language of torturers, Mayan prayers, and the words of the martyrs to represent the political struggle. Levertov contrasts an idealized precolonial Mayan culture, in which labor and prayer, human and natural life were in harmony, with a Western, money-driven economy of scientific "progress." While denying the possibility of a return to the earlier Mayan life, she presents the Christian vision of community held by those murdered, a community based on mutual respect and "listening," as a foundation for dignity and hope in society. A requiem rather than a documentary, the poem moves from pain and despair to search out a way from violence toward healing, finding in its commemoration of the dead "the knowledge / that grows in power / out of the seeds of their martyrdom."

Later, in *A Door in the Hive,* Levertov portrays the power of Christian belief as it is manifested in an individual life. In this collection, poems on the Christian themes of the Annunciation, the Nativity, and the Harrowing of Hell not only continue the rich illumination of Christian texts with humble, everyday detail that was begun in "The Showings" but, just as her Rilkean visions do, they seek to reveal the points at which divinity may become incarnate in the individual being. "Annunciation," for example, evokes the possibility of a divine incarnation that is imminent in the everyday world. "Aren't there annunciations / of one sort or another / in most lives?" Emphasizing the "compassion," "intelligence," and "courage" with which the Virgin Mary embraces her role as the mother of Jesus, Levertov seeks to translate a tradition of miracles into material and psychological circumstances more acceptable to the modern mind.

Even as Levertov affirms the activity of spirit in the daily life of the individual and society, *A Door in the Hive* betrays the uneasy relationship that exists between heightened vision and actual history. "Flickering Mind" explores the tension between the individual's desire to contemplate God's presence in all being and the individual mind's earthbound "wander[ing]." Although Levertov has said that she intends no particular relation between the two poems, a poem ending one section praises a blind man who is living at the edge of a cliff for breathing "face to face with desire," while the first poem of the next section suggests the limitations of such a private vision. "Distanced" is a poem that contrasts the witnessing of life from afar with the actuality of immediate experience, by presenting an image of shepherds in the mountains who "marvel" and "sorrow" at the sack of a city below them. They feel the "pity and dread" of tragic drama but perceive the people fleeing the city as a "river" without faces or blood. "Where Is the Angel?" seeks an angry wrestling by which to break the gentle September beauty, which, like glass, separates Levertov from the turbulence of history: "History / mouths, volume turned off." Questioning the value of her beautiful images, the poet feels isolated from the wounding engagement in history that mars such perfection, "so curses and blessing flow storming out / and the glass shatters, and the iron sunders."

Levertov's most recent book of poems, *Evening Train* (1992), records the experience of settling in her new home in Seattle, her dialogue with representations of nature created by poets of the Pacific Northwest, her struggle as an aging woman to understand the difficult meanings of love, and her response to the Persian Gulf War that pitted the United States against Iraq in 1991. In one poem, still conscious of mystery and delighted by descriptions, she nevertheless finds herself enjoying "the leisure of mind / to lean on the fence and simply look" and is thereby reluctant to synthesize or assign meaning — whether to the neighboring mountain, a photo of a friend, or barnyard doves and chickens. In another poem torn between the "two magnets" of nature and art, "Rock Simple or Rock Wrought," and "tools of Geology or tools of Art," she initiates a dialogue that contrasts the American tradition of immersion in nature and her European love of ancient cultural traditions. As in her earlier writing, some of Levertov's best poems emerge when she weaves the different strands of her writing into the evolving situations of personal experience. The longer line in many of these poems, the line she used in her earlier works inspired by Pavese, serves as a formal signal of her thematic return to Pavese's integration of person and place.

While the book's first section, "Lake Mountain Moon," finds the pulse of the poet's new environment, both in its natural and its man-made dimensions, subsequent sections interpret human creations through metaphors of the mist, the ancient rock, and the shadow of this landscape. "Stele," a response to a stone funerary relief, also describes the moments between a man and woman parting in terms of the "land of shadow" and "road of cloud" each is about to inhabit. In a later sequence, the speaker reprimands herself for falling in love just

*Dust jacket for Levertov's 1993 book, which includes poems
about the Persian Gulf War (courtesy of the Lilly Library,
Indiana University)*

when she had decided that she was too old for its demands; then she turns to her landscape for its "stoic" wisdom. "Shameless heart! Did you not vow to learn / stillness from the heron, / quiet from the mists of fall, / and from the mountain — what was it? / Pride? Remoteness?" "Witnessing from Afar" addresses the problem of identifying with or speaking for victims who are far away by focusing on the nearer effects of war and ecological disasters at home. Whether in swimmers' denial that a lake is seriously polluted, or in the dehumanization of the language of high-technology war and video games, or even in the substitution of *may* for *might* in contemporary speech, the poet recognizes and deplores the tendency to deny the real and final effects of human actions, and, thus, of responsibility for those actions. Whether her subject is the burial of Iraqi soldiers while they are still alive, a neighboring heron, or the stone of a medieval cathedral, Levertov, as she does in her earlier work, makes whatever is vitally important to her vivid and compelling.

Through her many writings and her abounding creativity, Levertov's ability to create luminous representations of the material world in its sensuous existence remains her greatest talent and the distinguishing feature of her mature poetic vision. By poetry that finds epiphanies in the concrete world of experience, and by her theory of "organic form," which emerges from a grounding of form in the object and an appreciation for the poetic possibilities of colloquial language, Levertov is linked both to William Carlos Williams and to the Black Mountain poets; but the increasingly romantic direction in which she develops her poetics has kept her from continuing the avant-garde's challenge to linguistic conventions, thereby significantly distancing her from one major legacy of the Black Mountain poets. Especially in her later work, Levertov aspires to translate the high calling and visionary power of the romantic and modernist poet into forms and terms comprehensible to a scientifically skeptical mass culture.

This effort sharply distinguishes her from such contemporaries as the Language poets — Charles Bernstein and Susan Howe, for example — who believe that genuine creativity requires a radical formal experimentation that challenges the traditional lyric forms and voice. Levertov's focus on the individual imagination as the source of political change further contrasts with these poets' desire to expose and disrupt the power of linguistic conventions, a disruption they assume will ultimately undermine other institutions they oppose. For critic Cary Nelson, the confidence that Levertov places in the power of individuals seems naive; for others, such as Albert Gelpi, her focus on the individual's potential to effect change, and her distinctively articulate personal voice, are sources of power and beauty.

Levertov's writing is perhaps most successful when she focuses the rays of its different subjects and styles through the lens of her personal, lived experience, sensitively revealing in her scrupulously crafted poems the vital relationship between the individual self and the world. Meanwhile, her ongoing efforts to fathom and express the problematic intersections between the public and private realms of society, between a Christian cosmology and the world of strictly scientific fact, and between literary tradition and the darknesses of contemporary history have helped build important new bridges across the difficult cultural landscape of contemporary poetry.

Interviews:

David Ossman, "An Interview with Denise Levertov," in *The Sullen Art* (New York: Corinth Books, 1963), pp. 73–76;

Walter Sutton, "A Conversation with Denise Levertov," *Minnesota Review*, 5 (October–December, 1965): 322–328;

E. G. Burrows, "An Interview with Denise Levertov," *Michigan Quarterly Review*, 7 (1968): 239–242;

Ian Reid, "'Everyman's Land': Ian Reid Interviews Denise Levertov," *Southern Review: Literary and Interdisciplinary Essays, South Australia*, 5 (1972): 231–236;

William Heyen and Anthony Piccione, "A Conversation with Denise Levertov," *Ironwood*, 4 (1973): 21–34;

William Packard, ed., "Craft Interview with Denise Levertov," *New York Quarterly*, 7 (1974): 79–100;

John K. Atchity, "Denise Levertov: An Interview," *San Francisco Review of Books*, no. 4 (March 1979): 5–8;

Sybil Estess, "An Interview with Denise Levertov and a Biographical Note," *American Poetry Observed: Poets and Their Work*, edited by Joseph David Bellamy (Chicago: University of Illinois Press, 1984), pp. 155–167;

Lorrie Smith, "An Interview with Denise Levertov," *Michigan Quarterly Review*, 24 (1985): 596–604.

Bibliographies:

Robert A. Wilson, *A Bibliography of Denise Levertov* (New York: Phonix Book Shop, 1972);

Liana Sakelliou-Schultz, *Denise Levertov: An Annotated Primary and Secondary Bibliography* (New York: Garland Publishing, 1988).

References:

Charles Altieri, "Denise Levertov and the Limits of the Aesthetics of Presence," in *Denise Levertov: Selected Criticism*, edited by Albert Gelpi (Ann Arbor: University of Michigan Press, 1993), pp. 126–147;

Robert Bly [Crunk], "The Work of Denise Levertov," *Sixties*, 9 (Spring 1967): 48–65;

Susan Stanford Friedman, "Creativity and the Childbirth Metaphor: Gender Difference in Literary Discourse," *Feminist Studies*, 13, no. 1 (1975): 328–341;

Gelpi, ed., *Denise Levertov: Selected Criticism* (Ann Arbor: University of Michigan Press, 1993);

Sandra Gilbert, "Revolutionary Love: Denise Levertov and the Poetics of Politics," in *Denise Levertov: Selected Criticism*, edited by Gelpi (Ann Arbor: University of Michigan Press, 1993), pp. 201–217;

Joan Hallisey, "Denise Levertov's 'Illustrious Ancestors': The Hassidic Influence," in *Denise Levertov: Selected Criticism*, edited by Gelpi (Ann Arbor: University of Michigan Press, 1993), pp. 260–267;

Linda A. Kinnahan, "Denise Levertov: The Daughter's Voice," *Poetics of the Feminine: Authority and Literary Tradition in William Carlos Williams, Mina Loy, Denise Levertov, and Kathleen Fraser* (Cambridge: Cambridge University Press, 1994), pp. 125–182;

Harry Marten, *Understanding Denise Levertov* (Columbia: University of South Carolina Press, 1988);

James F. Mersmann, "Denise Levertov: Piercing In," in *Out of the Vietnam Vortex: a study of poets and poetry against the war* (Lawrence: University Press of Kansas, 1974), pp. 77–106;

Peter Middleton, *Revelation and Revolution in the Poetry of Denise Levertov* (London: Binnacle Press, 1981);

Dorothy M. Nielson, "Prosopopoeia and the Ethics of Ecological Advocacy in the Poetry of Denise Levertov and Gary Snyder," *Contemporary Literature*, 34 (Winter 1993): 691–713;

Deborah Pope, "Homespun and Crazy Feathers: The Split–Self in the Poems of Denise Levertov," in *Critical Essays on Denise Levertov*, edited by Linda Welshimer Wagner (Boston: G. K. Hall, 1991), pp. 73–97;

Audrey Rodgers, *Denise Levertov: The Poetry of Engagement* (Rutherford: Fairleigh Dickinson University Press, 1993);

Leonard Schwartz, "Guillevic/Levertov: The Poetics of Matter," *Twentieth Century Literature,* 38 (Fall 1992): 290–298;

Nancy Sisko, "*To Stay Alive:* Levertov's Search for a Revolutionary Poetry," *Sagetrieb,* 5 (Fall 1986): 47–61;

Wagner, *Denise Levertov* (New York: Twayne Publishers, 1967);

Wagner, ed., *Critical Essays on Denise Levertov* (Boston: G. K. Hall, 1991);

Wagner, ed., *Denise Levertov: In Her Own Province* (New York: New Directions, 1979);

Edward Zlotowski, "Levertov and Rilke: A Sense of Aesthetic Ethics," *Twentieth Century Literature,* 38 (Fall 1992): 324–342.

Papers:
The Denise Levertov papers are housed in Special Collections, Green Library, Stanford University. Significant Levertov correspondence and manuscripts are also included in the Creeley papers at Stanford University, the Duncan papers in the Poetry/Rare Books Collection of the Lockwood Library at the State University of New York at Buffalo, and the Williams papers at the Beiniecke Library of Yale University.

Bernadette Mayer

(12 May 1945 –   )

Peter Baker
Towson State University

BOOKS: *Ceremony Latin* (New York: Angel Hair, 1964);

Story (New York: 0 to 9 Books, 1968);

Moving (New York: Angel Hair, 1971);

The Basketball Article, by Mayer and Anne Waldman (New York: Angel Hair Books, 1975);

Memory (Plainfield, Vt.: North Atlantic Books, 1975);

Studying Hunger (Berkeley, Cal.: Adventures in Poetry/Big Sky, 1975);

Poetry (New York: Kulchur Foundation, 1976);

Eruditio Ex Memoria (New York: Angel Hair, 1977);

The Golden Book of Words (Lenox, Mass.: Angel Hair, 1978);

Midwinter Day (Berkeley, Cal.: Turtle Island Foundation, 1982);

Incidents Reports Sonnets (New York: Archipelago Books, 1984);

Utopia (New York: United Artists Books, 1984);

Mutual Aid (New York: Mademoiselle de la Mole Press, 1985);

The Art of Science Writing, by Mayer and Dale Worsley (New York: Teachers & Writers Collaborative, 1989);

Sonnets (New York: Tender Buttons, 1989);

The Formal Field of Kissing (New York: Catchword Papers, 1990);

A Bernadette Mayer Reader (New York: New Directions, 1992);

The Desires of Mothers to Please Others in Letters (Stockbridge, Mass.: Hard Press, 1994).

OTHER: "The Obfuscated Poem" and "from the *Studying Hunger Journals,*" in *A Code of Signals: Recent Writings in Poetics,* edited by Michael Palmer (Berkeley, Cal.: North Atlantic, 1983): 164–171;

"Experiments," in *The L=A=N=G=U=A=G=E Book,* edited by Bruce Andrews and Charles Bernstein (Carbondale: Southern Illinois University Press, 1984), pp. 80–83;

"From: A Lecture at the Naropa Institute" in *0 / two: An Anthology,* edited by Leslie Scalapino (Oakland, Cal.: O Press, 1991): 89–97;

"Studying Hunger," in *Out of This World: The Poetry Project at St. Mark's Church-in-the-Bowery: An Anthology 1966–1991,* edited by Anne Waldman (New York: Crown, 1991).

Bernadette Mayer is a poet whose experiments in form and in language have attracted favorable critical reaction and the attention of numerous fellow poets and writers, leading some observers to consider her one of the most important experimental writers of recent years. Her most important work features a startling inclusivity by which the poet tries to re-create the innumerable objects, events, memories, and dreams that range into the field of an alert consciousness. Mayer has lived many years in New York City, the setting for many of her poems. In 1972 she burst onto the New York performance art scene with her experimental piece *Memory*. In the following years she has continued to write and publish. Perhaps one of her most important works is the book-length poem *Midwinter Day* (1982), which describes a day in the poet's life in 1978 when she was living in Lenox, Massachusetts.

Mayer's work is closely associated with New York City, in part through her long affiliation with the St. Mark's Poetry Project in Greenwich Village. At various times over more than twenty years, she has directed workshops in experimental writing; she also served as the Poetry Project's resident director for four years (1980–1984). Her early workshops (1971–1975) brought together several younger poets, among them Charles Bernstein, Bruce Andrews, Peter Seaton, and Nick Piombino, who later helped create what has come to be called the "Language" movement. Partly because of her distrust of labels, partly because she has always tried to write poetry across the full range of expressive possibilities, Mayer's interactions with members of the Language group have been somewhat troubled. Despite

Bernadette Mayer (photograph by Marie Warsh)

the fact that Mayer considers herself and the poet Clark Coolidge to be among the movement's "forebears," leading advocates of the movement have sometimes tended to minimize Mayer's role in developing this particular style of experimental writing. Her close affiliations with other leading experimental poets – such as Coolidge, whom she first met in 1969 in California – have, however, provided her with ongoing creative support. Of Coolidge, Mayer has said: "I think Clark's work and my work happening simultaneously in the world when we first both began to be aware of it was a major moment for both of us. I think Clark and I gave each other confidence, and I don't know that we could believe that it was possible to attempt to write in these weird ways that we were writing."

Mayer was born in 1945 in Brooklyn, New York, to Theodore and Marie Ann Bernadette Stumpf Mayer. Her early life was profoundly marked by the deaths of both parents: her father died in 1957 and her mother in 1959. Mayer's difficulties were then compounded by her being raised by her grandfather and a guardian uncle, who, in turn, died when she was seventeen. Although references to these early experiences of death tend to be elided in the published works, they are an underlying muted force in texts such as *Studying Hunger*

(1975) and *Midwinter Day*. An important turning point in Mayer's life was marked in the year 1965, when she attended the New School for Social Research, in part to take advantage of government benefits for orphaned children who remained in school. A formative class at the New School was her poetry workshop with poet Bill Berkson in 1965 and 1966. Through Berkson, Mayer was introduced to Frank O'Hara and John Ashbery. Mayer has been closely involved with poet Lewis Warsh, with whom she ran the United Artists publishing series, and with whom she had three children, Marie, Sophia, and Max, born in 1975, 1977, and 1980. When her children were very young, Mayer lived in various places in New England. Mayer has taught poetry not only at the St. Mark's Poetry Project, but also the New School for Social Research and many other institutions. She has a sister, Rosemary Mayer, a sculptor and watercolorist, with whom she collaborates on classical translation projects.

It was *Memory* that first attracted serious attention to Mayer's work. In her book *Studying Hunger,* she describes how the project originated:

You see, the whole thing had already had a beginning with a project called MEMORY which turned into a show which turned into a dream or returned to a dream that enabled me to walk. Before this I couldnt walk, I had street fantasies like any normal prostitute. Anyway, MEMORY was 1200 color snapshots, 3 X 5, processed by Kodak plus 7 hours of taped narration. I had shot one roll of 35-mm color film every day for the month of July, 1971. The pictures were mounted side by side in row after row along a long wall, each line to be read from left to right, 36 feet by 4 feet. All the images made each day were included, in sequence, along with a 31-part tape, which took the pictures as points of focus, one by one & as taking-off points for digression, filling in the spaces between.

Photography critic A. D. Coleman, reviewing the 1972 installation at Holly Solomon's 98 Greene Street gallery for the *Village Voice,* observed, "What resulted from this combination of methods and media was a unique and deeply exciting document. . . . [It] touches on a number of intrinsic, extra-aesthetic aspects of photography which are no less significant to our understanding of life for falling outside the boundaries of what is generally considered to be photographic art." Coolidge recently wrote that "The original gallery installation, grid of photos on the wall with the spoken text constantly playing on tape, was amazing: you felt like no matter what photo you were momentarily focusing on the voice was commenting on exactly that image, until finally you were enveloped in a dream continuum of total contingency." Mayer's startling *Memory* installation, although an important early influence on the performance-art movement in New York City and elsewhere, has never been reproduced in its entirety in book form; the written text, published in 1975, is generally considered one of her most experimental works. Reviewer Simon Schuchat said of the published text, "I think that this book in particular, and Mayer's work in general, is as important as any literary work since [William] Burroughs' cut-up novels." *Memory,* both as the installation and the printed book, significantly helped establish Mayer as one of the leading experimental writers of her time.

The text of *Memory* is challenging; indeed, Mayer herself has said that a common response — even from her most committed experimental writer friends — was that they could not finish it. The following passage suggests the flavor of the piece:

Colors & colors they're yellow blue brick grey white green pink words taxi lights my things tag $2.19 people radio balloon baby chair bright blue car l'escargot the chimes the boardwalk 3rd ave el baronet & coronet king movies can move backwards diamond ice cubes co. maneuvering not able to maneuver true sea & ski & rheingold beer the woman drive defensively from the

canadian rockies up on the roof violins horn & hardarts black white up down shoes clothes rear view mirror love a guy gets out of his car, looks around a kid gets out he gets back in he parked in the middle of the street, flashers, all the way to texas if you want, stirring up dust, if any.

In Peter Baker's book *Obdurate Brilliance* (1991), two problems for analyzing a text such as this are identified: "For one, the level of recorded reality is so insistent that there seems to be only that level — surface meaning and nothing more. The second, and more difficult, problem is the extent to which the text already embeds its own self-commentary, rendering secondary criticism unnecessary." Despite these interpretive problems, such a text succeeds in creating a space of movement, a headlong dive into words and images. Residents and cognoscenti of New York can gain great enjoyment from the specific references to landmarks, billboards, and the names of specific and distinctive New York business establishments. Although *Memory* is to some extent sui generis, an "unrepeatable work," as Mayer herself has called it, it may also stand as paradigmatic of both the tremendous energy of her writing and its firm basis in the poet's actual, lived experience.

Studying Hunger represents only part of a much longer work that Mayer refers to as the "Studying Hunger Journals." The journals are evidently a direct extension of the project that produced *Memory,* as Mayer describes in the opening section of *Studying Hunger:*

Listen.

I began all this in April, 1972. I wanted to try to record, like a diary, in writing, states of consciousness, my states of consciousness, as fully as I could every day, for one month. A month always seems like a likely time-span, if there is one, for an experiment. A month gives you enough time to feel free to skip a day, but not so much time that you wind up fucking off completely.

I had an idea before this that if a human, a writer, could come up with a workable code, or shorthand, for the transcription of every event, every motion, every transition of his or her own mind, & could perform this process of translation on himself, using the code, for a 24-hour period, he or we or someone could come up with a great piece of language/information.

The full text of the journals, which remains unpublished, runs to 310 pages of writing on single-spaced, legal-sized paper, mainly in prose, with some sections written in poetic lines. The published text of *Studying Hunger,* perhaps no more than 20 percent of the full journals, is in itself a compelling work that has been widely anthologized. Coolidge says of his and Mayer's work from this period: "We wanted endless works, that would zoom on & on and include everything ultimately, we'd talk about the 'Everything work,' which would use every possible bit flashing through our minds." Mayer recalls that she wrote the journals over several years when she was involved in Freudian psychoanalysis with Dr. David Rubinfine. Rubinfine contributed an introduction to *Memory,* in which he says of Mayer: "Her writing is sensory prose poetry with immense evocative power. If the reader is able to suspend his usual waking daytime logic he will have a unique and stirring experience, and perhaps discover something important about himself." This observation aptly applies to the work *Studying Hunger,* and will likely characterize the "Studying Hunger Journals" if and when the full text is published.

Mayer's next two significant collections, *Poetry* (1976) and *The Golden Book of Words* (1978), utilize more of the traditional conventions of poetry than she had previously used. In fact, some poets associated with the Language circle and experimental poetry generally regarded these works as a serious departure, even a betrayal of the movement. As Mayer recalls in an interview, one leading poet told her she was "a failed experimentalist," a remark that she says "hit me kind of hard." Even Mayer's friend Coolidge, she noted, "was getting a little worried." Despite his worry, he himself nevertheless turned toward a more personal style of expression in his book *Own Face* (1978), which bears the dedication "For Bernadette Mayer." Mayer described her book *Poetry* as being half "old poems" and half "poems I'd written in the last two weeks" and added in one lecture, somewhat inexplicably, "I resent the book in a way." Many of the poems in *Poetry* and *The Golden Book of Words* have been republished in a widely available volume by New Directions, *A Bernadette Mayer Reader* (1992), which allows readers to make their own judgments about the value of this part of Mayer's poetry.

The earliest poem in *Poetry,* "Corn," written when Mayer was nineteen, is an early example of her highly experimental mode. The poem begins:

Corn is a small hard seed.

Corn from Delft
is good for elves.

White corn, yellow, Indian
Is this kernel a kernel of corn?

In an interview with Ken Jordan, Mayer described this poem as "a real dictionary poem," indicating thereby her participation in the French surrealist practice of the "found poem." The simplicity of the diction in an experimental context also indicates an affinity with the work of Gertrude Stein. In the interview with Jordan, Mayer recounted a humorous anecdote about Bill Berkson, her teacher at the New School in 1966, who told her she had been "reading too much Gertrude Stein." But, she said, "I had never read her and never heard of her! So I guess it was shortly after that that I started reading her work." Accordingly, the similarities between Stein's and Mayer's techniques are not so much a question of influence as a matter of shared temperament and a shared range of interests in different kinds of language practices. One suspects, nonetheless, that humorous anecdotes such as this one may hide some of the "anxiety of influence" poets inevitably experience.

The body of Mayer's work reveals her clear allegiance to certain practices of surrealism, as well as to the experimental techniques of Stein, William Carlos Williams, and other writers in the American tradition. In poems from *The Golden Book of Words* Mayer's deep immersion in literary tradition is evident, as Molly Bendall says in an interview, "in a poem like 'Eve of Easter' in which the speaker faces her inheritance from literary forefathers." "Eve of Easter," a clever and moving poem, begins:

Milton, who made his illiterate daughters
Read to him in five languages
Till they heard the news he would marry again
And said they would rather hear he was dead
Milton who turns even Paradise Lost
Into an autobiography, I have three
Babies tonight, all three are sleeping:
Rachel the great great great granddaughter
Of Herman Melville is asleep on the bed
Sophia and Marie are sleeping
Sophia namesake of the wives
Lewis Freedson the scholar and Nathaniel Hawthorne. . . .

This setup, besides displaying wit and energy, allows Mayer to use Melville and Hawthorne as metonyms for the sleeping children, when, as she says, she "stole images from Milton to cure opacous gloom." It is a quaint conceit, as the Elizabethans might say, to allow this woman — a mother and poet — to explore her consciousness on this occasion, as her thoughts move in and out of literary culture and the acts and emotions related to caring for small children. Mayer's "Bernadette" persona is a free

Two pages from Mayer's notebook (courtesy of the author)

spirit, but also a critical consciousness, as the poem's conclusion shows:

I return a look to all the daughters and I wink
Eve of Easter, I've inherited this
Peaceful sleep of the children of men
Rachel, Sophia, Marie and again me
Bernadette, all heart I live, all head, all eye, all ear
I lost the prejudice of paradise
And wound up caring for the babies of these guys. . . .

Mayer's relatively rare use of end rhyme and literary diction allows her to enact the interpenetration of areas of experience that she lightly thematizes in the poem. Again, as Bendall notes, "Mayer's work shows that a writer can experiment with language, redetermine syntax, and refashion logos without abandoning voice and personality." Given Mayer's interests in this and other poems about children, gender, and sexual relations, it is suprising that her work has not received more attention from mainstream feminist critics, who presumably share at least some of the poet's major concerns.

"Eve of Easter" is a preparation for *Midwinter Day,* a text that some admirers consider one of the unacknowledged masterpieces of late-twentieth-century writing in English. Andrei Codrescu praised Mayer's book-length poem when it was published in 1982:

The long poem is the American poet's measure of greatness. We measure him or her with it, and ourselves by comparison. If we are in the presence of a vast body of words and find that, indeed, there is a reason for it to be there, we abandon ourselves to it and swim in it as if it were the ocean. . . . Mayer's *Midwinter Day* goes directly into the exalted company of the ocean-makers, without any hesitation. Partly verse, partly prose paragraphs, this sweep through the consciousness of a mother, a woman, a writer, a dreamer, a citizen, goes as far and as deep as anything attempted on this scale. With her babies around, with a million things to do, amid a swirl of people, memories and books, she makes her speech out of all of it, with a sure-footed and graceful bravado.

Codrescu's unrestrained response is also a fair summary of Mayer's poem. The conceit of this 119-page book is that it was written on a single day, 22

December 1978, in Lenox, Massachusetts (a claim reiterated on the book's back cover). Mayer has said in one lecture, "Nobody ever believes me when I tell them that it was written in one day, but it almost was."

The text is divided into six sections, with the second and fourth sections written in the dense poetic prose of *Memory* or *Studying Hunger* that Mayer typically uses to record the more quotidian aspects of existence. The first section is the dream section, with the dreaming preceding, and in some sense allowing for, the richness of the day's consciousness. The third section is also written in Mayer's beautifully stylized poetic line. The fifth section alternates between prose and verse, and the final section represents the poet-speaker's meditative writing time. Section three details a midday walk down Lenox's main street and begins:

> The dark brown stairs
> Towards the doors
> Of this house
>   Wisdom's gray sky remembers
> Snow is white crystals
> Hall mirror,
> Misaligned and broken strollers,
>   Sex and going out
> What there is of snow icing
> The path plowed over the ground
> Which is a story
>   Earth's surface, lovers' intentions
> Astounded as no one's around us
>   A woman two children a man[.]

For comparisons to the verse-writing skill exemplified in these lines, one might point to Charles Olson's projective measure or Robert Creeley's nuance of line and syllable, the most personal poems of Williams, or the strangely affective line of John Ashbery at his expressive best. One might have to turn to such distinguished French practitioners of the free verse line as Pierre Reverdy to find the balance of image and versification that Mayer achieves here with such apparent ease. And again there is the specifically personal and familial consciousness that makes Mayer's work valuable as a compelling example of a woman's writing in late-twentieth-century, real-world America.

Recognizing Mayer's achievement in *Midwinter Day,* Fanny Howe, writing in the *American Book Review,* says: "In a language made up of idiom and lyricism, which cancels the boundaries between prose and poetry, Bernadette Mayer's aesthetic intent is moral and theological in dimension. Her search for patterns woven out of small actions confirms the notion that seeing *what is* is a

radical human gesture. Doctrine is irrelevant here to the moral — and solitary — courage displayed by this act of writing, and sharing of that writing." The moral and ethical dimension of Mayer's work that Howe identifies is a dimension often overlooked in discussions of experimental writing. Mayer's work continues to be radical, as Howe suggests, even or especially when her poetic line borrows from the expressive geniuses of the recent past — not just Reverdy, but Antonin Artaud, Henri Michaux, and others, as well. In the penultimate section of the text, Mayer herself explains her intentions in *Midwinter Day:*

> I had an idea to write a book that would translate the detail of thought from a day to language like a dream transformed to read as it does, everything, a book that would end before it started in time to prove the day like the dream has everything in it, to do this without remembering like a dream inciting writing continuously for as long as you can stand up till you fall down like in a story to show and possess everything we know because having it all at once is performing a magical service for survival by the use of the mind like memory.

With this intention, Mayer's work thus relates to the tradition in which the poet is a visionary whose work may express what has formerly been unexpressed. The task she sets herself of producing the "unrepeatable work" (again and again) would seem to be impossible, but as Gertrude Stein is said to have said: "If it is possible why do it?"

Some readers believe that Mayer's work after *Midwinter Day* becomes less compelling. It may be that the published texts do not adequately represent Mayer's full production in this later period. A work that was published in 1994, for example, is *The Desires of Mothers to Please Others in Letters.* This book is a collection of prose letters — similar to the poetic prose of *Memory, Studying Hunger,* and the prose sections of *Midwinter Day* — that was written during Mayer's pregnancy with her third child (1989–1990). In an interview Mayer said of this time: "Then when I found out I was pregnant with Max, I decided to write the letters until he was born, which is a very congenial structure for me. I mean not in terms of the giving birth thing, but in terms of any kind of time structure happening." It may be that when the publishing process begins to match up to Mayer's actual production a clearer picture will emerge of her more recent work.

Mayer's next major work after *Midwinter Day* was *Utopia* (1984), a work that lightly takes on social issues and intermixes these with collaborative poems and texts by other people, thereby producing her own contribution to the collaborative literary genre. In her lecture at the Naropa Institute Mayer described the form of the text: "I wanted to make *Utopia* tongue-in-cheek like a text book with a table of contents, a preface, and an index." In a biographical statement in the *Out of this World* anthology, Mayer describes the political and social content that comes to the fore: "It was while I was working as the director of the Project that I decided to write a utopia because at last poetry (and my having at the same time thrust my children into P.S. 19) had situated me in the world not just cosmologically, which I already knew about from the muse, but also momentarily in a way that previous political work or thought and understanding of human nature had never mentioned to me." A book-jacket blurb by André Breton gives a sense of the verve and humor of the work: "I do believe Mayer is one of the few humans living (as I am not) who has read my 'Ode to Charles Fourier.'" Michael Palmer records one kind of response to Mayer's work in a poem published in his volume *Sun* (1988):

Mei-mei, here is the table
Who knows the word for it

Sikhs today are dancing in the streets,
some say a dance of death
Bernadette has written *Utopia* [.]

One of Mayer's most significant contributions to contemporary poetry may prove to be the authorization for others to experiment fully in whatever forms she may have invented or encouraged others to discover.

In a note to her *Sonnets* (1989), Mayer says: "I didn't realize I had written these sonnets much less that I had written them for such a long time but one year recently without anticipation I found that I was writing sonnets all the time and after a while I began to expect to write them and soon in the midst of all this contemporary sonnet writing going on I looked through my past poems in the morning and discovered I'd been writing the always somehow peripheral sonnet all along without understanding the forms of brief conclusive thought the poems had been taking so often in 14 lines without me." This statement gives a sense of the continuity of Mayer's writing project, how it seems to emerge from a process that is both ongoing and accessible to reflection. The tonality of some of the sonnets borrows from the classical translations of Catullus and others that she published in *The Formal Field of Kissing* (1990). One sonnet, for example, begins:

You jerk you didn't call me up
I haven't seen you in so long
You probably have a fucking tan
& besides that instead of making love tonight
You're drinking your parents to the airport
I'm through with you bourgeois boys[.]

One might compare this to a sample of the translation Mayer titles "Hendecasyllables on Catullus #33" that begins:

You have the balls to say you will be with me
but you hardly ever are, then you say you're scared
of your parents' opinion, they pay your rent
I wouldn't mind that if they didn't think I
was a whore ridden with Aids disease & worse things
but I am I and my little dog knows me[.]

The revelation of these sonnets and adaptations from the classical authors – as well as Gertrude Stein – is the way that the emotional setting is filtered through a language that is both tough and accurate, the language that people actually speak and, in speaking, use to create their quotidian realities.

Poet David Shapiro has responded enthusiastically to Mayer's sonnets, comparing them favorably to other recent works by Mayer's contemporaries, such as Coolidge's *The Crystal Text* (1986) and Michael Palmer's *Sun*. Shapiro writes: "Often her poems delight in a photographic sense of New York that does seem to come out of the dense love of [Edwin] Denby, Rudy Burckhardt, and [Ted] Berrigan. . . . The happiness in Mayer's poetry is a happiness of the city and its proletariat, with the marginal poet throwing in her lot, though without sentimentality. . . . There is a constantly teasing anarchism throughout the sonnets, and an audacity that permits her this kind of marriage of politics and love, urban photography and the whimsies of an anarchist sonnet. . . . Mayer's New York City *is* maximalism." Such a response helps reinforce the idea of the continuity of Mayer's later work with her early work, such as *Memory,* that also celebrated her rootedness in urban New York. Shapiro also sounds the theme of social marginality that gives Mayer's poetry some of its tough vision. In *Obdurate Brilliance* it is suggested that the social marginality displayed in Mayer's work may be less important in the long term than the textual marginality that her work explores and out of which it works.

The publication in 1992 of *A Bernadette Mayer Reader* gave reason for those who admire her work to rejoice and gave some hope that her work might reach a wider audience. Peter Gizzi trumpeted in a *Poetry Project Newsletter* review that "*The Reader* sold

1,000 copies in one month!" The *Reader* also works well as an introduction to Mayer's work, although there are inevitable limitations to any such volume. Her important book *Midwinter Day* is represented only by a five-page prose sequence; and, in general, as Gizzi points out: "The only real regret about this collection is that there aren't longer selections from any of her longer projects." The *Reader* nonetheless provides samples of Mayer's work over the full course of her remarkable career, especially with shorter poems that would otherwise be hard to find, such as "Corn" and "Eve of Easter." At the end of the volume, there is also an excellent selection of "New Poems," including "First turn to me . . . ," which may be one of the most fiercely erotic poems in the language.

What the future holds for this poet who is committed to an ethos of the "unrepeatable work" is uncertain, but some hints about her future direction can be discerned. It is to be hoped, first, that there will be the publication of volumes that have already been written, following the example of *The Desires of Mothers To Please Others in Letters,* finished in 1980 but only recently published. Mayer's success with the *Reader* bodes well for her relationship with the New Directions Press, which is trying to reestablish a commitment to the literary avant-garde. A work in progress that promises to extend the sequence of works such as *Memory, Studying Hunger,* and *Midwinter Day* is one Mayer refers to as the "Ethics of Sleep," a work that incorporates dream journals and delineates methods for readers to participate in the activity of recovering their own dreams. This work corresponds to Mayer's ongoing work of teaching, as she recently explained: "That's what I think I'm most concerned with. I explain to people how they can resuscitate their dreams; people who say they don't remember their dreams or people who say that they don't even have them. I think it's a much more valuable thing than saying, here is the sonnet form."

Interviews:

Ken Jordan, "The Colors of Consonance," *Poetry Project Newsletter,* 146 (October/November, 1992): 5–9;

Michael Gizzi, "Interview with Bernadette Mayer," *Lingo,* 1 (1993): 3–9, 139–143.

References:

Peter Baker, "Language, Poetry and Marginality: Coolidge, Palmer and Mayer," " 'Language' Theory and the Languages of Feminism," and "Afterword," in his *Obdurate Brilliance: Exteriority and the Modern Long Poem* (Gainesville: University of Florida Press, 1991), pp. 150–161; 162–175; 176–7;

William Corbett and Michael Gizzi, eds., *Writing for Bernadette* (Great Barrington, Mass.: The Figures, 1995).

James Merrill

(3 March 1926 – 6 February 1995)

Willard Spiegelman
Southern Methodist University

See also the Merrill entry in *DLB Yearbook: 1985*.

BOOKS: *Jim's Book: A Collection of Poems and Short
Stories* (New York: Privately printed, 1942);

The Black Swan and Other Poems (Athens: Icaros,
1946);

First Poems (New York: Knopf, 1951);

Short Stories (Pawlet, Vt.: Banyan Press, 1954);

The Seraglio (New York: Knopf, 1957; London:
Chatto & Windus, 1958);

*The Country of a Thousand Years of Peace and Other
Poems* (New York: Knopf, 1959; revised edition, New York: Atheneum, 1970);

Selected Poems (London: Chatto & Windus/Hogarth
Press, 1961);

Water Street (New York: Atheneum, 1962);

The Thousand and Second Night (Athens: Christos
Christou Press, 1963);

The (Diblos) Notebook (New York: Atheneum, 1965;
London: Chatto & Windus, 1965);

Violent Pastoral (Cambridge, Mass.: Adams House &
Lowell House, 1965);

Nights and Days (New York: Atheneum, 1966; London: Chatto & Windus/Hogarth Press, 1966);

The Fire Screen (New York: Atheneum, 1969; London: Chatto & Windus, 1970);

Braving the Elements (New York: Atheneum, 1972;
London: Chatto & Windus/Hogarth Press,
1973);

Two Poems: From the Cupola and The Summer People
(London: Chatto & Windus, 1972);

Yannina (New York: Phoenix Book Shop, 1973);

The Yellow Pages: 59 Poems (Cambridge, Mass.: Temple Bar Bookshop, 1974);

Divine Comedies (New York: Atheneum, 1976; London: Oxford University Press, 1977);

Metamorphosis of 741 (Pawlet, Vt.: Banyan Press,
1977);

Mirabell: Books of Number (New York: Atheneum,
1978; Oxford: Oxford University Press,
1979);

Ideas, Etc. (Brooklyn: J. Davies, 1980);

James Merrill

Samos (Los Angeles: Sylvester & Orphanos, 1980);

Scripts for the Pageant (New York: Atheneum, 1980);

The Changing Light at Sandover (New York: Atheneum, 1982);

Marbled Paper (Salem, Oreg.: Seluzicki, 1982);

Peter (Old Deerfield, Mass.: Deerfield / Dublin: Gallery, 1982);

Santorini: Stopping the Leak (Worcester, Mass.:
Metacom, 1982);

From the Cutting-Room Floor (Omaha: University of
Nebraska, 1983);

Heroes and Other Enlisted Men (Bryn Mawr, Penn.:
Dorrance, 1983);

Bronze (New York: Nadja, 1984);

Occasions & Inscriptions (New York: Davies, 1984);

Plays of Light (Ann Arbor, Mich.: Laurence Scott,
1984);

Rendezvous / JM (New York: Peter Hooten, 1984);

Souvenirs (New York: Nadja, 1984);

Late Settings (New York: Atheneum, 1985);

The Image Maker: A Play in One Act (New York: Sea Cliff, 1986);

Recitative: Prose (San Francisco: North Point, 1986);

Japan: Prose of Departure (New York: Nadja, 1987);

The Inner Room (New York: Knopf, 1988);

Three Poems (Child Okefore, Dorset: Words, 1988);

A Different Person: A Memoir (New York: Knopf, 1993);

A Scattering of Salts (New York: Knopf, 1995).

Collections: *From the First Nine: Poems 1946–1976* (New York: Atheneum, 1982);

Selected Poems, 1946–1985 (New York: Knopf, 1992).

With the completion of *The Changing Light at Sandover* (1982), which presents the revised "sacred books" of his philosophical verse trilogy with the addition of a coda, James Merrill earned his place as one of the most original and major poets of the twentieth century. This epic poem — a vast cosmology that tackles such topics as subatomic particle physics, the history of God's plan for the universe, reincarnation and population control, and the role of art — also takes place at the "salon level" as a series of communiqués from disembodied spirits who reach the poet via a Ouija board. That a major poem has such an outrageously peculiar basis is one of the great stories of American poetry; the story proves even more interesting when seen in the light of the progress of a basically fastidious poet whose wit and playfulness have come to include openness, seriousness, and revelation.

Born in New York City to Charles Edward and Hellen Ingram Merrill, James Ingram Merrill attended the Lawrenceville School and graduated with a B.A. from Amherst College in 1947. Much of his childhood has been recorded in his poetry, and in 1993 he examined his early maturity in the prose memoir titled *A Different Person,* which deals with the period (1950–1952) when he lived in Europe and came of age poetically, psychologically, and sexually. For many years Merrill divided his time between Athens, Greece, and Stonington, Connecticut, where he shared houses with his longtime companion, David Jackson. In the last decade of his life Merrill more or less abandoned Athens in favor of Key West, Florida, although he continued to travel widely in the United States as well as abroad.

At the beginning of his career Merrill's poetry was recognized for its elegance and rococo presentation of artful objects and fanciful scenes; subsequently, his themes became more personal, more deeply plumbed, and more historically based, and

critics and general readers began to take it more seriously. Two National Book Awards, in 1967 for *Nights and Days* (1966) and in 1979 for *Mirabell: Books of Number* (1978), and a Pulitzer Prize in 1977 for *Divine Comedies* (1976) augmented four early prizes from *Poetry* magazine (1947, 1949, 1951, and 1965); an award from the Bollingen Foundation (1972), the National Book Critics Circle Award in 1983 for *The Changing Light at Sandover,* and the Bobbit National Prize for Poetry from the Library of Congress in 1989 for *The Inner Room* (1988) rounded out the poet's many other honors and honorary degrees.

Three gifts distinguish Merrill's achievement. First, he was a master of verse technique and standard poetic forms. Second, the recognition that "life was fiction in disguise," which he recorded in "Days of 1935" from *Braving the Elements* (1972), has enabled Merrill to accommodate apparent autobiographical details (which may or may not come from his own life) to the excitement of narrative. He discovered what many lyric poets, confessional or merely personal, fail to find: a context for presenting autobiography in lyric verse through the mediation of myth and fable. Significantly, Northrop Frye, the theorist who adapted Jungian ideas about myth to criticism and showed that all literature is a system of interrelated correspondences, is cited at the start of "The Book of Ephraim," the first book of *The Changing Light at Sandover,* which was originally published in *Divine Comedies.* An heir of Proust, Merrill achieves a scope in poetry comparable to the work of major novelists; his great themes are the recovery of time (in spite of loss) through willed or automatic memory and the alternating erosions and bequests of erotic experience. He focuses on what is taken, what abides, in love and time, and considers how to handle them. Third, the major phase of Merrill's career, highlighted by *The Changing Light at Sandover,* offers his readers a model, or perhaps a metaphor, for the universe. His "poems of science" flagrantly mingle chatty séances with the dead and serious investigations of molecular biology, genetic evolution, and human history.

Only the elegance of Merrill's early poems points to his future. What Richard Howard deftly calls the "patinated narcissism" of *First Poems* (1951) is, in *The Country of a Thousand Years of Peace and Other Poems* (1959), "literally roughed up, and the resulting corrugation of surface corresponds ... to a new agitation of the depth." From the opening lines of the title poem of *The Black Swan and Other Poems* (1946) the reader can sniff the bouquet, rarefied but intense, of Merrill's language and rhythms: "Black

Merrill's parents, Hellen Ingram Merrill and Charles Edward Merrill

on flat water past the jonquil lawns / Riding, the black swan draws / A private chaos warbling in its wake." Nor is there any recklessness in *First Poems;* they are measured, reined in of feeling and, consequently, of meaning. The Keatsian lushness of "The Eve of St. Agnes" is joined with the Stevensesque archness of "The Comedian as the Letter C" in Merrill's "Portrait": "A lute, cold meats, a snifter somewhat full / Like a crystal ball predicting what's unknown; / Ingots of nougat, thumbsized cumquats sodden / With juice not quite their own."

Such poems of cold perfection lack a human center or moral wisdom. They are reticent and mannerly (in an interview Merrill commented: "Manners for me are the touch of nature, an artifice in the very bloodstream") but purposefully so. The holding back encourages the use of the pathetic fallacy. In a poem such as "Willow" the speaker invests nature with meaning in order to understand his own passions. He finds "that branches lent, though covertly, / Movements more suave, grinding what pangs there be / Into a bearable choreography." And reticence encourages equally the creation of imaginary lives for real animals in a bestiary worthy of Marianne Moore. The pelican, for instance, is as-

sisted by "his postures foolish yet severe . . . in a courtesy nowadays / Only among artists fashionable."

In the last poem of *First Poems* Merrill alights upon an image and a subject that are to hold him throughout his career. In "The House," whose first line takes the title as its grammatical subject, Merrill explores human fragility as a central theme. While day is comfort, "Night is a cold house" whose "west walls take the sunset like a blow." Houses confer meaning, not just protection; the "listener" described in the poem learns "soberly" at dusk that "a loss of deed and structure" is his plight. Things fade and fall, ownership and actions fail, and day is a flattering illusion, while the house of night "no key opens." In the poem's conclusion, the speaker has gained access to the house:

> I have entered, nevertheless,
> And seen the wet-faced sleepers the winds take
> To heart; have felt their dreadful profits break
> beyond my seeing. At a glance they wake.

The open ending, whether a revelation or a submission, captures a moment full of possibilities.

Between *First Poems* and *The Country of a Thousand Years of Peace* David Kalstone has written, "the solitary speaker had become a world traveller," setting his subjects in various foreign landscapes. Merrill's primary tone is elegiac, as he laments in "A Dedication" the early death of his friend Hans Lodeizen in Switzerland, the country alluded to in the book's title, and tries "to drink from the deep spring of a death / That freshness [it does] not yet need to understand." Orpheus and the Phoenix, types of rebirth, are subjects of longer poems, since Merrill wishes to reinvent Lodeizen or lead him from the millennial quiet of his Swiss grave. No one sees, however, "that starry land / Under the world . . . / Without a death" (Virgil's "*sed revocare gradum . . . hoc opus, hic labor est*"). In retrospect one can see the volume as equivalent to both Milton's *Lycidas,* as the poet is steeling himself for survival in a world indifferent to poets' voices, and to the *nekyia*s (or descents into hell) of Homer, Polydore Virgil, and Dante, which ready Merrill for the grandeur of epic revelation.

The ardor of seeing is the reason for following the title poem with "The Octopus," a dazzling demonstration of Merrill's metaphysical energy and prosodic daring. In alternating five- and four-stress lines, with rhymes on the first syllable of feminine endings and the second of masculine ones (for example, *translucence / unloose, fervor / observe*), Merrill makes an elaborate comparison between "vision asleep in the eye's tight translucence" and a sleepy, caged octopus, only rarely coaxed out by the light into a waking dance, uncurling its tentacles like the arms of a Hindu god toward the object of its attraction:

> He is willing to undergo the volition and fervor
> Of many fleshlike arms, observe
> These in their holiness of indirection
> Destroy, adore, evolve, reject —
> Till on glass rigid with his own seizure
> At length the sucking jewels freeze.

The last lines summarize Merrill's early poetic stances. "Holiness" suggests the sacerdotal function of art in this century, and "indirection" recalls T. S. Eliot's remarks on the need for artistic subtlety and opacity in a modern, disjointed society.

Because of its inevitable failure, the poem's enterprise is both sterile and disturbing. Greedy for experience and escape, vision enclosed in the eye is imprisoned like the octopus and doomed never to attain what attracts it. The predation motif, in Merrill's later poetry, will find a recognizably human corollary when it is translated into an erotic

quest. Its failure is stated as Proust's law in "Days of 1971" from *Braving the Elements:* "(a) What least thing our self-love longs for most / Others instinctively withhold; / (b) Only when time has slain desire / Is his wish granted to a smiling ghost / Neither harmed nor warmed, now, by the fire."

At this point in Merrill's career, however, the frozen jewels of attack are thwarted in their godlike wreath of wrath as they push toward accomplishment, seizure, control. Stasis, or the cold perfection of visual luster, is accepted as second best to entrapment. Hence, all the poems are about things ("The Olive Grove," "Thistledown," "A Time Piece," "Mirror," "Stones") because things, at least, are permanent. It is instructive to remember that *The Country of a Thousand Years of Peace* was published in the same year as *Life Studies,* Robert Lowell's turning volume. Although Lowell had found his major voice, Merrill still had seven years to go, but the fixation on the past and its stillness is common to both. In "91 Revere Street," Lowell announces what he and Merrill, alone among midcentury poets, were to make their obsession: in memory "the vast number of remembered *things* remains rocklike. Each is in its place, each has its function, its history, its drama. There, all is preserved by that motherly care that one either ignored or resented in his youth. The things and their owners come back with life and meaning — because finished, they are endurable and perfect." It is ironic that a critic in the *Hudson Review* singled out Merrill's volume for "scrupulously avoiding the ordinary" and for its "drier tone, discriminating and exact," while excoriating *Life Studies* as "lazy and anecdotal . . . more suited as an appendix to some snobbish society magazine." Later critical opinion would probably reverse the preference.

Merrill instinctively recognized his early limitations. In "The Book of Ephraim" (section A), attempting to decide how to form his material, he confesses, "My downfall was 'word-painting,' " but he opts for poetry over fiction since "in verse the feet went bare." In the titillating seminarrative poems in *The Country of a Thousand Years of Peace,* too much is withheld, and the reader never knows exactly what is happening, or why, to whom. Cleverness, like manners, betrays. One of these poems, "A Narrow Escape," starts with a commonplace, but baffling, admission: "During a lull at dinner the vampire frankly / Confessed herself a symbol of the inner / Adventure." These lines lead to the eerie, chatty giggle at the end: "It was then Charles thought to wonder, peering over / The rests of venison, what on earth a vampire / Means by the inner adventure. Her retort / Is now a classic in our particular circle."

Richard Howard has suggested, "it is not the story, not even the retort, but the notation of a world in which the retort is possible that matters to him: these poems are concerned to create a climate of opinion, a variable weather of discourse."

Another word for the poems might be Merrill's own: they are *doodles*. "The Doodler," a signature piece, exemplifies Merrill's accomplishments and warns self-consciously against his limitations. Doodles are children, "the long race that descends / From me," and also icons that grow like lichens. Inflated and comic, they are both art and preparations for it, excuses, symbols for paintings yet to come. A doodle traces the gap between intention and execution; it is an earnest, the young artist might hope, of future things. Looking at a page of designs, one confronts the equivalent of one's past, where the retrieval of meaning can be equally frustrating and fruitful: "Shapes never realized, were you dogs or chains?" Like the voices he hears in his later volumes, the art here is at first an unclear and unwilled antidote to the neat perfections of his more tightly organized poems: "Indeed, nothing I do is at all fine / Save certain abstract forms. These come unbidden." All the poet can do is to look hopefully forward to future outbursts of stories, designs, and better human figures ("I have learned to do feet," he announces wryly): portraiture in which the outlines are fleshed out. Like the Phoenix, his image of rebirth and withdrawal, Merrill's poetry constantly transforms itself, preening and steadying before a possible ritual conflagration. He begins "About the Phoenix," "But in the end one tires of the high flown." The bird, "keyed up for ever fiercer / Flights between ardor and ashes, back and forth," repeats its dazzling display until, "in the end, despite / Its pyrotechnic curiosity, the process / Palls." Like Theodore Roethke, Merrill learns by going where he has to go.

He goes to a new house and to his own past. *Water Street* (1962) celebrates the Stonington, Connecticut, residence; it marks, as well, a new candor about his life. In its final poem, "A Tenancy," he greets some guests and looks to his poetic future, with the fruits of his own life, the tonic of his major phase: "If I am host at last / It is of little more than my own past. / May others be at home in it." Futurity and benediction combine with a coming home and a coming to terms.

There is a new ease in many of these poems, starting with two important reminiscences, "An Urban Convalescence" and "Scenes of Childhood," and reaching even to specimens of Merrill's earlier style, where it is deployed in the service of subjects not fully realized. "Poem of Summer's End," for example, is about the termination of a ten-year love affair, with crucial narrative detail omitted. In its opening it shows how Merrill has absorbed the model of poet Elizabeth Bishop, grafting her deceptive austerity onto the archness of his former manner. The change occurs exactly in the sardonic, un-Bishop-like third sentence:

> The morning of the equinox
> Begins with brassy clouds and cocks.
> All the inn's shutters clatter wide
> Upon Fair Umbria. Twitching at my side
> You burrow in sleep like a red fox.

The theme is like a cloak hanging on a rack instead of a human body. But upon reconsideration, the teasing vagueness of the poem is apposite to the mysteries of our lives. Who, really, are we when we love, and whom are we loving? What does one see but himself in a lover's eyes? Repetition dulls experience ("Sun / Weaker each sunrise reddens that slow maze / So freely entered"), but the next turn, or path, may lead only to "the springs we started from," both a source and the "bed of iron and lace" where the poem began.

Themes of loss and return emerge from Merrill's yearning for compensation, for accepting in "An Urban Convalescence" "the dull need to make some kind of house / Out of the life lived, out of the love spent." In "For Proust" he weighs the need for retrenchment, as into a cork-lined room, against the requirement to "go into the world again" (Valéry's "*il faut tenter de vivre*" echoes throughout his poetry), because "over and over something would remain / Unbalanced in the painful sum of things." In "Scenes of Childhood," home movies reawaken consciousness and recapture a still-terrifying past. Memory, through repetition, is here controlled. It may revive original feelings of dismay or help to subjugate the dead whom it resurrects. The dead feed upon the living but are controlled by them — as Merrill will demonstrate in the prophetic books — through machines like a movie "projector" (an appropriately Freudian word). The poet realizes he is "sun and air" and also "son and heir" by comparison to his dead father. The child is father of the man, in Wordsworth's aphorism; for Merrill, the man, especially if childless, is still child himself. "The loved one always leaves," he remarks in "For Proust," but memory restores what life often denies.

The motifs of recollection and repetition are enlivened by Merrill's mirrors, which reflect a major concern: exactly how much does a resemblance replace, transform, or surpass its original? In

Merrill with a friend (photograph by Rolf Tietjens)

"The Water Hyacinth" the poet looks down at a dying woman's body: "I watch your sightless face / Jerked swiftly here and there, / Set in a puzzling frown. / Your face! it is no more yours / Than its reflected double / Bobbing on scummed water." He tries to correct her jumbled details from stories so long repeated that he knows them by heart, his inheritance from the woman who is now confused by chronology and circumstance. The "craft" to take her where she is going is storytelling, a barge to the next world. The water hyacinth of the title, a rootless new arrival sixty years earlier, has now vividly congested the river on which she rode during her honeymoon. These legacies from parents to children, or from one's past selves to his present one, become in Merrill's later work the commerce between the dead and the living. In "A Tenancy," although repetition enhances (it spurs his creativity), it also diminishes: "The body that lived through that day / And the sufficient love and relative peace / Of those short years, is now not mine. Would it be called a soul?"

Bodily decrepitude is wisdom: Merrill's poems from the mid 1960s onward enact Yeats's great theme. In *Nights and Days,* his first prizewinning volume, the soul is formed by the days of experience and the nights of imaginative recall, by the witty Cavafian manner (Constantin Cavafy, 1863–1933, the Alexandrian poet whose clarity of characterization and multileveled diction are models for Merrill's), and by the acceptance of those illusions on which human life depends. Another word for illusion is myth, and in the long poems, seminarrative, semimeditative, semilyric (Ezra Pound's description of his *Cantos*), which Merrill begins here and in which he finds his truest voice, one can appreciate Ernst Cassirer's remarks about the necessary filters through which one experiences reality in the modern age:

No longer can man confront reality immediately; he cannot see it, as it were, face to face. Physical reality seems to recede in proportion as man's symbolic activity advances. Instead of dealing with things themselves, man is in a sense constantly conversing with himself.

> He has so enveloped himself in linguistic forms, in artistic images, in mythical symbols or religious rites that he cannot see or know anything except by the interposition of the artistic medium.

Induction, subterfuge, fiction: these are Merrill's equivalents to Stephen Dedalus's silence, exile, and cunning. They explain his precision of manner and passion for manners, as well as the occasional reticence in even the autobiographical poems. As he said in a 1972 interview: "You hardly ever need to *state* your feelings. The point is to feel and keep your eyes open. Then what you feel is expressed, is mimed back at you by the scene. A room, a landscape. I'd go a step further. We don't *know* what we feel until we see it distanced by this kind of translation." Or, as he puts it in a mock lecture in "Days of 1964," "Form's what affirms." Art and life, in other words, sustain one another; they are never rival dispensations.

Merrill's two great themes – time and eros and the relationships between them – flower in this volume. "Time" (as the title of the poem elliptically slides into the first line) is "Ever that Everest / Among Concepts." It is measured by the tedium of the daily round, by a son caring for a dying father and playing endless games of patience and by the heroic effort to gain independence, the pinnacle of the mountain: "Arriving then at something not unlike / Meaning relieved of sense, / To plant a flag there on that needle peak / Whose diamond grates in the revolving silence."

Love, with its erotic energies of masking and unmasking, is the arena where illusion and reality perform their ritual matings and combats. In "Days of 1964" the poet in Greece is both foreign and surprisingly comfortable because the stranger is always thought a god in disguise. The Homeric world lives in a modern, comic suit, and Aphrodite is reborn as Kyria Kleo, the poet's cleaning woman, who masks despair and age with the prostitute's cosmetics and tight clothing, at the same time revealing precisely those ravages of time she is so desperate to conceal. In love himself, the poet thinks the maid *"was* Love," glistening with pain and love, which are twins, not opposites. He pays her generously because "Love [the goddess as well as his current affair] makes one generous," although, ironically, she is trolloping on the hills in search of more. Is love, deity or emotion, an illusion? Kleo's makeup is "the erotic mask / Worn the world over by illusion / To

weddings of itself and simple need." All oppositions are united at the end:

> If that was illusion, I wanted it to last long;
> To dwell, for its daily pittance, with us there,
> Cleaning and watering, sighing with love or pain.
> I hoped it would climb when it needed to the heights
> Even of degradation, as I for one
> Seemed, those days, to be always climbing
> Into a world of wild
> Flowers, feasting, tears – or was I falling, legs
> Buckling, heights, depths,
> Into a pool of each night's rain?
> But you were everywhere beside me, masked,
> As who was not, in laughter, pain, and love.

Through memory, the past clarifies. Distance confers a perspective on life's slowly evolving experiences. So it is in "The Broken Home," which proves that growing up is just another word for displacement and that all homes are broken but recoverable through memory. Guiding himself through recollections of childhood, the speaker recalls his parents, "Father Time and Mother Earth, a marriage on the rocks," who, like one's past, determine one's present. Returning to his old house, now a boarding school, where he hopes someone, at last, may learn something, the poet poignantly but wittily combines a memory of his old Irish setter and Wordsworth's clouds surrounding the setting sun at the close of "Ode: Intimations of Immorality" as a symbol of mortality and wisdom: "from my window, cool / With the unstiflement of the entire story, / [I] Watch a red setter stretch and sink in cloud." The puns on "setter" and "story" demonstrate Merrill's wit. Kalstone writes, "All conversational ease and, at the end, outrageous humor, Merrill's wit allows us momentary relaxation and then plants its sting . . . [it] is there to reveal patterns that vein a life: a precarious and double use of ordinary speech." Just as the ordinariness of daily life covers depths of passion and moment, so the virtuosity of Merrill's diction reveals possibilities in speech that the reader may not have previously considered. In fact, he once referred to his language as " 'English' in its billiard-table sense – words that have been set spinning against their own gravity."

The Fire Screen (1969) marks a defensive retreat, in middle age, from ardors and passions better enjoyed when young. Even grand opera, about which a series of poems revolves, seems too strenuous to confront, as he acknowledges half-jokingly in "Matinees," where the real thing, whether art or life, seems "too silly or solemn": it is "Enough to know the score / From records or transcriptions / For our four hands." Sometimes, even, "it seems /

Kinder to remember than to play." The fire screen of the collection's title is a protection, which in its French translation, *contre-coeur*, applies equally to love's flames. Merrill's prose footnote to "Mornings in a New House" shrugs cavalierly at the Brunhild-like protection offered by the fancy screen: "Oh well, our white heats lead us no less than words do. Both have been devices in their day." One's "household opera," the heroic passions unknown to children, develops in time and is recorded by memory. Life imitates art, however, as a child, confronting Wagnerian passion at the Met, must thereafter arrange for his "own chills and fever, passions and betrayals, / Chiefly in order to make song of them."

The defensiveness against debilitating passions in life and art is reflected most stunningly in the book's longest poem, "The Summer People," a ballad of chilling and disingenuous simplicity that dramatizes an aphorism from Merrill's experimental novel, *The (Diblos) Notebook* (1965): "After a certain age, the heart gives itself, if at all, too easily: the gift can be taken back." A quartet of summer residents in a fishing village enthusiastically welcomes a mysterious millionaire into their midst. He, his cat, and his Japanese houseboy assume year-round residency and enchant their adopters. After one of them is bitten by the cat, who is then destroyed, the millionaire, Jack Frost, leaves for the Orient; the summer people lose their infatuation; the house and garden fall into disrepair; and the houseboy dies. It is an uneventful narrative, with an eerie disjunction between style and subject. The narrator comments upon this spookiness:

> The meter grows misleading.
> Given my characters.
> . . . .
> For figures in a ballad
> Lend themselves to acts
> Passionate and simple.
> . . . .
> But I have no such hero,
> No fearful deeds – unless
> We count their quiet performance
> By Time or Tenderness.

The weirdness is like that of Edward Gorey or the macabre textures of pornography, a tone Merrill had captured well in the postcard section of "The Thousand and Second Night" in *Nights and Days*. In this suspended narrative, isolated events in the lives of the summer people are intersected by the mysterious stranger who comes from and returns to nowhere. Origins and ends are equally fathomless. The blessings of summer – dinners, musicales,

amusing distractions – are magical and illusory; underneath lurks something sinister, evoked even in the halting rhythm of the ballad stanza:

> Andrew at the piano
> Let the ice in his nightcap melt.
> Mendelssohn's augmentations
> Were very deeply felt.

How? By whom? Such questions are no more to be answered than the mysteries of the heart's extensions to, and withdrawals from, a visitor from somewhere beyond. Only transience abides.

The title *Braving the Elements* suggests tactics for survival, perhaps gaining heroic stature through risking exposure. Often, the poems begin with the enervation following a physical or emotional crisis, which increases sensitivity. At the same time, one can see clearly Merrill's metaphysical mind in poems that elaborate a many-stranded conceit into a fugal pattern. "Willowware Cup," for example, works through the association, amplification, and cross-referencing of art, politics, and biology, in an updating of Yeats's "Lapis Lazuli," a commentary on the interweavings of art and life. Levels of diction touch smoothly, like layers on the ocean floor; technical vocabulary from pottery or genetics mixes easily with the pseudoserious or the archly cryptic ("You are far away. The leaves tell what they tell").

In his middle age, Merrill becomes more aware of the constancy beneath the surface of change. A proud, strutting Athenian, the classical ideal still glowing through the debased, modern flesh, extra kilos, and a moustache, is his old friend Strato in "Strato in Plaster," just as Kyria Kleo both was and was not Love. The title seems to refer to a statue, but the reader learns soon that it is about a broken arm. The trick is meaningful since the poem deals with the ways man tends to stabilize the past and how life always resists art's attempts at finality. People are never, yet are somehow always, what they used to be. The return to a new beginning is eternally the same, as in "After the Fire," when Merrill visits his Athens apartment after a conflagration to learn that "everything changes, nothing does." Kleo is still a whore; her son Noti still cruises for lovers; all become parodies of what they once were. Even objects are merely "translated," and nothing ever fully disappears since in Merrill's universe, as in Freud's, a divine economy keeps everything moving and useful: "Life, like the bandit Somethingopoulos / Gives to others what it takes from us." Total disappearance is impossible; there is only displacement and shifting. Love is not wholly wasted, only metamorphosed by its own mysterious laws.

The denial of love, Merrill's compulsive fear as a child of a broken home, finds imaginative consolation in "Days of 1935," which revolves around a double fantasy: that of the adult for childhood innocence and bravado and that of the child for attention through victimization. The young boy dreams he is kidnapped by a pair of Bonnie and Clyde look-alikes, Floyd and Jean, movie stars right out of central casting or from the pages of the Lindbergh case. They are coarse, sexual creatures but also parent substitutes. The boy spins out tales for Jean all afternoon, realizing that he is Scheherazade and she the real child and that the whole escapade, now separate from, now connected to, life past and present, proves that there is neither end nor beginning. The child returns to normal life after the supposed capture of the criminals; the adult recalls a Proustian moment when the child goes off to bed as his parents prepare for a party:

> She kisses him sweet dreams, but who –
> Floyd and Jean are gone –
> Who will he dream of? True to life
> He's played them false. A golden haze
> Past belief, past disbelief . . .
> Well, those were the days.

Life is fiction in disguise, he knew even as a child; the poet teaches that fiction is equally life transformed and feeling translated.

Divine Comedies begins Merrill's supreme fiction, a self-mythologizing epic program that J. D. McClatchy has called, varying Samuel Taylor Coleridge's phrase, "The Other Life within Us and Abroad." Merrill combines his masters with graceful fluency in a creation entirely his own: the reader finds Proust's social world and his analysis of the human heart and the artist's growth, Dante's organizational genius, and Yeats's spiritualism, for which the hints in the earlier volumes gave only small promise. Added to these are the offhand humor of George Gordon, Lord Byron, and W. H. Auden, a Neoplatonic theory of reincarnation, a self-reflectiveness about the process of composition, and a virtual handbook of poetic technique. "The Book of Ephraim," the volume's long poem, is the first part of Merrill's central statement.

Traditionally, a poet writes one great epic for which his entire career is a preparation. The half-dozen smaller poems surrounding "The Book of Ephraim" like chapels around a great cathedral adumbrate the larger work's concerns. "Chimes for Yahya," like "Verse for Urania," echoes Milton's

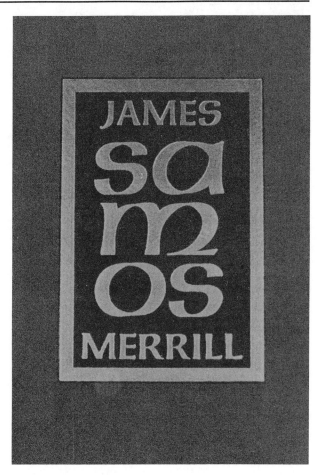

Cover for a limited edition of Merrill's six-stanza poem that begins the "&" section in Scripts for the Pageant

Nativity Ode; it also reworks Yeats's "The Second Coming" and revives Merrill's concern with surrogate fathers, the Near East, the collision of cultures, and inheritance and bequests. The impressive "Lost in Translation" pinpoints, more succinctly than any of Merrill's other short poems, the issues of loss and possession. Recalling a childhood jigsaw puzzle with one missing piece, Merrill is led to consider as well his vain attempts to retrieve a translation by Rainer Maria Rilke of Valéry's "Palme": "So many later puzzles had missing pieces" that he finds compensation in cosmic housekeeping:

> But nothing's lost. Or else: all is translation
> And every bit of us is lost in it
> . . . .
> And in that loss a self-effacing tree,
> Color of context, imperceptibly
> Rustling with its angel, turns the waste
> To shade and fiber, milk and memory.

Poetry, said Robert Frost, is what is lost in translation; Merrill's poem proves the adage wrong, since loss through translation is the motive for the poem itself.

Memory and vision are the milk of instruction in "The Book of Ephraim," as the poet pieces together past and present, with occasional sidelong glances at an unfinished novel he once worked on and with information about the universe supplied by his psychopomp, the poem's title character. The medium is a Ouija board, on which he and David Jackson had been experimenting since 1955, the second year of their Stonington tenancy. Their familiar spirit turns out to have been a Greek Jew, coincidentally from a broken home, who died in 36 A.D. He instructs "JM" and "DJ" through the twenty-six capital letters of the board. (The poem's twenty-six sections begin with the letters of the alphabet in sequence.) Ephraim is a smiling, chatty schoolmaster, less stern than Dante's Virgil (another major difference between the universes of Dante and Merrill is that the latter lacks a hell) and an epitome of worldly wit and skepticism who chides when necessary ("WILL / U NEVER LEARN LOOK LOOK LOOK LOOK YR FILL / BUT DO DO DO DO / NOTHING"), but more frequently adopts an affable, cooing tone. ("U ARE SO QUICK MES CHERS I FEEL WE HAVE / SKIPPING THE DULL CLASSROOM DONE IT ALL / AT THE SALON LEVEL.") Ephraim gilds the philosophic pill, as Merrill does the poem: "huge tracts of information / Have gone into these capsules flavorless / And rhymed for easy swallowing." A good thing, too, since JM and DJ, as stand-ins for their own reading audience, go in fear of abstractions: they have already slept through

> our last talk on Thomist
> Structures in Dante. Causes
> Were always lost – on us. We shared the traits
> Of both the dumbest
> Boy in school and that past master of clauses
> Whose finespun mind "no idea violates."

"The Book of Ephraim" is as worthy of Henry James as of Dante. In Heaven and Earth, the stage is set for a congregation of sociable spirits, with Ephraim as guide to what is past and passing and to come. The dramatis personae (section D) include friends, family, strangers, and fictional characters, striated and structured in manifold relationships. Every living person is the earthly representative of some otherworldly patron, who may not, however, intervene for him (only when there is "SOME POWERFUL MEMORY OR AFFINITY" may a spirit interfere with earthly arrangements, as Plato was permitted to do for Wallace Stevens). Borrow-

ing from the most shadowy of Orphic legends, filtered through Plato and Vergil, Merrill invests his living souls with repeated incarnations, and he arranges the otherworldly spirits upon a ladder of nine stages of patronage ("with every rise in station / Comes a degree of PEACE FROM REPRESENTATION"), which provoke the return of the taken-leave-of senses "LIKE PICTURES ON A SCREEN / GROWN SOLID THAT AT FIRST ARE MERELY SEEN."

Lacking a conventional plot, the poem wheels steadily down parallel paths: speculation, lyricism, self-analysis, history, fiction. Aware of the potentially absurd wrongheadedness of it all, Merrill sensibly steps back occasionally to behold the strangeness of his poem and the world it mirrors. His skepticism, like Ephraim's heuristic methods, is an educational tool: one is readier to accept the spiritualism for the very doubts with which it is offered. In a visit to a psychiatrist (section I), JM proffers the old Wildean epigram, "given a mask we'll tell the truth," to the fear that he and DJ are engaged in a harmless "folie à deux." What are they to make of "these odd inseminations by psycho-roulette?" His answer: "Somewhere a Father Figure shakes his rod / At sons who have not sired a child?" is certainly a reasonable Freudian explanation. Or, there may be an alternative, Jungian one: Ephraim's "lights and darks were a projection / Of what already burned, at some obscure / Level or another, in our skulls." Yeats's spirits told him they came to bring metaphors for poetry, and one may choose to take Ephraim's fables as a fictive construction, remembering, as Stevens says, that God and the imagination are one, or, as Jung would have it, that God and the unconscious are one:

> *He* was the revelation
> (Or if we have created him, then we were).
> The point – one twinkling point by now of
>   thousands –
> Was never to forego, in favor of
> Plain dull proof, the marvelous nightly pudding.

The poem can never say who is the creator, who the creation: perhaps its readers are all characters in some superplot by divine powers, or perhaps they are projections of our deepest desires. The mirror on the book's dust jacket reminds the reader of Merrill's habitual doubling: an abiding image is now a major theme.

The admixture of worldly wit and spiritual revelation resolves itself in fanciful moments: Mozart is "A BLACK ROCK STAR / WHATEVER THAT IS," assures Ephraim; he was allowed re-

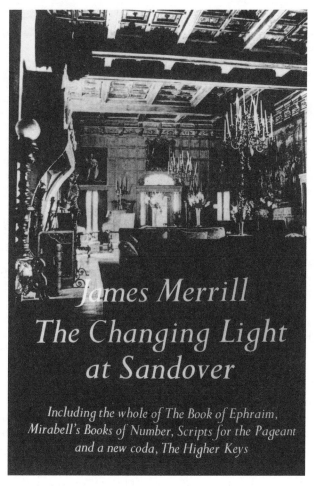

Dust jacket for Merrill's acclaimed philosophical verse trilogy

birth instead of promotion because "HE PREFERS / LIVE MUSIC TO A PATRON'S HUMDRUM SPHERES" (Mirabell corrects this misinformation in the next volume). More important than his wit, however, is the sureness of Merrill's tone in the poem. "The Book of Ephraim" is encyclopedic as much by virtue of calibrations along a tonal scale as by the scope of its information. Merrill admits to having cared for music long before literature, and in a 1968 interview with Donald Sheehan he used a word for tone that might explain his sympathy with the disembodied visitors he never sees: " 'Voice' is the democratic word for 'tone.' 'Tone' always sounds snobbish, but without a sense of it, how one flounders." "The Book of Ephraim" is a literal and figurative sounding of depths and scaling of heights throughout the universe and within its microcosm, the human voice.

Both "The Book of Ephraim" and its book-length sequel, *Mirabell: Books of Number,* the second part of the trilogy, dispel the earlier charges against

Merrill's "mere" artfulness. (After Merrill won the Bollingen Award, a *New York Times* editorial criticized the foundation for making an award in troubled times to a genteel poet.) They add depth to Stevens's phrase about the "essential gaudiness of poetry," because their essential vision is elaborate, comic, deliberate, and spacious. Merrill asked in the 1968 interview: "How can you appreciate the delights of concision unless you abuse them?"

The "GREAT GENETIC GOD" who figures dimly in "The Book of Ephraim" as a kind of Shavian Life Force, seeing to the gradual improvement of the universe and the human species, is more centrally located, but still offstage, in *Mirabell.* Ephraim (section P) says that he has seen souls from before the flood, nuclear in origin, compared with whom he is merely a shadow. In section U a new message is cut off: "MYND YOUR WEORK SIX MOONES REMAIN." This is the voice of Mirabell, which now, in his own book, overwhelms all the others: JM's, Ephraim's, plus the added commentaries of

W. H. Auden and Merrill's Greek friend Maria Mitsotaki, both recently gone, his spiritual parents, "father of forms and matter-of-fact mother," whose common sense keeps DJ and JM from despair after their communications with the angels. The voices blend in harmonious chorus, a music corresponding to a new focus away from the individual self.

The self begins its path toward opacity in "The Book of Ephraim." In sections W and X, as life and poem approach closure, Merrill opens himself to change: "So Time has – but who needs that *nom de plume?* I've – / We've modulated . . . We've grown autumnal, mild." He compares the Jacksons, crazy and quarrelsome but still "serenely holding hands" in old age, with his own condition: "Already I take up less emotional space than a snowdrop." We are all different selves: "Young chameleon, I used to / Ask how on earth one got sufficiently / Imbued with otherness. And now I see."

The twentieth century has destroyed what D. H. Lawrence called the old stable ego; otherness is the theme of *Mirabell,* the condition of its world. Ultimately, all of one's former lives run together (MM tells JM that "AS WITH THE OLD LOVES ONE FORGETS A FEW"). No longer is the poem's form the abecedarian used in "Ephraim"; here, discreteness and repetition nod toward Ludwig Wittgenstein's decimal arrangements. There are ten chapters, numbered from 0 to 9, each with ten similarly numbered sections. The living and the dead, a great society, meet on the Ouija board, the dead spirits anchored by the living (hence the importance of Cabel Stone, the spirit Merrill contacted even before Ephraim: Stone was his first cable to the other world), who accumulate and internalize knowledge. Heaven is "BOTH REALITY AND A FIGMENT OF THE IMAGINATION," a machine that Auden says "MAKES THE DEAD AVAILABLE TO LIFE." And although JM feels he is merely a "vehicle in this cosmic carpool," he is again reminded by Auden "WHAT A MINOR / PART THE SELF PLAYS IN A WORK OF ART." Fact is fable; creation is merely the correct reception and interpretation of signals; the universe is a whole organism in which the angel Michael says, at the book's end: "GOD IS THE ACCUMULATED INTELLIGENCE IN CELLS SINCE THE DEATH OF THE FIRST DISTANT CELL. / WE RESIDE IN THAT INTELLIGENCE."

The voices of *Mirabell* sing solo or in chorus; its technique serves its vision. "You sound like E," says JM, "maybe you are E?" To which Mirabell makes the cryptic reply: "WE ARE U YOU ARE WE EACH OTHERS DREAM." The new spirits speak in fourteeners, the older ones in decasyllables, Merrill and fellow mortals in a variety of living human speech. Who could guess that the teatabling opening lines – "Oh very well, then. Let us broach the matter / Of the new wallpaper in Stonington" – would expand to major discoveries or even follow from the epigraph drawn from Laura Fermi's memoir of her husband's atomic experiments: "They were the first men to see matter yield its inner energy, steadily, at their will." The occasion for the new book is the death and burial in Athens of David Jackson's parents. Having been out of touch with Ephraim for some time, DJ and JM contact him for "sense, comfort, and wit," as compensation for loss. But the new voice intervenes, demanding "poems of science." In "The Book of Ephraim," the poet felt initially inadequate to his task; here, he positively balks at what he always considered boring and obfuscating matters. But he plunges in, asking, "Why couldn't Science, in the long run, serve / As well as one's uncleared lunch-table or / *Mme X en culotte de Matador?*" Proton and neutron become metaphors for poetry, repeating an eclogue and "orbited by twinkling flocks."

"The Book of Ephraim" took twenty years to write; the whole of *Mirabell* was composed in Stonington during the summer of 1976. The former work was prologue, long in coming; the main body was assembled in a period of intense concentration. Ephraim was the first leader, witty and frivolous because his listeners were; the new voice, initially a number and named Mirabell by the heroes halfway through, is more serious, befitting their new maturity and higher station on the ladder of spiritual perfection. Mirabell and his peers serve God Biology (there is another god named Chaos – the universe seems more Manichean or Lucretian than previously); they are fallen, for having once trifled with creation (the result was black holes), but were forgiven. They must now "WARN MAN AGAINST THE CHAOS," which began in 1934 with atomic fission and threatens the five-hundred-million-year-old greenhouse of nature. They appear, according to the choral report of Auden, Maria, and Ephraim, as bats (the figures on Merrill's new carpet and also a skeptic's way of seeing anything as sense-defying as these spirits.)

The lesson of the universe may be briefly put. God Biology is a good, although distant, force, working eugenically with a very few souls (a biological version of spiritual election) who are cloned and recloned in his Research Lab for the gradual improvement of the race. The majority of lives is animal in nature and returns to the great genetic

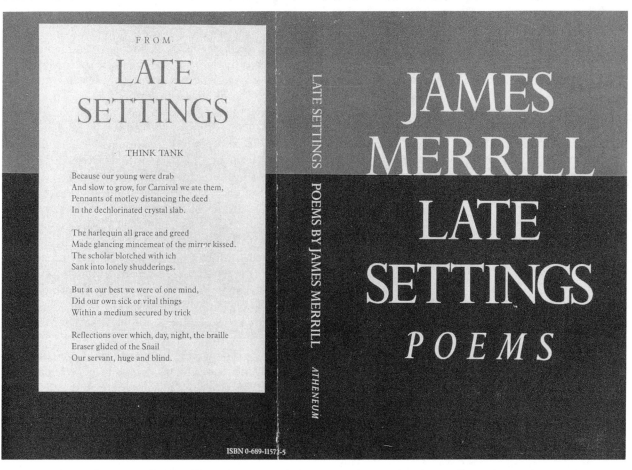

FROM

LATE SETTINGS

THINK TANK

Because our young were drab
And slow to grow, for Carnival we ate them,
Pennants of motley distancing the deed
In the dechlorinated crystal slab.

The harlequin all grace and greed
Made glancing mincemeat of the mirror kissed.
The scholar blotched with ich
Sank into lonely shudderings.

But at our best we were of one mind,
Did our own sick or vital things
Within a medium secured by trick

Reflections over which, day, night, the braille
Eraser glided of the Snail
Our servant, huge and blind.

LATE SETTINGS

POEMS BY JAMES MERRILL

ATHENEUM

ISBN 0-689-11572-5

JAMES MERRILL
LATE SETTINGS
POEMS

Dust jacket for Merrill's 1985 book, in which he returns to some of the themes of his earliest work

pool for general use. Nothing has ever been lost, except the souls of people killed at Hiroshima, and there are almost no mistakes (RNA = REMEMBER NO ACCIDENTS), which troubles Merrill's liberal belief in human choice and freedom: "All, all, it sinks in gradually, was meant / To happen, and not just the gross event. / But its minutest repercussion." Or, as Maria says of heaven: "ONE / BIG DATING COMPUTER MES ENFANTS GET WISE: / TO BE USED HERE IS THE TRUE PARADISE."

Apparent freedoms that entrap are but half the picture. As a poem of instruction, *Mirabell* both explains and dramatizes the symbiotic relationship between worlds, the accessibility of the dead to the living. Dependence is all; the main metaphor, harmony, is another word for the high hum of spiritual commerce. Mirabell is like Keats's Moneta, the priestess of history who makes futurity pastness, but he is also Merrill's creation. One is chosen to serve or to create, and Mirabell is as much JM's servant as God's. The ego is as fluid as the atom. Mind

and nature are wedded, as Wordsworth announced in his own epic plans: the result is the universe as we know it, or an image of the relationship between the conscious and unconscious minds.

Just as Mirabell is an information bank, JM is the receptacle without which the angelic knowledge would lodge useless, unrealized. The role of the scribe is to speed acceptance of God's work. This is nothing new in Western literature, but Merrill emphasizes the mutuality of scribe and master. The angels lack two humanizing gifts, language and feeling. For these they depend upon the living (the bats are just a little vampirish). Metaphor may be vulgar or negative, but the alternative, within a heavenly sphere, is pure formula. Since language is of human origin, God B has no words for his own power and grace: "Who, left alone, just falls back on flimflam / Tautologies like *I am that I am* / Or *The world is everything that is the case.*" The complex mathematical truths of the angels, both frightening and incomprehensible, must be translated by the scribes into their own "vocabulary of manners." Early in the book,

Mirabell, still known as 741, is granted feeling to love his translators. His own identity, and certainly his name, depend on humanization: "I HAVE ENTERED A GREAT WORLD I AM FILLED / WITH IS IT MANNERS?" Eternity, as Blake wrote, is in love with the productions of Time.

If the gift to Mirabell in this exchange is a human name, the price to his spellers is loss of individuality. Just as souls are cloned and reborn (Ephraim's system of patronage, the reader learns now, was a simplification, a fussy bureaucracy still part of God's lab), the progress toward revelation is marked by the breakdown of identity. JM and DJ merge with MM, WHA, and 741, five souls and five elements, into a psychic atom around the nucleus of the two living men. Completeness is loss of personality, as Mirabell pronounces in the tones of Wallace Stevens:

> JM THE STRIPPING IS THE POINT YR POEM
> WILL PERHAPS
> TAKE UP FROM ITS WINTRY END & MOVE
> STEP BY STEP INTO
> SEASONLESS & CHARACTERLESS STAGES TO
> ITS FINAL
> GREAT COLD RINGING OF THE CHIMES SHAPED
> AS O O O O O

Merrill wants to know why God has chosen him and Jackson, homosexuals, for his work. Why not heterosexuals like Hugo or Yeats? The answer is a tongue-in-cheek, semipornographic self-defense:

> Erection of theories, dissemination
> Of thought – the intellectual's machismo.
> We're more the docile takers-in of seed.
> No matter what tall tale our friends emit,
> Lately – you've noticed? – we just swallow it.

Homosexuality, assures Mirabell, was a late product (four thousand years ago) to encourage poetry and music. In another twist, Merrill realizes that this quartet was chosen because, like the spirits themselves, they are childless. Likewise, type is set backward but appears correctly on the page. Reversion, or inversion, when set straight, is correctness, and creation is "a reasoned indirection."

The last third of the trilogy, *Scripts for the Pageant* (1980), followed in the completed *The Changing Light at Sandover* by a coda entitled "The Higher Keys," is the longest and most difficult part but also in some ways is the simplest and most lucid. No summary can account for the depth and variety of information and revelation made by the new speakers here, primarily a pair of angels – Michael and Gabriel – who represent the universal forces of cre-

ation and destruction, light and darkness, respectively. *Scripts for the Pageant* is organized around the Ouija categories of *Yes, &,* and *No.* All affirmation is countered by negation. At the same time, Merrill reduces his enormous cast of characters: identities that have multiplied turn out to be versions of a sacred few. One of Merrill's perennial themes – masking and unmasking – here receives its highest, most dramatic, and moving treatment. Finally, the epic has both the heft of a scientific treatise and the energy of a mystery novel, as readers proceed through a series of discoveries to learn, at last, the simple, essential identities of the poem's characters, bringing the poem back to its beginning. Having completed his great life's work, JM now arises to perform it, before an audience composed of the living and the dead, the real and the imagined, although it is to the former that he owes his strongest allegiance: "For *their* ears I begin: 'Admittedly. . . .' " The poem has come full circle, ending with the first word of "The Book of Ephraim."

After completing his masterpiece, Merrill gathered together three further volumes of lyric poems – *Late Settings* (1985), *The Inner Room,* and *A Scattering of Salts* (1995), which was published posthumously. In them he returned to many of his earliest themes with the maturity and simplicity that come from years of honing one's art. Like his syntax, his diction dexterously careens between the ornate, the baroque, and the simple, the plain. In Merrill's ear, one that takes in all levels of language, the lapidary coexists with the colloquial. In *A Scattering of Salts* Merrill acknowledges mortality while never forgoing his characteristic lambent wit. His autobiographical memoir, *A Different Person,* continues the openness and self-examination begun in his epic. The defense of homosexuality in *Mirabell* is deepened and personalized, as Merrill writes about his psychoanalysis in Rome between 1950 and 1952, when he was breaking away from his family in America, coming to grips with his sexual identity, and making his first serious efforts at poetry. What this moving book proves, like the vast epic it succeeded, is that difference and sameness may turn out to be two names for the same thing. The "different" person of the distant past is also – *mutatis mutandis* – the James Merrill writing in the present. One may be reminded of a telling remark in one of Keats's letters: "We are like the relict shirt of a Saint: the same and not the same: for the careful Monks patch it and patch it until there's not a thread of the original garment left, and still they show it for St. Anthony's shirt." Merrill's great theme turns out to have been all along that most basic of human questions: how does one become a person, changing but simultaneously staying true to one's self?

Interviews:

Ashley Brown, "An Interview with James Merrill," *Shenandoah,* 19 (Summer 1968): 3–15;

Donald Sheehan, "An Interview with James Merrill," *Contemporary Literature,* 9 (Winter 1968): 1–14;

David Kalstone, "The Poet: Private," *Saturday Review,* 55 (2 December 1972): 43–45;

Christopher Buckley, "Exploring *The Changing Light at Sandover:* An Interview with James Merrill," *Twentieth Century Literature,* 38 (1992): 415–435.

References:

Harold Bloom, ed., *James Merrill* (New York: Chelsea House, 1985);

Richard Howard, *Alone With America: Essays on the Art of Poetry in the United States Since 1950* (New York: Atheneum, 1971), pp. 327–348;

David Kalstone, *Five Temperaments* (New York: Oxford University Press, 1977), pp. 77–128;

Ross Labrie, *James Merrill* (Boston: Twayne, 1982);

David Lehman and Charles Berger, eds., *James Merrill: Essays in Criticism* (Ithaca, N.Y.: Cornell University Press, 1983);

J. D. McClatchy, "Lost Paradises," *Parnassus,* 5 (Fall/Winter 1976): 305–320;

Judith Moffett, *James Merrill: An Introduction to the Poetry,* revised edition (New York: Columbia University Press, 1984);

Robert Polito, *A Reader's Guide to James Merrill's The Changing Light at Sandover* (Ann Arbor: University of Michigan Press, 1994);

Willard Spiegelman, *The Didactic Muse: Scenes of Instruction in Contemporary American Poetry* (Princeton: Princeton University Press, 1989), pp. 192–246;

Stephen Yenser, *The Consuming Myth: The Work of James Merrill* (Cambridge, Mass.: Harvard University Press, 1987).

George Oppen

(24 April 1908 – 7 July 1984)

Jeffrey Peterson
Ohio Wesleyan University

See also the Oppen entry in *DLB 5: American Poets Since World War II, First Series.*

BOOKS: *Discrete Series* (New York: Objectivist Press, 1934);

The Materials (New York: New Directions/San Francisco Review, 1962);

This in Which (New York: New Directions/San Francisco Review, 1965);

Of Being Numerous (New York: New Directions, 1968);

Alpine: Poems (Mount Horeb, Wis.: Perishable Press, 1969);

Seascape: Needle's Eye (Fremont, Mich.: Sumac Press, 1972);

Collected Poems (London: Fulcrum Press, 1972);

The Collected Poems of George Oppen (New York: New Directions, 1975);

Primitive (Santa Barbara, Cal.: Black Sparrow Press, 1978);

Poems of George Oppen, 1908–1984, selected and introduced by Charles Tomlinson (Newcastle upon Tyne, U.K.: Cloud, 1990).

OTHER: Ezra Pound, ed., *Active Anthology* (London: Faber & Faber, 1933) – includes five poems by Oppen;

Charles Reznikoff, *Poems 1937–1975: Volume II of the Complete Poems,* edited by Seamus Cooney, with a foreword by Oppen (Santa Barbara, Cal.: Black Sparrow Press, 1977).

SELECTED PERIODICAL PUBLICATIONS – UNCOLLECTED:

POETRY

"Discrete Series, 1–4," *Poetry,* 39 (January 1932): 198–199;

"Four Uncollected Poems from *Discrete Series,*" *Ironwood,* 26 (Fall 1985): 69–72.

NONFICTION

"Three Poets," *Poetry,* 100 (August 1962): 329–333;

George Oppen, circa 1955

"The Mind's Own Place," *Kulchur,* 3 (Summer 1963): 2–8;

"A Letter from George Oppen," *Elizabeth,* 10 (December 1966): 22–23;

"On Armand Schwerner," *Stony Bridge,* 3–4 (1969): 72;

"A Letter," *Agenda,* 11 (Spring/Summer 1973): 58–59;

"Non Resistance, etc. Or: Of the Guiltless," *West End,* 1 (Summer 1974): 5;

"My Best to Him" *New Directions 34: An International Anthology of Prose and Poetry,* edited by James Laughlin (New York: New Directions, 1979), p. 150;

"Pound in the U.S.A., 1969," *Sagetrieb,* 1 (Spring 1982): 119;

"Statement on Poetics," *Sagetrieb,* 3 (Winter 1984): 25–27;

"An Adequate Vision: A George Oppen Daybook," edited by Michael Davidson, *Ironwood,* 26 (Fall 1985): 5–31;

"'Disasters': Versions and Notes," edited by Cynthia Anderson, *Ironwood,* 26 (Fall 1985): 146–151;

"'Meaning Is to Be Here': A Selection from the Daybook," edited by Anderson, *Conjunctions,* 10 (1987): 186–208;

"*Primitive*: An Archeology of the Omega Point," edited by Anderson, *Ironwood,* 31/32 (Spring/ Fall 1988): 306–323;

"Selections from George Oppen's *Daybook*," edited by David Young, *Iowa Review,* 18 (Fall 1988): 1–17;

"The Circumstances: A Selection from George Oppen's Uncollected Writing," edited by Rachel Blau DuPlessis, *Sulfur,* 25 (Fall 1989): 10–43;

"The Anthropologist of Myself: A Selection from Working Papers," edited by DuPlessis, *Sulfur,* 26 (Spring 1990): 135–164;

"'The Philosophy of the Astonished': Selections from the Working Papers," edited by DuPlessis, *Sulfur,* 27 (Fall 1990): 202–220.

In "Route" – a poem from George Oppen's *Of Being Numerous* (1968), which won the 1969 Pulitzer Prize and whose title-poem critics regard as his major work – Oppen modestly states his aesthetic, philosophical, and political aims: "I might at the top of my ability stand at a window / and say, look out; out there is the world." Venturing out across the threshold of received knowledge, past the "window" of artistic preconception and social privilege – these are the paradigmatic moves of Oppen's life and work: entering the landscape "out there," through the ostensibly simple, though existentially complex, activity of naming "the world." This activity Oppen grounds in the contingent particulars of life and language, for the sake of affirming not only the referential power of words but also the world's ineluctable thereness. With a phenomenologist's attention to the mysterious interplay of subject and object, a socialist's concern for the individual's vulnerability to the determining pressures of class and history, and a craftsman's dedication to the materiality of the poem-as-object, Oppen refashioned the poetics of Imagism – as developed by such modernist forebears as Ezra Pound, Marianne Moore, and William Carlos Williams – into his own version of Objectivism, the loosely formulated movement with

which he, Louis Zukofsky, Charles Reznikoff, Carl Rakosi, and Lorine Niedecker were associated in the early 1930s.

As a member of the Objectivists, a group that reemerged in the 1960s after decades-long gaps in the writing lives of its various members, Oppen managed to make a slim (fewer than three hundred pages in fifty years) but remarkable contribution to twentieth-century American poetry, notable both for its breadth of experiential reference and its depth of philosophical and political reflection. Built of the complex refusal to take for granted either words or the world, Oppen's work confronts and records the contingencies of its own struggle to "construct a meaning," as he puts it in his 1969 interview with L. S. Dembo, "from moments of conviction." As Michael Heller observes in *Conviction's Net of Branches* (1985): "Oppen's entire body of work can be seen as a modern test of the poet's capacity to articulate. The terms of his poetry are the common meanings of words as they attempt to render the brute givens of the world of appearance."

George Oppen (né Oppenheimer) was born on 24 April 1908 in New Rochelle, New York, into a middle-class Jewish family. Of his boyhood home on Wildcliff Road, near Long Island Sound, George remarks in Mary Oppen's memoir, *Meaning a Life* (1978): "I lived in a house on the water, near the harbor, in a small village." When Oppen was four, and his sister, Elizabeth (Libby), seven, his mother, Elsie Rothfeld, suffered a nervous breakdown and committed suicide. As Rachel Blau DuPlessis notes in her introduction to *The Selected Letters of George Oppen* (1990), the best source of biographical information on the poet currently available, "his mother left a suicide note (not apparently extant) whose terms haunted Oppen." When Oppen was nine, his father, George August Oppenheimer, son of a diamond wholesaler and, by Oppen's account, a witty and charming if sometimes difficult man, married Selville Shainwald, a woman whose family wealth was considerable. Oppen was apparently tragically abused by his stepmother. In a selection from his working papers published as "'Meaning Is to Be Here': A Selection from the Daybook" Oppen writes: "My father's second marriage opened upon me an attack totally murderous, totally brutal, involving sexual attack, [and] beatings." In 1918 Oppen's half sister, June, was born, and the family moved to San Francisco, where Oppen spent the rest of his boyhood and adolescence.

Just before his high school graduation in 1925, Oppen was the driver in a car accident that involved one fatality. Accused of drinking, he was ex-

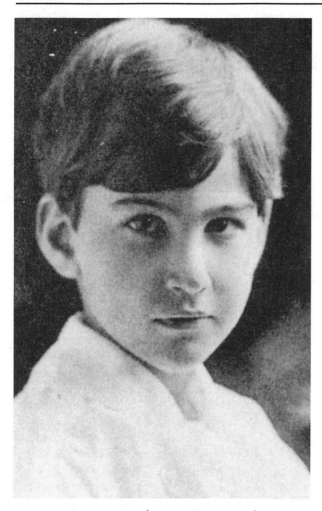

Oppen in 1914 (courtesy of Mary Oppen)

pelled from the Warren Military Academy. Oppen then traveled in Europe; after his return he attended and graduated from a small prep school. In the fall of 1926 he entered what is now Oregon State University at Corvallis. Shortly thereafter, in a course on modern poetry, he met Mary Colby. Both eighteen at the time, they would remain together, in league as artist-companions, for the rest of their lives. In response to official punishments for violating curfew on their first night together – an occasion that is movingly rendered in Oppen's "The Forms of Love" – they left college. Mary Oppen records the moment in *Meaning a Life:* "I found George Oppen and poetry at one moment, but the college expelled me and suspended George as a result of our meeting. Choice may not have been apparent to someone outside our situation, but what happened to us, our joined lives, seems to us both choice and inevitability." Willed as well as fated, then, George and Mary's meeting emblematizes the owned contingency of their "joined lives."

From 1927 to 1929 – until Oppen's twenty-first birthday, when he began receiving an inheritance from the estates of his mother and maternal grandmother, furnishing him with a monthly income of $500 – the couple sought to resist the oppressive social expectations of Oppen's wealthy family. Hitchhiking across the West, the couple were married in Dallas, Texas, on 7 October 1927. Underage and afraid of family interference, Oppen used an alias in the ceremony: "David Verdi." As DuPlessis suggests, the Oppens later took a playful kind of pride in this fact, "claiming, in semiteasing fashion, not to be really married, which seemed to give them a sense of continual and renewed choice in their deep commitment."

After returning for a time to San Francisco, the couple hitchhiked to Detroit in 1928, and – reveling in the fact that, as Mary puts it, "the wind was that free" – sailed a catboat through the Great Lakes, the Erie Canal, and the Hudson River to New York City. According to Mary, such travels – and hitchhiking in particular – "became more than flight from a powerful family – our discoveries themselves became an esthetic and a disclosure." "We were in search of an esthetic in which to live," Mary recalls: "We had learned in college that poetry was being written in our own times, and that in order to write we did not have to ground ourselves in the academic; the ground we needed was the roads we were travelling." In 1928 those roads (not to mention rivers and lakes) led the Oppens to meetings with two decisively influential writers: Louis Zukofsky and Charles Reznikoff. For Oppen these became friendships and poetic affiliations of lifelong consequence. The Oppens returned by ship to San Francisco and spent another year there, renting a house in Belvedere – across the bay from Oppen's parents.

Oppen began writing *Discrete Series* (1934), his first book, in 1929. He summons the scene in the last poem, "Till Other Voices Wake Us," of his last book, *Primitive* (1978): "writing // thru the night (a young man, / Brooklyn, 1929) I named the book // series empirical / series all force." In the same year the Oppens moved to France, settling in Le Beausset, where they formed a short-lived but productive press called TO, Publishers. By 1932, with Oppen serving as publisher and Zukofsky as editor, TO had published three important modernist texts: Pound's *How to Read,* Williams's *A Novelette and Other Prose (1921–1931),* and Zukofsky's *An "Objectivists" Anthology* (1932).

Before returning from Europe, the Oppens met Pound in Rapallo, Italy, and on Pound's suggestion visited Constantin Brancusi's studio in Paris. Mary Oppen's account of their visit with Pound captures the Oppens' sharply critical, if outwardly deferential, posture as upstart young artists:

> Walking with us on the waterfront, Ezra pointed with a grand gesture of his cape and his cane in the wrong direction and said, "From there came the Greekships." He was telling us, "Read, study the languages, read the poets in their own tongues."
>
> Our message to him would have been just as clear: "You are too far away from your roots." But we were twenty and Pound was forty, and respect for him as a poet forbade our telling him that we lacked respect for his politics and that he should go home.

During this period Oppen had also begun publishing and rearranging poems from his own work-in-progress. Under the title "1930'S," one poem appeared in Zukofsky's anthology, and under the same title a two-part sequence had appeared in the February 1931 "Objectivist" number of *Poetry*. In the January 1932 issue of *Poetry*, "Mr. George A. Oppen, of Belvedere, Cal." had placed a four-part sequence called "Discrete Series." The first three of these did not appear in the book *Discrete Series* and remained uncollected during Oppen's lifetime; the fourth, which Williams praised for its "craftsman-like economy of means" in his July 1934 review of *Discrete Series* in *Poetry*, was titled "Cat-Boat." Five of Oppen's early poems were also published in Pound's *Active Anthology* (1933); four reappeared in *Discrete Series*; the fifth, an uncharacteristically listlike lyric, titled "Brain," was omitted and was not collected by Oppen.

Strikingly, the opening poem of *Discrete Series* is an oblique tracing of Oppen's journey outward, from an interior space of social enclosure, into the larger landscape of social and historical immediacy, the "weather-swept" world of American modernity. The poem turns on an allusion to Maud Blessingbourne, a character in Henry James's "The Story in It" (1903), whose very name bespeaks social privilege. The Blessingbourne of the story, as quoted in the poem, "'approached the window as if to see / what really was going on'" – the act that Oppen would later suggest was the essential gesture of his work. She is prepared for her moment of revelation by the condition of "boredom," for Oppen the essential precondition of art that discloses the unelaborated bedrock of being. As he told Dembo, "the mood of boredom is the knowledge of what *is*." Later recognized by Oppen as an auspicious, if coincidental, allusion to Martin Heidegger's contemporaneous use of the word, *bore-*

dom as a philosophical concept held special significance for the poet.

A selection of Oppen's working papers published in the Fall 1988 *Iowa Review* provides a glimpse of the political motives behind Oppen's allusion to James, as well as a clear sense of his ironic distance from writers on the Left:

> Hemingway's style, the model of all the left-wing writers of the thirties, an essentially and incorrigibly right-wing style, – Whereas H James, the very symbol of 'snobbery' to such writers, displayed a style and a sensibility which made possible a political and social critique. In acknowledgment of this, I placed on the first page of Discrete Series the quotation from James: 'Maude Blessingbourne, it was' – and then the quotation, ending: 'As if to see what, really, was going on'[.]

Mary Oppen also remarks on James's importance to her developing critical consciousness: "Henry James opened the world around me by making the life of Europe and his society an example for me of a way to think and analyze; to find meaning in the social world around, to penetrate and understand it and to value the contribution of the U.S."

What Oppen's Blessingbourne finally participates in, then, is a world-opening act of witness. At the window, she sees:

>   rain falling, in the distance
>   more slowly,
> The road clear from her past the window-
>   glass ––
> Of the world, weather-swept, with which
>   one shares the century.

Within this clarified natural prospect, which opens out onto the broadened historical perspective of a shared century, Oppen methodically arranged his initiating series of thirty-one imagist statements. As Oppen describes his early Objectivist work for Dembo, "I learned from Louis [Zukofsky], as against the romanticism or even the quaintness of the imagist position, the necessity of forming a poem properly, for achieving form. That's what 'objectivist' really means. There's been tremendous misunderstanding about that. People assume it means the psychologically objective in attitude. It actually means the objectification of the poem, the making an object of the poem.... The other point for me, and I think for Louis, too, was the attempt to construct meaning, a method of thought from the imagist technique of poetry.... I was attempting to construct a meaning by empirical statements, by imagist statements."

Oppen's "method of thought" in *Discrete Series,* as the work's title suggests, relies both on discontinuity and implicit interconnection, on the "discrete" separateness of the particular observation and on the elliptical unity of the series-in-process. At its most tractable, the work proceeds by means of socially critical juxtapositions, playing alienated enclosures of class-privilege on the one hand, against more immediate sites of urban construction and natural contact on the other. Exemplary is the contrast between two of the book's most significant poems, the eighth and ninth in the series, Oppen's prized "Cat-Boat" (here untitled) and the poem beginning "Closed car – closed in glass –– ." The latter ends by contemplating the car's externally alien – and internally alienating – presence in the urban landscape:

> Moving in traffic
> This thing is less strange ––
> Tho the face, still within it,
> Between glasses – place, over which
>   time passes – a false light.

Glossing the poem for Dembo, Oppen remarked, "There is a feeling of something false in overprotection and over-luxury – my idea of categories of realness."

In sharp contrast and arguably more "real" was Oppen's spartan and salvific "Cat-Boat":

> The mast
> Inaudibly soars; bole-like, tapering:
> Sail flattens from it beneath the wind.
> The limp water holds the boat's round
>   sides. Sun
> Slants dry light on the deck.

As both the vertical thrust of "The Mast" and the sibilant zigzag of "sides. Sun / Slants" suggest, this poem graphically embodies its Sheeleresque visual content, demonstrating Oppen's aim of "making an object of the poem." Affirmatively of and in the natural, the poetic construction of "Cat-Boat" – as both a structure of wood and a structure of words – is explained by the description of the poem-as-object from the last poem of the volume:

> Written structure,
> Shape of art,
> More formal
> Than a field would be
> (existing in it) –– [.]

The poems of *Discrete Series* were short, depended on one another's thematic import, and

could be presented, evocatively, on a single page, or in pairs, dialectically, across facing pages (as were "Cat-Boat" and "Closed car"). Unfortunately, this calculated structural effect is obscured by their run-together presentation in *The Collected Poems of George Oppen* (1975). Mindful of this textual problem and its larger biographic and thematic implications, Joseph M. Conte has argued: "Like the steel cables that are at once the structural support and the aesthetic appeal of the Brooklyn and Golden Gate Bridges (landmarks of two of Oppen's [residences] . . .), an essential structural tension of the serial poem occurs between the series as relational system and the autonomy of each poem: the whole must act as a taut mechanism, just as the parts must have their independent sway. Oppen chose not to number his poems consecutively . . . so it is critical to the book as a discrete series that his decision be respected to isolate the poems, each to its own page."

In his 1968 interview with Dembo, Oppen explains the structural logic of the volume's title image as well as its fragmentary character: "My book, of course, was called *Discrete Series.* That's a phrase in mathematics. A pure mathematical series would be one in which each term is derived from the preceding term by a rule. A discrete series is a series of terms each of which is empirically derived, each one of which is empirically true. And this is the reason for the fragmentary character of those poems." In the effort to avoid tainting their "empirical" truth Oppen intended to resist any principle that would determine his poems aprioristically.

In a 4 October 1965 letter to DuPlessis, Oppen regretted not having furnished a more accessible gloss for his scientistic title: "(I thought too late – 30 years too late – that the flyleaf should have carried the inscription 14, 28, 32, 42, which is a discrete series: the names of the stations on the east side subway." The organizing principle for his "imagist statements," Oppen claimed, was thus cultural-historical contingency itself. And although his poems were addressed to the concerns of his times – he tacitly but persistently criticizes modern alienation throughout – Oppen chose not to foreground his political concerns. As critics have noted, the refusal to adopt an accessible rhetorical agenda – in keeping with the antirhetorical imperative of imagist-objectivist poetics – rendered work like Oppen's *Discrete Series* so neutral as to seem politically suspect to the Left in the 1930s.

However problematic it may have been at the time, such a refusal proved a source of pride in Oppen's later career. As he explained to his sister June Oppen Degnan in a letter of early 1959, the aesthetic problem with such ideologically driven poetry was its instrumentalism. From the perspective of Oppen's Objectivist stake in writing as an act of existentially fraught self-discovery, ideologically premeditated verse amounted to a betrayal of the art. This insight is crucial for understanding both Oppen's politics of perception and his profound reservations about "political" poetry in its conventional sense: "Maybe I admire myself more . . . for simply not attempting to write communist verse. That is, to any statement already determined before the verse. Poetry has to be protean; the meaning must begin there. With the perception."

In outtakes from his interview with Dembo published in 1981 Oppen describes the importance of his perceptions in "Party on Shipboard," the last poem he composed for *Discrete Series*. In this proto-poem for "Of Being Numerous" Oppen records what he remembers as a crisis of representation for his imagist-derived poetics:

> Wave in the round of the port-hole
> Springs, passing, –– arm waved,
> Shrieks, unbalanced by the motion ––
> Like the sea incapable of contact
> Save in incidents (the sea is not
>   water)
> . . . .
> The shallow surface of the sea, this,
> Numerously –– the first drinks ––
> The sea is constant weight
> In its bed.

Oppen remarks on this passage: "I may be encountering . . . (no, I was going to say the 'limitations') not the limitations, but the difficulties of imagist sincerity. Because one does have to know a wave is just a wave; one doesn't experience 'the sea.'" This seemingly idiosyncratic analogy, Oppen explains, is the crux of the poem's social "symbolism," a figure for the paradox of the many and the one:

> D[embo]. You said that the whole of "Of Being Numerous" was contained in [this] poem.

> O[ppen]. Yes, that was my first attempt. I don't know whether it's clear as symbolism. . . . The waves are the individual person. Humanity can't be encountered as an incident or something that has just happened. But all one has is "this happened," "that happened"; and out of this we try to make a picture of what a man is, who these other people are, and even, what humanity is. . . . I know there is such a thing as "the sea," the whole. But the poem doesn't manage to see it, and it records the poet's – my own – inability to see it.

Oppen decided to give up poetry for political activism in 1934 and did not write again until 1958. Michael Davidson observed in 1990 that the reasons for Oppen's long hiatus from writing were doubtless more complex than is usually acknowledged: "Hugh Kenner has provided the most convenient explanation of Oppen's silence by observing that '. . . it took twenty-five years to write the next poem,' a remark that Oppen has given assent to in various interviews. However elegant, Kenner's formulation dehistoricizes Oppen's silence by ignoring the challenges it was trying to meet during the politically charged 1930s." By the same token one should not depoliticize – or re-aestheticize – Oppen's early work on account of the poet's subsequent turn to activism. As Oppen's gloss on the crisis poem "Party on Shipboard" makes clear, confronting the limits of the individual's powers of perception was as much an artistic matter as it was a political one.

In 1933, after problems with distribution and a reduction in Oppen's income put an end to TO, Publishers, the Oppens returned to New York. They participated in yet another short-lived publishing venture, a co-op called the Objectivist Press, among whose self-financed publications in 1934 were Oppen's *Discrete Series*, Williams's *Collected Poems 1921–31*, and three books by Reznikoff: *Jerusalem the Golden*, *Testimony*, and *In Memoriam: 1933*. Pound had written a "Preface" to *Discrete Series*, and Williams wrote a review that appeared in *Poetry*. As DuPlessis remarks, these texts became "talismanic documents for Oppen's future literary career."

Moved by widespread poverty and unemployment, the Oppens in 1935 joined the Communist Party, "working as organizers for a social change," according to DuPlessis, "which was democratic socialist and populist in its ultimate contours, but also committed to the class analysis of Marxism." Feeling that his poetic work had exhausted its experiential basis, and unwilling to submit to the instrumentalism the party required of its artists and writers, Oppen concealed his identity as a poet and stopped writing. This decision, Oppen told Dembo, was informed both by political exigency and his desire for life experience:

> If you decide to do something politically, you do something with political efficacy. And if you write poetry, you write poetry, not something you hope, or deceive yourself into believing, can save people who are suffering. That was the dilemma of the 'thirties. In a way I gave up writing because of the pressures of what for the moment I'll call conscience. But there were some things I had to live through, some things I had to think my way

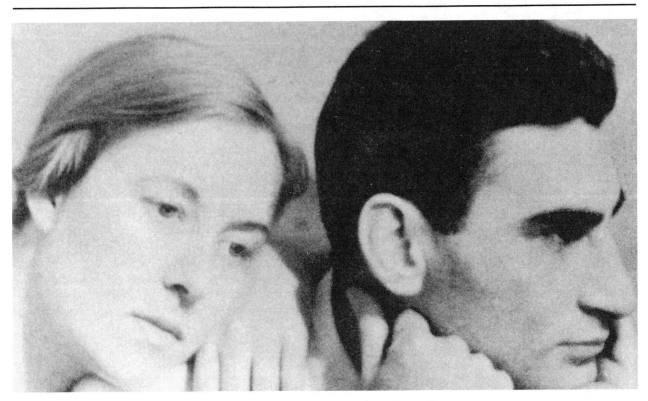

Mary and George Oppen, 1928 (courtesy of Mary Oppen)

through, some things I had to try out – and it was more than politics, really; it was the whole experience of working in factories, of having a child, and so on.

In this dramatic transition from avant-garde poetics to the radicalism of the Popular Front, the young couple had enacted what DuPlessis calls "one of the motifs of the Oppens' lives": "a kind of existential decidedness in which insight is attained, and one immediately, even radically, readjusts and sets one's course by that piercing knowledge." And as DuPlessis suggests, "there were complex and overlapping reasons" for Oppen's decision to initiate and maintain a silence that spanned much of the midcentury: "a critique of modernism which ran counter to contemporary critical, poetic, and academic thinking, a choice of activism in a deeply felt political crisis, a process of self-testing, a war injury, and recovery; later these were joined by a set of taboos and inhibitions around parenthood, and a fear of his own power."

The Oppens were active party members from 1936 to 1941. They worked as organizers for the Workers' Alliance and after training in a party school helped the Farmers' Union conduct a milk strike in Utica, New York, in 1937. DuPlessis reveals that according to his FBI file Oppen in 1936 was "Kings County election campaign manager for

Communist Party elections." After the war, Mary remembered in a fall 1988 *Iowa Review* interview, the Oppens were "a little bit active" but "very uncomfortable" and "ready to leave."

On 27 November 1942, two years after the birth of his daughter, Linda, and despite the work exemption he held as a pattern maker for Grumman Aircraft, Oppen moved the family to Detroit, thus provoking his induction into the U.S. Army. Trained in an antitank company, Oppen served in the Rhineland campaign between October 1944 and 1945, fighting in the Battle of the Bulge. He also fought in the Central Europe campaign, crossing the Rhine River into Germany in late March 1945, six weeks before Germany's surrender. In Alsace on 22 April 1945, following the shelling of a convoy in which he was driving, Oppen was seriously wounded.

Just after Oppen had taken cover in a make-shift foxhole, a second soldier piled in on top of him. "He was followed by an artillery shell," David McAleavey reports in "The Oppens: Remarks Toward Biography" (1985), "which landed close enough to send shrapnel through the one soldier into George." Pinned down by enemy fire, Oppen was unable to help his dying companion; further, fearing capture, Oppen buried the dogtags that identified him as Jewish. Much of Oppen's later work meditates on the guilt of this harrowing experience: "Blood from the Stone" and "Survival: Infantry," in *The Materials* (1962); sections of "Of Being Numerous" and "Route," in *Of Being Numerous;* "Of Hours" and section 3 of "Some Francisco Poems," in *Seascape: Needle's Eye* (1972); as well as "Myth of the Blaze" and "Semite," in *Collected Poems* (1972). Oppen received full disability benefits and was awarded, among several other medals, the Purple Heart.

After World War II the Oppens moved to Redondo Beach, California, where Oppen worked as a housing contractor and custom carpenter. In 1949 – in the wake of national hearings by the House Committee on Un-American Activities, which had been held in 1947 to rid the movie industry of Communist "infiltrators" – the Oppens were visited twice by the FBI. In June 1950, fearful they would be jailed for refusing to inform on their friends, the Oppens moved to Mexico, beginning a period of political exile that would last until 1958. In partnership with a Mexican craftsman Oppen oversaw the manufacture of furniture; however, his status as a resident alien barred him from manual labor. The Oppens had genuinely hoped to enter Mexican life, but such restrictions kept them at an uncomfortable remove. During this period Oppen studied at a distinguished art school and became an accomplished wood-carver, although he apparently wrote no poems or letters.

Several pivotal events for the Oppens occurred in 1958. Early that year Linda was admitted to Sarah Lawrence College, a transition that permitted a loosening-up of Oppen's "complex protective sense of fatherhood." According to DuPlessis, Oppen's protectiveness, "exacerbated by the family's life in exile . . . made him mute and censor the possibility of writing to protect Linda from his skepticism and apocalyptic fears of the atomic age when Linda was a 'child.'" Also in 1958, while visiting a therapist who had been working with Mary to relieve symptoms of depression, George analyzed a dream that held profound significance for his return to poetry. As DuPlessis describes it, "this was a dream connected with his father's instructions for preventing rust in copper; the dream's punch line, delivered in therapy – 'you were dreaming that you don't want to rust' – and Oppen's strained, even suicidal, hilarity that rust was supposed, ridiculously, to be in copper – formed a complex depth charge that unblocked the poet." Just fifty, Oppen began writing again in May and a year later was reestablishing contact with publishers: Henry Rago of *Poetry,*

James Laughlin of New Directions, and June Oppen Degnan, of the *San Francisco Review.*

The way to return to the United States was cleared in August 1958, when after a seven-year delay their passports were granted, signaling an end to McCarthyite harassment of U.S. citizens. In January 1960 Oppen's sister Libby died. (While the cause of death is debated within the family, Oppen suspected suicide.) The Oppens resumed permanent residence in the country in 1960, renting an apartment in Columbia Heights in Brooklyn. As a work space Oppen rented a room beneath the Brooklyn Bridge.

One of the remarkable things about *The Materials* is the tremendous body of Oppen's intervening life experience that informs its pages. *The Materials* is a book legitimately freighted with the themes of survival, return, and renewed self-making. As has often been noted, an epigraph from Jacques Maritain announces the book's unifying insight: "We awake in the same moment to ourselves and to things." Oppen's aim of staging such perceptual awakenings is evident in "Eclogue," the opening poem. Turning again from the "window" of social confinement and "the uproar" of dubious discourse, Oppen looks "outside," onto the world's humbling vastness, and finds an image of natural growth – and poetic rebirth:

> Beyond the window
> Flesh and rock and hunger
>
> Loose in the night sky
> Hardened into soil
>
> Tilting of itself to the sun once more, small
> Vegetative leaves
> And stems taking place
>
> Outside – O small ones,
> To be born!

As Oppen's friend John Crawford remarked in his 1975 essay, "If *this* is Marxism, it is the 'radicalism' of the very earth – the push of new things, which will not be denied; for the plants are the earth's own children."

In *The Materials* Oppen poses broadly political questions grounded in his experience as an activist. Flatly refusing the consolations of rhetorical "invention," Oppen raises the central question of his art in "Blood from a Stone," the first poem he wrote in his return to verse, which itself returns to the political scene of the 1930s:

As thirty in a group –
To Home Relief – the unemployed –
Within the city's intricacies
Are these lives. Belief ?
What do we believe
To live with? Answer.
Not invent – just answer – all
That verse attempts.
That we can somehow add each to each other?

As the next section of the poem makes clear, the answer to Oppen's overarching ethical question – "What do we believe / To live with?" – must be articulated against the worst the twentieth century has to offer, war:

More than we felt or saw.
There is a simple ego in a lyric,
A strange one in war.
To a body anything can happen,
Like a brick. Too obvious to say.
But all horror came from it.

Such is the matter of *The Materials:* bricks and bodies – firmly constituted yet absolutely vulnerable – recur as figures throughout the work.

Oppen's stake in the natural is by no means simplistically redemptive. As he writes in the final section of "Blood from a Stone" – in lines that may well be informed by Oppen's rage over maternal abandonment (if not also abuse) – nature's stony indifference is the tragic ground of community:

The planet's
Time.
Blood from a stone, life
From a stone dead dam. Mother
Nature! because we find the others
Deserted like ourselves and therefore brothers. Yet

So we lived
And chose to live

These were our times.

In "Time of the Missile" Oppen confronts the omnipresent risk of the nuclear age, rendering the notion of refuge-in-nature a "stone dead" fantasy:

My love, my love,
We are endangered
Totally at last. Look
Anywhere to the sight's limit: space
Which is viviparous:

Place of the mind
And eye. Which can destroy us,
Re-arrange itself, assert
Its own stone chain reaction.

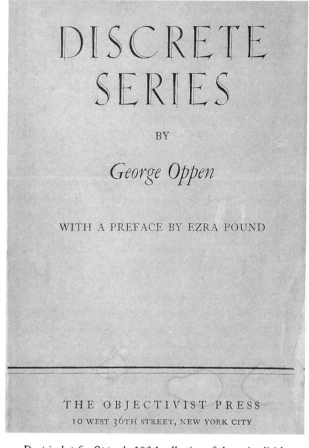

DISCRETE
SERIES

BY

George Oppen

WITH A PREFACE BY EZRA POUND

THE OBJECTIVIST PRESS
10 WEST 36TH STREET, NEW YORK CITY

Dust jacket for Oppen's 1934 collection of short, implicitly connected poems (courtesy of the Lilly Library, Indiana University)

The defining encounter in the collection is technological man's taking stock of himself in the mirror of the "things" he lives among. Emptying out Whitman's egotistical sublime in "Myself I Sing," Oppen uneasily observes, "I think myself / Is what I've seen and not myself."

The reemergence of the Objectivists in the 1960s, as critics such as Charles Altieri, David Antin, Ron Silliman, and Marjorie Perloff note, holds profound significance for the literary history of postwar American poetry. Silliman, for instance, argues that Oppen's return is the defining characteristic of what he calls "Third Phrase Objectivism." In Silliman's revisionary account Objectivism's "second phase" – that is, its period of absence during the 1940s and 1950s – contributes to the "extremism of form and content" resorted to by the poets represented in Donald Allen's *The New American Poetry: 1945–1960* (1960), many of whom were attempting innovations within the "rigorous, open-form, speech-based" poetics of Pound and Williams. What third phase objectivism offered to contemporary poetry, then, was "not so much a neo-objectivism," but what Silliman describes as the foundation of the ensuing "middle road": a historically self-reflective corrective "half-way between the New Americans and the academics who'd moved on their own toward a poetry founded on speech, both in open form and syllabics."

Oppen wrote two important pieces of critical writing in the early 1960s: "Three Poets," his only extended review article, which measures Oppen's differences from Allen Ginsberg, Charles Olson, and Michael McClure; and "The Mind's Own Place," his only published essay on poetics. In the latter Oppen articulates the poetic values that inform his critiques in "Three Poets" and proposes a "populist" poetic lineage, anticipating the sort of oppositional literary history later elaborated by Silliman and others. "Lindsay, Sandburg, Kreymborg, Williams," Oppen argues, "the poets of the little magazine *Others* which came off a hand press in a garage somewhere in New Jersey about 1918 – were almost a populist movement." As such these first-generation moderns "restored to poetry" something essential and fundamentally "populist" in origin and implication: "the sense of the poet's self among things." In a key passage in "The Mind's Own Place," Oppen provides a summation of his views:

It is possible to find a metaphor for anything, an analogue: but the image is encountered, not found; it is an account of the poet's perception, of the act of perception; it is a test of sincerity, a test of conviction, the rare poetic quality of truthfulness. They meant to replace by the data of experience the accepted poetry of their time, a display by the poets of right thinking and right sentiment, a dreary waste of lies. That data was and is the core of what "modernism" restored to poetry, the sense of the poet's self among things. So much depends upon the red wheelbarrow. The distinction between a poem that shows confidence in itself and in its materials, and on the other hand a performance, a speech by the poet is the distinction between poetry and histrionics. It is part of the function of poetry to serve as a test of truth.

Oppen's third book, *This in Which* (1965), while sustaining many of the themes of *The Materials,* focuses on the project of finding what Oppen refers to in the closing lines of "A Narrative" as "a substantial language / Of clarity, and of respect." In "The Gesture" Oppen continues his assault on instrumentalism and poetic contrivance, or what he calls in "The Mind's Own Place" the "trick of gracefulness":

How does one hold something
In the mind which he intends

To grasp and how does the salesman
Hold a bauble he intends

To sell? The question is
When will there not be a hundred

Poets who mistake that gesture
For a style.

In lieu of such gestural salesmanship, the fourth section of "A Language of New York" suggests a more cautious, even fearful, approach to language:

Possible
To use
Words provided one treat them
As enemies.
Not enemies – Ghosts
Which have run mad
In the subways
And of course the institutions
And the banks. If one captures them
One by one proceeding

Carefully they will restore
I hope to meaning
And to sense.

In an important parallel passage from a 21 October 1965 letter to DuPlessis, Oppen distinguishes his sense of the poem as an existentially fraught encounter from the confident physicality of Williams's poem-as-machine:

One's awareness of the world, one's concern with existence – they were not already in words – And the poem is not built out of words, one cannot make a poem by sticking words into it, it is the poem which makes the words and contains their meaning. One cannot reach out for *roses* and *elephants* and *essences* and put them in the poem – the ground under the elephant, the air around him, one would have to know very precisely one's distance from the elephant or step deliberately too close, close enough to frighten oneself.

When the man writing is frightened by a word, he may have started.

Stepping "close enough to frighten oneself," Oppen sidles up to words. Later, in "Some San Francisco Poems" he will remark, "One writes in the presence of something / Moving close to fear."

Oppen's suspicion about the relation between words and things informs his celebrated regard for "the little words" as well as his abiding interest in serial form. Oppen's understanding of serial form is expressed in the third section of the serial poem "A Narrative": "In which things explain each other / Not themselves." As in *Discrete Series* Oppen continues to explore the tensions between process and particularity, between the network of explanatory relations and the embedded particular thing. An often-cited example of the latter is to be found in "Psalm," the poem that contains the volume's title phrase. After affirming the existential givenness of the poem's wild deer – "In the small beauty of the forest / That they are there!" – Oppen turns in his last stanza to an affirmation of language itself:

> Their paths
> Nibbled thru the fields, the leaves that shade them
> Hang in the distances
> Of sun
>
> The small nouns
> Crying faith
> In this in which the wild deer
> Startle, and stare out.

In his talk with Dembo, Oppen explained his "faith" in "small nouns": "It is still a principle with me, of more than poetry, to notice, to state, to lay down the substantive for its own sake.... All the little nouns are the ones I like the most: the deer, the sun, and so on. You say these perfectly little words and you're asserting that the sun is ninety-three million miles away, and that there is shade because of shadows.... It's a tremendous structure to have built out of a few small nouns.... I do think that consciousness exists and that it is consciousness of something, and that is a fairly complete but not very detailed theology, as a matter of fact." Oppen's belief "that the nouns do refer to something; that it's there, that it's true, the whole implication of these nouns; that appearances represent reality, whether or not they misrepresent it: that this in which the thing takes place, this thing is here" is cradled in the volume's title phrase.

Between 1963 and 1977 the Oppens summered in Maine, even after they moved from Brooklyn to San Francisco in 1966, residing first on Little Deer Isle and later on Eagle Island. Oppen writes of their connection with Maine in the anthology *Maine Lines* (1970): "since 1963 we have come to Little Deer Isle every summer, coming now from San Francisco, not from New York, to sail through every passage and into every inlet and around every island in Penobscot Bay in a very small and very fast sailboat, sleeping on the boat in a boom tent. Not much claim on the State. But Pound said:

'What a man loves, is his heritage.'" The cover of *This in Which* features a photograph taken from the air of clouds, the sea, and a small island.

In the summer of 1965 Oppen began reworking the eight-part sequence "A Language of New York," circulating revisions among correspondents, and in the fall he read a version called "Another Language of New York" at the Guggenheim Museum. By early 1966 the poem had been retitled "Of Being Numerous" and was developing into a forty-part sequence. The influence of the Oppens' Maine experience is clear in the closing lines of the last poem of the collection, "Ballad": "What I like more than anything / Is to visit other islands[.]"

The question posed by *Of Being Numerous,* Oppen told Dembo, was "whether or not one will consider the concept of humanity to be valid, something that is, or else have to regard it as being simply a word." Oppen was concerned with the stark evidence of inhumanity in his culture, as the eighteenth section of the title poem makes clear, from the war in Vietnam ("A plume of smoke, visible at a distance / In which people burn") to the assassination of President Kennedy ("the air of atrocity, / An event as ordinary / As a President"). Moreover, the erosion of public discourse through rampant consumerism seemed not only to exceed the word's purchase but also undermined its philosophical grounding in the tradition of humanism.

In the face of such social-historical crises Oppen remains keenly aware of the precariousness, if not impossibility, of his desire "to speak," to affirm meaning amid meaninglessness, writing in section 17:

> There is madness in the number
> Of the living
> 'A state of matter'
> . . . .
> He wants to say
> His life is real,
> No one can say why
>
> It is not easy to speak
>
> A ferocious mumbling, in public
> Of rootless speech[.]

Granting the tenuousness of his own position as poetic speaker, Oppen proceeds in "Of Being Numerous" by the disjunctive "routes" of metonymy and seriality, rather than by the more contrived schemes of linear premeditation and metaphorical closure. As he writes of his representational aims in the tenth section of "Route," the other major series

Oppen with his daughter, Linda, in 1958

in the volume, the companion poem to "Of Being Numerous": "Not the symbol but the scene this pavement leads / To roadsides – the finite // Losing its purposes / Is estranged." With the purpose of keeping such "scenes" provisionally unestranged, "Of Being Numerous" and "Route" both evade the finitude not only of the single lyric poem but also that of the singular poetic voice.

Oppen acknowledges on the collection's copyright page that "phrases, comments, cadences of speech" have been "derived from friends, among them: Rachel Blau, John Crawford, Steven Schneider, Armand Schwerner, Phyllis Rivera, Christina Torrey." One of the compositional ironies of Oppen's meditation on the "numerous," then, is that his distinctively personal voice is openly animated by one or more "other voices," his lyric "singularity" already an intimate multiplicity. Fittingly, "Of Being Numerous" opens with a declaration of the reciprocity that exists between individual subjects and the "things" that surround them (like a group of informing friends) and between particular occasions and the myriad of events:

> There are things
> We live among 'and to see them

Is to know ourselves'.

> Occurrence, a part
> Of an infinite series[.]

From this reciprocally determined notion of identity and event follows the poem's crisis of political vision: the separation of the observer and the observed that is paradoxically enforced by the power of perception. As Oppen recognizes in section 9, quoting a letter from Rachel Blau Du Plessis, the question is

> 'Whether, as the intensity of seeing increases, one's distance from Them, the people, does not also increase'
> I know, of course I know, I can enter no other place

> Yet I am one of those who from nothing but man's way of thought and one of his dialects and what has happened to me
> Have made poetry[.]

In Oppen's poetics of contingency there is no alternative to the social; one "can enter no other place." And yet, in section 17 Oppen argues that "one may honorably keep // His distance / If he can," from those "ghosts that endanger // One's soul": privileged and unreflective "shoppers, / Choosers, judges."

Characteristically self-reflective, existentially ruminative, Oppen in section 14 reconsiders this proposal, granting that such separation is not wholly feasible, much less desirable:

> I cannot even now
> Altogether disengage myself
> From those men
>
> With whom I stood in emplacements, in mess tents,
> . . . .
> Among them many men
> More capable than I ——
>
> Muykut and a sergeant
> Named Healy,
> That lieutenant also ——
>
> How forget that? How talk
> Distantly of ' The People'[.]

For Oppen complete social withdrawal is as perilous as unself-conscious social immersion. As an ironic emblem of the conflict between self-identity and meaningful community, Oppen employs the image of shipwreck as a recurrent figure. On the one hand, the potentially affirmative "meaning / of being numerous" emerges from what the poet refers to as "the shipwreck of the singular," the death of isolated individualism. On the other hand, the end of such isolation means the loss of the potentially redemptive advantage of perspectival remove, of intense sociopolitical vision. As Oppen wryly notes in section 6, given the oppressiveness of mass society, Crusoe's isolation looks enviable:

>   Crusoe
> We say was
> 'Rescued'.
> So we have chosen.

Paul Zweig in the spring 1973 *Partisan Review* observed that "Crusoe, for Oppen, is the perceiver and the poet who knows that strong experience requires separateness, that seeing isolates." Thus it follows that "the poem moves between two shadowy figures that organize its themes," Kierkegaard and Whitman: one, "the lonely street-wanderer, who dramatized the 'shipwreck' of the singular self; [another], that other street-wanderer, whose self became a community of all the selves, a transparent city of the spirit."

The poetry of "Of Being Numerous" is adamantly urban and insistently critical of the city's ob-

durate reifications. Without posing the natural as a redemptive source of value ("the pure joy / Of the mineral fact / . . . is impenetrable"), from the outset Oppen's aim, as it was in *Discrete Series,* is to assail "over-protection and over-luxury." The critical target is announced in section 2:

> A city of corporations
>
> Glassed
> In dreams
>
> And images —— [.]

Critics debate the influence of Marxism in "Of Being Numerous." In "Forms of Refusal: George Oppen's 'Distant Life,'" Michael Davidson summarizes the conflict and endeavors both to take Oppen's politics seriously and to eschew what he sees as politically uncritical readings: "I agree with [Marjorie] Perloff that 'Of Being Numerous' has been read uncritically as a polemic in favor of the social, but I don't think that because Oppen acknowledged the alienation of the modern city, that his commitment to Socialism is thereby impugned. I feel that he was more than acutely aware that in a world of binary choices (the 'shipwreck of the singular' versus the 'rescue' of a social contract) one is left speechless. I see 'Of Being Numerous' as a polemic for clear distinction lest a renewed Stalinism further reify the liberatory possibilities of Socialism."

Of Being Numerous was published in March 1968, and in April, Oppen was interviewed by Dembo at the University of Wisconsin–Madison. In May 1969 the collection was awarded the Pulitzer Prize; in June, Oppen met with Ezra Pound again for the first time in thirty-five years. Despite winning the Pulitzer and giving several readings in 1968 and 1969, Oppen suffered a crisis of confidence in the fall of 1969 and canceled an extensive reading tour. In the early 1970s he experienced frustrating delays in the publication of his works. In December 1972, more than three years after signing his contract with Fulcrum Press, Oppen's *Collected Poems* was finally published in England. And in November 1972, after Oppen had withdrawn the work from another publisher, Sumac Press published *Seascape: Needle's Eye,* a book that contained the significant sequence "Some San Francisco Poems," which he had begun in 1967. During this period Oppen also began his friendship with Michael Cuddihy, editor of *Ironwood* magazine. Cuddihy devoted two special issues to Oppen's work, *Ironwood 5* (1975) and *Ironwood 26* (1985), which were consequential in advancing the poet's critical reputation.

Oppen's work undergoes marked formal and thematic changes in his final collections: *Seascape: Needle's Eye, Collected Poems,* and *Primitive.* According to Eleanor Berry's definition of Objectivism for the *New Princeton Encyclopedia of Poetry and Poetics* (1994), Oppen's late work is distinguished by its "multiple possibilities for parsing." In "Language Made Fluid: The Grammetrics of Oppen's Recent Poetry" (1984), Berry argues that the changes in Oppen's prosody of the 1970s accompany a shift in thematics, that "the more recent poetry is concerned with language, music, song, the poem"; whereas "the poetry of the four earlier books was concerned with naming and praising things of this world": "An imagery dominated by hard, unitary objects, typified by rock, has given way to an imagery of the liquid, of light; a conception of the world as external has been superseded by a vision of interpenetration."

In Oppen's later work Berry notes "frequent use of fragments; almost complete absence of conventional punctuation and capitalization; [and] frequent intralinear syntactic boundaries together with frequent enjambment, including enjambment of the final lines of line-groups, these last two features combining to undermine and submerge both line and line-group as units." Berry suggests that the first poem of *Seascape,* "From a Phrase of Simone Weil's and Some Words of Hegel's," dramatizes this conjunction of Oppen's new prosody and thematics:

> In   back   deep the jewel
> The treasure
> No   Liquid
> Pride of the living life's liquid
> Pride in the sandspit wind this ether this other this element all
> It is I or I believe
> We are the beaks of the ragged birds[.]

Another significant aspect of Oppen's late work, all the more interesting given his embrace of perceptual flux, is his use of allusion. As Norman Finkelstein observes in his essay on *Primitive* in *George Oppen: Man and Poet* (1981): "The series of allusions we encounter in *Primitive* (and Oppen has made spare use of this self-consciously literary technique up until now), suspended, as it were, amidst less mediated objects of experience, betokens a lasting tradition of which Oppen has unquestionably become a part." In the opening of "Disasters," for example, Oppen fuses an allusion to "O Western Wind" with an ironic inversion of Shelley's infa-

mous claim that "poets are the unacknowledged legislators of the World":

> of wars o western
> wind and storm
>
> of politics I am sick with a poet's
> vanity   legislators
>
> of the unacknowledged
> world.

In his last published lines, closing "Till Other Voices Wake Us," Oppen revises T. S. Eliot's "The Love Song of J. Alfred Prufrock" with an ironic turn: replacing an "and" with an "or," and converting the very source of Prufrock's fatality to the "other voices" of a saving, awakening human community:

> in events the myriad
>
> lights have entered
> us it is a music more powerful
>
> than music
>
> till other voices wake
> us or we drown[.]

In October 1975 New Directions published *The Collected Poems of George Oppen.* In a selection of his working papers published in *Sulfur 26* (1990), Oppen remarks on the occasion and gives a straightforward synopsis of his extraordinary life:

> My *Collected* poems were created by childhood, by my mother's death, by New Rochelle and sail-boats, by marriage to Mary, by hitch-hiking across the country with no money, by the depression, by the political movement demanding relief for the unemployed and the hungry, by the second World War, by the Fascist Threat, by the childhood of our daughter, by our life in France and in Mexico. If I live long enough, I will have more to tell of, and to understand.
>
> ((*If* I should write another Collected poems, I would be rather startled.[))]

The ironic afterthought is characteristic of an aspect of Oppen's personality and poetry not often noted: his sense of humor. As Eliot Weinberger playfully insists in his 1981 tribute to the poet in *Paideuma:* "It should be said, once, that Oppen can be very funny. (In conversation, gnomic one-liners alternate with ironic anecdotes, all punctuated by a bobbing of

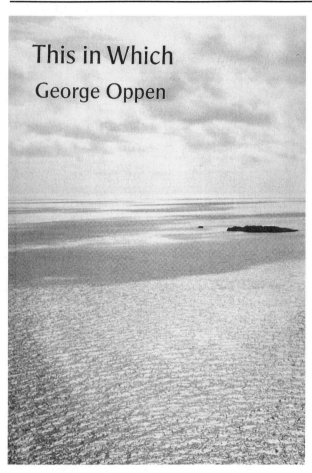

This in Which
George Oppen

Dust jacket for Oppen's 1965 book, in which he writes in "A Language of New York" of the need to choose words carefully, "One by One proceeding / Carefully" (courtesy of the Lilly Library, Indiana University)

those unavoidable eyebrows: a gesture that might have been invented by Groucho Marx.)"

In the fall of 1975 the Oppens traveled to Jerusalem. Between their return and the last summer they spent in Maine in 1977 Oppen's health began to decline. In the fall of 1977, with Mary's assistance, Oppen completed *Primitive;* in 1978 *Primitive* and *Meaning a Life* were published by Black Sparrow Press. In the early 1980s Oppen received the PEN/West Rediscovery Award and was honored by the American Academy and Institute of Arts and Letters and by the National Endowment for the Arts. Two collections devoted to Oppen, edited by Burton Hatlen, appeared in 1981: a special issue of *Paideuma* and *George Oppen: Man and Poet.* In 1982 the seventy-four-year-old Oppen was diagnosed with Alzheimer's disease. Sponsored by the Poetry Center at San Francisco State University and Intersection for the Arts, a George Oppen Tribute was held on the poet's seventy-fifth birthday. Oppen

died on 7 July 1984 at the Idlewood Convalescent Home in Sunnyvale, California.

In 1985, with a donation from Frances Jaffer and Mark Linenthal, the George Oppen Memorial Lecture was founded by James Hartz and Frances Phillips, directors of the Poetry Center at San Francisco State University. In 1988 Director Robert Glück established the George Oppen Memorial Lecture Endowment as a means of seeking continued support for the program. The annual lecture has been delivered by such distinguished poets and critics as Michael Heller, Rachel Blau DuPlessis, John Taggart, Hugh Kenner, Marjorie Perloff, David Bromige, August Kleinzahler, Mark Linenthal, Carl Rakosi, and Lyn Hejinian.

While in the decade since Oppen's death important developments have been made in Oppen studies – notably DuPlessis's edition of Oppen's *Letters* and the publication of various selections of his working papers – as yet no critical biography exists to articulate fully the pivotal significance of Oppen's lifework in the history of twentieth-century American poetry. Heller, an Oppen correspondent, suggests in *Sulfur 28* (1991) the importance Oppen's letters hold for such a study: "Oppen's poetry was intimately concerned with, as he put it, 'the order of disclosure,' with 'literature as a process of thought.' So too the correspondence. Taken together the poetry and the letters form not only an array, but a complex feedback loop by which the complexities of the work are tested fugally and dialectically: poems arise out of scraps of language formulated in response to others or in self-questionings and then are quoted again as answers to yet other questions."

Oppen's working papers also provide a rich field for critical work. Michael Davidson has described Oppen's manuscript "pages" and raised the confounding question of their textual status. Oppen's often-praised "craftsmanship" was more than metaphorical; it was an insistently "material" fact of the poet's process of composition, and his papers have an almost three-dimensional character. Davidson reports in *Ironwood 26* that among the thousands of loose pages, gatherings are often held together by "pipestem cleaners, pins or wires or other household items" or even "by means of a nail driven through the pages into a plywood backing." Moreover, it was also Oppen's regular practice "to glue fragments of writing on top of one another, so that in some cases a 'page' would become thick with layers upon layers of writing." Davidson observes in his 1988 "Palimtexts: Postmodern Poetry and the Material Text": "What we see in such collections is the degree to which writing is archeological, the

Mary Oppen, George Oppen, and Charles Reznikoff (courtesy of Mary Oppen)

gradual accretion and sedimentation of textual materials, no layer of which can ever be isolated from any other. George Oppen's page ... is part of a much larger 'conversation' for which the published poem is a scant record."

According to Heller's and Davidson's accounts, Oppen's letters and working papers pose the same daunting interpretive problem. As Davidson recognizes, the ultimate question is "can we speak of 'poetry' at all when so much of it is embedded in other quotations, prose remarks and observations? Does Oppen's *oeuvre* end in the work we know as *The Collected Poems* or does it end on the page on which it began?" The availability of Oppen's letters and working papers certainly shows that the terms of what constitutes "Oppen's work" have been dramatically enlarged in recent years, providing a boon to scholars.

Perhaps the best index of Oppen's importance is provided by the tributes to his work in *Ironwood 26,* which indicate that he has long been highly regarded among contemporary poets. Robert Hass writes, "what's extraordinary about

George Oppen's poetry is, moment after moment in his work, line by line, syllable by syllable, you have a sense of an enormous ethical pressure brought to bear on the act of perception, and a sense that the ethical pressure on the act of perception is for him the same thing as the writing of the poem." "What Oppen actually rescues for me is the conviction that art is crucial," Louise Glück affirms: "These poems speak a moral language, a language of salvation and contempt; they have the force of true passion, but none of the smarmy definitiveness, none of the self-righteousness. Their beauty always seemed to me the beauty of logic, the 'virtue of mind,' whose end is vision." For Charles Bernstein, "At his most resonant, Oppen creates a magnificent, prophetic, imaginary language – less voice than *chiselled sounds.* His writing evokes not the clamor of the streets or the windiness of conversation or the bombast of the 'dialogic' but the indwelling possibilities of words to speak starkly and with urgency." And Michael Palmer, writing in *Sulfur 26* (1990), prizes Oppen's refusal of received "poetic" values: "By speaking against literary contrivance, Oppen argues both for the possibility, or necessity, of an immediacy of poetic engagement or intervention, and against the 'poetic,' that is, against the devices of a passive and acculturated representation. He argues as well for a gaze turned outward, a responsibility of the self to find its realization, its form as thinking subject, in its relation to the visible and the invisible things of the world."

Letters:

The Selected Letters of George Oppen, edited, with an introduction, by Rachel Blau DuPlessis (Durham: Duke University Press, 1990).

Interviews:

L. S. Dembo, "The 'Objectivist' Poet: Four Interviews," *Contemporary Literature,* 10 (Spring 1969): 159–177;

Ruth Gruber, "An Interview with George Oppen and Ted Berrigan," *Chicago,* 1 (October 1973);

Charles Amirkhanian and David Gitin, "A Conversation with George Oppen," *Ironwood 5,* 3, no. 1 (1975): 21–24;

Kevin Power, "An Interview with George and Mary Oppen," *Montemora,* 4 (1978): 186–203;

Power, "Conversation with George and Mary Oppen, May 25, 1975," *Texas Quarterly,* 21 (Spring 1978): 53–52;

Dembo, "Oppen on his Poems: A Discussion," in *George Oppen: Man and Poet,* edited by Burton Hatlen (Orono, Maine: National Poetry Foundation, 1981), pp. 197–213;

Hatlen and Tom Mandel, "Poetry and Politics: A Conversation with George and Mary Oppen," in *George Oppen: Man and Poet,* edited by Hatlen (Orono, Maine: National Poetry Foundation, 1981), pp. 23–50;

Amirkhanian, "George and Mary Oppen; Memorial Broadcast for Charles Reznikoff," *Sagetrieb,* 3 (Winter 1984): 29–35;

Reinhold Schiffer, "Interview with George Oppen," *Sagetrieb,* 3 (Winter 1984): 9–23;

Michel Engelbert and Mike West, "George and Mary Oppen: An Interview," *American Poetry Review,* 14 (July/August 1985): 11–14;

David McAleavey, "The Oppens: Remarks towards Biography," *Ironwood 26,* 13 (Fall 1985): 309–318;

McAleavey, "Oppen on Oppen: Extracts from Interviews," *Sagetrieb,* 5 (Spring 1986): 59–93;

McAleavey, Interview with Oppen, *Sagetrieb,* 6 (Spring 1987): 109–135.

Bibliographies:

David McAleavey, "A Bibliography of the Works of George Oppen," *Paideuma,* 10 (Spring 1981): 155–169;

McAleavey, "A Bibliography of Discussions of George Oppen's Work: Reviews, Articles, Essays, and Books," in *George Oppen: Man and Poet,* edited by Burton Hatlen (Orono, Maine: National Poetry Foundation, 1981), pp. 451–462;

Hatlen and Julie Courant, "Annotated Chronological Bibliography of Discussions of George Oppen's Work: Reviews, Articles, Essays, and Books," in *George Oppen: Man and Poet,* edited by Hatlen (Orono, Maine: National Poetry Foundation, 1981), pp. 463–504;

Rachel Blau DuPlessis, "A Bibliography of Interviews of George and Mary Oppen Chronologically Arranged," *Sagetrieb,* 6 (Spring 1987): 137–139;

Vincent Prestianni, "George Oppen: An Analytic List of Bibliographies," *Sagetrieb,* 8 (Spring/Fall 1989): 261–262.

Biography:

Mary Oppen, *Meaning a Life: An Autobiography* (Santa Barbara, Cal.: Black Sparrow Press, 1978).

References:

Charles Altieri, "From Symbolist Thought to Immanence: The Ground of Postmodern American Poetics," *boundary 2* (Spring 1973): 605–641;

Altieri, "The Objectivist Tradition," *Chicago Review,* 30 (Winter 1979): 5–22;

David Antin, "Modernism and Postmodernism: Approaching the Present in American Poetry," *boundary 2* (Fall 1971): 98–133;

Eleanor Berry, "The Grammetrics of George Oppen's Recent Poetry," *Contemporary Literature,* 25 (Fall 1984): 305–322;

Berry, "The Williams-Oppen Connection," *Sagetrieb,* 3 (Fall 1984): 99–116;

Joseph M. Conte, "The Subway's Iron Circuit: George Oppen's *Discrete Series,*" in his *Unending Design: The Forms of Postmodern Poetry* (Ithaca, N.Y. & London: Cornell University Press, 1991), pp. 121–141;

John Crawford, "An Essay on George Oppen," *New: Canadian and American Poetry,* 25 (1975): 131–140;

Crawford, "A Letter on Oppen," *American Poetry,* 5 (Winter 1988): 87–91;

Andrew Crozier, "Inaugural and Valedictory: The Early Poetry of George Oppen," in *Modern American Poetry,* edited by R. W. Butterfield (London: Vision, 1984), pp. 142–157;

Michael Davidson, "Forms of Refusal: George Oppen's 'Distant Life,'" *Sulfur 26,* 10 (Spring 1990): 127–134;

Davidson, "Palimtexts: Postmodern Poetry and the Material Text," in *Postmodern Genres,* edited by Marjorie Perloff (Norman & London: University of Oklahoma Press, 1988), pp. 75–95;

L. S. Dembo, "The Existential World of George Oppen," *Iowa Review,* 3 (Winter 1972): 64–91;

W. S. Di Piero, "Public Music," in *The Columbia History of American Poetry,* edited by Jay Parini (New York: Columbia University Press, 1993), pp. 564–580;

Rachel Blau DuPlessis, "'The familiar / becomes extreme': George Oppen and Silence," *North Dakota Quarterly,* 55 (Fall 1987): 18–36;

Ross Feld, "Some Thoughts about Objectivism," *Sagetrieb,* 12 (Winter 1993): 65–77;

Norman Finkelstein, "Political Commitment and Poetic Subjectification: George Oppen's Test of Truth," *Contemporary Literature,* 22 (Winter 1981): 24–41;

Finkelstein, "What Was Objectivism?," in his *The Utopian Moment in Contemporary American Poetry,* second edition (London & Toronto: Associated University Presses, 1993), pp. 35–46;

John Freeman, ed., *Not Comforts // But Vision: Essays on the Poetry of George Oppen* (Devon, U.K.: Interim Press, 1985);

Laszlo Géfin, "Sincerity and Objectification," in his *Ideogram: History of a Poetic Method* (Austin: University of Texas Press, 1982), pp. 49–67;

Alan Golding, "George Oppen's Serial Poems," *Contemporary Literature,* 29 (Summer 1988): 221–240;

Burton Hatlen, "'Feminine Technologies': George Oppen Talks at Denise Levertov," *American Poetry Review,* 22 (May/June 1993): 9–14;

Hatlen, ed., *George Oppen: Man and Poet* (Orono, Maine: National Poetry Foundation, 1981);

Michael Heller, *Conviction's Net of Branches: Essays on the Objectivist Poets and Poetry* (Carbondale & Edwardsville: Southern Illinois University Press, 1985);

Heller, "Encountering Oppen," *Ohio Review,* 51 (1994): 75–88;

Heller, "A Mimetics of Humanity: Oppen's *Of Being Numerous,*" *American Poetry,* 4 (Spring 1987): 19–33;

Heller, "Oppen and Stevens: Reflections on the Lyrical and the Philosophical," *Sagetrieb,* 12 (Winter 1993): 13–32;

Heller, "Utopocalypse: American Poetry in the 1930s," in *A Profile of Twentieth-Century American Poetry,* edited by Jack Myers and Wojahn (Carbondale & Edwardsville: Southern Illinois University Press, 1991), pp. 84–101;

Eric Homberger, "Communists and Objectivists," in his *American Writers and Radical Politics, 1900–39: Equivocal Commitments* (Houndmills & London: Macmillan, 1986), pp. 163–186;

Ironwood 5, special issue on Oppen, 3 (1975);

Ironwood 26, special issue on Oppen, 13 (Fall 1985);

Hugh Kenner, "Classroom Accuracies," in his *A Homemade World: The American Modernist Writers* (New York: Knopf, 1975), pp. 158–193;

Kenner, "Further Thoughts: Little Words," in *The State of the Language,* edited by Christopher Ricks and Leonard Michaels (Berkeley & Los Angeles: University of California Press, 1990), pp. 62–65;

Kenner, "Oppen, Zukofsky, and the Poem as Lens," in *Literature at the Barricades: The American Writer in the 1930s,* edited by Ralph F. Bogardus and Fred Hobson (University: University of Alabama Press, 1982), pp. 162–171;

August Kleinzahler, "Out the Corner of the Minimalist's Window," *Threepenny Review,* 52 (Winter 1993): 12–16;

David McAleavey, "If to Know Is Noble: The Poetry of George Oppen," dissertation, Cornell University, 1975;

Paul Kenneth Naylor, "The Pre-Position 'Of': Being, Seeing, and Knowing in George Oppen's Poetry," *Contemporary Literature,* 32 (Spring 1991): 100–115;

Paideuma, special issue on Oppen, 10 (Spring 1981);

Michael Palmer, "On Objectivism," *Sulfur 26,* 10 (Spring 1990): 117–126;

Marjorie Perloff, "Against Transparency: From the Radiant Cluster to the Word as Such," in her *Radical Artifice: Writing in the Age of Media* (Chicago & London: University of Chicago Press, 1991), pp. 54–92;

Jeffrey Peterson, "The Siren Song of the Singular: Armantrout, Oppen, and the Ethics of Presentation," *Sagetrieb,* 12 (Winter 1993): 89–104;

Ezra Pound, "Preface to *Discrete Series,*" reprinted in *Sagetrieb,* 10 (Spring 1981): 13;

Carl Rakosi, "George Oppen, the Last Days," *Talisman: A Journal of Contemporary Poetry and Poetics,* 2 (Spring 1989): 82–89;

John Shoptaw, "Lyric Incorporated: The Serial Object of George Oppen and Langston Hughes," *Sagetrieb,* 12 (Winter 1993): 105–124;

Ron Silliman, "Third Phase Objectivism," in his *The New Sentence* (New York: Roof Books, 1987), pp. 136–141;

Louis Simpson, "Poetry in the Sixties – Long Live Blake! Down with Donne!," *New York Times Book Review,* 28 December 1969, p. 18;

John Taggart, "To Go Down To Go Into," *Ironwood 31/32,* 16 (Spring/Fall 1988): 270–285;

Charles Tomlinson, "Objectivists: Zukofsky and Oppen," in his *Some Americans: A Personal Record* (Berkeley & Los Angeles: University of California Press, 1981), pp. 45–73;

Henry Weinfield, " 'A Thousand Threads' and 'The One Thing': Oppen's Vision (A Reply to Ross Feld)," *Sagetrieb,* 12 (Winter 1993): 79–87;

William Carlos Williams, *Something to Say: William Carlos Williams on Younger Poets,* edited by James E. B. Breslin (New York: New Directions, 1985), pp. 55–59;

Dennis Young, "The Possibilities of Being: The Poetry of George Oppen," dissertation, University of Iowa, 1989.

Papers:

The George Oppen papers are housed in the Archive for New Poetry, Mandeville Department of Special Collections, Library of the University of California, San Diego. The literary executor of the estate of George Oppen is Linda Oppen Mourelatos.

Kenneth Rexroth

(22 December 1905 – 6 June 1982)

Linda Hamalian
William Paterson College

See also the Rexroth entries in *DLB 16: The Beats: Literary Bohemians in Postwar America; DLB 48: American Poets, 1880–1945, Second Series;* and *DLB Yearbook 1982.*

BOOKS: *In What Hour* (New York: Macmillan, 1940);

The Phoenix and the Tortoise (New York: New Directions, 1944);

The Art of Worldly Wisdom (Prairie City, Ill.: Decker Press, 1949);

The Signature of All Things (New York: New Directions, 1950);

Beyond the Mountains (New York: New Directions, 1951);

The Dragon and the Unicorn (Norfolk, Conn.: New Directions, 1952);

A Bestiary for My Daughters Mary and Katharine (San Francisco: Bern Porter, 1955);

Thou Shalt Not Kill: A Memorial for Dylan Thomas (Sunnyvale, Cal.: Goad, 1955);

In Defense of the Earth (New York: New Directions, 1956);

Birds in the Bush: Obvious Essays (New York: New Directions, 1959);

Assays (New York: New Directions, 1961);

The Homestead Called Damascus (New York: New Directions, 1963);

Natural Numbers: New and Selected Poems (New York: New Directions, 1963);

The Collected Shorter Poems (New York: New Directions, 1966);

An Autobiographical Novel (Garden City, N.J.: Doubleday, 1966; revised and enlarged, edited by Linda Hamalian (New York: New Directions, 1991);

The Heart's Garden, The Garden's Heart (Cambridge, Mass.: Pym–Randall Press, 1967);

The Spark in the Tinder of Knowing (Cambridge, Mass.: Pym–Randall Press, 1968);

The Collected Longer Poems (New York: New Directions, 1968);

Kenneth Rexroth (Gale International Portrait Gallery)

Classics Revisited (Chicago: Quadrangle Books, 1968);

The Alternative Society: Essays from the Other World (New York: Herder & Herder, 1970);

With Eye and Ear (New York: Herder & Herder, 1970);

Sky Sea Birds Trees Earth House Beasts Flowers (Santa Barbara, Cal.: Unicorn Press, 1971);

American Poetry in the Twentieth Century (New York: Herder & Herder, 1971);

The Kenneth Rexroth Reader, edited by Eric Mottram (London: Cape, 1972);

The Elastic Retort: Essays in Literature and Ideas (New York: Seabury Press, 1973);

Communalism: From its Origins to the Twentieth Century (New York: Seabury Press, 1974);

New Poems (New York: New Directions, 1974);

On Flower Wreath Hill (Burnaby, British Columbia: Blackfish Press, 1976);

The Silver Swan (Port Townsend, Wash.: Copper Canyon Press, 1976);

The Love Poems of Marichiko (Santa Barbara, Cal.: Christopher Books, 1978);

The Morning Star (New York: New Directions, 1979) — includes *The Silver Swan, On Flower Wreath Hill, The Love Poems of Marichiko;*

New and Selected Poems, edited by Edith Shiffert (Buffalo, N.Y.: White Pine Press, 1979);

Saucy Limericks and Christmas Cheer (Santa Barbara, Cal.: Morrow, 1980);

Excerpts from a Life (Santa Barbara, Cal.: Conjunctions Press, 1981);

Between Two Wars, edited by Richard Bigus (San Francisco: Iris Press, 1982);

Selected Poems, edited by Bradford Morrow (New York: New Directions, 1984);

World Outside the Window: The Selected Essays of Kenneth Rexroth, edited by Morrow (New York: New Directions, 1987);

More Classics Revisited, edited by Morrow (New York: New Directions, 1989).

RECORDINGS: *San Francisco Poets,* New York, Evergreen Records, 1, n.d.;

Poetry Readings in "The Cellar," San Francisco, Fantasy Records, 7002, 1957;

Kenneth Rexroth at the Black Hawk, San Francisco, Fantasy Records, 7008, 1960;

A Sword in a Cloud of Light, Washington, D.C., Watershed Foundation, 1977.

OTHER: D. H. Lawrence, *Selected Poems of D. H. Lawrence,* edited, with an introduction, by Rexroth (New York: New Directions, 1947);

The New British Poets: An Anthology, edited by Rexroth (New York: New Directions, 1949);

"Chidori," in *The Ark: For Rexroth 14,* edited by Geoffrey Gardner (New York: The Ark, 1980).

TRANSLATIONS: O. V. de L. Milosz, *Fourteen Poems by O. V. de L. Milosz* (San Francisco: Peregrine Press, 1952);

One Hundred Poems from the French (Highlands, N.C.: Jargon Society, 1955);

One Hundred Poems from the Japanese (New York: New Directions, 1955);

One Hundred Poems from the Chinese (New York: New Directions, 1956);

Thirty Spanish Poems of Love and Exile (San Francisco: City Lights, 1956);

Poems from the Greek Anthology (Ann Arbor: University of Michigan Press, 1962);

Pierre Reverdy, *Pierre Reverdy: Selected Poems* (New York: New Directions, 1969);

Love in the Turning Year: One Hundred More Poems from the Chinese (New York: New Directions, 1970);

The Orchid Boat: Women Poets of China, with Ling Chung (New York: McGraw-Hill, 1972);

One Hundred More Poems from the Japanese (New York: New Directions, 1974);

The Burning Heart: Women Poets of Japan, with Ikuko Atsumi (New York: Seabury Press, 1977);

Kazuko Shiraishi, *Seasons of Sacred Lust: Selected Poems of Kazuko Shiraishi,* with Carol Tinker, Atsumi, John Solt, Yasuyo Morita (New York: New Directions, 1978);

Li Ch'ing Chao, *Li Ch'ing Chao: Complete Poems,* with Chung (New York: New Directions, 1979);

Tu Fu, *Thirty-Six Poems by Tu Fu* (New York: Peter Blum Edition, 1987).

SELECTED PERIODICAL PUBLICATIONS —
UNCOLLECTED: "Chidori," with six drawings by Robert Graves, *The Ark,* 14 (1980): 113–125;

"Vivienne Renaud," *Conjunctions,* 2 (Spring/Summer 1982): 54–59;

"Excerpts from a Life," *Conjunctions,* 4 (Spring 1983): 96–114;

"Excerpts from a Life," *Sagetrieb,* 2 (Winter 1983): 9–17;

"A Crystal Out of Time and Space: The Poet's Diary," *Conjunctions,* 8 (Spring 1985): 62–85.

A caustic but erudite commentator on art and politics for more than half a century, Kenneth Rexroth published nineteen volumes of poetry, a collection of verse plays (produced by the Living Theater during its opening season), thirteen volumes of translations from the Chinese, Japanese, French, Spanish, and Greek, eight volumes of criticism (on subjects as diverse as the paintings of Mark Tobey, the notebooks of Simone Weil, and jazz poetry), and an autobiography covering the first forty-five years of his life. But while his achievements earned him many awards and fellowships, until recently Rexroth was relegated, particularly by East Coast critics, to the rank of a minor writer, one who was *on* the scene rather than *of* the scene. With few exceptions, his poems were ignored by anthologists. He did not fit neatly into the so-called high modernist movement, and his accomplishments – which, in retrospect, illustrate the way modernism itself would be redefined by the end of the century – were seemingly overshadowed by younger poets, some of whom had earlier turned to him for advice and encouragement. Among his most immediate contemporaries, the poets who attained the status that eluded Rexroth were Theodore Roethke, Langston Hughes, Robert Penn Warren, and Elizabeth Bishop.

Yet until he left San Francisco in 1968 to accept a post as lecturer of poetry and song at the Santa Barbara campus of the University of California, Rexroth was never far from the public eye. For one thing, he was the prototype of several American fictional characters: Kenny, the skittish drugstore clerk in James T. Farrell's *Studs Lonigan;* the "proletarian poet" in Mary McCarthy's *Groves of Academe* ("I was the IWW organizer with a red shirt who came on a freight train. I apparently made Mary hotter than hell," Rexroth boasted in a 1971 interview); and Reinhold Cacoethes, the cranky anarchist poet of the San Francisco literary scene in Jack Kerouac's *The Dharma Bums* (1958). He was also a painter who had one-man shows in Los Angeles, New York, Chicago, Paris, Santa Barbara, and San Francisco. He regularly aired his views in weekly columns in the *San Francisco Examiner,* in articles as a correspondent for *The Nation,* and also during his Sunday radio broadcasts in San Francisco on KPFA.

From the mid 1940s through the early 1960s, Rexroth's San Francisco apartments (first on Wisconsin Street, then Potrero Hill, Eighth Avenue, then Scott Street) served as meeting places for poets, anarchists, and artists. Younger writers such as Robert Duncan, Jack Spicer, James Broughton, Lenore Kandel, Gary Snyder, and Michael McClure met Friday evenings at Rexroth's apartment to read poems and talk about literature and politics. It was to Rexroth's home that William Carlos Williams sent Allen Ginsberg (with a letter of introduction) when Ginsberg made his youthful pilgrimage to San Francisco. An inspiring force behind the San Francisco Renaissance, Rexroth was among the first American poets, along with Kenneth Patchen and Lawrence Ferlinghetti, to recite poetry to jazz, reciting in such places as the Cellar, the Black Hawk, and the Five Spot (in New York City). He played an influential role in helping James Laughlin's New Directions Press promote fresh voices such as those of Denise Levertov, Michael McClure, and Jerome Rothenberg. During the final decade of his life he was especially supportive of younger women poets:

he conducted workshops for them, read their manuscripts, and suggested ways for them to get their writings into print.

Many people, however, remember Rexroth for the irascibility and fiery temperament that engaged him in emotional and psychological confrontations that would have destroyed a weaker individual. He could be a difficult opponent who, at times, alienated even his family and his friends. His extreme candor, which he cultivated to the very end of his life – his speculation about Mary McCarthy's attraction to him is typical – probably dissuaded some critics from taking him seriously. He had been known to call Marianne Moore a racist, Charles Olson a fascist, and Leslie A. Fiedler a cow-college professor. In his frivolous moments he reduced the youth movement of the 1960s to nothing but "pot and pussy." He knew that he risked displeasing his readers by criticizing their taste and upsetting the standards that their teachers had passed down to them – Henry James was relegated to the status of "Ouida in a frock coat," and spoken French to "farting in lettuce" – but this was part of the public persona he had created for himself, the irreverent renegade blessed with culture and an encyclopedic memory. His remarks easily bruised people, including members of the academic community who might otherwise have been receptive to him. As a result he was ostracized. Only recently are new readers discovering the powerfully appealing qualities of his work.

Rexroth's life and work reflect his passionate dedication to living a literary life in twentieth-century America. Frequently ahead of his time, he yearned in the 1920s for fresh idioms and the breaking down of artificial boundaries between art forms. He wrestled with the dilemmas created by the social and political crises of the 1930s and later decades. He also helped pave the way for the fusion of Western pragmatism with Eastern contemplativeness that informs so much contemporary poetry. He had a remarkable ability to transform the raw material of his daily life into art, with the beauty of the natural world serving as his constant inspiration. The style of his most successful verse is marked by direct statement and clear images; it is a poetry that with uncanny, breathtaking precision reproduces his observations of the physical world. Within the context of his art, Rexroth's perceptions appear unmistakably authentic – whether about love, loneliness, political commitment and disillusionment, hope, courage, despair, or transitory moments of revelation. His introduction to these emotions and experiences came at an extraordinarily early age.

Rexroth in 1935 (photograph by John Ferren)

Kenneth Charles Marion Rexroth was born 22 December 1905 in South Bend, Indiana. His father, Charles, was a pharmaceuticals businessman whose fortunes rose and fell according to the fluctuations of his alcoholism. His mother, Delia, a beautiful, passionate woman whom Rexroth compared to the fashionable women in the paintings of Gustav Klimt, created a life for herself as the cultured companion to her husband. Charles Rexroth's work often took him to various parts of the Midwest and New York City, where he and his wife enjoyed the bohemian atmosphere of meeting places in Greenwich Village such as Polly's Restaurant and the Lafayette Hotel Café. Their young son, who frequently traveled with them, retained vivid memories of New York City and a trip to central and eastern Europe, where his father searched for new suppliers for herbs, oils, and perfumes.

The family moved often, from South Bend to Elkhart, Indiana, where Delia's parents lived, then to Battle Creek, Michigan, and Chicago. Charles and Delia Rexroth were an elegant, sophisticated couple, decorating their sometimes palatial homes with Art Nouveau objets d'art and crystal chandeliers. Their residences were open to entertainers

and social reformers alike. Rexroth's public-school education was supplemented with music, dance, and art lessons, and tutoring in the rudiments of earth science. Delia was frequently his mentor. Rexroth's childhood, however, was neither as refined nor as precious as it might have appeared to be.

By the time the Rexroths moved to Chicago in 1915, when Rexroth was ten, his parents' marriage had deteriorated badly. Charles Rexroth was drinking heavily and had turned philanderer. Although the couple tried to reconcile, too much anger burned between them, and the young Rexroth witnessed not only violent arguments, but also sordid scenes in hotel rooms between his mother, father, and another woman. Delia Rexroth took an apartment for herself and her son in a Chicago suburb. At the end of the year she suffered a severe hemorrhage, and her illness proved fatal in 1916. She spent the last months of her life reading to her son, who was at her bedside, truant from school with her blessing. She encouraged him to be a writer and an artist, to be independent, and to recognize that the pursuit of knowledge was a moral activity. Caught up by the passion of her advice and by a boy's love for his dying mother, Rexroth listened carefully, and remained haunted by her early death throughout his life. In these lines from "Delia Rexroth," written for the thirty-first anniversary of her death, he celebrates Delia's independence, the tenderness that existed between them, and his deep gratitude to her for making the world of art and literature come alive:

> I took down a book of poems
> That you used to like, that you
> Used to sing to music I
> Never found anywhere again —
> Michael Field's book, *Long Ago.*
> Indeed it's long ago now —
> Your bronze hair and svelte body.
> I guess you were a fierce lover,
> A wild wife, an animal
> Mother. And now life has cost
> Me more years, though much less pain
> Than you had to pay for it.

Reminiscent of the elegiac, almost erotic poems D. H. Lawrence wrote about his mother, Rexroth offered this poem as a public homage to his mother's struggle to control her "distraught life." (Rexroth edited and wrote an introduction to the *Selected Poems of D. H. Lawrence* for New Directions in the same year that this poem was published.) Rexroth's sensual evocation of Delia's physical presence suggests that his passionate memory of her affected his relationships with other women. Indeed, his first two wives also prized their independence, possessed a strong self-image, and cared deeply about art and literature. They also provided him with the kind of emotional and material support that mothers provide their sons. Even in physical appearance – light-complexioned, regular-featured, red-haired – they must have called up comforting memories of Delia. However, they could hardly fill the role that Delia assumed in Rexroth's imagination.

After his mother's death, Rexroth was cared for by his grandmother in Toledo. This was a gruesome period for the boy. A retired teacher, Mary Moore Rexroth had grown eccentric in her old age, and her house barely contained the old books, newspapers, and disintegrating canned food that she refused to throw out. Far worse, however, was her belief in corporal discipline. The regular canings she gave Rexroth went undetected until a neighbor saw the boy being beaten. Rexroth's father found an apartment for himself and his son, and Rexroth's ordeal ended.

He spent most of the next two years playing hooky from school. Usually amusing himself in unorthodox ways, he joined a gang of boys who stole bicycles and terrorized the caddies on the golf courses; more important, taking his cue from his mother, he explored the flora and fauna around Ten Mile Creek, watching the birds and bathing for hours at a time. Another child might have retreated into irrevocable sadness, but Rexroth turned to nature for a sense of stability and peace, a resource he would tap later for his art. In "Gic to Har" he writes:

Suddenly I remember
Coming home from swimming
In Ten Mile Creek,
Over the long moraine in the early summer evening,
My hair wet, smelling of waterweeds and mud.
I remember a sycamore in front of a ruined farmhouse,
And instantly and clearly the revelation
Of a song of incredible purity and joy,
My first rose–breasted grosbeak,
Facing the low sun, his body
Suffused with light.
I was motionless and cold in the hot evening
Until he flew away, and I went on knowing
In my twelfth year one of the great things
Of my life had happened.

Thanks to friends of his father – three women who lived on a farm where Rexroth passed two summers – he was also introduced to political and imaginative literature rather sophisticated for a boy

his age: works by Upton Sinclair, Max Eastman, Herbert Read, Eugene Debs, and H. G. Wells. Back in Toledo he started attending High Mass, cultivated a taste for Tudor music, and pursued his private education at the public library by reading Arnold Bennett and Bernard Shaw. Such precocity gave him the fortitude to meet further tragedy. Three years after Delia died, Charles Rexroth died from cirrhosis of the liver, ulcers, and pneumonia, or, as Rexroth described it in "Proust's Madeleine," of "crooked cards and straight whiskey / slow horses and fast women." After a traumatic two weeks in the home of his father's brother, who confiscated the boy's journal of poems and pad of watercolors and tried to appropriate Rexroth's small inheritance for himself, Delia's sister rescued Rexroth. She and her family welcomed him back to Chicago and to the way of life so colorfully described in Farrell's Studs Lonigan series.

Rexroth returned to Chicago during the height of the Chicago Renaissance, that long burst of literary activity from approximately 1912 to 1925. This creative period was partly the delayed aftermath of a memorable event in the world of visual arts – the World's Columbian Exposition of 1893, an exhibition of classical masterpieces. Twenty years later, in 1913, the famous New York Armory Show came to Chicago. Although the works by Pablo Picasso, Georges Braque, Wassily Kandinsky, and other Expressionists and Cubists were received with more ridicule than praise, the seeds of modernism were planted. Midwest writers such as Theodore Dreiser, Sherwood Anderson, and Carl Sandburg moved to Chicago, where they thought they had a better chance to express their opposition to an American Dream they believed was reserved for the exclusive few, as well as their belief that urban, industrial life was dehumanizing. Magazines such as *The Dial, Little Review,* and *Poetry* all provided outlets for twentieth-century poets, and literary groups and salons sprang up.

At best Rexroth could only appreciate this phenomenon from afar, floating around its fringes; but, recalling that period, he captured the loneliness of an orphaned adolescent sensitive to the literary and social concerns that permeated the atmosphere of a big city. In "The Bad Old Days," he writes that after his father died and his aunt took him to live in Chicago:

The first thing I did was to take
A streetcar to the stockyards.
In the winter afternoon,
Gritty and fetid, I walked
Through the filthy snow, through the

Squalid street, looking shyly
Into the people's faces.
Those who were home in the daytime.

The ethos of the poem comes from a favorite book of Rexroth's at the time, *The Jungle* (1906), Upton Sinclair's imaginative exposé of the Chicago stockyards. The tone and imagery could be traced to T. S. Eliot's "Preludes" or, for that matter, *The Waste Land* (1922), first published in *The Dial,* a poem whose influence on Rexroth persisted into *The Homestead Called Damascus* (1963), although he tried to expurgate it as he developed his craft.

Rexroth was hardly a stellar student in Chicago; in fact, he dropped out of Englewood High School. He preferred to hang out at Bughouse Square in Washington Square, opposite the Newberry Library and the Bug Club in Washington Park, where he listened to professional intellectual soapbox orators speak out on a variety of radical and unorthodox causes. He frequented the North Side, especially the Dill Pickle Club and the Radical Bookstore, where he could watch a No play by William Butler Yeats or listen to Sandburg sing and play the guitar. He also wrangled his way into the burlesque houses such as the Green Mask, where the honky-tonk appealed to him as much as the impassioned speeches that he heard in the parks. By carefully budgeting the tiny trust that had been set up for him and by taking odd jobs, he eventually struck out on his own. Barely eighteen, he lived in a series of small studio apartments. Then he met the first true love of his life and the inspiration for one of his best-known love poems.

Legal problems concerning Rexroth's small trust and his lengthening record of truancy led to a visit from Leslie Smith, a social worker in juvenile research. Rexroth became infatuated with her: in his eyes she was a Katherine Mansfield look-alike. Instead of rebuffing his overtures, Smith yielded to the attraction that she felt for her young charge, clearly an artist-writer type far more advanced in social graces than his years would suggest. A romance blossomed, and Rexroth followed her to Smith College in 1923. He commemorated the fresh sensuous passion he felt for her in the poem "When We with Sappho":

> We lie here in the bee filled, ruinous
> orchard of a decayed New England farm,
> Summer in our hair, and the smell
> Of summer in our twined bodies,
> Summer in our mouths, and summer
> In the luminous, fragmentary words
> Of this dead Greek woman.

> Stop reading. Lean back. Give me your mouth.
> Your grace is as beautiful as sleep.
> You move against me like a wave
> That moves in sleep.
> Your body spreads across my brain
> Like a bird filled summer;
> Not like a body, not like a separate thing,
> But like a nimbus that hovers
> Over every other thing in all the world.

The lyrical energy of these lines is maintained throughout the poem, and typifies the love poetry that Rexroth wrote throughout his life, especially to his first three wives, Andrée, Marie, and Marthe. In these poems the world takes on a sensual and erotic component. As critic Donald Gutierrez has remarked about Rexroth's love poems, "the realized love experience is also a realization of one's unity with the living, circumambient universe." As an example of how love and sexuality become "forms of dynamic nature" in Rexroth's poems, Gutierrez cites the third section of "Inversely, As the Square of Their Distances Apart," where Rexroth and his companion make love at the "wood's edge," reaching their climax like falling meteors, "dark through black cold / Toward each other, and then compact / Blazing through air into earth." Rexroth described spectacular sex in many poems as an earthy communion of passion and spirit. His overt celebration of heterosexual love was a rare occurrence in twentieth-century American poetry.

Smith eventually broke off with her young lover in search of a man her own age who could provide her with the solid, middle-class respectability toward which Rexroth showed little inclination. During the next three years Rexroth assumed a vagabond life, hitchhiking to the West Coast, landing one job writing for *The Industrial Worker* in Seattle and another as a lookout at a ranger station near Marblemount, Washington. He felt a deep connection with the western parts of the United States. The people he met spoke in the tones and patterns that made sense to him, and their voices awakened part of his own authentic idiom. But when he returned to Chicago in 1924, he resumed his interest in the more rarefied avant-garde theories of André Breton and Tristan Tzara; he also immersed himself in the work of the French anarchist Pierre-Joseph Proudhon and the philosophers Alfred North Whitehead and Ludwig Wittgenstein. Soon his restlessness led him to the Southwest and Mexico. He also earned passage as a mess steward on a ship bound for the ports on the English Channel, then managed to live for a time in New York City, staying in the same Grove Street apartment house

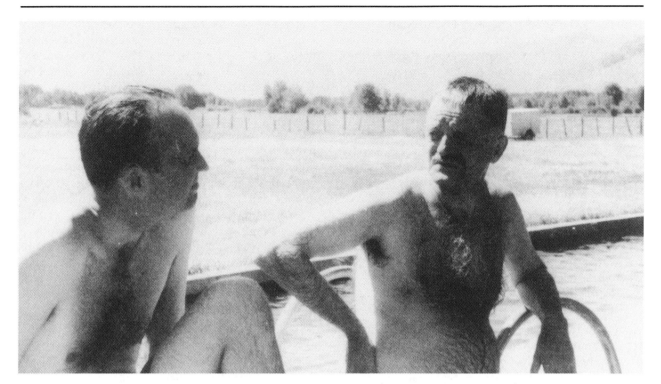

James Laughlin and Rexroth in Wilson, Wyoming (photograph by Ann Laughlin)

that Hart Crane had lived in. For a while Rexroth stayed at Holy Cross Monastery in Poughkeepsie, New York, as a guest leading the life of a penitent permitted to paint and write. During his two winter months there he made substantial progress on his first long philosophical poem, "The Homestead Called Damascus" (part of it set on a nearby private estate).

This long poem tracks the careers of two brothers who take their own measure amid conflicting philosophies and try to establish a connection with the drift of human history from biblical times through the Middle Ages and the Renaissance, finally up to their own time in the "New World." The poem not only reflects Rexroth's intellectual concerns, but it also furnishes a stage for the writers who had instructed and inspired him, among them John Duns Scotus, Jakob Böhme, Tu Fu, Guillaume Apollinaire, T. S. Eliot, Conrad Aiken, and H. G. Wells.

Back in Chicago by 1926, Rexroth continued his writing and painting and met his first wife, Andrée Schafer. Andrée was an artist whose politics, like Rexroth's, were strongly left-wing. The two often painted together on one canvas, creating Piet Mondrian–inspired geometrical patterns in primary colors. Rexroth showed her drafts of his poetry, which they would revise together. They married in January 1927; after a long, impoverished winter, they decided to go west to climb the mountains Rexroth had earlier learned to love and to start a life in California. Although a perfectly respectable couple and practicing Anglicans, he and his wife were hardly conventional. Hitchhikers, obviously without steady employment, each carrying a huge backpack loaded with camping supplies as well as writing pads and drawing paper, they were strangers who represented a warning to the natives that their Pacific paradise might not last exclusively for them forever. Indeed, Rexroth and Andrée were forerunners of the Beats and the flower children who, drawn to the mild climate and the freewheeling lifestyle, flocked to northern California during the 1950s and 1960s.

From 1927 to 1929 Andrée and Rexroth shaped a life in San Francisco that revolved around their commitment to writing, painting, and their love of the natural environment. They also became increasingly involved in leftist organizations. After a brief spell in a dank basement apartment and a few other equally unsavory places, they rented a studio in the famous Montgomery Block, sometimes known as the Monkey Block, a low-rent haven for writers and artists who were poor and needed space and light to work. Ambrose Bierce, Sadakichi Hartmann, Frank Norris, Jack London, Margaret

Anderson, Diego Rivera, and Frieda Kahlo were some of the better known occupants. To get a sharper sense of the change of seasons, Rexroth and his wife escaped from time to time to Yosemite and the Sierra Nevada. An excerpt from "Andrée Rexroth" illustrates the harmony the couple felt in natural settings:

> We were alone, twenty
> Miles from anybody;
> A young husband and wife,
> Closed in and wrapped about
> In the quiet autumn,
> In the sound of quiet water,
> In the turning and falling leaves,
> In the wavering of innumerable
> Bats from the caves, dipping
> Over the odorous pools
> Where the great trout drowsed in the evenings.

They also spent more than a year together in southern California, in Santa Monica Canyon, where, despite their small income, they fell into an idyllic routine, taking vegetables from neighbors' gardens and swimming every day. This period is vividly described in Rexroth's long poem *The Dragon and the Unicorn* (1952).

In 1927, with Andrée's encouragement, Rexroth began submitting poetry to ephemeral publications. With the exception of "Saint Joan," printed in a church bulletin in 1925, the first published works by Rexroth were four poems and one letter to the editor (wherein he criticizes his former hero William Carlos Williams for not writing a clear enough rebuttal to the "neoclassical polemics" of Yvor Winters). The poems were printed by Charles Henri Ford in the April, June, and Fall 1929 issues of *Blues*. Ford reported in a letter to Rexroth that he caught flak for printing the poem titled "When you asked for it." This poem resurfaced twenty years later, in *The Art of Worldly Wisdom* (1949), along with two other *Blues* poems and several poems written between 1927 and 1932. Examples of Rexroth's Cubist poetry, they mark the beginnings of his career as a published poet. He enjoyed a brief burst of popularity with this Cubist style when three versions of a long poem, "Prolegomena to a Theodicy," appeared in *An "Objectivists" Anthology,* a special edition of *Poetry* magazine edited by Louis Zukofsky in 1932; but he soon abandoned the Cubist style in search of a more suitable idiom.

Zukofsky and Rexroth's correspondence between 1930 and 1932 reveals a shared enthusiasm for the French avant-garde artists, for Alfred North Whitehead's systematic attempt to give the universe coherence, and for Marxism. But Rexroth was only tangentially connected to the Objectivist Movement that Zukofsky inspired, even if his "Prolegomena" was given ample space in *An "Objectivists" Anthology*. (Other contributors included Williams, Basil Bunting, George Oppen, Carl Rakosi, Lorine Niedecker, and Charles Reznikoff.) Like Zukofsky, Rexroth wanted to banish sentimentality and flippancy from poetry and release poetry from being limited only to so-called great and noble subjects.

Although he disapproved of artists who rigidly molded their work to suit a particular ideology, Rexroth himself conceived of his own writing within a political context. He wanted to reintroduce into poetry, he told Zukofsky in a 1931 letter, a seriousness, "a respect for ends . . . a consciousness of all the implications, the final issues, the guiding purpose." A poetry of responsibility would deal with subjects "worthy of writing, as an integral part of that vast complexus of vital significance we call the universe." But many of his poems in the Objectivist mode had an obsessive, perseverating quality, as in the following section from "Prolegomena to a Theodicy":

> The grammar of cause
> The cause of grammar
> The being of grammar
> The magnificent being of division
> The gradient of change
> The invisible triangle of difference
> Of division
> The parsed challenge
> If the extended injunction remains it will be almost
>   possible
> to observe the dispersion of the closing and unclosing follicles.

In his preface to *The Art of Worldly Wisdom,* Rexroth places these poems in the tradition of abstract art, comparing the elements of each poem to the "elementary shapes of a cubist painting." These poems, he advised, had to be understood on an intuitive level as well as on a rational one – a variation on T. S. Eliot's contention in a 1929 essay that genuine poetry communicates emotionally before it is understood intellectually. Rexroth asked his readers to consider these poems self-referential and not to expect conventional signals such as linear coherency, transitions, and symbols. He argued that he was divorcing the means of representation from what was presented, just as Cubist painters dispensed with shading and foreshortening.

Even when parodying the Surrealists Tzara and Breton, as in "Fundamental Disagreement with Two Contemporaries," Rexroth was not writing the

LAMENT FOR DYLAN THOMAS

I

He is dead.
The bird of Rhiannon.
He is Dead.
In the winter of the heart.
He is dead.
In the canyons of death.
They found him dumb at last,
In the blizzard of lies.
He never spoke again.
He died.
He is dead.
In their antiseptic hands,
He is dead.
The little spellbinder of Cader Idris.   *He is dead.*
He is dead.   *The sparrow of Cardiff.*
The canary of Swansea.
Who killed him?
Who killed the bright headed bird?
You did, you son of a bitch.
You drowned him in your cocktail brain.
He felldown and died in your synthetic heart.
You killed him,
Oppenheimer the Million-Killer.
You killed him,
Einstein the Grey Eminence.
You killed him,
Havanahavana, with your Nobel Prize.
You killed him,
Benign Lady on the postage stamp.
He was found dead at a New Republic luncheon.
He was found dead on the cutting room floor.
He was found dead at a Times policy conference.
Henry Luce killed him with a telegram to the Pope.
Mademoiselle strangled him with a padded brassiere.
Old Possum sprinkled him with a tea ball.
After the wolves were done, the vaticides
Crawled off with his bowels to their classrooms and quarterlies.
When the news came over the radio
You personally rose up shouting, "Give us Barrabas!"
In your lonely crowd you swept over him.
Your custom built brogans and your ballet slippers
Pummelled him to death in the gritty street.
You hit him with an album of Hindemith.
You stabbed him with stainless steel by Isamu Noguchi.
He is dead.
He is Dead.
Like Ignacio the bullfighter,
At four o'clock in the afternoon.
At precisely four o'clock.

Draft for Rexroth's poem published as "Thou Shalt Not Kill"

kind of poetry he himself would have defined as vitally significant. The bravado with which he wrote the preface to *The Art of Worldly Wisdom* belied his struggle to invent a style that did not sacrifice a central aspect of both his poetry and prose: his own, idiosyncratic, personal voice. He later told Babette Deutsch in a 1949 letter that his so-called Objectivist poems were a "literary parallel to the early Eisenstein movie technique, and a prosody which owed much to the short, abrupt cadences of primitive song [and to] non-European languages." He knew that he could not reach a wide audience with this kind of poetry. What he really wanted to write were love poems, political poems, poems that reflected his spiritual yearnings and deep sympathy for the natural world, and poems that would reach the ordinary reader. That meant for him that he had to develop a style grounded in his beloved West Coast landscape and written in a common yet lyrical syntax.

During the 1930s especially, but throughout his life, Rexroth sympathized with efforts to encourage writers and readers to identify strongly with the region where they lived and to resist social injustice and oppression wherever they encountered it. As a member of the Federal Writers' Project, he was engaged in activities that promoted these principles. One was a literary magazine that never saw publication, although a projected sample (with a geometric design on the cover probably designed by Rexroth) caught the attention of a San Francisco journalist who urged collectors in a 1936 news story to get their hands on a copy. The editors of *Material Gathered on the Federal Writers Project,* Rexroth among them, claimed that the Works Progress Administration (WPA) should offer writers more regional journals that would not be subject to the whims of skittish advertisers, an idea far ahead of its time: one has only to look at annual listings of the Coordinating Council of Literary Magazines to get a sense of how essential this concept is to sustain poets and their audiences.

Under the pseudonym of J. Rand Talbot, a name he sometimes used during his days as a Chicago juvenile delinquent, Rexroth wrote an essay for this magazine arguing that creative magazines of a regional nature would tap a large source of potential readers who were "too poor or too illiterate" to waste time and money on glossy national publications filled with stories and poems that had little to do with them. Under his own name he contributed a few poems, among them "Hiking on the Coast Range," written to commemorate the maritime general strike of 16 July 1934 and to deplore institution-

alized violence, represented here by police brutality. In this poem he composed lines of vivid imagery and contemplative lyricism, combining an acute, intense observation of the natural environment with a radical social conscience:

> The skirl of the kingfisher was never
> more clear than now, nor the scream of the jay
> as the deer shifts her covert at a footfall,
> nor the wild rose-poppy ever brighter
> in the white spent wheat, nor the pain
> of a wasp stab ever an omen more sure,
> the blood alternately dark and brilliant,
> of the blue and white bandana pattern.

The poem continues in this vein, skirting the Objectivist style that he had earlier tried to emulate. The poem gently asserts that the moral sense cannot remain intact when one feels and sees the shock of violence, anticipating some contemporary psychological theories about the origins of violence. When the poem appeared in *In What Hour* (1940), Rexroth changed the "wild rose-poppy" to a "butterfly tulip," saving the color red to emphasize bloodshed only.

As a member of the League of American Writers, Rexroth attended the Western Writers Conference in November 1936, where he delivered a paper, "The Function of the Poet in Society." Here he spelled out the minimal condition that artists needed to work. He declared that he was a radical, "a social outcast [who] identified . . . with forces striving for a better social system, a system in which humanity and leisure for vital appreciation of the arts would be the common property of all men." Neither he nor any other writer, he argued, deserved to live a life of semistarvation. He did not want to write with what he called the divided personality that characterized modernist writers such as Yeats and Eliot, whose poetry, although "truly revolutionary in its final implication," was in his opinion socially ineffective. Yeats and Eliot had evolved for themselves, not necessarily anyone else, systems of theosophy and Anglo-Catholicism that were deeply critical of the middle-class values that he, too, held in contempt. However, if the United States were to remain part of the "civilized world," Rexroth argued that he and his colleagues had to reach out to "all producing classes of the west," the workers and the farmers whom the country depended on, using the words used in the factories, farms, and trades. He was ultimately pleading for the recognition of regional literary magazines committed to good writing. More basically, he was stating that in order for people to tap into their creative

Lawrence Ferlinghetti, Bruce Lippincott, and Rexroth at the Cellar in San Francisco, circa 1957

energy, and to respect, seek, and support the poetry and art of others, they had to feel deeply connected to their own immediate environment. In a sense he was defining democracy in dynamic terms by asserting that a free country was a country that nurtured and validated an artistic sensibility in all people, irrespective of race, region, or class, a position that Walt Whitman had articulated more than fifty years earlier in *Democratic Vistas* (1871).

Ironically, *In What Hour,* a volume rich with the kind of poetry Rexroth extolled in his speech, was received harshly by critics during the years following its publication in 1940. Many of the political poems, love lyrics, and elegies had appeared in *New Masses, The New Republic,* and *Partisan Review.* Rexroth's intimate communion with the natural universe, especially the world of the High Sierra, remained paramount, as in this excerpt from "Falling Leaves and Early Snow":

In the years to come they will say,
"They fell like leaves
In the autumn of nineteen thirty-nine,"
November has come to the forest,
To the meadows where we picked the cyclamen.
The year fades with the white frost
On the brown sedge in the hazy meadows,
Where the deer tracks were black this morning.
Ice forms in the shadows;
Disheveled maples hang over the water;
Deep gold sunlight glistens on the shrunken stream.
Somnolent trout move through pillars of brown and
    gold.
The yellow maple leaves eddy above them,
The glittering leaves of the cottonwood,
The olive, velvety alder leaves,
The scarlet dogwood leaves,
Most poignant of all.

Exemplifying the kind of poetry that Rexroth would write best during the next thirty years, the poem mourns a terrible and tragic event – the German invasion of Poland – yet it unfolds against a landscape whose beauty never ceased to inspire him. The tone is contemplative; the measured rhythms are graceful; the reverence for nature is expressed in sharp-edged imagery; the circumstances and events of his own life are delicately meshed with larger, graver issues; and the unabashed idealism is reined in short of sentimentality.

In a 12 August 1940 review of *In What Hour* for *New Masses,* Rolphe Humphries refers to Rexroth as a "simpleminded man, with a liking for the outdoors" and advised him to avoid the pose of an "erudite indoor ponderer." In the November 1940 issue of *Poetry,* William Fitzgerald dismissed Rexroth's political perspective as "presumably Marxian" and a sign of his bewilderment with world events and ridiculed him for his "facile free association." In *A History of American Poetry* (1946), Horace Gregory and Marya Zaturenska dismissed the poems in the collection as little more than "regional verse that reflected the charms of the Pacific Coast."

Twenty years later, however, in the Spring 1962 issue of *The Minnesota Review,* Richard Foster described Rexroth's view of world events in the 1930s and 1940s as "chillingly prophetic." And more than twenty years after that Rexroth's volume received further acknowledgment. In his book *Twentieth Century Pleasures: Prose on Poetry* (1984), Robert Hass declared that *In What Hour* was the "first readable book of poems ever produced by a resident of [San Francisco]," adding that it seemed to "have invented the culture of the West Coast." This praise suggests the ways in which Rexroth's work fits more readily into the contexts that shaped much of the poetry of the second half of the twentieth century. Rexroth's work redefined regionalism as a vital aspect of composition, not a quaint and picturesque shortcoming; it incorporated politics and the personal voice within the setting of a specific locale; it stimulated the creation of small, local literary magazines that would provide a forum for talented but struggling writers; and it created new readers among people who did not ordinarily turn to poetry for pleasure or intellectual stimulation.

The cultural perspective that flourished in San Francisco at the end of World War II, in what became known as the San Francisco Renaissance, was one in whose creation Rexroth played a vital and essential role. At the same time, profound changes were occurring in Rexroth's life. As they worked their way into his poetry, he continued to refine his skills as a poet who steadfastly grounded his work in political conscience, personal vision, and his direct experience at home on the West Coast.

In October 1940, at the age of thirty-eight, Andrée Rexroth died from a massive epileptic seizure. She had been afflicted with this illness most of her adult life, and Rexroth had grown expert at administering to her whenever she suffered an attack. Several years prior to 1940 the marriage had collapsed, however, because of sexual infidelity, tempestuous arguments, and a widening difference between their perceptions about the moral integrity of the Communist Party. In 1936, the year before Rexroth filed for divorce on the grounds that Andrée had deserted him in 1934, he fell in love with Marie Kass, a lively, vivacious public health nurse whom he had met at an organizational meeting of the Nurses Association (he was still involved with Communist front organizations). He and Marie soon made a life together. They married in July 1940 and rented an apartment on Potrero Hill, where they spent many pleasant evenings with neighbors and visitors such as William Saroyan, Dorothy Van Ghent, George Hitchcock, John Ferren, Hilaire Hiler, and James Laughlin. Marie Rexroth was a skillful musician, and guests passed the evening singing, dancing, and arguing about literature and politics. Although Rexroth seemed to adjust smoothly to a new and fulfilling life with Marie, he was deeply distraught at the news of Andrée's death.

Rexroth did not attend Andrée's funeral, but he created a private myth that compensated for the failure of a once impassioned relationship. During the next few years he wrote three elegies to Andrée: two appeared in *The Phoenix and the Tortoise* (1944), the third in *The Signature of All Things* (1950). All three poems are set in Mount Tamalpais, one of their favorite haunts, where, according to Rexroth, Andrée's ashes were scattered. Each poem bursts with sharp and poignant observations that evoke great sorrow for a lost and idyllic innocence.

But outwardly, at least, Rexroth did not grieve long for Andrée, and he was already finding Marie Rexroth a devoted wife and amanuensis. Meanwhile, as an avowed anarchist and pacifist, he faced the immediate possibility that he might be drafted into the U.S. armed services, especially as the so-called Phony War in Europe began to intensify. After a grueling process that included a year-long investigation by the FBI, his initial application as a conscientious objector 4-E was confirmed. In the meantime, he worked as an orderly on the psychiatric ward of a San Francisco hospital, where he spent the quiet early morning hours translating poems from the *Greek Anthology*. It was mainly Marie Rexroth's salary that supported the couple at this time. Once war broke out, Rexroth and Marie transformed their Wisconsin Street apartment into a halfway house for Japanese Americans forced to evacuate their homes. He later recalled the terrified Japanese nationals who were being shipped to camps in Montana, certain that they would be shot. In his long poem "The Phoenix and the Tortoise," he heightened the tragedy by describing the reaction of children being confronted by the corpse of an enemy who once resembled their Japanese American neighbors:

> A group of terrified children
> Has just discovered the body
> Of a Japanese sailor bumping
> In a snarl of kelp in a tidepool.
> While the crowd collects, I stand, mute
> As he, watching his smashed ribs breathe
> Of the life of the ocean, his white
> Torn bowels braid themselves with the kelp.

Meanwhile, in a war that changed most pacifists into fighting men, Rexroth redoubled his effort to make his stand against the war a consistent position of integrity.

When his second volume of verse was published by New Directions at the end of 1944, Rexroth and his wife celebrated with a book party. Ostensibly it was a happy occasion. Marie Rexroth had recently returned from Washington, D.C., where she had been training to work as a nurse in European refugee camps for the United Nations. But the marriage had begun to fail under the pressure of Rexroth's draft appeal. Furthermore, Marie was growing increasingly irritated by her role as the major wage earner, and both she and Rexroth had begun to have affairs. Rexroth dedicated the book to Marie and wrote passionate love poetry to her, but within four years, the marriage ended. Rexroth and Marie nevertheless remained lifelong friends.

A rich mixture of love lyrics, political poems, satire, and translations from Latin and Japanese, *The Phoenix and the Tortoise* won the California Literature Award, as *In What Hour* had four years earlier. To Rexroth's delight the book was reviewed enthusiastically in the *Quarterly Review of Literature* by William Carlos Williams, to whose home in Rutherford, New Jersey, Rexroth had made a pilgrimage in 1931. Rexroth recalled this visit in "A Letter to William Carlos Williams," a homage to both the man and his disarmingly earthy writing style, first published in 1946:

> Remember years ago, when
> I told you you were the first
> Great Franciscan poet since
> The Middle Ages? I disturbed
> The even tenor of dinner.
> Your wife thought I was crazy.
> It's true, though. And you're 'pure', too[.]

Rexroth did not receive the same favorable reception from Yvor Winters, whose advice he continued to seek, despite the fact that Winters had rejected his overtures of friendship nearly fifteen years before. Winters preferred traditional metrical forms to the more organic rhythms that Rexroth chose for his poems, rhythms exemplified in "Floating," which describes his making love to Marie in a canoe as it slowly drifts down a stream thick with lily pads:

> Move softly, move hardly at all, part your thighs,
> Take me slowly while our gnawing lips
> Fumble against the humming blood in our throats.
> Move softly, do not move at all, but hold me,
> Deep, still, deep within you, while time slides away,
> As this river slides beyond this lily bed,
> And the thieving moments fuse and disappear
> In our mortal, timeless flesh.

Although the meter is fluid, the lines are finely crafted, and the rhythms and imagery fuse with the poem's subject, creating an inextricable, complex union of form and content.

After the war ended in 1945, Rexroth's creative energy surged into other genres. Besides lyrical poetry, he wrote four verse plays, two set in the Greek heroic age, "Phaedra" and "Iphegenia at Aulis," and two in Hellenized Bactria, "Hermaios" and "Berenike." The plays were published collectively in 1951 under the title *Beyond the Mountains;* they formally premiered in 1952 at the Living Theater in New York, in productions directed by Julian Beck and Judith Malina. Other projects included a selection of poems by D. H. Lawrence, which New Directions published in 1947. Rexroth had been drawn to Lawrence's ability to enter and identify with the natural world and write about that world as if from the inside out. He was fascinated, too, by the exuberance and vitality of Lawrence's sexually charged poetry. Rexroth also edited an anthology of British poets that appeared two years later, featuring Denise Levertov as one of the newest voices. By 1947 Rexroth's reputation as a man of letters was established on the West Coast, and his home became a mecca for local and visiting writers and artists.

America since the Bomb

(8) The Beat Generation

by Kenneth Rexroth

TLO 62/TE 108
43'40"
P 1

Please return to
O. G. Bridson
7083 BH

Trans: 26th Oct 66 T.P. 2210-2255

as soon
as poss

In the winter of 1954-55 America was in an economic, social
and cultural interregnum. One style of life, one mood -- like
Victorianism or Edwardianism -- was giving way to another. An
industrial age based on the mechanical *exploitation* of coal and iron was
giving way to electronics, computers, automation -- with all the
social and intellectual results such a basic revolution implies --
but as yet few indeed understood what was happening. The country
was in a minor economic depression following the end of the Korean
War. The Korean war *itself* represented a qualitative leap forward in
technology and a lag in all other factors. Morale broke down
however for a more simple reason. You can fight only one such war
every 25 years. The Korean war took place within the socially
effective memory of the Second World War. The academic and
intellectual establishment, Left, Right and Center, was shattered,
demoralized and discredited by the years of McCarthyism. Young
men by the thousands were returning from the Korean War to the
colleges disillusioned and contemptuous of their elders. They said
to each other, "Keep your nose clean and don't volunteer." "Don't
believe anybody over thirty." Communication between groups broke
down. Only those of the elder generation who had remained defiant
were respected, listened to, questioned. Just as the Army took
years to discover the almost total breakdown of morale in Korea,
so the older intellectuals were unaware that a volcano was building
up under them.

McCarthyism itself was an expression of breakdown of an older

First page for a 1966 radio script (The Estate of Kenneth Rexroth, courtesy of the Lilly Library, Indiana University)

These gatherings at Rexroth's home became a sort of freewheeling literary salon. Writers, artists, and a small core of local anarchists joined together for poetry readings and literary and philosophical discussions. Many who attended these evenings, including William Everson and Adrian Wilson, had recently come from Waldport, Oregon, where, as conscientious objectors, they had been confined to work camp. They brought with them the little magazines and printing presses that helped create new outlets for linking the life of the imagination with a pacifist-anarchist consciousness. Robert Duncan, Jack Spicer, and Robin Blaser, all students of poet Josephine Miles, crossed the bay to Rexroth's home to join others who were not particularly impressed by academic institutions and credentials. Rexroth contributed to various magazines that were launched or given fresh transfusions, including *The Illiterati, Circle,* and *The Ark.*

By his early forties Rexroth was the model literary figure – a wise, productive, sophisticated, and inspirational, if sometimes intimidating, mentor. Ruggedly handsome, he had a lion-sized head that seemed well suited to his status. The breadth of his knowledge could be astounding – the result, in part, of his reading the entire *Encyclopedia Britannica.* He appeared to be the epitome of the new, post–World War II poet described by Everson in *Archetype West: The Pacific Coast as a Literary Region* (1976). Everson redefined the role of poet as a kind of prophet, a refresher and invigorator of stultified literary and social forms, who rejected the poetics of the established New Criticism, especially its emphasis on detachment and impersonalism.

Much of this emerging sensibility was grounded in a profound respect for the natural world, and, to a large extent, the work of Jakob Böhme, the German mystic whose writings Rexroth had studied and urgently encouraged others to read. Rexroth accepted both the political and aesthetic implications of Böhme's thinking: Nature was a sacred paradigm of harmony, and, in such a universe, human beings themselves were responsible for creating good and for knowing God or the spiritual world. Böhme was an appropriate figure to study, Rexroth thought, for artists and activists attempting to work out for themselves an applied philosophy that might make the world a more humane place. Böhme also provided Rexroth with an explanation for the revelatory moments that he himself had experienced since childhood and described in his poems.

For poetry that was compatible with Böhme's perspective, Rexroth looked to Tu Fu, the re-

nowned Chinese poet of the T'ang dynasty whose poetry expresses a reverence for life, a mystical communion with nature, and a compassion for humanity. In often dense and compressed language, Tu Fu's poetry also articulates the poet's feelings of loneliness or frustration – moods that permeate Rexroth's poetry as well. From Tu Fu, Rexroth learned to dramatize moods, moving from one to the other by breaking them with an image vitally connected to the natural world. His poetry in the late 1940s and afterward demonstrated his allegiance to both Böhme and Tu Fu, most obviously in the title poem of *The Signature of All Things,* named after one of Böhme's greatest works, and also in Rexroth's translations of the works of Tu Fu and other Chinese and Japanese poets, books that for some readers were the easiest entry into Rexroth's work.

As Rexroth's position in the literary world of San Francisco grew more secure, his personal life grew more tumultuous. The troubles that he and Marie had buried after the end of World War II resurfaced. His earnings did not signficantly improve with his rising fame, and Marie sometimes despaired at being the major breadwinner, as well as the secretary for her husband's various projects. Rexroth had also begun to cultivate a rakish image – sometimes sporting a long, black cape – that did little to quell Marie's misgivings about his sexual fidelity. Marie eventually formed her own liaisons, and violent arguments ensued. When he was awarded a $3,000 Guggenheim Fellowship in 1948, Rexroth felt that he had been given a chance to set his life in order. The money temporarily freed him from his financial dependency on Marie, and a poetry circuit tour around the United States and a trip to Europe provided him with both a physical and psychological distance from places that had become poisoned with jealousy and anger. However, by the time he returned to San Francisco in late 1949 – the grant had been extended another year – his marriage to Marie had finally failed.

Throughout the time that Rexroth was traveling he corresponded with Marie, but he was also writing to Marthe Larsen, a recent Mills College graduate who had occasionally attended Rexroth's literary soirees. A romance blossomed between them despite the twenty-two-year age difference, and after much pleading Marthe joined Rexroth in Europe. He captured some of their time together in his 1952 collection, *The Dragon and the Unicorn:*

We camp on the Loire, the vélos
Parked under a rose bush, the

Sleeping bags under acacia,
And careen down the swift current,
Impossible to stand, much less
Swim against it. Two owls chatter
In the trees as the twilight
Comes, lavender and orange
Over the white reaches of
Water and the white sandbars,
And the first starlight dribbling
On the rushing river.

A disquisition of sorts on Rexroth's anarchist politics and a paean to erotic communion, the poem is also exquisite, if sometimes irreverent, travel writing: the prehistoric art in the Lascaux caves become "Sid Grauman's Cro-Magnum Theatre"; the medieval castle at Carcassonne turns into a "tiresome visite"; the atmosphere over Avignon is contaminated by the "Stink of the Papacy and / The present stink of English tourists." Rexroth's impressions are lively and intense. Selecting details with an unerring eye, he makes his readers hunger for the food that he and Marthe consume with gusto. Meanwhile, by the end of the trip, Marthe became pregnant. After great anguish for all parties concerned, Marie Rexroth found a new place to live, and Rexroth and Marthe made what preparations they could for their first child. Mary Delia Andrée was born 26 July 1950. Marie Rexroth, still legally married to Rexroth, agreed to be her godmother.

During the early 1950s Rexroth was totally immersed in San Francisco literary life. Besides writing poetry, he inaugurated a weekly book review program on KPFA, a public radio listener-sponsored station that he helped found. According to the form letter he sent to publishers requesting review copies, he specialized in "mature non-fiction, highbrow literature, scholarly works, fine arts, orientalia, poetry." Some listeners tuned in for information; others wanted to hear Rexroth's latest, sometimes outrageous pronouncements on the state of contemporary intellectual life, which he delivered in a voice that sounded as if it came right out of a second-rate gangster movie. He was also writing reviews for *The New Republic, Art News, The New York Times Book Review,* and *The Nation.* He also resumed his Friday night literary evenings.

Rexroth continued to seek solitude and inspiration in the mountains, most frequently in a lean-to hut in Devil's Gulch in nearby Marin County. Marthe Rexroth worked at various secretarial jobs at San Francisco State College and joined him only occasionally. The relationship had been troubled from the start, and frequent arguments arose from the tensions created by Marthe's role of wife, mother, breadwinner, and her husband's secretary/editor and also by Rexroth's possessiveness. Periods of peace, however, recurred; and if Marthe could not always accompany him to the mountains, two-year-old Mary was available for trips to Sequoia National Park.

Over the years, Mary's presence became the source for some of Rexroth's most poignant poems, including his autobiographical "A Living Pearl," "Halley's Comet," a celebration of a father's love for his daughter and the great sense of continuity she represents for him, and "The Great Nebula of Andromeda" all three of which appeared in the 1956 volume *In Defense of the Earth.* In "The Great Nebula of Andromeda," Rexroth's political attitudes surface, not in the didactic fashion that sometimes mars a long poem like *The Dragon and the Unicorn,* but as pointed observation. Wakened in the middle of the night by horses stumbling around a campsite, Rexroth stares at Mary, whose sleeping face he compares to a "jewel in the moonlight." He picks up his "glass" to observe "the Great Nebula / Of Andromeda swim like / A phosphorescent amoeba / Slowly around the Pole." But he speculates that man-made world events will prevent Mary from seeing the twenty-first century, and he expresses the fear that far away from this idyllic scene, "fat-hearted men" are plotting her murder. Rexroth had not abandoned his pacifist politics, and he became involved in helping young men to acquire conscientious objector status during the Korean War.

Rexroth's famous poem of this period was "Thou Shalt Not Kill," to commemorate the death of Dylan Thomas in 1953. An indictment of society at large, the poem is not necessarily an example of Rexroth's finest work, but its undisguised social protest is memorable:

You killed him! You killed him.
In your God damned Brooks Brothers suit,
You son of a bitch.

In a June 1957 review in *Poetry,* William Carlos Williams declared that copies of the poem should have been posted in college campuses across the country. Although the poem can intermittently sound like a recitation of clichés and can be offensive, as in the line "I want to slit the bellies of your frigid women," it nevertheless succeeds in communicating one poet's profound grief by its sheer force of energy and clear vision of where to place the blame for the death of a fellow poet – on a society that corrupts creative energy in the name of progress.

> Who killed the bright-headed bird?
> You did, you son of a bitch.
> You drowned him in your cocktail brain,
> He fell down and died in your synthetic heart.
> You killed him,
> Oppenheimer the Million-Killer,
> You killed him,
> Einstein the Gray Eminence.
> You killed him
> Havanahavana, with your Nobel Prize.

In a 1955 lecture on Dylan Thomas in San Francisco, Karl Shapiro ridiculed the poem as overblown with conviction. Yet the poem was published by three different presses. Rexroth often read it to jazz accompaniment at North Beach clubs like the Hungry I, the Black Hawk, and the Cellar. The powerful sense of outrage in "Thou Shalt Not Kill" arose partly from Rexroth's feeling that his own destiny was woven into the poem, that his own voice would be wiped out by a capitalist society that looked upon art and literature as commodities.

In later years Rexroth was growing slowly resigned to the realization that the world would never come close to his ideal. The execution of Nicola Sacco and Bartolomeo Vanzetti, the Moscow trials, the Spanish Civil War, the internment of Japanese Americans during World War II, the Cold War of the 1950s, and the Korean War all indicated the shrinking possibilities for the world community he had envisioned. He was not entirely embittered and did not regret the course he had chosen, but he began to doubt seriously that he would see substantial change in his lifetime. Through the following years he expressed his perspective in poems such as "For Eli Jacobsen," "The Bad Old Days," "Portrait of the Artist as a Young Anarchist," and also in these lines from the "Fish Peddler and Cobbler":

> We thought that soon all things would
> Be changed, not just economic
> And social relationships, but
> Painting, poetry, music, dance,
> Architecture, even the food
> We ate and the clothes we wore
> Would be ennobled. It will take
> Longer than we expected.

Yet while the political climate of the Silent Decade remained largely stagnant, Rexroth refused to surrender hope.

In October 1955 Rexroth acted as master of ceremonies at a major event in San Francisco literary history, a poetry reading at the Six Gallery on Fillmore Street. Gary Snyder, Michael McClure, Philip Lamantia, Philip Whalen, and Allen Ginsberg were the featured poets, and Jack Kerouac was the most visible, audible, and appreciative member of the audience. The highlight of the evening was Ginsberg's recitation of "Howl," part of which Ginsberg had shown Rexroth earlier that year. (It has been speculated that "Thou Shalt Not Kill" was one of the models for "Howl.") The media immediately announced the arrival of the "Beat Generation," and hailed Rexroth as its patron and elder statesman, a position he seemed glad to assume at first, with an essay that contributed to the success of a whole new generation of poets. In "Disengagement: The Art of the Beat Generation," first published in *New World Writing* in 1957, Rexroth rearticulated many of the values that he honored in his own poetry and that he saw emerging in the next generation's work: the creative act is an effective de-

The Collected Shorter Poems of Kenneth Rexroth

Cover for Rexroth's 1967 collection, with a photograph of Rexroth and his daughters, Katharine and Mary

fense against despair; twentieth-century artists cannot maintain their integrity if they curry favor with the establishment; poetry is personal communication based on clear images and simple language; poets should be antiwar and proecology; contemporary poets should emulate the works of William Blake, William Carlos Williams, D. H. Lawrence, Walt Whitman, and Ezra Pound, not those poets belonging to the "official high-brow culture."

When the 9 September 1957 issue of *Life* magazine ran a story about the San Francisco scene, Rexroth was prominently featured in a photograph that showed him reading poetry to the accompaniment of jazz; he was also described as a poet of national reputation and an "elder statesman" among the city's poets. *Time* magazine had reported that when Rexroth first read "Thou Shalt Not Kill" to jazz at the Cellar, five hundred fans tried to push their way into the club, which had a seating capacity of forty-three. Rexroth's fame on the West Coast peaked during the period that came to be known as the San Francisco Renaissance.

However, East Coast critics writing for *The New Republic, Commentary,* and *The Reporter* had a field day with Rexroth for supporting, promoting, and encouraging this new generation of poets. (He testified for the defense in the obscenity trial against Lawrence Ferlinghetti and City Lights Books for publishing "Howl.") He was accused of having "publicistic impulses" and of writing "intellectually irresponsible" essays. Meanwhile, although he did not break into the academic circles east of the Rockies, he accepted many of the invitations he began to receive from institutions up and down the West Coast, invitations to participate in poetry readings, workshops, and conferences. Eventually he distanced himself from the Beat writers and harshly reviewed Jack Kerouac, especially his volume of poetry, *Mexico City Blues* (1959). But the label "Father of the Beats" followed Rexroth to his last days.

His enhanced status as a literary figure did little to quell the domestic crises rocking the Rexroth household. A second daughter, Katharine Ann Helen, had been born in 1954, and Marthe Rexroth, determined not to return to work as quickly as she had after Mary was born, took a six-month leave from her job. The family scraped by, aided by gifts from Marie Rexroth, still legally married to Rexroth and now his second child's godmother. When Marthe did return to work, she had reached the breaking point. Rexroth still expected her to serve as amanuensis. He was inordinately jealous of Marthe's friends yet saw no reason she should resent his attachment to Marie and the various people

he invited to their home, despite the fact that these guests often kept her up long after she should have retired for the night. Moreover, Rexroth boasted about his sexual conquests to their friends and Friday-evening guests, a pastime that Marthe regarded as humiliating and that some Bay Area writers resented. More and more, Marthe wanted to leave Rexroth, and on two occasions, taking the children with her, she did leave. She went to Seattle at the end of the summer of 1955, and a year later she went to live with poet Robert Creeley in New Mexico. Rexroth threatened suicide, and, distraught, Marthe returned home. Certain changes resulted, and Rexroth and his second wife, Marie, were legally divorced in September 1955. With an award from the Amy Lowell Foundation, the Rexroth family spent 1958–1959 abroad in France, in Aix-en-Provence. Rexroth and Marthe hoped – in vain – that a change of scene might mend the deep rifts in their relationship.

Ironically, some of Rexroth's finest love poetry dates from this period. "Seven Poems for Marthe," which first appeared in the October 1956 issue of *Poetry,* and then *In Defense of the Earth,* both brim with an immediacy of heartfelt emotion and sexual yearning. Their lines for the most part sound deeply genuine because the emotion is described with precision and clarity and is related evocatively to the natural universe. In the poem "Quietly," Rexroth measures the pace of his and Marthe's lovemaking with the sure progression of a setting sun, the rhythms of their heartbeats absolving the daily traumas. In this and other poems of this time, he accomplished a harmony of thought and action that he seemed incapable of creating in the actual sphere of his intimate relationships. The writing remains hopeful and optimistic, although elegiac. After Marthe divorced him on the grounds of extreme cruelty in 1961, Rexroth scrambled the sequence of these poems for *The Collected Shorter Poems* (1966) and removed their original dedication to Marthe.

During the 1960s he remained a popular figure in San Francisco cultural life. He had a regular column in the *Examiner,* wrote book reviews and articles for national magazines and journals, gave readings at colleges and universities across the country, and taught a freewheeling course at San Francisco State. He also had a new companion and secretary in Carol Tinker, a young painter and poet who had moved to San Francisco in 1962 to observe the "renaissance" firsthand. (They married in 1974.) As before, Rexroth made his home available to young writers looking for advice and encourage-

Manuscript for Rexroth's "140 Syllables" (The Estate of Kenneth Rexroth, courtesy of the Lilly Library, Indiana University)

ment. Then, with a grant from the Rockefeller Foundation in 1965, Rexroth, Carol, and Mary (who had chosen to live with her father) traveled around the world. By 1968 San Francisco had palled for Rexroth, and he accepted a teaching post at the University of California, Santa Barbara.

Rexroth's poetry from this period is characterized by a dedicated shift toward the culture of the East. Although allusions to the landmarks and highlights of his life continued to enliven his work and his concern for social justice remained steady, Rexroth entered a new stage in which he felt less inclined to mourn lost causes and more interested in cultivating a vision that led to tangible results. Now Rexroth rarely used European settings or European myths. With the exception of a few fine poems in *New Poems* (1974), poems such as "The Family" and "Bei Wansee," the East dominated his creative impulses.

Rexroth's long poems are a kind of cardiogram of his arduous journey from Christian conviction through agnostic doubt toward a highly individualistic interpretation of Buddhist equanimity. In "The Heart's Garden, The Garden's Heart," he writes:

> What is the secret,
> The reward of the right contemplation?
> The revelation that it is all
> Gravel and moss and rock and clipped
> Shrubbery. That it doesn't
> Symbolize anything at all.

The search for enlightenment that informs *The Homestead Called Damascus* (1963), *The Phoenix and the Tortoise,* and particularly *The Dragon and the Unicorn* seems wedded to the imperatives of Western metaphysics. In "The Heart's Garden," the quest becomes a vision that makes abstract discourse superfluous. Here is a landscape where life is acted out not as a mere worldly occurrence, divorced from the inner life, but as a human experience in which the outward and the inward merge.

On another level, these are the thoughts of a man who feels himself approaching the end of his years. Emotional and psychological crises are now muted. He has even resolved to tame his obsession with visionary experience: "the desire for vision is / The sin of gluttony," he writes. Yet his love of nature is as intense as ever, and he is "still wandering / Through the wooded hills," and women in various forms – goddesses, prostitutes, dancing virgins – haunt the poems as though Rexroth could not forget his quest for romantic and erotic love. His ability to articulate a Buddhist perspective coincided with his recognition that his physical powers were waning, that his social and political commentary had limited influence, and that at sixty-three he could no longer easily accommodate the struggles, challenges, and contradictions that had once fired him. This perspective also informed the eight contemplative poems titled *On Flower Wreath Hill* (1976).

Rexroth continued to appear at various conferences – nasty and angry one moment, tenderly reading a poem the next. He made two more trips to Japan in 1972 and 1974 and continued his translations, producing, among other works, *One Hundred More Poems from the Japanese* (1974) and *The Burning Heart: Women Poets of Japan* (1977). During the last full decade of his life, he devoted an increasing amount of time and energy to translating the poems of Chinese and Japanese women poets. He had already won great respect for his translations of Chinese and Japanese poetry during the 1950s and 1960s; he had also written a significant essay in 1961 on the art of translating, titled "The Poet as Translator."

It could be argued that Rexroth decided at this time to focus on women poets because he wanted to ride the wave of the new feminist consciousness in the 1960s; more likely, he was trying to understand why his first three marriages had failed disastrously and why his relationship with his daughters had grown distant. Perhaps he thought that if he could enter the psyche of women poets, he would learn more about women than he had learned while living with them. Written by courtesans, Tao women priests, and contemporary Chinese women, the highly imagistic poems in *The Orchid Boat: Women Poets of China* (1972) are about heartbreak and sexual longing, the excitement of a secret tryst, the contentment of a lasting relationship. They can be witty and sexually explicit, as in the poetry of Huang O (1498–1519), but more often they express a yearning for the unity created by sexual passion, a recurrent theme in Rexroth's own poetry. In one series of poems, he goes so far as to adopt a female persona for himself, identifying the writer of the poems he was translating, poems actually his, as Marichiko, presumably a contemporary woman poet living near a Kyoto temple. By this mask Rexroth explored what he imagined to be one woman's psyche and attempted to come to terms with the way that he who had professed great love for women could at last acquire a rudimentary appreciation of woman's true nature.

In 1978 Rexroth received the $10,000 Copernicus Award, which recognizes the lifetime achievement of a poet older than forty-five years of age. This year was more than a watershed for Rexroth: it represented a new peak of achievement. His powers as a poet had been restored in Japan; his skills as a translator had become sharpened and refined. His poetic landscape widened, too, so that his own garden in Santa Barbara merged in his poetry with the landscape that so deeply touched him in Japan – the *Higashiyama,* the Eastern Hills. Poem "XVII" of *The Morning Star* (1979) clearly and beautifully suggests the spirit of a Buddhist setting:

> I go out
> In the wooded garden
> And walk, nude, except for my
> Sandals, through light and dark banded
> Like a field of sleeping tigers.
> Our raccoons watch me from the
> Walnut tree, the opossums
> Glide out of sight under the
> Woodpile. My dog Ch'ing is asleep.

Later in the poem, the long-dead princess whose burial mound was close to the farmhouse where Rexroth lived in Kyoto appears as an agent, both erotic and spiritual, who helps the poet transcend the limitations of mundane life without losing the joy the natural world provides. Her body enters his, his "self vanishes," and he achieves "another kind of knowing / Of an all encompassing / Love" where time, space, "grasping and consequence" do not exist. Yet immediately after his revelation, the poet becomes gloriously conscious of the brilliance of the morning sun that has just risen. His erotic pleasures have become etherealized, but he expresses his spiritual ecstasy with sense-ridden images of nature.

Rexroth died 6 June 1982. He remains one of *the* radical poets in the United States, with his productive career spanning six decades of the twentieth century. This extraordinary man lived a life that was full of the stuff of his poems, not always with wisdom and grace when it came to his private affairs, but always with a tremendous historical and political consciousness. Although he was not a people's poet, his deep sympathy for the oppressed of all races was genuine. He was a deeply contemplative man who immersed himself in both Western and Eastern philosophy and theology in his intense search for spiritual fulfillment. But he was also very much a man of the world, who took great delight in the beauty and harmony of the natural world, his love for his wives and daughters, and the plastic arts. He resolved the great conflicts of his life by making the writing of poetry his vocation. He provided a model for what a twentieth-century bard

could be – an imperfect but dedicated artist, eager to serve as model and mentor, a poet who wanted to move into interpersonal communication. Ultimately his goal was to create acts of imaginative identification between the poet and the men and women who lived nearby and afar. Rexroth never stopped believing that poets were indispensable to the rediscovery of a world community and a common literary sensibility.

Letters:

Kenneth Rexroth and James Laughlin: Selected Letters, edited by Lee Bartlett (New York & London: Norton, 1991).

Interviews:

Cyrena Pondrum, "Interview with Kenneth Rexroth," *Contemporary Literature,* 10 (Summer 1969): 313–331;

David Meltzer, "Kenneth Rexroth," in *Golden Gate: Interviews with 5 San Francisco Poets* (Berkeley, Cal.: Wingbow Press, 1976): 19–65;

James J. McKenzie and Robert W. Lewis, "That Rexroth – He'll Argue You into Anything," *North Dakota Quarterly,* 44 (Summer 1976): 7–33;

Paul Portuges and Paul Vangelisti, "Kenneth Rexroth," *Invisible City,* nos. 21–22 (November 1977): 25–29;

Bradford Morrow, "An Interview with Kenneth Rexroth," *Conjunctions,* 1 (Winter 1981–1982): 48–67;

Linda Hamalian, "On Rexroth: An Interview with William Everson," *Literary Review,* 26 (Spring 1983): 423–426;

Hamalian, "Robert Duncan on Kenneth Rexroth," *Conjunctions,* 4 (1983): 85–95;

John Tritica, "Regarding Rexroth: Interviews with Thomas Parkinson and William Everson," *American Poetry,* 7 (Fall 1989): 71–87.

Bibliographies:

James Hartzell and Richard Zumwinkle, *Kenneth Rexroth: A Checklist of His Published Writings* (Los Angeles: Friends of the University of California at Los Angeles Library, 1967);

Bradford Morrow, "An Outline of Unpublished Rexroth Manuscripts, with an introductory note to three chapters from the sequel to *An Autobiographical Novel,*" *Sagetrieb,* 2 (Winter 1983): 135–144.

Biography:
Linda Hamalian, *A Life of Kenneth Rexroth* (New York & London: Norton, 1991).

References:
Daniel Aaron, *Writers on the Left* (New York: Harcourt, Brace & World, 1961);

Lee Bartlett, *Kenneth Rexroth* (Boise, Idaho: Boise State University, 1988);

Bartlett, *The Sun Is But a Morning Star: Studies in West Coast Poetry and Poetics* (Albuquerque: University of New Mexico Press, 1989);

Walter Cummins, ed., *The Literary Review* (San Francisco Renaissance Issue), 32 (Fall 1988);

Michael Davidson, *The San Francisco Renaissance: Poetics and Community at Mid-Century* (Cambridge: Cambridge University Press, 1989);

William Everson, *Archetype West: The Pacific Coast as a Literary Region* (Berkeley, Cal.: Oyez, 1976);

Richard Foster, "The Voice of the Poet: Kenneth Rexroth," *Minnesota Review,* 2 (Spring 1962): 377–384;

Geoffrey Gardner, ed., *The Ark: For Rexroth 14* (New York: The Ark, 1980);

Morgan Gibson, *Kenneth Rexroth* (New York: Twayne, 1972);

Gibson, *Revolutionary Rexroth: Poet of East–West Widsom* (Hamden, Conn.: Archon, 1986);

Elsa Gidlow, *I Come with My Songs* (San Francisco: Booklegger Press, 1986);

Richard Gray, *American Poetry of the Twentieth Century* (New York: Longman, 1990), pp. 168–172;

Donald Gutierrez, "Kenneth Rexroth: *The Signature of All Things,*" *American Poetry,* 7 (Fall 1989): 31–37;

Gutierrez, "Kenneth Rexroth: A Tissue of Contradictions," *Literary Review,* 37 (Fall 1993): 134–138;

Gutierrez, "Natural Supernaturalism: The Nature Poetry of Kenneth Rexroth," *The Literary Review,* 26 (Spring 1983): 405–422;

Leo Hamalian, "Scanning the Self: The Influence of Emerson on Kenneth Rexroth," *South Dakota Review,* 27 (Summer 1989): 3–14;

Linda Hamalian, "Early Versions of *The Homestead Called Damascus,*" *North Dakota Quarterly,* 56 (Winter 1988): 131–147;

Sam Hamill, "The Poetry of Kenneth Rexroth," in *A Poet's Work* (Seattle: Broken Moon Press, 1990), pp. 149–161;

Robert Hass, "Some Notes on the San Francisco Bay Area As a Culture Region: A Memoir," in *Twentieth Century Pleasures: Prose on Poetry* (New York: Ecco Press, 1984);

Ken Knabb, *The Relevance of Rexroth* (Berkeley, Cal.: Bureau of Public Secrets, 1990);

Sanehide Kodama, *American Poetry and Japanese Culture* (Hamden, Conn.: Archon, 1984);

Lawrence Lipton, *The Holy Barbarians* (New York: Messner, 1959);

Lipton, "Notes Towards an Understanding of Kenneth Rexroth," *Quarterly Review of Literature,* 9 (1957), 37–46;

Thomas Parkinson, *Poets, Poems, Movements* (Ann Arbor: University of Michigan Research Press, 1987);

Janet Richards, *Common Soldiers* (San Francisco: Archer Press, 1979);

Sagetrieb, special issue on Rexroth, edited by Burton Hatlen, 2 (Winter 1983);

Larry Smith, "The Poetry-and-Jazz Movement in the United States," *Itinerary,* 7 (Fall 1977): 89–104;

Third Rail, special issue on Rexroth, edited by Doren Robbins, 8 (1987).

Papers:

The major repositories for Kenneth Rexroth's papers are the Department of Special Collections, University Research Library, UCLA, and Special Collections, University Library, University of Southern California. Additional materials are located in the Poetry/Rare Books Collection, University Libraries of the University of Buffalo; Harry Ransom Humanities Research Center, University of Texas at Austin; Special Collections, Washington University Libraries, St. Louis; Special Collections, Morris Library, Southern Illinois University at Carbondale; Ryerson and Burnham Libraries, The Art Institute of Chicago; and Special Collections, University of Wyoming.

Stephen Sandy

(2 August 1934 –   )

Phoebe Pettingell

BOOKS: *Caroms* (Groton, Mass.: Groton School
    Press, 1960);
Mary Baldwin (Cambridge, Mass.: Dolmen Press,
    1962);
The Destruction of Bulfinch's House (Cambridge, Mass.:
    Identity Press, 1963);
The Norway Spruce (Milford, N.H.: Ferguson Press,
    1964);
Wild Ducks (Milford, N.H.: Ferguson Press, 1965);
Stresses in the Peaceable Kingdom (Boston: Houghton
    Mifflin, 1967);
Roofs (Boston: Houghton Mifflin, 1971);
The Austin Tower (San Francisco: Empty Elevator
    Shaft, 1975);
The Difficulty (Providence, R.I.: Burning Deck,
    1975);
End of the Picaro (Pawlet, Vt.: Banyan Press, 1977);
The Hawthorne Effect (Lawrence, Kans.: Tansy Press,
    1980);
*The Raveling of the Novel; Studies in Romantic Fiction
    from Walpole to Scott* (New York: Arno Press,
    1980);
After the Hunt (Brattleboro, Vt.: Moonsquilt Press,
    1982);
Flight of Steps (Binghamton, N.Y.: Bellevue Press,
    1982);
Riding to Greylock (New York: Knopf, 1983);
To A Mantis (North Hoosick, N.Y.: Plinth Press,
    1987);
Man in the Open Air (New York: Knopf, 1988);
The Epoch (North Bennington, Vt.: Plinth Press,
    1990);
Thanksgiving Over the Water (New York: Knopf,
    1992);
Vale of Academe (Spartanburg, S.C.: Holocene,
    1996).

TRANSLATION: Lucius Annaeus Seneca, *A Cloak
    for Hercules,* verse translation of Seneca's

Stephen Sandy (courtesy of the author)

Hercules Oetaeus in *The Complete Roman Drama in
Translation,* volume 2 (Baltimore: Johns Hopkins University Press, 1994).

Stephen Sandy's importance in contemporary
poetry rests on his ability to wed an always engaging and controlled prosody to luminous insights
about the environment and the nature of experience. Disparities such as those between what happens to an individual and the way the experience af-

229

fects his feeling, or between the incompatible ideals of Western and oriental culture, are the kinds of subjects Sandy explores in his work. In "Letter from Stony Creek," from *Man in the Open Air* (1988), he expresses his conviction that

> Experience itself is a cul de sac.
> Depths in the rock beckon. Lichens peel, and you
> See in. The light on the water trembles, rises.

Characteristically, Sandy's poems investigate what he calls in the title poem of *Thanksgiving Over the Water* (1992) "ordinary experiences on a higher plane." Despite the delicacy of his insights and his intriguingly subtle perspectives, his work has not yet attracted widespread critical attention. Commenting on the manuscript of *Man in the Open Air,* James Merrill remarked that the qualities of Sandy's verse are "easy to overlook, but (once taken in) hard to forget." Indeed, over the years Sandy has won high praise from fellow poets such as Amy Clampitt, Richard Eberhart, Robert Creeley, Peter Davison, Dave Smith, and Alfred Corn.

Sandy was born in Minneapolis, Minnesota, on 2 August 1934, the child of Alan Francis and Evelyn Merrill (Martin) Sandy. Several poems allude to his midwestern childhood. His undergraduate work was done at Yale University. In 1955, the year he received his B.A., he was drafted into the army. At the conclusion of his tour of duty in 1957, Sandy began graduate studies at Harvard, both in classics and in English literature. He finished his M.A. in 1959 and his Ph.D. in 1963, then stayed at Harvard until 1967 as an instructor of English. His first major collection, *Stresses in the Peaceable Kingdom,* was published in 1967, on the eve of his leaving for Japan. The academic year of 1967–1968 was spent as a visiting professor of American literature at the University of Tokyo (Tokyo Daigaku) and visiting professor of English at the Tokyo University of Foreign Studies. His experiences in Japan profoundly affected his poetry, particularly at this time. Upon his return to the United States, he taught for a year at Brown University, where he was the university's 1969 Phi Beta Kappa poet. In that same year he married Virginia Scoville. The next fall the couple moved to Vermont, where Sandy had been hired by Bennington College to replace poet Howard Nemerov in the school's department of languages and literature. Except for brief sabbaticals, he has remained since that time at Bennington, where the small community of town and college suits his intensely private nature. He has been a leading proponent and exemplar of Bennington's progressive tradition of having import-

ant creative writers teach in their own genre. A dedicated instructor, he has inspired his students with some of his own intense dedication to poetry. A shrewd, perceptive critic of the writing of others, he firmly points out weaknesses but can be generous when the work merits praise. When he reads his own poems in class or at public performances, his manner is incantatory, his voice and body emphasizing the rhythm and cadences of the lines.

In retrospect, *Stresses in the Peaceable Kingdom* appears to be mainly an apprentice work, but at its appearance in 1967 it seemed a tour de force. Its reception was shaped in part by the book's two principal influences. W. H. Auden was the tyro's mentor for prosody, and the English master had an apt pupil. The word *stresses* in the title is, in fact, an Audenesque pun, suggesting both the anxiety that attends difficult situations and the metrical system that predated poetic feet and rhyme. Although he began his writing and teaching career just at the time when the modernist movement was ebbing, his poetry demonstrates certain affinities for the modernist ideals. At heart he is a formalist, and his intoxication with cadences and lyric arpeggios is often apparent:

> A real dodo in a green-
> house of smilax and excelsior, a sort of proto-
> gewgaw, if you please, it was so dada
> in that museum of small cheers.

In this playful remark in "The Woolworth Philodendron," the poet juggles vowel sounds like crystal balls spinning and refracting in the air. Sandy absorbed Auden's virtuosity more than his style or tone; nevertheless, this volume contains several effective pieces written in the master's voice.

Sandy's classical background formed the second important influence on his work. A title such as "Et Quid Amabo Nisi Quod Aenigma Est" or an epigram from the Greek might have seemed no more than fashion in the late 1960s; the giveaway is the poet's tendency to experiment with quantitative meter and his close attention to syllabic values—traits that help burnish his well-crafted stanzas. Indeed, from time to time, classical themes appear, as in the poem "Catullus and Clodia":

> Buds. Recurring splinters from
> the straight grain. Each line,
> stem from the frayed end of passion.
>
> Her carelessness a shaft that ground
> down splintering into flesh. Unspoken wounds.
> But they worked back, for him, to his surface,

each wound the first, each difficult
in the way that every autumn is the first
and unremembered in the grain when sharp buds vault
toward sun

probing their speechless twig.

By combining some of the Latin imagery with his own and taking Catullus's ardor for the fickle Clodia as an example of the interrelationship between erotics and inspiration, Sandy builds a subtle poem that wears its considerable learning lightly.

Another piece in this collection makes use of the poet's childhood in the upper Midwest. "Hiawatha," a poem Barry Spacks lauded in *Poetry* for its significant, complex theme and "solidly muscular" language, considers the mystique of the Indian in modern American culture. Sandy begins with an examination of the contents of a museum case at Harvard that contains ceremonial Native American artifacts. "Pale / *lares* and *penates* of tribes gone / to our reward. The painted bits call up / my bringing up in Minneapolis / (*city of water,* Ojibway & Greek), / haunt of Hiawatha / and his Minnehaha, whose stream once fell / dark past our home to its thundering fall." From memories of playing braves with his brother, he moves to consider the way in which white settlers felt it was their right to appropriate not only the land but also the symbolic attributes of the people they displaced. Henry Wadsworth Longfellow's poem made Hiawatha "the sign of a profitable / treaty with wildness; of something / within, beyond us, too essential / ever to be entertained in life." Meanwhile, Hiawatha's modern descendant and "tubercular, alcoholic," worked as a hunting and fishing guide for the white settlers' descendants and "drank whiskey round the fire with the men, / who chipped in twenty for the tip." By robbing Native Americans of their environment, "the essential / stream of our youth," Sandy concludes, later Americans dispossessed themselves of their innocence, "a truth, a childhood of us gone." This poem operates on multiple levels, combining literary and cultural commentary. Although its stage machinery may be too visible at times, it forecasts the intricate, contemplative verses that later became Sandy's hallmark, and it certainly justified William Alfred's appraisal on the dust jacket of *Stresses in the Peaceable Kingdom,* where he calls the book "truthfully sensitive and strongly compassionate."

Sandy also has a gift for conveying sensuous particulars. His retentive eye might be called "painterly," were it not so animated. In the poem "The Grasshopper" he describes the tiny subject:

Huddled, crouched there on the cement
it looked as if the highway hurt
    him, the braided brown
    left leg one half inch
farther left than the right was right.
Each vault the grasshopper took ahead he took
two left – or right – or backward. All
his progress seemed to lack a goal.
    Did he fear cars–
humped there like a crunched horse chestnut?

"Thanksgiving in the Country" begins with a twilight in which "Clouds swim into themselves: / one cloud." In "Two Dimensional" the poet tells how a rather whimsical personification of the sun edged around a window shade, "flopped in and splashed orange, / a shape with movement, but no sound." Many of these poems provide a stage for similar minidramas.

This technical strength turns out to be a liability as well, when some of the tricks are too obviously secondhand. The wraiths of Wallace Stevens and Marianne Moore glimmer across the backdrops of certain poems. Closer to the foreground, Anne Sexton swishes her witch's cape in a sequence of rather menacing dreamscapes. Attitudes that remind one of Robert Lowell appear. Auden's hand lies heavy on "The Ballad of Mary Baldwin" (although its author had the wit to eschew the common meter the English poet employed in "Victor" and "Miss Gee"). Occasionally Sandy produces a deliberate parody. "Can" is a kind of homage to the masterful Romantic light versifier Thomas Hood.

One important specter actually bolsters the effectiveness of "The Circular in the Post Office." This narrative records futile attempts to discover the identity of a murdered child. In the familiar conversational singsong of Robert Frost's *North of Boston* (1914) or *Steeple Bush* (1947) Sandy considers the way

The state's police declare
his height, his weight, the color of
    blue eyes, blond hair.

But all the authorities
who can't detect his killer, or what
    his name might be,

admit they cannot say
who thrust him into the world, or who
    forced him away.

Frost's capacity to raise moral implications in the course of what seems a simple report stands

```
late worksheet, Alleghany Front
```

Out of the dark from a field over the valley a cow calls.
From the quiet, the hoarse lowing crumbles from her throat
And fades. Silence again; each barn and star holds still.
Perhaps that voice the Alleghany hills echoed
Told of some dairy matter; or did it, late on the Sabbath
As the midnight was drawing near, declare a purge from the simple
Darkness of the traditions of men, the passing away
Of laws that had come to pass? He sensed the 1880

Human town devout, how near each felt: to self,
To the night, to God, each channel with no interference
From printed circuits, nor from the unborn tube not yet
Giving the eye to everyone, nonbiodegradable
Imagery. In the glass negatives from the house on Main
That Christopher printed, half the town--and two cows--pose,
The set jaws sweet. Those clumsy Chaucerian Baptists loved
Their fun but haven't much; each gent his own Chanticleer.

But justification burgeons like sheaves gathered in the rich
September of their fields, enough to make homes rosy
Through bellowing winters from Canada. The girls from scrubbing
Have changed, come, sat, stifling giggles; hands palm down
On taffeta skirts as if wiping, or spreading patterns;
The shopowner's coat, an upholstered tent, hangs off his body;
Mothers in pleats and urchings of jet and blue cohere
In the chevrons of their blood. With no rouge or powder, faces

Draft for a poem Sandy included in his 1988 collection (courtesy of the author)

his admirer in good stead both here and in later verses.

A few poems in *Stresses in the Peaceable Kingdom* break into the mature voice to which readers of later volumes have become accustomed. The outstanding example is "A Tree In My Memory," which could indeed blend into Sandy's latest collection. It describes the poet's discovery of a shagbark hickory. Dazed by literary allusions to this tree and its fruit, he looks forward to an October windfall. Alas, he writes:

> someone, who took no chances with weathers
> or other harvesters,
> had stripped each nut, picked up the drops, and stored
> his crop for winter. He
> was in the habit: I was not — and found
> my nature with a book.

This conclusion cannot be patronized as "a promising debut." It represents full-fledged achievement of a high order.

In *Roofs* (1971) the young poet apparently lost faith in the pyrotechnics and exuberance of forms that decked out his earlier work. The manner and subject of the poems in this second collection are affected by the period Sandy spent teaching in Japan. Most strive for an oriental simplicity. Some verses snake down the page like a single flower stem standing in a tall vase. Vernon Young described them in the *Hudson Review* as "distilled to a purity of form which itself celebrates the Japanese graphic art — ordered chaos in a bamboo room." While none actually breaks into haiku, a few seem about to do so. Yet some of these poems might disappoint other readers. Often Sandy's distinctive voice fades out amid so much Japonaiserie. Certain pieces confirm the earlier promise. "Peephole" exploits with a fine comic flair the poet's gift for making the most of odd visual images:

> Holding my breath
> to see who this may be out in the hall
> just sauntering to and fro
> I wonder if this body came for me
> appearing at first a giant
> then a pea
> in the lens that embraces and distorts him so.
> Holding my breath to see who this may be. . . .

At certain moments Sandy's new, stripped-down style yields pithy lines. "Screen for a Radical Friend" describes how "stones / even after generations / well up to snag the plow / almanacs tell us / it is the stars pull up the rocks / skyward by night / even as moons suck / at the heavy heart of the sea."

But W. S. Merwin generally does this kind of thing better. One misses not only Sandy's expansive rhetoric but also his generous vision. Only "Shore" manages to achieve a complete synthesis of the new style with this poet's most authentic voice as it evokes the way

> gulls strain
> on the sea-groin,
> adze trawling their cries between stars
> and white foam.

> Their lone song
> does, does belong
> on this delta of the dark world.
> All, they ring

> out, they roam
> pluming the stream
> of wind, dervish of storm, shriven
> of sensed doom.

One remarkable poem, "From the Fastest Train," actually seems closer to the dash and spirit of the earlier book. Reliving a journey from Kyoto to Tokyo, Sandy revels in the sun-drenched countryside that confers a sense of "seamless / identity, time with space, imagine / heaven that state / of final assurance locked in a trance of light like this / lone farmer carrying sticks of fuel / down snow drift toward his gate." The diction and short lines, with their images piling one on top of the next as they flash past, suggest the rapidity of the high-speed train as the moving panorama transforms into a kaleidoscope of fleeting impressions.

Not content to rest on laurels garnered for *Stresses in the Peaceable Kingdom*, Sandy continued his explorations in forms, and *Roofs* was undoubtedly a necessary experiment. In a poetic milieu increasingly dominated by the voices of poets such as Merwin, the Robert Lowell of *Notebook* (1969), and Sylvia Plath, modernist techniques could easily become stale. Besides, like most writers at the outset of their careers, Sandy needed to shake certain overbearing influences in his language. Harold Bloom praised the "grave, brooding, highly individualized style of *Roofs,* and the way it relates" the sensibility of the current era to "the larger contents of history and widely variant imaginative traditions." As it turned out, however, Sandy's Japanese phase did not prognosticate the future direction of his poetry. Indeed, no publisher was willing to bring out another collection by him for the next twelve years. This fact probably indicated more about the state of publishing at the time than it did about the quality of the poems

Sandy was composing, because much of this verse ultimately appeared in his third volume and was favorably reviewed. Reading the chapbooks Sandy brought out during those unpublished years provides an insight into the way he worked to discover his own voice. The journey began with poetic lines so minimal as to seem anorectic, but ultimately his language regained a rich, musical polyphony of meaning and sound.

During this period he also revised and published his Harvard Ph.D. thesis as *The Raveling of the Novel; Studies in Romantic Fiction from Walpole to Scott* (1980), believing, as he said, that it would be prudent to have a scholarly book in his résumé in case his teaching position at Bennington College should end. As with many student writings, the style of this treatise seems a bit pallid; nonetheless, the relation between its intelligent, carefully reasoned argument and the course its author was pursuing in his own poems is apparent. Sandy envisions the gothic novel as an attempt to freshen a genre that had bogged down by the early nineteenth century into formulaic drawing-room comedies. Luxuriant descriptions of scenery, which form a prominent feature of gothic stories, together with their episodic character, helped build a bridge to a new kind of fiction, one that combined the social commentary common to eighteenth-century plots with the psychological insights of Romanticism. In a kind of parallel journey, Sandy began combining the kind of revealing images he had perfected in *Roofs* with more resonant levels of feeling; at the same time, he began to recapture the rhetorical playfulness that characterized *Stresses in the Peaceable Kingdom,* while discarding the volume's imitative tendencies.

In *Riding to Greylock* (1983) Sandy's mature style has fully emerged. Even those familiar with the chapbooks from the interim period were unprepared for the full force of this new, stronger, and more distinctive voice. "End of the Picaro," which begins this collection, seems distinctly influenced by the author's work in *The Raveling of the Novel*. Indeed, the picaresque and the gothic are closely related in this collection. In the former, structure is dictated solely by the adventures and exploits of a rogue. Sandy limns the relationship between the writer at his desk and the rascal hero who is his creator's "youth / Stymied at the stricken plot of the world." Sooner or later, the two must merge, as the fictional character "effaces himself and doubles back / And homeward, down tangled banks, to your first need." This poem – one of the most striking fruits from Sandy's chapbooks during the un-

published years – illustrates the poet's fascination with loss of innocence and the way nostalgia influences a writer's bond with his creation. "End of the Picaro" burgeons with lush evocations of landscape and flora, bringing to mind Sandy's observation about gothic romance, where, he argues, "nature is so active and effective, landscape assumes agency, and nature's busy elements take the role of an actor. Hence . . . it does not seem unreasonable to compare a description with an episode." Similarly, descriptions in his poems frequently transmogrify into actions.

As always, Sandy's pictorial eye is in evidence, but now it complements an ear attuned to the nuances of sound and rhythm (in the earlier work, the visual and aural elements did not always work well together). In "At Peak's Island," one of several seascapes in the new book,

> someone had left
> Beside a patch of lichen and a square of moss
> A box of Binney & Smith Crayola crayons, *carnation*
> *Pink, sea green, periwinkle, burnt sienna*
> Half a *maize,* a stub of *sky*
> *Blue.* They looked
> Ready to use again
> After a musing child had colored in a lichen
> Or dotted the nightshade with purple dots;
> The box of colors seemed to lie there ready
> To turn a pebble red or blue, to heighten a petal;
> but not
>
> To spray "Lucy Grillo Loves George Rockwood"
> In dumb letters on the face of the concrete
> Bunker down the shore, this dated rockery
> For men to spot the Nazi U-boats from.

This passage illustrates Sandy's familiar whimsy. Readers owning the sixty-four-crayon set specified in the text may reproduce what the poet sees: a shimmering spectrum blending hues of ocean, sky, and beach, "Those minimal, burning edges / Of magnitude." He really does possess an artist's eye, and rolls his tongue appreciatively over the seductive list of color names. Such enchantment becomes the poem's true subject.

Many of these works achieve their effects by evoking the qualities of their sensuous particulars. In the poem "When April," that month's proverbial showers are compared to "blown Venetian glass / beads of rain," in whose reflection

> already the purple
> or golden para-
> chutes of crocus droop.
>
> The pinstripe lavenders

and saffron soaked through,
limp.

Texture appears palpable. "A cat no one can see is sleeping in the blue / Corduroy of weeds" in "Cyanotype." "End of the Picaro" describes a woodland trail that "fails in breaks where kudzu / Wild grape and raspberry lashes rope and knot." The poet's still lifes can be as delicate as an impressionist landscape, or, in the following stanza from "Flight of Steps," as bleak as an Edward Hopper painting:

> For aftermath, the catatonic apartment.
>   In the roominghouse yard a scrap of snow in mud.
> A big arm hanging out of a window, or one
>   Dirty big toe, cold at the mouth of a broken
> Shoe. Budweiser cans, three grapefruit skulls under the
>   Window of the girl painter.

The center section of *Riding to Greylock* pivots around the birth of Sandy's daughter, Clare, in 1976. "Nativity" is spoken by the poet in the delivery room. He tells his wife of "the dazzled retina, then the Persian blue / sky I saw that shone above your head," presumably in the circular mirror over the hospital's accouchement couch. "Stars and planets gleamed, spun / in one / boreal candelabrum, / shone out far from the saddle and the sheet / lighting a way, this exile from / ourselves, this passing through." The distorted reflection of the infant's emerging head in the convex surface provides this fractured perspective. It is also the kind of fragmented vision one experiences in states of euphoria or shock — joy at the new arrival, coupled with the sudden realization that this new person will be a separate being. "With distance doubled by the brilliant shield / we watched it yield / no stone, no harm, but suffered bliss. / Hard looking has afforded this." The dimension of fatherhood inspires a subtle change in Sandy's poetic sensibility, broadening his concern for the life of the world around him and introducing a connectedness and sense of engagement where once he inclined to detachment.

The title poem employs the grim Mount Greylock, hulking "like a beached whale / flooded by air" as a backdrop for the poet's intimations of mortality. During a tedious bus trip, he tries to read a nature book for children — the kind that anthropomorphizes small animal behavior by attributing to it motives akin to human citizenship. However, he cannot stop fretting about the keys he just dropped, then could not find again: "Are mice unreconciled as us to losing things in the snow?" Gradually, a more disturbing recollection intrudes. Back at the bus station, he saw an old woman collapse in the throes of a fatal heart attack. Now, gazing through the windows at New England's uncompromising winter landscape, he abandons childish pathetic fallacies about rodents and considers whether humans are able to face the inevitable in the matter-of-fact way other creatures can:

> Maybe the lady chose
> it this way, ready to shed
> Her frilly skin; to lie back,
> savaged. The willingness
> of an animal to be dead
> when it must; a flower's.

The bus is carrying the poet toward the destination where he must still hunt for his keys, when a red fox runs across a white field — a manifestation of a further wild epiphany of nature. As the poet observes in "Declension," which immediately precedes "Riding to Greylock," "In the chorus of memories a blessing in disguise."

Riding to Greylock draws much of its imagery and subject matter from the scenery around southwestern Vermont, western Massachusetts, and upper New York State — evidence of Sandy's years of involvement with the Bennington community. Such efforts as "Waiting for the Warden" (after a doe is hit by a passing car), "Air for Air," "Balance," and many others evoke the ground-down mountains of the Berkshires, a country of valleys that look up toward a rockbound skyline. Poems that depart from this milieu, such as "The Austin Tower" (a monologue unconvincingly spoken in the voice of the Texas tower sniper) generally work less well. Sandy reaches his lyrical heights in passages such as this conclusion to "Flight of Steps":

> Through fur-twigged sumac
> One jay rules. Jay, jay, brainy
> Bird, you hammer out
> Your protocols unheard. One
> Jag of blue against
> Greens; loud at strewn umbers, at
> Rifle green, greens deeper still!

These incantatory repetitions of the bluejay's name, which it cries out so insistently in northern forests (establishing the "protocols" of its territorial boundaries, according to some theories) also can suggest Emily Dickinson's "Bird / Who sings the same unheard / As unto crowd." Her trope for the poet has been appropriated by Sandy as a poignant reminder of those years when he could not get a book published but continued to compose. Taut, musical rhetoric in this collection owes much to that hidden period. The volume concludes with a vale-

draft / 'Fort Burial'

Bennington College

To   Date

From

Long mole, plump prodigal,
~~A long, plump, handsome mole~~ with pelt
of (glossy) midnight fur like velvet
In a Holbein portrait, ~~and~~ clenched cruel feet
With ~~Meissen~~ Meissen claws

Minute
~~Tiny~~, white, and fragile; yet
Ferocious in the power I ~~could~~ felt
They barely now had given up,
    This ~~animal~~ — time — worker lump — gds —
        moorless life   sendon
                                          digger
Both very soft and ~~somehow~~ scrappy cruel.
My son considered ~~the/mole~~ it meant on its bier,
With modest fingers stroked the fur
    Sweet to him now

As ~~one of the~~ stuffed, toy animals ~~toys~~ on his bed.
~~On his pillow. But~~ ~~it~~ its scurry now was slack
~~was stuck it~~ tight knit frame
That silken economy in black
    Meant business only.

I fetched the spade; we buried it
In a corner of the field, nearby
The bower my boy had named ~~its~~ Fort.
    He found a crate slat

                            on the pine
To mark the grave: with a nail ~~he scribbed~~
He scribed A legend: ~~with fire~~; " In this hole
Lies my mole." Verily, he
            Inscribed the grave!

He scored the words in deep & laughed.
In less than ½ a twilight hour
He took the strange mole to himself,
    and random death.

Draft for a poem describing a father who helps his son bury a mole (courtesy of the author)

236

diction to the Sandys' onetime home at Eagle Bridge. In the poem, now that their second child, Nathaniel, has been born (in 1980), they are moving back to the Bennington College campus. Though somewhat sorry to leave a beloved house, the poet is hopeful:

> Whatever we leave, the blue plate of this time
> Is wiped clean. After night, the tunnel of a day.

Despite this strong collection, hailed as "the renaissance of a fascinating poet" by *The New Leader,* Sandy did not receive many reviews – a fate that has generally befallen his books. The reviews that have appeared tend to be highly favorable.

Man in the Open Air blossoms into a strong transcendental perspective, hinted at in certain earlier poems but not a dominant feature until this book. Sandy's descriptive brilliance remains, often embellished with zaftig metaphors. An onion gone to seed in "Egyptian Onions" is called "a little temple / Sprouting the ruin of itself," as if the dome of a mosque or Oriental shrine had shot up into a chive plant's lavender pompon. In the piece "Spider," the poet notices that the arthropod's legs form "small girders, arching" like those of bridges or the buttressed ceilings of Gothic cathedrals.

These architectural tropes are more than decorative trimmings – they create a framework to uphold poems that celebrate the delights of artistic intuition. In the title poem a man anthropomorphizes the natural objects damaged by the thunderstorm that has wrecked havoc on the landscape:

> To Bingham Hill's unposted corners
> The stripping westerlies reveal
> Ebony wristbones of the apple,
> The schist ribcage of an elm.
> Creases of unmaking in a face.

Throughout *Man in the Open Air,* disintegration's skeletal presence propels the poet toward his most lyric moments, as if there were something liberating in the tearing down to basic elements. The death of Sandy's parents provides the catalyst; suddenly it seems that old certainties are melting away into newborn insights, fresh resurrections. In a moving sequence he probes the grief and shock when the death of a family member forces him to face his own mortality. "Station 41" describes the poet's deplaning in Minneapolis as he travels to his father's hospital bed. While waiting to retrieve his luggage at the airport, Sandy feels "shaken to see, when bags of mine / Crash down the chute, how time the foreman picks / And chooses from the line / Of travelers in Minnesota at the Styx." "Last Days at York Manor" jumps back in time to report a revealing conversation about poetry he had with his father when both were trying to take their minds off his mother's last illness. The older man argued that rhyme is merely sound, but circumstances inspired Sandy to realize that prosody is actually an artistic way to mirror the repetitions of one's existence. At his father's deathbed, in "Station 41," he must not only wrestle with parting but also come to terms with the needs of the survivor and the artist:

> How I came slowly to his going then!
> I heard the nurse long-distance telling me
> The mottling and the cyanosis had begun.
> I would not comprehend the urgency,
> He was so strong, headstrong; strongest of men,
> He'd stay among his three at least till one
> At bedside, daughter or son,
> Hugged him to speech, to bless
> From his high wilderness
> His child; but toiled then, now with joke, now rage.
> At last it was mine to be next; to disengage
> And sing, as the tenor, called to his loveliest
> Work, brightens the stage
> Alone and sings, by the dark hall possessed.

Ralph Waldo Emerson spoke of becoming a "transparent eyeball" and focusing on the truth of nature, a truth unblurred by inner confusion. Sandy achieves something of this clarity and truth here with his "hard looking."

Other valedictory poems abound: "Command Performance," a respectful elegy for Robert Lowell; another for the critic I. A. Richards; "Rural Affairs," for a Bennington colleague; and so forth. Yet none evokes absence so poignantly as "The White Oak of Eagle Bridge," in which, after a storm has knocked over a favorite tree, the poet cries out, "I walked, I walked / in tears, as if a friend had died." The influence of Frost, visible as imitation in *Roofs,* now is fully absorbed, a part of Sandy's natural voice, as is evident in this evocation of an abandoned field growing over:

>   I watched
> the field go white with daisies, yellow with buttercups;
> lavender off to the left, chicory mixing with purple
> clover; mallow, splotches of vetch; and soon the popple
> saplings, blinking with light: no good for haying now,
> or not until someone plowed, if someone wanted to.

The sublime "Allegheny Front" invokes American self-reliance and freshness of vision in the face

I watch the pod musroom. Coleridge, despairing
Because he'd blown it with his ~~oldest~~ friend; had ~~dropped~~ turned
~~From~~ ~~Dropped~~ Sara; ill
And numb with opium, en route to the Siberia
Of tacky Malta, found comfort, found what he ~~wanted~~   hoped
To find in St Michael Cave; in the depths the same
Chambers, pillars, the same chasm he had pictured   the
      ~~Writing~~ Osorio.

It was all to his liking, despite the lofty wells;
And I grew chummy with the sudden swelling,
      ~~What's happened unfolding~~
To Hello, there, sensing whatever it was

      What's happened hare
Unfolding to hellow, there, sesning whatever
It was was me now; acceptance; the familiar;
A sad, shy reflexive welcome to this
Unpremediàated addition to my
      Anatomy.

~~Unaccounted for addition to my~~
This unaccounted for addition to
      My anatomy

to find in the depths of

to find in the deep recess of St Micahel

to find in the deep recess of St Michel's cave the same

Chambers, the pillars, the same chasm he'd ~~imagined~~
      Imagined writing

Osorio. It was thus to his liking, the lofty wells.

Found terror the found what he hoped

was frightened till he found what he8d hoped

Of tacky Malta, found

Of tacky Malta, was terrified, then found what he

Of tacky Malta, found teror, then found what
he'd hoped to find, in St Michael's cave, the same
chambers, the pillars, the same chasm he'd
      Imagined writing

Osorio. It was thus to his liking, those lofty wells.

Draft for a section of "The Tack," which Sandy included in his 1992 book (courtesy of the author)

of received wisdom. Coming out of the tradition of the American Transcendentalists, the poem may well remind some of Henry David Thoreau or Emerson. Here, the speaker wanders into a rural church service in a building that resembles "a barn with Greek trim nailed to the front, hulks, / A canal barge beached at an intersection of country roads / To which through the waves of heat some forty or fifty souls / Carefully file." His description of this dirt-poor house of worship is respectful, but he cannot shake feelings of alienation. Too much the stranger in the insular rite of this place, he returns to the road, where

> The highway sings,
> A prism, the waxed gut of morning up from dreams
> Out of the cushioned pews of cloud in rivering olive
> Light. Carnelian hills! It is the Lord's Supper
> The rough hand draws the dirty cloth from.

Stunned by the magnificent cloud banks of a weather front, the speaker is finally moved to devotion:

> I kneel down, I begin to pray, I hear
> My own authority, cool voice which says that beauty
> Bears the numen, spirit rider. I am numb,
> I am deaf. Mine are not laws, but feelings that earn
> No bread in the milky valley, the pastel poverties
> With their electric crosses and rayon memories
> Saying grace from vestal mouths. At home, I wash and watch
> The water braid to the marble basin, circle and pool.

Having baptized himself, as it were, Sandy becomes truly a "man in the open air," as receptive to nature's grandeur as to its destructive powers. Robert Creeley commented that "the curiously down-home feelings of [such] poems meld with an apt classicism." "Allegheny Front" ends with the sense of calm one experiences after a thunderstorm.

Again and again, one notices that many poets reach a turning point in their middle age. Some start repeating themselves, rearranging the same elements, until eventually their creativity sputters and fails, or develops rigor mortis. Others burgeon into new eloquence. *Man in the Open Air* definitely marks Sandy's transition into this latter camp. The strength of this book was much commented on by those who had read its poems-in-progress or seen the manuscript. Dave Smith praised its "technical mastery" and called it "poetry that sounds like no other, but is as familiar as breath." Gerald Stern acknowledged that Sandy's difficult style could be obscure but added, "The obscurity is made acceptable – available – by the vivid, clear, and unexpected details." Kurt Heinzelman was

"amazed by the unlooked-for details, the sudden logical swerves, and the sheer range of stuff that Sandy gets into his poems while working in a formally conservative, essentially classical mode." He also admired how "in the magical final poem, 'The Heart's Desire of Americans,' it is 'Squally Election Day, a few drops pebbling / The hood,' and before long we are at Walden Pond, splitting granola bars, making up proverbs with a friend, changing wiper blades . . . , buying ice cream, and stopping to watch 'late / Twilight gleaming' under the sign of the poem's astonishing, proverbial sounding commandment: 'When you've seen / One perfect spot, you want to see them all.'" Heinzelman concluded, "There are a lot of perfect spots in this book."

Sandy's fifth collection of poems, *Thanksgiving Over the Water,* further expands his strengths. The title is borrowed from a prayer during the Service for Baptism in *The Book of Common Prayer.* By this stage in his career his short lyrics have acquired a luminescent polish. They convey what Amy Clampitt characterized as "the outer voice, the interior shifts of feeling." She also praised "his eye for the strangeness in the everyday." Such poignantly delicate works as the radiant elegy, "Around Our Table," or "Abandoned Houses South of Stafford" become part of the sympathetic reader's own mental furniture. However, the long poems best illustrate Sandy's intentions. The sequence composed of the poems "Trifid," "Twenty After," "Tyros," "Pledges," and "Jade" assembles a series of military, snapshot-like scenes, each suggesting some aspect of the moral ambiguities inherent in the recent wars of the United States. "Pledges" comments on the unintentional destructiveness of certain ostensibly helpful ventures in American foreign policy, underlining the innocent thoughtlessness of Americans by comparing them to "the first little pig" of the familiar fairy tale, "grasping at straws in the gust of change."

"Place and Fame" examines the character of Robert Frost. Sandy's own reminiscences move from his student days at Yale, where the elder statesman of American poetry used to spend time, to a much later party at which Frost and John Berryman engaged in an ambiguous exchange. Sandy is that rare writer who can perfectly convey these less-than-climactic remarks that great figures are often overheard making to one another. The particular incident Sandy describes is all the more telling for its inconclusiveness. Through the poet's eyes, one sees Frost as a guest that night might have seen him – not as an archetype, but as an old man having trouble making conversation at the end of a long evening of drinking. The concluding section of "Place and Fame" reminds the reader that its previous vignettes have evoked the elderly Frost – revered by the literary world, although long past his poetic prime. Now Sandy reconstructs a touching picture of the middle-aged laureate at the period of his best work, as he tries to help out his increasingly depressed son with his floral business by delivering orders around southern Vermont. Those familiar with firsthand accounts of Frost's life and character will appreciate Sandy's portrayal of his subject's canniness, his fierce sense of privacy, role-playing, and deep compassion. By the end, the younger poet seems to have crawled inside the mind of the elder poet.

"Mammal Pavilion" describes a father's excursion with his children to one of those "sea world" exhibits where whales, dolphins, and seals perform. This spectacle arouses contradictory feelings of admiration for the grace of these intelligent creatures and pity that they should be forced into entertaining their audience of fellow mammals. Watching a noble sea lion play its part, Sandy imagines that it

> Ignores the children in the bleachers,
> The tourist's flash, the science teachers.
> Alone in his midnight marbly pelf
> He dreams of a day he'll find himself
> Sniffing the breeze along the gleaming
> Foreshore of a rockbound bay,
> Hailing his lioness, the screaming
> Of the screaming children washed away.

With the poet the reader can imaginatively enter the ocean environment and "wipe the sea spray from my face, enthralled." The cooperation that the dolphins grant their trainers becomes a kind of benediction conferred by their species on the human species. At another level, "Mammal Pavilion" explores the conflict between the artist's role as entertainer and his desire for a secret, private existence. In this respect, it bears some affinity to "Place and Fame."

Two memorable pieces in *Thanksgiving Over the Water* plumb a depth of feeling new to Sandy's work. In "Fort Burial" a father helps his eight-year-old son compose a funeral for a dead mole the boy has found. The depiction of the animal's "pelt / of midnight-glossy fur, like a ruff / Engraved by Hollar, clenched coral feet / With Meissen claws" is a particularly felicitous meld of visual associations, as the tiny body takes on the dignity of a baroque burgher. Sandy delicately evokes his child's emotions in all their complexity: excitement in planning the burial, pity and sorrow for the dead thing, and religious solemnity, together with pride in the artistry

needed to put together an appropriate rite. "Fort Burial" brims with the poignancy of an innocence all the more valuable because it is soon to be outgrown. "The Tack" can best be described as a kind of Coleridgean "conversation poem," like "Frost at Midnight," "This Lime Tree Bower My Prison," or the great "Dejection" ode. A painful bite from a deerfly provokes in the poet a chain of images tossed up as he attempts to distract himself from his swelling arm, which he is watching in the convex surface of a thumbtack on the bulletin board over his desk. Anxiety about a possible allergic reaction makes him think about

> Coleridge, despairing
> Because he'd fallen from his friend and turned
> From Sara; ill
> And opium-numb – en route to the Siberia
> Of tacky Malta – found terror, then found what
> He'd hoped to find: in St. Michael's cave, the same
> Chambers, the columns, the same chasm he'd
> Imagined, writing
>
> *Osorio.* It was thus to his liking, those lofty wells;
> So the stung pruner grew chummy with his swelling,
> *What's happened here?*
> Unfolding to *hello, there!,* finding whatever
> It was, was him now. Acceptance. The familiar.

Having come to terms with his injury, the poet conjures up his own memory of a subterranean experience. On a platform in the cavernous New York subway system, he once encountered a panhandler who blessed him for the money he gave. This derelict must be a spiritual grandchild of the Leech-gatherer from another poem of the Romantic canon, "Resolution and Independence." Just as William Wordsworth's depression was lifted by the steadfastness of the old man who could follow such a distasteful and poorly remunerative trade, so Sandy's poetic persona learns better how to confront life's mercies from a street person able to offer thanksgiving for so little. No trace of sentimentality mars the portrayal of this beggar "from the homeless land" of underground tunnels. He is the epitome of the street people many people have encountered – filthy, obsequious, and stoned. Nevertheless, he stands as one of those guardians meant to direct the mythic hero on his path.

> His last words died in the roar
> Of the train arriving; I left him to wander, to con
> Or bless more travelers;
> Yet watching the burnished thumbtack, tunnel mirror,

I caught his rushy odor still, the white wine
Of his urine; understood that blessings were; that I
Had been chosen, even as I was punctured by
    The awaited fly.

The poet captures the raveling network of associations that attend nearly every experience, no matter how trivial. By parsing them, "The Tack" gleans insights into the way the self comes to terms with what lies outside. Chard de Niord notes in *The New England Review* that "Sandy combines an account of empathetic practice with intellectual selflessness in this poem, thus subverting the romantic apotheosis of individual heroism in favor of selfless identification with the other – in this case, a beggar." He also characterizes this poet as cultivating "the right objectivity for disinterested inspiration." The growing capacity to express an almost religious intensity of feeling, added to the increased vulnerability of his poems, will undoubtedly strengthen and expand Sandy's future work.

Since the appearance of *Thanksgiving Over the Water,* Sandy has produced a number of prose pieces: a short story, reviews, and reminiscences of other writers. The second volume of *Seneca: The Tragedies, Volume II* (1994), in Johns Hopkins University's Complete Roman Drama in Translation series, contains Sandy's version of *Hercules Oetaeus,* which he has titled *A Cloak for Hercules.* This straightforward yet mellifluous translation illustrates again how much he has been affected by the cadences of Latin verse. Moreover, his own poems continue to evolve; recently there has been a spate of fine, taut sonnets, a new direction for him.

Sandy's reputation continues to be less widespread than one would expect for a poet of his caliber. Such neglect too often becomes the lot of "quiet" poets whose work does not publicize a catchy persona. There also remains an ambivalence in the current culture toward the lyric. Bruce Bennet complained in a review of *Riding to Greylock* (in *The New York Times Book Review* of 17 July 1983) that Sandy's "language interposes itself to the point where it becomes the poem's entire subject." Such a criticism might be equally applicable to the work of most lyric poets from Gerard Manley Hopkins through Wallace Stevens to Amy Clampitt, if one accepts its criteria. In many cases it is only after a writer has achieved the cult following of a James Merrill or a John Ashbery that the public builds up an enthusiasm for the musical and incantatory aspects of the verse; but as Sandy's voice gains in lucidity and powerful emotion, he may yet win a wider, more appreciative following. He continues to impress discerning critics and fellow lyricists. For those attuned to his graces of form, which are wed to a compassionate and transcendent temperament, Sandy is a poet who sings strongly, with striking riches of nuance and beauty.

Bibliography:

Contemporary Authors, New Revision Series, volume 22 (Detroit: Gale Research, 1985).

References:

Kurt Heinzelman, "The Year in Poetry, 1988," *Massachusetts Review,* 30 (Spring 1989): 169–171;

Chard de Niord, "In the Divide: Skeptic Master, Stung Pilgrim," *New England Review, Middlebery Series,* 16 (Spring 1994);

Terence Diggory, "Witnesses and Seers," *Salmagundi* (Fall 1983);

Margo Jefferson, "The Pleasures of Craft, Honesty and Intelligence," *The New York Times,* 16 November 1994;

Phoebe Pettingell, "Coloring Emotions," *New Leader* (11–25 July 1983): 15–16;

Pettingell, "Poetry in Review," *Yale Review,* 80 (October 1992): 111–113;

Pettingell, "Stages of Growth," *The New Leader* (11–25 January 1988): 17–18;

Barry Spacks, "Four Poets," *Poetry,* 112 (April 1968);

Richard Tillinghast, "The Everyday and The Transcendent," *Michigan Quarterly Review,* 32 (Summer 1993);

Vernon Young, "Roofs," *Hudson Review* (Winter 1971).

Armand Schwerner

(11 May 1927 –   )

Arthur J. Sabatini
Arizona State University West

BOOKS: *The Domesday Dictionary,* by Schwerner and
    Donald Kaplan (New York: Simon & Schuster,
    1963);
The Lightfall (New York: Hawk's Well Press, 1963);
(if personal) (Los Angeles: Black Sparrow Press,
    1968);
The Tablets I–VIII (West Branch, Iowa: Cum-
    mington Press, 1968);
Seaweed (Los Angeles: Black Sparrow Press, 1969);
The Tablets I–XV (New York: Grossman, 1971);
The Bacchae Sonnets (Omaha, Nebr.: Abbatoir Edi-
    tions, 1974);
Redspel: Eleven American Indian Adaptations (Mount
    Horeb, Wis.: Perishable Press, 1975);
Tablets XVI–XVIII (Boston: Heron Press, 1976);
This Practice: Tablet XIX and Other Poems (London:
    Permanent Press, 1976);
Triumph of the Will (Mount Horeb, Wis.: Perishable
    Press, 1976);
the work, the joy and the triumph of the will (New York:
    New Rivers Press, 1978);
Sounds of the River Naranjana and *The Tablets I–XXIV*
    (Barrytown, N.Y.: Station Hill, 1983);
Tablets I–XXVI (London: Atlas Press, 1989);
*The Ogre of Information / the Fiend of Silence: Selected Es-
    says, Interviews, Letters* (Albuquerque: Univer-
    sity of New Mexico Press, 1996).

PERFORMANCES: *"Everything You're Giving Me is
    Just Things You're Giving Me,"* by Schwerner
    and Ellen Zweig, San Jose, California, Works
    Gallery, September 1987;
The Tablets, The Living Theater Company, U.S.
    and European tour (Italy, Germany, Spain),
    1989–1990;
Solo Reading/Performance, "Voci nell'acqua," Spoleto,
    Italy, Festival Dei Due Mondi, June 1989;
Teratophany, by Schwerner and Zweig, Marseille,
    France, Centre International de Poésie à Mar-
    seille, 1990;
Solo Reading/Performance, San Diego, University of
    California at San Diego, May 1992;

Armand Schwerner (photograph © 1985 Felver)

Solo Reading/Performance, Orono, Maine, University
    of Maine, National Poetry Foundation Poetry
    Festival, June 1993.
Solo Reading/Performance, Boulder, Colorado, Naropa
    Institute, July 1993.

SELECTED PERIODICAL PUBLICATIONS –
UNCOLLECTED:
FICTION
"The Lot Pit," *Colorado Review,* 19 (1992).

POETRY

"ground figures, light cells," *Poetry New York* (1989);

"Tablet XXVII," *Conjunctions, Semi-Annual Volumes of New Writing,* 17 (1991);

"Storehouse," *Sulfur, A Literary Bi-Annual of the Whole Art,* 30 (Spring 1992);

"Dreamers' Transport," *Talisman, A Journal of Contemporary Poetry and Poetics,* 8 (Spring 1992);

"All in the Family," *Tyuonyi,* 11 (1992);

"Everything You're Giving Me is Just Things You're Giving Me," by Schwerner and Ellen Zweig, *The Kenyon Review,* 16, no. 1 (1994).

NONFICTION

"Taking up the Thread: on the Poetry of Michael Heller," *Talisman* (Winter 1993–1994);

"Toby Olson's 'Unfinished Buildings' Songs," *TO,* 2 (Spring 1994);

"Spencer Holst, Fabulous Geometrician," *American Book Review,* 16 (Summer 1994);

"The Anxiety Capers: Wander; No Loveport: Dusk," *American Poetry Review,* 24 (September 1995);

"The Aquarium Fancies," *Pequod,* 39 (1995).

By the late 1950s Armand Schwerner, then in his thirties, was evolving as a poet and musician. Living in Manhattan and studying anthropology at Columbia University, he began a close association with the city's overlapping circles of experimental poets, innovative scholars, translators, publishers, artists, actors, and performers. With the editors and contributors to the journal *Alcheringa* and the poets who read at the St. Mark's poetry series in Greenwich Village or who published with Black Sparrow Press, Schwerner engaged in formative discussions of ideas that have become central to the contemporary era's fin de siècle literary discourse. Crucial issues, both then and now, have been the poetics of ordinary speech and poetic language; native poetries, aleatoric operations, ethnopoetics, and translation; and open-field poetry, poetic genres, and performance. Schwerner's own writings, translation projects, and approaches to performances derived significantly from the multiplicity of concerns within his community. Simultaneously, he urgently pursued personal psychological and spiritual investigations. As his career developed, his individual poetic voice and particular thematic intensities became more distinctive. Through the 1970s and 1980s he expanded his collaborations with other artists and cooperated in having his work adapted as performance for theater, dance, and recordings. In 1968 he began writing an open-ended poem, *The Tablets.*

To date, there are twenty-seven sections of this work, which has been critically praised as the postmodern successor to Ezra Pound's *Cantos* and Charles Olson's *Maximus Poems.* The reception of *The Tablets* has drawn attention to Schwerner's other poetry and prose and to the remarkable variety of his creative work.

Schwerner's importance is twofold. Although associated with the oral performance and ethnopoetic traditions, his work is often characterized by an uncompromising linguistic density that serves complex expressions of personalized utterance and inner speech. Schwerner's texts exude an Olsonian urgency to commit to orality and complex oral poetic forms. His texts reflect being in the world, the complexity of one's relationships to others, the interpenetration of the human and natural worlds, and the problematics of authorship and selfhood. He has deeply absorbed non-Western teachings, particularly through Tibetan and Zen Buddhism, and has produced many translations, performance texts, and workings of tribal and archaic materials. As Rachel Blau Duplessis has noted, Schwerner is part of a second generation of ethnopoets, whose work engages theory, multiculturalism, and technology. In recent interviews Schwerner has remarked that, while he is aware of the trajectory of his own ideas and work, he did not intentionally pursue a career that, in retrospect, has crossed so many significant terrains. Schwerner's career, nevertheless, is a paradigm of the way, during the past three decades, poets and poetry have become enmeshed in the many forms of discourse and performance that characterize contemporary art.

Schwerner was born in Antwerp, Belgium, in 1927. In 1935 his father, immigrating to the United States, settled in New York City; the next year Armand, two siblings, and his mother followed. Reared with a "loosely traditional Jewish upbringing," Schwerner spoke only French until the age of nine; mastering English therefore became central to his adolescent development. In 1945 he entered Cornell University as a premed student, and shortly after served for a year as a U.S. Navy musician. He returned to Cornell, then attended the Université de Genève for one year. In 1950 he received a bachelor of arts in French from Columbia University. After two years of graduate work at Columbia in the subject of anthropology, he changed his major, earning a master of arts degree from the Department of English and Comparative Literature in 1964. Married from 1961 to 1974, he has two sons, Adam, born in 1961, and Ari, born in 1964. A recipient of fifteen grants and fellowships, Schwerner taught at Staten Island Community College from 1964 to 1976 and has been a professor of English at the College of Staten Island, City University of New York, since 1976.

A convenient and not wholly irrelevant analogy for Schwerner's poetry, writings, and performances is a hypertext program for computers. On such a program, imagine simultaneously calling onto the screen written texts, graphic images, the poet reading, and audio and video performances. With keywords, it would then be possible to pursue connections among the materials with an interpretive schema that identifies formal, technical, thematic, linguistic, psychological, and philosophical concerns. Some of the operative terms for such an approach to Schwerner's work would be orality, visual poetry, performance, translation, voices, divagations, wordplay, chant, song, fragmentation, narrative, nonsense, and sound poetry. Broad thematic terms to use in assessing the writing would be presence and absence, disintegration, separation, light and darkness, openness and closings; also joy, fatherhood, thought and meditation, the nonnuclear self, Buddhism and spirituality, animism, pain, the body, laughter, poetics, the gratuitous, transformations of the self, teachings, pleasure, love, and otherness. Since Schwerner's poems are frequently nonlinear, his various texts are imbricated with multiple thematic concerns. In addition, they are formally structured to represent the processes of the poem's transmission. That is, the shifting textures, tonalities, patterns of concentration, and voices often give way to a poetry of open form, most notably in (*if personal*) (1968), "Constellations," and *The Tablets.*

Moreover, lines or word clusters or pure graphic arrangements in his poems (including computer-generated glyphs and graphics) are themselves evocative visually and verbally. Schwerner's career-long investigation of poetic and printed form underlies his sense of the slippages or discontinuities among oral, written, visual, performative, and ideographical meanings. Thus, even in his earliest work, Schwerner anticipates several key postmodern problematics. His poetry displays a struggle, which can be in metaphysical or playful modalities, with language and signification. His texts also become a series of contests to say the unsayable and represent temporalities. They register dialogues between voices in the prevailing culture, especially between self and others. Schwerner's work, which he often performs, directly engages readers and audiences — a fact especially true in his most noted series, *The Tablets.* As the source for many forms of

live performance, this series has been conceived of and presented as dance, dialogue, drama, full-length opera, and theatrical production. Schwerner has been an active participant in many of these adaptations.

In sum, on a hypertext screen, Schwerner's work would appear as a rich but unsettling palimpsest of images, texts, sounds, voices, and performances that demand serious play. The hypertext player (who might be a scholar or reader or participant or all these simultaneously) could follow an abundance of vectors in order to unravel Schwerner's linguistic complexities, coordinate his oral/graphic/visual patterns, probe the epistemological suggestions in his writings, and enjoy the depth of his poetic language and understandings and his invitations to become involved in the performance.

Schwerner began to contribute to poetry journals around 1960. Oddly, his first book, *The Domesday Dictionary* (1963), was a collaboration with psychoanalyst Donald Kaplan. In the spirit of *Dr. Strangelove,* the book is a formidable satire of Cold War machinery and Cold War states of mind. Entries range from sociotheological commentaries (for example, "Deadly Sins") to extended technical discussions of the effects of atomic and chemical warfare. The critic Sherman Paul has suggested that *The Domesday Dictionary,* like the translation of Sophocles' *Philoctetes* (1978), discloses the manner in which Schwerner addresses artistic themes in terms of psychology, morality, suffering, and political awareness — concerns that reappear throughout his work.

Schwerner's first volume of poetry, *The Lightfall,* appeared in 1963. A thirty-two-page book, its fifteen poems swerve between darkly imaged interior probings and dialogic commentaries on poetry and poetics. In these poems Schwerner focuses upon asserting a personal aesthetic, even if the process, evident in the poems themselves, is confusing and painful. Several poems concerning his wife and children betray anxieties about loss — of life, of light, of pleasure, of knowing, of identity. Simultaneously, loss becomes the foundation for creativity, joy, and love. In a later poem, "Sounds of the River Naranjana," this theme is stated explicitly: "how I love loss," Schwerner says; "loss is the mother of the beautiful." In a telling note in *The Lightfall* Schwerner remarks, "The poet is a creature of process and risks disintegration every time the things he has learned fall away from the real to whose radiance he slowly and patiently submits himself." The title poem of *The Lightfall,* a cautionary allegory about the hazards of the poetic vocation, is ad-

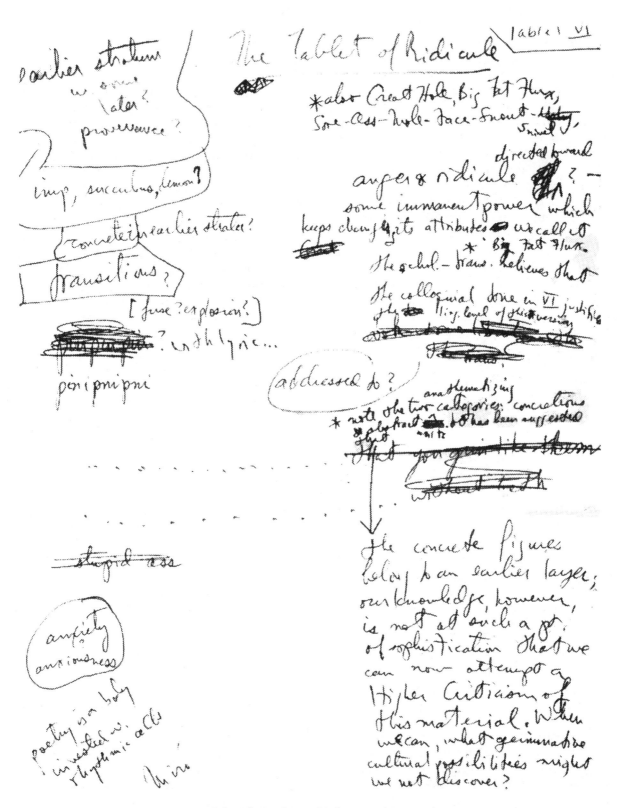

Draft for "Tablet of Ridicule" (courtesy of the author)

dressed to anonymous "poor women" in a mountainous region; "poor fools," it begins, "waiting for the light to surrender / on a falling leaf poor / crickets afraid of falling / they turn endlessly to the tune within their ears." The women ignore the "pressing / lightfall behind their eyes." That is, for Schwerner, illumination — a lightfall, with all the puns intended — occurs within the psyche. It must be sought after and seized. Other poems also consider poetry. "The Other" (dedicated to Jackson MacLow) asks and affirms, "and of what can he be the maker / whispering up there is the absence / of desire; his hand / cover his quiet thighs" only to acknowledge tenderly that, regardless of the wounding, "all poems are some power."

But such directness is rarely sustained through an entire poem. Schwerner's voicings move rapidly. Plain utterances alternate with syntactically knotted lines, lexical pyrotechnics, and grotesque imagery. The poetry is everywhere earthy, vegetative, thick with animal motion. As he does in later work, Schwerner imparts harsh images of the body and the natural world. "My eyes are a vast curved film, an elliptical skin of liquid tension: there the ants drag themselves up and down," he says in "The Door." One poem, "The Magic Runner," pursues the theme of multiple selves. It opens: "in the heart of the dark ground." The runner of the poem is the transformative shadow of the psyche, who is aware that "everything / is other." So it is for Schwerner, who, through the darkness of this book, affirms a poetry of sun, light, radiance, lightfalls, light falling.

(if personal) is an inventive booklet that physically and thematically reveals several of Schwerner's lifelong concerns. The book is a "window" poem consisting of four, unbound yellow tinted pages and five pages of text, each of which features cutout rectangular areas. The text is spread in lines and rows over each page. Readers are instructed to "play the yellow leaves ad lib," so as to produce different arrangements of the poem. The effect, which becomes central to *The Tablets,* is an interplay among visible and invisible lines, words, and sections. (In the latter work, the Scholar-Translator character identifies passages as untranslatable or missing.) Regardless of the combinations, the meaning of *(if personal)* remains enigmatic. The words *orange, Japan, trembling, children,* and the question *"why do the innocent suffer?"* contribute to the reader's sense that the poem is a piecing together of personal or historic or imaginary destructions. The shattered syntax, seemingly aleatoric combinations of words, and hesitations suggested by the patterns disclose an unsettled state of mind. Nevertheless, the text invites readers to formulate associations. Of course, any meaning grasped in *(if personal)* can only be tentative, as a turned or reinserted page offers other versions of the text.

Ellen Zweig provides an intricate reading of *(if personal)*. She elaborates on the theme of the open and closed in Schwerner's work and shows how surprise and discovery draw the reader into the poem. Zweig segues from a discussion of *(if personal)* to *The Tablets,* which first appeared about the same time. In *The Tablets,* she argues, the dialogue between the open and the closed becomes more structurally complex and philosophically sophisticated.

The most complete and penetrating critical study of Schwerner's work is Sherman Paul's *In Love with the Gratuitous: Rereading Armand Schwerner* (1986). Among other themes, Paul emphasizes Schwerner's archetypal responses to "primitive" psychic needs. Beginning with *The Domesday Dictionary* and Schwerner's *Philoctetes,* Paul traces the poet's processes of "soul-making." Citing Philoctetes' wound as a metaphor for the artist's pain, which is compensated for by a depth of self-understanding, Paul shows how many of Schwerner's texts artfully and playfully explore a "yielding to the most profound needs of the psyche." Paul also lucidly indicates the affinities between Schwerner's work and that of Charles Olson, Robert Duncan, and Wallace Stevens. Stevens is the subject of a rich essay by Schwerner, written in 1965 and published in the seminal magazine *KULTURE*. Paul acknowledges the importance of the essay. In it Schwerner "reclaims" Stevens as a meditative poet who provides a version of the "yielded self." He also contends that Stevens's last book shows him to be a poet in the Buddhist tradition. Paul consistently contextualizes Schwerner in relation to his contemporaries, particularly Jackson MacLow, Jerome Rothenberg, and David Antin. They, like Olson, are poets who employ "process-as-style," in Schwerner's words. Their work ceaselessly moves, but never reaches a reconciliation between the self and the world. Paul characterizes these poets as being "in love with the gratuitous," which speaks to their regard for aleatoric phenomena, their sense of wordplay, and their spirit of self-journeying.

Paul's book progressively assesses Schwerner's publications. He writes at length of Schwerner's evolving artistry in his 1969 collection, *Seaweed.* Of *Seaweed* Paul finds that Schwerner's public and performative experiments "challenge our assumptions about language." He cites the book's occasionally savage tone and its poems of disgust, desperation, and passionate grief, and he notices how the poet's several selves are on display. Three dominant clusters of poetic and thematic attention describe this collection. The first is represented in six of the twenty-six poems that involve Schwerner's children, who provide the inspiration for reflections on language and mischievous activity. An innocent request in "Daddy, can you staple these two stars together to make an airplane?" leads the poet toward a surreal concatenation of couplings, including "cement two pears together to make a country." A barbed rhyme, "Muck the Fuck," contains lines such as "Bees in the Mouth" and "Rat moose cowlick prick." A second type of energy, then, revolves around the gleeful use of language in texts determined by chance and in open texts. Thus, "zoology 1" has thirty-one vertical lists, such as: "vicuna / cow / hyena." The title poem and "Language is Poetry" are take-offs on found texts. In the latter Schwerner quotes from a 1900 handbook on writing poetry. Ignoring directions to avoid vague and high-sounding words or undignified talk, the poem revels in a mocking dispersion of words such as *quaff, crank, thing, chloride, blubber, emolumentum, naughty, daddy,* and *dolly.* These poems further develop Schwerner's aesthetic.

A third thematic notion carried through *Seaweed* is also evident in poems that mention Schwerner's contemporaries. Several make overt statements or pointedly demonstrate Schwerner's concerns as a poet and thinker. This is most evident in longer poems that Paul calls "showpieces." These poems, "Constellations" and "Prologue in Six Parts," are open texts that follow the typographic expansiveness of *(if personal)* (although without the feature of the "windows"). Thematically, they are both sustained meditations on the journeying and grounding of the poetic imagination. The former is a Beckettian rustle of fragments ("withdraw nothing / out the window / doors or door"), splayed among quotations such as "art prepares the world in some sense to receive the soul, and the soul to master the world."

Through the 1970s Schwerner produced versions of poems from Hawaiian, American Indian, and other tribal and archaic sources. These translations have appeared in forty-five anthologies (see, especially, his poems in *Technicians of the Sacred* [1968], *Shaking the Pumpkin* [1972], and *The New Open Poetry* [1973]), as well as *Alcheringa,* the major journal of the ethnopoetic group. The deep, often ritualistic seriousness, sacred playfulness, and unconscious integration of the body and nature present in the poetries of native peoples permeates Schwerner's own work and thought. From translating he

also gathered a sense of poetic forms (dirge, litany, chant, insult, mythic narration) and learned ways to incorporate modes of animistic experiences. Moreover, Schwerner's translations are stamped with his own skill in demotic expressiveness. Cumulatively, these elements inform his other work and indicate how Schwerner's oeuvre is not easily assessed as the articulations of a single consciousness.

Since the 1960s Schwerner has worked simultaneously on *The Tablets* while also producing poetry, essays, translations, audiotapes, and collaborative performance pieces. Chronologically, *The Tablets* have appeared since 1968, both individually and in their own volumes. *The Bacchae Sonnets* (1974) were published in a similar manner. For the sake of clarity, *The Tablets* will be discussed in their entirety after remarks on *the work, the joy and the triumph of the will* (1978) (and the translation of *Philoctetes*) and the poems in *Sounds of the River Naranjana* (1983), which includes *The Bacchae Sonnets, The Tablets I–XXIV* (1983), and *Tablets/Journals/Divagations,* a revealing text that reflects upon the development of *The Tablets.*

There are eleven poems and a translation of Sophocles's *Philoctetes* in *the work, the joy and the triumph of the will.* Thematically, the volume investigates pain, spiritual growth, and artistic and personal evolution. Charles Doria considers the central issue in this book to be survival: "Not merely physical survival, but the more fundamental survival of the person as living, feeling witness of that helplessness imposed as limit on everyone by time, as far as recovering and making our peace with the past." Poems with titles such as "The Teaching" and "The Knowledge," probe the emptying of the self, separation, and death (in this case, of Schwerner's father) with a desire for discipline and understanding. Many poems reference Buddhism, mystical practices, and teachers ("so many teachers!"). Eschewing irregular or open-field arrangements, the poems viscerally capture transient emotional states in quasi narratives marked by Schwerner's signature disjunctive style. "The work is broken into fragments . . . in often very tense phrases that are forced to flow into each other," writes Harry Lewis. He adds, "Connectives are often lost and the surface logic of language is sometimes dropped. Yet the work makes very clear and precise sense." As Schwerner progresses from loss and pain toward joy and triumph, the poems turn whimsical, lyrical, ecstatic — as in the orgiastic chant that erupts near the close of "The Triumph of the Will": "impossible / to not sing in the song body . . . in the sing in the sing in

of low-tide decay invades his rust nostrils, he inhales

aroma of singed hair he shudders with pleasure

....................++++++++++++++++++ stiff as a penis, ~~warm~~ on the river ~~surface~~

sees inside to the shoal of sea-robins and flounder and porgies

which never ~~touch~~ Ahanarshi sees them never touch

under the chocolate river, his head turns warm, he ~~distinguishes~~ *tells*

well among the ⌈species⌉ ~~~~~~~~ a while and the ~~movement~~ *telling*

~~confuses him~~, Ahanarshi .... a ~~drive~~ of red ~~pumping~~

.... rest ++++++++++++++++++++++++++++++

is it clear is it clear are you enveloping, Ahanarshi, *are you,*

or riding at the ~~core~~ of an envelopment?

the ~~bronze~~ ~~canals of his right foot freeze~~, the ~~right foot frozen~~,

~~tucked in~~ behind the left knee. He says 'pain, pain'

Ahanarshi says ' pain, pain' he reenters his activity

he is present no longer concentrating he hears

the Teacher ~~breathing~~ he splinters into a ~~mass~~

of ~~keen shards~~, thousands of painful wisps

ride him, tiny throats, the Teacher says :

                              'we will work together.'

~~Ahanarshi has managed to invent his Teacher.~~

Draft for "Tablet XVII" (courtesy of the author)

the song / sing body sing speech sing arrow star-body / sing in the arrow star song in the / dream body."

The poems in *the work, the joy and the triumph of the will* constitute half the volume. The other half is Schwerner's widely acclaimed translation of Sophocles' *Philoctetes*. Sophocles's play, as Edmund Wilson, Robert Duncan, and others have recognized, is a metaphor for the artist's predicament. Suffering, alienation, and the struggle for recognition are among its themes. That Schwerner couples it with his poetry further emphasizes his concerns with matters of soul making and the vocation of the poet. Even beyond its thematic issues, the translation itself is extraordinary. For Doria, Schwerner's translation "goes so far beyond the literal meanings of the Greek that it penetrates the play's core: how a hero, though wounded, can surmount his accidental/fated crippling and still achieve destiny." Without acknowledging his other translations, Doria applauds the "immensity of Schwerner's achievement" in rescuing translation from its often stodgy, formulaic renderings. Hugh Kenner is more straightforward, calling Schwerner's *Philoctetes* "a speakable version . . . as it were, after 25 years, a sequel to Pound's *The Women of Trachis* . . . and Pound did not have Schwerner's sure feel for the demotic."

Speaking with Schwerner in person confirms critical observations about the sounds and sense of his poetry. In conversations, and when performing live, Schwerner is tenacious, deeply serious, comedic, ruminative, querulous, surprising, attentive, and idiosyncratically demotic. Kathryn Van Spanckeren recalls that on a fishing trip, Schwerner "would shift into a jovial performance mode, one moment a stentorian Sumerian prophet, the next a wizened idiot nattering over worms, then a French aesthete with his nose up a snorkle." His word choice and sentence structure are richly varied, yet exact. He has a sure feel for language as performance, dialogistics, and parody, and he has a musician's sense of intonation. Schwerner is an accomplished reed player (he studied improvisation on clarinet with Lennie Tristano), and music is often incorporated into his performances. Thus, when Paul writes that Schwerner's "phrases create aural eddies, derive from jazz and contribute to the conspicuous lyricism," he is also speaking, in part, about the poet's actual voice. These qualities are evident in audio tapes of Schwerner (where, incidentally, audience reactions indicate how appealing the work is). Fortunately, throughout his career, Schwerner has given many interviews that capture the spirit of his conversation and the fluidity of his thought. The significance of these interviews cannot be underestimated. They provide commentaries on Schwerner's creative practice, reveal the extent of his research and use of sources, and trace his study and assessment of the poetry around him.

"If the poems can be said to be about anything," Schwerner says of *The Bacchae Sonnets,* they "are about duality and the excruciating pain and difficulty of our situation in duality in samsara, the realm of confusion and bewilderment and suffering . . . the sonnets . . . have a texture of a very particular intensely condensed order." They were written, he adds, after a long involvement with readings and translations of Mahayana texts, Tibetan sacred texts, mystical materials, and Hawaiian rituals and spells. Interestingly, and appropriately, the seven formally structured sonnets are included in Schwerner's mostly gentle and personal collection, *Sounds of the River Naranjana* and *The Tablets I–XXIV.* These thirty lyrical and reflective poems (plus the sonnet sequence) are addressed to friends, family, poets, and voices from literary and spiritual traditions. With the inclusions of *The Tablets* and *Tablets/Journals/Divagations,* this is Schwerner's most representative book. It provides samplings of nearly every aspect of his artistic temperament, ability, and conception of poetry, except for his translations. Thus, the harsh, earthy tonality of *The Bacchae Sonnets* ("first you burn your hair, its spider filaments,") is counterbalanced with antic wordplay and aleatoric energy in a poem with "materials from Milarepa and . . . American and Italian computer-generated Shakespearean monkeys," which includes the line "to dea not nat to be will and them be does doesorns." The title poem, with its allusion to Buddhism, and other poems are introspective, spiritual castings for peace and poetic practice as a form of understanding and action. Yet, as with previous and later work, Schwerner's restless inquisitions are woven into experiences of others and the natural world. Air, mist, water, and gardens predominate in these poems. Schwerner also pursues poetry's doings with commentaries on utterances by Leonard Crowdog, Duncan, and MacLow, among many others. "Old Dog Sermon," for MacLow, begins, "the poet reads," then wonders "that the sounds matter, how?" How, Schwerner asks, do "our poems body the 'task,?' / Rilke calls it"? This is a large question, never far from the surface of Schwerner's writing and thought. An answer in the poem, "the empty center / is poetry in action, us in this voicing, no feathers / if now, right now. I'm hippo. whatever. 'energy is eternal delight,' " comes close to being emblematic for all his work. These swiftly moving lines spark attention to soul work, spiritual teachings, the body, animal forces, voices, and poetic inheritance from, for example, William Blake. They display Schwerner's fundamental orientation toward performance, his courage, and distinctive wit: "if now, right now. I'm hippo. whatever."

In some instances critics of Schwerner's work (up to *Sounds of the River Naranjana*) have interpreted his intellection, high play, multivocality, and rapid music as evidence of an impersonal stance that eludes the possibility of authentic poetic lyricism. Paul Christensen summarizes this sentiment when he notes that "None of Schwerner's critics want to say outright that his language is tentative, that it deflates selfhood by its indecision and its casual assimilation of almost anything lying near that could be turned to speech." Christensen contends that Schwerner's "avoidance" of a graspable style or a singular, emotional voice has been coolly received. In hindsight, many early readers doubtless took Schwerner's texts as not wholly successful reactions to tradition-bound modernist poetry, rather than as the incipient texts of an ethnopoetically informed, spiritual, philosophical postmodern performance poetry that insists on its own originality and evolution. For his part, Schwerner has said that even as his poetry "tracks and embodies modes of postmodernism, the work embodies the complex and obdurate persistencies of soul-making, in an on going attempt to generate such processes through their appropriate musics." His statement emphatically reminds the reader (as do the writings of Sherman Paul, Christensen, and Van Spanckeren) that Schwerner's deepest concern is, as he says in "Sounds of the River Naranjana": "the holiness of the heart's puzzling affections," which are sometimes painful, and which are "impossible / not to sing in the song-body," wordwise, performance-wise.

About Schwerner's thirty-year project, the long poem, *The Tablets,* there is critical agreement. It is an "important *poetic* find," (Diane Wakoski), "a profound and intricate poem" (John Shawcross), and "ambitious and monumental" (Kathryn Van Spanckeren). *The Tablets,* commentators immediately notice, follow in the tradition of Ezra Pound's *Cantos,* Charles Olson's *Maximus Poems,* William Carlos Williams's *Paterson,* and Robert Duncan's *Passages,* all of which were sequences published throughout the authors' careers. But *The Tablets* supersede any comparison with mere literary texts. Conceived by Schwerner in the context of his interactions with the poetry and performance exper-

iments in the late 1960s, *The Tablets* revise and challenge poetic and literary categories. They add to existing notions of genre authoritative conceptions of the possibilities for creating mythic, oral, and graphic imaginings of consciousness and manifestations of mind and body in performance. Although often approached through themes common to our postmodern sensibility, "*The Tablets* give a fundamental poetry," according to Paul. Shawcross, another critic adds, they are "an epic of the aesthetic spirit which has quickened man through history."

The Tablets are spectacularly representative of Schwerner's learning and understanding, as well as his artistry, joy, and fearlessness. Wakoski observes that *The Tablets* (presently numbering twenty-seven), are "a startling conception, a full giving of a man to his whole life and consequently the creation that comes out of a whole vision." She adds that the work "is inexhaustible. It is immense in scope, intimate in voice." Were it not for the latter quality — voicings, which are audible or indelible in every text of Schwerner's — the huge, complex meanings and effect of *The Tablets* could be expeditiously glossed. But Schwerner tenaciously sustains such a voiced attention to "flesh and spirit" and "the stuff of life" that the resonance of *The Tablets* is, as Van Spanckeren states, "becoming increasingly important."

The 106-page 1989 Atlas Press volume of *The Tablets I–XXVI* includes *Tablets/Journals/Divagations.* As presented by a character called the Scholar-Translator, *The Tablets* are "translations" of recently discovered Sumero-Akkadian clay tablets, supposedly inscribed more than four thousand years ago (the oldest known writings are dated from about 3600 B.C.). Of course, there are no original tablets and each one is printed as a mix of "translated" sections (of one to four pages) to which are added scholarly annotations, intrusive commentaries, and graphic images. On the page, the typography recalls the layout of the *Cantos* or the *Maximus Poems.* Upon inspection, however, *The Tablets* are far more eccentric. They are replete with boldface and italicized words, multilingual phrases, odd orthographies, invented words, and the following keys supplied by the Scholar-Translator: .... means untranslatable, +++++++ means missing, (?) means variant reading. Recent *Tablets* contain "glyphs" created on a Macintosh computer.

Since the conceit of *The Tablets* involves an awareness of the process of "translation," with all its scholarly encumbrances, readers and/or audiences are immediately plunged into Schwerner's

TABLET IV

Most large fragments are the result of horizontal breaks. This Tablet (IV) and the next (V), however, are vertically fractured. The reconstruction of V is almost certainly correct. Doubt lingers about IV. The edges do not meet in three places; otherwise it is a good tight fit. Whether the idiosyncratic continuity derives from accident or design is a problem which only time and further studies and excavations will resolve. Note the cesuras.

is the man a bush on fire?	like one drop of quartz, two cold onyx beads
is the man four-legged and with teeth?	like one piece of petrified wood
is the man a hot woman?	like one hard-finger-bone, one moonlight on iron
is he mud, of solid mud?	in the shape of one clay tablet in frost
is the man a bird?	. . . . like bronze eyes
is the unhappy man on all fours?	in the shape of bronze statues of something wood
is the man all blood, all bile?	like menstrual blood congealed in cold mud
is the woman a fat belly?	like the world, a five-year-old's bloody . . .
is the man sleeping in a god?	like a frog stuffed with small white stones
is the man's head aching?	like . . . . . . empty + + + + + maggots
does the man play with her lips?	like amber + + + + + + + running pus
can the man make himself come?	like a . . . . cold onyx beads
can the woman come on top of the man?	. . . . dead trees
when does the man sacrifice his hands?	like sheep draped in cold mud
does the man wipe her belly with sperm?	like stories about ice, about frozen wheat
does the man put good leaves under his testicles?	+ + + + + + + + + of maggots
does the man put his lips on the sheep's udder?	in the shape of a clay tablet in frost
does the man put hand and elbow in his cow's vagina?	like death in blossoms when . . . . .
does he ram his penis into soft earth?	like the death in petrified wood
does he touch his woman's . . . . ?	like the death in two cold onyx beads
does the man pray to her vulva for rain?	like stories about ice, about frozen wheat
does he lament the sickness in his groin?	like a frog stuffed with small white pebbles
it is night; does he swim in the river?	like sheep draped by cold mud
+ + + + + + + + + + +	like hail
+ + + + + + + + + + + + +	like a leg burning on the pyre
+ + + + + + + + + + + +	like ants, a rotten cadaver, the dead trees

67

A page from Schwerner's 1989 collection, Tablets I – XXVI

playful, or gamelike, structurings. The first line of "Tablet I" is: "All that's left is pattern* (shoes?) / *doubtful reconstruction." Superficially, *The Tablets* seem humorous and open-ended. Playfulness, however, is quickly offset by the gravity of the poetry's archetypal themes and a recognition that the language, the speakers, and the archaic world imagined in the text are deeply conflicted. In the first place, there are many speakers in the poems. They often engage in obscure, pain-drenched, sexually heated encounters and rituals. Voices seem curiously intermingled in what Schwerner calls a "plurilogue." A single "voice" may be many people praying, chanting, or telepathically communicating. This is also an emerging world full of terror and insecurity. Anonymous utterances are, by turns, primitive, grotesque, and comic. In *Tablet V* voices ask of man, "is his mighty penis fifty times a fly's wing?" Voices answer, "what pleasure!" In later *Tablets* distinct indi-

viduals appear, and the initial theme of the origins of community and/or communication recedes before the traumatic joy of the awakening of consciousness and selfhood. Thus Schwerner, as he has always done, dwells upon the questions of the nuclear self, creativity, and relationships.

The Scholar-Translator, readers soon discover, is not a neutral figure. Part savant, part idiot, and personally troubled, he glosses passages with peculiar variants and extended comments. Pompous and erudite, like Vladimir Nabokov's "Kinbote" in *Pale Fire* (1962), he is funny, but hardly reliable. With this character Schwerner ups the ante on scholarly pretensions to interpretation, translation, and the problematics of an archaic anthropology. The Scholar-Translator engages in polemics and, in the manner of Jorge Luis Borges, cites actual and bogus sources. (Paul's invaluable book and Van Spanckeren's essays annotate the plethora of allusions in *The Tablets.*) In performance the Scholar-Translator has been played as both severe and mysterious, and also as a doddering fool.

Each "Tablet" varies in its emotionality, generic orientation, mythic overtones, and the interplay between linguistic, visual, and auditory materials. "Tablet XII" contains a lost Sumerian hymn of creation. It is followed by a "design-tablet" in the form of a mandala. Pictographs and "glyphs" in Tablets XXVI and XXVII are supplemented by long inquiries into the nature of nascent, perhaps imaginary states of consciousness, the study of which has transformed the Scholar-Translator.

On one level, *The Tablets* are clearly a postmodern scholar's delight. Yet, recalling Wakoski and Paul, there is an intimate, felt voice throughout the text and an inescapable depth created by Schwerner's pursuits in this primordial, archetypal, spiritual, and artistic journey. In this dual sense, *The Tablets* are a palimpsest that reveal all the technical skills, themes, and intellectual concerns of Schwerner throughout his career. As critics and audiences have begun to recognize, *The Tablets* are of vital significance. They probe – and play with – the most unsettling issues of the contemporary era and illuminate paths that readers and audiences might well consider making their own.

Through the 1990s Schwerner has produced a series of essays that address his learnings and career as a poet. He has also begun translating Dante. *The American Poetry Review* (September 1995) contained a special supplement on Schwerner, which included Schwerner's essay "The Anxiety Capers: Wander; No Loveport: Dusk"; his translation of Canto 15 from the *Inferno;* a poem, "The Work"; and an interview. Schwerner's translation of Dante is rich with a demotic feel for language and the complexities of Dante's pain. It is conceived, like most of his poetry, architecturally on the page. The effect is to reveal a Dante whose journey appears more humble, fragmented, modern. In the essay on anxiety, Schwerner opts for a historical view that tracks the subject from the mid seventeenth century to the "third decade of the twenty-first century." In the future he satirically invokes a universe of anxiousness provoked by excessive information. Working with Middle Eastern alphabets and his own graphics, Schwerner invents fonts to convey our futuristic malaise.

It might be suggested, in returning to the analogy of a hypertext program, that to experience the multifariousness and profundity of Schwerner's work fully is to acknowledge that it is steeped in the most primitive and ancient of human activities, while it also creates expressive meanings among the most advanced forms of art and technology. That one would need a hypertext program (or its image) to return one to the original energies of the body, voice, song, spirit, writing, and the performance of the self and others is an irony for which there is not resolution – except, perhaps, in the always elusive realm of poetry itself.

Interviews:

Barry Alpert, "Armand Schwerner: An Interview," *VORT,* 8 (1975): 101–125;

Lee Bartlett, "A Conversation with Armand Schwerner," *American Poetry,* 4 (Spring 1987);

Guy de Bièvre, "Armand Schwerner," in *Logos Blad, Institute for Contemporary Poetry and Music* (Gent, Belgium, 1989);

Alan Drake, "Armand Schwerner. Interview: *The Tablets* and the Path of the Poet. A Conversation," *Archae,* 2, no. 2 (1991): 61–92;

Drake, "A Conversation: Dialogue with Philip Corner," *Conjunctions,* 8 (1991);

Willard Gingerich, "Interview #1 with Armand Schwerner," *Hambone,* 11 (Spring 1994);

Gingerich, "Interview #2 with Armand Schwerner," *American Poetry Review* (September/October 1995): 27–32.

References:

Barry Alpert, ed., *Jackson MacLow, Armand Schwerner: Interviews and Critical Essays* (Silver Spring, Md.: Vort Works Ink, 1975);

David Antin, "The Stranger at the Door," *Genre,* 20 (Fall/Winter 1987);

D. J. R. Bruckner, "Illusion vs. Reality in *The Tablets,*" *New York Times,* 11 June 1989;

Paul Christensen, "Ethnopoetics," *Parnassus,* 15 (1989): 154–159;

Charles Doria, "The Poetry of Memory: Armand Schwerner's *the work the joy & the triumph of the will, with a translation of Sophocles' Philoctetes,*" *Parnassus,* 7 (Fall/Winter 1979): 257–266;

Rachel Blau Duplessis, "Armand Schwerner," *Sulfur* (Fall 1991): 212;

Jesse Glass Jr., "Notes Towards a Reading of *The Tablets, *" *Salthouse* (1986): 14–17;

Michael Heller, "Schwerner's Poetry," *Sagetrieb,* 3, no. 3 (1984);

Hugh Kenner, "Schwerner's *the work, the joy & the triumph of the will,* with a translation of Sophocles' *Philoctetes," New York Times Sunday Book Review,* 12 February and 4 June 1978;

Richard Kostelanetz, *Performing Arts* (Winter 1978);

Thomas Lavazzi, "Editing Schwerner: Versions of Armand Schwerner's 'Design Tablet,'" *TEXT* (1994);

Lavazzi, "Textual Performance/Performing the Text: Armand Schwerner's *The Tablets*" and "Editing Schwerner: Versions of Armand Schwerner's 'design-tablet,' " in "Performing Criticism: Reading as Bricolage," dissertation, City University of New York, 1994;

Brian McHale, "Archaeologies of Knowledge: Geoffrey Hill's Hymns, Seamus Heany's Bog-People, Schwerner's *Tablets*," in *The Obligations Toward a Difficult Whole* (Durham, N.C.: Duke University Press, 1996);

George Oppen, "On Armand Schwerner," *Stony Brook*, 3, no. 4 (1969);

Sherman Paul, *In Love with the Gratuitous: Rereading Armand Schwerner* (Grand Forks: University of North Dakota Press, 1986);

Allen Planz, "Poetry by Schwerner," *Nation* (19 June 1972);

Hanon Reznikov, *Living on Third Street* (New York, Paris, Tokyo, Singapore, Camberwell & Australia: Harwood Academic Press, 1994);

Jerome Rothenberg, "Noticings: Armand Schwerner," *Sulfur* (Winter 1990);

Ed Sanders, "Path of the Glyph," *American Book Review*, 13 (October/November 1991): 13;

John Shawcross, "Schwerner's *The Tablets*," *American Poetry Review* (March 1973): 16–17;

Stanley Sultan, "Son of the Cantos?," *Chelsea* (1971);

Christine Tamblin, "Armand Schwerner & Ellen Zweig's 'Everything You're Giving Me is Just Things You're Giving Me,' " *High Performance*, 40 (September 1987);

Kathryn Van Spanckeren, "Moonrise in Ancient Sumer: Armand Schwerner's *The Tablets*," *American Poetry Review*, 22 (July/August 1993): 15–18;

Van Spanckeren, "Schwerner's *The Tablets*," *Dialectical Anthropology*, 2 (Winter/Spring 1986): 381–388;

Diane Wakoski, "A Satirist in the Avant-Garde," *Parnassus* (Fall/Winter 1972): 148–151;

Mark Weiss, "*The Tablets*," Bluefish, 1 (Spring 1984);

Ellen Zweig, "Armand Schwerner, The Problem of the 'Text': Process and Indeterminacy: 1. The Open Poem; 2. The Dialogue Between the Open and the Closed," in "Performance Poetry: Critical Approaches to Contemporary Intermedia," dissertation, University of Michigan, 1980.

Gary Snyder

(8 May 1930 –)

Kevin McGuirk
Queen's University

See also the Snyder entries in *DLB 5: American Poets Since World War II, First Series* and *DLB 16: The Beats: Literary Bohemians in Postwar America.*

BOOKS: *Riprap* (Kyoto, Japan: Origin Press, 1959);

Myths & Texts (New York: Totem Press/Corinth Books, 1960; London: Centaur, 1960);

Riprap & Cold Mountain Poems (San Francisco: Four Seasons Foundation, 1965);

Six Sections from Mountains and Rivers without End (San Francisco: Four Seasons Foundation, 1965; London: Fulcrum Press, 1967); enlarged and republished as *Six Sections from Mountains and Rivers without End Plus One* (San Francisco: Four Seasons Foundation, 1970);

A Range of Poems (London: Fulcrum Press, 1966);

Three Worlds, Three Realms, Six Roads (Marlboro, Vt.: Griffin Press, 1966);

The Back Country (London: Fulcrum Press, 1967; New York: New Directions, 1968);

The Blue Sky (New York: Phoenix Book Shop, 1969);

Earth House Hold: Technical Notes & Queries for Fellow Dharma Revolutionaries (New York: New Directions, 1969; London: Cape, 1970);

Regarding Wave (Iowa City: Windhover Press, 1969; enlarged edition, New York: New Directions, 1970; London: Fulcrum Press, 1972);

Manzanita (Bolinas, Cal.: Four Seasons Foundation, 1972);

The Fudo Trilogy (Berkeley: Shaman Drum, 1973);

Turtle Island (New York: New Directions, 1974);

The Old Ways: Six Essays (San Francisco: City Lights, 1977);

He Who Hunted Birds in His Father's Village: The Dimensions of a Haida Myth (Bolinas, Cal.: Grey Fox, 1979);

Gary Snyder

The Real Work: Interviews & Talks 1964–1979, edited by William Scott McLean (New York: New Directions, 1980);

True Night (North San Juan, Cal.: Bob Giorgio, 1980);

Axe Handles (San Francisco: North Point Press, 1983);

Passage through India (San Francisco: Grey Fox Press, 1983);

Good Wild Sacred (Madley, U.K.: Five Seasons, 1984);

The Fates of Rocks & Trees (San Francisco: James Linden, 1986);

Left Out in the Rain: New Poems 1947–1985 (San Francisco: North Point Press, 1986);

The Practice of the Wild (San Francisco: North Point Press, 1990);

No Nature: New and Selected Poems (New York: Pantheon, 1992);

North Pacific Lands & Waters: A Further Six Sections (Waldron Island: Brooding Heron Press, 1993);

A Place in Space: Ethics, Aesthetics, and Watersheds: New and Selected Prose (Washington, D.C.: Counterpoint, 1995).

OTHER: *The New American Poetry,* edited by Donald M. Allen (New York: Grove, 1960), pp. 420–421;

Naked Poetry, edited by Stephen Berg and Robert Mezey (New York: Bobbs-Merrill, 1969);

On Bread & Poetry: A Panel Discussion with Gary Snyder, Lew Welch, & Philip Whalen, edited by Donald Allen (Bolinas, Cal.: Grey Fox Press, 1977);

Kent Johnson and Craig Paulenich, ed., *Beneath a Single Moon: Buddhism in Contemporary American Poetry,* introduction by Snyder (Boston: Shambhala, 1991).

As Wendell Berry writes in his contribution to *Gary Snyder: Dimensions of a Life* (1991), "One thing that distinguishes Gary Snyder among his literary contemporaries is his willingness to address himself, in his life and in his work, to hard practical questions." Snyder's work is informed by anarchist and union politics, Amerindian lore, Zen Buddhism, and a pragmatic commitment to and delight in the daily work that sustains community. It is important to emphasize the integrity but insufficiency of Snyder's poetry to his total cultural project. As is suggested by his title *The Practice of the Wild,* a 1990 essay collection, he wants to heal the division between practice, a cultural activity, and the wild by reading the wild itself as a culture. His aim in his work and in his life has been to envision and enact the reinhabitation of the American land on a sustainable basis. One of the most highly regarded postwar American poets, Snyder has produced a large body of poetry intelligible to the political and spiritual aspirations of many readers not normally concerned with poetry.

Snyder was born in San Francisco and raised in a poor family on a farm just north of Seattle during the Depression. His family tradition was radical on both sides – socialist and atheist. His mother studied writing at the University of Washington and introduced him to poetry. He attended Lincoln High School in Portland, where he spent

his adolescent years with his younger sister, Anthea, and his mother, who worked as reporter. During these years he had his first experience of wilderness as a member of the Mazama Mountain Climbers. In 1957 he went to Reed College in Portland on a scholarship, where he met the poets Philip Whalen and Lew Welch, who became his lifelong friends, and majored in English and anthropology.

Although his literary education reflected the formalist criticism of the time, anthropology exposed him to other traditions and conceptions of the cultural role of literature. Already at this time he was recognized for his independence, unconventionality, industry, and learning. The 159-page honors thesis he wrote in 1951, *He Who Hunted Birds in His Father's Village: The Dimensions of a Haida Myth* (1979), examined the West Coast tribe's mythology from different methodological points of view and set him on the cross-cultural path he has followed in his work ever since. From 1950 to 1952 he was married to Alison Gass. In 1951 Snyder hitchhiked east to attend graduate school at Indiana University but dropped out after one semester, heading west again to enroll in Japanese and Chinese courses at the University of California at Berkeley in order to prepare himself for a trip to Japan to study Zen. He worked summers as a U.S. Forest Service lookout (1952–1953), a logging crewman in Oregon (1954), and a trail crewman in Yosemite National Park (1955), experiences that would inform his first published books.

In November 1955 Snyder participated in the famous Six Gallery reading in San Francisco, where his friend Allen Ginsberg read "Howl" publicly for the first time, a scene replayed in Jack Kerouac's Beat novel *The Dharma Bums* (1958). This novel, in which Snyder is fictionalized as Dharma hero Japhy Ryder, inaugurated Snyder's career as public figure well before he became famous as a poet and stamped him with a lingering, and ultimately limiting, Beat identity. The Beat writers' apparently freewheeling religiosity, their casual dress and manners, their adoption of jazz, and their experiments with sex and mind-altering drugs set them deliberately at odds with the establishment intelligentsia and cultural elite of the 1950s. One reviewer called them "the know-nothing Beats," but such a view belies the serious spiritual and political commitments of Snyder and many Beat figures.

The poems of *Riprap* (1959) present the young seeker-worker divesting himself of civilization – "All the junk that goes with being human / Drops away" – but an alternative vision is not clearly artic-

Snyder with his sister, Althea, circa 1946 (photograph from the Gary Snyder Collection)

ulated as yet. In "Piute Creek" he encounters the sublime otherness of austere nature but is still unsure of his welcome there. What he is sure of is his deep respect for ordinary manual work and for his teachers among ordinary workers, to whom he dedicates the book. On the title page he defines the word *riprap* as "a cobble of stone laid on steep slick rock to make a trail for horses in the mountains." He makes it the central metaphor of the collection in the beginning of the title poem that is often taken as an *ars poetica*:

> Lay down these words
> Before your mind like rocks.
>   placed solid, by hands
> In choice of place, set
> Before the body of the mind.

"Poetry," as Snyder writes in *Myths & Texts* (1960), is "a riprap on the slick rock of metaphysics." "Riprap" is significant first because it presents Snyder's solution to the Romantic problem of the relation between mind and nature, though his solution may be read as either advancing or diverging from that tradition: to give words in poems the qualities of things in nature. The poem is also important be-

cause it links the poetic solution to a life problem through a key Snyder concept: *work*. Snyder's "nature poetry" is not about aesthetic perception of a pristine nature but about work as an activity that mediates between humans and the material world. For Snyder the acts of the mind are grounded in physical activity. As he noted in his contribution to the classic anthology *The New American Poetry* (1960), "I've just recently come to realize that the rhythms of my poems follow the rhythms of the physical work I'm doing . . . at any given time."

Snyder writes in the American tradition articulated by William Carlos Williams in *Paterson* (1963), a poetry that discovers "no ideas but in things," or better, poetry as "a reply to Greek and Latin with the bare hands." Although as a West Coast poet he looks to Asia for supplements to his American experience rather than to Europe, he occasionally invokes the Western tradition to define his difference from it. In "Milton by Firelight," Satan is compared to the poet's trail-crew leader, Roy Marchbanks. The poem juxtaposes Satan's exclamation of despair upon seeing the unfallen Adam and Eve in the garden – "O hell, what do mine eyes / with grief behold?" – and a "Singlejack miner, who can sense / The vein and cleavage / In the very guts of rock." The juxtaposition provokes a question: "What use, Milton, a silly story / Of our lost general parents, eaters of fruit?" The crisis that captures Milton's imagination is rejected in favor of the grounded selves of the miner and an Indian boy who live in the context of the ancient sierras: "No paradise, no fall, / Only the weathering land." While Snyder finds among workers types of the poet-sage, he also looks to history. At Berkeley he translated the work of Han Shan (650–727), a hermit who lived during the T'ang dynasty, which he includes as "Cold Mountain Poems" in the collection *Riprap & Cold Mountain Poems* (1965). Han Shan "and his sidekick," Snyder writes, "became great favorites with Zen painters of later days – the scroll, the broom, the wild hair and laughter." Han Shan disdained ambition and the usual run of social life; instead, he chose a place in "a tangle of cliffs," where he reveled in "the pearl of the Buddha-nature." Cold Mountain becomes a metaphor for a life lived free and an expression of Buddhist metaphysics:

Cold Mountain is a house
Without beams or walls.
The six doors left and right are open
The hall is blue sky.
The rooms all vacant and vague
The east wall beats on the west wall
At the center nothing.

Myths & Texts, which was begun in 1952 and finished in 1956, is a more systematic and ambitious volume. Except for the still unfinished "Mountains and Rivers without End," published in six sections in 1965, it is the only volume of his work conceived as a whole rather than as a collection. The book was written under the influence of Ezra Pound's *Cantos,* which Snyder read as an undergraduate. Snyder shares Pound's stress on concision, on the natural object as the adequate symbol, and on presentation rather than expression. Image-line units similar to Pound's – for example, a line such as "Thick frost on the pine bow" – are standard. The influence is structural as well as stylistic, most obviously in the organization of a variety of texts, modes, documents, and anecdotes according to the principle of juxtaposition, or collage, rather than narrative or exposition.

Myths & Texts has received less critical attention than either *Riprap* or subsequent books. It is more forbidding partly because of the absence of a consistent subjective center, or lyric "I" – the likable, straightforward speaker of the typical Snyder poem – and partly because of the inconclusiveness of its radically allusive poetics. It is less interesting as poetic autobiography than as technical experiment reflecting Snyder's early work experience and preoccupations. As Patrick Murphy observes in his essay on *Myths & Texts* in the collection *Critical Essays on Gary Snyder* (1991), which he edited, critics have observed two principals of structure underlying the poem: it is a quest, or, according to Lee Bartlett in "Gary Snyder's *Myths & Texts* and the Monomyth" (also published in *Critical Essays*), it is a three-part progression adding up to what Joseph Campbell calls a "monomyth." The book's three sections, "Logging," "Hunting," and "Burning," correspond, Bartlett argues, to "separation – initiation – return," a journey from an Apollonian vision of experience to a Dionysian one. Murphy argues that the volume is better understood as structured by the alternation and interpenetration of "texts," or phenomenal experience, and "myths," or cultural interpretations.

Part 1, "Logging," is based on Snyder's own logging experience in Oregon, but its thematic core is not personal. It comments on the exploitative and ultimately *culturally* destructive logging enterprise by juxtaposing different levels of experiences, texts, and myths. Thoreau declared that "The sun is but a morning star," but Snyder opens with a literalizing counter, stating that "the morning star is not a star"; he then cites a second position, that "The May Queen / Is the survival of / A pre-human rutting season" and tacitly relates this to images of contemporary San Francisco through juxtaposition: "Green comes out of the ground / Birds squabble / Young girls run mad with the pine bough." The second poem tells a different story in *its* selected myths and texts. Exodus 34:13 – "But ye shall destroy their altars, break their images, and cut down their groves" – stands as a metonym for Western attitudes to the wild and to the investment of the wild with sacred meaning by premodern peoples. The "text" of this "myth" is that both in China and elsewhere ancient forests have long since been logged; "San Francisco 2 x 4s / were the woods around Seattle." In this poem the poet is waking "from bitter dreams" to the real world of logging: "250,000 board-feet a day / If both Cats keep working / & nobody gets hurt."

The second section, "Hunting," initiates a process of healing. Hunting describes a relationship with the natural world that may be either merely destructive or productive of integral relations. It is closely linked to shamanism, which is in turn linked to poetry. All three are cultural activities – forms of meditation or ritual – that aim to bring the hunter-

Snyder at Sourdough Mountain Lookout, summer 1953

shaman-poet into intimate contact with animals. "The shaman-poet," as Snyder writes in *Earth House Hold: Technical Notes & Queries for Fellow Dharma Revolutionaries* (1969), "is simply a man whose mind reaches easily out into all manners of shapes and other lives, and gives song to dreams." Shamanism is Snyder's metaphor for imagining an ideology of human-animal-wild relations to replace the mainline Western ideology.

The first poem of the Hunting section, *"first shaman song,"* situates Snyder on an apparent vision-quest, fasting in isolation to achieve a dislocation of the self and open a chink to shamanistic wisdom. The section then enacts textually a shamanistic experience. In *"this poem is for bear"* Snyder retells a local native tale – shamanistic lore – about the union of a woman and a bear. Commenting on the story, the poet debunks his own potential, as if he is not yet ready for transformation. The critical piece in the section is *"this poem is for deer."* It depicts first the ugly practice of shooting deer from cars, in which Snyder has apparently been involved at least once, and moves toward an experience of expiation or *kenosis:* "Deer don't want to die for me. / I'll drink sea-water / Sleep on beach pebbles in the rain / Until the deer come down to die / in pity for my pain."

The third section opens with *"second shaman song,"* in which the speaker initiates a second phase

of his wilderness quest, "Quivering in nerve and muscle / Hung in the pelvic cradle / Bones propped against roots / A blind flicker of nerve . . . . /A mud-streaked thigh." The section then presents a series of purgative confrontations with evil, fear, and death that include *"Maudgalyayana saw hell"* and *"Maitreya the future Buddha."* One poem describes John Muir on Mount Ritter. Despairing of finding a foothold or handhold to lead him from the rock face, Muir discovers that "life blaze[es] / Forth again with a preternatural clearness. . . . every rift and flaw in / The rock was seen as through a microscope." Snyder achieves a vision of the Earth as feminine Buddhist Prajna: "The Mother whose body is the Universe / Whose breasts are Sun and Moon, / the statue of Prajna / From Java: the quiet smile, / The naked breasts."

The volume ends by juxtaposing the literal and mythical versions of an event. The final poem describes a fire on Sourdough Mountain that is fought all night. In the morning the firefighters "saw / the last glimmer of the morning star." Snyder gives the event mythical significance by alluding to the ancient city of Troy burning. He asserts that the "mountains are your mind" and sees "the last wisp of smoke float up / Into the absolute cold / Into the spiral whorls of fire / The storms of the Milky Way" as "'Buddha incense in an empty world.'" With this successful conclusion to the "alternation and interpenetration" of myth and text, he is able to say with Thoreau in the last line that "the sun is but a morning star" and look forward to regeneration.

Between 1956, when he won a First American Zen Centre scholarship, and 1968, when he returned to the United States permanently, Snyder spent most of his time in Kyoto, Japan, where he studied as a lay monk in the rigorous Rinzai sect of Zen under his beloved teacher Oda Sesso Roshi, who died in 1966. He was married to the poet Joanne Kyger between 1960 and 1964. *The Back Country* (1967) charts his experience of living in Japan, his visit to India with Kyger and Allen Ginsberg in 1962, and his first return to the United States in 1966. Along with *Regarding Wave* (1969) and *Earth House Hold,* a collection of notes, reviews, and essays, *The Back Country* established Snyder as a poet and extended his fame as a countercultural hero. The first critical article on his work was published in 1968.

Studying Zen as a lay monk in Kyoto, Snyder gradually came into contact with a Japanese Beat scene, a group of people calling themselves the Bum Academy, and developed an important friendship with the wandering poet and teacher Nanao Sakaki.

He also met, in 1966, Masa Uehara, a graduate student in English at Ochanomizu Women's University. Following Sakaki with several others, Snyder and Masa settled on a sparsely populated volcanic island off the Japanese coast called Suwanose in 1967, where they established the Banyan Ashram, an experiment in communal living. With Sakaki acting as priest, Snyder and Masa were married on 6 August 1967 at 6:30 A.M. on the lip of the active volcano. The Suwanose experience is described in the last essay of *Earth House Hold,* concluding the movement from solitary seeker of *Riprap* to marriage and community. "It is possible at last," he writes, "for Masa and me to imagine a little what the ancient – archaic – mind and life of Japan were. And to see what could be restored to the life today." In December 1968 Snyder, Masa, and their new son, Kai, returned to the United States and set up residence in San Francisco. A second son, Gen, was born in 1969.

In some ways Snyder's least political volume, *The Back Country* covers about a decade of his life. The title can be read as referring to the wilderness, the unconscious, and the so-called backward countries of the East. The book is divided into four sections, "Far West," "Far East," "Kali," and "Back," which correspond roughly to Snyder's experiences in the American West, Japan, India, and to his return to the United States – or, in different terms, a journey from home, to otherness, to chaos and dread, and back to home on a different plane. As Charles Molesworth suggests in his book on Snyder, "If we realize the fourth section refers, among other things, to a return to America, and if we recognize in 'Kali' that much of the imagery and incidents are drawn from Snyder's visit to India in 1962, then obviously place becomes the central metaphor of the book." Place will increasingly form the basis for cultural vision in Snyder's work, and *The Back Country* as a whole traces his transformation from traveler to dweller, from alienated American to inhabitant of what he will call "Turtle Island."

"Far West" contains several of Snyder's best-known poems. "A Walk" seems like merely a casual anecdotal narrative of a hike in the woods, but it is significant in the way it concretizes values, encouraging engagement and satisfaction through its simple accumulation of particulars that, as Charles Altieri notes in *Enlarging the Temple* (1978), "require one another if they are to be appreciated fully":

> The tent flaps in the warm
> Early sun: I've eaten breakfast and I'll
> take a walk
> To Benson Lake. Packed a lunch,
> Goodbye. Hopping on creekbed boulders

> Up the rock throat three miles
> Piute Creek –
> In a steep gorge glacier-slick rattlesnake country
> Jump, land by a pool, trout skitter,
> The clear sky. Deer tracks.

Details accumulate, jostle, both in the walk and in the poem; they are completed in the arrival "At last," where he eats by the old cookstove of a trail crew. Not merely sensory, the process is in an ordinary and important sense customary: he repeats the basic but sacramental satisfactions of others before him.

The juxtaposition of such images is not merely reportorial; it should be emphasized that Snyder uses techniques he learned jointly from Pound and from Chinese poetics. As far back as his "Lookout's Journal," the opening piece in *Earth House Hold,* he noted a technical strategy based on a principal akin to Zen philosophy:

> form – leaving things out at the right spot
> ellipse, is emptiness[.]

Snyder uses gaps and spaces expressively to score the reading of the poem and give it a visual rhythm. Silences or gaps also admit the essential emptiness out of which, according to Zen, phenomena arise and into which they return.

"Burning the Small Dead" illustrates various potentials of the strategy:

> Burning the small dead
> branches
> . . . .
> a hundred summers
> snowmelt rock   and air

> hiss in a twisted bough.

> sierra granite;
> mt. Ritter –
> black rock twice as old.

> Deneb, Altair

> windy fire[.]

Elisions, juxtapositions, spacing – these are as important as the words themselves. While the speaker is apparently burning branches, the poem seems to go on without him, more as a function of the activity itself. The relations configured in the poem, seemingly random, actually articulate an ethos, a view of relations in the world. The star Deneb and Altair and windy fire are set in apposition to one another, inviting the reader to discover identi-

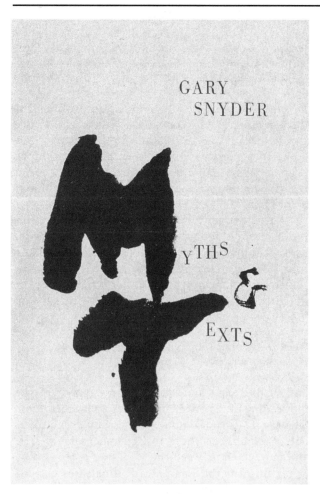

*Cover for Snyder's 1960 book, in which he draws on his work
experiences to create a mythology*

lege. He concludes the last, "I feel ancient, as
though I had / Lived many lives. // And may never
now know / If I am a fool / Or have done what my /
karma demands." The second section also includes
"Six Years," a picture of one phase of his life in
Japan reshuffled into a twelve-poem cycle representing a year, in which Snyder takes his predilection
for the metonymic list to an extreme. The next section, "Kali," presents images of danger and evil that
provoke an uncharacteristic yearning for "the safe
place in a blanket burrow." "This Tokyo" represents Snyder at his bleakest. The meditation is
opened and, more important, closed by the refrain
"Peace war religion revolution / will not help." But
"Back" elaborates a more positive vision, notably in
"Through the Smoke Hole," a poem based on Hopi
Indian cosmology. The kiva, a ceremonial structure, serves as an analogue for Snyder's own vision
of a multiworld universe, while the kiva rituals for
ensuring the continuity of community through life
and death offer structures for Snyder's own movement beyond, if not exclusive of, the vision of
"Kali" and toward the real work of building community in his native place.

Regarding Wave, written under the influence of
his Japanese anarchist-visionary friends, sets Snyder
firmly on a new communitarian course, celebrating
a countercultural hero's version of family values.
The collection begins with a poem titled "Wave," a
meditation that associates the words *wave* and *wife.*
The poem is a self-delighted unfolding of what it
means to have a wife: the word, the woman, the
"wyfman," the erotic, spiritual adventure that is
"'veiled; vibrating; vague'":

> Ah, trembling spreading radiating wyf
> 　　　　　racing zebra
> 　catch me and fling me wide
> To the dancing grain of things
> 　　　　　　　　of my mind!

The last phrase, "dancing grain of things / of my
mind," nicely articulates the repetitions Snyder affirms as generated out of *wyf,* the repetition that
occurs at once in things and in the things of the
mind.

An exuberant formalism, or in Charles
Olson's phrase, representation "by the *primitive-
abstract,*" dominates the book. Many poems elaborate a basic perception of formal and spiritual correspondences between different ontological planes. In
"Song of the Tangle" lovers who "sit all folded" formally "repeat" the ancient temple and landscape at
the center of which they sit: "Two thigh hills hold
us at the fork / round mount center." Both the over-

ties and differences between them. Deneb and Altair are windy fire at the same time that they obviously have different references. As Altieri notes,
"The process of the poem up to the last line is a
continual pushing outward in time and space until
the contemplative mind reaches the stars Deneb
and Altair. . . . The last line then creates a fusion
of two forces: it is a return to the limited space of
the burning branches, but it is also a continuation
beyond the stars to a kind of essence of fire."
Phenomena are placed in relations that are local
and cosmic, but the basis of their existence is
emptiness.

The subsequent three sections of *The Back
Country* chart Snyder's emotional and spiritual journey out and his return. In "Far East" Snyder appears as an observer in a strange culture, prompted
by dislocation to a degree of self-reflection and ret-
rospective meditation unusual in his poetry. In
"Four Poems for Robin" he remembers an important relationship during his early years at Reed Col-

grown archaic temple and crotches of lovers are forms for discovery: "the tangle of the thigh // the brush / through which we push." "Song of the Slip," a poem arranged with every line centered on the page, proposes that the male's lovemaking completes a physical and spiritual harmony: "seed-prow // moves in and makes home in the whole." When a son is born the poet stays home and discovers a new center: "From dawn til late at night / making a new world of ourselves / around this life."

Such formal design may seem to displace politics, as if the intuition of correspondence was also an intuition of a sufficient world. Thus, in "Everybody Lying on their Stomachs, Head Toward the Candle, Reading, Sleeping, Drawing," as the poet's household forms a circle whose "plank shutter" is "set / Half-open on eternity," the social world is bypassed. But such intuitions of formal and spiritual shapeliness, as partly realized in erotic, family, and natural experience, provide the basis for a militant politics and poetics that envision such harmonies realized in society. *Regarding Wave* lays groundwork for the overtly political verse of later volumes. "Revolution in the Revolution in the Revolution" displays its formal repetition in a revisionary statement of political ideology:

> If the capitalists and imperialists
>   are the exploiters, the masses are the workers.
>   and the party
>   is the communist.
>
> If civilization
>   is the exploiter, the masses is nature.
>   and the party
>   is the poets.
>
> If the abstract rational intellect
>   is the exploiter, the masses is the unconscious.
>   and the party
>   is the yogins.
>
> & POWER
> comes out of the seed-syllables of mantras.

This is a politics based on a kind of formalist logic — the substitution of new elements within the same formula. Mantras themselves are forms — more than contents — that produce a kind of elementary power through repetition. It is the kind of power that Snyder believes will drive political change.

In 1966 Snyder had bought with Allen Ginsberg one hundred acres of land on the San Juan Ridge near Nevada City in northern California. In 1970, with the help of a crew of ten, he built a home for his family there, naming it Kitkitdizze after some local vegetation. In "Buddhism and the Coming Revolution," an essay first written in 1961 and collected in *Earth House Hold,* Snyder states: "The mercy of the West has been social revolution; the mercy of the East has been individual insight into the basic self/void. We need both." Kitkitdizze and its region would be Snyder's place to develop a grounded Buddhism. Buddhism's essential perception of emptiness, its aim to look into the nature of things without prejudice, would be put to the service of a local, ecological politics informed by a planetary perspective.

Turtle Island (1974), Snyder's most successful and highly regarded book, won the Pulitzer Prize for 1975. The first complete book written after his permanent return to the United States, it has generated the most criticism of any of his books, partly because it marks a major turn in his career. The volume as a whole sets forth an explicit, sometimes militant ecopolitics, made urgent on one hand by the sense that a virtual war is being waged against the environment and on the other by the vision of sustainable life on Earth. Snyder's use of form changes as well, shifting away from his earlier emphasis on visual presentation to a more straightforward rhetorical mode. The fourth section of the book, called "Plain Talk," consists of four polemical or didactic essays. Instead of letting the images of nature "speak for themselves," Snyder now wishes "to bring a voice from the wilderness, my constituency. I wish to be a spokesman."

The book is prefaced by an opening prose salvo that explains the title and the poet's purpose in using it. Turtle Island is "the old/new name for the continent, based on many creation myths of the people who have been living here for millenia, and reapplied by some of them to 'North America' in recent years." The name must be changed, he argues, so "that we may see ourselves more accurately on this continent of watersheds and life-communities — plant zones, physiographic provinces, culture areas: following natural boundaries." Snyder calls for nothing less than the undoing of such confounding territorial markers as state lines and national borders, metonymies for civilization.

The poems, written in the service of what he calls "the real work," are revisionist histories, prophecies, spells, chants, prayers, jeremiads, and visions, as well as personal lyrics. "I Went into the Maverick Bar" describes his infiltration of a conservative establishment during a rest from the road: "My long hair was tucked up under a cap / I'd left the earring in the car." Cowboys, country music, a couple dancing, holding each other "like in High

School dances / in the fifties" – Snyder acknowledges the innocent appeal of this world: "The short-haired joy and roughness – / America – your stupidity. / I could almost love you again." But out on the road "under the tough old stars" he "came back" to himself, "to the real work, to / 'What is to be done.' " The revolutionary aim of Snyder's work – not just in poetry – is indicated in the citation from Lenin. "Work" in being qualified by the adjective "real" becomes a master term for his cultural project.

American "stupidity" is not "real" because it is complicit in the destruction of the wild. In "The Call of the Wild" the wild is figured as the Native American trickster figure Coyote: amoral, unpredictable, always ungainsayable by human design. But Snyder's coyote is a real animal as well as a figure. The old man who doesn't like coyote "songs" puts out traps; the acidheads from the cities shut him out from their "oil-heated / Geodesic domes, that / Were stuck like warts / In the woods"; the government wages all-out war, "Across Asia first, / And next North America." The coyote is not a spirit that can survive the devastation of the wild. There is "A war against earth. / When it's done there'll be / no place // A Coyote could hide." The envoy reads: "I would like to say / Coyote is forever / Inside you. // But it's not true."

The question posed by this poem is who will inhabit the land: "my sons ask, who are we? / drying apples picked from homestead trees / drying berries, curing meat, / shooting arrows at a bale of straw." Up above "military jets head northeast, roaring every dawn. / my sons ask, who are they?" The poet challenges: "WE SHALL SEE / WHO KNOWS / HOW TO BE." Against the abstract innocence of a country bar and an invasive government, Snyder in "The Bath" celebrates the religious values of his new life of family in nature. Like "Burning the Small Dead," "The Bath" traces a movement from the commonplace phenomena to the apprehension of cosmic significance and back to an immediate reality invested with a larger meaning but in a more elaborate, personal, and ecstatic manner. The bath here is the family soak in the sauna, poet-father-husband-lover, two young sons, and wife-lover-cosmic-mother. The poem depends on juxtaposition, but its principal structural feature is a refrain, "is this our body?," that in its final rendering becomes the declarative "this is our body." Consciously or not, Snyder echoes the Christian mass, which transforms ordinary bread and wine into the body of a dead savior by transforming the daily family bath into an event of religious significance.

Several of Snyder's most perceptive critics have seen the shift in *Turtle Island* as a problematic development. Either the political statements are not justified dramatically, as Altieri argues, or as Robert Kern suggests in *Critical Essays on Gary Snyder,* the statements seem like slogans because Snyder's style is made "for the quick, accurate, and reticent notation of metonymic detail that would provide no foothold for the subjective ego or analytic intellect." Michael Davidson cautions that in Snyder's turn toward a more explicit rhetorical intent "the attendant danger is that the poet will move from seer to prophet and begin to instruct where he might present." But this is only to beg the question of whether didacticism in general, and Snyder's didacticism in particular, must be considered intrinsically antipoetic.

Turtle Island, despite the limitations some critics find, can perhaps best be appreciated within its historical context. Snyder wrote the book after the bloom had gone off 1960s radicalism and in the midst of the first widely perceived ecological crisis, the oil shortage of the early 1970s. His trust in the body, in the goodness of natural impulses, in the ability of poetry to share in that goodness – a poetics of immediate experience – gives way in the 1970s to a more rhetorical style capable of dealing with the disappointments and complexities of new kinds of politics. At the same time, Snyder acknowledges both the temptation of rhetoric and its dangers, because, as he told Ekbert Faas, it may afford only a quick-fix of emotion and ideas "as against the work of doing it structurally. Convincing people with ideas is one system, the other is to change its structural basis."

Many critics have noted Snyder's tendency to elide the pronoun "I" in his poetry. For example, in "Six-Month Song in the Foothills" from *The Back Country* the preparation of tools for the spring is described. Instead of stating, "*I* am sharpening the saws," the "I" is elided, leaving only the participle: "In the cold shed sharpening saw." The speaker is a function of the work, a belief that can be related to Snyder's more general sense of how human subjectivity is derived. In *The Practice of the Wild* he writes:

how could we *be* were it not for this planet that provided our very shape? Two conditions – gravity and a livable temperature range between freezing and boiling – have given us fluids and flesh. The trees we climb and the ground we walk on have given us five fingers and toes. The 'place' . . . gave us far-seeing eyes, the streams and

Allen Ginsberg and Snyder doing calligraphy, summer 1963 (photograph from the Gary Snyder Collection)

breezes gave us versatile tongues and whorly ears. The land gave us a stride, and the lake a dive. The amazement gave us our kind of mind.

Snyder reverses the priority given to human subjectivity in Western philosophy; subjectivity is a derivative of natural processes. As Davidson suggests, the presentation of the natural ground of subjectivity would seem to be the appropriate mode for the poetry. Snyder observes in his contribution to the anthology *Naked Poetry* (1969) that "Each poem grows from an energy-mine-field-dance, and has its own inner grain. To let it grow, to let it speak for itself, is a large part of the work of the poet." A problem arises in *Turtle Island* because political activism in a modern nation-state is not given by nature. Nature lacks rhetorical skills, and this is why Snyder is compelled to assume a "legislative role" with the wild as his constituency. If the poets are the party of nature in a defensive war against civilization, they must marshal their rhetorical powers.

Underlying the rhetoric, however, is a perception both "primitive" and Buddhist that, as he says in "It Pleases," "The world does as it pleases."

"Knowing that nothing need be done," he writes in "Plain Talk," "is where we begin to move from." As he suggests in "As For Poets," there is an earth poet, air poet, fire poet, water poet, and space poet, all with their peculiar gifts, but the ultimate place to be what Buddhists call "original mind," which encompasses matter and spirit, is the house without walls on Cold Mountain:

> A Mind Poet
> Stays in the house.
> The house is empty
> And it has no walls.
> The poem
> Is seen from all sides,
> Everywhere,
> At once.

Such freedom from anxiety – knowing that nothing *need* be done – permits one of Snyder's achievements, a lyric poetry outside the Romantic tradition. Snyder produces lyric speakers who, rather than exercise a lyric crisis of subjectivity in isolation, participate, with good humor and compassion, in collective and political endeavors.

Cover for Snyder's 1967 collection, which is structured by his experiences in Japan, India, and the American West

edge and the knowledge of knowledge, or culture. Snyder recalls Pound and quotes to his son: "When making an axe handle / the pattern is not far off ": "And he sees." Now he recalls also Lu Ji of the fourth century A.D.: – "in making the handle / Of an axe / By cutting wood with an axe / The model is indeed near at hand" – and his Chinese teacher, Shih-hsiang, who translated it years ago:

> And I see: Pound was an axe,
> Chen was an axe, I am an axe
> And my son a handle, soon
> To be shaping again, model
> And tool, craft of culture,
> How we go on.

Two poems in the collection especially speak to the poles of Snyder's career, wandering and dwelling. "True Night," Robert Schultz and David Wyatt suggest in "Gary Snyder and the Curve of Return" from *Critical Essays on Gary Synder,* articulates "the tension between the urge to be out and away and the need to settle and stay." Awakened from sleep to chase away raccoons from the kitchen, Snyder is arrested by the moment of stillness and emptiness: "I am all alive to the night. / Bare foot shaping on gravel / Stick in the hand forever." "Fifty years old," he reflects sardonically, "I still spend my time / Screwing nuts down on bolts." But he is pulled back, in Wyatt's words, by "a contrary motion," realizing that "One cannot stay too long awake / In this dark." Life is back with his family, "the waking that comes / Every day // With the dawn." The final poem, "For All," elaborates that insight as a statement of faith and purpose. Snyder is not primarily an ironic writer, but the light irony in this version of the pledge of allegiance to the American flag provides enough tension to make the poem more than a political program. It moves from exclamation, "ah to be alive" – the mind's amazement – to illustration through metonymic description of fording a stream. This delighted kinetic experience of contiguity – not alienation, not fusion – opens to the single line, "I pledge allegiance":

> I pledge allegiance to the soil
>   of Turtle Island,
> and to the beings who thereon dwell
>   one ecosystem
>   in diversity
>   under the sun
> With joyful interpenetration for all.

In the nine years that passed between *Turtle Island* and his next major volume of poems, *Axe Handles* (1983), Snyder was building a life on the San Juan Ridge with his wife and sons, an activity honored in the new collection's dedication: "This book is for San Juan Ridge." The didacticism of the previous collection is tempered even as it becomes a central theme of *Axe Handles.* "From/For Lew," a poem dedicated to his Reed College friend Lew Welch, exemplifies the content of instruction. Snyder, surprised Welch has not killed himself after all, sees his friend in a dream; but Welch actually is dead and has appeared only to ask Snyder to teach him the wisdom of cycles. Welch's appearance is itself one turn in the cycling of life, death, and knowledge.

In "Axe Handles" Snyder recalls teaching his son Kai how to shape a handle for his hatchet from a broken-off axe handle. The poem becomes a reflection on the transmission of both practical knowl-

A broadside of "for all" is posted on one wall of the North Columbia Cultural Center on San Juan Ridge.

In the spring of 1986 Snyder became a faculty member at the University of California at Davis, two hours' drive from his home. He has taught creative writing, literature, and wilderness thought and has been actively involved in bringing writers to the campus and in developing a program in nature and culture. This position freed him from the arduous poetry-reading circuit and gave him another area of activity, a broad scholarly community, and the encouragement to produce *Practice of the Wild,* a sustained work of prose distinct from his previous collections of occasional essays and talks. In 1991 Snyder's many friends and colleagues contributed to *Gary Snyder: Dimensions of a Life,* a book honoring the poet's sixtieth birthday. They testify to Snyder's worth as a teacher of Zen and as a model of pragmatism, courtesy, good sense, and leadership. He is praised for making his home a center for the recreative life of the San Juan community and for his generosity and honesty.

Although he has not produced a major volume of poetry since *Axe Handles,* Snyder in the fifteen-poem final section of *No Nature: New and Selected Poems* (1992), titled "No Nature," continues his "real work." Snyder seems to be looking back over his career in such poems as "On Climbing the Sierra Matterhorn Again After Thirty-One Years":

> Range after range of mountains
> Year after year after year.
> I am still in love.

"The cultural revolution is over," he says in "Building," a poem dedicated to his neighbors. But "this dance with Matter / Goes on: our buildings are solid, to live, to teach, to sit, / To sit, to know for sure the sound of a bell – / This is history. This is outside history." Snyder again articulates a Buddhist perception: nothing need be done, yet it will be done:

> Buildings are built in the moment,
>> they are constantly wet from the pool
>>> that renews all things
>> naked and gleaming.

The last poem of the volume, "Ripples on the Surface," may reflect Snyder's exposure to poststructuralist thought at Davis, showing the latest inflection of Snyder's thinking on the relations between nature and culture:

> "Ripples on the surface of the water –
> were silver salmon passing under – different
> from the ripples caused by breezes"

Snyder asserts that nature has a signifying practice; because the ripples signify, Snyder concludes: " – Nature not a book, but a *performance,* a / high old culture." Culture is not a category of society only, not a structure set off from the wild: there is in a sense "No nature," only "Both together, one big empty house" – Cold Mountain.

Recent developments in cultural studies have made possible a less literary assessment of Snyder's work. Tim Dean's *Gary Snyder and the American Unconscious: Inhabiting the Ground* (1991) is the most ambitious work on Snyder to date, both in the critical, cultural, and theoretical materials it brings to a reading of a small selection of representative poems and in the claims it makes, not so much for Snyder's greatness as a poet but for his important role in the construction of American culture in the late twentieth century. For Dean, American culture is defined both by the central role of the land in its development and by the repression of its real relation to that land, which is one of exploitation. Snyder is significant because his principal address as poet and thinker is to that very relation, and his principal goal as cultural worker is the reinhabitation of the ground according to a different relation. His work reminds us over and over, as in *The Practice of the Wild,* that "It is not enough just to 'love nature' or to want to 'be in harmony with Gaia.' " In his 1990 interview with David Robertson, Snyder indicated that his next project would be the completion of his long poem begun in the late 1950s, "Mountains and Rivers without End."

Interviews:

Ekbert Faas, ed., *Towards a New American Poetics: Essays and Interviews* (Santa Barbara: Black Sparrow Press, 1978), pp. 105–142;

William Scott McLean, ed., *The Real Work: Interviews & Talks 1964–1979* (New York: New Directions, 1980);

Julia Martin, "Coyote-Mind: An Interview with Gary Snyder," *Triquarterly,* 79 (Fall 1990): 148–172;

David Robertson, "Practicing the Wild – Present and Future Plans: An Interview with Gary Snyder," in *Critical Essays on Gary Snyder,* edited by Patrick D. Murphy (Boston: G. K. Hall, 1991), pp. 257–262.

Bibliographies:

Katherine McNeil, *Gary Snyder: A Bibliography,* Phoenix Bibliographies Series, 8 (New York: Phoenix Bookshop, 1983);

Tom Lavazzi, "Gary Snyder: An International Checklist of Criticism," *Sagetrieb,* 12 (Spring 1993): 97–128.

Biographies:

David Kheridan, *A Biographical Sketch and a Descriptive Checklist of Gary Snyder* (Berkeley: Oyez, 1965);

Jon Halper, ed., *Gary Snyder: Dimensions of a Life* (San Francisco: Sierra Club Books, 1991).

References:

Charles Altieri, *Enlarging the Temple: New Directions in American Poetry during the 1960s* (Lewisburg, Pa.: Bucknell University Press, 1978);

Altieri, "Gary Snyder's *Turtle Island*: The Problem of Reconciling the Roles of Seer and Prophet," *Boundary,* 2, 4 (1976): 761–777;

Christopher Beach, "Pound's Words in Their Pockets: Denise Levertov and Gary Snyder," in his *ABC of Influence: Ezra Pound and the Remaking of the American Poetic Tradition* (Berkeley & Los Angeles: University of California Press, 1992), pp. 190–216;

Michael Davidson, *The San Francisco Renaissance: Poetics and Community at Mid-Century* (New York: Cambridge University Press, 1989);

Tim Dean, *Gary Snyder and the American Unconscious: Inhabiting the Ground* (London: Macmillan, 1991);

Robert Kern, "Recipes, Catalogues, Open Form Poetics: Gary Snyder's Archtypal Voice," *Contemporary Poetry,* 18, no. 2 (1977): 173–197;

Charles Molesworth, *Gary Snyder's Vision: Poetry and the Real Work* (Columbia: University of Missouri Press, 1983);

Patrick D. Murphy, ed., *Critical Essays on Gary Snyder* (Boston: G. K. Hall, 1991);

Jody Norton, "The Importance of Nothing: Absence and its Origins in the Poetry of Gary Snyder," *Contemporary Literature,* 28 (Spring 1987): 41–66;

Thomas Parkinson, "The Poetry of Gary Snyder," *Southern Review,* 4 (Summer 1968): 616–632;

Bob Steuding, *Gary Snyder* (Boston: Twayne, 1976).

Papers:

The Gary Snyder Collection, including more than one hundred thousand items, is housed at the University of California at Davis.

Charles Wright

(25 August 1935 –   )

James McCorkle

See also the Wright entry in *DLB Yearbook 1982*.

BOOKS: *The Voyage* (Iowa City: Patrician Press, 1963);

6 Poems (London: David Freed, 1965);

The Dream Animal (Toronto: Anansi, 1968);

Private Madrigals (Madison, Wis.: Abraxas Press, 1969);

The Grave of the Right Hand (Middletown, Conn.: Wesleyan University Press, 1970);

The Venice Notebook (Boston: Barn Dream Press, 1971);

Backwater (Santa Ana, Cal.: Golem Press, 1973);

Hard Freight (Middletown, Conn.: Wesleyan University Press, 1973);

Bloodlines (Middletown, Conn.: Wesleyan University Press, 1975);

China Trace (Middletown, Conn.: Wesleyan University Press, 1977);

Colophons (Iowa City: Windhover Press, 1977);

Wright: A Profile (Iowa City: Grilled Flowers Press, 1979);

Dead Color (Salem, Oreg.: Charles Seluzicki, 1980);

The Southern Cross (New York: Random House, 1981);

Country Music: Selected Early Poems (Middletown, Conn.: Wesleyan University Press, 1982);

Four Poems of Departure (Portland, Oreg.: Trace Editions, 1983);

The Other Side of the River (New York: Random House, 1984);

Five Journals (New York: Red Ozier Press, 1986);

Halflife: Improvisations and Interviews 1977–87 (Ann Arbor: University of Michigan Press, 1988);

Zone Journals (New York: Farrar, Straus & Giroux, 1988);

Xionia (Iowa City: Windhover Press, 1990);

The World of the Ten Thousand Things (New York: Farrar, Straus & Giroux, 1990);

Chickamauga (New York: Farrar, Straus & Giroux, 1995);

Charles Wright (photograph by Nancy Crampton)

Quarter Notes: Improvisations and Interviews (Ann Arbor: University of Michigan Press, 1995).

OTHER: Mark Strand, ed., *The Contemporary American Poets,* includes a poem by Wright (New York: World, 1969);

Daniel Halpern, ed., *The American Poetry Anthology,* includes poems by Wright (New York: Avon, 1975);

Stuart Friebert and David Young, eds., *The Longman Anthology of Contemporary American Poetry,* includes poems by Wright (New York: Longman, 1983);

A. Poulin Jr., ed., *Contemporary American Poetry*, includes poems by Wright (Boston: Houghton Mifflin, 1985);

David Lehman, ed., *Ecstatic Occasions, Expedient Forms*, includes a poem and commentary by Wright (New York: Collier, 1987);

J. D. McClatchy, ed., *The Vintage Book of Contemporary American Poetry*, includes poems by Wright (New York: Vintage, 1990).

TRANSLATIONS: Eugenio Montale, *The Storm and Other Poems* (Oberlin, Ohio: Oberlin College, Field Translation Series, 1978);

Dino Campana, *Orphic Songs* (Oberlin, Ohio: Oberlin College, Field Translation Series, 1984).

RECORDING: *Poets In Person: Charles Wright with J. D. McClatchy,* Modern Poetry Association, Chicago, 1991.

The insistence on the radiant image and line, a line that traces the sacred dimension of the natural world and offers a space of contemplation, is a central and defining quality of the poetry of Charles Wright. More than most poets of his generation, he has written poetry that has increasingly explored the overlay of sensual and sacred beauty. Although he generally eschews narrative and expository elements in his work, most of his poems have an autobiographical grounding; in fact, the poems almost always emerge from specific images of particular places, whether they be Tennessee, Italy, or California. Rigorously constructed, Wright's poems emphasize the possibilities of associative connections between images. In counterbalance to this visual element, Wright's lines stress musicality and the richness of shifting rhythms. In describing the objective of poetry, Wright essentially defines himself: in his *Halflife: Improvisations and Interviews 1977–87* (1988), he states that "the ultimate duty and fate of the poet is visionary."

Born in 1935 in Pickwick Dam, Tennessee, Wright grew up in eastern Tennessee and western North Carolina. After graduating from Davidson College in 1957, he served in the army's Intelligence Service for four years (1957–1961), three of which he spent in Verona, Italy, where he began to write poems. He later studied at the Writers Workshop at the University of Iowa, receiving an M.F.A. in 1963, then returned to Italy as a Fulbright Scholar to teach at the University of Rome and begin his translations from the Italian of Eugenio

Montale, Pier Paolo Pasolini, and Cesare Pavese. From 1965 to 1966 Wright returned to the University of Iowa. In 1968 he taught in Padua as a Fulbright lecturer, and in the following year he married the photographer Holly McIntire (they have one son, Luke). From 1966 to 1983, Wright taught at the University of California at Irvine and, since 1983, he has taught at the University of Virginia in Charlottesville.

Wright's poetry won early acclaim. His second book, *Hard Freight* (1973), was nominated for a National Book Award; he then received a National Endowment for the Arts Grant in 1974 and a Guggenheim Fellowship in 1975. Wright's third book, *Bloodlines* (1975), won the Edgar Allan Poe Award from the Academy of American Poets and the Melville Cane Award from the Poetry Society of America in 1976. Wright also received an Academy-Institute Grant from the American Academy and Institute of Arts and Letters in 1977. His translation of Montale's *The Storm and Other Poems* (1978) won the 1979 P.E.N. Translation Prize, and his collected early poems, *Country Music: Selected Early Poems* (1982), won the 1983 National Book Award. In 1987 he received the Brandeis University Creative Arts Citation for Poetry.

As Wright has recalled in his rare interviews, his impetus to write began while he was stationed in Verona, where he first read Ezra Pound's *Selected Poems* (1928) and the poems of Montale while reveling in the surrounding landscape of Sirmione and Lake Garda. The formal demands of Pound's *Cantos* — both in the use of the line and image, as well as in the developing architectural form of the whole — have exerted an influence throughout Wright's career. Through Pound, Wright was introduced to the work of Ovid and Dante and the spiritual and aural sensibility of poetry. Like many poets of his generation and the one before his, he regarded translation as an important task and discipline, and his beginnings as a poet are intertwined with his translations of Montale, his work in both areas beginning in earnest while he was at the University of Iowa in 1961.

Significantly, Wright has emphasized in interviews his indebtedness to his teachers, particularly to his poet-teacher at the University of Iowa, Donald Justice, who was profoundly influential in his development. Justice, in particular, provided Wright with a history of poetry and poetics, and Justice's attention to the music of the poem is evident in Wright's work, albeit in Wright's own distinct poetic idiom. In his study of Pound, Montale, and Justice, Wright learned to connect language with landscape and with a history both public and intimate. Justice's importance as a teacher to Wright can hardly be overstated. Wright's insistence on the line as the primary and defining structure of poetry derived from Justice's teaching; indeed, Wright states in a 1987 interview that "I was the blackboard and he was the chalk." In another interview Wright states that while on his first Fulbright trip to Rome, he studied with "the second of two wonderful teachers I've had, Maria Sampoli," who guided him through Montale and Dante. Through the influence of such teachers, Wright developed a sense of poetic continuity and genealogy.

In 1970 Wright's first book of poems, *The Grave of the Right Hand,* was published in the distinguished poetry series from Wesleyan University Press. The poems are as precise and enigmatic as the paintings by the Italian Surrealist Giorgio De Chirico: "Someone is crossing the square / Nailed to a door / There is a pair of gloves" ("Self-Portrait"). The poems often employ an American version of Surrealism as it is found in the work of such contemporaries of Wright as Mark Strand, Charles Simic, and W. S. Merwin. The enigmatic, however, is never allowed to become obscure. As in "Self-Portrait," Wright establishes a direct connection, indeed a translation, of several of De Chirico's motifs, as found in such paintings as *The Song of Love* (1914), *Portrait of Guillaume Apollinaire* (1914), or *The Mystery and Melancholy of a Street* (1914). Like De Chirico's paintings, the poems allude to a narrative, but it remains undisclosed, only glimpsed at, unsettling the reader or listener by the juxtaposition of ordinary objects. Wright draws an emptiness from the landscape, a sense of exhaustion and fatality, that again parallels many of De Chirico's paintings; in "To a Friend Who Wished Always to Be Alone," the poet writes, "you begin to recede . . . into yourself, like / Some fountain turned off at dusk." The arrangement of *The Grave of the Right Hand* into five distinct sections reveals Wright's early sense of the construction or architecture of a book. His poems are not solely separate entities but belong to a larger ordering or composition. Far from being diminished by their placement in a larger design, the individual poems are enriched: Wright emphasizes their interconnections and the dialogues between different poems not only by their differing treatments of similar themes but also through their careful arrangement in the book. In *The Grave of the Right Hand,* Wright orders the poems primarily by thematic and tonal demands. For example, the first section, "The Night Watch," is elegiac; the next section, "Departures," explores the theme of memory. This sensi-

tivity to the architecture of the book becomes more significant with each subsequent collection, as well as with the development of Wright's longer, journal-like poems.

Although Wright has dismissed *The Grave of the Right Hand* as his apprenticeship collection, his most commanding themes and concerns find their initial expressions here. He begins his meditations on mortality – the fear of dying rather than the abstraction of death – in such poems as "Private Madrigals" or "Homecoming." Mortality is acknowledged through sequences of images. In "Homecoming," the progression of the evening darkness is counterbalanced by a sequence of light: the cape jasmine blossoms give way to the Milky Way, which in turn gives way to fireflies. In this Dantean play of light against the ensuing darkness, Wright creates both an elegy and a lyrical evocation of his own fear of dying. The evidence of decay presents itself as an aspect of mortality. It is this erosion of life and, hence, of expression, that Wright works against. In the second of his "Private Madrigals," the blight on the fruit of an orange tree is "from something else which has / No name, and will not ever sing." While adhering to the madrigal's form, Wright rejects its traditional amatory subject matter and invokes the presence of mutability.

Mutability and loss, in fact, pervade the collection. Death is a presence that always attempts to silence; for the poet it is the struggle of language to move through and beyond that silence. Wright asks in "American Landscape," "What does one say? What *can* one say: / That death is without a metric, / That it has no metaphor?" The land remains, Wright answers: "The snow; the dark pines, their boughs / Heavy with moisture, and failing." In life and death we are part of this nature and process: "We enter into the earth like shoots, / throwing off tendrils . . . working / Toward some improbable center." This integration with the landscape – almost a Romantic version of the life force – is further elaborated in Wright's later books. The accentual process of naming and the transposition of noun and image, as in lines such as "The otter and wolverine, the elk," or "The ghost-weed and Indian paintbrush," exemplify the sacred element of names. Implicitly, for Wright, language is the material by which one maintains a connection to the sacredness of the landscape. Unlike William Wordsworth or Ralph Waldo Emerson, however, he does not find transcendence in nature; one is ultimately severed from the natural world, despite the yearning toward some form of union with it. Death – metaphoric or literal – is a cutting off, a snapping of

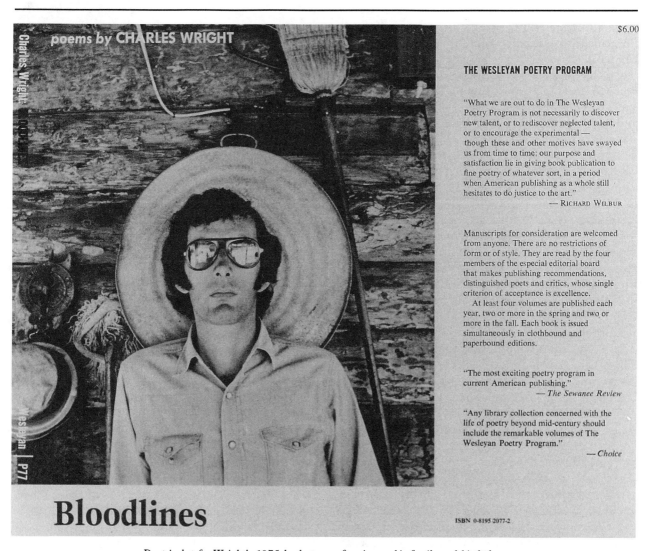

Dust jacket for Wright's 1975 book, poems focusing on his family and birthplace

the cord. At the close of "American Landscape," even what remains, as in the lines "clearings we might have crossed; / The footprints we do not leave?" is cast as an absence and placed in question.

Also present in these poems is the aesthetic of exhaustion, replete with the irony and sarcasm that is evident in the second section of "The Bolivar Letters": "Siegfried Sassoon is dead. . . . / Did you read him? Do you care? / — Nobody ever does." The poems in this series are ostensibly sent to Bolivar, Tennessee, where, as Wright notes, the state institution for the insane is located. With the circumstances of the deaths of Guy de Maupassant, Jonathan Swift, and Sassoon as examples, Wright questions the usefulness and efficacy of writing. Construed as letters, these poems ironically have no addressee; hence, they are sent into silence. Social connection is withdrawn, as Wright places a large X on

the fourth poem of the sequence, giving the reader both the poem and its rejection.

In the final poem, "Black Sonnet," Wright transmutes the sonnet form into an arbitrary list that begins with "0. Psittacosis" and ends with "13. Carthago delenda est." The subversion of the accepted convention, which appears in this antipoem, also appears in Wright's second collection, *Hard Freight,* in the *ars poetica* of "The New Poem," which is similarly constructed as a list, in three-line stanzas, each line beginning with "It will not." By utilizing the device of the anaphora, the poet creates an arbitrariness, where arguably form and procedure generate the poem.

From *The Grave of the Right Hand* only the five prose poems that compose the section "Departures" are reprinted in the later gathering of Wright's early poems, *Country Music: Selected Early Poems.* That other poems are excluded is not a repudiation of his first book; rather, Wright has stated that the publication of *Country Music* provided him the opportunity to gather in one book what he considers a triptych – *Hard Freight, Bloodlines,* and *China Trace* (1977). Instead of the more literary term, trilogy, which implies an interrelatedness on a strictly textual level, Wright prefers "to think of the books as a triptych, three different and separate instances in the same life. . . . The linkage is my life." The prose poems from *The Grave of the Right Hand* provide a point of departure. In volumes after *The Grave of the Right Hand,* Wright explores the integrity of the long line – the way it can be freighted with images without collapsing into prose. Thus, these early prose poems, set in counterpoint to the lyric poems in his first collection, suggest the direction the later poetry takes: an increasingly longer line, carrying within it image and implicit narrative.

The prose poems of Wright's first book offer a mapping of Italy and the poet's imagination; *Hard Freight,* Wright's second book, initiates the poet's explicit autobiographical mapping. Like those in *The Grave of the Right Hand,* the poems of this collection demonstrate a concern with a highly wrought surface and technical virtuosity. Such poems as "Homage to X," "The New Poem," "Nouns," "Slides of Verona," or "Synopsis" test the limits of composition by their emphasis on irony and strict formal arrangements. In contrast, however, "First-born," "Dog Creek Mainline," "Sky Valley Rider," and "Congenital" start Wright's autobiographical explorations. The local setting, evinced through names and their resonances, provides in the opening poem, "Homage to Ezra Pound," a map of Pound's walks through Venice:

Past San Sebastiano, past
The Ogni Santi and San Trovaso, down
The Zattere and left
Across the tiered bridge to where
– Off to the right, half hidden –
The Old Dogana burns in the spring sun:
This is how you arrive.

In the name of a place, as Pound's own work attests, is condensed a history as well as a field of associations. For Wright, Pound is the necessary poet, whose work teaches the demands of the art. With this opening stanza, Wright literally follows Pound's footsteps, even stepping into Pound's gait and poetic rhythm. Wright is not an apologist for Pound but understands Pound's belief that poetry should sing through palimpsest-like images, as in the visionary overlay of Homer and Venice in the

lines "leans to the signal, the low / Rustle of wings, the splash of an oar."

Pound's observation that "rhythm is a form cut into time" profoundly informs Wright's poetic practice. Wright in fact seeks to create an image that is not so much symbolic as it is rhythmic. The poem's language – the very materiality of words – is a stay against the erosiveness of time. In "Congenital," Wright counterbalances continuity with mortality ("These hands are my father's hands") and creation with absence:

Here is where it begins here
In the hawk-light in the quiet
The blue of the shag spruce
Lumescent
          night-rinsed and grand[.]

The presence of language is established and sustained through the heavily stressed lines, the use of epanalepsis in the opening line, and enjambment. Wright implicitly asks what endures: it is not the individual identity but lineage, history, and language. The self is continually effaced in the process of writing and in the movement of life. Any definition of the self in social or political terms collapses in Wright's vision; instead, one's identity exists within the matrices of connection and the recognition of the materiality of the world and word.

Wright's poetry, however, offers a metaphysics that should be read, as Bonnie Costello writes, from "within a Dickinsonian countersublime rather than an Emersonian sublime," and she advises: "measure it not by the confirmation of being in the infinite but by the alienation of being *from* the infinite." What emerges in *Hard Freight* is a struggle between an ironic, deprecatory vision, as in "The New Poem," and a poetry that, while admitting the defeat of transcendence, nonetheless posits that the most genuine form of consciousness is experienced in the activity of representation and characterized by the aesthetic desire for beauty. This struggle is, in fact, not oppositional because neither vision, to paraphrase "The New Poem," will console or attend to the sorrows of the individual; and the desire for beauty through representation comes to dominate Wright's poetry. Yet, for Wright, beauty is not redemption; instead, the aesthetic is the only way to apprehend our utter transience. To contemplate this transience is to attempt to apprehend mortality and to question, as the poet does in "Negatives," "what awaits us, amorphous." To know is not possible; the condition of mortality can only be evoked in the diminishing light of negatives or through the knowledge, although limited and displaced, afforded by similes and other rhetorical devices.

Such meditations find their source in the hermeticism of the Italian poet Eugenio Montale's work, which Wright has brilliantly translated. Montale's influence is seen literally in the translation and transposition of some of his lines into Wright's poetry. A comparison of the concluding lines of "Blackwater Mountain" and Montale's "From a Swiss Lake" demonstrates Wright's affinity with Montale. The elegiac "Blackwater Mountain" ends:

> I stand where we stood before and aim
> My flashlight down to the lake. A black duck
> Explodes to my right, hangs, and is gone.
> He shows me the way to you;
> He shows me the way to a different fire
> Where you, black moon, warm your hands.

As he does in "Negatives," Wright seeks to represent absence. No longer duck hunting, he is hunting memory. What he finds becomes an emblem of the trace of presence. Wright's translation of Montale's poem, included in *The Storm,* concludes:

> Is it you who shines in the darkness? I enter
> the pulsing furrow of night on a sizzling pathway,
> hot on the trail of your light
> predator's tracks (a mark
> almost invisible, star-shaped), and tumble,
> I, outsider; suddenly a black duck
> beats upward on the clotted air from far out on the
>   lake;
> he leads the way to the new fire, where he will burn.

Montale's poem, addressed to an unnamed woman, is a hermetic evocation of desire. Wright translates this desire, established through imagery and metaphor, into an apprehension of mortality.

The most important poem of this collection is "Dog Creek Mainline." In it Wright establishes his connections to a particular landscape. The poem is constructed as a series of liminal movements set off from each other through colons and stanza breaks. The language becomes tauter and more highly stressed, evoking the sprung rhythms of Gerard Manley Hopkins's poetry – an influence Wright shares with Montale. The preponderance of stresses in the opening lines creates a terrain, a high relief map of sound, that issues from the mnemonic qualities of a place-name: "Dog Creek: cat track and bird splay, / Spindrift and windfall; woodrot." The landscape is sacred but does not provide access to transcendence. Landscape and the body are connected in that they share primordial materials: "Dog

Creek" begins "in the leaf reach and shoal run of the blood; / Starts in the falling light just back / Of the fingertips."

"Dog Creek Mainline" presages the experiments in sound and narrative compression present in his third collection, *Bloodlines* (1975). Wright distills his autobiography throughout the poems of this collection so that narrative almost disappears into emblem and image. Nonetheless, in the collection's genealogical title and in the opening poem, "Virgo Descending," Wright indicates that a personal mapping of family and birthplace will be the focus of these poems. The title, *Bloodlines,* alludes to kinship and generational connections; it also suggests the body's own physiological tracery as well as the organic physicality of the poetic line. Time and history are layered into the lines of these poems. The opening stanza of "Virgo Descending" exemplifies these concerns. The first two lines suggest a painterly aesthetic linked to ritual and primordial origins: "Through the viridian (and black of the burnt match), / Through ox-blood and ochre, the ham-colored clay." The reader travels with the poet – under his sign of Virgo – through the pure pigment of aesthetic representation and the blood and clay of matter. The journey moves into Wright's memories of his family and the unfinished house his father was always building. The house is both literal and cosmological, both memory and future.

The house, the cosmos, the family, and the book are constructed: "Through arches and door jambs, the spidery wires / And coiled cables, the blueprint takes shape." *Bloodlines* continues to display Wright's acute architectonic sensibility: its five parts are symmetrically balanced, with the opening and closing sections containing three poems apiece and the second and fourth sections being devoted to a single long poem. The middle section contains two elegies: "Hardin County" is dedicated to Wright's father, and "Delta Traveller" elegizes his mother. This collection establishes Wright as a southern writer, although one could argue that he is actually a writer of southern lights, whether those of Tennessee and the Carolinas or of Italy or of southern California. *Bloodlines,* however, grounds Wright in the lushness and, paradoxically, the sense of endemic loss that is suggested by the landscape and sensibility of the American South.

"Tattoos" and "Skins" are the two central poems of the collection. Each is a twenty-part poem that embeds accumulative autobiographical meditations. "Tattoos" includes notes that indicate the particular autobiographical event underpinning each section. Each section elegizes past moments and be-

Dust jacket for Wright's 1990 book, which includes four collections: The Southern Cross, The Other Side of the River, Zone Journals, *and* Xionia

comes, as the title suggests, a ritualized music; each section is also dated, although the sequence is not arranged chronologically. This book is less an accounting of Wright's life than it is an accumulation of events signaling the difficulty of writing songs of remembrance:

> So light the light that fires you
> – Petals of horn, scales of blood – ,
> Where would you have me return?
> What songs would I sing,
> And the hymns . . . What garden of wax statues.

In this opening section of "Tattoos," Wright attempts to recall his mother, years after her death. In each section Wright questions faith, redemption, mortality, and desire through a compressed recounting of a past incident. Like a tattoo, each of these incidents, memories, or dreams is incised into Wright's consciousness, just as it is incised into the lines of the poem.

"Skins," the parallel sequence of poems, is more abstract than "Tattoos." Each of its twenty

sections is a fourteen-line block, rather than the arrangement of the three five-line stanzas for each section of "Tattoos." This formal distinction emphasizes the movement from meditation to meditation in "Skins." The title suggests the shedding of outward appearances and the ongoing process of moving toward a center of belief and identity. While each section of "Tattoos" has the integrity of a single poem, every section of "Skins" belongs to a larger process. In an interview at Oberlin College in 1977, Wright explained that "Skins" moves up a scale of ten sections and then down ten. He also designates the topics of each section: the first section is introduced by the precept "what you are is what you will be"; section 2 explores the theme of beauty; section 3 refers to truth; section 4 refers to the beginning and end of the universe; section 5, Wright states, is organized religion. In section 6, Wright uses the image of the mayfly to convey metamorphosis. Sections 7, 8, and 9 refer to the four elements – air, fire, earth, and water – or their combinations. The tenth section, the top of the scale, is aether, or what the Greeks called the fifth element, the air above the air. Ending with a colon, this section opens to the descent: section 11 concerns primitive magic; section 12 is about necromancy; section 13 is about black magic; section 14 is concerned with alchemy; and section 15 portrays knowledge as allegorical. All these ways of knowing are rejected. The next four sections, Wright states, are acceptances of what he has previously ascended the scale with: the elements of earth, air, fire, and water. The final section returns to the initial situation of the poem, but this situation appears now in a different light, a changed perspective created by the movement through the preceding positions. Wright does not include notes in *Bloodlines;* however, he does in *Country Music,* thus providing further symmetry between "Tattoos" and "Skins."

While "Tattoos" describes Wright's relation to his past, "Skins" explores his relation to the present. Wright's vision proposes that all is "Procedure and process, the one / Inalterable circulation." This "inalterable circulation," unlike William Butler Yeats's vision of the gyres of history, is wholly individual but also the condition that connects all people to each other. Transience defines the human condition. This situation is depicted by regenerative cycles, where "the sparks / That rise, the cinders, / Rework you and make you new, burned to an ash." Literally, figuratively, and rhythmically, Wright evokes a rising and falling, often offering his insights through the vehicles of paradox and oxymoron. He does not allow for an unbridled integrative, organic vision; he evokes, instead, a sense of the limitations of expression and a final exhaustion of belief:

> And what does it come to, Pilgrim,
> This walking to and fro on the earth, knowing
> That nothing changes, or everything;
> And only, to tell it, these sad marks,
> Phrases half-parsed, ellipses and scratches across the
>   dirt?
> It comes to a point. It comes and it goes.

The poet attempts to represent this relentless movement and, as Wright acknowledges, to realize that in "all beauty there lies / Something inhuman, something you can't know."

In "Link Chain," one of the three closing poems of *Bloodlines,* Wright reiterates the primordial connection between himself and the earth: "Circle by circle, link chain / And hair breath, I'm bound to the oak mulch." This description of regeneration reemphasizes the vision of such a poem as "Firstborn," in *Hard Freight,* where he instructs his young son to "Indenture yourself to the land," because "All things that are are lights." *Bloodlines* also commences Wright's Augustinian view of the world as being filled with luminous alphabets. In "Rural Route," the final poem of the collection, Wright sees "the smears of light / Retrench and repeat their alphabet" on the holly leaves.

With the publication in 1977 of *China Trace,* Wright's triptych completes itself; but the triptych is not an absolute formal arrangement. Wright has stated that *Hard Freight, Bloodlines,* and *China Trace* "are supposed to work together in a smudgy sort of way and are part of an idea I started out with about seven years ago and that I'm about to finish with in *China Trace.*" *Bloodlines* serves as a hinge in the triptych, as the long poem "Tattoos" "hooks up with *Hard Freight* and the past, and 'Skins' hooks up with *China Trace* and the future." *Hard Freight* is composed of discrete poems, whereas two long sequences define *Bloodlines.* With *China Trace,* Wright stated in a 1981 interview, he has created a "long poem with fifty chapters," where "each poem is individual and stands on its own, but there is a span from the goodbye in 'Childhood' to the 'he' — whoever the 'he' is — rising up partially to heaven, or as far as the constellations, which is as far as he gets." The collection is divided into two sections, each prefaced by the same passage from the Italian novelist Italo Calvino's *Invisible Cities* (1972). Their repetition serves to maintain the focus on yearning and pilgrimage, or the desire to apprehend the unknowable, and thus to initiate regeneration.

Each poem in *China Trace* is restricted to a maximum of twelve lines, a limit that underscores the poet's concern with compression. The collection is an implicit homage to Pound's *Cathay* (1915), a seminal work for Wright; it is also an experiment with the compression and economy of form found in classical Chinese poetry and painting. The accumulative process found in *Bloodlines* is present here, but it has assumed the looser, more journal-like quality that Wright will radically develop in later volumes. However, this journal-like approach resembles *pensées,* which are more than daily jottings, as critic Helen Vendler has observed in her *Part of Nature, Part of Us* (1980). In fact, daily experience, at least insofar as it is construed in linear, social narratives, is suppressed in *China Trace.* "By its visionary language," Vendler writes, "it assumes the priority of insight, solitude, and abstraction, while remaining beset by a mysterious loss of something that can be absorbed and reconstituted only in death." While Vendler's statement describes Wright's poetry in general, it is especially applicable to *China Trace,* as illustrated in the opening poem, "Childhood," where the narrator says goodbye to his past: "Shrunken and drained dry, turning transparent, / You've followed me like a dog." The poem concludes with a series of repetitions that, as they accumulate, also subtract:

I'm going away now, goodbye.
Goodbye to the locust husk and the chairs;
Goodbye to the genuflections. Goodbye to the clothes
That circle beneath the earth, the names
Falling into the darkness, face
After face, like beads from a broken rosary.

The poem begins by establishing the fact of loss and the act of journeying toward the poet's apprehension of death, described in the third poem, "Self-Portrait in 2035:" "Darkness, erase these lines, forget these words. / Spider recite his one sin."

Although Wright had a Christian upbringing, it has been, in his words, "something to work against . . . [a] brooding background to get out from under." Moreover, he maintains that "Christianity is very much like childhood," in that it is a memory of "rituals, symbols, processions, songs and circumstance." Intimations of this past resurface throughout the poems; indeed, the myths and symbols of Christianity form an apparatus for questioning the possibility of transcendence and for locating, at least for Wright, the source of the yearning for transcendence, as expressed in the lines in "Clear Night":

I want to be bruised by God.
I want to be strung up in a strong light and singled out.
I want to be stretched, like music wrung from a
    dropped seed.
I want to be entered and picked clean.

The desire for revelation is physical and results in annihilation. Furthermore, the self becomes an obstacle that must be erased to fulfill this desire. The poet is further checked in this aim, because in response to it, "the wind says 'What?' to me." Thus, the world intervenes.

The "he" of each poem in *China Trace* is a pilgrim, akin to Dante in *The Divine Comedy* or "Christian" in John Bunyan's *Pilgrim's Progress* (1678). *China Trace*, however, does not employ allegory; instead, the collection examines the condition of the quotidian self that seems at times exhausted by the world and longs for oblivion – an exhaustion evident in the poem "Next," where the poet states, "I am weary of daily things / . . . How the ice moans and the salt swells." But it is the daily details, such as the luminosity of familiar landscapes, that over-

rides the narrator's sense of exhaustion. More accurately, it is the actual activity of representing the landscape that is luminous. It is the act of discovering and representing beauty that counterbalances the fatigue of the self; and, while the self may indeed be lost in the making of the luminous image, that image is also the trace of the self's presence.

Wright signals the importance of representation by including meditations on the poets Gerard de Nerval, Dino Campana, and Georg Trakl and the painters Giorgio Morandi and Edvard Munch. As it is in previous collections, the addressing of dead poets and artists is an attempt to learn something of their secret knowledge. In "Morandi," Wright gives voice to the painter's aesthetic intentions, which become the basis for Wright's own *ars poetica:* "I'm talking about stillness, the hush / Of a porcelain center bowl, a tear vase, a jug." Morandi painted landscapes and still lifes of bottles and bowls that became abstract, interiorized landscapes. If De Chirico's paintings serve as the painterly analogy to Wright's early work, and Paul Cézanne's to his later work, then it is Morandi's landscapes that parallel Wright's in *China Trace*. It is through the process of representation that he begins to apprehend death: "I'm talking about bottles, and ruin, / And what we flash at the darkness, and what for."

Against the potentially destructive yearning expressed in "Next," Wright posits a pantheistic and agonistic vision that is no less visionary. Wright trains his eye on the more-minute and transitory particulars of the landscape, as in "April": "The plum tree breaks out in bees. / A gull is locked like a ghost in the blue attic of heaven." Time has become less panoramic; the world moves quickly, as do these poems, through discrete and irretrievable moments (except through art): "A downfall of light in the pine woods, motes in the rush, / Gold leaf through the undergrowth." Wright suggests that one's life is caught briefly in these liminal moments before disappearing. Knowing this, he wants to come back "As another name, water / Pooled in the black leaves and holding me there, to be / Released as a glint, as a flash, as a spark." The poem trails off with an ellipsis, as does "Morandi," thereby accentuating the transitory and yet intimating a continuum of regeneration.

With the subdued reaction to *China Trace*, especially after the acclaim that greeted *Bloodlines*, Wright waited until 1981 to publish *The Southern Cross*. Although he has stated that he had reached a conclusion to his triptych, the poetic experiment of *China Trace* is developed in *The Southern Cross* and also in the collections that followed. The landscapes of *China Trace* are to be *read,* as in the closing poem, "Him":

> Look for him in the flat black of the northern Pacific sky,
> Released in his suit of lights,
>   lifted and laid clear.

Each element of the landscape offers illumination as well as a space (both temporal and spatial) for reflection. The poet's meditations on death and regeneration continue in *The Southern Cross;* however, they begin to encompass a larger — or more social — world than the interiorized landscapes of *China Trace.* Self-scrutiny, as indicated by the many images of reflection, mirroring, and self-portraiture in *China Trace,* is continued in *The Southern Cross.* But by developing a more extended, journal-like poetry, Wright moves away from the deep imagist poetics of *China Trace,* where such poetics, as practiced by Galway Kinnell or W. S. Merwin, emphasize a synonymity of image and thing and depend on free association rather than metaphor.

The Southern Cross opens with a single long poem, "Homage to Paul Cézanne." As Wright describes in his 1981 interview with Sherod Santos, the opening lines of "Homage to Paul Cézanne" came to him several months after completing *China Trace.* Seeing three scraps of blank paper catch first the late afternoon light and then moonlight in a field near his home was the inspiration for the poem, which subsequently motivated his interest in Cézanne's painterly techniques. The poem's composition suggests the nonlinear accumulation of lines or layers and blocks of paint and even points to this process: "The dead are a cadmium blue. / We spread them with palette knives in broad blocks and planes." The poem, however, is Wright's most sustained meditation on the influences of the dead; whether they be artists or family, for Wright the dead are always present: "The dead are with us to stay. / Their shadows rock in the back yard, so pure, so black, / Between the oak tree and the porch." They are those to whom we answer and to whom we turn for knowledge and inspiration. The dead are also reminders of our own mortality and transience. While we may long for immortality — "We're out here, our feet in the soil, our heads craned up at the sky, / The stars streaming and bursting behind the trees" — the dead remind us that there is no immortality, except in the world's continual regeneration and our representation of that renewal.

The second section is composed of five self-portraits of the poet at different periods of his life.

Each expresses a state of confession as the poet announces in the first "Self-Portrait": "Some day they'll find me out." Counterbalancing these self-portraits are four poems that reiterate, as in "Mount Caribou at Night," his vision of "Everything on the move, everything flowing and folding back / And starting again." The twenty poems of the third section are all based on specific technical instructions that Wright imposed upon himself when composing each poem. In an interview with Elizabeth McBride in 1985, Wright recounts how this practice came about:

> It was a John Cage concert. Afterwards, during a question and answer period ... someone asked a serious question: "Mr. Cage, when you are up there fiddling with your score paper or looking out the window or tapping your finger on the piano, or shifting around on the stool, what are you really doing?" And Cage said, "I'm giving myself instructions and carrying them out." Now I thought that was pretty interesting and Don [Justice] thought that was pretty interesting and we discussed it. And what I did in that section was give myself instructions and carry them out, in every one of those poems.

These poems may be constructed, for example, without verbs, as in "Dog Yoga," or with each line a complete sentence, as in "California Spring." Some of the self-imposed instructions are more esoteric: the instruction for "Spring Abstract" was to write an abstract of a poem that was not there. Others were based on photographs, images from Dante, portraits with poets Wright could never meet, or were required to be composed within a given period of time.

These instructions underscore Wright's economy of language, as well as his technical virtuosity. These twenty poems, as a group, are elegiac in that they attempt to recompose what has been lost: "Spring Abstract" retrieves the absent poem; "Bar Giamaica, 1959–60" repopulates a photograph by Ugo Mulas of a bar Wright visited in Milan with old friends. Through the catalogue of names in this poem, Wright insists on the precision of memory; and memory, the poem demonstrates, is the basis for representation. Furthermore, salvation exists only through representation, whether through the poem or the photograph. Art saves one from oblivion. In "Portrait of the Artist with Li Po," Wright draws the absent poet close, and in so doing saves the poet, himself, and the reader from the void:

> Over a 1000 years later, I write out one of his lines in a notebook,
> *The peach blossom follows the moving water,*

And watch the October darkness gather against the hills.
All night long the river of heaven will move westward while no one notices.
The distance between the dead and the living
               is more than a heart beat and a breath.

Wright, through his poem, enacts the entwined processes of remembrance and renewal.

"The Southern Cross" achieves the painterly techniques of layering in blocks of color more fully than does "Homage to Paul Cézanne." The poem, the last poem written for this collection, was motivated in part by the poet Mark Jarman's urging Wright to write a long, abstract poem. What resulted was an expansive, luminous poem that defies narrative exposition. This accumulative, autobiographical poem reveals the tenuous process of memory: again and again, Wright states "I remember," which is counterbalanced by "I can't remember" or "What's hard to remember." "Who can ever remember enough?" Wright asks; yet the poem's authority resides in Wright's hypnotic naming, his exact descriptions, and his certainty of place. The desire to remember is always resisting the erosiveness of time and loss. Indeed, the title refers to presence and absence, the otherworldly, and what one might navigate by: although the Southern Cross is invisible in the Northern Hemisphere, the constellation is there waiting to be seen. No less fabulously, the South is also evoked in the title: "It's what we forget that defines us, and stays in the same place, / And waits to be rediscovered."

The poem is divided into twenty-five unnumbered sections of varying lengths. Abandoning conventional stanzaic arrangements, Wright intends the lines to move through space: they extend to the edge of the page, or are enjambed, or slip to the next line. The lines are more fluid and seem effortless. They assume, however, a greater lyric authority than the controlled poetic line of earlier collections. Paradox, oxymoron, and exact but startling images weave through the poem: "The morning is dark with spring. / The early blooms on the honeysuckle shine like maggots after the rain." Death seems to shine through everything, but it does not, for Wright, mean the cessation of speculation: "Thinking of Dante is thinking about the other side, / And the other side of the other side."

Wright's poetry is in fact an ongoing speculation about the other side and the ways through to that zone. Everywhere Wright senses clues to this life:

I watched, as I've watched before, the waters send up their smoke signals of blue mist,
And thought, for the 1st time,
      I half-understood what they keep on trying to say.

But now I'm not sure.
      Behind my back, the spider has got her instructions
And carries them out.
Flies drone, wind back-combs the marsh grass, swallows bank and climb.
Everything I can see knows just what to do,

Even the dragonfly, hanging like lapis lazuli in the sun.

In these concluding lines of the twentieth section of "The Southern Cross," Wright's language shines with a concentrated light like an illuminated manuscript. While Wright's descriptions are precise, they are not an imitation of a naturalist's exactitude. Instead, they represent permanence drawn out of sheer transience. The world's particulars serve as exempla for him: the spider's work parallels the poet's work; each trace and glimmer is a signal of an undisclosed truth. And perhaps because these truths remain secret they can be, in fact, truth.

The Southern Cross was greeted with critical acclaim and it may be that the response to *The Other Side of the River* (1984), Wright's next collection, was slightly muted by the earlier volume's acclaim. The fluid and spatial lines that marked the preceding volume as a significant departure become Wright's signature in *The Other Side of the River*. After a hiatus of nearly twenty years, Wright also resumed translating from the Italian and in 1984 *Orphic Songs,* his book of translations of the singular poetry of Dino Campana, was published.

In his introduction to Wright's translation of Campana, Jonathan Galassi's concluding comments on Campana's poetry may also describe Wright's poetry: "Campana's obscurity, when he is obscure, is in homage to his own peculiar perception of what surrounds him. It is impossible for him to 'understand' and thus codify and de-nature the Other. Instead, naked and alone, he confronts the irreducible difference, the final unknowability, of what is out there." Wright's affinity with Campana is spiritual; both share in that keen perception of the luminous mystery of their surrounding. This fact is apparent in this brief passage from Campana's long prose poem, "Night": "Which bridge, we asked silently, which bridge have we thrown across to the infinite, so that everything appears to us as a shadow of eternity? To which dream have we raised the nostalgia of our beauty? The moon rose in her old robe behind the Byzantine church." Through translating Montale, Wright found ways

JESUIT GRAVES

Midsummer. Irish overcast. Oatmeal-colored sky.
The Jesuit pit. Last mass
For hundreds whose names are incised on the marble wall
Above the dirt and small stones ~
Just dirt and the small stones -
                                    how strict, how self-effacing.

Not suited for him, however, Father Bird-of-Paradise,
Whose plumage of far wonder is not formless and not faceless,
Whatever he might have hoped for once.
Glasnevin Cemetery, Dublin, 3 July 1995.
For those who would rise to meet their work,
                                    that work is scaffolding.

Sacrifice is the cause of ruin.
The absence of sacrifice is the cause of ruin.
Thus the legends instruct us,
North wind through the flat-leaved limbs of the sheltering trees,
Three mounds in the small, square enclosure,
                            souls God-gulped and heaven-hidden.

P. Gerardus Hopkins, 28 July 1844 - 8 June 1889, Age 44.
And then the next name. And then the next,
Soldiers of misfortune, lock-step into a star-colored tight dissolve,
History's hand-me-ons. But

Draft for "Jesuit Graves" (courtesy of the author)

of moving his own words; however, Campana is not the instructor that Montale was. Instead, in Campana's voice Wright hears his own luminescent and elegiac voice.

The Other Side of the River, more than any past volumes, is filled with friends, with different landscapes – oddly similar when it is Wright's memory that draws them onto the same page – and with his reading of such poets as Dante, Li Po, William Blake, and Emily Dickinson. Reading is a way of mapping this world, because the world fills continuously with momentary traces, as is evident in "Three Poems for the New Year":

> All day with the knuckle of solitude
> To gnaw on,
>   the turkey buzzards and red-tailed hawk
> Lifting and widening concentrically over the field,
> Brush-tails of the pepper branches
>   writing invisibly on the sky.

Paradoxically the writing is known to exist, but it is invisible, and also not yet understood nor read. Like subatomic physics or Zen koans, Wright's poetry represents paradox – but unlike science or meditative theology, such paradoxes are not problems to solve but necessary passages to move through in order to understand, as he states at the end of "Italian Days," "What gifts there are are all here, in this world."

Reading becomes elegy and homage in *The Other Side of the River.* "T'ang Notebook" and "To Giacomo Leopardi in the Sky" demonstrate two distinct responses to his reading. "T'ang Notebook," as the title implies, consists of gathered fragments that in their accretion build up a nacreous surface. Based on poems from an anonymous translation of T'ang dynasty poetry, this poem contains images from the T'ang poets that are layered onto Wright's perceptions so that innumerable voices occupy the same lines.

Echoing several of Leopardi's poems, "To Giacomo Leopardi in the Sky" is an homage that employs both the didactic and elegiac voices. Leopardi becomes Wright's poetic alter ego; as Calvin Bedient states, "the Italian poet focuses for Wright the displaced condition of our existence." The practice of poetry – or of any art – risks futility: "Not one word has ever melted in glory not one. / We keep on sending them up, however." Nonetheless, intimacy arises from the act of reading, because one's words touch, respond, or take from another's words: a communion is struck between the living and the dead in their shared thought and words.

Despite his abandonment of conventional narrative and reliance on the accumulation of fragments, Wright insists on the necessity of connection. As he writes in the title poem,

> It's linkage I'm talking about,
>   and harmonies and structures
> And all the various things that lock our wrists to the past.
>
> Something infinite behind everything appears,
>   and then disappears.

Wright's staggered, cantilevered lines suggest the accumulation of connections where absence and presence are counterbalanced. As each object or memory is held suspended, one can glimpse the "infinite," some prime-mover, or a deepening but ever-secret truth.

Although most certainly a visual poet, Wright also thinks musically and insists on the Neoplatonic ideal of music as a series of harmonies that lead to revelatory knowledge. These harmonics are most powerful when they enfold the visual, as in the closing image of "To Giacomo Leopardi in the Sky": Wright thinks of Leopardi when "the moon's like a golden tick on the summer sky / Gorged with light," then "you're part of my parts of speech." When Wright transforms the dichotomy of the lowly and the heavenly, the tick becomes golden, because to be "Gorged with light" is to enfold the very "or/e" of golden: the "or" of "gorged" becomes the "ore" of golden. Thus, there is a visual, musical, and philosophical harmony established, where one resonates with the goldenness of the other.

With the publication of *Zone Journals* (1988), Wright is in full command of his singular poetic process. The journal-poem allows for seemingly random inclusion as well as a peripatetic "eye/I." His exquisite but controlled early lyrics and his sequential poems are not discarded but embedded in each journal-poem. *Zone Journals* is divided into three sections, the middle section consisting of the "A Journal of the Year of the Ox." As long as *China Trace,* this central poem is also a journey, but one that traverses the year 1985 rather than a metaphysical pilgrimage. Though composed within a year's chronological limit, it is not a strict daily record. In his interview with the poet J. D. McClatchy, Wright stated that the "structural elements – the four entries about the Cherokees and the Long Island of the Holston, and the long sojourn in northern Italy – of 'sacred places,' as well as the natural one of the four seasons, plus the visits to the two great American medieval writers, Poe and Dickinson, and the two great Italian ones, Petrarch and Dante, et cetera, all combine to both hide and expose the story line, which is, like most story lines, circular." The poem creates and moves through spatial and temporal zones, a poem that traverses boundaries while also mapping widening circumferences. As Wright states later in the interview, the poem is both epiphanic and oceanic – thus, identifiably American.

The recovery of history is perhaps the most pervasive element in American poetry. "A Journal of the Year of the Ox" exemplifies this desire to invoke lost or transgressed histories, particularly of local or personal habitations. The sacred grounds of the Cherokee on the Holston River's Long Island have become a golf course, and the river's name has been corrupted from its Cherokee name, Hogoheegee. Wright maps the landscape of the eastern Tennessee of his childhood and its dismal history of the breaking apart of the Cherokee Nation. The West is opened with the Holston Peace Treaty, where the Cherokee agreed to give away "What wasn't assignable, / The ground that everyone walked on" and with it the "Wind in the trees, sunlight, all the magic of water." With this treaty the wilderness in European eyes becomes a possession; thus, this moment encapsulates the history of the European colonization of the continent.

Counterbalancing this history of loss is the center sequence that describes the Renaissance frescoes in the Schifanoia Palace of the dukes of Este in Ferrara. These frescoes detail an allegorical ordering of the cosmos that moves from the gods, to the zodiac, to the civic and social order of the dukes and their domains. If the historical fact of the loss of the wilderness, as evidenced by the dispersal of the Cherokee, represents the loss of Eden, then these frescoes detail the underpinnings of the European culture that could not recognize that unassignable beauty of the Holston River, of that entire new world. Wright is able to capture the lit beauty of these frescoes:

> Up there, in the third realm,
> 　　　　　　　　light as though under water
> Washes and folds and breaks in small waves
> Over each month like sunrise:
> 　　　　　　　　triumph after triumph
> Of pure Abstraction and pure Word, a paradise of
> 　　white cloth
> And white reflections of cloth cross-currented over the
> 　　cars

> With golden wheels and gold leads,
> 　　　　　　　　all Concept and finery.

Implicit in this description is Blake's critique of purely abstract reasoning. Wright, however, refuses to settle into a simple oppositional mode in this complex, long poem. The history that Wright writes is that of the soul as it moves from place to place, from Dickinson's house and Edgar Allen Poe's Baltimore, to the interior heavens of the lush frescoes in Ferrara, to the landscape of the Holston River. Thus, the poem enacts the soul's recovery of what is sacred.

In the volume's opening poem, "Yard Journal," Wright states that "the more luminous anything is, / The more it subtracts what's around it," thus "making the unseen seen: / Body by new body they all rise into the light / Tactile and still damp." The poem conjoins the intuitive intelligence, which is expressed through paradox, and phenomenal or sensory perception. The yard is transformed into "Dantescan gloom" where a bumblebee rises like Geryon out "the rain gutter's tin *bolgia*" and then spirals out of sight as a hummingbird. This fluidity of allusion, time, and space reflects an overlay of readings, which always circles back to the physical and vernacular world. The inclusion of references to Dante, Issa, or Dickinson underscores Wright's reading of the world, but as with each of these poets, he also works to trace the limits of the zone of language. Words move slowly, Wright states in the first "Night Journal," "trailing their dark identities." "Caught in their finitude," words, like all things, "start here, they finish here, / No matter how high they rise."

In these last three volumes of poetry, Wright has been steadily evolving a poetics of luminous intensity where the moment's surface slips over mnemonic surfaces and landscapes overlay other landscapes. This becomes readily apparent in *The World of the Ten Thousand Things* (1990), which gathers the entirety of *The Southern Cross, The Other Side of the River,* and *Zone Journals.* Additionally, it includes the poems from *Xionia* (1990), available otherwise only in a fine-press, limited edition. *The World of the Ten Thousand Things* suggests a project as sustained as Wright's earlier triptych. However tempting it is to view *The World of the Ten Thousand Things* as a single accumulative journal-poem, it is more accurate to see the poems as forming a jeweled net where each is distinct but also knotted to the others.

The poems in *Xionia* form a coda or envoi. While they self-reflectively name themselves as

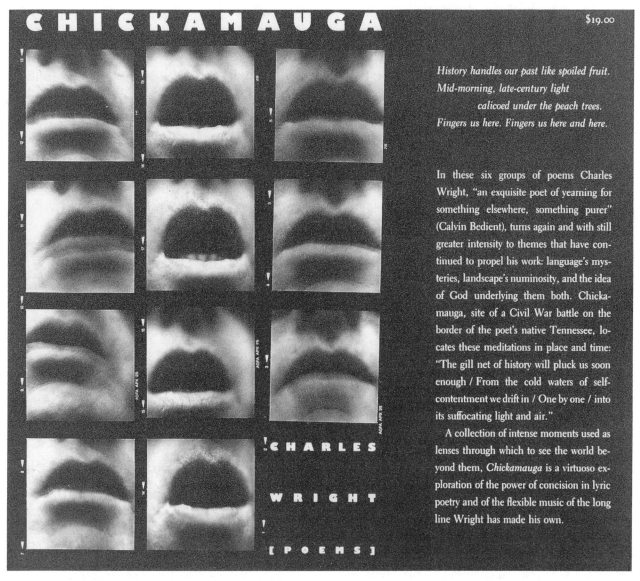

History handles our past like spoiled fruit.
Mid-morning, late-century light
*   calicoed under the peach trees.*
Fingers us here. Fingers us here and here.

In these six groups of poems Charles Wright, "an exquisite poet of yearning for something elsewhere, something purer" (Calvin Bedient), turns again and with still greater intensity to themes that have continued to propel his work: language's mysteries, landscape's numinosity, and the idea of God underlying them both. Chickamauga, site of a Civil War battle on the border of the poet's native Tennessee, locates these meditations in place and time: "The gill net of history will pluck us soon enough / From the cold waters of self-contentment we drift in / One by one / into its suffocating light and air."

A collection of intense moments used as lenses through which to see the world beyond them, *Chickamauga* is a virtuoso exploration of the power of concision in lyric poetry and of the flexible music of the long line Wright has made his own.

CHARLES

WRIGHT

[POEMS]

Dust jacket for Wright's 1995 collection of poems, in which he invokes one of the crucial battles of the Civil War

journals, they are also pointing away from the extended journal form exemplified by "A Journal of the Year of the Ox." These poems move toward a concentrated lyric moment, even in the poems that are several pages in length. They also sharply focus on Wright's belief in the physical, mutable world – his belief that Being is in this world. He writes in "A Journal of Southern Rivers" that "In awe and astonishment we regain ourselves in this world. / There is no other." A repudiation of his religious upbringing shadows these lines, but, more important, it is from that upbringing that Wright is able to contemplate so fully the possibilities of revelation and salvation.

Perhaps more than any other poet in the United States writing after World War II, a time of widespread disbelief, Wright has pursued the questions of revelation and resurrection and fashioned a powerful vision of the renewing power of the natural world. Within this vision, words are as material and finite as anything else in this world. With each successive volume of poetry, transience and mutability become more and more the defining qualities of contemporary life and the world itself, as the poet states in the closing lines of "A Journal of Southern Rivers": "Whose shadows are dancing upside down in the southern rivers? / Fifty-two years have passed / like the turning of a palm." If the hard, muscular words of the poems of *Bloodlines* suggested a material permanence, this feature has been refuted in the fluid lines of his later poems. With the use of slipped half lines, for example, words become transitory; the poem slides through layers of shifting language. This is not to say that Wright has adopted a poetics based on Jacques Derrida's analysis of the modes of deconstruction; to reconstruct is Wright's desire. The process of representation is not, however, a form of replacing the world but a tracing of perceptions or a sensing of what is there and what is not. Wright's poetry offers his pilgrimage toward solitude, tracing the world's circumference, and, as he says in "A Journal of Southern Rivers": "The nearness of nothingness, / The single spirit that lies at the root of all things."

Interviews:

"An Interview with Charles Wright," *Skywriting,* 3 (September 1973): 6–10;

"Charles Wright at Oberlin College," *Field,* 17 (Fall 1977): 46–85;

Sherod Santos, "An Interview with Charles Wright," *Quarterly West,* 12 (Spring/Summer 1981): 18–45;

Elizabeth McBride, "Charles Wright: An Interview," *Ohio Review,* 34 (1985): 14–41;

Santos, "An Interview with Charles Wright," *Missouri Review,* 10, 1 (1987): 73–95;

J. D. McClatchy, "The Art of Poetry XLI: Charles Wright," *Paris Review,* 113 (Winter 1989): 184–221.

Bibliography:

Stuart Wright, "Charles Wright: A Bibliographic Chronicle, 1963–1985," *Bulletin of Bibliography,* 43 (March 1986): 3–12.

References:

Tom Andrews, *The Point Where All Things Meet: Essays on Charles Wright* (Oberlin, Ohio: Oberlin College Press, 1995);

Calvin Bedient, "Side-Wheeling Around the Curves," *Southern Review,* 27 (January 1991): 221–234;

Bedient, "Tracing Charles Wright," *Parnassus: Poetry in Review,* 10 (Spring/Summer 1982): 55–74;

Floyd Collins, "Metamorphosis Within the Poetry of Charles Wright," *Gettysburg Review,* 4 (Summer 1991): 464–479;

Bonnie Costello, "The Soil and Man's Intelligence: Three Contemporary Landscape Poets," *Contemporary Literature,* 30 (Fall 1989): 412–433;

Mark Jarman, "The Pragmatic Imagination and the Secret of Poetry," *Gettysburg Review,* 1 (Autumn 1988): 647–660;

Paul Lake, "Return to Metaphor: From Deep Imagist to New Formalist," *Southwest Review,* 74 (Autumn 1989): 515–529;

James McCorkle, "'Things that Lock Our Wrists to the Past:' Self-Portraiture and Autobiography in Charles Wright's Poetry" in his *The Still Performance: Writing, Self and Interconnection in Five Postmodern American Poets* (Charlottesville: University Press of Virginia, 1989), pp. 171–211;

Nance Van Winkel, "Charles Wright and the Landscape of the Lyric," *New England Review,* 12 (Spring 1990): 308–312;

Helen Vendler, "Charles Wright," in her *The Music of What Happens: Poems, Poets, Critics* (Cambridge, Mass.: Harvard University Press, 1988), pp. 388–397;

Vendler, "Charles Wright: The Transcendent 'I'," in her *Part of Nature, Part of Us* (Cambridge, Mass.: Harvard University Press, 1980).

Louis Zukofsky

(23 January 1904 – 12 May 1978)

Mark Scroggins
Florida Atlantic University

See also the Zukofsky entry in *DLB 5: American Poets Since World War II, First Series.*

BOOKS: *Le Style Apollinaire,* French translation by René Taupin (Paris: Presses Modernes, 1934);

First Half of "A"-9 (New York: Privately printed, 1940);

55 Poems (Prairie City, Ill.: Decker, 1941);

Anew: Poems (Prairie City, Ill.: Decker, 1946);

A Test of Poetry (New York: Objectivist Press, 1948; London: Routledge & Kegan Paul, 1952);

Some Time / Short Poems (Highlands, N.C.: Jargon, 1956);

5 Statements for Poetry (San Francisco: San Francisco State College, 1958);

Barely and Widely (New York: Celia Zukofsky, 1958);

"A" 1-12 (Kyoto: Origin Press, 1959; London: Cape, 1966; Garden City, N.Y.: Doubleday, 1967);

It Was (Kyoto: Origin Press, 1961);

16 Once Published (Edinburgh: Wild Hawthorn Press, 1962);

I's Pronounced "Eyes" (New York: Trobar Press, 1963);

Bottom: on Shakespeare (Austin: Ark Press/University of Texas Press, 1963);

Found Objects 1962–1926 (Georgetown, Ky.: H. B. Chapin, 1964);

After I's (Pittsburgh: Boxwood Press/Mother Press, 1964);

Finally A Valentine (Stroud, U.K.: Piccolo Press, 1965);

An Unearthing: A Poem (Cambridge, Mass.: Adams House & Lowell House Printers, 1965);

I Sent Thee Late (Cambridge, Mass.: Privately printed, 1965);

"A" Libretto (New York: Privately printed, 1965);

Iyyob (London: Turret, 1965);

"A"-9 (Stuttgart: Edition Hansjörg Mayer, 1966);

"A"-14 (London: Turret, 1967);

Louis Zukofsky, 1976 (photograph by Hugh Kenner)

Prepositions: The Collected Critical Essays of Louis Zukofsky (London: Rapp & Carroll, 1967; New York: Horizon, 1968; expanded edition, Berkeley: University of California Press, 1981);

Little, a fragment for Careenagers (San Francisco: Black Sparrow, 1967);

From Thanks to the Dictionary (Buffalo, N.Y.: Gallery Upstairs, 1968);

Ferdinand, Including It Was (London: Cape, 1968; New York: Grossman, 1968);

Catullus Fragmenta, with Celia Zukofsky (London: Turret, 1968);

"A" 13–21 (London: Cape, 1969; Garden City, N.Y.: Doubleday, 1969);

Catullus, with Celia Zukofsky (London: Cape Goliard, 1969; New York: Grossman, 1969);

The Gas Age (Newcastle upon Tyne: Ultima Thule, 1969);

Autobiography (New York: Grossman, 1970);

An Era (Santa Barbara: Unicorn, 1970);

Initial (New York: Phoenix Book Shop, 1970);

Little; for Careenagers (New York: Grossman, 1970);

"A"-24 (New York: Grossman, 1972);

Arise, arise (New York: Grossman, 1973);

"A" 22 & 23 (New York: Grossman, 1975; London: Trigram, 1977);

"A" (Berkeley & London: University of California Press, 1978);

80 Flowers (Lunenburg, Vt.: Stinehour Press, 1978).

Collections: *All: The Collected Short Poems 1923–1958* (New York: Norton, 1965; London: Cape, 1966);

All: The Collected Short Poems 1956–1964 (New York: Norton, 1966; London: Cape, 1967);

Collected Fiction (Elmwood Park, Ill.: Dalkey Archive, 1990);

Complete Short Poetry (Baltimore: Johns Hopkins University Press, 1991).

OTHER: *Poetry,* special *"Objectivists" 1931* issue, edited by Zukofsky, 37 (February 1931): 235–298;

An "Objectivists" Anthology, edited by Zukofsky (Le Beausset, France, & New York: TO, Publishers, 1932);

Jonathan Williams, *Amen / Huzza / Selah,* with a preface by Zukofsky (Highlands, N.C.: Jargon, 1960);

"To Basil," with Celia Zukofsky, in *Madeira & Toasts for Basil Bunting's 75th Birthday,* edited by Williams (Dentdale, U.K.: Jargon Society, 1975);

"Discarded Poems," in *Louis Zukofsky: Man and Poet,* edited by Carroll F. Terrell (Orono, Maine: National Poetry Foundation, 1979), pp. 145–162.

SELECTED PERIODICAL PUBLICATIONS –
UNCOLLECTED: "The Writing of Guillaume Apollinaire: Le Flâneur, (I) – Il y a," *Westminster Magazine,* 22 (Winter 1933): 9–50;

"The Writing of Guillaume Apollinaire: (II) – Le Poète Ressucité, (III) – & Cie," *Westminster Magazine,* 23 (Spring 1934): 7–46;

Review of *The Whip,* by Robert Creeley, *Poetry,* 92 (September 1958): 387–388;

Reply to Questionaire on Poetic Method, *Agenda,* 11 (Spring/Summer 1973): 66.

Louis Zukofsky, who died in 1978 at the age of seventy-four largely unknown to the majority of critics and readers of American poetry, was one of the century's most fascinating and accomplished poets. Physically and personally unprepossessing – an apparitionally thin, chain-smoking hypochondriac, Zukofksky in his later years saw visitors only with extreme reluctance and would refuse to speak above a whisper when he thought he might be overheard – this child of non-English-speaking immigrants came to master the English language and to create a large corpus of writings of unsurpassed aural delicacy, emotional subtlety, and intellectual rigor.

In or about 1950 Zukofsky in "A"-12 defined his poetry in mathematical terms: "An integral / Lower limit speech / Upper limit music." While Zukofsky's verse spends more time in the upper than in the lower reaches of this equation, proposing an order of pleasure that is more dependent on sound than meaning, his poetry is never meaningless, even at its most seemingly recondite: in Wallace Stevens's words, it "resists the intelligence almost successfully." It is characteristic that Zukofsky would define his poetry in terms of calculus, for he admired the constructive minds of engineers and scientists, seeing his own work as closer to theirs than to that of most poets; in the composer he most admired, Johann Sebastian Bach, he saw a similar interest in precision and mathematical structure. But even with this emphasis on the structural, the formal, and the mathematical, Zukofsky never forgets what his *A Test of Poetry* (1948) defines as the proper measure of verse: "The test of poetry is the range of pleasure it affords as sight, sound, and intellection. This is its purpose as art."

Until recently it was customary to begin critical examinations of Zukofsky's work with a lament about the poet's status as the great undiscovered American modernist poet. This situation is less true than it once was; while Zukofsky suffered acutely from his public obscurity and the vacuum into which it seemed his works vanished as soon as they appeared, since the poet's death it has become clear that one's picture of twentieth-century American writing is impoverished if one has not come to terms with Zukofsky's writings and influence. Critics often speak of Zukofsky as a "disciple" of Ezra Pound's, and it is true both that he and Pound enjoyed a decades-long (if at times strained) friendship and that Zukofsky's poetics are grounded in the imagistic, juxtapositional mode that Pound pioneered. But Zukofsky, who maintained friendships with many of the major modernists – Pound, E. E. Cummings, William Carlos Williams, and Marianne Moore – would late in life assert a deep-seated kinship with Stevens, prominent representative of a poetic tradition that some have seen as the diametric opposite of Pound's, and was also greatly influenced by the visual poetics and wordplay of French poet Guillaume Apollinaire, whose work Pound offhandedly dismissed. The young poets who came to learn from and pay homage to Zukofsky in the 1960s, unlike his first critics – and many critics today – were well aware that the writer they admired was no belated follower of Pound. While Zukofsky deeply admired Pound's poetry, the content, style, and formal invention of his poems are not those of anyone's disciple; his poetics are his own.

Perhaps most important to an assessment of Zukofsky's place in twentieth-century writing is the recognition that during his half-century career he pressed past the boundaries of the modernist poetics from which his work sprang. In the process he laid the groundwork for a whole range of contemporary, postmodernist writing practices that neither Pound nor Williams could have foreseen. At the end of the century there is a growing consensus in the poetic community that Zukofsky is at the very least an important figure, and there are many poets, ranging from such exponents of the "New American Poetry" as Allen Ginsberg and Robert Creeley to experimentalists such as the Language poets Bob Perelman, Charles Bernstein, and Ron Silliman who look to Zukofsky and Gertrude Stein as the central figures of American modernism.

The range of Zukofsky's accomplishments are impressive. He exhaustively explores the aural qualities as well as the meanings of words in combination in his carefully constructed short lyrics. His translations, especially his ambitious rendering (with his wife, Celia) of the entire works of Catullus, are a profound theoretical examination of the practice of translation itself. And Zukofsky's "poem of a life," *"A"* (1978), an epic equal in length to Pound's *Cantos* – and, unlike *The Cantos,* actually completed – is a compendium of both forms and subject matter. It demonstrates a whole new range of ways in which the constitutive elements of the long poem might be articulated one with another. The academy, decades behind the community of practicing poets, is only now beginning to realize the importance of this poet once dismissed as a minor epigone and to revise its map of Ameri-

Zukofsky in 1941 (photograph by Dushan Hill)

can modernism to accommodate his remarkable achievements.

Zukofsky was born on Manhattan's Lower East Side in 1904, the same year the novelist Henry James revisited America for the last time; the poet would later enjoy drawing attention to this coincidence, explaining in his *Autobiography* (1970) that "The contingency appeals to me as a forecast of the first-generation American infusion into twentieth-century literature." "Infusion" is delicately put, but it serves to emphasize Zukofsky's awareness of his own anomalous position as a Jew in the midst of a modernist movement in literature whose heroes, such as James himself, would portray Western culture as fundamentally endangered by Jewish influences.

Zukofsky's parents, Pinchos and Chana Pruss Zukofsky, were born in the part of Russia that is now Lithuania; Pinchos immigrated to the United States in 1898, working as a pants presser and night watchman until he could send for his wife in 1903. These immigrant parents are important presences in Zukofsky's work: the figure of his mother is central to his early "Poem beginning 'The,'" written in 1926, and he mourns her 1927 death in the play *Arise, arise* (1973), various early sections of his long poem *"A,"* and in "A Song for the Year's End," written in 1945. Pinchos Zukofsky's Orthodox faith was a tradition against which his son reacted early – he would later claim that his own period of religious crisis lasted "from the age of 10 to 13 and no more" – but by 1950 and 1951, when he came to write "A"-12, the longest section at that time of his epic poem, his father's dedication to work, faith, and family had come to represent for him an ideal akin to that of his favorite image of the poet, the blinkered horse who patiently pursues his back-breaking task with a resigned calm and a subdued hopefulness.

Zukofsky grew up in a Yiddish-speaking household; while he would not learn English until he began elementary school, his brother Morris took him to the Yiddish theater, where he saw Yiddish versions of many of Shakespeare's plays (he would proceed to read all of William Shakespeare by the time he was eleven), along with those of Henrik Ibsen, August Strindberg, and dramatizations of Leo Tolstoy's novels. Shakespeare, to whom he came so early, is in many ways the tutelary spirit of Zukofsky's work, though Zukofsky's poems – discontinuous, imagistic, above all *lyrical* rather than narrative – seem worlds away from the Englishman's fundamentally dramatic work. The Jewish immigrant culture of turn-of-the-century New York, which afforded a wealth of cultural opportunities for a boy as intelligent and curious as Zukofsky, was also a powerful influence.

Zukofsky's parents made the financial sacrifice to send their promising son to Columbia University, though he could have gone to City College for free. At Columbia Zukofsky belonged to the student literary society and saw his poems published in the student literary magazines; his student works, some of which were skillful enough to merit publication in Harriet Monroe's *Poetry,* are in a fairly conventional romantic vein. At times, however, they show evidence of the whimsical lyricism combined with an almost astringent diction that would become one of the hallmarks of the mature poet's work.

Zukofsky studied philosophy and English at Columbia, where one of his best friends was Whittaker Chambers, the future accuser of Alger Hiss and author of *Witness* (1952), perhaps the most famous anticommunist document of the century. Chambers spent the 1920s as a member of the Communist Party (he was expelled from Columbia in 1922 for publishing a "atheistic" play in a student magazine), and he offered to sponsor his friend Zukofsky for membership in his own cell; the party higher-ups rejected the nattily attired young poet,

perhaps rightly suspecting that this nascent intellectual would not lightly suffer party discipline. Though he never became a member of the Communist Party, Zukofsky's political alignments at least through the end of the 1930s were firmly on the Left. Many of the early sections of *"A"* incorporate sophisticated expositions of Marxist philosophy and economics, and even when he no longer believed in the inevitable victory of the proletariat, Zukofsky still admired the quality of Marx's thought.

By the time he was awarded his master's degree in English in 1926 (he never received the baccalaureate, having dropped out of the required physical education course), Zukofsky had studied with some of Columbia's most prominent scholars, including the poet Mark Van Doren, the philosopher John Dewey, and the novelist John Erskine, whose "Great Books" approach to literature he would lampoon in "Poem beginning 'The.'" He had also written as his M.A. thesis the earliest version of his long essay "Henry Adams: A Criticism in Autobiography." Zukofsky's fascination with Adams, scion of perhaps the first family of Anglo-Saxon Boston, a self-proclaimed decadent representative of a heroic tradition and like his contemporary Henry James a culture hero for American modernism, was to persist through much of his career. The essay, published in *Prepositions: The Collected Critical Essays of Louis Zukofsky* (1967) in an abbreviated form, is also a significant forecast of the mature Zukofsky's concerns and working methods.

The great majority of the text of "Henry Adams" is quotation from Adams's own works, looking forward both to the method of Zukofsky's long critical work *Bottom: on Shakespeare* (1963), which is in large part a collage of quotations, and, more important, to the poetics of quotation that Zukofsky would extend and refine throughout his writing life. In his last completed work, *80 Flowers* (1978), as critic Michele J. Leggott has shown, almost every word of the eighty-one forty-word poems can be traced to some preexisting text. One of the primary conceptual thrusts of Zukofsky's work, early and late, is a reconceptualization of the notions of quotation and originality, a shifting of the hierarchy between composition as original writing and composition as arrangement, as *composing.*

Henry Adams's ideas would prove important to Zukofsky, in particular his adaptation of the physicist Willard Gibbs's theory of phase shifts in the equilibrium between substances. While Adams had adapted Gibbs to the study of history, analyzing historical forces as progressively "Mechanical,"

"Electrical," and "Ethereal," Zukofsky would adopt a similar set of terms — "solid," "liquid," and "gaseous" — to describe "states of language," in the process identifying those states closely with Pound's tripartite division of poetry into phanopoeia, melopoeia, and logopoeia — roughly speaking, imagistic, musical, and intellective.

Throughout his career, and most notably in his prose work *Bottom: on Shakespeare,* at once one of the most idiosyncratic and most important texts of American modernism, Zukofsky would stress the importance of "solid-state" language, poetic discourse based on the hard evidence of the physical senses (the eyes in particular). At the same time, as he would admit ruefully in his 1969 talk "About The Gas Age," Zukofsky was inescapably marooned in a "gas age," an era of intellectual abstractions: "I'd like to keep solid because I can't help myself, I was born in a gas age." His solution is in part to return to the senses by striving to make the poem itself as much a tangible object as possible, an impulse that lies behind the doctrine of "objectification," which Zukofsky formulated in his manifestoes for the Objectivist movement.

Zukofsky first brought himself to Ezra Pound's attention in 1927 by sending the older poet (who was by then living in Italy) his "Poem beginning 'The,'" which Pound published in 1928 in his short-lived periodical *The Exile.* It is an astonishingly precocious poem and demonstrates that Zukofsky had fully absorbed the modernist techniques of Pound, Cummings, and, perhaps most important, T. S. Eliot. Like other poems of its day, including Samuel Beckett's "Whoroscope" and Hugh MacDiarmid's *A Drunk Man Looks at the Thistle,* "Poem beginning 'The'" is in large part a response to Eliot's influential *The Waste Land,* first published in 1922.

While Zukofsky adopted Eliot's strategies of quotation and juxtaposition, of contrasting the discourse of high and low culture, common speech and literary discourse, he did so primarily in order to criticize Eliot's larger cultural project. In Zukofsky's eyes (and in those of his friend William Carlos Williams) Eliot, both in *The Waste Land* and in such critical works as *The Sacred Wood* (1920), was promulgating a version of literary tradition that in its Eurocentric emphasis excluded the possibility of a specifically American poetry. Perhaps closer to home, Eliot's tradition excluded and demonized Jews and Jewish culture, and lent itself to the anti-Semitism voiced in Eliot's early poetry — "Burbank with a Baedeker, Bleistein with a Cigar" and "Gerontion" are the most egregious examples — and

more virulently in much of Pound's political, economic, and poetic discourse.

"Poem beginning 'The'" counters Eliot on several fronts: where Eliot had numbered every tenth line of *The Waste Land,* Zukofsky numbers every line; and where Eliot had affixed to his poem several pages of pedantic (and often misleading) explanatory notes, Zukofsky conflates all of his multifarious references into a single, page-long "dedication," in which he lists all of his sources in alphabetical order, including such gnomic entries as "Modern Advertising – [line] 63" and "Obvious – Where the Reference is Obvious." Most important, where Eliot had drawn for the most part upon canonical works of classical and English literature, a significant part of Zukofsky's poem consists of translations from the contemporary Yiddish poet Yehoash (Solomon Bloomgarden), a poet himself fascinatingly protomodernist and author of orientalist poems that put one in mind of Pound's *Cathay. The Waste Land,* to its early readers, had lamented the post–World War I disintegration of Western culture; Zukofsky's "Poem beginning 'The'" castigates such modernist pessimism and looks forward to a new hopeful future: both in literature, as stimulated by the "first generation . . . infusion" of new blood into the American body politic, and in politics itself, as demonstrated by the brave new experiment then being carried forth in Soviet Russia, the homeland of Zukofsky's mother.

Pound was appropriately impressed, both by "Poem beginning 'The'" and by Zukofsky's critical sense, which he demonstrated in his 1929 essay on the *Cantos* (one of the first analyses of Pound's work-in-progress). He persuaded Harriet Monroe, editor of *Poetry,* to allow Zukofsky to edit the February 1931 issue of her journal. Titled *"Objectivists" 1931,* the issue marked the beginning of what would later come to be seen as the Objectivist movement, including Zukofsky, George Oppen, Carl Rakosi, William Carlos Williams, and one of Zukofsky's greatest influences, Charles Reznikoff.

Zukofsky would later deny that there ever existed anything that could be called Objectivism, claiming that Monroe had insisted that the issue be structured around a "movement," an "ism"; as he says in 1968, "objectivism . . . I never used the word; I used the word "objectivist." . . . I don't like any of those *isms.* I mean, as soon as you do that, you start becoming a balloon instead of a person." Objectivist doctrine, however, was clearly not just an ad hoc construction for Zukofsky, and there is some evidence that he regarded the movement as

Dust jacket for Zukofsky's 1946 book, which includes poems on family life and friends (courtesy of the Lilly Library, Indiana University)

more than an ex post facto umbrella under which to gather more-or-less like-minded writers.

Whatever the truth about the Objectivist school origins may be, it is clear that in order to provide the *Poetry* issue with a poetic manifesto, Zukofsky adapted an already-drafted essay on the work of his friend Reznikoff, fitting it with an elaborate theoretical apparatus. The resulting document, "Sincerity and Objectification: With Special Reference to the Work of Charles Reznikoff," is more important as a description of Zukofsky's own work than as a manifesto of an emergent movement. "Sincerity," in Zukofsky's usage, is the poet's extreme care for the specific particulars, both of observed phenomena and of his own words – their connotations, denotations, and perhaps above all their sounds, their "movement and tone." "Objectification" is the shaping by the poet of "minor units of sincerity" into a formal whole, an objectlike or tangible structure that will produce a sensation of "rested totality" in a reader's mind. (Zukofsky's concept differs from the later New Critical notion of the poem as "well wrought urn" in that it describes

the poem's reception by a reader, rather than the poem's own autonomous nature.)

While the extent to which the terms *sincerity* and *objectification* accurately describe Reznikoff's work is at best arguable (they certainly have little relationship to the work of many of the poets collected in *"Objectivists" 1931* and *An "Objectivists" Anthology* [1932]), as ideas they remain critical touchstones throughout Zukofsky's career, denoting both a scrupulous attention to the particulars of existence and of language and a continual awareness of the importance of poetic *form,* in its broadest sense, as simultaneously contingent yet indispensable. Zukofsky's poetry, while usually written in free verse, is always formal. The arbitrariness of his forms – in sections of *"A,"* for instance, recondite mathematical formulas determine the distribution of n and r sounds, and his later works feature word-count prosodies in which lines have seven or five words, regardless of the aural or metrical length of those words – only serves to heighten the reader's awareness that for Zukofsky form is always a conscious decision, never a received container.

The *"Objectivists" 1931* issue of *Poetry* was followed in 1932 by *An "Objectivists" Anthology,* edited by Zukofsky and published by TO, Publishers, a loose consortium of the Objectivists themselves, underwritten by George Oppen, the only member of the movement with the necessary financial resources. While the number of poets in the anthology was considerably diminished from the *Poetry* issue, there was still little firm commonality among them. Zukofsky at the time was writing (along with some short poems) both the prose work "Thanks to the Dictionary," a short story of sorts that through its largely aleatoric compositional method hearkens forward to the later works of John Cage and Jackson MacLow, and a critical study, *The Writing of Guillaume Apollinaire.* The bulk of the Apollinaire study, like the Henry Adams essay, consists of arranged and juxtaposed quotations from the subject's writings. It was published in 1934 as *Le Style Apollinaire,* in a translation by the French critic René Taupin, but with both Taupin and Zukofsky listed as authors; the bulk of the edition was almost immediately destroyed in a warehouse fire, and it remains one of the rarest documents of American modernism.

This "collaboration" with Taupin, the author of *L'Influence du symbolisme français sur la póesie américaine de 1910 à 1920* (1929), and a friend of Zukofsky's, was something of a ruse designed to help Taupin, a reluctant writer, along the tenure track at his academic position. It was one of several exigencies to which Zukofsky was forced in order to earn money to support himself in the lean Depression years. He taught for a year at the University of Wisconsin (1930–1931), drew a stipend as the editor of TO, Publishers for almost a year, and from 1935 until the spring of 1942 worked, as did so many other writers, artists, and intellectuals of the day, for the Federal Writers Project of the Works Progress Administration (WPA).

During much of his time at the WPA, he worked on *The Index of American Design,* a large-scale project that aimed to record and catalogue the entire range of American handicrafts and design from colonial times through the end of the nineteenth century. From 1936 to 1940 Zukofsky wrote essays and radio scripts on various aspects of American crafts for *The Index.* He assiduously researched these projects, learning the history of American kitchenware, tinsmithing, friendship quilts, and other types of material culture; this work strengthened his appreciation for the individual craftsman and cemented his own ideology of the poet as craftsman, rather than expressive vessel. The essays and

scripts themselves, far more wide-ranging in content than their ostensible subject matter might indicate, are documents of cultural criticism very much in the tradition of Henry Adams's *Mont Saint Michel and Chartres* (1904) or William Carlos Williams's *In the American Grain* (1925).

The 1930s were a crucial decade for Zukofsky, both personally and artistically. The Objectivists' issue of *Poetry* had made important connections for him. Pound's continuing interest brought him to Italy in 1933, where he met Basil Bunting, a poet included both in the *Poetry* issue and in *An "Objectivists" Anthology,* who is sometimes considered the sole English Objectivist. While Bunting would continually chide Zukofsky for the abstraction of his prose and the obscurity of his verse, there grew up between the two a lasting friendship. They remained close correspondents to the end of Zukofsky's life, and in the preface to his own *Collected Poems* Bunting would acknowledge Zukofsky as one of two living poets who, "in his sterner, stonier way," had taught him something. Pound would dedicate his 1938 *Guide to Kulchur* to Bunting and Zukofsky, "strugglers in the desert." Perhaps the most inspired reader of the *Poetry* issue was Lorine Niedecker, a young Wisconsin poet who initiated a correspondence with Zukofsky that continued for the forty years till her death, proving herself one of his earliest and most intelligent readers. Niedecker's own poetry, consisting for the most part of short lyrics and sequences, is at times heavily reminiscent of Zukofsky's, and her development was shaped in large part by her close personal association and intense correspondence with the older poet. In recent years she has been recognized as a major poetic talent.

Zukofsky began the decade by publishing the first installments of his long poem *"A";* much of *"A"*-1 through *"A"*-7, written between 1926 and 1930, had appeared in various little magazines, but their publication together in *An "Objectivists" Anthology* signaled that a major project was underway. Barry Ahearn dates to 1927 or 1928 Zukofsky's first overall schema for *"A,"* which specifies, among much else later abandoned, a twenty-four-movement length to the poem. The forms, themes, and subject matter of those movements were undefined at the outset of the project, and indeed there is considerable evidence that Zukofsky's conception of the poem shifted as the work progressed; while the early sections of *"A"* might be characterized as Poundian, in later movements Zukofsky effectively abandons Pound's poetics of the ideogram and opens his work to a whole range of formal experiments. But unlike Pound in *Cantos,* Williams in

Paterson, and Olson in *The Maximus Poems,* Zukofsky projected a clear – if flexible – armature for his poem and stuck to it.

The major question of the first sections of *"A,"* as Zukofsky phrases it in "A"-6, is *"Can / The design / Of the fugue / Be transferred / To poetry?"* The notion of "fugal" form, in which the poet deploys various "themes" in repeating and overlapping patterns, is one that Pound had toyed with in describing the mode of his ongoing *Cantos,* most notably in a famous conversation with William Butler Yeats, but Zukofsky takes the analogy far more literally and pursues it far more strictly in his own work. "A"-1 begins "A / Round of fiddles playing Bach"; it evokes a 1928 Carnegie Hall performance of Bach's *St. Matthew Passion* and juxtaposes it with the 1729 premiere of that work in Leipzig. The "black full dress" and jewels of the New York audience is contrasted with Bach's original auditors, "motley / Country people"; the religious, apocalyptic rhetoric of the *Passion*'s libretto is juxtaposed with the contemporary economic straits of the homeless and of striking miners.

The struggle between captains of industry and the working masses – the archetypal Marxist theme clearly presented in "A"-1 – informs the early section of *"A."* James Laughlin, publisher of New Directions Press, in 1936 called *"A"* an "epic of the class struggle," and while Zukofsky would downplay that aspect of his poem in a 1953 letter to Niedecker, it is undeniable that a Marxian formulation of the war between capital and labor is one of the overriding themes of all of Zukofsky's work of the 1930s. But the early sections of *"A,"* written in a paratactic, juxtapositional style closely akin to that of the *Cantos* and informed throughout by the analogy of the fugue and the themes and lyrics of the *St. Matthew Passion,* deal with far more than just class struggle.

In "A"-3, an elegy to the suicide of "Ricky," Whittaker Chambers's brother, Zukofsky positions himself as Joseph of Arimathea to Ricky's Christ. The theme of death and resurrection, unavoidably present in the Passion story, is laid out in the early sections. Zukofsky deploys the image of "liveforever" (an evergreen plant of the *Sedum* genus) as an emblem of immortality, whether a personal immortality for which one might hope or the vicarious immortality of artistic creation. In various guises, liveforever will recur up to the very end of Zukofsky's writing life. "A"-4, like "Poem beginning 'The,'" addresses the subject of origins, "[t]he courses we tide from," and explores Zukofsky's status as the partially assimilated son of Orthodox parents, able neither to accept his father's stringent culture and religion nor to claim as wholly his own a broader Western culture that regards him for the most part with hostility.

The animosity of Western culture was sometimes quite close at hand in his voluminous correspondence with Pound, who was frequently "instigating" Zukofsky to form "movements" and schools. When most exasperated with his at times recalcitrant younger colleague, Pound would chastise him for falling back into invidious "racial characteristics." (In Pound's correspondence with Bunting, the extent to which Pound's anti-Semitism poisoned his opinion of Zukofsky is uncomfortably evident; Bunting stood up to Pound on his friend's behalf in ways that Zukofsky himself rarely would.)

Significantly, Pound wholly failed to appreciate "A"-7, the section Zukofsky rightly regarded as his most substantial accomplishment. In "A"-7, a sequence of seven formally regular sonnets, Zukofsky contemplates a set of "street closed" wooden sawhorses, each of which, in shape, resembles a pair of capital *A*'s. Through a series of dazzling puns and shifts of linguistic register, Zukofsky transforms them into imaginary horses and puts them through a breathtaking set of paces, culminating in their self-revelation: "'words, words, we are words, horses, manes, / words.'" These seven sonnets fold in everything that has come before – the *St. Matthew Passion,* the struggles of the working masses, Ricky's death, and Zukofsky's own cultural identity – while taking as their focus language itself, the literal forms and shapes of words, the relationships between the sounds and motions of words and the concepts and objects to which they correspond. More clearly than any other text "A"-7 demonstrates that Zukofsky's Objectivist poetics do not limit him to what are commonly designated "objects." He is just as concerned with the objective, communal existence of language, the aural objects that constitute the social and human environment.

During the 1930s Zukofsky also pursued the concerns of *"A"* in various shorter poems, perhaps most notably in "To my wash-stand" (1932) and "'Mantis,'" along with its accompanying piece, "'Mantis,' An Interpretation" (1934), which were collected in *55 poems* (1941). "To my wash-stand" begins with a close physical examination of the poet's bathroom sink, one that acknowledges that the "song / of water" he hears "is a song / entirely in my head," and then moves into an imaginative recreation of the morning ablutions of the poor, "carefully attentive / to what they have / and to what they do not / have." The "flow of water" from the

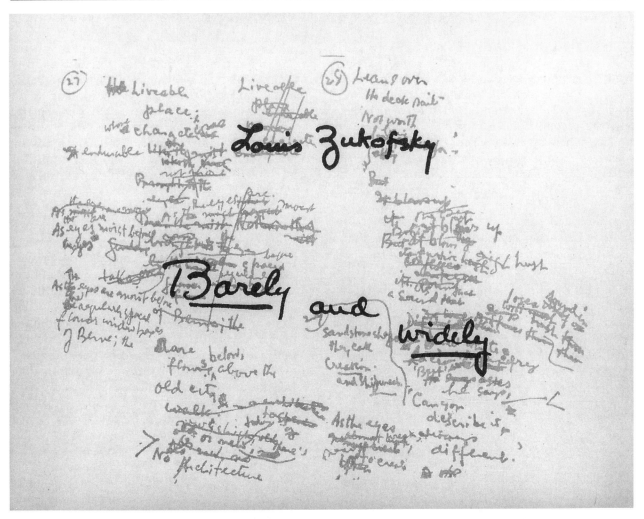

Dust jacket for Zukofsky's 1958 book, which includes poems about his family's vacation in Europe in 1957 (courtesy of the Lilly Library, Indiana University)

stand's two faucets "occasions invertible counterpoints," bringing forth in vivid detail the sordid realities and privations of the poor.

In "'Mantis,'" a sestina inspired by the poet's coming upon a praying mantis on a subway platform, Zukofsky ranges through the historical, etymological, and mythical backgrounds of the insect. He finds it a fitting analogue for the urban "poor," whose armies in the last stanza are encouraged to "arise like leaves" "And build the new world[.]" Largely through the influence of W. H. Auden the sestina, a Provençal form of daunting complexity, has become almost a cliché of twentieth-century poetry, a tour de force for poets to show off their technical abilities. Zukofsky seems to anticipate such a criticism in "'Mantis,' An Interpretation," an eight-page free verse disquisition in which he denies having appropriated the form "as an experiment," a "wicker-work" in which to "write up" his experi-

ence. On the contrary, Zukofsky argues that the sestina form, even when one takes into account its history of use (and Victorian misuse), is the *only* appropriate form for representing the "thoughts' torsion" occasioned by his encounter with the insect. That "'Mantis'" happens to take the form of a classical sestina, Zukofsky insists, does not mean that he set out to write a poem of that form: the poet can never in good conscience simply *accept* a form for his poem, but that does not mean that the internal pressures and recurrences of the poem's ideas cannot find themselves coalescing into the sestina form.

Zukofsky wrote briefer poems in the 1930s as well, including the delightful "It's a gay li - ife" and the political "This Fall, 1933" and "Song-3/4 Time (pleasantly drunk)," the last adapting phrases from Marx's *Capital* to a descending line that anticipates the later Williams. Working as a supervisor in 1933 on a WPA project, he met the musician and composer Celia Thaew. After a protracted friendship and courtship, they were married in August 1939. Celia Zukofsky would become Zukofsky's devoted collaborator, typing his manuscripts and assisting with the elaborate research he carried out for every project he undertook. She would take a directly collaborative role in his translation of *Catullus* (1969), and the second volume of *Bottom: on Shakespeare* (1963) consisted her operatic setting of Shakespeare's *Pericles, Prince of Tyre.* Her music became an integral part of many of Zukofsky's later works: his *Autobiography* consists mainly of Celia's musical settings of some of his short poems, and the concluding movement of *"A,"* "A"-24, is "Celia's L.Z. Masque," an arrangement of a myriad of Zukofsky texts, both poetry and prose, in four-voiced counterpoint to Handel's *Harpsichord Pieces.*

The Zukofskys' only child, Paul (born in 1943), was a child prodigy on the violin; he has gone on to become one of the world's foremost performers and conductors of twentieth-century music. In 1970 Zukofsky would publish a novel, *Little, A Fragment for Careenagers,* a roman à clef dealing with the upbringing of a young violin prodigy whose parents are a poet and a pianist. The novel, graceful, whimsical, and full of verbal wit, paints a charming picture of the Zukofskys' domestic life; it includes pseudonymous portraits of several of Zukofsky's acquaintances, including "R. Z. Draykup" as Ezra Pound, who by the time of the novel's action was incarcerated in St. Elizabeth's mental hospital in Washington, D.C. Despite their differences – during the course of the 1930s Zukofsky and Pound had increasingly fallen out over issues of politics and economics as well as Pound's anti-Semitism – Zukofsky still felt a strong bond to his older colleague. He, Celia, and Paul visited Pound in his confinement in 1954, where Paul played a concert for him on the lawn of the ward. Pound supplied a list of names of possible attendees at Paul's Carnegie Hall debut in 1956.

The 1930s marked the end of the period in which politics played a major role in Zukofsky's work. From 1935 to 1940 he worked on compiling *A Test of Poetry,* a teaching anthology that resembles Pound's *ABC of Reading,* though it includes far less of its author's commentary than does Pound's book; as always Zukofsky was inclined to let his material speak for itself. Significantly, *A Test of Poetry* followed directly on the heels of an aborted project, a "Workers' Anthology" that Zukofsky abandoned in 1935: the turn from the political to the more broadly aesthetic is indicative of the overall shift in Zukofsky's concerns. Throughout the 1930s he was involved with leftist organizations, in particular the Communist Party literary journal, *New Masses,* and he published two small fragments of "A"-8 there in 1936 and 1938. But he could find no leftist publishing venue for the whole of "A"-8, the most ambitious (and longest) section of *"A"* to that time, in large part because it did not clearly conform to the hortatory aesthetic of "socialist realism" that most of the party's official organs espoused. The *First Half of "A"-9,* which he published himself in 1940, was the last overtly leftist work he would write.

After "A"-8 the directions and forms of *"A"* grew more varied. The first half of "A"-9 was a translation of Guido Cavalcanti's canzone "Donna mi pregha" (a text to which Pound often returned), a translation that not only preserves the elaborate rhyme scheme of the Italian original but also simultaneously adapts phrases from Marx's *Capital.* The poem is an elaborate disquisition on the economic roots of use-value and exchange-value. When Zukofsky returned to "A"-9 in 1948, he completed it by translating the same canzone again, this time using phrases from Benedict de Spinoza's *Ethics,* making the poem into an analysis of love. Zukofsky had been fascinated with the ideas of this Jewish philosopher since "Poem beginning 'The,'" and Spinoza's categories of *natura naturans* and *natura naturata* ("nature naturing" and "nature natured") – roughly, the creator and the created, considered as moments of a single entity – recur throughout the early sections of *"A,"* but his turn from Marx to Spinoza at this crucial juncture of his poem is indicative of how the focus of *"A"* shifts from the public world of economics and revolution to the private sphere of familial love. ("A"-10, a public poem elegizing the 1940 fall of Paris to the Nazis, was written between the two halves of "A"-9.)

With his abandonment of what had at times bordered on political didacticism, Zukofsky is free to pursue more formally various and experimental modes. "A"-11 is a formal lyric, based on Cavalcanti's "Perch' io no spero," and addressed to the poet's wife and child after his death. "A"-12 is as long as the first eleven movements of the poem combined; it is a vast collage, incorporating themes from the earlier sections of the poem, materials from the then-in-progress *Bottom: on Shakespeare,* and, perhaps most important, quotations and anecdotes that draw attention to the Zukofsky family: this movement takes familial happiness as a more fitting "epic" subject than class struggle. The poem is a giant fugue that revolves around the theme of *B-A-C-H* (the letters standing for Baruch Spinoza,

Aristotle, Celia, and Paracelsus, whose real name was Hohenheim) and simultaneously a *Ulysses*-like odyssey, in which the poet travels through worlds of philosophy, history, and literature to return to the family enclosure, where his wife and son, like Penelope and Telemachus, await him. The movement also includes a moving elegy to Zukofsky's recently dead father and, as an analogue to Odysseus's descent into hell, the verbatim letters of the "poor pay pfc." Jackie, a semiliterate friend of the Zukofskys, now on his way to the Korean War. In contrast to the expansiveness of "A"-12, "A"-13 announces itself as a "partita," and its five sections formally imitate the rhythms of one of Bach's violin partitas. The "matter" of the movement is the daily life of the Zukofsky family, including the father and son's walk across the Brooklyn Bridge to the Duane Street Fire Museum and back to their Brooklyn Heights apartment.

It is easier to talk about formal structures, continuities, and discontinuities than about content when discussing Zukofsky's work. The reader has the distinct sense that the poet saw himself as planning structures in which the materials were less crucial than the formal shapes and their engineering. In the later sections of *"A"* Zukofsky winds all manner of personal and familial history, philosophy, literature, esoterica, and current events into these knotty but graceful poems: "A"-15, for instance, deals among much else with the death of John F. Kennedy; "A"-18 concerns itself off and on with the Vietnam War; and "A"-19 follows Paul Zukofsky to Genoa for his participation in the Paganini Competition while simultaneously cementing the poet's conceptual bonds with Stéphane Mallarmé, who is quoted, paraphrased, and transliterated.

"A"-14 announces itself as *"First of / eleven songs / beginning An,"* and indeed each movement from "A"-14 through "A"-24 begins with the letters *an*. Similarly, the first phrase of each movement plays with and permutes a similar set of phonemes: *"beginning"* ("A"-14), "An / hinny" ("A"-15), "An / inequality" ("A"-16), "Anemones" ("A"-17); "An unearthing" ("A"-18), "An other" ("A"-19), and so on. It is such continuities and shifts that readers learn to attend to in *"A,"* for the poem as a whole presents not a narrative or a continuously developed argument but a series of formal structures, instantiated with materials from all realms of Zukofsky's life, interlinked one with another and proceeding out of a common "fugal" impulse.

"A"-17 and "A"-20 are perhaps exemplary of Zukofsky's conception of what it means to *compose* a poem. "A"-17, "A CORONAL for Floss," is an hom-

age to Zukofsky's recently deceased friend William Carlos Williams; it consists wholly of quotations: quotations from Williams's letters to Zukofsky, from all of Zukofsky's writings (prose and poetry) that bear on Williams's work, and finally, a visual "quotation" of Williams's scrawled signature in Zukofsky's copy of *Pictures from Brueghel.* "A"-20 is a "Respond for P.Z.'s tone row / At twenty," and consists simply of a list of the titles of twelve compositions that Paul had written up to the age of twenty, repeated four times in different orders, and a short poem that Paul had written at age nine in response to a poem of Henry VIII's included in *A Test of Poetry.* "Composition," for Zukofsky, is as much the arrangement of previously written texts as it is the wholesale invention of new ones.

A lifelong New Yorker, Zukofsky in 1947 took a job as an instructor in the English department of the Polytechnic Institute of Brooklyn, a position he would hold until 1966, when he retired at the rank of associate professor. It was not a particularly congenial atmosphere for a poet, but Zukofsky made the best of it, teaching a wide range of literature and acting as faculty adviser to the poetry club. At least one fledgling engineer, Hugh Seidman, went on to pursue poetry as a vocation; but in the main Zukofsky thought of his students as "my plumbers."

Just as the parallels that can be drawn between Pound's *Cantos* and the early movements of *"A"* break down as Zukofsky's poem progresses and diversifies, the place of the epic poems within the two poets' respective careers also diverged. Once the *Cantos* were well underway, they became the center of Pound's poetic production; while he wrote large amounts of prose, except for translation (and there were many of those) Pound wrote no substantial poetry outside the *Cantos.* Zukofsky, on the other hand, was continually adding to his corpus of short poems. The collections *Anew: Poems* (1946) and *Some Time / Short Poems* (1956) include many delicate occasional poems — birthday poems, wedding poems, valentines — and such important sequences as "Light" and "Chloride of Lime and Charcoal." These poems reflect the Zukofsky family's physical circumstances, their friendships, and the milieu of artists, musicians, and writers within which they gingerly moved. "Four Other Countries" and "Stratford-on-Avon," from the volume *Barely and Widely* (1958), record the family's 1957 vacation in Europe and show them to be assiduous literary tourists, seeking out the sites of Shakespeare's plays, classical poets' haunts, and the various "luminous details" of Italy and Provence that Pound presented so memorably in his poetry.

"Stratford-on-Avon" reflects Zukofsky's ongoing fascination with Shakespeare. From 1947 to 1960 much of his energies were devoted to his massive prose work *Bottom: on Shakespeare*. This text is more than a grand act of homage by one poet to another; it in effect lays out Zukofsky's poetics and epistemology on a fuller scale than any other work save *"A"* itself. In a brief explanatory note to *Bottom* written in 1961, Zukofsky describes the text as "A long poem built on a theme for the variety of its recurrences." *Bottom* argues repeatedly and from a variety of perspectives and approaches that Shakespeare's poems and plays, considered as "one work, sometimes poor, sometimes good, sometimes great," in effect display and reinforce the fundamental tenets of Objectivist poetics, that the evidence of the physical senses is always more reliable than the a posteriori rationalizations of the abstracting intellect.

Zukofsky pursues this theme through all of Shakespeare's works, finding a "singular and simple" "formula" to the plays: "when the passions [that is, the irrational meddlings of the intellect] tend to constitute the least possible part of the mind of the characters, the result is 'comedy'; when the passions are irresolute for them, the result is 'tragedy'; when either 'comedy' or 'tragedy' or blends of both involve the passions of historical characters, the result is history." Zukofsky does more than simply trace this formula through all the works of Shakespeare's canon: he explores the theme of passion and the senses as it is discussed in Western philosophy up to the twentieth century (and especially in Aristotle and Spinoza). He also compiles an enormous body of quotations from all periods and genres of Western literature, quotations that deal with – or can be construed to deal with – the theme of love and vision.

Decidedly heterodox, *Bottom* has created scarcely a ripple of interest in the Shakespeare-criticism community. On its own grounds both *Bottom*'s doctrine and its method – the obsessive ferreting out of quotations that might be made to support the theme that Zukofsky finds running throughout Shakespeare, often without regard to those quotations' original context or implications – have been severely criticized by such otherwise sympathetic readers as the poets David Melnick and Charles Bernstein. But, as Bernstein points out, it is as "long poem" in prose that *Bottom* is most important in Zukofsky's oeuvre as a whole. Precisely through its concatenation of quotations, divorced from their original occasions and recontextualized according to the logic of Zukofsky's overall thesis, *Bottom* can

be read as a large-scale playing out of the poetics of quotation, a technique that is pervasive in his later writings.

Melnick faults *Bottom* for a failure to deal with Shakespeare's characters as if they were human beings in human situations. *Bottom,* he claims, abstracts various phrases, themes, and images from their contexts within the plays and fits them into the logic of Zukofsky's "love : reason :: eyes : mind" analogy; in so doing, it drains the plays of their human values, their appeal to our emotions and experience. In this most "thematic" reading of Shakespeare, Zukofsky presses the ideology of the individual sensorium so far that he verges upon solipsism and ignores the human community.

Despite the acuteness of such a criticism of *Bottom,* Zukofsky's work on the whole is too deeply grounded in the concrete realities of experience to fall into solipsism; an important midperiod work, the title poem of *I's Pronounced "eyes"* (1963) deploys a witty sequence of brief stanzas whose ultimate import is not merely to emphasize the integrity of perception and identity (*I* equals *eye*) but to show how one's perception is always grounded in a socially shared context and environment in which the evidence of the senses is continually tested through linguistic interchange. One section, "Tree – see," consists merely of the statement "I see / by / your tree" and the response, "What / do you / see[?]" While perception itself is ultimately grounded in the individual – the I/eye – the truth and perhaps even the shape of that perception is to be created in interpersonal exchange. (This poem, of course, also exemplifies Zukofsky's poetics of quotation, since its lines are taken from two letters between Zukofsky and Lorine Niedecker.)

I's Pronounced "eyes" and its sequel, *After I's* (1964), are two slim volumes of typically angular, oblique poems, many of which have about them an air of occasionality. There are valentines here, a response to younger poets' recognition, and even a sequence celebrating the family's removal from their longtime abode, "The Old Poet Moves to a New Apartment 14 Times" (1962). In 1966, after carefully calculating his and Celia's combined incomes, Zukofsky retired from teaching to devote himself full-time to his poetry. The couple would eventually move to Port Jefferson, Long Island, where Zukofsky could plan and write his works and Celia could compose and (among other pursuits) cultivate the plants on which Zukofsky would focus so intensely in *80 Flowers*.

It was not until 1966, when the first volume of *All: The Collected Short Poems* was published by Nor-

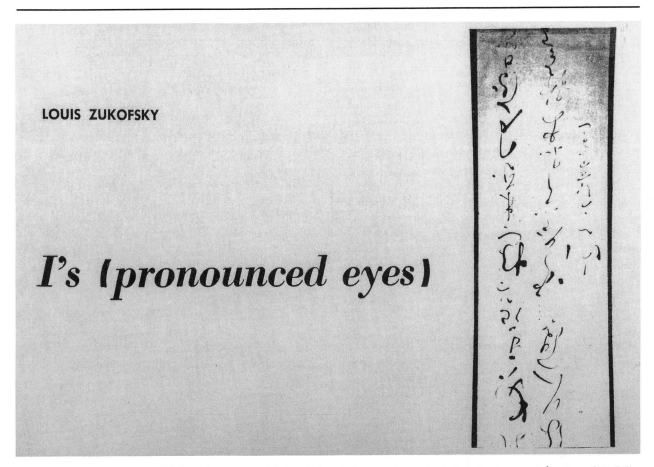

LOUIS ZUKOFSKY

I's (pronounced eyes)

Dust jacket for the collection of Zukofsky's poems published by Robert Kelly, one of many poets Zukofsky influenced (courtesy of the Lilly Library, Indiana University)

ton, that Zukofsky saw his poems in print by a major publisher. His career had begun auspiciously back in 1931, with his own issue of *Poetry* and his own anthology; but in the years since, he had watched his elders and contemporaries, such poets as Cummings and Oppen, go on to attain a degree of the recognition that he felt was his due while he remained in obscurity. While Oppen, who had ceased writing poetry altogether for some twenty-five years, returned to print immediately with *The Materials* from New Directions in 1962, neither Zukofsky nor his friend Williams could interest New Directions publisher James Laughlin in a volume of Zukofsky's work. In the years before *All* – a volume that signaled a gradual opening-up of medium and large presses to his work – Zukofsky became irremediably bitter, convinced that he had somehow been unreasonably passed over by the powers that conveyed poetic recognition. This bitterness, combined with an increasingly debilitating series of illnesses and hypochondriac "aches," made Zukofsky more and more the recluse. When Basil Bunting, among the very oldest of his friends, came

to New York in 1967 he found Zukofsky "very bitter and, strangely, very jealous." Bunting was riding high on the success of his *Briggflatts,* but Zukofsky declined to attend his New York reading, complaining of "drafts."

Zukofsky, however, was by no means without friends, nor as the 1960s progressed without admirers among younger poets. Edward Dahlberg, his contemporary and colleague at Brooklyn Polytechnic, became close friends with Zukofsky, and a succession of young poets made their way to his apartment: Paul Blackburn, Jerome Rothenberg, Jonathan Williams, Denise Levertov, Gilbert Sorrentino, and Allen Ginsberg. The eclectic Robert Duncan, at the time writing a medievalist-cum-modernist verse, had added Zukofsky's influence to an aesthetic that already counted Stein, Edith Sitwell, Hilda Doolittle (H. D.), Williams, and Alexis Saint-Léger Léger among its household gods. Ronald Johnson, whose early work was in the much "looser" vein of Charles Olson, would go on to write *ARK,* a long poem that made use of many of Zukofsky's compositional procedures. Cid Corman, who lived in Japan and edited the groundbreaking journal *Origin,* published *"A" 1-12* in a limited edition in 1959 and was an indefatigable supporter of Zukofsky's work. Perhaps most influenced by Zukofsky was the young Robert Creeley, who marveled not merely at the older poet's craft, but at the personal kindness he showed his impecunious young colleague. As welcome as such recognition was, in the end it failed to compensate Zukofsky for thirty years of obscurity.

Bottom was published in 1963 by the University of Texas as part of a deal in which Zukofsky agreed to donate his papers to the Harry Ransom Humanities Research Center in Austin. This first edition was a two-volume work, the second being Celia Zukofsky's operatic setting of Shakespeare's *Pericles.* Zukofsky's next major project, begun in 1958 and completed in 1966, was also a collaboration with his wife. The Zukofskys' complete translation of *Catullus* was a conceptual tour de force that baffled and angered classicists much as Pound's "Homage to Sextus Propertius" (1919) had a half-century earlier. Its purpose, Zukofsky writes, is "to breathe the 'literal' meaning" of the Latin original, adhering as closely as possible to the sounds and rhythms of Catullus, and letting the meaning take a distant backseat. The famous statement "Odi et amo. Quare id faciam, fortasse requiris," for instance, which literally means "I hate and I love. Perhaps you want to know why I do this," in Zukofsky's hands becomes "O th'hate I move love. Quarry it fact I am, for that's so re queries." (While the book is credited to both Louis and Celia Zukofsky, Celia prepared the literal translations and notated the sounds of the Latin, and Louis alone was responsible for the final form of the translations.)

While some readers have found it to be a long, tedious joke, *Catullus,* beyond its real merits of wit and invention, is important in Zukofsky's work as a whole, exemplifying at least two central elements of his poetics. There is the notion of the word, as Zukofsky puts it in an interview, as a "physiological" thing, a tangible shaping of air and sound by an embodied person; in that sense, it is clear that the way to get closest to the historical Catullus would be to produce poems that shape sound and air as closely as possible to the ways in which he shaped them in his poetry in the first century B.C. When one reads the Zukofskys' *Catullus* one experiences the Roman poet in a way that one reading a translation more faithful in literal "meaning" cannot.

Beyond his fidelity to the physiological word, Zukofsky employs a method of phonetic translitera-

tion as an active technique. By using as a template the sounds and rhythms of a non-English text, he generates a new English text that sometimes does and often does not bear a "meaningful" relationship to the original. The poet-translator is thereby freed from the burden of formal originality in a way perhaps analogous to how the Provençal poet explored formal permutations, knowing that his conventional themes freed him from any need to dream up original subject-matter. Zukofsky uses such transliteration often in his later work, drawing on texts in Greek, Hebrew, Latin, Ojibwa, and Welsh, among others: *"A"*-15 begins with passages from the Book of Job, *"A"*-22 and -23 include stretches of phonetically transliterated material, and large portions of *80 Flowers* (Guy Davenport claims all) are written over foreign templates.

Such a transliteration is *"A"*-21, a full-length translation of Titus Maccius Plautus's *Rudens* (*The Rope*), a play in which Zukofsky saw suggestive parallels to Shakespeare's *Pericles.* What makes the verse of *"A"*-21 even more knotted than mere transliteration would have it is the fact that Zukofsky translates line-for-line, one five-word English line for each line of Latin hexameter. The sound of the verse is alien, and the compressed syntax often reads as fragments. Sections *"A"*-21, -22, and -23 are all composed of five-word lines, and in other sections of the poem Zukofsky had used three-word and even one-word lines. Traditional English accentual-syllabic prosody, of course, takes no notice of the number of words to a line, and Zukofsky's relentless pursuit of word-count forms is a full-scale assault on the time-honored norms of what constitutes a meter.

A problem that Zukofsky no doubt found more pressing perhaps even than such questions of form was that of closure; in 1967, with *"A"*-21 finished and *"A"*-22 and -23 planned out, how was he to bring an end to his poem? How does one finish a long poem that is in large part a series of formal experiments, rather than a narrative or argument that might be brought to some sort of a logical close? What was to constitute *"A"*-24? Celia Zukofsky solved that problem when she presented him in 1968 with the gift of the "L.Z. Masque," a 240-page arrangement to music (Handel's *Harpsichord Pieces*) of various of Zukofsky's texts. Zukofsky promptly named this work *"A"*-24 and designated it the closing movement of his "poem of a life." By naming Celia's composition the final movement of his own poem, Zukofsky characteristically carries out the ultimate destabilization of textual authority, render-

Dust jacket for Zukofsky's Objectivist criticism of Shakespeare, which he described as "A long poem built on a theme for the variety of its recurrences" (courtesy of the Lilly Library, Indiana University)

ing the attribution of authorship problematic in a way that even his wholesale quotation had not.

"A"-22 and -23, the last-composed movements of *"A,"* are also perhaps the densest. Each is comprised of one thousand five-word lines, and each winds within it six thousand years of history: in "A"-22 the history is geological and botanical, and in "A"-23 it is literary. There are passages of these two thousand lines that are readily apprehensible – perhaps most memorably, a 150-line stretch of "A"-23 that translates the Gilgamesh myth, renaming Gilgamesh "Strongest" and Enkidu "One Kid" – but for the most part the reader is hard-pressed to find the principle of continuity in these baffling but sonically exquisite lines. "History's best emptied of names' / impertinence," Zukofsky writes (or quotes, or transliterates) in "A"-22, and these movements indeed lack any proper names that might provide signposts for readers. Many of these lines are clearly transliterated or translated; most of them, one suspects, are quotations; but in the end, for all the evident care and labor that went into their composition, they remain obdurately other, refusing to

"mean" in conventionally circumscribed manners, and they thereby might be seen as proposing a new democracy of interpretation. Perhaps readers should not hunt after source texts or Poundian arcana or a meaning *behind* the text but should concentrate on the words themselves: as Zukofsky's alter ego in *Little* says, "I too have been charged with obscurity, tho it's a case of listeners wanting to know too much about me, more than the words say." Or as "A"-22 puts it, more simply, "why deny what you've not / tried: read, not into, it: / desire until all be bright."

The poetics that produced "A"-22 and -23 are similar to those used to generate *80 Flowers,* Zukofsky's last completed collection. This volume of eighty-one poems, each of eight five-word lines, takes to new extremes of density Zukofsky's methods of composition by quotation, transliteration, and compression. Each poem focuses on a particular flower (or class of flowers) and each aims to draw in and allude to as much knowledge as possible pertaining to that flower: botanical, commercial, historical, alchemical, literary, etymological, and personal knowledge are all compacted into these resonant little poems. What they in the end suggest – though Zukofsky himself was probably not wholly conscious of working toward such a goal – is the possibility of the word set free from the determinate meaningful context, liberated to interact with its neighbors in any or all of the combinations possible. The compression and foreshortening of syntax in *80 Flowers,* far from making the poems meaningless, open them up to a far broader range of potential meanings and connotations. Even an exhaustive ferreting out of the source texts and original contexts from which the words of the poems are drawn, such as Michele J. Leggott has carried out, does not pin the poems down to a determinate meaning or set of meanings, but serves to enrich and expand our multidirectional, polysemic experience of the text.

When Zukofsky died in 1978, *80 Flowers* was at the printer awaiting publication in a limited edition, and the first complete edition of *"A,"* undoubtedly the poet's major work, was being readied for publication by the University of California Press. Zukofsky had planned the release of *80 Flowers* to coincide with his eightieth birthday in 1984 but had finished the work early and begun taking notes for his next project, *Gamut: 90 Trees.* His last work was the index to the California *"A."* He had originally indexed only the words *a, an,* and *the,* reiterating a conviction he had first voiced in 1946:

> a case can be made for the poet giving some of his life to the use of the words *the* and *a:* both of which are weighted with as much epos and historical destiny as one man can perhaps resolve. Those who do not believe this are too sure that the little words mean nothing among so many other words.

His wife persuaded him to let her index the book more fully, and he in turn revised her index to produce the final version. It is fitting that his last completed work was such a formal one and that it was to be a collaboration with his partner of thirty-eight years.

In the years since Zukofsky's death readers have come more and more to recognize the extraordinary strengths of his work. Zukofsky's ear was unparalleled, though his poetry's music is rarely mellifluous; his writings, both poetry and prose, press the boundaries of their respective genres, proposing provocative models for such contemporaries as Charles Bernstein and Susan Howe; and his work explores complex philosophical and epistemological issues with an admirable rigor, his logic that of what he once called the "finer mathematician." *"A,"* in its simultaneous ambition of means and hu-mility of purpose, has caused contemporary poets to rethink the formal aesthetics of the modernist long poem, with its seemingly inevitable incompletion: long projects by Ron Silliman, Ronald Johnson, and Frank Samperi, among many others, owe significant debts to Zukofsky's example. Perhaps most significantly, Zukofsky's later works – works pursued, as he tragically saw it, almost wholly without recognition or in the face of uncomprehending scorn – pushed brusquely past the boundaries of Zukofsky's modernist heritage, the works of his mentors and contemporaries, and laid the groundwork for an entirely new range of poetic approaches and practices.

Letters:

"Three letters to Cid Corman," *Origin,* second series, 1 (April 1961);

"Letters between Zukofsky and Ezra Pound," edited by Barry Ahearn, *Montemora,* 8 (1981): 158–165;

Pound/Zukofsky: Selected Letters of Ezra Pound and Louis Zukofsky, edited by Ahearn (New York: New Directions, 1987);

"Three letters to Cid Corman," *Line,* 14 (Fall 1989): 3–10.

Interview:

"[Sincerity and Objectification]," interview with L. S. Dembo, in *Louis Zukofsky: Man and Poet,* edited by Carroll F. Terrell (Orono, Maine: National Poetry Foundation, 1979), pp. 265–281.

Bibliographies:

Celia Zukofsky, *A Bibliography of Louis Zukofsky* (Los Angeles: Black Sparrow Press, 1969);

Marcella Booth, *A Catalogue of the Louis Zukofsky Manuscript Collection* (Austin: Harry Ransom Humanities Research Center, University of Texas, 1975);

Booth, "The Zukofsky Papers: The Cadence of a Life," in *Louis Zukofsky: Man and Poet,* edited by Carroll F. Terrell (Orono, Maine: National Poetry Foundation, 1979), pp. 393–400;

Zukofsky, "Year by Year Bibliography of Louis Zukofsky," in *Louis Zukofsky: Man and Poet,* edited by Terrell (Orono, Maine: National Poetry Foundation, 1979), pp. 385–392;

Cathy Henderson, "Supplement to Marcella Booth's 'A Catalogue of the Louis Zukofsky Manuscript Collection,'" *Library Chronicle of the University of Texas,* 38–39 (1987): 106–181.

References:

Barry Ahearn, "Two Conversations with Celia Zukofsky," *Sagetrieb,* 2, no. 1 (1983): 113–131;

Ahearn, *Zukofsky's "A": An Introduction* (Berkeley: University of California Press, 1983);

Neil Baldwin, "The Letters of William Carlos Williams to Louis Zukofsky: A Chronicle of Trust and Difficulty," *Library Chronicle of the University of Texas,* 23 (1983): 36–49;

Charles Bernstein, "Words and Pictures," in *Content's Dream: Essays 1975–1984* (Los Angeles: Sun & Moon, 1986), pp. 114–161;

George F. Butterick, "With Louis Zukofsky in Connecticut," *Credences,* 1, nos. 2–3 (1981–1982): 158–163;

Don Byrd, "Getting Ready to Read *'A',*" *Boundary 2,* 10 (1982): 291–308;

Bruce Comens, *Apocalypse and After: Modern Strategy and Postmodern Tactics in Pound, Williams, and Zukofsky* (Tuscaloosa: University of Alabama Press, 1996);

Comens, "From A to An: The Postmodern Twist in Louis Zukofsky, *Sagetrieb,* 10 (Winter 1991): 37–62;

Comens, "Soundings: The 'An' Song Beginning 'A'-22," *Sagetrieb,* 5 (Spring 1986): 95–106;

Kenneth Cox, "Louis Zukofsky," *Agenda,* 16, no. 2 (1978): 11–13;

Cox, "The Poetry of Louis Zukofsky: *'A',*" *Agenda,* 9 (1971–1972): 80–89;

Cox, "Zukofsky and Mallarmé: Notes on 'A'-19," *MAPS,* 5 (1973): 1–11;

Guy Davenport, "Zukofsky," in his *The Geography of the Imagination* (San Francisco: North Point Press, 1981), pp. 100–113;

Michel Davidson, "Dismantling 'Mantis': Reification and Objectivist Poetics," *American Literary History,* 3 (Fall 1991): 521–541;

Charlene Diehl-Johnes, "Sounding *'A',*" *Line,* 14 (Fall 1989): 32–51;

Lisa Pater Faranda, ed., *"Between Your House and Mine": The Letters of Lorine Niedecker to Cid Corman, 1960 to 1970* (Durham, N.C.: Duke University Press, 1986);

Harry Gilonis, ed., *Louis Zukofsky, Or Whomever Someone Else Thought He Was: A Collection of Responses to the Work of Louis Zukofsky* (Twickenham & Wakefield, U.K.: North & South, 1988);

Alan Golding, "The 'Community of Elements' in Wallace Stevens and Louis Zukofsky," in *Wallace Stevens: The Poetics of Modernism,* edited by Albert Gelpi (Cambridge: Cambridge University Press, 1985), pp. 121–140;

Burton Hatlen, "Art and/as Labor: Some Dialectical Patterns in 'A'-1 through 'A'-10," *Contemporary Literature,* 25 (1984): 205–234;

Hatlen, "From Modernism to Postmodernism: Zukofsky's 'A'-12," *Sagetrieb,* 11 (Spring & Fall 1992): 21–34;

Hatlen, "Zukofsky, Wittgenstein, and the Poetics of Absence," *Sagetrieb,* 1, no. 1 (1982): 63–93;

Michael Heller, *Conviction's Net of Branches: Essays on the Objectivist Poets and Poetry* (Carbondale: Southern Illinois University Press, 1985);

Erica Hunt, "Beginning at 'Bottom,'" *Poetics Journal,* 3 (May 1983): 63–66;

Udo Kasemets, *Z for Zuk for Zukofsky: A Celebration of 80 Flowers* (Toronto: Sun, 1995);

Hugh Kenner, "Loove in Brooklyn," *Paideuma,* 7 (1978): 413–420;

Kenner, "Oppen, Zukofsky, and the Poem as Lens," in *Literature at the Barricades: The American Writer in the 1930s,* edited by Ralph Bogardus and Fred Hobson (Tuscaloosa: University of Alabama Press, 1982), pp. 162–171;

Michele J. Leggott, *Reading Zukofsky's 80 Flowers* (Baltimore: Johns Hopkins University Press, 1989);

David Melnick, "The 'Ought' of Seeing: Zukofsky's *Bottom,*" *MAPS,* 5 (1973): 55–65;

Robert Mittenthal, "Zukofsky's Love's Song a Circle Sent: The Valentine Written To-Two: Initial Period of 'A'-22 and its Correspondence," *Line,* 14 (Fall 1989): 11–31;

Eric Mottram, "1924–1951: Politics and Form in Zukofsky," *MAPS,* 5 (1973): 76–103;

Lorine Niedecker, "The Poetry of Louis Zukofsky," *Quarterly Review of Literature,* 8 (1956): 198–210;

Jenny Penberthy, *Niedecker and the Correspondence with Zukofsky* (Cambridge: Cambridge University Press, 1993);

Bob Perlman, *The Trouble with Genius: Reading Pound, Joyce, Stein, and Zukofsky* (Berkeley: University of California Press, 1994);

Peter Quartermain, *Disjunctive Poetics: From Gertrude Stein and Louis Zukofsky to Susan Howe* (Cambridge: Cambridge University Press, 1992);

Alison Rieke, *The Senses of Nonsense* (Iowa City: University of Iowa Press, 1992);

Edward Schelb, "The Exaction of Song: Louis Zukofsky and the Ideology of Form," *Contemporary Literature,* 31 (Fall 1990): 335–353;

Schelb, "Through Rupture to Destiny: Repetition in Zukofsky," *Sagetrieb,* 9 (Spring/Fall 1990): 25–42;

Mark Scroggins, "A 'Sense of Duration': Wallace Stevens, Louis Zukofsky, and 'Language,'" *Sagetrieb,* 11 (Spring/Fall 1992): 67–83;

Scroggins, "'To Breathe the "Literal" Meaning': Zukofsky's *Catullus," Talisman,* 6 (Spring 1991): 42–44;

Scroggins, "Zukofsky's *Bottom: on Shakespeare*: Objectivist Poetics and Critical Prosody," *West Coast Line,* 12 (Winter 1993–1994): 17–36;

Scroggins, ed., *Upper Limit Music: The Writings of Louis Zukofsky* (Tuscaloosa: University of Alabama Press, 1997);

Ron Silliman, "Z-Sited Path," in his *The New Sentence* (New York: Roof Books, 1987), pp. 127–146;

Sandra Kumamoto Stanley, *Louis Zukofsky and the Transformation of a Modern American Poetics* (Berkeley: University of California Press, 1994);

David Levi Strauss, "Approaching *80 Flowers,"* in *Code of Signals: Recent Writing in Poetics,* edited by Michael Palmer (Berkeley, Cal.: North Atlantic, 1983), pp. 79–102;

John Taggart, *Songs of Degrees: Essays on Contemporary Poetry and Poetics* (Tuscaloosa: University of Alabama Press, 1994);

Carroll F. Terrell, ed., *Louis Zukofsky: Man and Poet* (Orono, Maine: National Poetry Foundation, 1979);

Charles Tomlinson, *Some Americans* (Berkeley: University of California Press, 1981);

Jeffrey Twitchell, "Tuning the Senses: Cavalcanti, Marx, Spinoza and Zukofsky's 'A'-9," *Sagetrieb,* 11 (Winter 1992): 57–91;

Karen A. Weisman, "'Self-taunt' and 'The Courses We Tide From': A Note on Zukofsky's 'A'-4," *Sagetrieb,* 6 (Spring 1987): 75–80;

Celia Zukofsky, *American Friends* (New York: C. Z. Publications, 1979).

Papers:
Zukofsky's papers are held at the Harry Ransom Humanities Research Center, University of Texas at Austin; some of his letters to Cid Corman are held by the Special Collections department of the University Library at Simon Fraser University, Burnaby, British Columbia.

Books for Further Reading

Allen, Donald, and Warren Tallman, eds. *The Poetics of the New American Poetry*. New York: Grove, 1973.

Altieri, Charles. *Enlarging the Temple: New Directions in American Poetry During the 1960s*. Lewisburg, Pa.: Bucknell University Press, 1979.

Altieri. *Self and Sensibility in Contemporary American Poetry*. New York: Cambridge University Press, 1984.

Baker, Peter. *Obdurate Brilliance: Exteriority and the Modern Long Poem*. Gainesville: University of Florida Press, 1991.

Bartlett, Lee. *Talking Poetry: Conversations in the Workshop with Contemporary Poets*. Albuquerque: University of New Mexico Press, 1987.

Beach, Christopher. *ABC of Influence: Ezra Pound and the Remaking of American Poetic Tradition*. Berkeley & Los Angeles: University of California Press, 1992.

Bellamy, Joe David, ed. *American Poetry Observed: Poets on Their Work*. Urbana: University of Illinois Press, 1984.

Berke, Roberta Elzey. *Bounds Out of Bounds: A Compass for Recent American and British Poetry*. New York: Oxford University Press, 1981.

Bernstein, Charles. *A Poetics*. Cambridge, Mass.: Harvard University Press, 1992.

Blasing, Mutlu Konuk. *American Poetry: The Rhetoric of Its Forms*. New Haven: Yale University Press, 1987.

Bloom, Harold, ed. *Contemporary Poets*. New York: Chelsea House, 1986.

Boyers, Robert, ed. *Contemporary Poetry in America: Essays and Interviews*. New York: Schocken Books, 1974.

Breslin, James E. B. *From Modern to Contemporary: American Poetry, 1945–1965*. Chicago: University of Chicago Press, 1983.

Breslin. "Poetry: 1945 to the Present," *Columbia Literary History of the United States,* edited by Emory Elliott and others. New York: Columbia University Press, 1988, pp. 1079–1100;

Breslin, Paul. *The Psycho-Political Muse: American Poetry Since the Fifties*. Chicago: University of Chicago Press, 1987.

Carroll, Paul. *The Poem in its Skin*. Chicago: Follett, 1968.

Codrescu, Andrei, ed. *American Poetry Since 1970: Up Late*. New York: Four Walls Eight Windows, 1987.

Conte, Joseph M. *Unending Design: The Forms of Postmodern Poetry*. Ithaca, N.Y.: Cornell University Press, 1991.

Damon, Maria. *The Dark End of the Street: Margins in American Vanguard Poetry*. Minneapolis: University of Minnesota Press, 1993.

Davidson, Michael. *The San Francisco Renaissance: Poetics and Community at Mid-Century.* Cambridge: Cambridge University Press, 1989.

Dembo, L. S. *Conceptions of Reality in Modern American Poetry.* Berkeley: University of California Press, 1966.

Duberman, Martin B. *Black Mountain: An Exploration in Community.* Garden City, N.Y.: Doubleday, 1973.

Erkilla, Betsy. *The Wicked Sisters: Women Poets, Literary History and Discord.* New York: Oxford University Press, 1992.

Faas, Ekbert. *Towards a New American Poetics: Essays and Interviews.* Santa Barbara, Cal.: Black Sparrow Press, 1978.

Feirstein, Frederick, ed. *Expansive Poetry: Essays on the New Narrative and the New Formalism.* Santa Cruz, Cal.: Story Line Press, 1989.

Finch, Annie. *The Ghost of Meter: Culture and Prosody in American Free Verse.* Ann Arbor: University of Michigan Press, 1993.

Finch, ed. *A Formal Feeling Comes: Poems in Form by Contemporary Women.* Brownsville, Oreg.: Story Line Press, 1994.

Finkelstein, Norman. *The Utopian Moment in Contemporary American Poetry.* Lewisburg, Pa.: Bucknell University Press, 1988.

Frank, Robert, and Henry Sayre, eds. *The Line in Postmodern Poetry.* Urbana: University of Illinois Press, 1988.

Fredman, Stephen. *The Grounding of American Poetry: Charles Olson and the Emersonian Tradition.* Cambridge: Cambridge University Press, 1993.

Fredman. *Poet's Prose: The Crisis in American Verse,* second edition. Cambridge: Cambridge University Press, 1990.

Gardner, Thomas. *Discovering Ourselves in Whitman: The Contemporary American Long Poem.* Urbana & Chicago: University of Illinois Press, 1989.

Géfin, Laszlo K. *Ideogram: History of a Poetic Method.* Austin: University of Texas Press, 1982.

Gelpi, Albert. *A Coherent Splendor: The American Poetic Renaissance, 1910–1950.* New York: Cambridge University Press, 1987.

Gilbert, Roger. *Walks in the World: Representation and Experience in Modern American Poetry.* Princeton: Princeton University Press, 1991.

Gioia, Dana. *Can Poetry Matter?: Essays on Poetry and Culture.* Saint Paul, Minn.: Graywolf Press, 1992.

Glazier, Loss Pequeño. *Small Press: An Annotated Guide.* Westport, Conn.: Greenwood Press, 1992.

Gould, Jean. *Modern American Women Poets.* New York: Dodd, Mead, 1984.

Gray, Richard. *American Poetry of the Twentieth Century.* New York: Longman, 1990.

Hamilton, Ian, ed. *The Oxford Companion to Twentieth-Century Poetry.* New York: Oxford University Press, 1994.

Hartley, George. *Textual Politics and the Language Poets*. Bloomington: Indiana University Press, 1989.

Hartman, Charles O. *Free Verse: An Essay on Prosody*. Princeton: Princeton University Press, 1980.

Hass, Robert. *Twentieth Century Pleasures: Prose or Poetry*. New York: Ecco Press, 1984.

Heller, Michael. *Conviction's Net of Branches: Essays on the Objectivist Poets and Poetry*. Carbondale & Edwardsville: Southern Illinois University Press, 1985.

Henderson, Stephen, ed. *Understanding the New Black Poetry*. New York: Morrow, 1973.

Hoffman, Daniel, ed. *American Poetry and Poetics*. Garden City: Doubleday, 1962.

Holden, Jonathan. *The Fate of American Poetry*. Athens: University of Georgia Press, 1991.

Holden. *Style and Authenticity in Postmodern Poetry*. Columbia: University of Missouri Press, 1986.

Homberger, Eric. *The Art of the Real: Poetry in England and America Since 1939*. London: Dent, 1977.

Hoover, Paul, ed. *Postmodern American Poetry*. New York: Norton, 1994.

Howard, Richard. *Alone with America: Essays on the Art of Poetry in the United States Since 1950*. New York: Atheneum, 1980.

Howard, ed. *Preferences: 51 American Poets Choose Poems From Their Own Work and From the Past*. New York: Viking, 1974.

Ignatow, David, ed. *Political Poetry*. New York: Chelsea, 1960.

Ingersoll, Earl, Judith Kitchen, and Stan Sanvel Rublin, eds. *The Post-Confessionals: Conversations with American Poets of the Eighties*. Cranford, N.J.: Associated University Presses, 1989.

Jackson, Richard. *Acts of Mind: Conversations with Contemporary Poets*. Tuscaloosa: University of Alabama Press, 1983.

Jackson. *The Dismantling of Time in Contemporary Poetry*. Tuscaloosa: University of Alabama Press, 1988.

Juhasz, Suzanne. *Naked and Fiery Forms: Modern American Poetry by Women*. New York: Harper & Row, 1976.

Kalaidjian, Walter. *Languages of Liberation: The Social Text in Contemporary American Poetry*. New York: Columbia University Press, 1989.

Kalstone, David. *Five Temperaments: Elizabeth Bishop, Robert Lowell, James Merrill, Adrienne Rich, John Ashbery*. New York: Oxford University Press, 1977.

Keller, Lynn. *Re-making It New: Contemporary American Poetry and the Modernist Tradition*. Cambridge: Cambridge University Press, 1987.

Keller and Cristanne Miller, eds. *Feminist Measures: Soundings in Poetry and Theory*. Ann Arbor: University of Michigan Press, 1995.

Kostelanetz, Richard. *The Old Poetries and the New*. Ann Arbor: University of Michigan Press, 1981.

Lacey, Paul A. *The Inner War: Forms and Themes in Recent American Poetry*. Philadelphia: Fortress Press, 1972.

Larrissy, Edward. *Reading Twentieth-Century Poetry: The Language of Gender and Objects.* Oxford: Blackwell, 1990.

Lazer, Hank, ed. *What Is a Poet?: Essays from the Eleventh Alabama Symposium on English and American Literature.* Tuscaloosa: University of Alabama Press, 1987.

Leary, Paris, and Robert Kelly, eds. *A Controversy of Poets.* Garden City: Anchor, 1965.

Lehman, David. *Ecstatic Occasions, Expedient Forms: 65 Leading Contemporary Poets Select and Comment on their Poems.* New York: Macmillan, 1987.

Lehman. *The Line Forms Here.* Ann Arbor: University of Michigan Press, 1992.

Lensing, George S., and Robert Moran. *Four Poets and the Emotive Imagination: Robert Bly, James Wright, Louis Simpson, and William Stafford.* Baton Rouge: Louisiana State University Press, 1976.

Lepper, Gary M. *A Bibliographical Introduction to Seventy-Five Modern American Authors.* Berkeley, Cal.: Serendipity Books, 1976.

Libby, Anthony. *Mythologies of Nothing: Mystical Death in American Poetry, 1940–1970.* Urbana: University of Illinois Press, 1984.

Lieberman, Laurence. *Unassigned Frequencies: American Poetry in Review, 1964–77.* Urbana: University of Illinois Press, 1977.

Martin, Robert K. *The Homosexual Tradition in American Poetry.* Austin: University of Texas Press, 1979.

Mazzaro, Jerome. *Postmodern American Poetry.* Urbana: University of Illinois Press, 1980.

McClatchy, J. D. *White Paper: On Contemporary American Poetry.* New York: Columbia University Press, 1989.

McClure, Michael. *Scratching the Beat Surface.* San Francisco: North Point Press, 1982.

McCorkle, James. *The Still Performance: Writing, Self, and Interconnection in Five Postmodern American Poets.* Charlottesville: University of Virginia Press, 1989.

McCorkle, ed. *Conversant Essays: Contemporary Poets on Poetry.* Detroit: Wayne State University Press, 1990.

McCowell, Robert, ed. *Poetry After Modernism.* Brownsville, Oreg.: Story Line Press, 1991.

Mersmann, James F. *Out of the Vietnam Vortex: A Study of Poets and Poetry Against the War.* Lawrence: University Press of Kansas, 1974.

Messerli, Douglas, ed. *From the Other Side of the Century: A New American Poetry, 1960–1990.* Los Angeles: Sun and Moon Press, 1994.

Miller, James E. Jr. *The American Quest for a Supreme Fiction: Whitman's Legacy in the Personal Epic.* Chicago: University of Chicago Press, 1979.

Molesworth, Charles. *The Fierce Embrace: A Study of Contemporary American Poetry.* Columbia: University of Missouri Press, 1979.

Moss, Howard, ed. *The Poet's Story.* New York: Macmillan, 1973.

Myers, Jack, and David Wojahn, eds. *A Profile of Twentieth-Century American Poetry*. Carbondale & Edwardsville: Southern Illinois University Press, 1991.

Nelson, Cary. *Our Last First Poets: Vision and History in Contemporary American Poetry*. Urbana & Chicago: University of Illinois Press, 1981.

Nelson. *Repression and Recovery: Modern American Poetry and the Politics of Cultural Memory, 1910–1945*. Madison: University of Wisconsin Press, 1989.

Ossman, David. *The Sullen Art*. New York: Corinth Books, 1967.

Ostriker, Alicia Suskin. *Stealing the Language: The Emergence of Women's Poetry in America*. Boston: Beacon, 1986.

Packard, William, ed. *The Craft of Poetry: Interviews from the New York Quarterly*. Garden City, N.Y.: Doubleday, 1974.

Palmer, Michael, ed. *Code of Signals: Recent Writings in Poetics*. Berkeley, Cal.: North Atlantic Books, 1983.

Parini, Jay, and Brett C. Millier, eds. *The Columbia History of American Poetry*. New York: Columbia University Press, 1993.

Perelman, Bob. *The Trouble With Genius: Reading Pound, Joyce, Stein, and Zukofsky*. Berkeley: University of California Press, 1994.

Perkins, David. *A History of Modern Poetry: Modernism and After*. Cambridge, Mass.: Harvard University Press, 1987.

Perloff, Marjorie. *The Dance of the Intellect: Studies in the Poetry of the Pound Tradition*. Cambridge: Cambridge University Press, 1985.

Perloff. *Poetic License: Essays on Modernist and Postmodernist Lyric*. Evanston, Ill.: Northwestern University Press, 1990.

Perloff. *The Poetics of Indeterminacy: Rimbaud to Cage*. Princeton: Princeton University Press, 1981.

Perloff. *Radical Artifice: Writing Poetry in the Age of Media*. Chicago: University of Chicago Press, 1991.

Pinsky, Robert. *The Poet and the World*. New York: Ecco Press, 1988.

Pinsky. *The Situation of Poetry: Contemporary Poetry and Its Traditions*. Princeton: Princeton University Press, 1976.

Poulin, A. Jr., ed. *Contemporary American Poetry*. Boston: Houghton Mifflin, 1971.

Quartermain, Peter. *Disjunctive Poetics: From Gertrude Stein and Louis Zukofsky to Susan Howe*. Cambridge: Cambridge University Press, 1992.

Redmond, Eugene. *Drumvoices: The Mission of Afro-American Poetry: A Critical History*. Garden City, N.Y.: Anchor Press, 1976.

Reinfeld, Linda. *Language Poetry: Writing as Rescue*. Baton Rouge: Louisiana State University Press, 1992.

Richman, Robert, ed. *The Direction of Poetry: An Anthology of Rhymed and Metered Verse Written in the English Language Since 1975*. Boston: Houghton Mifflin, 1988.

Rosenthal, M. L., and Sally M. Gall. *The Modern Poetic Sequence: The Genius of Modern Poetry*. New York: Oxford University Press, 1983.

Rosenthal. *The New Poets*. New York: Oxford University Press, 1967.

Ross, Andrew. *The Failure of Modernism: Symptoms of American Poetry*. New York: Columbia University Press, 1986.

Schultz, Susan M., ed. *The Tribe of John: Ashbery and Contemporary Poetry*. Tuscaloosa: University of Alabama Press, 1995.

Shaw, Robert B., ed. *American Poetry Since 1960; Some Critical Perspectives*. Chester Springs, Pa.: Dufour, 1974.

Shetley, Vernon. *After the Death of Poetry: Poet and Audience in Contemporary America*. Durham, N.C.: Duke University Press, 1993.

Shucard, Alan, Fred Moramarco, and William Sullivan. *Modern American Poetry, 1865–1950*. Boston: Twayne, 1989.

Simpson, Eileen. *Poets in Their Youth: A Memoir*. New York: Random House, 1982.

Smith, Dave. *Local Assays*. Urbana: University of Illinois Press, 1985.

Sorrentino, Gilbert. *Something Said*. San Francisco: North Point Press, 1984.

Spiegelman, Willard. *The Didactic Muse: Scenes of Instruction in Contemporary American Poetry*. Princeton: Princeton University Press, 1989.

Steele, Timothy. *Missing Measures: Modern Poetry and the Revolt Against Meter*. Fayetteville: University of Arkansas Press, 1990.

Stepanchev, Stephen. *American Poetry Since 1945: A Critical Survey*. New York: Harper & Row, 1965.

Thurley, Geoffrey. *The American Moment: American Poetry in the Mid-century*. London: E. Arnold, 1977.

Vendler, Helen. *The Music of What Happens*. Cambridge, Mass.: Harvard University Press, 1988.

von Hallberg, Robert. *American Poetry and Culture, 1945–1980*. Cambridge, Mass.: Harvard University Press, 1985.

Young, David, and Stuart Friebert, eds. *A Field Guide to Contemporary Poetry and Poetics*. New York: Longman, 1980.

Contributors

Peter Baker ....*Towson State University*
Anne Day Dewey ....*Saint Louis University, Madrid, Spain*
John Ernest ....*University of New Hampshire*
Thomas Gardner ....*Virginia Polytechnic Institute & State University*
Roger Gilbert ....*Cornell University*
Farah Jasmine Griffin ....*University of Pennsylvania*
Linda Hamalian ....*William Paterson College*
Ruth Y. Hsu ....*University of Hawaii*
Burt Kimmelman ....*New Jersey Institute of Technology*
David W. Landrey ....*Buffalo (N.Y.) State College*
James McCorkle ....*Geneva, New York*
Kevin McGuirk ....*Queen's University*
Patrick Meanor ....*State University of New York College at Oneonta*
Miriam Nichols ....*University College of the Fraser Valley*
Jeffrey Peterson..*Ohio Wesleyan University*
Phoebe Pettingell .... *Three Lakes, Wisconsin*
Arthur J. Sabatini..*Arizona State University West*
Mark Scroggins ....*Florida Atlantic University*
Juliana Spahr ....*State University of New York at Buffalo*
Willard Spiegelman...*Southern Methodist University*

Cumulative Index

Dictionary of Literary Biography, Volumes 1-165
Dictionary of Literary Biography Yearbook, 1980-1995
Dictionary of Literary Biography Documentary Series, Volumes 1-13

Cumulative Index

DLB before number: *Dictionary of Literary Biography,* Volumes 1-165
Y before number: *Dictionary of Literary Biography Yearbook,* 1980-1995
DS before number: *Dictionary of Literary Biography Documentary Series,* Volumes 1-13

A

Abbey Press DLB-49

The Abbey Theatre and Irish Drama,
1900-1945 . . . . DLB-10

Abbot, Willis J. 1863-1934 . . . . DLB-29

Abbott, Jacob 1803-1879 . . . . DLB-1

Abbott, Lee K. 1947- DLB-130

Abbott, Lyman 1835-1922 . . . . DLB-79

Abbott, Robert S. 1868-1940 . . . DLB-29, 91

Abelard, Peter circa 1079-1142 . . . . . DLB-115

Abelard-Schuman DLB-46

Abell, Arunah S. 1806-1888 . . . . DLB-43

Abercrombie, Lascelles 1881-1938 . . . DLB-19

Aberdeen University Press
Limited DLB-106

Abish, Walter 1931- DLB-130

Ablesimov, Aleksandr Onisimovich
1742-1783 . . . . DLB-150

Abrahams, Peter 1919- DLB-117

Abrams, M. H. 1912- DLB-67

Abrogans circa 790-800 . . . . DLB-148

Abse, Dannie 1923- DLB-27

Academy Chicago Publishers DLB-46

Accrocca, Elio Filippo 1923- DLB-128

Ace Books DLB-46

Achebe, Chinua 1930- DLB-117

Achtenberg, Herbert 1938- DLB-124

Ackerman, Diane 1948- DLB-120

Ackroyd, Peter 1949- DLB-155

Acorn, Milton 1923-1986 . . . . DLB-53

Acosta, Oscar Zeta 1935?- DLB-82

Actors Theatre of Louisville DLB-7

Adair, James 1709?-1783? DLB-30

Adam, Graeme Mercer 1839-1912 . . . DLB-99

Adame, Leonard 1947- DLB-82

Adamic, Louis 1898-1951 . . . . DLB-9

Adams, Alice 1926- Y-86

Adams, Brooks 1848-1927 . . . . DLB-47

Adams, Charles Francis, Jr.
1835-1915 . . . . DLB-47

Adams, Douglas 1952- Y-83

Adams, Franklin P. 1881-1960 . . . . . . DLB-29

Adams, Henry 1838-1918 . . . . DLB-12, 47

Adams, Herbert Baxter 1850-1901 . . . DLB-47

Adams, J. S. and C.
[publishing house] DLB-49

Adams, James Truslow 1878-1949 . . . DLB-17

Adams, John 1735-1826 . . . . DLB-31

Adams, John Quincy 1767-1848 . . . . . DLB-37

Adams, Léonie 1899-1988 . . . . DLB-48

Adams, Levi 1802-1832 . . . . DLB-99

Adams, Samuel 1722-1803 . . . . . . DLB-31, 43

Adams, Thomas
1582 or 1583-1652 . . . . DLB-151

Adams, William Taylor 1822-1897 . . DLB-42

Adamson, Sir John 1867-1950 . . . . . . DLB-98

Adcock, Arthur St. John
1864-1930 . . . . DLB-135

Adcock, Betty 1938- DLB-105

Adcock, Betty, Certain Gifts DLB-105

Adcock, Fleur 1934- DLB-40

Addison, Joseph 1672-1719 . . . . DLB-101

Ade, George 1866-1944 . . . . DLB-11, 25

Adeler, Max (see Clark, Charles Heber)

Adonias Filho 1915-1990 . . . . DLB-145

Advance Publishing Company DLB-49

AE 1867-1935 . . . . DLB-19

Ælfric circa 955-circa 1010 . . . . DLB-146

Aesthetic Poetry (1873), by
Walter Pater DLB-35

After Dinner Opera Company Y-92

Afro-American Literary Critics:
An Introduction DLB-33

Agassiz, Jean Louis Rodolphe
1807-1873 . . . . DLB-1

Agee, James 1909-1955 . . . . . . DLB-2, 26, 152

The Agee Legacy: A Conference at
the University of Tennessee
at Knoxville Y-89

Aguilera Malta, Demetrio
1909-1981 . . . . DLB-145

Ai 1947- DLB-120

Aichinger, Ilse 1921- DLB-85

Aidoo, Ama Ata 1942- DLB-117

Aiken, Conrad 1889-1973 . . . DLB-9, 45, 102

Aiken, Joan 1924- DLB-161

Aikin, Lucy 1781-1864 . . . . DLB-144, 163

Ainsworth, William Harrison
1805-1882 . . . . DLB-21

Aitken, George A. 1860-1917 . . . . . . DLB-149

Aitken, Robert [publishing house] . . . DLB-49

Akenside, Mark 1721-1770 . . . . DLB-109

Akins, Zoë 1886-1958 . . . . DLB-26

Alabaster, William 1568-1640 . . . . . DLB-132

Alain-Fournier 1886-1914 . . . . DLB-65

Alarcón, Francisco X. 1954- DLB-122

Alba, Nanina 1915-1968 . . . . DLB-41

Albee, Edward 1928- DLB-7

Albert the Great circa 1200-1280 . . . DLB-115

Alberti, Rafael 1902- DLB-108

Albertinus, Aegidius
circa 1560-1620 . . . . DLB-164

Alcott, Amos Bronson 1799-1888 . . . . DLB-1

Alcott, Louisa May
1832-1888 . . . . DLB-1, 42, 79

Alcott, William Andrus 1798-1859 . . . DLB-1

Alcuin circa 732-804 . . . . DLB-148

Alden, Henry Mills 1836-1919 . . . . . DLB-79

Alden, Isabella 1841-1930 . . . . DLB-42

Alden, John B. [publishing house] . . . DLB-49

Alden, Beardsley and Company DLB-49

B

C

G

H

K

L

Mankiewicz, Herman 1897-1953 . . . . .DLB-26

Mankiewicz, Joseph L. 1909-1993 . . . .DLB-44

Mankowitz, Wolf 1924- DLB-15

Manley, Delarivière
1672?-1724 . . . . .DLB-39, 80

Mann, Abby 1927- DLB-44

Mann, Heinrich 1871-1950 . . . . .DLB-66, 118

Mann, Horace 1796-1859 . . . . .DLB-1

Mann, Klaus 1906-1949 . . . . .DLB-56

Mann, Thomas 1875-1955 . . . . .DLB-66

Mann, William D'Alton
1839-1920 . . . . .DLB-137

Manning, Marie 1873?-1945 . . . . . . .DLB-29

Manning and Loring DLB-49

Mannyng, Robert
flourished 1303-1338 . . . . .DLB-146

Mano, D. Keith 1942- DLB-6

Manor Books .DLB-46

Mansfield, Katherine 1888-1923 . . . .DLB-162

Mapanje, Jack 1944- DLB-157

March, William 1893-1954 . . . . . .DLB-9, 86

Marchand, Leslie A. 1900- DLB-103

Marchant, Bessie 1862-1941 . . . . . . .DLB-160

Marchessault, Jovette 1938- DLB-60

Marcus, Frank 1928- DLB-13

Marden, Orison Swett
1850-1924 . . . . .DLB-137

Marechera, Dambudzo
1952-1987 . . . . .DLB-157

Marek, Richard, Books DLB-46

Mares, E. A. 1938- DLB-122

Mariani, Paul 1940- DLB-111

Marie-Victorin, Frère 1885-1944 . . . . .DLB-92

Marin, Biagio 1891-1985 . . . . .DLB-128

Marincović, Ranko 1913- DLB-147

Marinetti, Filippo Tommaso
1876-1944 . . . . .DLB-114

Marion, Frances 1886-1973 . . . . .DLB-44

Marius, Richard C. 1933- Y-85

The Mark Taper Forum DLB-7

Mark Twain on Perpetual Copyright Y-92

Markfield, Wallace 1926- DLB-2, 28

Markham, Edwin 1852-1940 . . . . . . .DLB-54

Markle, Fletcher 1921-1991 . . .DLB-68; Y-91

Marlatt, Daphne 1942- DLB-60

Marlitt, E. 1825-1887 . . . . .DLB-129

Marlowe, Christopher 1564-1593 . . . DLB-62

Marlyn, John 1912- DLB-88

Marmion, Shakerley 1603-1639 . . . . . DLB-58

Der Marner
before 1230-circa 1287 . . . . DLB-138

The *Marprelate Tracts* 1588-1589 . . . . DLB-132

Marquand, John P. 1893-1960 . . . DLB-9, 102

Marqués, René 1919-1979 . . . . DLB-113

Marquis, Don 1878-1937 . . . . . . DLB-11, 25

Marriott, Anne 1913- DLB-68

Marryat, Frederick 1792-1848 . . DLB-21, 163

Marsh, George Perkins
1801-1882 . . . . DLB-1, 64

Marsh, James 1794-1842 . . . . DLB-1, 59

Marsh, Capen, Lyon and Webb DLB-49

Marsh, Ngaio 1899-1982 . . . . DLB-77

Marshall, Edison 1894-1967 . . . . DLB-102

Marshall, Edward 1932- DLB-16

Marshall, Emma 1828-1899 . . . . DLB-163

Marshall, James 1942-1992 . . . . DLB-61

Marshall, Joyce 1913- DLB-88

Marshall, Paule 1929- DLB-33, 157

Marshall, Tom 1938- DLB-60

Marsilius of Padua
circa 1275-circa 1342 . . . . DLB-115

Marson, Una 1905-1965 . . . . DLB-157

Marston, John 1576-1634 . . . . DLB-58

Marston, Philip Bourke 1850-1887 . . DLB-35

Martens, Kurt 1870-1945 . . . . DLB-66

Martien, William S.
[publishing house] DLB-49

Martin, Abe (see Hubbard, Kin)

Martin, Charles 1942- DLB-120

Martin, Claire 1914- DLB-60

Martin, Jay 1935- DLB-111

Martin, Violet Florence (see Ross, Martin)

Martin du Gard, Roger 1881-1958 . . . DLB-65

Martineau, Harriet
1802-1876 . . . . .DLB-21, 55, 159, 163

Martínez, Eliud 1935- DLB-122

Martínez, Max 1943- DLB-82

Martyn, Edward 1859-1923 . . . . DLB-10

Marvell, Andrew 1621-1678 . . . . DLB-131

Marvin X 1944- DLB-38

Marx, Karl 1818-1883 . . . . DLB-129

Marzials, Theo 1850-1920 . . . . DLB-35

Masefield, John
1878-1967 . . . . DLB-10, 19, 153, 160

Mason, A. E. W. 1865-1948 . . . . . . .DLB-70

Mason, Bobbie Ann 1940- Y-87

Mason, William 1725-1797 . . . . . . .DLB-142

Mason Brothers DLB-49

Massey, Gerald 1828-1907 . . . . .DLB-32

Massinger, Philip 1583-1640 . . . . . . .DLB-58

Masson, David 1822-1907 . . . . .DLB-144

Masters, Edgar Lee 1868-1950 . . . . .DLB-54

Mather, Cotton
1663-1728 . . . . .DLB-24, 30, 140

Mather, Increase 1639-1723 . . . . .DLB-24

Mather, Richard 1596-1669 . . . . .DLB-24

Matheson, Richard 1926- DLB-8, 44

Matheus, John F. 1887- DLB-51

Mathews, Cornelius
1817?-1889 . . . . .DLB-3, 64

Mathews, Elkin
[publishing house] DLB-112

Mathias, Roland 1915- DLB-27

Mathis, June 1892-1927 . . . . .DLB-44

Mathis, Sharon Bell 1937- DLB-33

Matoš, Antun Gustav 1873-1914 . . .DLB-147

The Matter of England
1240-1400 . . . . .DLB-146

The Matter of Rome
early twelfth to late fifteenth
century .DLB-146

Matthews, Brander
1852-1929 . . . . DLB-71, 78; DS-13

Matthews, Jack 1925- DLB-6

Matthews, William 1942- DLB-5

Matthiessen, F. O. 1902-1950 . . . . . . .DLB-63

Matthiessen, Peter 1927- DLB-6

Maugham, W. Somerset
1874-1965 . . . . .DLB-10, 36, 77, 100, 162

Maupassant, Guy de 1850-1893 . . . .DLB-123

Mauriac, Claude 1914- DLB-83

Mauriac, François 1885-1970 . . . . . . .DLB-65

Maurice, Frederick Denison
1805-1872 . . . . .DLB-55

Maurois, André 1885-1967 . . . . .DLB-65

Maury, James 1718-1769 . . . . .DLB-31

Mavor, Elizabeth 1927- DLB-14

Mavor, Osborne Henry (see Bridie, James)

Maxwell, H. [publishing house] DLB-49

Maxwell, John [publishing house] . . .DLB-106

S

Y

ISBN 0-8103-9360-3

Documentary Series